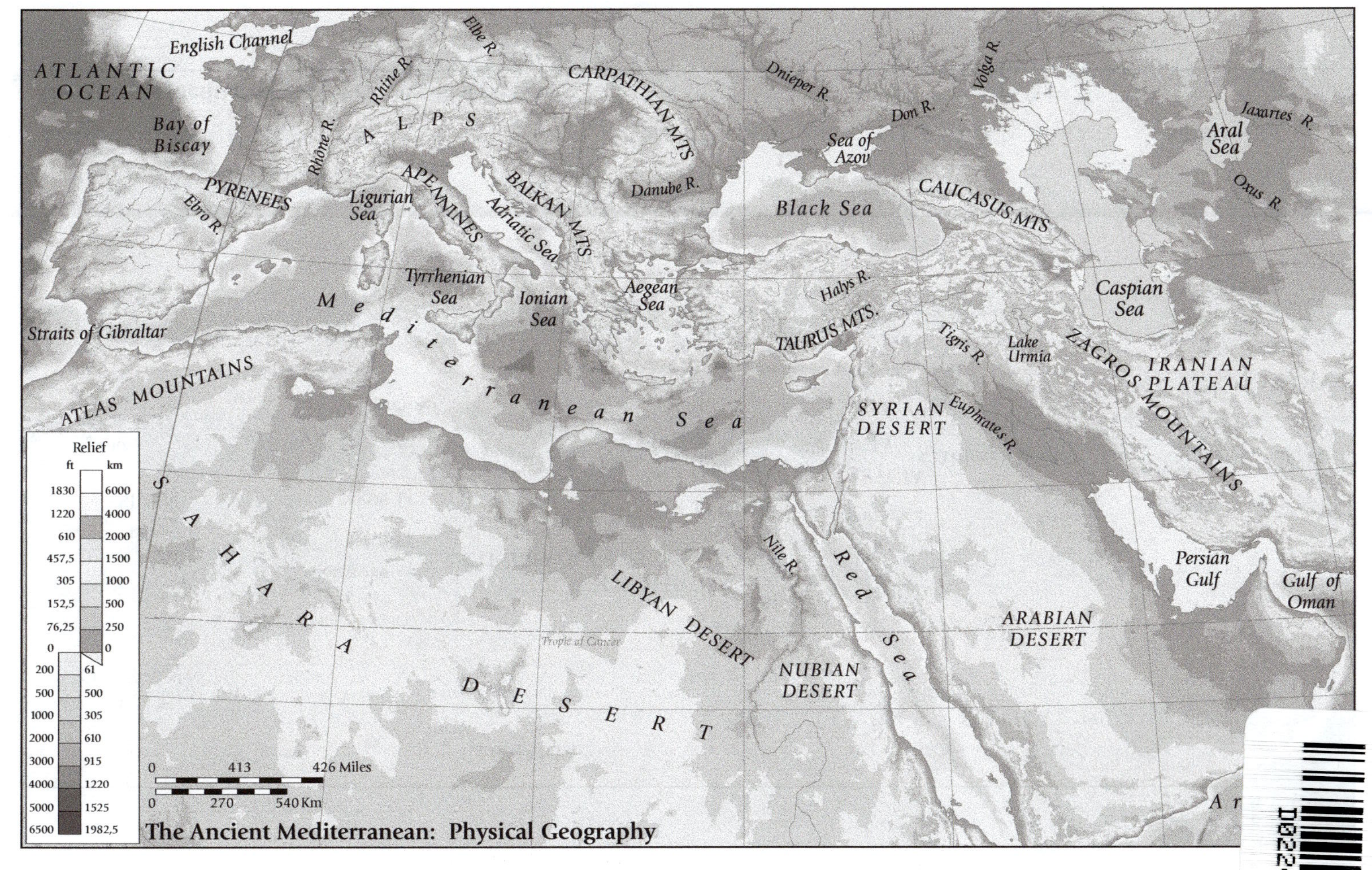
ATLANTIC OCEAN
English Channel
Bay of Biscay
PYRENEES
Ebro R.
Rhône R.
Rhine R.
Elbe R.
A L P S
CARPATHIAN MTS
Dnieper R.
Volga R.
Don R.
Sea of Azov
Jaxartes R.
Aral Sea
Oxus R.
Ligurian Sea
APENNINES
Adriatic Sea
BALKAN MTS
Danube R.
Black Sea
CAUCASUS MTS
Caspian Sea
Tyrrhenian Sea
Ionian Sea
Aegean Sea
Halys R.
TAURUS MTS.
Straits of Gibraltar
Mediterranean Sea
ATLAS MOUNTAINS
Tigris R.
Lake Urmia
ZAGROS MOUNTAINS
IRANIAN PLATEAU
SYRIAN DESERT
Euphrates R.
SAHARA DESERT
LIBYAN DESERT
Tropic of Cancer
Nile R.
Red Sea
NUBIAN DESERT
ARABIAN DESERT
Persian Gulf
Gulf of Oman
Relief
ft
km
1830
6000
1220
4000
610
2000
457,5
1500
305
1000
152,5
500
76,25
250
0
0
200
61
500
500
1000
305
2000
610
3000
915
4000
1220
5000
1525
6500
1982,5
0
413
426 Miles
0
270
540 Km
The Ancient Mediterranean: Physical Geography

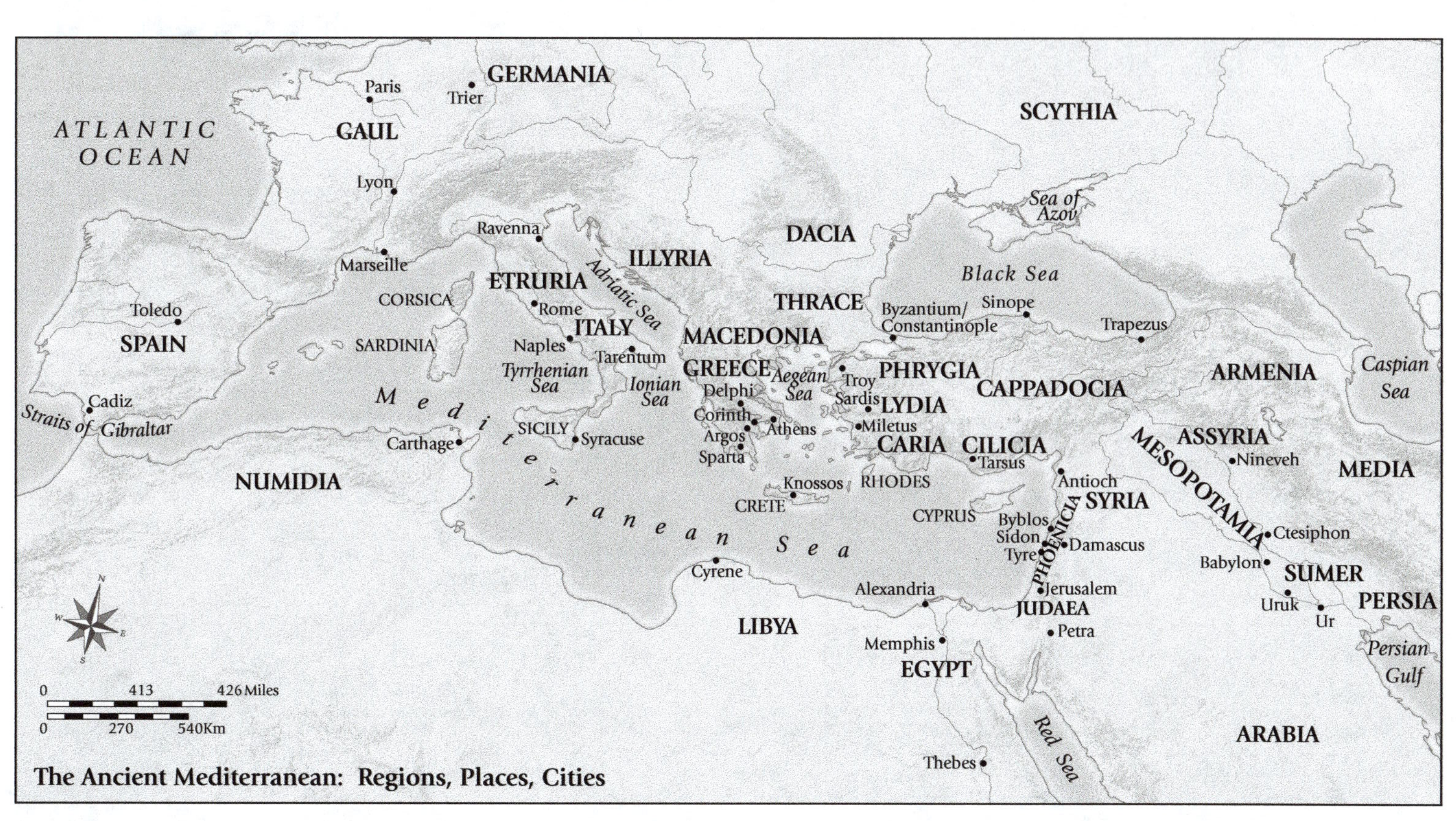

The Ancient Mediterranean: Regions, Places, Cities

SOURCES FOR ANCIENT MEDITERRANEAN CIVILIZATIONS

SOURCES FOR ANCIENT MEDITERRANEAN CIVILIZATIONS

Texts, Maps, and Images

Ralph W. Mathisen

New York Oxford
OXFORD UNIVERSITY PRESS

Oxford University Press is a department of the University of Oxford.
It furthers the University's objective of excellence in research, scholarship,
and education by publishing worldwide. Oxford is a registered trade mark
of Oxford University Press in the UK and certain other countries.

Published in the United States of America by Oxford University Press
198 Madison Avenue, New York, NY 10016, United States of America.

Library of Congress Cataloging-in-Publication Data
Names: Mathisen, Ralph W., 1947- | Mathisen, Ralph W., 1947- Ancient
Mediterranean civilizations.
Title: Sources for Ancient Mediterranean civilizations : texts, maps and images /
Ralph W. Mathisen.
Description: New York : Oxford University Press, 2017.
Identifiers: LCCN 2016018155 | ISBN 9780190280918 (acid-free paper)
Subjects: LCSH: Mediterranean Region—Civilization—Sources. | Mediterranean
Region—Antiquities—Sources. | Mediterranean Region—History—To 476—Sources. |
Mediterranean Region—History—476-1517—Sources.
Classification: LCC DE86 .M375 2017 | DDC 937—dc23
LC record available at https://lccn.loc.gov/2016018155

CONTENTS

MAPS

MAPS

PREFACE

Every civilization and culture has stories to tell. The written sources of antiquity generally survived until the present day only through special circumstances or by following circuitous routes. The most common writing material used in antiquity was made from papyrus, a hollow reed growing in the Nile River whose stalks were slit, flattened, and glued together to make sheets of writing material. Egyptian papyrus was shipped throughout the Mediterranean world. Papyrus books usually consisted of rolled-up scrolls made of papyrus sheets glued together into thirty-foot strips. The problem with papyrus was that it did not have a long shelf life. After about fifty years it became brittle and friable. In most places, papyrus documents thus needed to be recopied every so often if they were going to stand the test of time. The exception was Egypt itself, where tens of thousands of papyrus documents, some entire manuscripts but others just scraps, have been preserved in trash heaps in the desiccated sands of Egypt and continue to be discovered.

Other materials also were employed as writing materials. Clay tablets, used in the Near East and by the Minoans and Mycenaeans, were preserved only if they were baked, something that usually happened when a city was burned, perhaps as a consequence of a natural disaster such as an earthquake, or of a hostile attack, or, most usually, because of a domestic conflagration. Thus, paradoxically, the destruction of some or all of a city led to the preservation of its documents. Moreover, when used for writing, stone and bronze were virtually indestructible. But both often were reused, the stone serving as building material or the metal being melted down. In addition, stone, and even more so metal, were used for lengthy documents only in special cases.

During Late Antiquity, parchment, made from treated sheep or calf skins, replaced papyrus as the most common writing material outside of Egypt. The vast majority of textual sources surviving from antiquity have been preserved on parchment in manuscripts bound in codex form, that is, books with pages. Even though parchment is very sturdy and a significant number of parchment documents survive from as early as the fifth and sixth centuries, in most cases parchment manuscripts were recopied at least once or twice before making it to the modern day. As a result, issues can arise regarding just how faithful each successive copy is to the original text.

The sources included here represent all of these different kinds of materials. About two-thirds of these documents were preserved as parchment manuscripts. The remaining one-third include eighteen metal or stone inscriptions, fourteen clay tablets, and ten Egyptian papyri documents, thus providing a good cross-section of the different kinds of documents that survive from antiquity.

Ancient Mediterranean Civilizations: Texts, Maps, and Images not only serves as a companion volume to R. W. Mathisen, *Ancient Mediterranean Civilizations. From Prehistory to 640 CE*, second edition (Oxford University Press, 2015) but also stands alone in its own right as an all-purpose source book for ancient history. It provides not only 134 primary sources in translation but also 12 maps, and 118 illustrations. The entries are organized into the same chapters as in *Ancient Mediterranean Civilizations*, usually in chronological order.

This sourcebook differs from the generally available ancient history sourcebooks in several important regards. This volume avoids the "bit and snippet" presentation that characterizes so many sourcebooks, where the approach often is to cram in as many brief extracts as possible. This makes it difficult for instructors and students to discuss at length the significance of any particular source. The use of longer extracts—an average of well over four pages per document, more than in any other existing sourcebook—provides a self-contained venue where students can give reports or write papers based on a source that extends over several pages and can relate the source more effectively to material presented in class, in a textbook, or in ancillary secondary sources. Personal experience also suggests that longer source extracts are ideal for use in discussions, either in lecture or in a discussion venue, where an entire class period could be used to elucidate the significance of a passage.

In addition, this sourcebook provides a more equitable division of sources among the different periods of history to reflect the most current understanding of the nature of the ancient world. Existing sourcebooks are all heavily Greco-Roman–centric, with between 70% and 78% of their entries dealing with the traditional periods of Ancient Greece and the Roman Republic and Principate. This sourcebook is equally divided among the four periods of antiquity, that is, the Ancient Near East (3000–500 BCE), Ancient Greece (2500–31 BCE), the Roman Republic and Empire (753 BCE–192 CE), and Late Antiquity (192–640 CE), with additional chapters on "Accounts of the Creation of the Universe, Humans, and the Flood" and "Civilization beyond the Near East, Greece, and Rome," topics not covered in any existing sourcebook.

Moreover, unlike sourcebooks that merely lift documents verbatim out of previous translations, the sources presented here, most of which are out of copyright and in the public domain, are edited for readability, sense, consistency, and flow, with superfluous and repetitious information edited out. All documents are direct quotations of the original sources. There are no paraphrases or summaries. Furthermore, sources are fully annotated to explain names, terms, and concepts that students may be unfamiliar with and are not explicated in the document itself. Unattributed translations are by the author of this volume.

This volume eschews the "blocks of text" approach, in which a student is confronted by intimidating and daunting unrelieved textual material that does nothing to draw a student in. In this sourcebook, every chapter begins with a full-page-width map that helps to contextualize the material in place and time. Students thus can visualize where the action in each chapter is taking place. In addition, each document also is prefaced with an image, almost always of an ancient artifact or place, that gives students a visual context in which to place the content of the source. Each document also is introduced by a paragraph of commentary that establishes its authorship, historical context, and significance.

Finally, the volume also presents an internal consistency that goes beyond stand-alone sources presented in isolation from one another. Thus, similar concepts, often indicated by cross references, recur throughout the text and can be used by students for a comparative approach. Leitmotifs that permeate the volume include the following:

(1) Comparative sources on the creation of the world and humans and the primeval flood, from the Mesopotamian, Jewish, Greco-Roman, and Islamic traditions;
(2) So much law that this volume almost could be the reader for a course on ancient law: the Code of Ur-Nammu; the Code of Hammurabi; Hebrew Laws; the Great Rhetra of Sparta; the Constitution of Athens; the Constitution of Carthage; the Roman Twelve Tables; the Trial of Jesus before Pontius Pilate; Expanding the Membership of the Senate; the Antonine Constitution; Diocletian's Edict on Maximum Prices; the Edict of Milan; the Council of Nicaea; Roman Criminal Legal Process; the Theodosian Code; and the Code of Justinian;
(3) Women in history: Inanna; Enheduanna; Hatshepsut; Deborah; Judith; Sappho; The "Trojan Women"; Lysistrata; Lucretia; the Bacchanalians; Cleopatra; Turia; Boudicca; Roman Misogyny; Perpetua and Felicitas; Zenobia; Hypatia; Roman Criminal Legal Process; and Theodora;
(4) Humans' relations with the gods: *Epic of Gilgamesh*; "Exaltation of Inanna"; "Hymn to the Nile"; "Book of the Dead"; "Hymn to Aton"; selections from the Hebrew Bible; Anchises Prophesizes the Future of Rome; Horace's "Secular Hymn"; the "Vigil of Venus"; the Council of Nicaea; the Monastic Life; the Conversion of Clovis; and the rise of Islam;
(5) Judaism: the Hebrews in Egypt and the Legend of Moses (ca. 1300 BCE); Laws of the Hebrew Bible (ca. 1230 BCE); Deborah the Judge Defeats the Canaanites (ca. 1050 BCE); King Solomon Consolidates His Authority (ca. 950 BCE); the Assyrian Siege of Jerusalem (701 BCE); Judith and Holofernes (ca. 587 BCE); Revolt of the Maccabees (167 BCE); the Trial of Jesus before Pontius Pilate (ca. 28/37 CE); the Fall of Masada (74 CE); the Jews Confront Rome (133–180 CE); and Late Roman legislation on the Jews (313-436 CE);
(6) Christianity: the Trial of Jesus before Pontius Pilate (ca. 28/37 CE); Pliny's Letter to Trajan on the Christians (ca. 112 CE); the Martyrdom of Perpetua and Felicitas (203 CE); the "Great Persecution" (303–311 CE): the Edict of Milan (312/313 CE); the Council of Nicaea (325 CE); Late Roman Legislation on Christianity (313-436 CE); the Monastic Life on the Eastern Frontier (ca. 360/390 CE); the Late Roman Criminal Legal Process (ca. 370 CE); the Sack of Rome by the Visigoths in God's Plan (410 CE); the Murder of Hypatia of Alexandria (415 CE); and the Conversion of Clovis (496 CE);
(7) Human society and personal experiences: the Autobiography of Weni; the "Eloquent Peasant"; Egyptian Love Letters; the "Report of Wen-Amon"; Human Society in the Greek Archaic Age; Greek Personal Poetry; Greek Arētē; the "Sword of Damocles"; Spartan Education; the Young Alexander; Aristotle's Justification for Slavery; the Bacchanalian Scandal; Cato the Elder; Catullus's Poems; the "Praise of Turia"; the "Vigil of Venus;" Monastic Life; and the Conversion of Clovis;

(8) Poetry from Mesopotamia (Enheduanna), Egypt (Hymn to the Nile, Hymn to Aton), Greece (Sappho, Pindar, Euripides, Aristophanes), the Roman Republic (Catullus), the Roman Empire (Vergil, Horace), and Late Antiquity (the "Vigil of Venus"; the Poem of Eucheria);

(9) Rulers: the Legend of Sargon (ca. 2250 BCE); Hatshepsut's Expedition to Punt (ca. 1470 BCE); the Peace Treaty between Ramses II and Hattusilis III (1258 BCE); the "Victory Hymn" of Merneptah (1208 BCE); King Solomon Consolidates his Authority (ca. 950 BCE); the Black Obelisk of Shalmaneser III (825 BCE); the Prism of Sennacherib (ca. 689 BCE); the Cyrus Legend (ca. 550 BCE); the Behistun Inscription (ca. 520 BCE); the Sword of Damocles (ca. 360 BCE); the Young Alexander the Great (ca. 350–334 BCE); Alexander's Expedition into India (326–324 BCE); the Wars of the Successors (323–301 BCE); Cleopatra, Pharaoh and Queen of Egypt (48–31 BCE); the Deeds of the Divine Augustus (14 CE); the Emperor Caligula (37–41 CE); Zenobia and the Empire of Palmyra (266–274 CE); a Visigothic King and His Court (ca. 455/465 CE); the Conversion of Clovis (496 CE); and the Character of Justinian and Theodora (527–548);

(10) Parallel birth legends: Sargon; Moses; Cyrus; and Romulus and Remus;

(11) Philosophers: Pythagoras; Socrates; Epictetus; and Hypatia;

(12) Subversive activities: the Cursing of Agadē; Judith and Holofernes; Athenian Anti-War Sentiment (Euripides; *Trojan Women*; Aristophanes; *Lysistrata*); the Bacchanalian Scandal; the Land Law of Tiberius Gracchus; the Slave Revolt of Spartacus; the Trial of Jesus before Pontius Pilate; the Rebellion of Boudicca; and the Fall of Masada; the Jews Confront Rome; and Late Roman Heresies; and, yes,

(13) Wars and battles: Battles between the Gods and the Titans and Giants; the Peace Treaty between Ramses II and Hattusilis III (1258 BCE); the Victory Hymn of Merneptah (1208 BCE); the Invasion of the Sea Peoples (ca. 1180 BCE); the Trojan War (ca. 1185 BCE); the "Dorian Invasion" and the Origin of the Greek Peoples (ca. 1100 BCE); Deborah Defeats the Canaanites (ca. 1050 BCE); the Black Obelisk of Shalmaneser III (825 BCE); Victory Stele of Piye (731 BCE); the Prism of Sennacherib (ca. 689 BCE); Siege of Jerusalem (701 BCE); the Behistun Inscription (ca. 520 BCE); Battle of Salamis (480 BCE); Pericles's Funeral Oration (431/430 BCE); the Sacred Band of Thebes (375–338 BCE); the Battle of Hydaspes (326 BCE); the Wars of the Successors of Alexander (323–301 BCE); the Battle of Cannae (216 BCE); Revolt of the Maccabees (167 BCE); the Slave Revolt of Spartacus (73–71 BCE); Fall of Masada (73 CE); Hadrian Inspects the Troops (128 CE); the Battle of Adrianople (378 CE); the Battle of Ad Decimum (533 CE); and the Conquest of Egypt by Muslims (641–642 CE); including also several submotifs such as Greek and Roman wars with the Celts: the Expansion of the Celts into Greece (279–277 BCE); the Sack of Rome by the Gauls (390 BCE); Caesar's Siege of Alesia (52 BCE); the Rebellion of Boudicca (60–61 CE); and sacks of Rome: the Sack of Rome by Gauls (390 BCE); the Sack of Rome by Goths (410 CE); and the Sack of Rome by Vandals in (455 CE).

This "variations on a theme" approach can be used by students to investigate, in either discussions or research papers, the development, evolution, and similarities versus differences of similar phenomena over long periods of time. Several of the documents, such as the Greek drama, also would be ideally suited for classroom performances.

I now can take this opportunity to extend my thanks to the several referees of this volume at different stages of its production, including Bryan Givens (Pepperdine University); Craig M. Nakashian (Texas A&M University); Frances B. Titchener (Utah State University); and Jennifer Westerfeld (University of Louisville), not only for offering most helpful suggestions regarding balance, coverage, and content, but also for saving me from several embarrassing typos, not to mention outright errors. Finally, my utmost gratitude goes to Charles Cavaliere, Executive Editor for Classics, Classical Studies, and History at Oxford University Press, who, along with keeping me on my toes while shepherding two editions of *Ancient Mediterranean Civilizations* through the editorial process, first broached the subject of putting together an ancient history reader back in January 2013. Given that I often had thought of doing just that, this was a match made in heaven. Charles and the ever-active staff at OUP, and in particular Sara Birmingham, have made crafting this volume a real pleasure! So to Charles I can only say, "Divinitas te servet per multos annos, parens karissime atque amantissime!"

SOURCES FOR ANCIENT MEDITERRANEAN CIVILIZATIONS

CHAPTER 1

Civilization before Civilization (2,000,000–3000 BCE)

The entire extent of the human past covers more than a million years. But when we speak of "history" and "civilization," the time frame dwindles to merely the previous five thousand years. The very definition of history itself is based on the existence of written documents. This means, of course, that no textual sources survive from the prehistoric period. But this is not to say that early peoples of the historic period did not have accounts of what their earlier history had been. In particular, all of the civilizations discussed in this volume had accounts of how the universe and the living things in it, including humans, had been created. For them, these accounts were not "myths" or "legends," but what really happened.

Even though the accounts of different peoples reflected their own particular social or geographic circumstances, in many regards they had remarkable parallels with the tales of other peoples. Although the details differed, in every case all peoples saw creation being effected by some form of deity. Another common motif was the genesis of the universe from chaos or nothingness, with increasing particularization resulting from the creation of the earth and the sky, the land and the water. Yet another repetitious theme relates to an angry deity who decided to destroy humanity by sending a great flood but permitted a favored person and his family, along with representatives of many animal species, to survive. Presented here are creation stories that were current in the Mesopotamian, Egyptian, Greek, Jewish, and Islamic traditions.

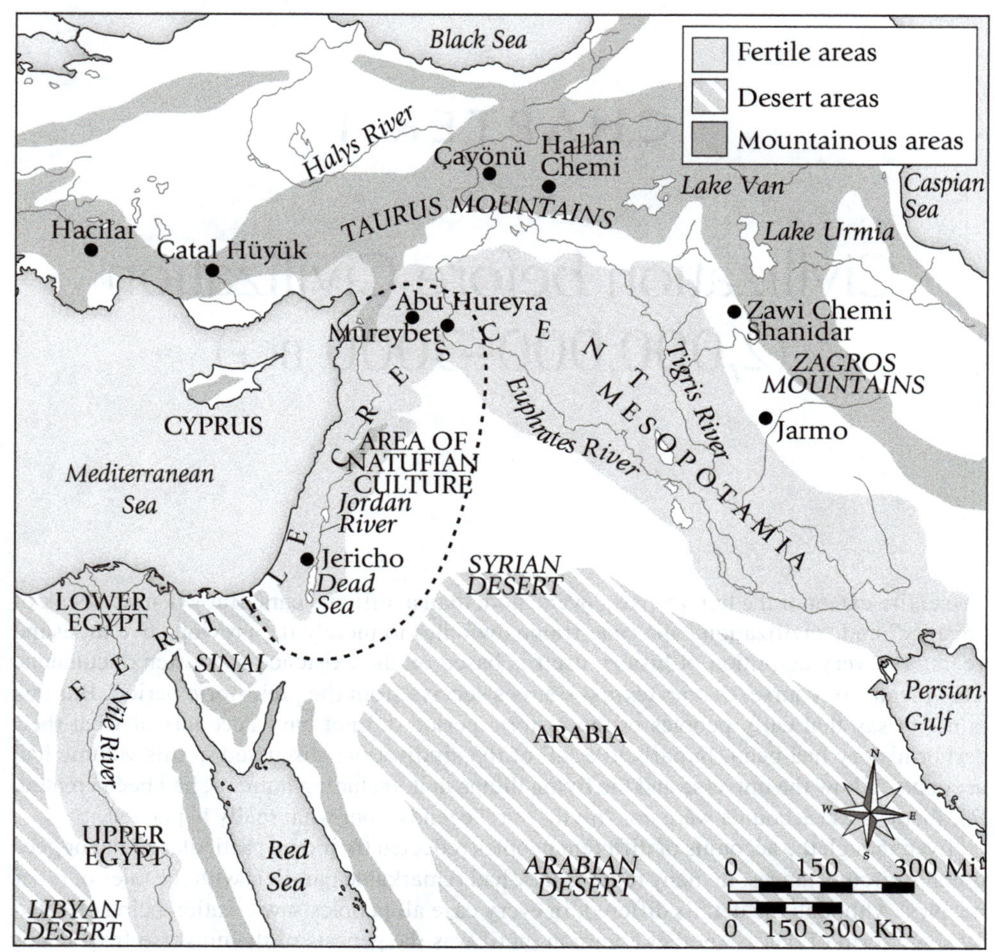

Map 1 Neolithic Sites of the Ancient Near East

Accounts of the
Creation of the Universe, Humans, and the Flood

I: MESOPOTAMIAN ACCOUNTS

Beginning around 2500 BCE, Mesopotamian accounts of creation and the early history of humanity are preserved on clay tablets. Some are in fragmentary condition and can only be conjecturally restored. Many of the gods mentioned in these accounts were known by several different names, which can make reading the accounts confusing.

1

THE CREATION STORY: THE "ENÛMA ELIŠ" ("ENUMA ELISH"), TABLETS 1–5[1]

A section of the cuneiform text of the "Enuma Elish," the Mesopotamian creation story, preserved in the British Museum, London.

[1] Edited summaries, using the original wording, of the much longer accounts are presented here.

The Mesopotamian creation myth the Enuma Elish, also known as "The Seven Tablets of Creation," is one of the oldest surviving stories in the world. Its title is derived from the opening lines of the piece, "When on High." It first was recovered, in a seventh-century BCE version, from the library of the Assyrian king Ashurbanipal at Nineveh (Mosul, Iraq). Other copies of tablets containing the myth have been found at Ashur, Kish, and Sultantepe. Their contents indicate that they are copies of much older original versions, dating to the Kassite (1500–1200 BCE) or, more likely, the Old Babylonian (2000–1500 BCE) period. Whereas in the original version the Sumerian god Enlil was the main actor, in the Babylonian version his name was changed to Marduk, the main god of the Babylonians. Assyrian versions had the Assyrian god Ashur in the title role.

Source: W. G. Lambert, "Mesopotamian Creation Stories," in Markham J. Geller and Mineke Schipper, eds., *Imagining Creation, IJS Studies in Judaica* 5 (Leiden: Brill, 2008), 17–59.

When the on high did not exist, and earth beneath had not come into being, there was Apsû,[2] the first in order, their begetter, and demiurge[3] Tiamat,[4] who gave birth to them all. They had mingled their waters together before meadow-land had coalesced and reed-bed[5] was to be found, when not one of the gods had been formed or had come into being, when no destinies had been decreed, the gods were created within them: Lahmu and Lahamu[6] were formed and came into being. While they grew and increased in stature Anšar[7] and Kišar,[8] who excelled them, were created.[9] They prolonged their days, they multiplied their years. Anu,[10] their son, could rival his fathers. Anu, the son, equalled Anšar, and Anu begat Nudimmud,[11] his own equal. Nudimmud was the champion among his fathers: profoundly discerning, wise, of robust strength; very much stronger than his father's begetter, Anšar had no rival among the gods, his brothers. The divine brothers came together, their clamor got loud, throwing Tiamat into a turmoil and by their dancing they spread alarm in Anduruna.[12] Thereupon Apsû, the begetter of the great gods, addressed Tiamat, "Their behavior has become displeasing to me and I cannot rest in the day-time or sleep at night. I will destroy and break up their way of life so that silence may reign and we may sleep." The gods heard this and were frantic. They were overcome with silence and sat quietly.

Ea,[13] who excels in knowledge, the skilled and learned, Ea, who knows everything, fashioned his pure incantation. He poured sleep upon Apsû as he was slumbering deeply. He split his sinews, ripped off his crown, carried away his aura and put it on himself. He bound Apsû and killed him. He set his dwelling upon Apsû.[14] He rested quietly in his chamber, he called it abzu, then he founded his living-quarters within it, and Ea and Damkina, his wife, sat in splendor. In the chamber of the destinies, the room of the archetypes, the wisest of the wise, Bêl[15] was conceived. In the abzu was Marduk[16] born. His figure was

[2] Representing sweet fresh water.

[3] A creator god.

[4] Representing salty water.

[5] A recollection of the marshlands of the Tigris and Euphrates rivers.

[6] These two always are mentioned together and sometimes are thought to represent riverbed silt.

[7] A sky god.

[8] An earth goddess.

[9] Most creation stories envisage a sequence of rulers in which power and authority are passed from parents to their offspring.

[10] The god of the heavens, An in Sumerian, Anu in Akkadian and Babylonian.

[11] Another name for the water god, Enki in Sumerian, Ea in Akkadian and Babylonian.

[12] The preworld world.

[13] Also Enki or Nudimmud.

[14] The sweet water that was the body of Apsû became the home of Enki.

[15] "Lord," another name for Marduk.

[16] Enlil in the original Sumerian version, changed to Marduk by the Babylonians, whose primary god was Marduk.

well developed, the glance of his eyes was dazzling, he was mighty from the beginning. Four were his eyes, four his ears, flame shot forth as he moved his lips, his four ears grew large, his figure was lofty and superior in comparison with the gods, he was Mari-utu, Mari-utu,[17] the Son, the Sun-god, the Sun-god of the gods. The Fifty Dreads were loaded upon him. Anu[18] formed and gave birth to the four winds, He delivered them to Marduk, "My son, let them whirl!"

Meanwhile the gods took no rest, they plotted evil, and addressed their mother Tiamat, "When Apsû, your spouse, was killed, you did not go at his side, but sat quietly. Now the four dreadful winds have been fashioned to throw you into confusion, and we cannot sleep. You sit alone and you do not love us! Make battle, avenge Apsû!" Tiamat heard, the speech pleased her. She said, "Let us make demons." The gods took the side of Tiamat, fiercely plotting, unresting by night and day, lusting for battle, raging, storming, they set up a host to bring about conflict. Mother Hubur,[19] who forms everything, supplied irresistible weapons, and gave birth to giant serpents. She created the Hydra, the Dragon, the Hairy Hero the Great Demon, the Savage Dog, and the Scorpion-man, Fierce demons, the Fish-man, and the Bull-man, carriers of merciless weapons, fearless in the face of battle. Among the gods, her sons, she exalted Qingu, and magnified him among them. The leadership of the army, supreme command she entrusted to him and she set him on a throne, saying, "I have cast the spell for you. Let your commands prevail over all the Anunnaki."[20] She gave him the Tablet of Destinies[21] and fastened it to his breast, saying, "Your order may not be changed." After Qingu was elevated and had acquired the power of Anuship,[22] He decreed the destinies for the gods, her sons: "May the utterance of your mouths subdue the fire-god."[23]

Henceforth Tiamat plotted evil because of Apsû. It became known to Ea that she had arranged the conflict. He entered the presence of the father of his begetter, Anšar, and related to him all of Tiamat's plotting: "My father, Tiamat our mother has conceived a hatred for us, She has established a host in her savage fury. All the gods have turned to her, Even those you begat took the side of Tiamat." Anšar heard. He cried, "Woe!" and bit his lip. His heart was in fury, his mind could not be calmed. Over Ea his son his cry was faltering: "My son, you who provoked the war, take responsibility for whatever you alone have done! You set out and killed Apsû, and as for Tiamat, whom you made furious, where is her equal?" The creator of wisdom, the god Nudimmud, gently answered his father Anšar: "My father, deep mind, who decrees destiny, who has the power to bring into being and destroy, consider that I performed a helpful deed. Before I killed Apsû who could have anticipated the present situation?" Anšar heard, the words pleased him. His heart relaxed to speak to Ea, "My son, your deeds are fitting for a god. Go before Tiamat and appease her, attack with your incantation."

Ea heard the speech of Anšar his father. He took the road to Tiamat, but he perceived her tricks, he fell silent, and turned back. He entered the presence of Anšar, penitently addressing him, "My father, Tiamat's deeds are too much for me. My incantation was not enough. Her strength is mighty, none can go against her. I became afraid of her cry and turned back. My father, do not lose hope, send a second person against her. Although a woman's strength is very great, it is not equal to a man's. Break up her plans before she lays her hands on us." Anšar cried out in intense fury, addressing Anu his other son, "Honored son, whose strength is mighty, whose attack is irresistible, hasten and stand before Tiamat, appease her rage that her heart may relax. Address to her words of petition that she may be appeased." Anu heard the speech of Anšar his father. He took the road to her, he perceived the tricks of Tiamat, he

[17] Marduk also was equated with Utu, the sun god.

[18] Marduk's grandfather.

[19] The underworld river, another name for Tiamat.

[20] The gods.

[21] The Tablets of Destinies legalize the rule of a god and control the fates.

[22] Kingship. In the usual Sumerian hierarchy, Anu was the king of the gods.

[23] Marduk.

fell silent, and turned back. He entered the presence of Anšar the father, penitently addressing him: "My father, Tiamat's deeds are too much for me. My incantation was not enough. Her strength is mighty, no one can go against her. I became afraid of her cry and turned back. My father, do not lose hope, send another person against her. Although a woman's strength is very great, it is not equal to a man's. Break up her plans before she lays her hands on us." Anšar lapsed into silence, staring at the ground. He nodded to Ea, shaking his head. The Igigi[24] and all the Anunnaki had assembled. No god would go to face Tiamat. The Lord Anšar, the father of the great gods, was angry in his heart, and did not summon anyone.

A mighty son, the warrior Marduk, Ea summoned to his private chamber, saying: "Marduk, give counsel, listen to your father. Go reverently before Anšar, ease him with your glance." Bêl drew near and stood in the presence of Anšar. Anšar saw him, his heart filled with satisfaction. He kissed his lips and removed his fear. "My father,[25] I will go and fulfill your desires! Soon you will tread on the neck of Tiamat!" "Go, my son, appease Tiamat with your pure spell. Drive the storm chariot without delay, and turn her back." With glad heart Bêl addressed his father, "Lord of the gods, destiny of the great gods, if I should bind Tiamat and preserve you, convene an assembly and proclaim for me an exalted destiny. Sit, all of you, in Upšukkinakku[26] with gladness, and let me, with my utterance, decree destinies instead of you. Whatever I instigate must not be changed, nor may my command be nullified or altered."

Anšar opened his mouth and addressed Kakka, his vizier[27]: "Have the gods, my fathers, brought to my presence. Let them decree the destiny for Marduk their avenger. Repeat to them all that I tell you: 'Anšar, your son, has sent me. Marduk, the sage of the gods, your son, has come forward, He has determined to meet Tiamat. Quickly, now, decree your destiny for him without delay, that he may go and face your powerful enemy.'" Kakka went. He directed his steps to Lahmu and Lahamu, the gods his fathers. When Lahmu and Lahamu heard, they cried aloud. They entered the presence of Anšar and became filled with joy. They conferred as they sat at table. They ate grain, they drank ale. They strained the sweet liquor through their straws. They drank beer and felt good. They became carefree, their mood was merry, and they decreed the fate for Marduk, their avenger. They set a Lordly dais for him and he took his seat before his fathers to receive kingship. Lahmu and Lahamu said, "Marduk, you are the most honored among the great gods, your destiny is unequalled, your command is like Anu's. Henceforth your order will not be annulled. You are Marduk, our avenger. We have given you kingship over the whole universe. Take your seat in the assembly, let your weapons slay your enemies." The gods rejoiced and offered congratulation: "Marduk is the king!" They presented to him a mace, a throne, and a rod, and they gave him an irresistible weapon that overwhelms the foe, saying, "Go, cut Tiamat's throat."

Marduk fashioned a bow and made it his weapon. He took up his club and held it in his right hand. He placed lightning before him, and filled his body with tongues of flame. He made a net to enmesh the entrails of Tiamat. He put beside his net the winds given by his father, Anu. He fashioned the Evil Wind, the Dust Storm, Tempest, Chaos-spreading Wind. Bêl took up the Storm-flood, his great weapon. He rode the fearful chariot of the irresistible storm. Four steeds he yoked to it and harnessed them to it, the Destroyer, the Merciless, the Trampler, the Fleet.[28] At his right hand he stationed raging battle and strife, on the left, conflict that overwhelms a united battle array. He set his face toward the raging Tiamat. In his lips he held a spell. He grasped a plant to counter poison in his hand.

Bêl drew near, surveying the maw of Tiamat. He observed the tricks of Qingu, her spouse. Tiamat cast her spell without turning her neck. Bêl lifted up the

[24] The senior gods.

[25] A term of respect; actually his grandfather.

[26] Assembly place of the gods.

[27] An executive official who often does the real work.

[28] Similar to the four horsemen of the Apocalypse, Conquest, War, Famine, and Death.

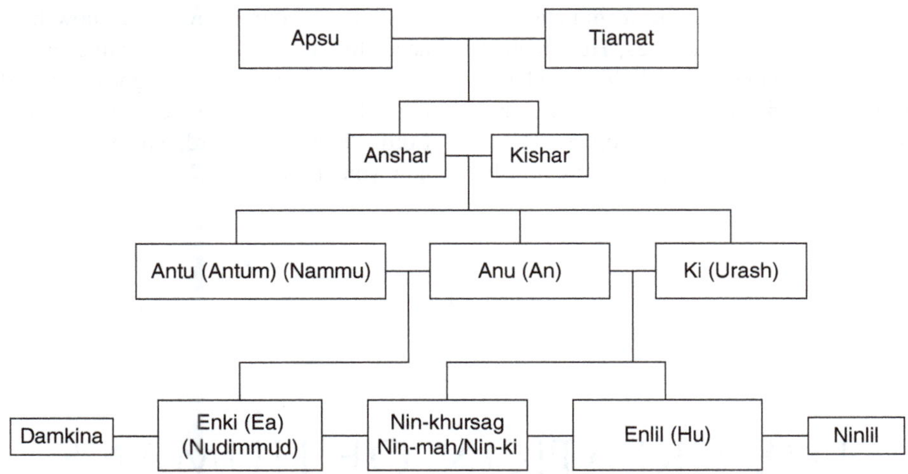

Figure 1 "A geneology of the Mesopotamia gods as presented in the Enuma Elish."

Storm-flood, his great weapon, and with these words threw it at the raging Tiamat, "Why are you aggressive and arrogant, and strive to provoke battle? The younger generation have shouted, outraging their elders, but you, their mother, hold pity in contempt. Qingu you have named to be your spouse, and you have improperly appointed him to the rank of Anuship. Against Anšar, king of the gods, you have stirred up trouble. Deploy your troops, gird on your weapons. You and I will take our stand and do battle." When Tiamat heard this she lost her reason. All her lower members trembled beneath her. She kept reciting her spell. Tiamat and Marduk, the sage of the gods, came together. Bêl spread out his net and enmeshed her; he let loose the Evil Wind in her face. Tiamat opened her mouth to swallow it, the fierce winds weighed down her belly, her inward were distended and she opened her mouth wide. He let fly an arrow and pierced her belly. He tore open her entrails and slit her inward. He bound her and extinguished her life. He threw down her corpse and stood on it. After he had killed Tiamat, the leader, her assembly dispersed, her host scattered. But they were completely surrounded, unable to escape. He bound them and broke their weapons, Now Qingu, who had risen to power among them, he bound. He took from him the Tablet of Destinies, which was not properly his, and fastened it to his own breast.

After the warrior Marduk had bound and slain his enemies, and returned to Tiamat, whom he had bound, Bêl placed his feet on the lower parts of Tiamat and with his merciless club smashed her skull. He severed her arteries and let the north wind bear up her blood to give the news. His fathers saw it and were glad and exulted. Bêl rested, surveying the corpse. He split her into two like a dried fish. One half of her he set up and stretched out as the heavens. He stretched the skin and appointed a watch with the instruction not to let her waters escape. He fashioned heavenly stations for the great gods, and set up constellations, the patterns of the stars. He appointed the year, marked off divisions, and set up three stars each for the twelve months. He placed the heights of heaven in Tiamat's belly. He created Nanna,[29] entrusting to him the night. He appointed him as the jewel of the night to fix the days. From her two eyes he let the Euphrates and Tigris flow. He heaped up the distant mountains on her breasts. He bored wells to channel the springs. He twisted her tail and wove it into the Durmahu.[30] He set up her crotch—it wedged up the heavens—thus the other half of her he stretched out and made it firm as the earth. After he had finished his work inside Tiamat, he surveyed the

[29] The god of the moon.

[30] The bond that holds the earth and the heavens in position.

heavens and the earth. After he had formulated his regulations and composed his decrees, He attached guide-ropes and put them in Ea's hands. The Tablet of Destinies that Qingu had taken and carried he presented to Anu. Lahmu and Lahamu opened their mouths and addressed the Igigi gods: "Previously Marduk was our beloved son, now he is your king, heed his command! His name is Lugaldimmerankia,[31] trust in him!" The gods bowed down, speaking to him, They addressed Lugaldimmerankia, their Lord, "Formerly, Lord, you were our beloved son, now you are our king."

2

THE CREATION OF HUMANS BY ENKI AND NINMAḪ

The Sumerian god of water, Enki, is recognized by the rivulets of water running off his shoulders.

In this myth, preserved on Mesopotamian cuneiform clay tablets, Enki, the god of water and civilization and the creator of forms, aided by Namma, an original mother of the gods, and Ninmaḫ, an ancient mother goddess, created the first humans to relieve the gods of their workload. Their efforts left something to be desired and explained why humans hence forward were afflicted with a range of disabilities.

Source: "Enki and Ninmah," in J. A. Black, G. Cunningham, J. Ebeling, E. Flückiger-Hawker, E. Robson, J. Taylor, and G. Zólyomi, "The Electronic Text Corpus of Sumerian Literature."

[31] "King of the Gods," incorporating the word "lugal," a Sumerian military leader or king of several cities.

In those days, in the days when heaven and earth were created, the gods were obliged to work for their food. The senior gods oversaw the work, while the minor gods were bearing the toil. The gods were digging the canals and piling up the silt in Harali.[32] The gods, dredging the clay, began complaining about this life. At that time, the one of great wisdom, the creator of all the senior gods, Enki[33] lay on his bed, not waking up from his sleep, in the deep engur,[34] in the flowing water, the place the inside of which no other god knows. The gods said, weeping: "He is the cause of the lamenting!" Namma,[35] the primeval mother who gave birth to the senior gods, took the tears of the gods to the one who lay sleeping: "Are you really lying there asleep? My son, wake up from your bed! Please apply the skill deriving from your wisdom and create a substitute for the gods so that they can be freed from their toil!" At the word of his mother Namma, Enki rose up from his bed.

And after Enki, the fashioner of designs by himself, had pondered the matter, he said to his mother Namma: "My mother, the creature you planned will really come into existence. Impose on him the work of carrying baskets. You should knead clay from the top of the apsû[36]; the birth-goddesses will nip off the clay and you shall bring the form into existence. Let Ninmaḫ[37] act as your assistant. My mother, after you have decreed his fate, let Ninmaḫ impose on him the work of carrying baskets." Enki brought joy to their heart. He set a feast for his mother Namma and for Ninmaḫ, An, Enlil,[38] and the Lord Nudimmud[39] roasted holy kids. All the senior gods praised him: "O Lord of wide understanding, who is as wise as you? Enki, the great Lord, who can equal your actions?" Enki and Ninmaḫ drank beer, their hearts became elated, and then Ninmaḫ said to Enki: "Man's body can be either good or bad and whether I make a fate good or bad depends on my will." Enki answered Ninmaḫ: "I will counterbalance whatever fate, good or bad, you happen to decide."

Ninmaḫ took clay from the top of the apsû in her hand and she fashioned from it first a man who could not bend his outstretched weak hands. Enki looked at the man who could not bend his outstretched weak hands, and decreed his fate: he appointed him as a servant of the king. Next, she fashioned one who could not hold back his urine. Enki looked at the one who could not hold back his urine and bathed him in enchanted water and drove out the Namtar[40] demon from his body. Then she fashioned a woman who could not give birth. Enki looked at the woman who could not give birth, and decreed her fate: he made her belong to the queen's household. Next, she fashioned one with neither penis nor vagina. Enki looked at the one with neither penis nor vagina and give it the name "Nibru[41] eunuch," and decreed as its fate to stand before the king. Ninmaḫ threw the pinched-off clay from her hand on the ground and a great silence fell.

The great Lord Enki said to Ninmaḫ: "I have decreed the fates of your creatures and given them their daily bread. Come, now I will fashion somebody for you, and you must decree the fate of the newborn one!" Enki devised a shape with head, and mouth in its middle, and said to Ninmaḫ: "Pour ejaculated semen into a woman's womb, and the woman will give birth to the semen of her womb." Ninmaḫ stood by for the newborn and the woman bore Umul[42]: its head was afflicted, its eyes were afflicted, its neck was afflicted. It could hardly breathe, its ribs were shaky, its lungs were afflicted, its heart was afflicted, its bowels were afflicted. With its hand and its lolling head it could not put bread into its mouth; its spine and head were

[32] A mythical site somewhere near ancient Sumeria.
[33] The water god.
[34] The great sea beneath the world and the underworld, also called apsû.
[35] An ancient water goddess said to be either the mother or the grandmother of Enki; eventually, Enki took over most of her functions.
[36] The underground source of fresh water, see Reading 1.
[37] Or Ninhursag, a mountain and fertility goddess, also goddess of pregnancy.
[38] The storm god, Babylonian Marduk, the only god who was in contact with his father An, the king of the gods.
[39] Another name for Enki.
[40] God of diseases.
[41] Nippur, the city of Enlil.
[42] A handicapped person.

dislocated. Enki fashioned it in this way. Enki said to Ninmaḫ: "For your creatures I have decreed a fate, I have given them their daily bread. Now, you should decree a fate for my creature, give him his daily bread too." Ninmaḫ looked at Umul and turned to him. She went nearer to Umul and asked him questions but he could not speak. She offered him bread to eat but he could not reach out for it. Standing up he could not sit down, could not lie down, he could not eat bread. Ninmaḫ answered Enki: "The man you have fashioned is neither alive nor dead. He cannot support himself." Enki answered Ninmaḫ: "I decreed a fate for the first man with the weak hands, I decreed a fate for the man who could not hold back his urine, I gave him bread. I decreed a fate for the woman who could not give birth, I gave her bread. I decreed the fate for the one with neither penis nor vagina on its body, I gave it bread." Ninmaḫ could not rival the great Lord Enki. Father Enki, your praise is sweet!

3

THE FLOOD STORY: *EPIC OF GILGAMESH*, TABLET XI

The Sumerian flood story, as reported in the *Epic of Gilgamesh*, is preserved on this cuneiform tablet written in the seventh century BCE and found in the nineteenth century in the library at the Assyrian capital city of Nineveh. Now preserved in the British Museum in London.

The Sumerian *Epic of Gilgamesh*, preserved on clay tablets inscribed with cuneiform text, is one of the oldest surviving works of literature. The earliest known examples of its current full form, written in cuneiform script on clay tablets, date to the Old Babylonian period, but its constituent parts go well back into the Sumerian period. Gilgamesh was an apparently historical king of the city of Uruk who reigned in the early third millennium BCE. A famous epic tale about him later developed. After the death of his friend Enkidu, Gilgamesh attempted to restore him to life by visiting Utnapishtim, who had survived a great flood and been granted immortality by the gods. Utnapishtim provided Gilgamesh with a lengthy discussion of the flood.

Source: Maureen Gallery Kovacs, *The Epic of Gilgamesh* (Stanford, CA: Stanford University Press, 1989), 95–110. Electronic edition by Wolf Carhanan (1998).

Utnapishtim spoke to Gilgamesh, saying, I will reveal to you, Gilgamesh, a thing that is hidden, a secret of the gods I will tell you! Shuruppak, a city that you surely know, situated on the banks of the Euphrates, that city was very old, and there were gods inside it. The hearts of the Great Gods moved them to inflict the Flood. Their Father An uttered the oath of secrecy, valiant Enlil[43] was their adviser, Ninurta[44] was their Chamberlain, Ennugi[45] was their Minister of Canals. Ea,[46] the Clever Prince, was under oath with them so he repeated their talk to the reed house:[47] "Reed house, reed house! Wall, wall! O man of Shuruppak, son of Ubartutu[48]: Tear down the house and build a boat! Abandon wealth and seek living beings! Spurn possessions and keep alive living beings! Make all living beings go up into the boat. The boat that you are to build, its dimensions must measure equal to each other: its length must correspond to its width. Roof it over like the abzu.[49]" I laid out her exterior. It was a field in area, its walls were each 10 times 12 cubits[50] in height, the sides of its top were of equal length, 10 times 12 cubits each. I provided it with six decks, thus dividing it into seven levels. The inside of it I divided into nine compartments. I drove plugs to keep out water in its middle part. I gave the workmen ale, beer, oil, and wine, so they could make a party like the New Year's Festival. The boat was finished by sunset. The launching was very difficult. All the living beings that I had I loaded on it, I had all my kith and kin go up into the boat, all the beasts and animals of the field and the craftsmen I had go up. Shamash had set a stated time: "Go inside the boat, seal the entry!" That stated time had arrived. The weather was frightful to behold! I went into the boat and sealed the entry. Just as dawn began to glow there arose from the horizon a black cloud. Adad[51] rumbled inside of it. Erragal[52] pulled out the mooring poles.

Ninurta made the dikes overflow, the Anunnaki[53] lifted up the torches, setting the land ablaze with their flare. Stunned shock over Adad's deeds overtook the heavens, and turned to blackness all that had been light. All day long the South Wind blew, submerging the mountain in water, overwhelming the people like an attack. No one could see his fellow, they could not recognize each other in the torrent. The gods were frightened by the Flood. Ishtar shrieked like a woman in childbirth, "How could I say evil things in the Assembly of the Gods, ordering a catastrophe to destroy my people? No sooner have I given birth to my dear people than they fill the sea like so many fish!" Six days and seven nights came the wind and flood, the storm flattening the land.

When the seventh day arrived, the storm was pounding, the flood was a war, struggling with itself like a woman writhing in labor. The sea calmed, fell still, the whirlwind and flood stopped. I looked around all day long. Quiet had set in and all the human beings had turned to clay. The terrain was as flat as a roof. I opened a vent and fresh air fell upon the side of my nose. I fell to my knees and sat weeping, tears streaming down the side of my nose. I looked around for coastlines in the expanse of the sea, and at twelve leagues[54] there emerged a region of land. On Mt.

[43] The storm god who governed life on earth.

[44] God of hunting and warfare.

[45] An attendant of Enlil.

[46] Another name for Enki, the water god.

[47] So as not to violate his oath not to tell anyone.

[48] The last king of Shuruppak before the flood.

[49] The underground watery dwelling place of the water god Enki.

[50] A unit of length about eighteen inches (forty-six centimeters).

[51] The storm god.

[52] A god of the underworld.

[53] The gods.

Nimush[55] the boat lodged firm. When a seventh day arrived I sent forth a dove and released it. The dove went off, but came back to me. No perch was visible so it circled back to me. I sent forth a swallow and released it. The swallow went off, but came back to me; no perch was visible so it circled back to me. I sent forth a raven and released it. The raven went off, and saw the waters slither back.

It eats, it scratches, it bobs, but does not circle back to me. Then I sent out everything in all directions and I offered incense in front of the mountain-ziggurat. The gods smelled the sweet savor, and collected like flies over a sacrifice. Just then Beletili[56] arrived and said, "The gods may come to the incense offering, but Enlil may not come to the incense offering, because without considering he brought about the Flood and consigned my people to annihilation." Just then Enlil arrived. He saw the boat and was filled with rage at the Igigi[57] gods: "Where did a living being escape? No man was to survive the annihilation!" Ea[58] spoke to Valiant Enlil, saying: "How, how could you bring about a Flood without consideration? Charge the violation to the violator. It was not I who revealed the secret of the Great Gods, I only made a dream appear to Atrahasis,[59] and thus he heard the secret of the gods." Enlil went up inside the boat and, grasping my hand, made me go up. He had my wife go up and kneel by my side. He touched our forehead and, standing between us, he blessed us: "Previously Utnapishtim was a human being. But now let Utnapishtim and his wife become like us, the gods! Let Utnapishtim reside far away, at the Mouth of the Rivers."

[54] A unit of distance, about 3.5 miles (5.6 km).

[55] Also called Mt. Nisir. Identified as Pir Magrun, a mountain in Kurdistan.

[56] The same as Ninmaḫ and Ninhursag, a mountain and fertility goddess.

[57] The senior gods.

[58] Enki.

[59] An alternate name for Utnapishtim.

II: EGYPTIAN ACCOUNTS

Several different Egyptian accounts of the creation are preserved, primarily on papyrus documents dating to 2500 BCE and later. Some have been found in the tombs that Egyptians believed would assist them in enjoying the afterlife, whereas others survived in trash heaps.

4

THE CREATION STORY: "A BOOK OF KNOWING THE EVOLUTIONS OF RA"

The god Ra, represented by the sun disk, with the falcon head of the god Horus and the ostrich feather of Ma'at, goddess of divine justice. Preserved in the Louvre Museum, Paris.

This version of the Egyptian creation story is only preserved in a sixteen-foot-long papyrus roll written in the late fourth century BCE and discovered near Thebes in the early 1860s. It now is in the British Museum. The story is told by the god Neb-er-tcher, the god of the universe, who was born out of Nu, the watery abyss.

Source: E. A. Wallis Budge, *Legends of the Gods* (London: Kegan Paul, 1912), 2–13.

These are the words of the god Neb-er-tcher[60] spoke after he had come into being: "I am the creator of what hath come into being, and I myself came into being under the form of the god Khepera,[61] and I came into being in primeval time. I came into being in the form of Khepera, and I am the creator of what did come into being, that is to say, I formed myself out of the primeval matter, and I made and formed myself out of the substance that existed in primeval time. I have done my will in everything in this earth. I have spread myself abroad therein, and I have made strong my hand. I was one by myself, for the gods had not been brought forth, and I had emitted from myself neither Shu[62] nor Tefnut.[63] I brought my own name into my mouth as a word of power, and I forthwith came into being under the form of things that are and under the form of Khepera. I came into being from out of primeval matter, and from the beginning I appeared under the form of the multitudinous things that exist; nothing whatsoever existed at that time in this earth, and it was I who made whatsoever was made.

I was one by myself, and there was no other being who worked with me in that place. I made all the things under the forms of which I appeared then by means of the Soul-God that I raised into firmness at that time from out of Nu,[64] from a state of inertness. I found no place whatsoever there whereon I could stand, I worked by the power of a spell by means of my heart, I laid a foundation for things by Ma'at,[65] and whatsoever was made, I made. I was one by myself, and I laid the foundation of things by means of my heart, and I made the other things that came into being, and the things of Khepera that were made were manifold, and their offspring came into existence from the things to which they gave birth. I it was who emitted Shu, and I it was who emitted Tefnut, and from being the one god I became three gods; the two other gods who came into being on this earth sprang from me, and Shu and Tefnut were raised up from out of Nu in which they were. Now behold, they brought my Eye[66] to me after two henti periods[67] since the time when they went forth from me.

I gathered together my members, which had appeared in my own body, and afterward I had sex with my closed hand, and my will came unto me from out of my hand, and the seed poured into my own mouth, and I emitted from myself the gods Shu and Tefnut, and so from being the one god, thus the two other gods who came into being on this earth sprang from me, and Shu and Tefnut were raised up from out of Nu in which they were.

My father Nu said: "Shu and Tefnut covered up my Eye[68] with the plant-like clouds that were behind them for very many henti periods." Then Shu and Tefnut rejoiced from out of the inert watery mass wherein they and I were, and they brought to me my Eye. Now after these things I gathered together my members, and I wept over them, and plants and creeping things sprang up from the tears that I let fall. I cried out to my Eye, and men and women sprang into being from the tears that came forth from my Eye.

Then I bestowed upon my Eye the uraeus[69] of fire, and it raged at me when another Eye[70] came and grew up in its place, whereupon I endowed the second Eye with some of the splendor that I had made for the first, and I made the first to occupy its place in my Face. Its vigorous power fell on the plants, on the plants that I had placed there, and it set order among them, and it took up its place in my face, and it does rule the whole earth.

---

[60] More usually called Atum.

[61] A sun god, the god of creation and rebirth.

[62] God of the air.

[63] Goddess of moisture.

[64] Or Nun, the watery abyss and chaos that existed before all time and from which the world and universe were created.

[65] Divine truth, justice, and order.

[66] The sun, which sees everything.

[67] Periods of sixty years each.

[68] The sun, which often is depicted as a large all-seeing eye, often equated with the god Ra.

[69] A rearing cobra, the sign of royalty and divine authority.

[70] The moon.

Then Shu and Tefnut brought forth Geb[71] and Nut;[72] and Geb and Nut brought forth brought forth Osiris,[73] and Heru-khenti-An-maa,[74] and Set,[75] and Isis,[76] and Nephthys[77] and behold, they have produced offspring, and have created multitudinous children in this earth, by means of the beings that came into existence from the creatures that they produced. They invoke my name, and they overthrow their enemies, and they make words of power for the overthrowing of Apep,[78] over whose hands and arms Aker[79] keeps ward. Apep's hands and arms shall not exist, his feet and legs shall not exist, and he is chained in one place while Ra inflicts upon him the blows that are decreed for him. He is thrown upon his accursed back, his face is slit open by reason of the evil that he has done, and he shall remain upon his accursed back."

[71] God of the earth.

[72] Goddess of the heavens.

[73] Subsequently the god of the underworld, who judged the dead.

[74] A form of the god Horus.

[75] A storm god and god of the red desert land, he killed and dismembered Osiris.

[76] The most worshipped goddess of ancient Egypt, wife of Osiris and mother of Horus; Isis symbolized life and rebirth and represented the throne of the pharaoh.

[77] A goddess involved in funeral ceremony.

[78] Apophis, an evil snake god, enemy of Ra.

[79] An ancient god, the god of the horizon.

III: GREEK ACCOUNTS

There are several Greek versions of the creation of the universe and humanity. Two of these versions are given by Hesiod and in "The Library."

5

THE CREATION OF THE UNIVERSE AND THE TITANS: HESIOD, *THEOGONY*, LINES 104–225

In this Roman copy of a Greek original relief sculpture, Gaia hands over one of her children to be eaten by Uranus.

Hesiod of Askra in Boeotia in east central Greece lived in the eighth century BCE and was one of the earliest Greek writers. He authored a long and detailed poem called the *Theogony* ("The Birth of the Gods") about the origin of the universe. Like similar stories told elsewhere, it embodies a succession of sons who either inherit or seize power from their fathers.

Source: Hugh G. Evelyn-White, *Hesiod, the Homeric Hymns and Homerica* (Cambridge, MA: Harvard University Press, 1924), 2–64.

Hail, children of Zeus![80] Tell how at the first gods and earth came to be, and rivers, and the boundless sea with its raging swell, and the gleaming stars, and the wide heaven above. These things declare to me from the beginning, ye Muses. Verily at the first Chaos[81] came to be, but next wide-bosomed Gaia.[82] From Chaos came forth Erebus[83] and black Night; and of Night were born Aether[84] and Day, whom Night conceived and bore from union in love with Erebus. And Gaia first bore starry Uranus,[85] equal to herself, to cover her on every side, and to be an ever-sure abiding-place for the blessed gods. Afterward she lay with Uranus and bore deep-swirling Ocean, Coeus and Crius, and Hyperion and Iapetus, Theia and Rhea, Themis and Mnemosyne, and gold-crowned Phoebe, and lovely Tethys.[86] After them was born Cronus[87] the wily, youngest and most terrible of her children, and he hated his lusty sire. And again, she bore the Cyclopes; in all else they were like the gods, but one eye only was set in the midst of their foreheads. And again, three other sons were born of Gaia and Uranus, Cottus and Briareos and Gyes.[88] From their shoulders sprang a hundred arms, and each had fifty heads upon his shoulders on their strong limbs. Of all the children, these[89] were the most terrible, and they were hated by their own father. And he used to hide them all away in a secret place[90] of Gaia as soon as each was born, and would not suffer them to come up into the light. But vast Gaia groaned within, and from grey flint she shaped a great sickle, and told her plan to her dear sons: "My children, gotten of a sinful father, we should punish the vile outrage of your father." But fear seized them all, and none of them uttered a word.

Then great Cronus the wily took courage and answered his dear mother: "Mother, I will undertake to do this deed, for I reverence not our father of evil name." Vast Gaia rejoiced and hid him in an ambush, and put in his hands the jagged sickle, and revealed to him the whole plot. And Uranus came, bringing on night and longing for love, and he lay about Gaia spreading himself full upon her. Then the son from his ambush took the great long sickle with jagged teeth and swiftly lopped off his own father's testicles and cast them away to fall behind him. And not vainly did they fall from his hand; for all the bloody drops that gushed forth Gaia received, and she bore the Furies,[91] to wit, Alecto, Tisiphone, and Megaera, and the great Giants[92] and the Nymphs.[93] And as soon as he had cut off the testicles with flint and cast them into the surging sea, a white foam spread around them and in it there came forth an awful and lovely goddess. Her gods and men call Aphrodite,[94] and with her went Eros.[95] Also she bore the ruthless avenging Fates,[96] Clotho and Lachesis and Atropos, who give men at their birth both evil and good to have, and they pursue the transgressions of men and of gods. Also deadly Night bore Nemesis[97] to afflict mortal men, and after her, Deceit and Friendship and hateful Age and hard-hearted Strife.[98]

[80] The Muses were the children of Zeus (Roman Jupiter), the king of the Olympian gods. They represented branches of the arts and brought inspiration to writers.
[81] The formless emptiness that existed before the universe was created.
[82] The Earth.
[83] Darkness.
[84] The upper atmosphere that was breathed by the gods.
[85] The Heavens.
[86] The Titans, several of whom gave their names to the moons of the planet Saturn.
[87] Saturn to the Romans.
[88] The Hecatonchires, that is, the "Hundred-Armed-Ones."
[89] That is, the Cyclopes and the Hecatonchires.
[90] Tartarus, a region deep below the underworld used for the imprisonment and punishment of the worst wrongdoers.
[91] Avenging goddesses who pursued and punished disrespectful people.
[92] A race that later engaged in war with the gods.
[93] Young Greek nature goddesses who inhabit the woods.
[94] Goddess of love; Roman Venus.
[95] Roman Cupid; the god of sexual desire.
[96] Goddesses depicted as elderly women who control human destiny: Clotho spun the thread of life, Lachesis measured how long it would be, and Atropos cut it off at the end.
[97] Goddess of divine retribution, who punishes mortals who are guilty of hubris (excessive pride).
[98] Eris, Roman Discordia; the cause of discord and warfare among the Greeks.

6

THE BATTLES BETWEEN THE GODS AND THE TITANS AND GIANTS: PSEUDO-APOLLODORUS, "THE LIBRARY"

In this section of the frieze depicting the Battle between the Gods and Giants on the great Altar of Pergamum, the Fates club to death the giant Agrius. Preserved in the Pergamon Museum in Berlin.

One of the classic accounts of Greek mythology was the defeat of the Titans and Giants by Zeus and the Olympian gods. In the "Titanomachy" ("Battle of the Titans"), the Olympians defeated the Titans and imprisoned them in Tartarus. Subsequently, the Olympians were attacked by the Giants, and in the great "Gigantomachy," or "Battle of the Giants," the Giants likewise were defeated. The story presented here is preserved in a massive summary of Greek myth and legend known simply as the Bibliotheca ("The Library") that often is attributed to an otherwise unknown Greek author, Apollodorus, although other sources attribute it to Castor of Rhodes. It was compiled sometime between the first century BCE and the second century CE. It picks up after Cronus has castrated his father Uranus and taken over the position of king of the gods (see Reading 5).

Source: James George Frazer, trans., *Apollodorus, The Library*, 2 vols. (Cambridge, MA: Harvard University Press; London, Heinemann, 1921).

Cronus again bound and shut up the Cyclopes and Hecatonchires in Tartarus,[99] and wedded his sister Rhea; and because both Gaia and Uranus foretold that he would be dethroned by his own son, he used to swallow his offspring at birth. His firstborn Hestia[100] he swallowed, then Demeter[101] and Hera,[102] and after them Hades[103] and Poseidon.[104] Enraged at this, Rhea repaired to Crete, when she was big with Zeus, and brought him forth in a cave of Dicte. She gave him to the Curetes[105] and to the nymphs Adrastia and Ida, daughters of Melisseus, to nurse. So these nymphs fed the child on the milk of the goat Amalthea; and the Curetes in arms guarded the babe in the cave, clashing their spears on their shields in order that Cronus might not hear the child's voice. But Rhea wrapped a stone in swaddling clothes and gave it to Cronus to swallow, as if it were the newborn child. But when Zeus was full-grown, he took Metis,[106] daughter of Ocean, to help him, and she gave Cronus a drug to swallow, which forced him to disgorge first the stone and then the children whom he had swallowed, and with their aid Zeus waged the war against Cronus and the Titans.

They fought for ten years, and Gaia prophesied victory to Zeus if he should have as allies those who had been hurled down to Tartarus. So he loosed their bonds. And the Cyclopes then gave Zeus thunder and lightning and a thunderbolt, and on Hades they bestowed a helmet and on Poseidon a trident. Armed with these weapons the gods overcame the Titans, shut them up in Tartarus, and appointed the Hecatonchires as their guards. They themselves cast lots for the sovereignty, and to Zeus was allotted the dominion of the sky, to Poseidon the dominion of the sea, and to Hades the dominion in the underworld.

[99] The deepest section of the underworld, where the most dangerous creatures were imprisoned.
[100] Goddess of the hearth; Roman Vesta.
[101] Goddess of the harvest; Roman Ceres.
[102] Queen of the gods, wife of Zeus; Roman Juno.
[103] God of the underworld; Roman Pluto.
[104] God of the sea; Roman Neptune.
[105] Nine mythical dancers of Crete.
[106] Goddess of wisdom, thought, and cunning.

Now Zeus wedded Hera and begat Hebe,[107] Ilithyia,[108] and Ares,[109] but he had intercourse with many women, both mortals and immortals. By Themis, daughter of Uranus, he had daughters, the Seasons, to wit, Peace, Order, and Justice; also the Fates, to wit, Clotho, Lachesis, and Atropos[110]; by Dione he had Aphrodite[111]; by Eurynome, daughter of Ocean, he had the Graces,[112] to wit, Aglaia, Euphrosyne, and Thalia; by Styx[113] he had Persephone[114]; and by Mnemosyne[115] he had the Muses, first Calliope, then Clio, Melpomene, Euterpe, Erato, Terpsichore, Urania, Thalia, and Polymnia.[116] And Alcmene was joined in love with Zeus who drives the clouds and bore mighty Hercules.[117] Hera gave birth to Hephaestus[118] without intercourse with the other sex. Zeus had intercourse with Metis, who turned into many shapes in order to avoid his embraces. When she was with child, Zeus swallowed her, because Gaia had said that, after giving birth to the maiden who was then in her womb, Metis would bear a son who should be the Lord of heaven. From fear of that Zeus swallowed her. And when the time

[107] Goddess of youth; Roman Juventas.
[108] Goddess of childbirth; Roman Lucina.
[109] The god of war; Roman Mars.
[110] In the version cited in Reading 5, Rhea was the mother of the Fates.
[111] In the version cited in Reading 5, Aphrodite was born out of sea foam.
[112] Graces, known in Greek as the Charites, were minor female goddesses connected to nature and fertility.
[113] The personification of one of the rivers of the underworld.
[114] Persephone more usually was thought to be the daughter of Zeus and the harvest goddess Demeter. She became the queen of the underworld, which created an association between her and the underworld river, the Styx.
[115] Memory.
[116] Respectively, the Muses of epic poetry, history, tragedy, elegiac poetry and music, lyric poetry, dance, astronomy, comedy, and sacred poetry.
[117] The most important of the Greek demi-gods, the offspring of gods and humans.
[118] God of craftsmanship.

came for the birth to take place, Prometheus[119] smote the head of Zeus with an axe, and Athena,[120] fully armed, leaped up from the top of his head. Latona for her intrigue with Zeus was hunted by Hera over the whole earth, until she came to Delos[121] and brought forth first Artemis,[122] by the help of whose midwifery she afterward gave birth to Apollo.[123]

But Gaia, vexed on account of the Titans,[124] released the Giants, whom she had had by Uranus. These were matchless in the bulk of their bodies and invincible in their might; terrible of aspect did they appear, with long locks drooping from their head and chin, and with the scales of dragons for feet. And they darted rocks and burning oaks at the sky. Now the gods had an oracle[125] that none of the giants could perish at the hand of gods, but that with the help of a mortal they would be made an end of. Learning of this, Gaia sought for a method to prevent the giants from being destroyed even by a mortal. But Zeus forbade the Dawn and the Moon and the Sun to shine, and then by means of Athena summoned Hercules to his help.[126] Hercules first shot Alcyoneus with an arrow. Zeus inspired Porphyrion[127] with lust for Hera, and when he tore her robes, she called for help, and Hercules shot him dead with an arrow. Ephialtes was shot by Apollo with an arrow in his left eye and by Hercules in his right; Eurytus was killed by Dionysus,[128] and Clytius by Hecate,[129] and Mimas by Hephaestus. Athena flayed Pallas and used his skin to shield her own body in the fight. Polybotes was chased to Cos; and Poseidon, breaking off that piece of the island that is called Nisyrum, threw it on him. And Hermes[130] slew Hippolytus, and Artemis slew Gration. And the Fates killed Agrius and Thoas. The other giants Zeus smote and destroyed with thunderbolts and all of them Hercules shot with arrows as they were dying.

When the gods had overcome the giants, Gaia, still more enraged, had intercourse with Tartarus[131] and brought forth Typhon in Cilicia,[132] a hybrid between man and beast. In size and strength he surpassed all the offspring of Gaia. As far as the thighs he was of human shape and of such prodigious bulk that he outtopped all the mountains, and his head often brushed the stars. One of his hands reached out to the west and the other to the east, and from them projected a hundred dragons' heads. From the thighs downward he had huge coils of vipers, which when drawn out, reached to his very head and emitted a loud hissing. His body was all winged: unkempt hair streamed on the wind from his head and cheeks; and fire flashed from his eyes. Such and so great was Typhon when, hurling kindled rocks, he made for the very heaven with hissings and shouts, spouting a great jet of fire from his mouth. When the gods saw him rushing at heaven, they made for Egypt in flight. But Zeus, riding in a chariot of winged horses, pelted Typhon with thunderbolts and pursued him to Thrace,[133] and in fighting at Mount Haemus Tryphon heaved whole mountains. But when these recoiled on him through the force of the thunderbolt, a stream of blood gushed out on the mountain. And when he started to flee through the Sicilian sea, Zeus cast Mount Etna[134] in Sicily upon him. That is a huge mountain, from which down to this day they say that blasts of fire issue from the thunderbolts that were thrown.

---

[119] The son of the Titan Iapetus; for revealing the use of fire to humans he was eternally punished by Zeus (see Reading 7).

[120] Goddess of wisdom.

[121] An island in the Aegean Sea.

[122] Goddess of hunting and the moon.

[123] God of music, prophecy, and the sun.

[124] Because they were her children and had been imprisoned.

[125] A prophecy.

[126] One by one the Giants then were killed.

[127] The greatest of the Giants.

[128] God of wine.

[129] A goddess of magic.

[130] The messenger of the gods.

[131] The personification of the deepest underworld.

[132] A region of southern Anatolia.

[133] A mountainous Balkan region northeast of Greece.

[134] A famous volcano in eastern Sicily.

7

THE CREATION OF HUMANS: PSEUDO-APOLLODORUS, "THE LIBRARY," BOOKS 1.1.5–1.6.3

A Greek vase of the fourth century BCE depicts Pandora, the first woman, who was created by Zeus to torment humanity. In other stories, Pandora opened the jar (often wrongly thought to be a box) that released all the evils that afflict humanity, including work and disease. Preserved in the Archaeological Museum of Catalonia in Barcelona, Spain.

The Greek version of the creation of humanity was recounted only in passing, in the context of another story, in the massive mythological compendium known as the "Bibliotheca" ("Library"). With typical ancient Greek misogyny, the same tale tells of the origin of human miseries.

Source: James George Frazer, trans., *Apollodorus,* "The Library, 2 vols. (Cambridge, MA: Harvard University Press; London, Heinemann, 1921).

Now to the Titans were born offspring: to Iapetus and Asia was born Atlas, who has the sky on his shoulders, and Prometheus, and Epimetheus, and Menoetius, he whom Zeus in the battle with the Titans smote with a thunderbolt and hurled down to Tartarus. Prometheus molded men out of water and earth but Zeus would not give the power of unwearying fire to the race of mortal men who live on the earth. But the noble son of Iapetus outwitted him and stole the far-seen gleam of unwearying fire in a hollow fennel stalk. When Zeus learned of it, he ordered Hephaestus to nail his body to Mount Caucasus,[135]

[135] The highest mountain in Europe, now Mt. Elbrus in the Caucasus Mountains, located between the Black and Caspian seas.

which is a Scythian[136] mountain. On it Prometheus was nailed and kept bound for many years. Every day an eagle swooped on him and devoured the lobes of his liver, which grew by night. That was the penalty that Prometheus paid for the theft of fire until Hercules afterward released him.

And Zeus who thunders on high was angered when he saw among men the far-seen ray of fire. Forthwith he made an evil thing for men as the price of fire, for, as the son of Cronus willed, the very famous Hephaestus formed of earth the likeness of a shy maiden, Pandora.[137] And the goddess bright-eyed Athena girded and clothed her with silvery raiment, and down from her head she spread with her hands a broidered veil, a wonder to see; and she, Pallas[138] Athene, put about her head lovely garlands, flowers of new-grown herbs. Also she put upon her head a crown of gold that the very famous Hephaestus made himself and worked with his own hands as a favor to Zeus his father. On it was much curious work, wonderful to see; for of the many creatures that the land and sea rear up, he put most upon it, wonderful things, like living beings with voices: and great beauty shone out from it. But when he had made the beautiful evil to be the price for the blessing, he brought her out, delighting in the finery that the bright-eyed daughter[139] of a mighty father had given her, to the place where the other gods and men were. And wonder took hold of the deathless gods and mortal men when they saw that which was sheer guile, not to be withstood by men. For from her is the race of women and female kind, of her is the deadly race of women who live among mortal men to their great trouble, no helpmeets in hateful poverty, but only in wealth. And as in thatched hives bees feed the drones whose nature is to do mischief—by day and throughout the day until the sun goes down the bees are busy and lay the white combs, while the drones stay at home in the covered hives and reap the toil of others into their own bellies—even so Zeus who thunders on high made women to be an evil to mortal men, with a nature to do evil. And he gave them a second evil to be the price for the good they had: whoever avoids marriage and the sorrows that women cause, and will not wed, reaches deadly old age without anyone to tend his years, and although he at least has no lack of livelihood while he lives, yet, when he is dead, his kinsfolk divide his possessions among them. And as for the man who chooses the lot of marriage and takes a good wife suited to his mind, evil continually contends with good; for whoever happens to have mischievous children lives always with unceasing grief in his spirit and heart within him; and this evil cannot be healed.

---

[136] For the Scythians, see Reading 68.

[137] A Greek word meaning "All Gifts."

[138] An epithet taken by Athena after she accidentally killed her childhood friend, Pallas.

[139] The goddess Athena, another of whose epithets was Glaukopis, or "bright-eyed."

8

THE FLOOD: PSEUDO-APOLLODORUS, "THE LIBRARY," 1.7.2

After being saved from Zeus's great flood by constructing a large floating chest, Deucalion and Pyrrha repopulated the world by throwing behind their backs stones that turned into women and men, as depicted in this nineteenth-century relief in the Parc del Laberint d'Horta in Barcelona, Spain.

"The Library" also includes a brief Greek version of the flood story that was so common in the ancient world, where a powerful god decides to destroy humanity but does not quite succeed.

Source: James George Frazer, trans., *Apollodorus,* "The Library, 2 vols. (Cambridge, MA: Harvard University Press; London, Heinemann, 1921).

And Prometheus had a son Deucalion. He reigning in the regions about Phthia,[140] married Pyrrha, the daughter of Epimetheus and Pandora, the first woman fashioned by the gods. And when Zeus would destroy the men of the Bronze Age, Deucalion by the advice of Prometheus constructed a chest, and having stored it with provisions he embarked in it with Pyrrha. But Zeus by pouring heavy rain from heaven flooded the greater part of Greece, so that all men were destroyed, except a few who fled to the high mountains in the neighborhood. It was then that the mountains in Thessaly parted, and that all the world outside the Isthmus and Peloponnese was overwhelmed. But Deucalion, floating in the chest over the sea for nine days and as many nights, drifted to Parnassus,[141] and there, when the rain ceased, he landed and sacrificed to Zeus, the god of Escape. And Zeus sent Hermes to him and allowed him to choose what he would, and he chose to get men. And at the bidding of Zeus he took up stones and threw them over his head, and the stones that Deucalion threw became men, and the stones that Pyrrha threw became women. Hence people were called metaphorically people (*laos*) from *laas*, "a stone." And Deucalion had children by Pyrrha, first Hellen, whose father some say was Zeus, and second Amphictyon, who reigned over Attica after Cranaus[142]; and third a daughter Protogenia, who became the mother of Aethlius by Zeus.

IV: JEWISH ACCOUNTS

Jewish tradition also included accounts of the creation of the world, the creation of humans, and a great flood, all preserved beginning around 400 BCE in the Hebrew Bible. It has many parallels with Mesopotamian accounts.

9

THE CREATION STORY: GENESIS 1–7

At the beginning of the book of Genesis in Jewish scripture are two different versions, presented back to back, of how God created the world and humans.

Source: The Hebrew Bible, Genesis 1–7.

[140] In northern Greece; the kingdom of the Greek hero Achilles.

[141] A mountain in central Greece.

[142] The legendary second king of Athens.

[First creation story, including creation of men and women together]

In the beginning God created the heaven and the earth. And the earth was without form, and void; and darkness was upon the face of the deep. And the Spirit of God moved upon the face of the waters. And God said, "Let there be light": and there was light. And God saw the light, that it was good, and God divided the light from the darkness. And God called the light Day, and the darkness he called Night. And the evening and the morning were the first day. And God said, "Let there be a firmament in the midst of the waters, and let it divide the waters from the waters." And God made the firmament, and divided the waters that were under the firmament from the waters that were above the firmament, and it was so. And God called the firmament Heaven. And the evening and the morning were the second day. And God said, "Let the waters under the heaven be gathered together unto one place, and let the dry land appear," and it was so. And God called the dry land Earth; and the gathering together of the waters he called the Seas, and God saw that it was good. And God said, "Let the earth bring forth grass, the herb yielding seed, and the fruit tree yielding fruit after its kind, whose seed is in itself, upon the earth," and it was so. And the earth brought forth grass, and herb yielding seed after its kind, and the tree yielding fruit, whose seed was in itself, after his kind, and God saw that it was good. And the evening and the morning were the third day. And God said, "Let there be lights in the firmament of the heaven to divide the day from the night; and let them be for signs, and for seasons, and for days, and years, and let them be for lights in the firmament of the heaven to give light upon the earth," and it was so. And God made two great lights; the greater light to rule the day, and the lesser light to rule the night; he also made the stars. And God set them in the firmament of the heaven to give light upon the earth, and to rule over the day and over the night, and to divide the light from the darkness, and God saw that it was good. And the evening and the morning were the fourth day. And God said, "Let the waters bring forth abundantly the moving creature that hath life, and fowl that may fly above the earth in the open firmament of heaven." And God created great whales, and every living creature that moveth, which the waters brought forth abundantly, after their kind, and every winged fowl after its kind, and God saw that it was good. And God blessed them, saying, "Be fruitful, and multiply, and fill the waters in the seas, and let fowl multiply in the earth." And the evening and the morning were the fifth day. And God said, "Let the earth bring forth the living creature after its kind, cattle, and creeping thing, and beast of the earth after its kind," and it was so. And God made the beast of the earth after his kind, and cattle after their kind, and every thing that creepeth upon the earth after his kind, and God saw that it was good.

And God said, "Let us make man in our image, after our likeness, and let him have dominion over the fish of the sea, and over the fowl of the air, and over the cattle, and over all the earth, and over every creeping thing that creepeth upon the earth." So God created man in his own image, in the image of God he created him; male and female, he created them. And God blessed them, and God said unto them, "Be fruitful, and multiply, and replenish the earth, and subdue it, and have dominion over the fish of the sea, and over the fowl of the air, and over every living thing that moveth upon the earth." And God said, "Behold, I have given you every herb bearing seed that is upon the face of all the earth, and every tree in which is the fruit of a tree yielding seed; to you it shall be for meat. And to every beast of the earth, and to every fowl of the air, and to every thing that creepeth upon the earth, wherein there is life, I have given every green herb for meat, and it was so." And God saw every thing that he had made, and, behold, it was very good. And the evening and the morning were the sixth day.

Thus the heavens and the earth were finished, and all the host of them. And on the seventh day God ended his work that he had made; and he rested on the seventh day from all his work that he had made. And God blessed the seventh day, and sanctified it, because that in it he had rested from all his work that God created and made.

[Second creation story, including creation of men and women separately]
These are the generations of the heavens and of the earth when they were created, in the day that the Lord God made the earth and the heavens, And every plant of the field before it was in the earth, and every herb of the field before it grew, for the Lord God had not caused it to rain upon the earth, and there was not a man to till the ground. But there went up a mist from the earth, and watered the whole face of the ground.

And the Lord God formed man of the dust of the ground, and breathed into his nostrils the breath of life; and man became a living soul. And the Lord God planted a garden eastward in Eden; and there he put the man whom he had formed. And out of the ground made the Lord God to grow every tree that is pleasant to the sight, and good for food; the tree of life also in the midst of the garden, and the tree of knowledge of good and evil. And the Lord God took the man, and put him into the garden of Eden to dress it and to keep it. And the Lord God commanded the man, saying, "Of every tree of the garden thou mayest freely eat, but of the tree of the knowledge of good and evil, thou shalt not eat of it, for in the day that thou eatest thereof thou shalt surely die." And the Lord God said, "It is not good that the man should be alone; I will make him a helpmeet for him." And out of the ground the Lord God formed every beast of the field, and every fowl of the air; and brought them unto Adam to see what he would call them, and whatsoever Adam called every living creature, that was the name thereof.

And Adam gave names to all cattle, and to the fowl of the air, and to every beast of the field; but for Adam there was not found a helpmeet for him. And the Lord God caused a deep sleep to fall upon Adam, and he slept, and he took one of his ribs, and closed up the flesh instead thereof, and the rib, which the Lord God had taken from man, made he a woman, and brought her unto the man. And Adam said, "This is now bone of my bones, and flesh of my flesh; she shall be called woman, because she was taken out of man. Therefore shall a man leave his father and his mother, and shall cleave unto his wife, and they shall be one flesh." And they were both naked, the man and his wife, and were not ashamed.

10

THE FLOOD STORY: GENESIS 8

The Jewish flood story preserved in the Hebrew Old Testament repeats many of the details in the much older Mesopotamian flood story.

Source: The Hebrew Bible, Genesis 8.

And God saw that the wickedness of man was great in the earth, and that every imagination of the thoughts of his heart was only evil continually. And it repented the Lord that he had made man on the earth, and it grieved him at his heart. And the Lord said, "I will destroy man whom I have created from the face of the earth; both man, and beast, and the creeping thing, and the fowls of the air; for it repenteth me that I have made them." But Noah found grace in the eyes of the Lord and God said unto Noah, "The end of all flesh is come before me, for the earth is filled with violence through them, and, behold, I will destroy them with the earth. Make thee an ark[143] of gopher wood; rooms shalt thou make in the ark, and shalt pitch it within and without with pitch. And this is the fashion that thou shalt make it of: The length of the ark shall be three hundred cubits,[144] the breadth of it fifty cubits, and the height of it thirty cubits. A window shalt thou make to the ark, and in a cubit shalt thou finish it above; and the door of the ark shalt thou set in the side thereof; with lower, second, and third storeys shalt thou make it. And, behold, I bring a flood of waters upon the earth, to destroy all flesh, wherein is the breath of life, from under heaven; and every thing that is in the earth shall die. But with thee will I establish my covenant; and thou shalt come into the ark, thou, and thy sons, and thy wife, and thy sons' wives with thee. And of every living thing of all flesh, two of every sort shalt thou bring into the ark, to keep them alive with thee; they shall be male and female. Of fowls after their kind, and of cattle after their kind, of every creeping thing of the earth after its kind, two of every sort shall come unto thee, to keep them alive. And take thou unto thee of all food that is eaten, and thou shalt gather it to thee; and it shall be for food for thee, and for them.

Thus did Noah; according to all that God commanded him. And the Lord said unto Noah, "Come thou and all thy house into the ark; for thee have I seen righteous before me in this generation. Of every clean beast thou shalt take to thee by sevens, the male and his female: and of beasts that are not clean by two, the male and his female. Of fowls also of the air by sevens, the male and the female, to keep seed alive upon the face of all the earth. For in seven days I will cause it to rain upon the earth forty days and forty nights, and every living substance that I have made will I destroy from off the face of the earth." And Noah did according unto all that the Lord commanded him. And Noah was six hundred years old when the flood of waters was upon the earth. And Noah went in, and his sons, and his wife, and his sons' wives with him, into the ark, because of the waters of the flood. Of clean beasts, and of beasts that are not clean, and of fowls, and of every thing that creepeth upon the earth, there went in two and two unto Noah into the ark, the male and the female, as God had commanded Noah.

And it came to pass after seven days that the waters of the flood were upon the earth, the same day were all the fountains of the great deep broken up, and the windows of heaven were opened. And the rain was upon the earth forty days and forty nights. In the selfsame day entered Noah, and Shem, and Ham, and Japheth, the sons of Noah, and Noah's wife, and the three wives of his sons with them, into the ark. They, and every beast after his kind, and all the cattle after their kind, and every creeping thing that creepeth upon the earth after his kind, and every fowl after his kind, every bird of every sort. And they that went in, went in male and female of all flesh, as God had commanded him, and the Lord shut him in. And the flood was forty days upon the earth, and the waters increased, and bore up the ark, and it was lifted up above the earth. And the waters prevailed exceedingly upon the earth; and all the high hills, that were under the whole heaven, were covered. Fifteen cubits upward did the waters prevail, and the mountains were covered. And every living substance was destroyed that was upon the face of the ground, both man, and cattle, and the creeping things, and the fowl of the heaven, and they were destroyed from the earth, and Noah only remained alive, and they that were with him in the ark.

And the waters prevailed upon the earth a hundred and fifty days. And God remembered Noah, and every living thing, and all the cattle that were with him in the ark: and God made a wind to pass over the earth, and the waters assuaged. The rain from heaven was restrained and the waters returned from off the earth continually, and after the end of the hundred and fifty days the waters were abated. And the ark

---

[143] The same word is used for the basket used to float Moses in the Nile River; see Reading 34.

[144] The Hebrew cubit was about twenty inches.

rested in the seventh month upon the mountains of Ararat.[145] And the waters decreased continually until the tenth month: in the tenth month, on the first day of the month, were the tops of the mountains seen.

And it came to pass at the end of forty days, that Noah opened the window of the ark. And he sent forth a raven, which went forth to and fro, until the waters were dried up from off the earth. Also he sent forth a dove from him, to see if the waters were abated from off the face of the ground. But the dove found no rest for the sole of her foot, and she returned unto him into the ark, for the waters were on the face of the whole earth. And he stayed yet another seven days and again he sent forth the dove out of the ark. And the dove came in to him in the evening, and, lo, in her mouth was an olive leaf plucked off, so Noah knew that the waters were abated from off the earth. And he stayed yet other seven days and sent forth the dove; which returned not again unto him any more. And it came to pass in the six hundredth and first year, in the first month, the first day of the month, that the waters were dried up from off the earth, and Noah removed the covering of the ark, and looked, and, behold, the face of the ground was dry. And in the second month, on the seven and twentieth day of the month, was the earth dried. And God spoke unto Noah, saying, "Go forth of the ark, thou, and thy wife, and thy sons, and thy sons' wives with thee. Bring forth with thee every living thing that is with thee, of all flesh, both of fowl, and of cattle, and of every creeping thing that creepeth upon the earth, that they may breed abundantly in the earth, and be fruitful, and multiply upon the earth." And Noah went forth, and his sons, and his wife, and his sons' wives with him. Every beast, every creeping thing, and every fowl, and whatsoever creepeth upon the earth, after their kinds, went forth out of the ark.

V: MUSLIM ACCOUNTS

Because the Muslim Qur'an is not written in narrative fashion like Jewish and Christian scripture, Muslim accounts of creation are found in several different sections of the text.

THE CREATION OF HUMANS: THE QUR'AN, SURAH 2/30–38, 7/11–19, 38/71–83

In the Muslim account of creation of humans, angels are under the authority of Adam, the first man, but the angel Iblis refused to submit to Adam.

Source: Yusuf Ali, trans, *The Holy Qur'an, Text, Translation and Commentary* (Lahore, Cairo, Riyadh, 1934).

[145] The highest mountain in Turkey, on the border of Armenia.

[2/30–38] Behold, thy Lord[146] said to the angels, "I will create a vicegerent on earth." They said, "Wilt thou place therein one who will make mischief therein and shed blood? While we do celebrate Thy praise and glorify thy holy name?" He said, "I know what ye know not." And he taught Adam the names of all things; then he placed them before the angels, and said, "Tell me the names of these if ye are right." They said, "Glory to thee. Of knowledge we have none, save what thou hast taught us; in truth it is thou who art perfect in knowledge and wisdom." He said, "O Adam! Tell them their names." When he had told them, Allah said, "Did I not tell you that I know the secrets of heavens and earth, and I know what ye reveal and what ye conceal?" And behold, we[147] said to the angels, "Bow down to Adam," and they bowed down. Not so Iblis.[148] He refused and was haughty; he was of those who reject faith. We said, "O Adam! Dwell thou and thy wife in the garden,[149] and eat of the bountiful things therein as ye will, but approach not this tree, or ye run into harm and transgression." Then did Satan make them slip from the garden, and get them out of the state of felicity in which they had been. We said, "Get ye down, all ye people, with enmity between yourselves. On earth will be your dwelling place and your means of livelihood for a time." Then learnt Adam from his Lord words of inspiration, and his Lord turned toward him, for he is oft-returning, most merciful. We said, "Get ye down all from here, and if, as is sure, there comes to you guidance from me, whosoever follows my guidance, on them shall be no fear, nor shall they grieve. But those who reject Faith and belie our signs, they shall be companions of the fire; they shall abide therein."

[7/11–19] It is we who created you and gave you shape. Then we bade the angels bow down to Adam, and they bowed down. Not so Iblis; he refused to be of those who bow down. Allah said, "What prevented thee from bowing down when I commanded thee?" He said, "I am better than he; thou didst create me from fire, and him from clay." Allah said, "Get thee down from this, it is not for thee to be arrogant here. Get out, for thou art of the meanest of creatures." He said, "Give me respite until the day they are raised up." Allah said, "Be thou among those who have respite." He said, "Because thou hast thrown me out of the way, lo!, I will lie in wait for them on thy straight way. Then will I assault them from before them and behind them, from their right and their left, nor wilt thou find, in most of them, gratitude for thy mercies." Allah said, "Get out from this, disgraced and expelled. If any of them follow thee, Hell will I fill with you all. O Adam! Dwell thou and thy wife in the garden, and enjoy its good things as ye wish, but approach not this tree, or ye run into harm and transgression."

[38/71–83] Behold, the Lord said to the angels, "I am about to create man from clay. When I have fashioned him and breathed into him of my spirit, fall ye down in obeisance unto him." So the angels prostrated themselves, all of them together. Not so Iblis. He was haughty, and became one of those who reject faith. Allah said, "O Iblis! What prevents thee from prostrating thyself to one whom I have created with my hands? Art thou haughty? Or art thou one of the high and mighty ones?" Iblis said, "I am better than he: thou createdst me from fire, and him thou createdst from clay." Allah said, "Then get thee out from here, for thou art rejected, accursed. And my curse shall be on thee until the Day of Judgment." Iblis said, "O my Lord! Give me then respite until the day the dead are raised." Allah said, "Respite then is granted thee, until the day of the time appointed." Iblis said, "Then by thy power, I will put them all in the wrong, except thy servants among them, sincere and purified by thy grace."

146 Allah.

147 Allah.

148 The devil.

149 The Garden of Eden.

12

THE FLOOD STORY: THE QUR'AN, SURAH 11/15–49

The story of Noah and the flood is found in a section of the Qur'an dealing with people who were destroyed because they ignored prophets telling them to follow Allah.

Source: Yusuf Ali, trans, *The Holy Qur'an, Text, Translation and Commentary* (Lahore, Cairo, Riyadh, 1934).

Those who desire the life of the present and its glitter, to them we shall pay the price of their deeds therein, without diminution. They are those for whom there is nothing in the hereafter but the fire. Vain are the designs they frame therein, and of no effect the deeds that they do! Can they[150] be like those[151] who accept a clear sign[152] from their Lord,[153] and whom a witness[154] from himself doth teach, as did the Book of Moses[155] before it, a guide and a mercy? Muslims believe therein, but as for those of the sects[156] that reject it, the fire will be their promised meeting place. Be not then in doubt thereon, for it is the truth from thy Lord, yet many among men do not believe! Who doth more wrong than those who invent a lie against Allah. They will be turned back to the presence of their Lord, and the witnesses will say, "These are the ones who lied against their Lord! Behold! the curse of Allah is on those who do wrong! Those who would hinder men from the path of Allah and would seek in it something crooked, these were they who denied the hereafter!" Without a doubt, these are the very ones who will lose most in the hereafter! But those who believe and work righteousness, and humble themselves before their Lord, they will be companions of the gardens, to dwell therein forever! These two kinds of persons may be compared to the blind and deaf, and those who can see and hear well. Are they equal when compared? Will you not then take heed?

We sent Noah[157] to his people with a mission, to say, "I have come to you with a clear warning, that you serve none but Allah. Verily I do fear for you the penalty of a grievous day." But the chiefs of the unbelievers among his people said, "We see in you

[150] Unbelievers.
[151] Muslims
[152] The Qur'an.
[153] Allah.
[154] The prophet Muhammad.
[155] From the Hebrew Bible.
[156] Christians, Jews, and other unbelievers.

[157] Nuh in the Qur'an.

nothing but a man like ourselves, nor do we see that any follow you but the meanest among us, in judgment immature, nor do we see in you any merit above us, in fact we think you are liars!" He said, "O my people, I have a clear sign from my Lord, and he hath sent mercy unto me from his own presence, but hath the mercy been obscured from your sight? Shall we compel you to accept it when you are averse to it? And O my people, I ask you for no wealth in return; my reward is from none but Allah. But I will not drive away those who believe, for verily they are to meet their Lord, and you I see are the ignorant ones! Will you not then take heed? I tell you not that with me are the treasures of Allah, nor do I know what is hidden, nor claim I to be an angel." They said, "O Noah, thou hast disputed with us, and much hast thou prolonged the dispute with us. Now bring upon us what thou threatenest us with, if thou speakest the truth!?" He said, "Truly, Allah will bring it on you if he wills, and then you will not be able to frustrate it! Of no profit will be my counsel to you, much as I desire to give you good counsel, if it be that Allah willeth to leave you astray. He is your Lord! And to him will you return!" It was revealed to Noah, "None of thy people will believe except those who have believed already! So grieve no longer over their evil deeds, but construct an ark under our eyes and our inspiration, and address me no further on behalf of those who are in sin, for they are about to be overwhelmed."[158] Forthwith he starts constructing the ark. Every time that the chiefs of his people passed by him, they threw ridicule on him. He said, "If you ridicule us now, we can look down on you with ridicule likewise! But soon will you know who it is on whom will descend a penalty that will cover them with shame, on whom will be unloosed a penalty lasting:" At length, behold!, there came our[159] command, and the fountains of the earth gushed forth! We said, "Embark therein, of each kind two, male and female, and your family, except those against whom the word has already gone forth, and the believers." But only a few believed with him.

So Noah said, "Embark you on the ark, In the name of Allah, whether it moves or is at rest! For my Lord is, be sure, oft-forgiving, most merciful!" So the ark floated with them on the waves towering like mountains, and Noah called out to his son, who had separated himself from the rest, "O my son, embark with us, and be not with the unbelievers!" The son replied, "I will betake myself to some mountain; it will save me from the water." Noah said, "This day nothing can save from the command of Allah any but those on whom he hath mercy!" And the waves came between them, and the son was among those overwhelmed in the flood. Then the word went forth,[160] "O earth, swallow up thy water, and O sky, withhold thy rain!" And the water abated, and the matter was ended. The ark rested on Mount Judi,[161] and the word went forth, "Away with those who do wrong!" And Noah called upon his Lord, and said, "O my Lord!, surely my son is of my family! And thy promise is true, and thou art the justest of judges!" He said, "O Noah, he is not of thy family, for his conduct is unrighteous. So ask not of me that of which thou hast no knowledge! I give you counsel, lest thou act like the ignorant!" Noah said, "O my Lord, I do seek refuge with thee, lest I ask you for that of which I have no knowledge. And unless thou forgive me and have mercy on me, I should indeed be lost!" The word came,[162] "O Noah, come down from the ark with peace from us, and blessing on you and on some of the peoples who will spring from those with thee, but there will be other peoples to whom we shall grant their pleasures for a time, but in the end will a grievous penalty reach them from us."

[158] That is, by the flood.
[159] Allah

[160] From Allah
[161] Often identified as a mountain on the upper Tigris River, in northern Mesopotamia.
[162] From Allah.

CHAPTER 2

Mesopotamia and the Bronze Age (6000–1200 BCE)

By the sixth millennium BCE, a high level of social, political, and technological culture based on an agricultural economy already existed in many places in Europe, western Asia, and North Africa. An agricultural economy permitted people to live in permanent villages and towns constructed from mud brick, stone, timber, and other materials. The amount of food produced could be expanded by bringing additional land under cultivation, and agricultural foodstuffs could be stored to provide a dependable food supply. Larger populations and the ability to remain in one place encouraged specialization of labor, with different people serving as potters, carpenters, basket makers, traders, and shepherds, not to mention fighters to protect the food surpluses and luxury items stored in the villages.

As in the case of the cultures of the Old Stone Age, the economic and technological developments of the Neolithic and Chalcolithic periods, and in particular the use of agriculture, eventually expanded to the point where there was no further room to expand based on contemporary social and technological levels of development. All of the geographical regions and economic niches suitable for this kind of society became occupied, even relatively marginal areas with little rainfall. Thus, if different kinds of societies and economies were going to develop, it probably would happen somewhere else. And this is exactly what happened.

The next significant social, economic, and cultural developments occurred in large Near Eastern river valleys, in Mesopotamia (modern Iraq, eastern Syria, and eastern Turkey) and Egypt, where huge tracts of rich alluvial soil were available for cultivation in the deltas at the mouths of the rivers. The problem that initially kept this soil from being exploited, however, was that these areas were very marshy, were subject to severe flooding from upstream, and had very little rainfall. Thus, before the soil could be cultivated, the marshes had to be drained, flood control systems had to be created, and elaborate irrigation systems had to be established. These endeavors required the organization and mobilization of huge amounts of human labor, something not available to most Neolithic and Chalcolithic societies.

The story of the development of ancient Mesopotamian society and culture is told by hundreds of thousands of clay tablets inscribed with cuneiform symbols usually written in the Akkadian language, the common language of much of the ancient Near East. The tablets are preserved in the ruins of ancient Mesopotamian cities: paradoxically enough, the only way that sun-dried clay tablets could be preserved for thousands of years was if they were baked in a fire that usually resulted from the destruction of a city. Although the vast majority of these tablets deal with administrative and commercial documents, a significant number, whose authors almost always are unknown, also preserve accounts of the history and mythology of Mesopotamian peoples.

Map 2 Sites of Early Mesopotamia

13

INANNA STEALS THE KNOWLEDGE OF CIVILIZATION FROM ENKI

The fertility goddess Inanna (Ishtar) is thought to be depicted in this Old Babylonian relief dated to ca. 1750 BCE and known as "The Queen of the Night." It is preserved in the British Museum.

A large six-column cuneiform tablet in the Nippur Collection at the University of Pennsylvania preserves the story, probably based on oral tradition, of how the fertility goddess Inanna (Ishtar) used her seductive powers to induce Enki (Ea), the god of water and civilization, to release the knowledge of civilization and of how Enki unsuccessfully tried to reclaim it. Implicit in this account is the connection between access to water and the development of civilization.

Source: "Inana and Enki," in J. A. Black, G. Cunningham, J. Ebeling, E. Flückiger-Hawker, E. Robson, J. Taylor, and G. Zólyomi, "The Electronic Text Corpus of Sumerian Literature."

Inanna put the šu-gura, the desert crown, on her head. Her genitals were remarkable. She praised herself, full of delight at her genitals, saying, "When I have gratified the Lord, when I have made myself beautiful, when I have made myself perfect, when I have made myself luxuriant, when I have made myself brilliant, I shall direct my steps to the abzu,[1] to Eridu,[2] I shall direct my steps to Enki, to the abzu,

[1] The underground dwelling place of the water god Enki located in Eridu.

[2] A Sumerian city southwest of Ur thought by some to be the oldest city in the world. It was the location of the E-Abzu, the main temple of the water god Enki.

to Eridu, and I myself shall speak coaxingly to him. I shall utter a plea to Lord Enki. Like the sweet oil of the cedar. It shall never escape me that I have been neglected by him who has had sex." On that day the maiden Inanna, holy Inanna, directed her steps all by herself toward Enki's abzu in Eridu. On that day, he of exceptional knowledge, who knows the divine powers in heaven and earth, who from his own dwelling already knows the intentions of the gods, Enki, the king of the abzu, who, even before holy Inanna had approached within six miles of the abzu in Eridu, knew all about her enterprise, Enki spoke to his man, gave him instructions, "Come here, my man, listen to my words. When the maiden Inanna has entered the abzu and Eridu, offer her butter cake to eat. Let her be served cool refreshing water. Pour beer for her, in front of the Lions' Gate, make her feel as if she is in her girlfriend's house. You are to welcome holy Inanna at the holy table, at the table of An."

After Enki had spoken thus to him, Isimud the minister followed his master's instructions closely. He let the maiden into the abzu and Eridu. She got butter cake to eat. They poured cool refreshing water for her, and they gave her beer to drink, in front of the Lions' Gate. He made her feel as if she was in her girlfriend's house. He welcomed holy Inanna at the holy table, at the table of An. So it came about that Enki and Inanna were drinking beer together in the abzu, and enjoying the taste of sweet wine. The bronze aga[3] vessels were filled to the brim, and the two of them started a competition, drinking from the bronze vessels of Uraš.[4]

[In a missing section, Inanna gets Enki drunk and induces him to give her the gifts of civilization.]

Enki said, "I will give them to holy Inanna, my daughter." Holy Inanna received heroism, power, wickedness, righteousness, the plundering of cities, making lamentations, rejoicing. "In the name of my power, in the name of my abzu, I will give them to holy Inanna, my daughter." Holy Inanna received deceit, the rebel lands, kindness, being on the move, being sedentary. "In the name of my power, in the name of my abzu, I will give them to holy Inanna, my daughter." Holy Inanna received the craft of the carpenter, the craft of the coppersmith, the craft of the scribe, the craft of the smith, the craft of the leather-worker, the craft of the fuller, the craft of the builder, the craft of the reed-worker. "In the name of my power, in the name of my abzu, I will give them to holy Inanna, my daughter." Holy Inanna received wisdom, attentiveness, holy purification rites, the shepherd's hut, piling up glowing charcoals, the sheepfold, respect, awe, reverent silence. "In the name of my power, in the name of my abzu, I will give them to holy Inanna, my daughter." Holy Inanna received the kindling of fire, the extinguishing of fire, hard work, the assembled family, descendents. "In the name of my power, in the name of my abzu, I will give them to holy Inanna, my daughter." Holy Inanna received strife, triumph, counselling, comforting, judging, decision-making.

[In another missing section, Enki sobers up, realizes what he has done, and has second thoughts.]

Enki spoke to the minister Isimud, "Isimud, my minister, my Sweet Name of Heaven!" "Enki, my master, I am at your service! What is your wish?" "Because Inanna said that she would not yet depart from here for Unug Kulaba,[5] can I still reach her?" But holy Inanna had gathered up the divine powers and embarked onto the Boat of Heaven.[6] The Boat of Heaven had already left the quay. As the effects of the beer cleared from Father Enki who had drunk beer, the great Lord Enki turned his attention to Eridu. Enki spoke to Isimud the minister, "Isimud, my minister, my Sweet Name of Heaven!" "Enki, my master, I am at your service! What is your wish?" "Where are the office of en priest,[7] the office of lagar priest,[8] divinity, the great and good crown, the royal throne?" "My master has given them to his daughter." "Where are

[3] A word meaning "diadem."

[4] An earth goddess, consort of An.

[5] Uruk, Erech in the Bible, the city of Inanna.

[6] The ship of Inanna, sometimes thought to be in the shape of a crescent.

[7] A Sumerian priest-king.

[8] A temple servant who made invocations.

the noble scepter, the staff and crook, the noble dress, shepherdship, kingship?" "My master has given them to his daughter." "Where are the office of egir-zid priestess, the office of nin-diĝir priestess,[9] the office of išib priest,[10] the office of lu-maḫ priest,[11] the office of gudug priest[12]?" "My master has given them to his daughter." "Where are constancy, going down to the underworld, coming up from the underworld, the kur-ĝara priest[13]?" "My master has given them to his daughter." "Where are the sword and club, the black garment, the colorful garment, the hair-style?" "My master has given them to his daughter." "Where are the standard, the quiver, sexual intercourse, kissing, prostitution?" "My master has given them to his daughter." "Where are forthright speech, deceitful speech, grandiloquent speech, the cultic prostitute, the holy tavern?" "My master has given them to his daughter." "Where are loud musical instruments, the art of song, venerable old age?" "My master has given them to his daughter."

The prince spoke to his minister Isimud, Enki addressed the Sweet Name of Heaven, "Isimud, my minister, my Sweet Name of Heaven!" "Enki, my master, I am at your service! What is your wish?" "Where has the Boat of Heaven reached now?" "It has just now reached the quay." "Go now! The enkum[14] are to take the Boat of Heaven away from her!" The minister Isimud spoke to holy Inanna, "My lady! Your father has sent me to you. What Enki spoke was very serious. His important words cannot be countermanded." Holy Inanna replied to him, "What has my father said to you, what has he spoken?" "Enki has said to me, 'Inanna may travel to Unug, but you are to get the Boat of Heaven back to Eridu for me.'" Holy Inanna spoke to the minister Isimud, "How could my father have altered his promise? Was it falsehood that my father said to me, did he speak falsely to me? Has he sworn falsely by the name of his power and by the name of his abzu? Has he duplicitously sent you to me as a messenger?" Now as these words were still in her mouth, he got the enkum to seize hold of the Boat of Heaven. Holy Inanna addressed her minister Ninšubur:[15] "Come, my good minister of E-ana![16] My fair-spoken minister! My envoy of reliable words! Water has never touched your hand, water has never touched your feet!" So Inanna got hold again of the divine powers that had been presented to her, and the Boat of Heaven. And then for the second time the prince spoke to his minister Isimud, Enki addressed the Sweet Name of Heaven, "Isimud, my minister, my Sweet Name of Heaven!" "Enki, my master, I am at your service! What is your wish?" "Where has the Boat of Heaven reached now?" "It has just now reached the holy [—]" "Go now! The fifty giants of Eridu are to take the Boat of Heaven away from her!" The minister Isimud spoke to holy Inanna, "My lady! Your father has sent me to you. What your father said was very serious. What Enki spoke was very serious." Holy Inanna replied to him, "What has my father said to you?" "My master has spoken to me, Enki has said to me, 'Inanna may travel to Unug, but you are to get the Boat of Heaven back to Eridu for me.'" Holy Inanna spoke to the minister Isimud, "How could my father have changed what he said to me? How could he have altered his promise?" Now as these words were still in her mouth, he got the fifty giants of Eridu to seize hold of the Boat of Heaven. Holy Inanna addressed her minister Ninšubur, "Come, my good minister of E-ana! My fair-spoken minister!" So Inanna got hold again of the divine powers that had been presented to her, and the Boat of Heaven

[Enki then made four more unsuccessful attempts, in the same words, to seize the Boat of Heaven. Inanna finally arrived home at Uruk.]

Her minister Ninšubur spoke to holy Inanna, "My lady, today you have brought the Boat of Heaven to

[9] "Divine lady"; a priestess supported at the temple of Enki.

[10] An exorcist.

[11] A generic word for priest.

[12] A generic word for priest.

[13] A cult performer.

[14] Guardian deities.

[15] A goddess who accompanied Inanna on her adventures.

[16] The temple of Inanna in Uruk.

the Gate of Joy, to Unug Kulaba. Now there will be rejoicing in our city." Holy Inanna replied to her, "Today I have brought the Boat of Heaven to the Gate of Joy, to Unug Kulaba. It shall pass along the street magnificently. The people shall stand in the street full of awe. The foreign lands shall declare my greatness. My people shall utter my praise."

14

"EPIC OF GILGAMESH" (CA. 2500 BCE), TABLETS I–VIII

In the course of their adventures, Gilgamesh and his trusty companion Enkidu defeated the monster Humbaba, who guarded the Cedar Forest where the gods lived, as depicted on this Assyrian cylinder seal of the seventh century BCE.

Not only is the *Epic of Gilgamesh,* originally written around 2000 BCE and preserved on clay tablets inscribed with cuneiform text dating to later periods, one of the greatest pieces of world literature, it also is one of the earliest, if not the earliest. In Sumerian history, Gilgamesh appears as the fifth king of the city of Uruk (see

Reading 15) and would have reigned around 2500 BCE. In the epic, Gilgamesh appears as a semidivine hero, two-thirds god and one-third human. The story, no doubt based on oral tradition, begins with the gods creating the wild man Enkidu to save the people of Uruk from Gilgamesh's oppressive rule. Enkidu and Gilgamesh become friends and have a series of adventures, but the gods eventually punish Gilgamesh by killing Enkidu. Gilgamesh then wanders the world looking for the secret of eternal life.

Source: William Ellery Leonard, trans., *Gilgamesh. Epic of Old Babylonia* (New York: Viking, 1934).

TABLET I [After a brief section describing Gilgamesh, the inhabitants of Uruk then complain to the gods about Gilgamesh's oppressive administration. The gods respond by creating the wild man Enkidu to challenge Gilgamesh.]

He built the walls of ramparted Uruk. He laid the foundations, steadfast as bronze, of the holy E-ana,[17] the pure temple. Two thirds of him is god, one third of him is man. There is none who can match the form of his body [—].

"Gilgamesh keeps the son from the father, Gilgamesh keeps the lover from the maiden." The great gods heard their outcries. The gods of heaven called the Lord Anu, "Was he not of thy making, this almighty wild bull, this hero Gilgamesh?" The great god Anu lent ear to their cries. Aruru[18] was summoned, she the great goddess, "Thou, Aruru, madest Gilgamesh; now make another like unto him. Let him come at Gilgamesh. Let them contend together, that Uruk may have peace." As Aruru heard this, she shaped in her heart a warrior of Anu. She pinched up some clay and spat on it. She molded Enkidu, fashioned a hero. His whole body was shaggy with hair. He knew naught of land and people, with the gazelles he eats the plants, with the wild beasts he drinks at the watering-place. He walked to the watering-place toward a hunter, a stalker of wild beasts. The hunter saw him, the hunter's face grew troubled. Without his quarry he turned back to his house. He was down-cast, troubled; he shrieked. The hunter says to his father, "My father, a man that came from the hills hath become strong indeed in the land, mighty in power like a fighter of Anu's. He is ever beside the wild beasts. I am afraid, I cannot go near to him. My traps that I laid he hath destroyed. No catch he allows me."

The father says to the hunter, "Seek out Gilgamesh, the Lord of Uruk. Beg for a priestess and lead her back with thee. When the wild beasts come to the watering-place, then let her cast her garment off. When he sees her, he will draw near." The hunter heard the counsel of his father. He started on the way, he entered into Uruk. He goes to Gilgamesh, and Gilgamesh says to him, "Go, my hunter, and get thee a priestess." The hunter went yonder and got him a priestess. They made themselves ready. The wild beasts come along and drink at the watering-place. So too comes he, Enkidu. Then the priestess saw him, the great strong one, the wild fellow, the man of the steppes. The hunter said, "There he is, woman! Loosen thy buckle, unveil thy delight. When he sees thee, he will draw near. Open thy robe that he may rest upon thee! Arouse in him rapture, the work of woman. His bosom will press against thee."

Then the priestess loosened her buckle, unveiled her delight. She aroused in him rapture, the work of woman. His bosom pressed against her. Enkidu forgot where he was born. For six days and seven nights was Enkidu given over to love with the priestess. When he had sated himself with the fill of her, he raised up his face to his wild ones. At sight of Enkidu, the wild beasts of the fields shrink back before him. Then Enkidu marveled. His body stood as in a spell. He turns about and sits down at the feet

[17] The temple of Ishtar (or Inanna) in Uruk.

[18] Goddess of the Earth and birth; in some versions, she created humanity.

of the priestess. And to what the priestess now speaks his ears give heed. "Enkidu, how beautiful thou, how like a god! Why must thou rush with animals over the steppes? Come, I will lead thee into ramparted Uruk, to a pure house, the dwelling of Anu and Ishtar, where Gilgamesh lives, matchless in might." She talks to him, until he likes her words. Knowing his own heart, he seeketh a friend. Enkidu says to her, to the priestess, "Woman, lead me to the pure, the holy house, the dwelling of Anu and Ishtar, where Gilgamesh lives, matchless in might. I will challenge him to a fight. I, born on the steppes, matchless in might, well I know what the outcome will be."

Then she stripped off one of her robes, and clothed him therewith. In the other robe she herself remained clad. She took him by the hand and led him like a bridegroom, and the shepherds foregathered around him. Then they set bread before him. He was bewildered. Enkidu understood not how to eat bread; to drink wine he had not learned. Then the priestess opens her mouth and says to Enkidu, "Eat bread, Enkidu, the glory of life, drink wine, Enkidu, the custom of the land." Then Enkidu ate bread until he was full. Then he drank wine, seven beakers. His spirit loosed itself, he grew merry. He took his weapon, he attacked lions, so that the great shepherds found rest at night, for Enkidu was their safeguard. Enkidu and the priestess arrived at ramparted Uruk. They go together to seek out Gilgamesh.

TABLET II [Enkidu picks a fight with Gilgamesh, and the two then become friends and embark on a series of adventures.]

Enkidu goes along the market-street of ramparted Uruk. Marvelling he looks at the mighty work. He bars the way of the warriors of Uruk; the couch had been spread for goddess Ishtar at the gates of her house. Enkidu barred the going-to, allowed not Gilgamesh that he enter in. They grappled each other at the gates of her house. They fought in the street. The doorposts quaked and the wall swayed. Gilgamesh crumpled his leg to the ground. His anger softened, he checked his onset. Says Enkidu to him, to Gilgamesh, "Thee, as one matchless, thy mother bore, the goddess Ninsun.[19] Enlil[20] to thee hath allotted the kingdom over mankind!"

[Gilgamesh suggests that he and Enkidu attack Humbaba, the giant that guarded the Cedar Forest, where the gods lived. Enkidu replies.]

"In the hills, my friend, I found it out, as I roamed with the wild beasts. Hither and thither ten thousand miles stretches that forest. Who could dare enter therein? Humbaba's bellow is a stormwind, his mouth is fire, his snort is death! Whence came thy resolve to dare this?" Gilgamesh says to Enkidu, "My heart hath its longing to conquer Humbaba." Enkidu says to Gilgamesh, "How against Humbaba can we make way to the Cedar Forest? Enlil hath set him therein, to the terror of men, for guarding the cedars." Gilgamesh says to Enkidu, "My friend, We both will strive against Humbaba. Thou art now afeared of death, and thy power is gone. I will go on before thee. Even if I fall, I will make myself a name. 'Gilgamesh,' so men will say, 'Hath gone forth against the almighty Humbaba.' "

[The city elders advise Gilgamesh before his departure to fight Humbaba.]

"Gilgamesh, trust not in thy powers. He who knoweth the way guardeth his companion. Let Enkidu go on before thee, he knoweth the way to the Cedar Forest. He is wise in fight, he understandeth combats. May Enkidu save the friend, may he guard the comrade. In the stream of Humbaba mayst thou bathe thy feet!"

Enkidu spoke to Gilgamesh, "Now start on thy way! Be thy heart fearless! Fix eye upon me! We will win against Humbaba."

TABLET III [Gilgamesh visits his mother Ninsun before departing.]

Gilgamesh says to Enkidu, "My friend, let us go to the splendid palace and stand before Ninsun, the great queen. The lady Ninsun, who knoweth all things, will lend goodspeed to our footsteps." They

[19] The wild cow goddess, daughter of Anu; see also Readings 17, 19.

[20] The Sumerian storm god, highest ranking of the gods on earth.

took each other by the hand; Gilgamesh and Enkidu went to the splendid palace, and stood before Ninsun, the great queen. She burnt much incense. She called Enkidu and said to him, "Enkidu, thou strong one, thou alone art my comfort, shelter for me now Gilgamesh, my son, From the day of his going, until the day of his coming home, until he reaches the Cedar Forest, yield not from his side!"

TABLET IV [Gilgamesh and Enkidu are climbing the mountain of the Cedar Forest. Gilgamesh has several dreams. After the second one, he says:]
"My friend, I had a second dream, and the dream that I saw was horrible. On the top of a mountain we two were standing when the mountain caved in." Then said Enkidu to his friend, "The dream thou hadst is good, my friend, the mountain thou saw'st is the Cedar Mountain! We are going to seize Humbaba and kill him, and cast his corpse into the plain!" After twenty miles they ate a little. After thirty miles they rested for the night. Gilgamesh sank on his knee, a sleep overtook him. At midnight he stood up and said to his friend, "My friend, I saw a third dream, and the dream that I saw was horrible. The heavens shrieked, the earth bellowed, a storm gathered, darkness came forth, a flash flamed, a fire shot up, the clouds thickened, it rained death. Then the brightness vanished, the fire went out, the blaze that had fallen turned to ashes. Let us climb down, that we may take counsel on the plain."

[But the two eventually press on and reach the great gate to the Cedar Forest. This time it is Enkidu who gets cold feet.]
Enkidu says to Gilgamesh, "My friend, let us not enter the forest; my hands are lamed!" Gilgamesh says to Enkidu, "My friend, thou shalt not act like a weakling! Art thou not wise in fight? Forget death! The laming of thy hands will be over, and thy faintness pass off! Let us enter, my friend, let us fight side by side—Did not thine own heart urge to the fight?" Then the two got into the Cedar Forest. Their words stood still, and they themselves stopped and stood.

TABLET V [Most of this tablet, in which Gilgamesh and Enkidu hunt down Humbaba, is destroyed, but by the end of it, Humbaba has been slain and the two heroes have returned to Uruk.]
They took their stand and gaze at the forest. They survey the height of the cedars. They survey the entrance to the forest, where Humbaba goes about, roving along [—]

TABLET VI [Gilgamesh rejects the erotic advances of Ishtar, who complains to Anu that Gilgamesh needs to be punished for this insult.]
Gilgamesh threw off his unclean garments and put on clean raiment. Gilgamesh set his crown on. Then Ishtar, sublime one, lifted her eyes to the beauty of Gilgamesh, "Go to it, Gilgamesh, be my consort, spend thy love upon me. Be thou my husband, be I thy wife! I will have a chariot harnessed for thee of lapis lazuli and of gold. Its wheels are golden, its horns of precious stones." Gilgamesh says to Ishtar, sublime one, "Keep thy gifts to thyself! Thou art like a back door that keeps not the storm out. For which of thy consorts has thy love lasted? Which of thy shepherds could bind thee forever? Go to, I will count off all thy paramours, I will hold a reckoning with thee. Tammuz,[21] the lover of thy youth, hast thou year after year made to wail.[22] *[Gilgamesh lists four more of Ishtar's rejected lovers, then continues:]* Thou fellest in love with Ishullanu, The gardener of thy father.[23] Thou liftedst thine eyes to him and lurèst him, 'Dear Ishullanu, let us enjoy love together.' Ishullanu spoke to thee, 'What dost thou want of me? Hath my mother not baked, and have I not eaten, that I should eat dishes of evil deeds and of curses?' As thou heardset this his talking, thou turnedst him into a bat. And now thou hast fallen in love with me, and wilt treat me as them."

As Ishtar heard this, she was wroth and mounted to heaven. Ishtar stepped up to Anu, her father, and to Antu,[24] her mother, she went, and she spoke, "My

[21] A vegetation god, Tammuz in Semitic and Dumuzi in Sumerian.

[22] Tammuz spent half the year on earth, then died and spent half the year in the underworld, then was reborn.

[23] That is, the great god Anu.

[24] The wife of Anu.

father, Gilgamesh hath curst me, Gilgamesh hath tallied up my evil deeds and my curses." Anu opened his mouth and spoke to Ishtar, sublime one, "And thou hast besought his love, and Gilgamesh hath tallied off thy evil deeds and thy curses." Ishtar says to Anu, her father, "My father, do thou create a Bull of Heaven that he may butt Gilgamesh down. And do thou fill the bull's body with fire!" Anu lent ear to her words, "Let a Bull of Heaven descend and come unto Uruk." At his first snort the bull kills three hundred warriors. And Enkidu grasped the Bull of Heaven by his horns. At his second snort two hundred warriors he knocks over. At his third snort Enkidu leaps on his back and grasps him by the thick of the tail. Then Enkidu says to Gilgamesh, "My friend, we have made our name glorious." And Gilgamesh thrusts his sword between nape and horns. When they had laid low the Bull of Heaven, their heart had peace. Then Ishtar mounted the walls of ramparted Uruk and shrieked down, "Woe unto Gilgamesh who affronted me, who killed the Bull of Heaven." As Enkidu heard these words of Ishtar, he tore loose a thigh-bone from the Bull of Heaven, and flung it into her face. Then Ishtar assembled the damsels of the temple, the harlots and the priestesses, over the thigh-bone of the Bull of Heaven they wailed a chant. The people of Uruk stand assembled. Gilgamesh speaks thus to the maid-servants of his palace, "Who is the most beautiful among the heroes?" "Gilgamesh is the most beautiful among the heroes!" Then Gilgamesh makes in his palace a feast of rejoicing.

TABLET VII [The gods punish Gilgamesh for killing the Bull of Heaven. Enkidu becomes ill and has a feverish dream of his own death.]

"Gilgamesh, my friend, I beheld dreams this last night, in the dark night I see a man with forbidding face. He is hideous to look on, his nails are eagle-talons. He made my arms into wings like a bird's, saying, 'Descend, descend, I say, into the house of darkness, to the dwelling of Irkaila,[25] to the house that none leave again who have betrodden it, to the house whose inhabitants do without light, where dust is their nourishment and clay their food. They are as birds clothed with wings, they see not the light, they dwell in the darkness.' In the house of dust that I entered are kings' crowns bowed down. There do dwell the mighty ones who from the days of old ruled the land. In the house of dust that I entered dwells the queen of the earth, Ereshkigal. She raised her head and saw me. She stretched out her hand and took me to herself."

[Gilgamesh replies:]

"My friend, who with me hast ranged through all hardships, my friend, the dream comes true!" On the day when he saw the dream his fate was fulfilled. Enkidu lies stricken. For one day, for a second day, Enkidu suffers pain in his bed. For a third day, and a fourth, Enkidu lies stricken. For a fifth, a sixth, and a seventh, for an eighth, a ninth, and a tenth day, Enkidu's pain grows great. For an eleventh and a twelfth day, Enkidu lies in his bed. He calls Gilgamesh and speaks, "A god hath cursed me, my friend. Not like one wounded in battle is it mine to die. I once feared the fight, but, my friend, he who falls in the fight is happy. As for me, I must die in my bed."

TABLET VIII [Gilgamesh laments the death of his friend.]

Then Gilgamesh assembles his nobles and says, "Hear me, ye elders, look upon me! For Enkidu, for my friend, I weep. Like a wailing woman I cry bitterly. An evil spirit hath risen up and cast me down into ruin." *[Gilgamesh speaks to Enkidu.]* "Enkidu, my young friend, who couldst do all things, So that we climbed the mountain, overthrew Humbaba, so that we seized and slew the Bull of Heaven. Dark is thy look, and thine ears take not my voice!" But he lifts up his eyes no more. Gilgamesh touched him on the heart, but the heart beats no more. Like as a lion, Gilgamesh raised his voice, like as a lioness, he roared out. He tears his hair and strews it forth." Soon as beamed the first shimmer of morning, Gilgamesh raised a new cry, "I will myself put on mourning for thee, will clothe myself in a lion's skin, and haste away over the steppes."

[25] The underworld, ruled by Ereshkigal, the older sister of Ishtar, and Nergal, the god of death.

[Distraught at the loss of his friend, Gilgamesh then sets out to find the secret of eternal life. He meets Utnapishtim (see Reading 3), who survived the Great Flood and who directs Gilgamesh to a life-preserving plant. But the plant is stolen by a serpent, and Gilgamesh returns home empty handed.]

15

THE SUMERIAN KING LIST (CA. 2500/1700 BCE)

This best surviving copy of the Sumerian King List is the Weld–Blundell prism now kept in the Ashmolean Museum in Oxford.

The Sumerian King List, preserved on clay blocks inscribed with cuneiform text, ostensibly was a sequential record of Sumerian kings who laid claim to hegemony in lower Mesopotamia in the years before and after 3000 BCE. It did not have a single author, but grew by accretion. As time went on, it was used to legitimate the claims of various cities to supremacy. Many of the dynasties cited, however, overlapped, making it difficult to use the document to establish a fixed chronology. The earliest reigns are clearly legendary, with lengths of tens of thousands of years. After the flood, the reign lengths gradually shorten to more realistic lengths. Eventually, the list enters historical times with kings whose existence is confirmed in other documents. Most of the kings are just names; only a few of them are credited with any particular accomplishment. The city names have been normalized here to more standard spellings. It is unclear when the King List was first created, but the latest entries run into the eighteenth century BCE.

Source: "The Sumerian King List," in J. A. Black, G. Cunningham, J. Ebeling, E. Flückiger-Hawker, E. Robson, J. Taylor, and G. Zólyomi, "The Electronic Text Corpus of Sumerian Literature."

After the kingship descended from heaven, the kingship was in Eridu. In Eridu, Alulim became king; he ruled for 28800 years. Alaljar ruled for 36000 years. 2 kings; they ruled for 64800 years. Then Eridu fell and the kingship was taken to Bad-tibira.[26]

In Bad-tibira, En-men-lu-ana[27] ruled for 43200 years. En-men-gal-ana ruled for 28800 years. Dumuzi, the shepherd, ruled for 36000 years. 3 kings; they ruled for 108000 years.

Then Bad-tibira fell and the kingship was taken to Larsa. In Larsa, En-sipad-zid-ana ruled for 28800 years. 1 king; he ruled for 28800 years. Then Larsa fell and the kingship was taken to Sippar.

In Sippar, En-men-dur-ana became king; he ruled for 21000 years. 1 king; he ruled for 21000 years. Then Sippar fell and the kingship was taken to Shuruppak.

In Shuruppak, Ubara-tutu became king; he ruled for 18600 years. 1 king; he ruled for 18600 years. In 5 cities 8 kings; they ruled for 241200 years.

Then the flood swept over. After the flood had swept over, and the kingship had descended from heaven, the kingship was in Kish.

In Kish, Jucur became king; he ruled for 1200 years. Kullassina-bel ruled for 960 years. Nanjiclicma ruled for 670 years. En-tarah-ana ruled for 420 years. Babum ruled for 300 years. Puannum ruled for 840 years. Kalibum ruled for 960 years. Kalumum ruled for 900 years. Zuqaqip ruled for 900 years. Atab ruled for 600 years. Macda, the son of Atab, ruled for 840 years. Arwium, the son of Macda, ruled for 720 years. Etana, the shepherd, who ascended to heaven and consolidated all the foreign countries, became king; he ruled for 1500 years. Balih, the son of Etana, ruled for 400 years. En-me-nuna ruled for 660 years. Melem-Kish, the son of En-me-nuna, ruled for 900 years. Barsal-nuna, the son of En-me-nuna, ruled for 1200 years. Zamug, the son of Barsal-nuna, ruled for 140 years. Tizqar, the son of Zamug, ruled for 305 years. Iltasadum ruled for 1200 years. En-men-barage-si,[28] who made the land of Elam submit, became king; he ruled for 900 years. Aga, the son of En-men-barage-si, ruled for 625 years. Then Kish was defeated and the kingship was taken to Uruk.

In Uruk Mec-ki-aj-gacer, the son of Utu, became Lord and king; he ruled for 324 years. Mec-ki-aj-gacer entered the sea and disappeared. Enmerkar, the son of Mec-ki-aj-gacer, the King of Uruk, who built Uruk, became king; he ruled for 420 years. 745 are the years of the dynasty of Mec-ki-aj-gacer; [—] Lugalbanda,[29] the shepherd, ruled for 1200 years. Dumuzi, the fisherman, whose city was Kuara,[30] ruled for 100 years. He captured En-me-barage-si[31] single-handed. Gilgamesh,[32] whose father was a phantom, the Lord of Kulaba,[33] ruled for 126 years. Ur-Nungal, the son of Gilgamesh, ruled for 30 years. Udul-kalama, the son of Ur-lugal, ruled for 15 years. La-ba'cum

[26] "Fortress of the Smiths," a Sumerian city of unknown location, perhaps modern Tel al-Madineh.

[27] Many names of rulers include the word "En," the title of a priest-king, also known as an "Ensi."

[28] The first king in the list to be historically attested; fragments found at Nippur and dated to ca. 2500 BCE name En-men-barage-si as the Lugal of Kish, and he was said to have built the first temple, the Ekur at Nippur, in honor of the god Enlil.

[29] The word "Lugal," literally "Big man," was a generic word for "ruler"; it also may refer to a military general or a ruler over several cities.

[30] Otherwise unknown.

[31] It is not clear whether this is the same En-me-barage-si who was king of Kish.

[32] The same Gilgamesh as in the "Legend of Gilgamesh," see Readings 3 and 14.

[33] An alternate name for Uruk.

ruled for 9 years. En-nun-tarah-ana ruled for 8 years. Mec-he, the smith, ruled for 36 years. Melem-ana ruled for 6 years. Lugal-kitun ruled for 36 years. 12 kings; they ruled for 2310 years. Then Uruk was defeated and the kingship was taken to Ur.

In Ur Mec-ane-pada became king;[34] he ruled for 80 years. Mec-ki-aj-Nanna, the son of Mec-ane-pada, became king; he ruled for 36 years. Elulu ruled for 25 years. Balulu ruled for 36 years. 4 kings; they ruled for 171 years. Then Ur was defeated and the kingship was taken to Awan.[35]

In Awan [—] became king; he ruled for [—] years, [—] ruled for [—] years [—], ruled for 36 years. 3 kings; they ruled for 356 years. Then Awan was defeated and the kingship was taken to Kish.

In Kish, Susuda, the fuller, became king; he ruled for 201 + X years. Dadasig ruled for 81 years. Mamagal, the boatman, ruled for 360 years. Kalbum, the son of Mamagal, ruled for 195 years. Tuge ruled for 360 years. Men-nuna, the son of Tuge, ruled for 180 years [—] ruled for 290 years. Lugalju ruled for 360 years. 8 kings; they ruled for 3195 years. Then Kish was defeated and the kingship was taken to Hamazi.[36]

In Hamazi, Hadanic became king; he ruled for 360 years. 1 king; he ruled for 360 years. Then Hamazi was defeated and the kingship was taken to Uruk.

In Uruk, En-cakanca-ana became king; he ruled for 60 years. Lugal-ure ruled for 120 years. Argandea ruled for 7 years. 3 kings; they ruled for 187 years. Then Uruk was defeated and the kingship was taken to Ur.

In Ur, Nani became king; he ruled for 120 + X years. Mec-ki-aj-Nanna, the son of Nani, ruled for 48 years, [—] the son of [—], ruled for 2 years. 3 kings; they ruled for 582 years. Then Ur was defeated and the kingship was taken to Adab.[37]

In Adab, Lugal-ane-mundu became king; he ruled for 90 years. 1 king; he ruled for 90 years. Then Adab was defeated and the kingship was taken to Mari.

In Mari, Anbu became king; he ruled for 30 years. Anba, the son of Anbu, ruled for 17 years. Bazi, the leatherworker, ruled for 30 years. Zizi, the fuller, ruled for 20 years. Limer, the *gudu*[38] priest, ruled for 30 years. Carrum-iter ruled for 9 years. 6 kings; they ruled for 136 years. Then Mari was defeated and the kingship was taken to Kish.

In Kish, Kug-bau, the woman tavern-keeper, who made firm the foundations of Kish, became king; she ruled for 100 years. 1 king; she ruled for 100 years. Then Kish was defeated and the kingship was taken to Akcak.[39]

In Akcak, Unzi became king; he ruled for 30 years. Undalulu ruled for 6 years. Urur ruled for 6 years. Puzur-Nirah ruled for 20 years. Icu-Il ruled for 24 years. Shu-Sin,[40] the son of Icu-Il, ruled for 7 years. 6 kings; they ruled for 99 years Then Akcak was defeated and the kingship was taken to Kish.

In Kish, Puzur-Sin,[41] the son of Kug-bau, became king; he ruled for 25 years. Ur-zababa, the son of Puzur-Sin, ruled for 400 years. 131 are the years of the dynasty of Kug-bau. Zimudar ruled for 30 years. Usi-watar, the son of Zimudar, ruled for 7 years. Ectar-muti ruled for 11 years. Icme-Camac ruled for 11 years. Cu-ilicu ruled for 15 years. Nanniya, the jeweler, ruled for 7 years. 7 kings; they ruled for 491 years. Then Kish was defeated and the kingship was taken to Uruk.

In Uruk, Lugal-zage-si became king; he ruled for 25 years. 1 king; he ruled for 25 years. Then Uruk was defeated and the kingship was taken to Akkad.

In Akkad, Sargon,[42] whose father was a gardener, the cupbearer of Ur-zababa,[43] became king, the King

[34] Mec-ane-pada was the grandson of Meskalamdug, the first historically attested king of Ur, in the twenty-sixth century BCE.

[35] In Elam, to the east of Sumeria in Iran.

[36] Location unknown; perhaps east of Assyria.

[37] Modern Bismaya.

[38] A generic word for "priest."

[39] Location unknown.

[40] Named after Sin, the sun god.

[41] The kingship of Puzur-Sin seems to overlap with that of the previous dynasty from Akcak.

[42] For the legend of Sargon, see Reading 16.

[43] The king of Kish, noted previously.

of Akkad, who built Akkad; he ruled for 56 years. Rimuc, the son of Sargon, ruled for 9 years. Man-icticcu, the older brother of Rimuc, the son of Sargon, ruled for 15 years. Naram-Sin, the son of Man-icticcu, ruled for 56 years. Car-kali-carri, the son of Naram-Sin, ruled for 25 years. 157 are the years of the dynasty of Sargon. Then who was king? Who indeed was king? Irgigi was king, Imi was king, Nanûm was king, Ilulu was king, and the 4 of them ruled for only 3 years. Dudu ruled for 21 years. Cu-Durul, the son of Dudu, ruled for 15 years. 11 kings; they ruled for 181 years. Then Akkad was defeated and the kingship was taken to Uruk.

In Uruk, Ur-nijin became king; he ruled for 7 years. Ur-gigir, the son of Ur-nijin, ruled for 6 years. Kuda ruled for 6 years. Puzur-ili ruled for 5 years. Ur-utu ruled for 6 years. 5 kings; they ruled for 30 years. Uruk was defeated and the kingship was taken to the army of Gutium.[44]

In the army of Gutium, at first no king was famous; they were their own kings and ruled thus for 3 years. Then Inkicuc ruled for 6 years. Zarlagab ruled for 6 years. Culme ruled for 6 years. Silulumec ruled for 6 years. Inimabakec ruled for 5 years. Igecauc ruled for 6 years. Yarlagab ruled for 15 years. Ibate ruled for 3 years. Yarla ruled for 3 years. Kurum ruled for 1 year. Apil-kin ruled for 3 years. La-erabum ruled for 2 years. Irarum ruled for 2 years. Ibranum ruled for 1 year. Hablum ruled for 2 years. Puzur-Sin, the son of Hablum, ruled for 7 years. Yarlaganda ruled for 7 years. [—] ruled for 7 years. Tiriga ruled for 40 days. 21 kings; they ruled for 124 years and 40 days. Then the army of Gutium was defeated and the kingship was taken to Uruk.

In Uruk, Utu-hejal became king; he ruled for 26 years, 2 + X months, and 15 days. 1 king; he ruled for 7 years, 6 months, and 15 days. Then Uruk was defeated and the kingship was taken to Ur.

[44] For the Gutians, see Reading 18.

In Ur, Ur-Nammu became king; he ruled for 18 years. Shulgi, the son of Ur-Nammu, ruled for 46 years. Amar-Sin, the son of Shulgi, ruled for 9 years. Shu-Sin, the son of Amar-Sin, ruled for 9 years. Ibbi-Sin, the son of Shu-Sin, ruled for 24 years. 4 kings; they ruled for 108 years. Then Ur was defeated. The very foundation of Sumer was torn out. The kingship was taken to Isin.

In Isin, Icbi-erra became king; he ruled for 33 years. Cu-ilicu, the son of Icbi-erra, ruled for 20 years. Iddin-Dagan, the son of Cu-ilicu, ruled for 21 years. Icme-Dagan, the son of Iddin-Dagan, ruled for 20 years. Lipit-ectar, the son of Icme-Dagan, ruled 11 years. Ur-Ninurta,[45] the son of Ickur—may he have years of abundance, a good reign, and a sweet life—ruled for 28 years. Bur-Sin, the son of Ur-Ninurta, ruled for 21 years. Lipit-enlil,[46] the son of Bur-Sin, ruled for 5 years. Erra-imitti ruled for 8 years. [—] ruled for [—] 6 months. Enlil-bani ruled for 24 years. Zambiya ruled for 3 years. Iter-pica ruled for 4 years. Ur-dul-kuga ruled for 4 years. Sin-magir ruled for 11 years. Damiq-ilicu, the son of Sin-magir, ruled for 23 years. 14 kings; they ruled for 203 years.

A total of 39 kings ruled for 14409 + X years, 3 months and 3 1/2 days, 4 times in Kish. A total of 22 kings ruled for 2610 + X years, 6 months and 15 days, 5 times in Uruk. A total of 12 kings ruled for 396 years, 3 times in Ur. A total of 3 kings ruled for 356 years, once in Awan. A total of 1 king ruled for 420 years, once in Hamazi. *[16 lines missing]*[47] A total of 12 kings ruled for 197 years, once in Akkad. A total of 21 kings ruled for 125 years and 40 days, once in the army of Gutium. A total of 11 kings ruled for 159 years, once in Isin. There are 11 cities, cities in which the kingship was exercised. A total of 134 kings, who altogether ruled for 28876 + X years.

[45] Named after Ninurta, god of hunting and warfare.

[46] Named after the supreme god Enlil.

[47] The missing sections of this consolidated summary can be recreated from the preceding enumerations.

16

THE LEGEND OF SARGON (CA. 2250 BCE)

A bust from Nineveh with the hair bound up for combat often is identified as Sargon, although this is by no means certain. The semiprecious stones used for the eyes were pried out when the tomb was looted in antiquity.

After the death of Sargon of Akkad, the creator of the greatest world empire up to that time, several legends circulated on clay tablets written in cuneiform script purporting to detail his origins. In one supposedly autobiographical version, he had an unknown father, was born in secret, and then was set adrift in a basket in the Euphrates River. The "infant set adrift" motif was popular in ancient folk literature and is found later in the stories of Moses (Reading 34) and Romulus and Remus (Reading 73).

Source: George A. Barton, *Archaeology and the Bible*, 3rd ed. (Philadelphia: American Sunday-School Union, 1920), 310.

Sargon, the mighty king, King of Agadē[48] am I. My mother was lowly; my father I did not know. The brother of my father dwelt in the mountain. My city is Azupiranu,[49] which is situated on the bank of the Purattu.[50] My lowly mother conceived me, in secret she brought me forth. She placed me in a basket of reeds, she closed my entrance with bitumen. She cast me upon the rivers that did not engulf me. The river carried me, it brought me to Akki, the irrigator. Akki, the irrigator, in the goodness of his heart lifted me out. Akki, the irrigator, as his own son brought me up. Akki, the irrigator, as his gardener appointed me. When I was a gardener the goddess Ishtar loved me, and for four years I ruled the kingdom. The black-headed peoples[51] I ruled, I governed. Mighty mountains with axes of bronze I conquered. I ascended the upper mountains, I burst through the lower mountains. The country of the sea I besieged three times; Dilmun[52] I captured. Unto the great Dur-ilu[53] I went up [—].

Whatsoever king shall be exalted after me, let him rule, let him govern the black-headed peoples. Mighty mountains with axes of bronze let him conquer. Let him ascend the upper mountains, let him break through the lower mountains. The country of the sea let him besiege three times. Dilmun let him capture. To great Dur-ilu let him go up from my city, Agadē.

[48] The newly built capital of the Akkadian Empire; see Reading 18.

[49] The location of Azupiranu is unknown; in Akkadian the word means "City of Saffron."

[50] The Euphrates River.

[51] The traditional means of describing the Sumerian people in particular and Mesopotamians in general.

[52] An area of eastern Arabia.

[53] Der, on the eastern frontier of Babylonia.

17

THE EARLIEST KNOWN AUTHOR (CA. 2190 BCE): ENHEDUANA, "THE EXALTATION OF INANNA"

The "Enheduana Disk," 25.6 centimeters in diameter and made of translucent alabaster (calcite), was found at Ur and now is preserved in storage at the University of Pennsylvania Museum. It dates to ca. 2200 BCE and depicts Enheduana as first in a religious procession with three other figures (her estate manager Adda, her hair dresser Palilis, and her scribe Sagadu) making a sacrifice to Nanna, the moon god. A cuneiform inscription on the back reads, "Enheduana, zirru-priestess, wife of the god Nanna, daughter of Sargon king of the world, in the temple of the goddess Innana."

Sargon, the founder of the Akkadian Empire, appointed his daughter Enheduana as priestess of the temple of the moon god Nanna at Ur. Enheduana is the earliest known named, single author from the ancient Near Eastern and Mediterranean worlds. She wrote several surviving poems in the Sumerian language and is the earliest known author of anything written in cuneiform and the first to write in the first person. Her most famous poem, in 153 lines, honored the goddess Inanna (or, in Semitic, Ishtar). It begins by listing the epithets of the goddess and then continues with Enheduana's personal pleas for Inanna's help in gaining the assistance of Nanna, also known as Sin and Acimbabbar, after she was exiled from the cities of Ur and Uruk by the rebellious king Lugal-ane.

Source: "The Exaltation of Inanna," in J. A. Black, G. Cunningham, J. Ebeling, E. Flückiger-Hawker, E. Robson, J. Taylor, and G. Zólyomi, "The Electronic Text Corpus of Sumerian Literature."

Lady of all the divine powers, resplendent light, righteous woman clothed in radiance, beloved of An and Uras![54] Mistress of heaven, with the great diadem, who loves the good headdress befitting the office of en priestess,[55] who has seized all seven of its divine powers! My lady, you are the guardian of the great divine powers! You have taken up the divine powers, you have hung the divine powers from your hand. You have gathered up the divine powers, you have clasped the divine powers to your breast. Like a dragon you have deposited venom on the foreign lands. When like Ickur[56] you roar at the earth, no vegetation can stand up to you. As a flood descending upon those foreign lands, powerful one of heaven and earth, you are their Inanna. Raining blazing fire down upon the land, endowed with divine powers by An, lady who rides upon a beast, whose words are spoken at the holy command of An! The great rites are yours: who can fathom them? Destroyer of the foreign lands, you confer strength on the storm. Beloved of Enlil, you have made awesome terror weigh upon the Land. You stand at the service of An's commands. At your battle-cry, my lady, the foreign lands bow low. When humanity comes before you in awed silence at the terrifying radiance and tempest, you grasp the most terrible of all the divine powers. Because of you, the threshold of tears is opened, and people walk along the path of the house of great lamentations. In the van of battle, all is struck down before you. With your strength, my lady, teeth can crush flint. You charge forward like a charging storm. You roar with the roaring storm, you continually thunder with Ickur. You spread exhaustion with the stormwinds, while your own feet remain tireless. With the lamenting balaj drum[57] a lament is struck up. My lady, the great Anuna[58] gods fly from you to the ruin mounds like scudding bats. They dare not stand before your terrible gaze. They dare not confront your terrible countenance.

Who can cool your raging heart? Your malevolent anger is too great to cool. Lady, can your mood be soothed? Lady, can your heart be gladdened? Eldest daughter of Sin,[59] your rage cannot be cooled! Lady supreme over the foreign lands, who can take anything from your province? If you frown at the mountains, vegetation there is ruined. Their palaces are set afire. Blood is poured into their rivers because of you, and their people must drink it. They must lead their troops captive before you, all together. They must scatter their elite regiments for you, all together. They must stand their able-bodied young men at your service, all together. Tempests have filled the dancing-places of cities. They drive their young men before you as prisoners. Your holy command has been spoken over the city that has not declared "The foreign lands are yours!", wherever they have not declared "It is your own father's!"; and it is brought back under your feet. Responsible care is removed from its sheepfolds. Its woman no longer speaks affectionately with her husband; at dead of night she no longer takes counsel with him, and she no longer reveals to him the pure thoughts of her heart. Impetuous wild cow, great daughter of Sin, lady greater than An, who can take anything from your province? Great queen of queens, issue of a holy womb for righteous divine powers, greater than your own mother, wise and sage, lady of all the foreign lands, life-force of the teeming people: I will recite your holy song! True goddess fit for divine powers, your splendid utterances are magnificent. Deep-hearted, good woman with a radiant heart, I will enumerate your holy divine powers for you!

I, Enheduana the en priestess, entered my holy jipar[60] in your service. I carried the ritual basket, and intoned the song of joy. But funeral offerings were brought, as if I had never lived there. I approached the light, but the light was scorching hot to me. I approached that shade, but I was covered with a storm.

[54] Uras was an earth goddess, sometimes the consort of An.

[55] The highest-ranking priestess.

[56] The storm god; also Adad.

[57] A large drum.

[58] The gods, also known as Anunnaki, see Reading 1.

[59] Or Nanna, the moon god.

[60] The temple of Inanna.

My honeyed mouth became scum. My ability to soothe moods vanished. Sin, tell An about Lugal-ane[61] and my fate! May An undo it for me! As soon as you tell An about it, An will release me. The Lady[62] will take the destiny away from Lugal-ane; foreign lands and flood lie at her feet. The Lady too is exalted, and can make cities tremble. I, Enheduana, will recite a prayer to you. To you, holy Inanna, I shall give free vent to my tears like sweet beer! I shall say to her "Greetings!" Do not be anxious about Acimbabbar.[63] In connection with the purification rites of holy An, Lugal-ane has altered everything of his, and has stripped An of the E-ana.[64] He has not stood in awe of the greatest deity. He has turned that temple, whose attractions were inexhaustible, whose beauty was endless, into a destroyed temple. While he entered before me as if he was a partner, really he approached out of envy. My good divine wild cow,[65] drive out the man, capture the man! In the place of divine encouragement, what is my standing now? May An extradite the land that is a malevolent rebel against your Nanna! May An smash that city! May Enlil curse it! May its plaintive child not be placated by his mother!

Lady, with the laments begun, may your ship of lamentation be abandoned in hostile territory. Must I die because of my holy songs? My Nanna has paid no heed to me. He has destroyed me utterly in renegade territory. Acimbabbar has certainly not pronounced a verdict on me. What is it to me if he has pronounced it? What is it to me if he has not pronounced it? He stood there in triumph and drove me out of the temple. He made me fly like a swallow from the window; I have exhausted my life-strength. He made me walk through the thorn bushes of the mountains. He stripped me of the rightful crown of the en priestess. He gave me a knife and dagger, saying to me "These are appropriate ornaments for you."

Most precious lady, beloved by An, your holy heart is great; may it be assuaged on my behalf! Beloved spouse of Ucumgal-ana,[66] you are the great lady of the horizon and zenith of the heavens. The Anuna have submitted to you. From birth you were the junior queen: how supreme you are now over the Anuna, the great gods! The Anuna kiss the ground with their lips before you. But my own trial is not yet concluded, although a hostile verdict encloses me as if it were my own verdict. I did not reach out my hands to the flowered bed. I did not reveal the pronouncements of Ningal[67] to anybody. My lady beloved of An, may your heart be calmed toward me, the brilliant en priestess of Nanna! It must be known! It must be known! Nanna has not yet spoken out! He has said, "He is yours!" Be it known that you are lofty as the heavens! Be it known that you are broad as the earth! Be it known that you destroy the rebel lands! Be it known that you roar at the foreign lands! Be it known that you crush heads! Be it known that you devour corpses like a dog! Be it known that your gaze is terrible! Be it known that you lift your terrible gaze! Be it known that you have flashing eyes! Be it known that you are unshakeable and unyielding! Be it known that you always stand triumphant! That Nanna has not yet spoken out, and that he has said "He is yours!" has made you greater, my lady; you have become the greatest! My lady beloved by An, I shall tell of all your rages! I have heaped up the coals in the censer, and prepared the purification rites. The E-ecdam-kug[68] shrine awaits you. Might your heart not be appeased toward me? Because it was full, too full for me, great exalted lady, I have recited this song for you. May a singer repeat to you at noon that which was recited to you at dead of night: "Because of your captive spouse, because of

[61] The rebellious king of Ur who expelled Enheduana from the temple of Nanna.

[62] Inanna.

[63] Nanna or Sin, the moon god.

[64] The temple of An in Uruk.

[65] Ninsun, daughter of An and Uras and mother of Gilgamesh.

[66] Dumuzi (Semitic Tammuz), a vegetation god, was a favorite lover of Inanna; see Reading 14.

[67] The goddess of marsh reeds, Ningal was the daughter of Enki and the consort of Nanna.

[68] A temple in the ancient Sumerian city of Girsu.

your captive child, your rage is increased, your heart unassuaged."

The powerful lady, respected in the gathering of rulers, has accepted her offerings from her. Inanna's holy heart has been assuaged. The light was sweet for her, delight extended over her, she was full of fairest beauty. Like the light of the rising moon, she exuded delight. Nanna came out to gaze at her properly, and her mother Ningal blessed her. The door posts greeted her. Everyone's speech to the mistress is exalted. Praise be to the destroyer of foreign lands, endowed with divine powers by An, to my lady enveloped in beauty, to Inanna!

18

"THE CURSING OF AGADĒ" (CA. 2050 BCE)

The Victory Stele of Naram-Sin commemorating the victory of Naram-Sin, the grandson of Sargon of Akkad, over the Lullubi, a mountain people. In the text known as "The Cursing of Agadē," it was Naram-Sin's looting of the Ekur, the temple of Enlil in Nippur, that caused Enlil to destroy Agadē, the capital of the Akkadian Empire.

The lamentation "The Cursing of Agadē," written by an unknown author and preserved written in cuneiform script on clay tablets, was composed less than a century after the destruction of the Akkadian capital city of Agadē. It relates that after Naram-Sin, the grandson of Sargon, had plundered the Ekur, the temple of Enlil in Nippur, the storm god Enlil retaliated by destroying the city, in much the same way that he already had attempted to destroy humanity with the great flood. In the modern day the curse has been connected to speculations about climate change.

Source: "The Cursing of Agade," in J. A. Black, G. Cunningham, J. Ebeling, E. Flückiger-Hawker, E. Robson, J. Taylor, and G. Zólyomi, "The Electronic Text Corpus of Sumerian Literature."

[Enlil threatens Agadē and causes the gods to depart.]
The shepherd Naram-Sin rose as the daylight on the holy throne of Agadē. Its city wall, like a mountain, reached the heavens. It was like the Tigris flowing into the sea as holy Inanna opened the portals of its city-gates and made Sumer bring its own possessions upstream by boats. The highland Martu,[69] people ignorant of agriculture, brought spirited cattle and kids for her. The Meluḫans,[70] the people of the black land, brought exotic wares up to her. Elam and Subir[71] loaded themselves with goods for her. Holy Inanna could hardly receive all these offerings. But the statement coming from the Ekur[72] was disquieting. Because of Enlil all Agadē was reduced to trembling, and terror befell Inanna in Ulmaš.[73] Holy Inanna abandoned the sanctuary of Agadē. Ninurta[74] brought the jewels of rulership, the royal crown, the emblem and the royal throne bestowed on Agadē, back into his E-šu-me-ša.[75] Utu[76] took away the eloquence of the city. Enki[77] took away its wisdom. An took away into the midst of heaven its fearsomeness that reaches heaven. Enki tore out its well-anchored holy mooring pole from the abzu. Inanna took away its weapons.

[69] The later Amorites, Semitic pastoralists of western Mesopotamia.
[70] Peoples of the Harappan civilization of ancient India.
[71] Subartu, an early name for Assyria.
[72] The temple of Enlil at Nippur, where heaven and earth met and from which divine laws were issued. Originally built ca. 2500 BCE by Enmebaragesi, king of Kish.
[73] The temple of Inanna in Agadē.
[74] God of hunting and warfare, proprietary god of Lagash
[75] The temple of Ninurta.
[76] The sun god, Shamash in Semitic.
[77] The water god, Ea in Semitic.

[Naram-Sin attempts to placate Enlil.]
Naram-Sin saw in a nocturnal vision that Enlil would not let the kingdom of Akkad occupy a pleasant, lasting residence, that he would make its future altogether unfavorable, that he would make its temples shake and would scatter its treasures. He put on mourning clothes. Naram-Sin persisted for seven years! Who has ever seen a king burying his head in his hands for seven years? In order to change what had been inflicted upon him, he tried to alter Enlil's pronouncement.

[When that fails, Naram-Sin attempts to take revenge on Enlil by looting the Ekur, probably because his treasury was short of cash.]
Like an athlete bent to start a contest, he treated the giguna[78] as if it were worth only thirty shekels. Like a robber plundering the city, he set tall ladders against the temple. To demolish Ekur as if it were a huge ship, to prostrate it like a city inundated by Iškur,[79] He set spades against its roots and it sank as low as the foundation of the Land. He put axes against its top, and the temple, like a dead soldier, bowed its neck before him. He ripped out its drain pipes. He struck the Gate of Well-Being with the pickaxe. The Akkadians could look into the holy treasure chest of the gods. The laḫama[80] deities of the great pilasters standing at the temple were thrown into the fire by Naram-Sin. He put its gold in containers and put its silver in leather bags. He filled the docks with its copper, as if it were a huge transport of

[78] The central shrine of the Ekur.
[79] Adad, the storm god.
[80] Lahmu and Lahama were the parents of the god An; see Reading 1.

grain. Large ships were moored at Enlil's temple and its possessions were taken away from the city.

[Enlil takes revenge of his own against Naram-Sin by destroying the city.]
Enlil, the roaring storm that subjugates the entire land, the rising deluge that cannot be confronted, was considering what should be destroyed in return for the wrecking of his beloved Ekur. He lifted his gaze toward the Gubin mountains,[81] and made all the inhabitants of the broad mountain ranges descend. Enlil brought out of the mountains those who do not resemble other people, who are not reckoned as part of the Land, the Gutians,[82] an unbridled people, with human intelligence but canine instincts and monkeys' features. Like small birds they swooped on the ground in great flocks. Because of Enlil, they stretched their arms out across the plain like a net for animals. Nothing escaped their clutches, no one left their grasp. The Gutians drove the trusty goats of Enlil out of their folds. Brigands occupied the highways. Those who lay down on the roof died on the roof; those who lay down in the house were not buried. People were flailing at themselves from hunger. Dogs were packed together in the silent streets; if two men walked there they would be devoured by them, and if three men walked there they would be devoured by them. Honest people were confounded with traitors, heroes lay dead on top of heroes, the blood of traitors ran upon the blood of honest men. The old women did not restrain the cry "Alas for my city!" The old men did not restrain the cry "Alas for its people!" Its young women did not restrain from tearing their hair. Its young men did not restrain from sharpening their knives.

[The gods curse the city.]
At that time, Sin, Enki, Inanna, Ninurta, Iškur, Utu, Nuska, and Nisaba, the great gods cooled Enlil's heart with cool water and prayed to him: "Enlil, may the city that destroyed your city be treated as your city has been treated! May the one that defiled your giguna be treated as Nibru![83] In this city, may heads fill the wells! May its young woman be cruelly killed in her woman's domain, may its old man cry in distress for his slain wife!" Again, Sin, Enki, Inanna, Ninurta, Iškur, Utu, Nuska, and Nisaba, all the gods whosoever, turned their attention to the city, and cursed Agadē severely: "City, you pounced on Ekur! May your holy walls, to their highest point, resound with mourning deities. May your giguna be reduced to a pile of dust! May your pilasters with the standing lahama deities fall to the ground like tall young men drunk on wine! May your grain be returned to its furrow, may it be grain cursed by Ezina![84] May your timber be returned to its forest, may it be timber cursed by Ninilduma[85]! May the cattle slaughterer slaughter his wife, may the sheep butcher butcher his child! May your pregnant priestesses and cult prostitutes abort their children. Agadē, may this make the city die of hunger! May your citizens lie hungry. May the evils of the desert, the silent place, howl continuously! May the ukuku,[86] the bird of depression, make its nest in your gateways! May the grass of mourning grow on your highways. May brackish water flow in the river, where fresh water flowed for you! If someone decides, "I will dwell in this city!," may he not enjoy the pleasures of a dwelling place!"

[The curse is fulfilled.]
And before Utu on that very day, so it was! On its highways laid for wagons, the grass of mourning grew. Moreover, wild rams and alert snakes of the mountains allowed no one to pass. On its plains, where fine grass grew, now the reeds of lamentation grew. Agadē's flowing fresh water flowed as brackish water. When someone decided, "I will dwell in that city!," he could not enjoy the pleasures of a dwelling place. Inanna be praised for the destruction of Agadē!

---

[81] Mountains north of lower Mesopotamia, known as a source of timber.

[82] A mountain people from north of lower Mesopotamia who invaded and destroyed the Akkadian Empire; see Readings 15 and 18.

[83] Nippur, where the looted Ekur was located.

[84] A Sumerian grain goddess.

[85] The god of carpenters.

[86] Owl.

19

THE LAW CODE OF UR-NAMMU (CA. 2040 BCE)

On this cylinder seal Ur-Nammu, seated, appoints Khashkhamer governor of Ishkun-Sin in northern Babylonia.

Because Mesopotamians believed that their gods were unreliable and unpredictable, Mesopotamian rulers served as stand-ins for the gods by issuing law codes, which generally were inscribed on stone in cuneiform script and set up in public places, that were intended to regulate the behavior of people on earth. Nevertheless, laws always were issued in the name of the gods, not of the individual rulers. Either Ur-Nammu (2047–2030 BCE), the founder of the Third Dynasty of Ur, or his son Shulgi (2029–1982 BCE) promulgated the earliest known Mesopotamian law code, which was intended to unify people in the different cities they controlled. The similarity to other law codes subsequently issued by other rulers attests to the common culture that united all the different Mesopotamian cities. The law codes begin with a prologue in which a ruler asserts his right to issue laws in the name of a god and promises to rule justly. These laws can be compared to those of Hammurabi cited in Reading 20.

Sources: J. J. Finkelstein, trans., in James Bennet Pritchard, ed., *Ancient Near Eastern Texts Relating to the Old Testament* (Princeton, NJ: Princeton University Press, 1950), 87–89; James Bennet Pritchard, ed., *The Ancient Near East, Volume I, An*

Anthology of Texts and Pictures (Princeton, NJ: Princeton University Press, 1958), 179–181; James Bennet Pritchard, ed., *Ancient Near Eastern Texts* (Princeton, NJ: Princeton University Press, 1969), 523–525; James Bennet Pritchard, ed., *The Ancient Near East: Supplementary Texts and Pictures Related to the Old Testament* (Princeton, NJ: Princeton University Press, 1969), 87–89.

After An and Enlil had turned over the kingship of Ur to Nanna, at that time did Ur-Nammu, son born of Ninsun, for his beloved mother who bore him, in accordance with his principles of equity and truth [—]. Then did Ur-Nammu the mighty warrior, King of Ur, King of Sumer and Akkad, by the might of Nanna,[87] Lord of the city, and in accordance with the true word of Utu,[88] establish equity in the land; he banished malediction, violence, and strife, and set the monthly Temple expenses at 90 gur[89] of barley, 30 sheep, and 30 sila[90] of butter. He fashioned the bronze sila-measure, standardized the one-mina[91] weight, and standardized the stone weight of a shekel[92] of silver in relation to one mina [—]. The orphan was not delivered up to the rich man; the widow was not delivered up to the mighty man; the man of one shekel was not delivered up to the man of one mina.

1. If a man commits a murder, that man must be killed.
2. If a man commits a robbery, he will be killed.
3. If a man commits a kidnapping, he is to be imprisoned and pay 15 shekels of silver.
4. If a slave marries a slave, and that slave is set free, he does not leave the household.
5. If a slave marries a native free person, he/she is to hand the firstborn son over to his owner.
6. If a man violates the right of another and deflowers the virgin wife of a young man, they shall kill that male.
7. If the wife of a man followed after another man and he slept with her, they shall slay that woman, but that male shall be set free.
8. If a man proceeded by force, and deflowered the virgin female slave of another man, that man must pay five shekels of silver.
9. If a man divorces his first-time wife, he shall pay her one mina of silver.
10. If it is a widow whom he divorces, he shall pay her half a mina of silver.
11. If the man had slept with the widow without there having been any marriage contract, he need not pay any silver.
13. If a man is accused of sorcery he must undergo ordeal by water[93]; if he is proven innocent, his accuser must pay 3 shekels.
14. If a man accused the wife of a man of adultery, and the river ordeal proved her innocent, then the man who had accused her must pay one-third of a mina of silver.
15. If a prospective son-in-law enters the house of his prospective father-in-law, but his father-in-law later gives his daughter to another man, the father-in-law shall return to the rejected son-in-law twofold the amount of bridal presents he had brought.
17. If a slave escapes from the city limits, and someone returns him, the owner shall pay two shekels to the one who returned him.
18. If a man knocks out the eye of another man, he shall weigh out 1/2 a mina of silver.
19. If a man has cut off another man's foot, he is to pay ten shekels.
20. If a man, in the course of a scuffle, smashed the limb of another man with a club, he shall pay one mina of silver.

[87] Or Sin in Semitic; the god of the moon and the proprietary god of Ur.
[88] Or Shamash in Semitic; the god of justice and therefore associated with lawmaking.
[89] A gur was about five bushels.
[90] A sila was about one quart (one liter).
[91] A mina was 1/60 of a talent, or about 1.25 pounds (0.57 kg).
[92] A shekel was 1/60 of a mina.
[93] A test of guilt or innocence where the accused were thrown into the Euphrates River. If they made it to shore they were presumed innocent. Whether they were bound or not made a big difference.

21. If someone severed the nose of another man with a copper knife, he must pay two-thirds of a mina of silver.
22. If a man knocks out a tooth of another man, he shall pay two shekels of silver.
24. [—][94] if he does not have a slave, he is to pay 10 shekels of silver. If he does not have silver, he is to give another thing that belongs to him.
25. If a man's slave-woman, comparing herself to her mistress, speaks insolently to her, her mouth shall be scoured with 1 quart of salt.
28. If a man appeared as a witness, and was shown to be a perjurer, he must pay fifteen shekels of silver.
29. If a man appears as a witness, but withdraws his oath, he must make payment, to the extent of the value in litigation of the case.
30. If a man stealthily cultivates the field of another man and he raises a complaint, this is however to be rejected, and this man will lose his expenses.
31. If a man flooded the field of a man with water, he shall measure out three gur of barley per iku[95] of field.
32. If a man had rented an arable field to another man for cultivation, but he did not cultivate it, turning it into wasteland, he shall measure out three gur of barley per iku of field.

[94] The crime is missing here; only the penalty is given.

[95] About 0.9 acres (0.35 hectares).

20

THE CODE OF HAMMURABI (CA. 1700 BCE)

Copies of the Code of Hammurabi were placed around the Babylonian Empire. Atop the stele shown here, Hammurabi, standing to the left, was depicted receiving the laws from the sun god Shamash. A copy from the Oriental Institute, Chicago.

The Law Code of Hammurabi, issued by the Old Babylonian king Hammurabi (1728–1686 BCE) and inscribed on stone stelai in cuneiform text, is the fullest surviving exposition of ancient Near Eastern law. As in the case of all Mesopotamian law codes, the kings who issued them based their authority not on themselves, but on the gods who appointed them and whom they represented. Although there are differentiations in civil and criminal law among the relative values of the different social classes, the law nevertheless purports to protect the interests of all of the people in Hammurabi's empire. For crimes, the laws prescribe various kinds of punishments that were carried out on the spot, ranging from economic compensation paid to the wronged party to execution, a punishment reserved mostly for slaves. In some cases, a test of guilt or innocence was performed, where the accused was thrown into the Tigris or Euphrates River. If the person made it to shore, he or she was presumed innocent. Whether the person was tied up or a good swimmer made a big difference.

The following extracts focus on what the laws tell us about the social and family structures of ancient Mesopotamia. The code embodies principles found in other Near Eastern law codes ranging from the Code of Ur-Nammu (Reading 19) to the Hebrew Bible (Reading 35).

Source: Robert Francis Harper, *The Code of Hammurabi, King of Babylon, about 2250 BC* (Chicago: University of Chicago Press, 1904).

[Prologue]

When the lofty Anu,[96] King of the Anunnaki,[97] and Bêl,[98] lord of heaven and earth, he who determines the destiny of the land, committed the rule of all mankind to Marduk,[99] the chief son of Ea; when they made him great among the Igigi[100]; when they pronounced the lofty name of Babylon; when they made it famous among the quarters of the world and in its midst established an everlasting kingdom whose foundations were firm as heaven and earth—at that time, Anu and Bêl called me, Hammurabi, the exalted prince, the worshiper of the gods, to cause justice to prevail in the land, to destroy the wicked and the evil, to prevent the strong from oppressing the weak, to go forth like the Sun over the black-headed people, to enlighten the land and to further the welfare of the people. When Marduk sent me to rule the people and to bring help to the country, I established law and justice in the land and promoted the welfare of the oppressed.

———

15. If a man aids a male or female slave of the palace, or a male or female slave of a freeman to escape from the city gate, he shall be put to death.
16. If a man harbors in his house a male or female slave who has fled from the palace or from a freeman, and does not bring the slave forth at the call of the commandant, the owner of that house shall be put to death.
17. If a man seizes a male or female slave, a fugitive, in the field and brings that slave back to his owner, the owner of the slave shall pay him two shekels of silver.
18. If that slave will not name his owner, he shall bring him to the palace and they shall inquire into his antecedents and they shall return him to his owner.
19. If he detains that slave in his house and later the slave be found in his possession, that man shall be put to death.
20. If the slave escapes from the hand of his captor, that man shall so declare, in the name of god,[101] to the owner of the slave and shall go free.

———

42. If a man rents a field for cultivation and does not produce any grain in the field, they shall call him to account because he has not performed the work required on the field, and he shall give to the owner of the field grain on the basis of the adjacent fields.
43. If he does not cultivate the field and neglect it, he shall give to the owner of the field grain on the basis of the adjacent fields; and the field that he has neglected he shall break up with hoes, he shall harrow and he shall return to the owner of the field.
44. If a man rents an unreclaimed field for three years to develop it, and neglects it and does not develop the field, in the fourth year he shall break up the field with hoes, he shall hoe and harrow it and he shall return it to the owner of

[96] Or An, the god of the universe, highest ranking of the gods.
[97] The gods; see Reading 1.
[98] "Lord," another name for Marduk.
[99] The Babylonian equivalent of Enlil, the Sumerian storm god.
[100] The chief gods.

[101] That is, he shall swear an oath.

the field and shall measure out ten gur[102] of grain per ten gan[103] of land.

———

52. If the tenant does not secure a crop of grain or sesame in his field, he shall not cancel his contract.[104]
53. If a man neglects to strengthen his dyke and do not strengthen it,[105] and a break is made in his dyke and the water carries away the farm-land, the man in whose dyke the break has been made shall restore the grain that he has damaged.
54. If he is not able to restore the grain, they shall sell him and his goods, and the farmers whose grain the water has carried away shall share (the results of the sale).
55. If a man opens his canal for irrigation and neglects it and the water carry away an adjacent field, he shall measure out grain on the basis of the adjacent fields.
56. If a man opens up the water and the water carries away the improvements of an adjacent field, he shall measure out ten gur of grain per gan of land.

———

108. If a female wine-seller does not receive grain as the price of drink, but if she receives silver by weight, or makes the measure for drink smaller than the measure for grain, they shall call that wine-seller to account, and they shall throw her into the river.
109. If outlaws collect in the house of a wine-seller, and she does not arrest these outlaws and bring them to the palace, that wine-seller shall be put to death.
110. If a priestess[106] who is not living as a bride opens a wine-shop or enters a wine-shop for a drink, they shall burn that woman.

———

128. If a man takes a wife and does not have intercourse with her, that woman is not a legal wife.
129. If the wife of a man is apprehended in bed with another man, they shall bind them and throw them into the river. If the husband of the woman would save his wife, or if the king would save his male servant, he may.
130. If a man violates the fiancée of another who has not known a male and is living in her father's house, and he lies in her bosom and they apprehend him, that man shall be put to death and that woman shall have no blame.
131. If a man accuses his wife and she has not been taken in lying with another man, she shall take an oath in the name of god and she shall return to her house.
132. If the finger has been pointed[107] at the wife of a man because of another man, and she has not been apprehended in lying with another man, for her husband's sake she shall throw herself into the river.
133. If a man is captured in war and there be maintenance in his house and his wife goes out of her house, she shall protect her body and she shall not enter into another house. If that woman does not protect her body and enters into another house, they shall call that woman to account and they shall throw her into the river.

———

137. If a man sets his face to put away a concubine[108] who has borne him children or a wife who has presented him with children, he shall return to that woman her dowry and shall give to her the income of field, garden, and goods and she shall bring up her children. From the time that her children are grown up, from whatever is given to her children[109] they shall

[102] A gur was about five bushels.
[103] The gan was a field of about 3,300 square yards, or 0.7 acres.
[104] That is, the rent still must be paid.
[105] For maintaining the irrigation system.
[106] Literally, a "sister of god."
[107] That is, an accusation of adultery has been made against her by a third party.
[108] An unmarried woman with whom the man has been living.
[109] By their father.

give to her a portion corresponding to that of a son and the man of her heart may marry her.

138. If a man would put away his wife who has not borne him children, he shall give her money to the amount of her marriage settlement[110] and he shall make good to her the dowry that she brought from her father's house and then he may put her away.
139. If there was no marriage settlement, he shall give to her one mina of silver for a divorce.
140. If he is a freeman, he shall give her one-third mina of silver.
141. If the wife of a man who is living in his house sets her face to go out and play the part of a fool, neglect her house, belittle her husband, they shall call her to account. If her husband says, "I have put her away," he shall let her go. On her departure nothing shall be given to her for her divorce. If her husband says: "I have not put her away," her husband may take another woman. The first woman shall dwell in the house of her husband as a maid servant.
142. If a woman hates her husband, and says: "Thou shalt not have me," they shall inquire into her antecedents for her defects, and if she has been a careful mistress and is without reproach and her husband has been going about and greatly belittling her, that woman has no blame, and she shall receive her dowry and shall go to her father's house.
143. If she has not been a careful mistress, has gadded about, has neglected her house and has belittled her husband, they shall throw that woman into the river.
144. If a man takes a wife and that wife gives a maid servant to her husband and she bears children, if that man sets his face to take a concubine, they shall not countenance him. He may not take a concubine.
145. If a man takes a wife and she does not present him with children and he sets his face to take a concubine, that man may take a concubine and bring her into his house.[111] That concubine shall not rank with his wife.
146. If a man takes a wife and she gives a maid servant to her husband, and that maid servant bears children and afterwards would take rank with her mistress, because she has borne children, her mistress may not sell her for money, but she may reduce her to bondage and count her among the maid servants.
147. If she[112] has not borne children, her mistress may sell her for money.

———

153. If a woman brings about the death of her husband for the sake of another man, they shall impale her.
154. If a man has intercourse with his daughter, they shall expel that man from the city.
155. If a man has betrothed a bride to his son and his son has intercourse with her, and if the father afterward lies in her bosom and they apprehend him, they shall bind that man and throw him into the river.[113]
156. If a man has betrothed a bride to his son and his son has not had intercourse with her but he himself lies in her bosom, he shall pay her one-half mina of silver and he shall make good to her whatever she brought from the house of her father and the man of her heart may marry her.
157. If a man lies in the bosom of his mother after his father, they shall burn both of them.

———

179. If there is a priestess or a devotee[114] to whom her father has given a dowry and written a deed of gift; if in the deed that he has written for her, he have written "after her death she may will to whomsoever she may please," and

[110] The amount paid by the wife's family to the husband.

[111] As a means of dealing with infertility.

[112] The maid servant.

[113] In extreme cases, an accused or convicted party would be bound before being thrown into the river; these unfortunate persons were not expected to survive.

[114] A temple servant; in some interpretations a temple prostitute.

he has granted her full discretion; after her father dies she may give it to whomsoever she may please after her death. Her brothers may not lay claim against her.

180. If a father does not give a dowry to his daughter, a bride or devotee, after her father dies she shall receive as her share in the goods of her father's house the portion of a son, and she shall enjoy it as long as she lives. After her death it belongs to her brothers.
181. If a father devotes a votary or a virgin to a god and does not give her a dowry, after her father dies she shall receive as her share in the goods of her father's house one-third of the portion of a son and she shall enjoy it as long as she lives. After her death, it belongs to her brothers.

———

195. If a son strikes his father, they shall cut off his fingers.[115]
196. If a man destroys the eye of another man, they shall destroy his eye.
197. If one breaks a man's bone, they shall break his bone.
198. If one destroys the eye of a freeman or breaks the bone of a freeman, he shall pay one mina of silver.
199. If one destroys the eye of a man's slave or breaks a bone of a man's slave he shall pay one-half its price.
200. If a man knocks out a tooth of a man of his own rank, they shall knock out his tooth.
201. If one knocks out a tooth of a freeman, he shall pay one-third mina of silver.
202. If a man strikes the person of a man[116] who is his superior, he shall receive sixty strokes with an ox-tail whip in public.
203. If a man strikes another man of his own rank, he shall pay one mina of silver.

———

[Epilogue]

The righteous laws that Hammurabi, the wise king, established and with which he gave the land stable support and pure government. Hammurabi, the perfect king, am I. I was not careless, nor was I neglectful of the black-headed people, whose rule Bêl presented and Marduk delivered to me.[117] I provided them with a peaceful country. I opened up difficult barriers and lent them support. With the powerful weapon that Zamama[118] and Nanna entrusted to me, with the breadth of vision that Ea allotted me, with the might that Marduk gave me, I expelled the enemy to the north and south; I made an end of their raids; I brought health to the land; I made the populace to rest in security; I permitted no one to molest them.

The great gods proclaimed me and I am the guardian governor, whose scepter is righteous and whose beneficent protection is spread over my city. In my bosom I carried the people of the land of Sumer and Akkad; under my protection I brought their brethren into security; in my wisdom I oversaw them, so that the strong might not oppose the weak, and that they should give justice to the orphan and the widow: in Babylon, the city whose turrets Anu and Bêl raised; in Ésagila,[119] the temple whose foundations are firm as heaven and earth, for the pronouncing of judgments in the land, for the rendering of decisions for the land, and for the righting of wrong, my weighty words I have written upon my monument, and in the presence of my image as King of Righteousness have I established.

The king, who is pre-eminent among city kings, am I. My words are precious, my wisdom is unrivaled. By the command of Shamash,[120] the great judge of heaven and earth, may I make righteousness to shine forth on the land. By the order of Marduk,

[115] The "lex talionis," or "law of retaliation," where the punishment is made to fit the crime, was a common feature of ancient law codes.
[116] That is, commit an assault.
[117] Bêl and Marduk being names for the same god.
[118] A war god.
[119] The temple of Marduk in Babylon.
[120] On the monument, Hammurabi receives the law code from the sun god Shamash, the god of justice.

my lord, may no one efface my statues, may my name be remembered with favor in Ésagila forever. Let any oppressed man who has a cause come before my image as King of Righteousness! Let him read the inscription on my monument! Let him give heed to my weighty words! And may my monument enlighten him as to his cause and may he understand his case![121] May he set his heart at ease, exclaiming: "Hammurabi indeed is a ruler who is like a real father to his people; he has given reverence to the words of Marduk, his lord. He has obtained victory for Marduk in north and south. He has made glad the heart of Marduk, his lord. He has established prosperity for the people for all time and given a pure government to the land." Let him read the code and pray with a full heart before Marduk, my lord, and Zarpanit,[122] my lady, and may the protecting deities, the gods who enter Ésagila, daily in the midst of Ésagila look with favor on his wishes in the presence of Marduk, my lord, and Zarpanit, my lady!

In the days that are yet to come, for all future time, may the king who is in the land observe the words of righteousness that I have written upon my monument! May he not alter the judgments of the land that I have pronounced, or the decisions of the country that I have rendered! May he not efface my statues! If that man have wisdom, if he wish to give his land good government, let him give attention to the words that I have written upon my monument! And may this monument enlighten him as to procedure and administration, the judgments that I have pronounced, and the decisions that I have rendered for the land! And let him rightly rule his black-headed people; let him pronounce judgments for them and render for them decisions! Let him root out the wicked and evildoer from his land! Let him promote the welfare of his people!

Hammurabi, the King of Righteousness, whom Shamash has endowed with justice, am I. My words are weighty; my deeds are unrivaled. If that man pay attention to my words that I have written upon my monument, do not efface my judgments, do not overrule my words, and do not alter my statues, then will Shamash prolong that man's reign, as he has mine, who am King of Righteousness, that he may rule his people in righteousness.

If that man do not pay attention to my words that I have written upon my monument; if he forget my curse and do not fear the curse of god; if he abolish the judgments that I have formulated, overrule my words, alter my statues, efface my name written thereon and write his own name; on account of these curses, commission another to do so,[123] but as for that man, be he king or lord, or priest-king or commoner, whoever he may be, may the great god, the father of the gods, who has ordained my reign, take from him the glory of his sovereignty, may he break his scepter, and curse his fate!

---

[121] By reading what the laws were, anyone would know where they stood under the law and whether they had a good case.

[122] A mother goddess, the consort of Marduk.

[123] Hammurabi is still addressing Marduk.

CHAPTER 3

Egypt and the Bronze Age (5000–1200 BCE)

As had occurred in Mesopotamia, a Bronze Age civilization likewise arose in the Nile River Valley, similar in its broad outlines to Mesopotamian civilization but very different in its specific manifestations. As in Mesopotamia, the manner in which civilization developed in Egypt and the role that people played in it were heavily influenced by geography, although the geographic characteristics of Egypt and Mesopotamia greatly differed. In particular, Egypt's geographic isolation created political unity, as opposed to the characteristic disunity of Mesopotamia. Being less affected than the rest of the Near East by either internal disruption or outside invasion, Egyptian history passed relatively smoothly through three periods, the Old Kingdom (2700–2200 BCE), the Middle Kingdom (2050–1786 BCE), and the New Kingdom (1534–1070 BCE), each with its own particular characteristics, with only occasional periods of disruption separating them.

Documents that survive from the earliest periods of ancient Egypt usually are written using the hieroglyphic writing system on stone, the walls of tombs, or papyrus. Stone, by its very nature, lasts for many centuries, whereas documents in papyrus and fresco have survived as a result of Egypt's dry and desiccated climate. Egyptian literature soon developed from inventories and terse catalogues of pharaohs to include a wide range of literary genres, including a significant number of first-person accounts. Thus, unlike most Mesopotamian records, the documents that survive from even the earliest times of ancient Egypt give personal accounts of named individuals.

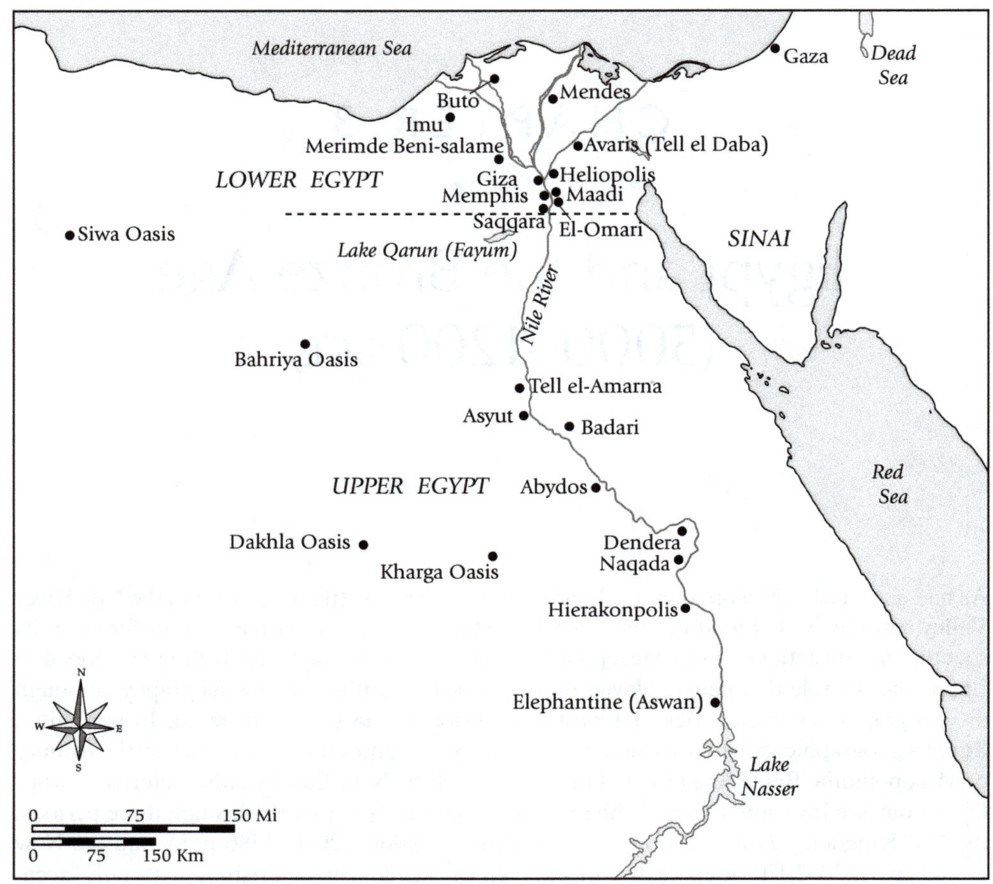

Map 3 Early Dynastic Egypt

21

THE AUTOBIOGRAPHY OF WENI (CA. 2275 BCE)

The autobiography of Weni, inscribed on a limestone slab, is preserved as inventory number 1435 in the Cairo Museum.

The autobiography of Weni, an Egyptian palace official during the Sixth Dynasty of the Old Kingdom, survives in a single copy carved on a large, damaged slab of limestone covering one wall of a tomb from Abydos. The tomb was misplaced after its original discovery in 1880 and not rediscovered until 1999. The inscription contains fifty-one columns of hieroglyphic text and demonstrates how Egyptian officials of this period were completely dependent on the good will of the pharaoh. Weni served under the pharaohs Teti (2345–2333 BCE), Pepi I

(2332–2283 BCE), and Merenre (2283–2278 BCE) and took great pride in his close, personal relationship with them.

Sources: Miriam Lichtheim, trans., *Ancient Egyptian Literature: A Book of Readings*, Vol. 1 (Berkeley: University of California Press, 1973, repr. 2006), 18–22; also James Henry Breasted, *Ancient Records of Egypt, Historical Documents from the Earliest Times to the Persian Conquest*, Vol. I (Chicago: University of Chicago Press, 1906), 134–150.

The Count, Governor of Upper Egypt, Chamberlain, Warden of Nekhen,[1] Mayor of Nekheb,[2] Sole Companion, honored by Osiris[3] Foremost-of-the-Westerners, Weni says: I was a fillet-wearing youth under the majesty of Pharaoh Teti,[4] my office being that of Custodian of the Storehouse, when I became Inspector of the Royal Tenants of the Palace. When I had become Overseer of the Robing-Room under the majesty of Pharaoh Pepi,[5] His Majesty gave me the rank of Companion and Inspector of Priests of his pyramid town. While my office was that of Palace [—] His Majesty made me Senior Warden of Nekhen, his heart being filled with me beyond any other servant of his. I heard cases alone with the chief judge and vizier, concerning all kinds of secrets. I acted in the name of the pharaoh for the royal harem and for the six great houses, because His Majesty's heart was filled with me beyond any official of his, any noble of his, any servant of his. When I begged of the majesty of my Lord that there be brought for me a sarcophagus of white stone from Tura,[6] His Majesty had a royal seal-bearer cross over with a company of sailors under his command, to bring me this sarcophagus from Tura. It came with him in a great barge of the court, together with its lid, a doorway, lintel, two doorjambs, and a libation-table. Never before had the like been done for any servant—but I was excellent in His Majesty's heart; I was rooted in His Majesty's heart; His Majesty's heart was filled with me.

[1] An ancient city of Upper Egypt, Hierakonpolis in Greek.

[2] Modern El Kab on the east bank of the Nile in Upper Egypt, on the other side of the river from Nekhen.

[3] God of the underworld.

[4] Pharaoh 2345–2333 BCE.

[5] Pharaoh 2332–2283 BCE.

[6] The most important Egyptian limestone quarrying site, located near modern Cairo.

While I was Senior Warden of Nekhen, His Majesty made me a sole companion and overseer of the royal tenants. I replaced four overseers of "royal tenants" who were there. I acted for His Majesty's praise in guarding, escorting the pharaoh, and attending. I acted throughout so that His Majesty praised me for it exceedingly. When there was a secret charge in the royal harem against Queen Weret-yamtes,[7] His Majesty made me go in to hear it alone. No chief judge and vizier, no official was there, only I alone, because I was worthy, because I was rooted in His Majesty's heart; because His Majesty had filled his heart with me. Only I put it in writing together with one other senior warden of Nekhen, while my rank was that of overseer of royal tenants. Never before had one like me heard a secret of the pharaoh's harem, but His Majesty made me hear it, because I was worthy in His Majesty's heart beyond any official of his, beyond any noble of his, beyond any servant of his.

When His Majesty took action against the Asiatic Sand-Dwellers,[8] His Majesty made an army of many tens of thousands from all of Upper Egypt: from Yebu[9] in the south to Medinet[10] in the north; from Lower Egypt: from all of the Two-Sides-of-the-House[11] and from Sedjer and Khen-sedjru[12]; and from Irtjet-Kushites, Medjay-Kushites, Yam-Kushites, Wawat-Kushites,

[7] Consort of the pharaoh Pepi.

[8] A generic term for desert peoples living to the east of Egypt.

[9] The island of Elephantine in the far Upper Nile River, now part of the city of Aswan.

[10] A city of the Fayum oasis in the northern part of Upper Egypt.

[11] The Nile delta region.

[12] Sedjer and Khen-sedjru are otherwise unknown places in the Nile delta.

Kaau-Kushites[13]; and from Tiemeh-land.[14] His Majesty sent me at the head of this army, there being counts, royal seal-bearers, sole companions of the palace, chieftains and mayors of towns of Upper and Lower Egypt, companions, scout leaders, chief priests of Upper and Lower Egypt, and chief district officials at the head of the troops of Upper and Lower Egypt, from the villages and towns that they governed and from the Kushites of those foreign lands. I was the one who commanded them, while my rank was that of Overseer of Royal Tenants, because of my rectitude, so that no one attacked his fellow, so that no one seized a loaf or sandals from a traveler, so that no one took a cloth from any town, so that no one took a goat from anyone. I led them from Northern Isle and Gate of Ly-hotep in the district of Horus-Lord-of-Truth[15] while being in this rank, I determined the number of these troops. It had never been determined by any servant.

This army returned in safety,
It had ravaged the Sand-Dwellers' land.
This army returned in safety,
It had flattened the Sand-Dwellers' land.
This army returned in safety,
It had sacked its strongholds.
This army returned in safety,
It had cut down its figs, its vines.
This army returned in safety,
It had thrown fire in all its mansions.
This army returned in safety,
It had slain its troops by many ten-thousands.
This army returned in safety,
It had carried off many as captives.

His Majesty praised me for it beyond anything. His Majesty sent me to lead this army five times, to attack the land of the Sand-Dwellers as often as they rebelled, with these troops. I acted so that His Majesty praised me for it beyond anything. Told there were marauders among these foreigners at the nose of Gazelle's-head,[16] I crossed in ships with these troops. I made a landing in the back of the height of the mountain range, to the north of the land of the Sand-Dwellers, while half of this army was on the road. I came and caught them all and slew every marauder among them.

[Weni becomes governor of Upper Egypt.]

When I was chamberlain of the palace and sandal-bearer, Pharaoh Merenre,[17] my Lord who lives forever, made me Count and Governor of Upper Egypt, from Yebu[18] in the south to Medinet in the north, because I was worthy in His Majesty's heart, because I was rooted in His Majesty's heart, because His Majesty's heart was filled with me. When I was chamberlain and sandal-bearer, His Majesty praised me for the watch and guard duty that I did at court, more than any official of his, more than any noble of his, more than any servant of his. Never before had this office been held by any servant. I governed Upper Egypt for him in peace, so that no one attacked his fellow. I did every task. I counted everything that is countable for the residence in this Upper Egypt two times, and every service that is countable for the residence in this Upper Egypt two times. I did a perfect job in Upper Egypt. Never before had the like been done in Upper Egypt. I acted throughout so that His Majesty praised me for it.

His Majesty sent me to Ibhat[19] to bring the sarcophagus "chest of the living" together with its lid, and the costly august pyramidion[20] for the pyramid "Merenre-Appears-in-Splendor."[21] His Majesty sent me to Yebu to bring a granite false-door and its libation stone and granite lintels, and to bring granite portals and libation stones for the upper chamber of my mistress, the pyramid "Merenre-Appears-in-Splendor." I traveled north with them to the pyramid

[13] The territory of Kush, immediately south of Egypt on the Nile River, was a favorite recruiting ground for soldiers and mercenaries. For the later Empire of Kush, see Reading 70.

[14] An arid region to the west of Kush; modern Libya.

[15] Three otherwise unknown places.

[16] Perhaps on the southern coast of Palestine.

[17] Pharaoh 2283–2278 BCE.

[18] The island of Elephantine on the Nile between Egypt and Kush.

[19] A quarry south of the second cataract of the Nile River.

[20] The capstone at the peak of the pyramid.

[21] Pyramids had names and were viewed as gods in their own right.

"Merenre-Appears-in-Splendor" in six barges and three tow-boats of eight ribs in a single expedition. Never had Yebu and Ibhat been done in a single expedition under any pharaoh. Thus everything His Majesty commanded was done entirely as His Majesty commanded. His Majesty sent me to Hatnub[22] to bring a great altar of alabaster of Hatnub. I brought this altar down for him in seventeen days. After it was quarried at Hatnub, I had it go downstream in this barge I had built for it, a barge of acacia wood of sixty cubits in length and thirty cubits in width. Assembled in seventeen days, in the third month of summer, when there was no water on the sandbanks, it landed at the pyramid "Merenre-Appears-in-Splendor" in safety. It came about through me entirely in accordance with the ordinance commanded by my Lord.

His Majesty sent me to dig five canals in Upper Egypt, and to build three barges and four tow-boats of acacia wood of Wawat.[23] Then the foreign chiefs of Irtjet, Wawat, Yam, and Medjay[24] cut the timber for them. I did it all in one year. Floated, they were loaded with very large granite blocks for the pyramid "Merenre-Appears-in-Splendor." Indeed I made a saving for the palace with all these five canals. As Pharaoh Merenre who lives forever is august, exalted, and mighty more than any god, so everything came about in accordance with the ordinance commanded by his ka.[25]

I was one beloved of his father, praised by his mother, gracious to his brothers. The count, true Governor of Upper Egypt, honored by Osiris, Weni.

22

"THE TALE OF THE ELOQUENT PEASANT" (CA. 2100 BCE)

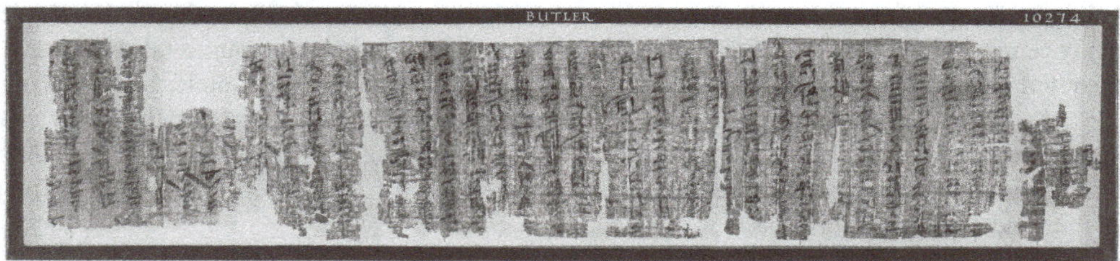

A section of the "Papyrus Butler," now in the British Museum, which preserves "The Tale of the Eloquent Peasant." It was written circa 1800 BCE.

[22] The location of alabaster quarries in the desert east of Egypt.

[23] The northernmost part of Kush, immediately south of Egypt on the Nile.

[24] All areas of Kush, south of Egypt.

[25] One of the souls of the pharaoh, a life force that left the body at death, but also regularly returned. Offerings were left in a tomb so the ka could be nourished.

"The Tale of the Eloquent Peasant," composed by an anonymous author, tells the story of Khunanup, who tries to recover his property that has been stolen by Nemtynakht. Khunanup addresses nine eloquent petitions to the pharaoh, who eventually orders the goods to be restored. The pharaoh Neb-kau-ra was a member of the Ninth or Tenth Dynasty, which ruled part of Egypt from Heracleopolis circa 2160–2025 BCE, during the First Intermediate Period, when centralized rule had broken down. The text illustrates newly emerging concepts of justice and the increasing rights of the common people at that time. As is usually the case with papyrus documents, there are missing parts in the text.

Source: George A. Barton, *Archaeology and the Bible*, 3rd ed. (Philadelphia: American Sunday School, 1920), 418–421.

There was a man, Khunanup by name, a peasant of Sechet-hemat, and he had a wife [—] by name. Then said this peasant to his wife, "Behold, I am going down to Egypt to bring back bread for my children. Go in and measure the grain that we still have in our storehouse [—] bushels." Then from this he measured for her eight bushels of grain. Then this peasant said to his wife, "Behold, two bushels of grain shall be left for bread for you and the children. But make for me the six bushels into bread and beer for each of the days that I shall be on the road." Then this peasant went down to Egypt after he had loaded his asses with all the good produce of Sechet-hemat. This peasant set out and journeyed southward to Ehnas.[26] He came to a point opposite Per-fefi, north of Medenit, and found there a man standing on the bank, Dehuti-necht by name, who was the son of a man named Iseri, who was one of the serfs of the chief steward, Meruitensi. Then said this Dehuti-necht, when he saw the asses of this peasant that appealed to his covetousness, "Oh that some good god would help me to rob this peasant of his goods!"

The house of Dehuti-necht stood close to the side of the path, which was narrow, not wide. It was about the width of a [—]-cloth, and upon one side of it was the water and upon the other side was growing grain. Then said Dehuti-necht to his servant, "Hasten and bring me a shawl from the house!" And it was brought at once. Then he spread this shawl upon the middle of the road, and it extended, one edge to the water, and the other to the grain. The peasant came along the path that was the common highway. Then said Dehuti-necht, "Look out, peasant, do not trample on my clothes!" The peasant answered, "I will do as you wish; I will go in the right of way!" As he was turning to the upper side, Dehuti-necht said, "Does my grain serve you as a road?" Then said the peasant, "I am going in the right way. The bank is steep and the path lies near the grain and you have stopped up the road ahead with your clothes. Will you, then, not let me go by?"

Upon that one of the asses took a mouthful of grain. Then said Dehuti-necht, "See, I will take away your ass because it has eaten my grain." Then the peasant said, "I am going in the right way. As one side was made impassable I have led my ass along the other, and will you seize it because it has taken a mouthful of grain? But I know the Lord of this property; it belongs to the chief steward, Meruitensi. It is he who punishes every robber in this whole land. Shall I, then, be robbed in his domain?" Then said Dehuti-necht, "Is it not a proverb that the people employ: 'The name of the poor is only known on account of his Lord?' It is I who speak to you, but the chief steward of whom you think." Then he took a rod from a green tamarisk and beat all his limbs with it, and seized his asses and drove them into his compound. Thereupon the peasant wept loudly on account of the pain of what had been done to him. Dehuti-necht said to him, "Do not cry so loud, peasant, or you shall go to the city of the dead." The peasant said, "You beat me and steal my goods, and will you also take the wail

[26] Heracleopolis in Greek; capital of the twentieth nome of Upper Egypt.

away from my mouth? O Silence-maker! Give me my goods again! May I never cease to cry out, if you fear!" The peasant consumed four days, during which he besought Dehuti-necht, but he did not grant him his rights.

Then this peasant went to the south, to Ehnas to implore the chief steward, Meruitensi. He met him as he was coming out of the canal-door of his compound to embark in his boat. Thereupon the peasant said, "Oh, let me lay before you this affair. Permit one of your trusted servants to come to me, that I may send him to you concerning it." Then the steward Meruitensi, sent one of his servants to him, and he sent back by him an account of the whole affair. Then the chief steward, Meruitensi, laid the case of Dehuti-necht before his attendant officials, and they said to him, "Lord, it is presumably a case of one of your peasants who has gone against another peasant near him. Behold, it is customary with peasants to so conduct themselves toward others who are near them. Shall we beat Dehuti-necht for a little natron and a little salt? Command him to restore it and he will restore it." The chief steward, Meruitensi, remained silent; he answered neither the officials nor the peasant.

The peasant then came to entreat the chief steward Meruitensi, for the first time, and said, "Chief steward, my Lord, you are greatest of the great, you are guide of all that is not and that is. When you embark on the sea of truth, that you may go sailing upon it, then shall your ship remain fast, then shall no misfortune happen to your mast, then shall you not be stranded. For you are the father of the orphan, the husband of the widow, the brother of the desolate, the garment of the motherless.[27] Let me place your name in this land higher than all good laws: you guide without avarice, you free from meanness, you who destroys deceit, who creates truthfulness. Throw the evil to the ground. I will speak. Hear me. Do justice, O you praised one, whom the praised ones praise. Remove my oppression. Behold, I have a heavy weight to carry. Behold, I am troubled of soul. Examine me, I am in sorrow."

[Meruitensi was so impressed with Khunanup's eloquence that he delayed making a ruling and compelled Khunanup to return again and again.]

This peasant came to implore him for the eighth time, and said, "Chief steward, my Lord, greed is absent from a good merchant. Your heart is greedy, it does not become you. You despoil: this is not praiseworthy for you. Your daily rations are in your house; your body is well filled. Fear of you has not deterred me from supplicating you; if you think so, you have not known my heart. The Silent One,[28] who turns to report to you his difficulties, is not afraid to present them to you. Your real estate is in the country, your bread is on your estate, your food is in the storehouse. Your officials give to you and you take it. Are you, then, not a robber? Do the truth for the sake of the Lord of Truth.[29] You god, Thoth,[30] you ought to keep yourself far removed from injustice. You, virtuous one, you should be really virtuous. Further, truth is true to eternity. It goes with those who perform it to the region of the dead. Does it then happen that the scales stand aslant?[31] Behold, if I come not, if another comes, then you host opportunity to speak as one who addresses the silent, as one who responds to him who has not spoken to you. You have not been sick. You have not fled, you have not departed. But you have not yet granted me any reply to this beautiful word that comes from the mouth of the sun god himself, 'Speak the truth; do the truth, for it is great,

[27] For the theme of government officials being the protectors of the poor and destitute, note also the prologue and epilogue of the "Code of Hammurabi," Reading 20.

[28] The theme of the "Silent One" recurs in Egyptian literature. It can refer to keeping silent in a temple, to a lord who does not reply to a petition, or even to the god Osiris. In this instance it apparently refers to the usual silence of the unprivileged in the face of authority.

[29] The god Ptah, a god of justice.

[30] The god of wisdom, Thoth weighs the hearts of deceased persons in the underworld to determine whether they had lived a just life.

[31] That is, the just person will not be cheated by the scales of justice, administered by Thoth, in the judgment after death.

it is mighty, it is everlasting. It will obtain for you merit, and will lead you to veneration.' For does the scale stand aslant? It is their scale-pans that bear the objects, and in just scales there is no wanting."

[After making a ninth appeal, Khunanup was summoned back to Meruitensi.]
Then the chief steward, Meruitensi, sent two servants to bring him back. Thereupon the peasant feared that he would suffer thirst as a punishment imposed upon him for what he had said. Then said the chief steward, Meruitensi, "Fear not, peasant! See, you shall remain with me." Then said the peasant, "I live because I eat of your bread and drink your beer forever." Then the chief steward, Meruitensi, caused them to bring, written on a new roll, all the addresses of these days. The chief steward sent them to His Majesty, the Pharaoh of Upper and Lower Egypt,[32] Neb-kau-ra,[33] the blessed, and they were more agreeable to the heart of His Majesty than all that was in his land. His Majesty said, "Pass sentence yourself, my beloved son!" Then the chief steward, Meruitensi, caused two servants to go and bring a list of the household of Dehuti-necht from the government office, and his possessions were six persons, with a selection from his [—] from his barley, from his spelt, from his asses, from his swine, from his [—].

[The rest of the tale is lost, but it would appear that these goods from the property of Dehuti-necht were given to the peasant and he went home victorious.]

[32] Rather an overstatement, as during the Intermediate Periods Egyptian unity had broken down.
[33] Neb-kau-ra Khety was a pharaoh of the Ninth or Tenth Dynasty who ruled from Heracleopolis between 2160 and 2025 BCE during the First Intermediate Period.

23

"THE HYMN TO THE NILE" (CA. 2000 BCE)

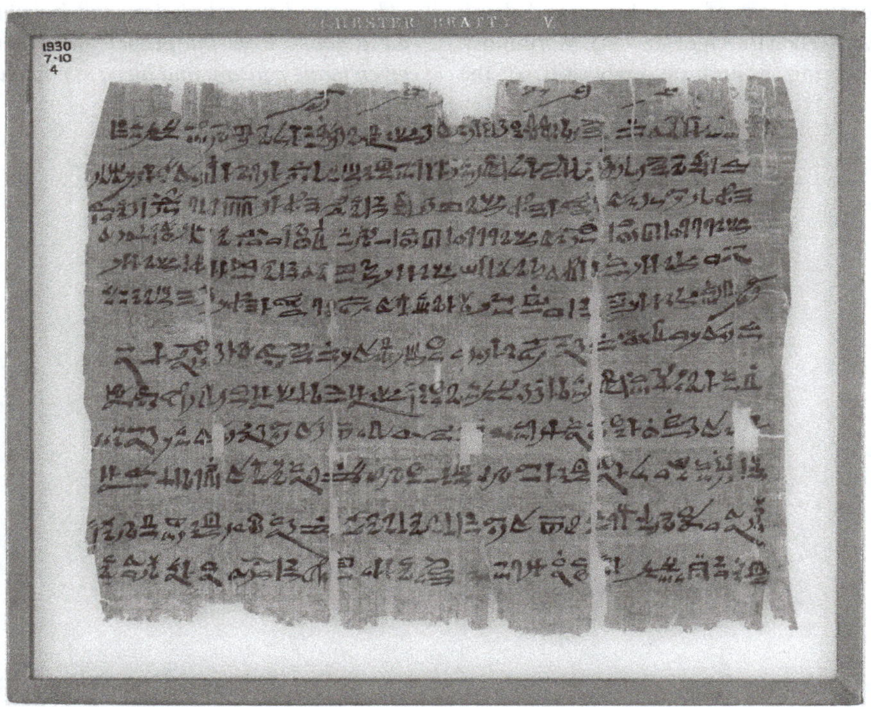

"The Hymn to the Nile" as written in hieratic script on the "Papyrus Chester Beatty" 5 in the British Museum in London.

The anonymously authored poem known as "The Hymn to the Nile" or "The Hymn to the Inundation," like much of Egyptian literature, demonstrates the great significance of the Nile River for life in Egypt. All good things in Egypt were attributed to the Nile, in particular to the annual flood, represented by the god Hapi. Although no temples were dedicated to the Nile, there were many festivals in its honor. Although the earliest surviving papyrus copies of the "Hymn to the Nile" date to the New Kingdom, its language suggests that it was originally composed shortly after 2000 BCE, at the beginning of the Middle Kingdom.

Source: Oliver J. Thatcher, ed., *The Library of Original Sources, Vol. I: The Ancient World* (Milwaukee: University Research Extension Co., 1907), 9–83.

Hail to thee, O Nile!, who manifests thyself over this land, and comes to give life to Egypt! Mysterious is thy issuing forth from the darkness, on this day whereon it is celebrated! Watering the orchards created by Ra,[34] to cause all the cattle to live, you give the earth to drink, inexhaustible one! Path that descends from the sky, loving the bread of Geb[35] and the first-fruits of Neper,[36] you cause the workshops of Ptah[37] to prosper!

Lord of the fish, during the inundation, no bird alights on the crops. You create the grain, you bring forth the barley, assuring perpetuity to the temples. If you cease your toil and your work, then all that exists is in anguish. If the gods suffer in heaven, then the faces of men waste away. Then he torments the flocks of Egypt, and great and small are in agony.

But all is changed for mankind when he comes. He is endowed with the qualities of Nu.[38] If he shines, the earth is joyous, every stomach is full of rejoicing, every spine is happy, every jaw-bone crushes its food.

He brings the offerings, as chief of provisioning. He is the creator of all good things, as master of energy, full of sweetness in his choice. If offerings are made it is thanks to him, he brings forth the herbage for the flocks, and sees that each god receives his sacrifices. All that depends on him is a precious incense. He spreads himself over Egypt, filling the granaries, renewing the markets, watching over the goods of the unhappy.

He is prosperous to the height of all desires, without fatiguing himself therefor. He brings again his Lordly boat. He is not sculptured in stone. He is not an image crowned with the uraeus serpent. He cannot be contemplated. No servitors has he, no bearers of offerings! He is not enticed by incantations! None knows the place where he dwells, none discovers his retreat by the power of a written spell.

No dwelling can contain you! None penetrates within your heart! Your young men, your children applaud you and render unto you royal homage. Stable are your decrees for Egypt before your servants of the north! He stanches the water from all eyes and watches over the increase of his good things.

Where misery existed, joy manifests itself; all beasts rejoice. The children of Sebek,[39] the sons of Neith,[40] the cycle of the gods that dwells in him, are prosperous. His reservoirs water the fields! He makes mankind valiant, enriching some, bestowing his love on others. None commands at the same time as himself. He creates the offerings without the aid of Neith, making mankind for himself with multiform care.

He shines when he issues forth from the darkness, to cause his flocks to prosper. It is his force that gives existence to all things; nothing remains hidden for him. Let men clothe themselves to fill his gardens. He watches over his works, producing the inundation during the night. The associate of Ptah, he causes all his servants to exist, all writings and divine words, and that which he needs in the north.

It is with the words that he penetrates into his dwelling. He issues forth at his pleasure through the magic spells. Your unkindness brings destruction to the fish. It is then that prayer is made for the seasonal water; that southern Egypt may be seen in the same state as the north, that each one is seen with his

[34] Initially, the primary sun god of ancient Egypt.

[35] God of the earth.

[36] God of grain.

[37] God of wisdom.

[38] Or Nun, the watery abyss and chaos that existed before all time and from which the world and universe were created.

[39] The crocodile god.

[40] An ancient goddess with many epithets, such as "The Great Flood" and the "Nurse of Crocodiles."

instruments of labor, that no one is left behind his companions. No one clothes himself with garments, the children of the noble put aside their ornaments.[41] His night remains silent, but all is changed by the inundation; it is a healing-balm for all mankind.

Establisher of justice! Mankind desires you, supplicating you to answer their prayers; you answer them by the inundation! Men offer the first-fruits of wheat; all the gods adore you! The birds descend not on the soil. It is believed that with your hand of gold you make bricks of silver! But we are not nourished on lapis-lazuli[42]; wheat alone gives vigor.

A festal song is raised for you on the harp, with the accompaniment of the hand. Your young men and your children acclaim you and prepare their long exercises. You are the august ornament of the earth, letting your boat advance before men, lifting up the heart of women in labor, and loving the multitude of the flocks.

When you shine in the royal city, the rich man is sated with good things, the poor man even disdains the lotus; all that is produced is of the choicest; all the plants exist for your children. If you have refused nourishment, the dwelling is silent, devoid of all that is good, the country falls exhausted.

O inundation of the Nile, offerings are made unto you, oxen are immolated for you, great festivals are instituted for you. Birds are sacrificed to you, gazelles are taken for you in the mountain, pure flames are prepared for you. Sacrifice is made to every god as it is made to the Nile. Incense ascends unto heaven, Oxen, bulls, fowls are burnt! The Nile has made its retreats in southern Egypt, its name is not known beyond the Tuau.[43] The god does not manifest his forms, he baffles all conception.

Men exalt him like the cycle of the gods, they dread him who creates the heat,[44] even him who has made his son[45] the universal master in order to give prosperity to Egypt. Come and prosper! Come and prosper! O Nile, come and prosper! O you who make men to live through your flocks and your flocks through your orchards! Come and prosper, come, O Nile, come and prosper!

[41] That is, during the prayers for the Nile flood.

[42] A blue semiprecious stone, obtained in trade from Afghanistan, used for jewelry and, in powdered form, for cosmetics.

[43] One of two lions, representing "today," that delineated the horizon.

[44] The sun god Ra.

[45] The pharaoh, who was both the son of Ra and Ra himself.

24

"THE ADMONITIONS OF IPUWER" (CA. 1700 BCE)

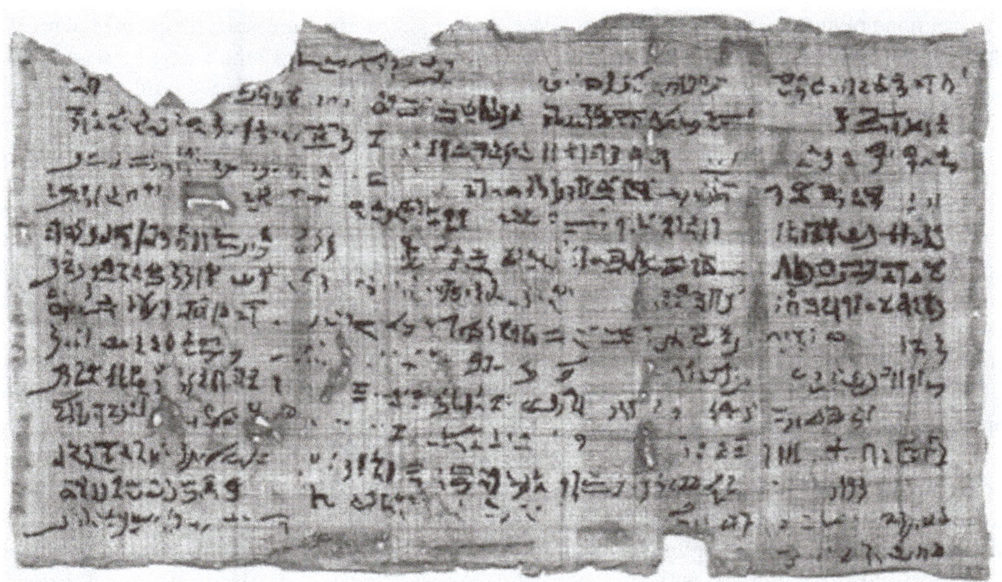

The "Lament of Ipuwer" is preserved on only a single papyrus document, now in Leiden in the Netherlands. Both the beginning and the end are missing. The orthography suggests that this copy was made in the thirteenth century BCE, during the Nineteenth Dynasty.

The "Admonitions of Ipuwer," written on papyrus, describes how Egypt faced troubled times when the area was beset by natural disasters, social disruption, internal disorder, and foreign attacks. Ipuwer advises the pharaoh to placate the gods so that they will restore order. The rambling narrative usually is thought to depict conditions during either the First or the Second Intermediate Period, when internal unity in Egypt had broken down. The references to incursions of foreigners would seem to be more suited to the Second Intermediate Period, when the Hyksos made their way into Egypt. Fringe theorists see the account, which refers to a "river of blood," as an Egyptian version of the "plagues of Egypt" that preceded the Hebrew Exodus. Still others suggest that the tale is completely fictional.

Source: Alan H. Gardiner, *The Admonitions of an Egyptian Sage, from a Hieratic Papyrus in Leiden* (Leipzig: Hinrichs, 1909).

The door keepers say: "Let us go and plunder." A man regards his son as his enemy. The virtuous man goes in mourning because of what has happened in the land. The peoples of the desert have become Egyptians everywhere. The bowman is ready, wrongdoing is everywhere. Indeed, the plunderer is everywhere, and the servant takes what he finds. Indeed, the Nile overflows, yet none plough for it. Everyone says, "We do not know what will happen throughout the land." Indeed, the women are barren and none conceive. Indeed, poor men have become owners of wealth, and he who could not make sandals for himself is now a possessor of riches. Indeed, pestilence is throughout the land, blood is everywhere, death is not lacking. Indeed, many dead are buried in the river; the stream is a sepulcher. Indeed, noblemen are in distress, whereas the poor man is full of joy. Every town says, "Let us suppress the powerful among us."

Indeed, the land turns around as does a potter's wheel; the robber is a possessor of riches. The poor man complains, "How terrible! What am I to do?" Indeed, the river is blood,[46] yet men drink of it. Men shrink from human beings and thirst after water. Indeed, gates, columns and walls are burnt up; towns are destroyed and Upper Egypt has become an empty waste. Indeed, the desert is throughout the land, the nomes are laid waste, and barbarians from abroad have come to Egypt. Good things are throughout the land, yet housewives say, "Oh that we had something to eat!" Indeed, noblewomen are in sad plight by reason of their rags, and their hearts sink when greeting one another. Indeed, none shall sail northward to Byblos[47] today; what shall we do for cedar trees for our mummies, and with the produce of which priests are buried and with the oil of which chiefs are embalmed as far as Keftiu[48]? All is ruin! Indeed, laughter is perished; groaning is throughout the land, mingled with complaints. Those who were Egyptians have become foreigners and are thrust aside, and the man of rank can no longer be distinguished from him who is nobody. Indeed, great and small say, "I wish I might die." Little children say, "He should not have caused me to live." Indeed, the children of princes are dashed against walls. Indeed, all female slaves are free with their tongues,[49] and when their mistress speaks, it is irksome to the maidservants. The roads are watched; men sit in the bushes until the benighted traveler comes in order to plunder his burden,[50] and what is upon him is taken away. He is belabored with blows of a stick and murdered.

Would that there were an end of men, without conception, without birth! Then would the land be quiet from noise and tumult be no more. Indeed, everywhere barley has perished and men are stripped of clothes, spice, and oil; everyone says, "There is none." The storehouse is empty and its keeper is stretched on the ground; a happy state of affairs! Would that I had raised my voice at that moment, that it might have saved me from the pain in which I am. Indeed, public offices are opened and their inventories are taken away; the serf has become an owner of serfs. Indeed, scribes are killed and their writings are taken away. Woe is me because of the misery of this time! Indeed, the laws of the council chamber are thrown out; indeed, men walk on them

[46] A theme that also appears in the Biblical account of the plagues brought on Egypt by Moses.

[47] A trading city in Lebanon later belonging to the Phoenicians and a source of cedar, for which see Readings 33 and 38.

[48] The Egyptian term for the Minoans of Crete.

[49] Compare Reading 19, entry no. 25.

[50] Compare the complaints of the "eloquent peasant," Reading 22.

in public places, and poor men break them up in the streets. Indeed, the great council-chamber is a popular resort, and poor men come and go to the Great Mansions.[51]

Behold, the fire has gone up on high, and its burning goes forth against the enemies of the land. Behold, things have been done that have not happened for a long time past; the pharaoh has been deposed by the rabble.[52] Behold, it has befallen that the land has been deprived of the pharaohship by a few lawless men. Behold, men have fallen into rebellion against the Uraeus. Behold, the Serpent is taken from its hole, and the secrets of the Pharaohs of Upper and Lower Egypt are divulged. Behold, the land has knotted itself up with confederacies,[53] and the coward takes the brave man's property. Behold, the magistrates of the land are driven out throughout the land, are driven out from the palaces. Behold, noble ladies are now on rafts and magnates are in the labor establishment whereas he who could not sleep even on walls is now the possessor of a bed. Behold, the possessor of wealth now spends the night thirsty whereas he who once begged his dregs for himself is now the possessor of overflowing bowls. Behold, the possessors of robes are now in rags whereas he who could not weave for himself is now a possessor of fine linen. Behold, he who was ignorant of the lyre is now the possessor of a harp whereas he who never sang for himself now vaunts the Songstress-Goddess. Behold, he who had no loaf is now the owner of a barn, and his storehouse is provided with the goods of another. Behold, he whose hair is fallen out and who had no oil has now become the possessors of jars of sweet myrrh. Behold, she who had no box is now the owner of a coffer, and she who had to look at her face in the water is now the owner of a mirror. Behold, a man is slain beside his brother, who runs away and abandons him to save his own skin. Behold, he who had no yoke of oxen is now the owner of a herd, and he who could find for himself no ploughman is now the owner of cattle. Behold, he who had no grain is now the owner of granaries, and he who had to fetch loan-wheat for himself is now one who issues it. Behold, he who had no dependents is now an owner of serfs, and he who was a magnate now performs his own errands. Lower Egypt weeps; the pharaoh's storehouse is the common property of everyone, and the entire palace is without its revenues.

Destroy the enemies of the august Residence, splendid of magistrates.[54] Remember to fumigate with incense and to offer water in a jar in the early morning. Remember to offer god's offerings to the gods. Remember to erect flagstaffs and to carve offering stones. Remember to observe regulations, to fix dates correctly, and to remove him who enters on the priestly office in impurity of body. Remember: the things to remember are the duties of the priests, first among them the Pharaoh as High Priest. Men say, "He is the herdsman of mankind, and there is no evil in his heart." Where is he today? Is he asleep? Behold, his power is not seen. If we had been fed, I would not have found you, I would not have been summoned in vain. Authority, knowledge, and truth are with you, yet confusion is what you set throughout the land. Oh that you could taste a little of the misery of it!

It is indeed good when the hands of men build pyramids, when ponds are dug and plantations of the trees of the gods are made. It is indeed good when men are drunk; they drink myt[55] and their hearts are happy. It is indeed good when the magnates of districts are clad in a cloak, cleansed in front and well-provided within. It is indeed good when fine linen is spread out on New Year's Day on the bank.

Everyone fights for his sister and saves his own skin. Is it Kushites?[56] Then will we guard ourselves;

[51] The main law courts in the most important cities, as opposed to local law courts.

[52] A characteristic of the Intermediate Periods, when pharaohs were not able to maintain their power.

[53] During the Intermediate Periods, Egyptian unity collapsed and several individuals claiming to be "pharaoh" controlled different regions.

[54] Here Ipuwer pauses in his laments and suggests to the pharaoh what he needs to do to make things better.

[55] A drink perhaps made from pressed dates.

[56] For Kush, south of Egypt, see Reading 70.

warriors are made many in order to ward off foreigners. Is it Libyans?[57] Then we will turn away. The Medjay[58] are pleased with Egypt. How comes it that every man kills his brother? The troops whom we marshaled for ourselves have turned into foreigners and have taken to ravaging. What has come to pass through it is informing the Asiatics of the state of the land.

What Ipuwer said when he addressed the Majesty of the Lord of All: "You have done what was good and you have nourished the people. They cover their faces through fear of the morrow. That is how a man grows old before he dies, while his son is a lad of understanding; he does not open his mouth to speak to you, but you seize him in the doom of death."

25

"THE BOOK OF THE DEAD" (CA. 1500 BCE)

The "Book of the Dead of Neferini," written on papyrus ca. the third century BCE. Here, Osiris, seated and depicted as the pharaoh, judges the woman in front of him, who conciliates him with a pile of offerings. To the left, the gods Anubis, depicted with a jackal's head, and Horus, with a falcon's head, hold their hands on the scales-chain, and at far left Thoth records the verdict. Now in the Neues Museum, Berlin.

[57] From the desert area west of Egypt.

[58] A people of northern Kush; also mentioned in the Autobiography of Weni, Reading 21.

During the Middle Kingdom (ca. 2000–1730 BCE), the Egyptian afterlife became open to all Egyptians. In order to ensure a smooth entry into the underworld, Egyptians who were wealthy enough to be able to do so had their corpses accompanied by or even wrapped in a long document known as the "Book of the Dead." It included all of the rituals and spells that Egyptians believed would ensure them a happy life after death with the sun god Ra. For example, there were sections that provided the proper ways to address the gods the deceased would encounter, such as Osiris and Ra. Osiris, as the judge of the dead, was especially important because he would question the deceased to determine whether the person had led a life worthy of an afterlife. The "Book of the Dead" therefore also included the proper answers to the questions that would be asked. In sum, the whole judgment of the dead was rigged. Not only did the deceased have, in the "Book of the Dead," all of the proper rituals necessary for entry into the underworld, but also when his or her heart was weighed against justice, the god Anubis kept his hand on the weighing pan to ensure that no one's heart was found wanting. Thus, even though the Egyptians did believe that the "Eater of the Dead" would consume anyone who had lived an unjust life, they never thought that it would apply to themselves.

Source: E. A. Wallis Budge, *Ancient Egyptian Religion* (Allen and Faulkner, 1895).

[Hymn to Osiris.]

Homage to thee, Osiris,[59] Lord of eternity, King of the Gods, whose names are manifold, whose forms are holy, thou being of hidden form in the temples, whose ka[60] is holy. Thou art the governor of Tattu,[61] and also the mighty one in Khem.[62] Thou art the Lord to whom praises are ascribed in the nome of Ati,[63] thou art the Prince of divine food in Anu.[64] Thou art the Lord who is commemorated in Maati,[65] the Hidden Soul, the Lord of Qerrt,[66] the Ruler supreme in White Wall.[67] Thou art the Soul of Ra, his own body, and hast thy place of rest in Henensu.[68] Thou art the beneficent one, and art praised in Nart.[69] Thou makest thy soul to be raised up. Thou art the Lord of the Great House in Khemenu.[70] Thou art the mighty one of victories in Shas-hetep,[71] the Lord of eternity, the Governor of Abydos.[72] The path of his throne is in Ta-tcheser.[73] Thy name is established in the mouths of men. Thou art the substance of Two Lands.[74] Thou art Tem, the feeder of Kau,[75] the Governor of the Companies of the gods.[76] Thou art the beneficent Spirit among the spirits. The god of the

[59] The god of the underworld who judged the dead to determine whether they had lived a just life; if they had, they were permitted to enjoy a happy life in the underworld.

[60] One of the Egyptian eternal souls.

[61] Also known as Tetut, Busiris in Greek, a city of Lower Egypt and early center of the worship of Osiris.

[62] Letopolis in Greek; a center of the worship of the god Horus.

[63] Or Anetch, the ninth nome in Lower Egypt, capital city Tattu (Busiris).

[64] The capital of the thirteenth nome in Lower Egypt, better known as On and Iunu in Egyptian, Heliopolis in Greek.

[65] The first nome of Lower Egypt, embodying the word "truth"; capital at Memphis.

[66] Elephantine, an island in the Nile on the southern frontier of Egypt.

[67] Memphis.

[68] Also known as Ehnas, Heracleopolis in Greek, in the twentieth nome of Upper Egypt.

[69] Heracleopolis.

[70] Hermopolis in Greek.

[71] Location of the great battle between Horus, lord of Lower Egypt, and his uncle, the brother of Osiris, Set, lord of Upper Egypt.

[72] One of the oldest cities in Egypt, capital of the eighth nome of Upper Egypt.

[73] A section of Abydos.

[74] One of the Egyptian names for Egypt.

[75] The plural of ka, one of the Egyptian immortal souls.

[76] All of the gods.

Celestial Ocean[77] draweth from thee his waters. Thou sendest forth the north wind at eventide, and breath from thy nostrils to the satisfaction of thy heart. Thy heart reneweth its youth, thou producest the tchef food.[78] The stars in the celestial heights are obedient unto thee, and the great doors of the sky open themselves before thee.

Hail to you, you having come as Khepri,[79] even Khepri who is the creator of the gods. You rise and shine on the back of your mother the sky, having appeared in glory as king of the gods. Your mother Nut[80] shall use her arms on your behalf in making greeting. The Manu-mountain[81] receives you in peace. Ma'at[82] embraces you at all seasons. May you give power and might in vindication—and a coming forth as a living soul to see horakhty[83]—to the ka of N. May you be gracious to me when I see your beauty, having departed from upon earth. May I smite the Ass, may I drive off the rebel-serpent, may I destroy Apep[84] when he acts, for I have seen the abdju-fish[85] in its moment of being and the bulti-fish[86] piloting the canoe on its waterway. I have seen Horus[87] as helmsman with Thoth[88] and Ma'at beside him, I have taken hold of the bow-warp of the Night-boat and the stern-warp of the Day-boat.[89] May he grant that I see the sun-disc and behold the moon unceasingly every day; may my soul go forth to travel to every place that it desires; may my name be called out, may it be found at the board of offerings, may there be given to me loaves in the Presence like the Followers of Horus, may a place be made for me in the solar boat on the day when the god ferries across, and may I be received into the presence of Osiris in the Land of Vindication.

[The Declaration of Innocence.]

What should be said when arriving at the Hall of Justice, of Two Truths, purging N[90] of all the forbidden things he has done, and seeing the faces of all the gods. The spell for descending to the broad hall of Two Truths[91]:

"Hail to you, great god, Lord of Justice![92] I have come to you, my Lord, that you may bring me so that I may see your beauty, for I know you and I know your name, and I know the names of the forty-two gods of those who are with you in this Hall of Justice, who live on those who cherish evil and who gulp down their blood on that day of the reckoning of characters in the presence of Wennefer.[93] Behold the double son of the Songstresses; Lord of Truth is your name. Behold I have come to you, I have brought you truth, I have repelled falsehood for you."

"Hail Far-strider[94] who came forth from Heliopolis,[95] I have done no falsehood. Hail Fire-embracer who came forth from Kheraha,[96] I have not robbed. Hail Nosey[97] who came forth from Hermopolis, I have not been rapacious. Hail Swallower of shades who came forth from the cavern, I have not stolen.

Hail Dangerous One who came forth from Rosetjau,[98] I have not killed men. Hail Double Lion who came forth from the sky, I have not destroyed food-supplies. Hail Fiery Eyes who came forth from

[77] Nu, the original ocean.
[78] The food of the soul, the ka.
[79] God of sunrise and rebirth.
[80] Goddess of the sky; with Geb, god of the earth, she produced Osiris, Isis, and Set.
[81] The western mountain peak that helped support the sky.
[82] Goddess of justice.
[83] The horizon associated with the rising and setting sun.
[84] Or Apophis; the god of chaos, enemy of Ma'at.
[85] A Nile fish, and the pilot for the boat of Ra.
[86] A Nile fish, and a symbol of eternal life.
[87] The falcon god, son of Osiris and Isis, who defended deceased people in the final judgment before Osiris.
[88] The baboon god who recorded Osiris's judgments of the dead.
[89] The two boats that took Ra through the sky and the underworld during the daily journey of the sun.
[90] The name of the deceased person was inserted here.
[91] In these declarations the deceased makes a series of negative confessions, that is, assertions of what she or he has not done.
[92] Osiris.
[93] An epithet of Osiris.
[94] One of the epithets of Osiris.
[95] The main cult center of the gods Atum and Ra, the god of the noonday sun.
[96] Greek and Roman Babylon, modern Old Cairo.
[97] Thoth.
[98] Or Rostau; the underworld.

Letopolis, I have done no crookedness. Hail Flame that came forth backwards, I have not stolen the god's offerings. Hail Bone-breaker who came forth from Heracleopolis,[99] I have not told lies. Hail Green of Flame who came forth from Memphis, I have not taken food. Hail You of the cavern who came forth from the west, I have not been sullen. Hail White of teeth who came forth from the Fayum,[100] I have not transgressed. Hail Blood-eater who came forth from the shambles, I have not killed a sacred bull.

Hail Eater of entrails who came forth from the House of Thirty, I have not committed perjury.

Hail Lord of Truth who came forth from Maati,[101] I have not stolen bread

Hail Wanderer who came forth from Bubastis, I have not eavesdropped.

Hail Pale One who came forth from Heliopolis, I have not babbled.

Hail Doubly evil who came forth from Andjet,[102] I have not disputed except concerning my own property.

Hail Wememty-snake[103] who came forth from the place of execution, I have not fornicated with a child.

Hail You who see whom you bring who came forth from the House of Min,[104] I have not misbehaved.

Hail You who are over the Old One who came forth from Imau,[105] I have not made terror.

Hail Demolisher who came forth from Xois,[106] I have not transgressed.

Hail Disturber who came forth from Weryt, I have not been hot-tempered.

Hail Youth who came forth from the Heliopolitan nome,[107] I have not been deaf to words of truth.

Hail Foreteller who came forth from Wenes,[108] I have not made disturbance.

Hail You of the altar who came forth from the secret place, I have not hoodwinked.

Hail You whose face is behind him who came forth from the Cavern of Wrong, I have neither misconducted myself nor copulated with a boy.

Hail Hot-foot who came forth from the dusk, I have not been neglectful.

Hail You of the darkness who came forth from the darkness, I have not been quarrelsome.

Hail Bringer of your offering who came forth from Saïs,[109] I have not been unduly active.

Hail Owner of faces who came forth from Nedjefet,[110] I have not been impatient.

Hail Accuser who came forth from Wetjenet, I have not transgressed my nature, I have not washed out the picture of a god.

Hail Owner of horns who came forth from Zawty,[111] I have not been voluble in speech.

Hail Nefertum[112] who came forth from Memphis, I have done no wrong, I have seen no evil.

Hail Tempsep who came forth from Busiris, I have not made conjuration against the pharaoh.

Hail You who acted according to your will, who came forth from Tjebu,[113] I have not waded in water.

Hail Water-smiter who came forth from the Abyss, I have not been loud-voiced.

Hail Prosperer of the common folk who came forth from your house, I have not reviled mankind.

Hail Bestower of good who came forth from the Harpoon nome,[114] I have not been puffed up.

Hail Bestower of powers who came forth from the City, I have not made distinctions for myself.

---

[99] Egyptian Ehnas; capital of the twentieth nome of Upper Egypt.

[100] An oasis in the northern part of Upper Egypt.

[101] The first nome of Lower Egypt, embodying the word "truth"; capital at Memphis.

[102] The ninth nome of Lower Egypt.

[103] One of the Egyptian judgment deities.

[104] God of male sexual potency; god of Akhmim, the ninth nome of Upper Egypt.

[105] Capital of the third nome of Lower Egypt.

[106] Khasut in Egyptian, an ancient city of the Nile delta, the capital city of the Fourteenth Dynasty, which preceded the Hyksos.

[107] Iunu in Egyptian; the thirteenth nome of Lower Egypt.

[108] Hermopolis in Greek; the fifteenth nome of Upper Egypt, center of the worship of Thoth

[109] Capital of the fifth nome of Lower Egypt, Zau in Egyptian; origin of the Saïte Dynasty of the sixth century BCE.

[110] The fourteenth nome of Upper Egypt.

[111] Lycopolis in Greek, modern Asyut; the thirteenth nome of Upper Egypt.

[112] A healing god of Memphis, son of Ptah and Sekhmet.

[113] Aphroditopolis in Greek; capital of the tenth nome of Upper Egypt.

[114] The seventh nome of Lower Egypt.

Hail Serpent with raised head, who came forth from the cavern, I am not wealthy except with my own property.

Hail Carrier-off of His Portion who came forth from the Silent Land, I have not blasphemed god in my city.

26

HATSHEPSUT'S EXPEDITION TO PUNT (CA. 1470 BCE)

An illustration from Hatshepsut's mortuary temple depicts Queen Ati of Punt receiving the embassy from Egypt.

Hatshepsut (1479–1458 BCE) was easily the greatest and most able of all the native Egyptian female pharaohs. She asserted that she was the daughter not of Pharaoh Thutmose I, but of the god Amon himself. She portrayed herself wearing all of the regalia of a male pharaoh, including the beard, and referred to herself using masculine pronouns. In the temple of Amon at Karnak she recalled her achievements. In a temple she built in honor of Pakhet, the lioness goddess of war, Hatshepsut spoke of her role in the Egyptian recovery after the expulsion of the Hyksos. A lengthy text, preserved carved and painted on the walls of her mortuary (memorial) temple and accompanied by illustrations, discussed the naval expedition that she sent to Punt, a mysterious land south of Egypt on the coast of the Red Sea, in the ninth year of her reign. The text perhaps overstates the importance of a simple trading expedition, making it into a statement of the extent of Hatshepsut's authority. After her death, Hatshepsut's stepson and successor, Thutmose III (1458–1425 BCE), attempted to erase her name and image from history. It was not until the early twentieth century that many monuments telling of her deeds were discovered.

Source: E. Naville, "The Life and Monuments of the Queen," in Theodore M. Davis, ed., *The Tomb of Hâtshopsîtû* (London, Constable: 1906), 25–41.

[Inscription from the temple of Amon in Karnak][115]
I have done this with a loving heart for my father Amon, I did not forget whatever he had ordained, now, my heart turns to and fro, in thinking what will the people say, they who will see my monument in after years, and shall speak of what I have done. I swear, as I am loved of Ra, as I wear the white crown, as I appear in the red crown, as I rule this land like the son of Isis, so as regards these two great obelisks, in order that my name may endure in this temple.

[Inscription from the temple of Pakhet, known to the Greeks as Speos Artemidos, at Beni Hasan]
Hear, all ye nobles and common folk in their multitudes! I did these things by the design of my heart, and no indolent one could sleep because of me! I restored what had decayed; I annulled the former privileges that existed since the time the Asiatics[116] were in the region of Avaris[117] of Lower Egypt! The immigrants among them disregarded the tasks that were assigned to them, thinking that Ra would not consent when the deified Thutmosis I assigned the rulership to my majesty.[118] When I was established over the thrones of Ra, I became known through a period of three years as a born conqueror. And when I came as pharaoh my uraeus threw fire against my enemies!

[115] James Henry Breasted, ed., *Ancient Records of Egypt: The Eighteenth Dynasty* (Chicago: University of Chicago Press, 1906), 131–132.

[116] The Hyksos.

[117] The capital city of the Hyksos, in the northeastern Nile delta.

[118] Hatshepsut blames the opposition to her when she came to the throne on foreign immigrants.

[The Expedition to Punt: Brief inscriptions from Hatshepsut's burial temple at Deir el-Bahri accompany the illustrations of the voyage.]

[Hatshepsut begins by claiming she was the wife not of Thutmose I but of the god Amon.]
Amon took the form of the noble Pharaoh Thutmose and found the queen sleeping in her room. When the pleasant odors that proceeded from him announced his presence she woke. He gave her his heart and showed himself in his godlike splendor. When he approached the queen she wept for joy at his strength and beauty and he gave her his love.[119]

[Hatshepsut reports that Thutmose I made her his heir.]
Then His Majesty said to them: "This daughter of mine, Khnumetamon[120] Hatshepsut—may she live!—I have appointed as my successor upon my throne. She shall direct the people in every sphere of the palace; it is she indeed who shall lead you. Obey her words, unite yourselves at her command." The royal nobles, the dignitaries, and the leaders of the people heard this proclamation of the promotion of his daughter, the Pharaoh of Upper and Lower Egypt, Ma'at-ka-Ra[121]—may she live eternally! His daughter, the Pharaoh of Upper and Lower Egypt, Ma'at-ka-Ra—may she live eternally.

[119] Similar to the story that Alexander the Great was the son not of King Philip II, but of the god Zeus (see Reading 62).

[120] One of Hatshepsut's names, incorporating the name of the god Amon.

[121] Another of the names of Hatshepsut, incorporating the names of Ma'at, goddess of justice, and Ra, god of the sun.

[The fleet, led by Nehasi, a word meaning "the Nubian," moors at the mouth of a river that empties into the Red Sea.]
The navigation on the sea, the starting on the good journey to the divine land, the landing happily in the land of Punt by the soldiers of the pharaoh, according to the prescription of the Lord of the gods, Amon, Lord of the thrones of the two lands, in order to bring the precious products of the whole land, because of his great love toward Hatshepsut. Never did such a thing happen to the pharaohs who were in the land eternally.

[Nehasi lands with nine soldiers and presents for the queen of Punt are displayed on a table.]
The landing of the royal messenger in the divine land, with the soldiers who accompany him, in the presence of the chiefs of Punt, to bring all goods from the sovereign, to Hathor the lady of Punt, in order that she may grant life, strength and health to Her Majesty.

[King Parohu and Queen Ati of Punt then appear.]
The coming of the chiefs of Punt, bowing and stooping in order to receive these soldiers, they give praise to Hatshepsut. They say in asking for peace, "You have arrived here on what way, to which land that the Egyptians did not know. Have you come through the way of the sky or have you travelled on water to the green land, the divine land to which Ra has transported you? For the pharaoh of Egypt there is no closed way, we live in the breath that he gives us."

[King Parohu reappears with gifts that the Egyptians exaggeratedly call "tribute."]
"The coming of the chief of Punt, bringing his tribute on the shore of the sea, in the presence of the royal messenger."

[Nehasi prepares a reception.]
The preparing of the tent for the royal ambassador and the soldiers in the harbors of frankincense of Punt, on the shore of the sea, in order to receive the chiefs of this land and to present them with bread, beer, wine, meat, fruits and all the good things of the land of Egypt, as has been ordered by the sovereign.

[The Egyptian ships are loaded with trade goods.]
The loading of the cargo boats with great quantities of the marvels of the land of Punt, with all the good woods of the divine land, heaps of pieces of ani,[122] and trees of green ani, with pure ivory, with pure gold of the land of Amu,[123] with cinnamon wood, khesit wood, with balsam, resin, antimony, with cynocephali,[124] monkeys, greyhounds, with skins of panthers of the south, with inhabitants of the country and their children. Never were brought any such things to any pharaoh since the beginning of the world.

[The fleet returns to Thebes.]
The navigation, the landing at Thebes with joy by the soldiers of the pharaoh. With them are the chiefs of the land, they bring such things as were never brought to any pharaoh, in products of the land of Punt, through the power of the venerable god Amon-Ra, the Lord of the thrones of the two lands.

[Hatshepsut greets the fleet.]
The pharaoh himself, Pharaoh Ma'at-kara,[125] takes a bushel; she stretches forth her hand to measure the heaps the first time; it is an object of rejoicing to measure the fresh ani of Amon, the Lord of the Throne of the Two Lands, the Lord of the Sky. The first day of the summer [—] The good things of the land of Punt, the Lord of Shmun[126] records them in writing, Safekhabui[127] makes up the accounts. His Majesty herself put with her own hands oil of ani on all her limbs. Her fragrance was like a divine breath, her scent reached as far as the land of Punt, her skin is made of gold, it shines like the stars in the hall of festival, in view of the whole land. The rekhiu[128] are rejoicing, they give praises to the Lord of the gods, they celebrate Ma'at-kara in her divine

[122] Myrrh.
[123] Perhaps in Arabia.
[124] Apes.
[125] One of Hatshepsut's names.
[126] The god Thoth.
[127] Wife of Thoth.
[128] Initiates into sacred mysteries.

doings, as she is such a great marvel. She has no equal among the gods who were before since the world was. She is living Ra eternally."

[Hatshepsut appears before Amon, who gives his approval and support to the mission.]
His royal majesty[129] repaired toward the staircase of the pharaoh of the gods, hearing his orders in the palace, the speech of the god who investigates the roads to Punt, and who opens the ways to the harbors of incense, who leads the soldiers on water, and on land, that they may bring the good things from the divine land to this god who created her person, so that all should be done as was ordered by the venerable god, and according to the wish of her majesty. Said by Amon, the Lord of the Thrones of the Two Lands, "Come, come in peace my daughter, the graceful, who art in my heart, Pharaoh Ma'at-kara who makest for me fine buildings. I will give thee Punt, the whole of it, as far as extend the divine lands. The divine land has never been explored, the harbors of incense had never been seen by the men of Egypt; it had been heard from mouth to mouth, through the saying of the ancestors; its good things were brought, they were brought to thy fathers, the pharaohs of Lower Egypt, one after the other, since the age of the forefathers, and to the pharaohs of Upper Egypt, who were before, in exchange for large payments; nobody had reached these lands except a stray messenger. Henceforth I will cause them to be walked over by thy soldiers. I will lead thy soldiers by land and by water, on mysterious shores, which join the harbors of incense, the sacred territory of the divine land, my abode of pleasure. I will convey them myself; and thy mother Hathor and Urert, the lady of Punt, and Urheketu the queen of the gods. They will take incense as much as they like. They will load their ships to the satisfaction of their hearts with trees of fresh incense, and all the good things of the land. The Puntites who did not know the Egyptians, the cultivators of the divine land, I will win their hearts in order that they give thee their praises and that they adore thy will, which reigns over this land. I know them, for I am their master."

[Hatshepsut summarizes her own accomplishment.]
My majesty put before her eyes to reach the harbor of incense, to open its way, to throw open its roads, according to the orders of my father Amon. Says my majesty, I let you know what was ordered to me. I was obedient to my father. He put before me to establish Punt in his house, digging up fruit trees in the divine land, for the two sides of his divine dwelling, in his garden. As he ordered, so it was, in order to increase the offerings that I vowed to him. I have not neglected what he ordered, which was accomplished according to my prescriptions, there was no transgressing of what my mouth gave out on that subject, he opened me a place in his heart, to me who know all he loves. What he loves, he takes hold of. I brought to him Punt in his garden, as he put it before me, to Thebes, he enlarged it, he walked in it.

[129] Hatshepsut, referred to using masculine forms.

27

"HYMN TO ATON" (CA. 1350 BCE)

In this relief the pharaoh Akhenaton, his wife Nefertiti, and their children bask in the rays emanating from their god Aton, represented by a sun disk with rays terminating in hands. Preserved in the Neues Museum, Berlin.

One of the greatest social and religious upheavals in the history of ancient Egypt occurred when the pharaoh Akhenaton (1351–1334 BCE) attempted to make the sun god Aton, who was represented as a solar disk from which rays ending in hands emanated, into the primary god of Egypt. Akhenaton's devotion to Aton was manifested in the suppression of the worship of other gods, a massive building program, the foundation of a new city, Akhetaton ("Horizon of Aton"), in honor of his god, a new "Amarna" style of art, and literature praising Aton. In his "Hymn to Aton," which is preserved inscribed on the walls of at least five courtiers' tombs and would have been part of the religious rituals honoring the god, Aton is portrayed as the primary god of Egypt, to the exclusion of all the other gods. Some scholars have seen parallels between this hymn and Psalm 104 from the Hebrew Bible.

Source: Miriam Lichtheim, ed., *Ancient Egyptian Literature: A Book of Readings*, Vol. 2. *The New Kingdom* (Berkeley/London: University of California Press, 1976), 96–100.

You rise beautiful from the horizon to heaven,
living disk, origin of life.
You are arisen from the horizon, you have filled
every land with your beauty.
You are fine, great, radiant, lofty over and above
every land.
Your rays bind the lands to the limit of all you
have made,
You are the sun, you have reached their limits.
You bind them for your beloved son.
You are distant, but your rays are on earth.
You are in their sight, but your movements are
hidden.
You rest in the western horizon, and the land is
in darkness in the manner of death,
sleepers in chambers, heads covered, no eye can
see its other.
Anything of theirs can be taken from under their
heads, they would not know.
Every lion goes out from its den, every snake
bites.
Darkness envelops, the land is in silence, their
creator is resting in his horizon.
At daybreak, arisen from the horizon, shining as
the disk in day,
you remove the darkness, you grant your rays,
and the two lands are in festival, awakened and
standing on their feet.
You have raised them up, their bodies cleansed,
clothing on,
their arms are in adoration at your sunrise.
The entire land carries out its tasks, every herd
rests in its pastures,
trees and plants are sprouting, birds flying up
from their nests,
their wings in adoration for your spirit.
Every flock frolics afoot, all that fly up and
alight, they live when you have shone for
them.
Boats sail north and south too, every road is
opened at your sunrise,
and the fish on the river leap at the sight of you.
Your rays penetrate the Great Green.[130]

[130] The Mediterranean Sea.

You who cause the sperm to grow in women,
who turns seed into people, who causes
the son to live in the womb of his mother, who
silences him in stopping him crying.
Nurse in the womb, who gives breath to cause all
he has made to live,
when he goes down from the womb to breathe on
the day of his birth,
you open his mouth in form, you make his needs.
When the chick in the egg speaks in the shell,
you give it breath within to cause it to live,
you have made him, he is complete, to break out
from the egg,
and he emerges from the egg to speak to his
completion,
and walks on his legs, going out from it.
How numerous are your works, although hidden
from sight.
Unique god, there is none beside you.
You mould the earth to your wish, you and you
alone:
All people, herds and flocks,
All on earth that walk on legs,
All on high that fly with their wings.
And on the foreign lands of Khar[131] and Kush,[132]
the land of Egypt.
You place every man in his place, you make
what they need,
so that everyone has his food, his lifespan
counted.
Tongues are separated in speech, and forms
too—
Their skins are made different, for you make
foreign lands different.
You make a Flood in the underworld, and bring
it at your desire
to cause the populace to live, as you made them
for you,
Lord of all they labor over, the Lord of every
land.
Shine for them, O disk of day, great of dignity.

[131] Syria.

[132] Located on the Nile River immediately south of Egypt; see Reading 70.

All distant lands, you make them live,
you place a Flood in the sky, to descend for them,
to make waves over the mountains like the Great Green,
to water their fields with their settlements.
How effective they are, your plans, O Lord of Eternity!
A Flood in the sky for foreigners, for the flocks of every land that go on foot,
and a Flood to come from the underworld for Egypt,
your rays nursing every meadow, you shine and they live and grow for you.
You make the seasons to nurture all you make,
winter to cool them, heat so they may taste you.
You have made the far sky to shine in it,
to see what you make, while you are far, and shining in your form as living disk.
Risen, shining, distant, near, you make millions of forms from yourself, lone one,
cities, towns, fields, the road of rivers.
Every eye sees you in their entry.
You are the disk of day, master of your move, of the existence of every form.
You create alone what you have made.
You are in my heart, there is none other who knows you
beside your son Neferkheperura-Sole-One-of-Ra.[133]
You instruct him in your plans, in your strength.
The land comes into being by your action, as you make them,
and when you have shone, they live, when you rest, they die.
You are lifetime, in your body, people live by you.
Eyes are on your beauty until you set.
All work is stopped when you set on the west.
Shine, and strengthen all for the pharaoh.
Motion is in every leg, since you founded the earth,
you raise them for your son who come from your body,
the pharaoh who lives on Right, Lord of the Two Lands, Neferkheperura-Sole-One-of-Ra,
son of Ra who lives on Right, Lord of Risings, Akhenaton, great in his lifespan,
and the great pharaoh's wife whom he loves, lady of the two lands,
Neferneferuaton[134] Nefertiti, eternally alive.

[133] The Throne Name of Akhenaton.

[134] Another name of Nefertiti, who may have ruled jointly with Akhenaton.

28

EGYPTIAN LOVE LETTERS (CA. 1300 BCE)

A statuette of ca. 1425 BCE from Karnak, now preserved in the Neues Museum in Berlin, depicts the administrator Amenhotep-User seated with his wife, Tendwadj, in a typical affectionate pose.

Ancient Egyptian men and women were not shy about expressing their personal and even erotic feelings toward each other, as attested in a great number of surviving documents. The following expressions of attraction, love, and devotion, all composed, primarily on papyrus, by anonymous authors, date to the Middle and New Kingdoms.

Source: Translated from Johanna Margarete *Kellner, Unter dem Schutze der* Hathor. *Ägyptische Märchen und Hymnen* (Weimar: Gustav Kiepenheuer Verlag, 1954).

(Woman:)
Come, my brother, swim to me!
The water is deep in my love
That carries me to you.
We are in the midst of the stream,
I clasp the flowers to my breast
That is naked and drips with water.
But the moon makes them bloom like the lotus.
I give you my flowers
because they are beautiful,
And you are holding my hand
In the middle of the water.
(Man:)
The little sycamore
That she planted with her own hand
Opens its mouth to speak.
Its rustling is as sweet
As a draught of honey.
How beautiful its graceful branches
In their greenness.
On it hangs young fruit and fruit that is ripe,
Redder than the blood-red jasper.
The love of my loved one is on the other shore.
An arm of the river lies between us,
And crocodiles lurk on the sand-banks.
But I enter the water, I plunge into the flood;
My eager heart carries me swiftly over the waves;
I swim as surely as though I were walking on solid ground.
Love, it is love that gives me strength,
Averting the perils of the river.

Source: J. E. Manchip White, trans., in Samivel [pseudonym], *The Glory of Egypt* (London: Thames & Hudson, 1955).

(Man:)
My loved one is unique, without a peer,
More beautiful than any other,
See, she is like the star that rises on the horizon
At the dawn of an auspicious year.
She moves in a shimmer of perfection, her complexion is superb,
Her eyes are marvellously seductive,
On her lip linger persuasive words.
Never does she speak one word too many!
Her neck is slender, ample her breast,
Her hair is lapis-lazuli;
Her arms more splendid than gold
And her fingers like lotus petals.
Her robe is tightly caught in around her waist.
Revealing the most beautiful legs in all the world.
You cannot help following her with your eyes wherever she goes,
She is such an unrivalled goddess in appearance.

Source: J. E. Manchip White, trans., in Samivel [pseudonym], *The Glory of Egypt* (London: Thames & Hudson, 1955).

(Woman:)
Am I not here with [you]?
Where have you set your heart (upon going)?
Should you not embrace [me]?
Has my deed come back [upon me]?
If you seek to caress my thighs
[—]
Is it because you have thought of eating that you would go forth?
Is it because you are a slave to your belly?
Is it because you [care about] clothes?
I have a bedsheet!
Is it because you are hungry that you would leave?
(Then) take my breasts
That their gift may flow forth to you.
Better a day in the embrace [of] my brother
Than a thousand myriads while [—]

Source: Michael V. Fox, *Song of Songs and the Ancient Egyptian Love Songs* (Madison: University of Wisconsin Press, 1983).

29

THE PEACE TREATY BETWEEN RAMSES II AND HATTUSILIS III (1258 BCE): EGYPTIAN AND HITTITE VERSIONS

The text, on a clay tablet, of the Akkadian version of the treaty between Ramses II and Hattusilis III is preserved in the Istanbul Archaeology Museum.

In 1258 BCE, following the great Battle of Kadesh in 1274 BCE, where Ramses II (1279–1212 BCE), Pharaoh of Egypt, and the Hittite king Muwatalli II (ca. 1295–1272 BCE) fought to a draw after decades of intermittent warfare, Hattusilis III (ca. 1267–1237), the grandson of Muwatalli, and Ramses finally made peace. Their treaty, which survives in both its Egyptian and its Akkadian (a commonly used diplomatic language) versions, is the first surviving international peace treaty, and a copy of it hangs on the walls of the United Nations in New York. The versions are essentially the same with regard to the fundamental clauses, although each side claimed that the other had first sued for peace, and both versions include longer elaborations or patriotic sections that are not in the other. This suggests that the versions were not meant to reproduce a single master copy. The two powers established the boundary between them; promised not to attack each other; entered into a mutual defense alliance, including assistance in civil wars; agreed to return refugees and fugitives (the first attested extradition agreement); and permitted free trade across the border. To seal the bargain, Ramses married Maathorneferure, the daughter of Hattusilis. The incomplete Egyptian version is preserved both on a stele at Karnak and at Ramses's mortuary temple, the Ramesseum near Luxor, and the Hittite version began to be uncovered in 1906 in excavations at the Hittite capital city of Hattusa (modern Boğazköy) and now is preserved in Istanbul. All of the clauses in the Hittite version appear in the Egyptian version; a sense of the missing part of the Egyptian version can be gained from the surviving Hittite version.

Source: C. W. Goodwin, trans., *Records of the Past, Being English Translations of the Assyrian and Egyptian Monuments*, Vol. 4 (London: Bagster, 1875), 27–34.

[The section numbers are not part of the original documents but have been added to help to identify similar sections. The numbers refer to similar topics; different sections can refer to the same topic, and single sections can refer to different topics. Sections without numbers in one version do not appear, as such, in the other version.]

(a) Egyptian Version

[prologue]

The twenty-first year, the twenty-first day of Tybif, in the reign of Pharaoh Ra-User-Ma,[135] approved by the Sun,[136] Son of the Sun, Ramessu-Meriamen,[137] endowed with life eternal and for ever; lover of Amon-Ra,[138] Harmachu,[139] Ptah[140] of Memphis, Mut Lady of Asheru,[141] and Khonsu Neferhotep[142]; invested upon the throne of Horus, among the living, like his father Harmachu, eternally and for ever. On this day behold His Majesty was in the city of the House of Ramessu-Meriamen, making propitiations to his father Amon-Ra, to Harmachu, to Atum Lord of On,[143] to Amon of Ramessu-Meriamen, to Ptah of Ramessu-Meriamem, to Set[144] the most glorious son of Nut[145]; may they grant him an eternity of thirty-years' festivals, an infinity of years of peace, all lands, all nations, being bowed down beneath his feet for ever.

1. There came a royal herald.[146] The King of Kheta,[147] Kheta-Sira,[148] had sent to the Pharaoh to beg for peace of Pharaoh Ra-User-Ma,[149] approved of the Sun, Son of the Sun, Ramessu-Meriamen, endowed with life for

[135] Ramses II, the pharaoh of Egypt.

[136] Here Ramses lists all the gods whose support he has.

[137] Another name for Ramses.

[138] A union of the gods Amon and Ra; the most important god during the Middle and New Kingdoms.

[139] A manifestation of the sun god.

[140] A creator god; also a god of justice.

[141] The consort of the god Amon of Thebes; Asheru was the sacred lake in the temple of Mut at Karnak.

[142] The god of time.

[143] Heliopolis, capital of the thirteenth nome of Lower Egypt, center of the worship of the gods Ra and Atum.

[144] The god of the red desert as opposed to Horus, god of fertile black land.

[145] The goddess of the sky.

[146] An ambassador.

[147] "Hatti" in the Hittite version.

[148] The Egyptian name for Hattusilis, the Hittite king.

[149] Ramses II, the pharaoh of Egypt.

ever and ever, like his father the Sun continually. Copy of the plate of silver that the King of Kheta, Kheta-Sira, sent to the Pharaoh by the hand of his herald Tartisbu, and his herald Rames, to beg for peace of His Majesty Ra-User-Ma, approved of the Sun, Son of the Sun, Ramessu-Meriamen, Chief of Rulers, whose boundaries extend to every land at his pleasure, the covenant made by the King of Kheta, Kheta-Sira, the powerful, son of Marassa,[150] the King of Kheta, the powerful, grandson of Sapalala, the King of Kheta, the powerful; upon the plate of silver, with Ra-User-Ma, approved of the Sun, the great ruler of Egypt, the powerful, son of Amon-Ma[151] the great ruler of Egypt, the powerful, grandson of Ra-Men-Peru.[152] The great ruler of Egypt, the powerful: The good conditions of peace and fraternity [—] to eternity, which were aforetime from eternity.

2. This was an arrangement of the great ruler of Egypt with the great Prince of Kheta, by way of covenant, that god might cause no hostility to arise between them. Now it happened in the time of Mautenara,[153] the King of Kheta, my brother, that he fought with [—] the great ruler of Egypt. But thus it shall be henceforth, even from this day. Behold, Kheta-Sira the King of Kheta, covenants to adhere to the arrangement made by the Sun, made by Set, concerning the land of Egypt, with the land of Kheta, to cause no hostility to arise between them for ever.

2/3/7. Behold, this it is: Kheta-Sira the King of Kheta covenants with Ra-User-Ma, approved by the Sun, the great ruler of Egypt from this day forth, that good peace and good brotherhood shall be between us for ever.

4/7. He shall fraternize with me, he shall be at peace with me, and I will fraternize with him, I will be at peace with him for ever. It happened in the time of Mautenara the King of Kheta, my brother, after his decease, Kheta-Sira sat as King of Kheta upon the throne of his father. Behold, I am at one in heart with Ramessu-Meriamen, the great ruler of Egypt [—] of peace, of brotherhood; it shall be better than the peace and the brotherhood, which was before this.

5. Behold, I the King of Kheta with Ramessu-Meriamen the great ruler of Egypt, am in good peace, in good brotherhood; the children's children of the King of Kheta shall be in good brotherhood and peace with the children's children of Ramessu-Meriamen the great ruler of Egypt. As our treaty of brotherhood, and our arrangements with the land of Kheta, so to them also shall be peace and brotherhood for ever; there shall no hostility arise between them for ever.

6. The King of Kheta shall not invade the land of Egypt for ever, to carry away anything from it; nor shall Ramessu-Meriamen the great ruler of Egypt invade the land of Kheta for ever to carry away anything from it for ever. The treaty of alliance that was even from the time of Sapalala,[154] the King of Kheta, as well as the treaty of alliance that was in the time of Matenara, the King of Kheta, my father, if I fulfill it, behold Ramessu-Meriamen the great ruler of Egypt shall fulfill it together with us, in each case, even from this day, we will fulfill it, executing the design of alliance.

8. If any enemy shall come to the lands of Ramessu-Meriamen the great ruler of Egypt, and he shall send to the King of Kheta saying, "Come and give me help against him," then shall the King of Kheta [—] the King of Kheta to smite the enemy; but if it be that the King of Kheta shall not come himself, he shall send his infantry and his cavalry [—] to smite his enemy [—] of the anger of Ramessu-Meriamen.

11. [—] the slaves of the gates, and they shall do any damage to him, and he shall go to smite them, then shall the King of Kheta together with [—]

[150] Mursili III, Hittite king ca. 1272–1267, predecessor of Hattusilis III.

[151] Seti I (1290–1279) BCE.

[152] Ramses I (1292–1290 BCE).

[153] The Hittite king Muwatalli II (ca. 1295–1272 BCE).

[154] The Hittite king Suppiluliuma I (ca. 1344–1322 BCE).

9/12. [—] to come to help to smite his enemies, if it shall please Ramessu-Meriamen the great ruler of Egypt to go, he shall [—]

10. [—] to return all answer to the land of Kheta. But if the servants of the King of Kheta shall invade him, namely Ramessu-Meriamen [—]

15/18/22. [—] from the lands of Ramessu-Meriamen the great ruler of Egypt and they shall come to the King of Kheta, then shall the King of Kheta not receive them, but the King of Kheta shall send them to Ra-User-Ma, approved of the Sun, the great ruler of Egypt [—] and if they shall come to the land of Kheta to do service to anyone, they shall not be added to the land of Kheta, they shall be given up to Ramessu-Meriamen the great ruler of Egypt. Or if there shall pass over [—]

13/17/21. [—] coming from the land of Kheta, and if they shall come to Ramessu-Meriamen the great ruler of Egypt, then shall not Ra-User-Ma, approved of the Sun, the great ruler of Egypt [—] and if they shall come to the land of Egypt to do service of any sort, then shall not Ra-User-Ma, approved of the Sun, the great ruler of Egypt, claim them; he shall cause them to be given up to the King of Kheta [—].

24.[155] [—] the tablet of silver, it is declared by the thousand gods, the gods male, the gods female, those that are of the land of Kheta, in concert with the thousand gods, the gods male, the gods female, those that are of the land of Egypt, those [—] Set of Kheta, Set of the city of A [—], Set[156] of the city of Taaranta, Set of the city of Pairaka, Set of the city of Khisasap, Set of the city of Sarasu, Set of the city of Khirabu, Set [of the city of], Set of the city of Sarapaina, Astarata[157] of Kheta, the god of Taitatkherri, the god of Ka [—], the goddess of the city of [—], the goddess of Tain [—], the god of [—] of the hills of the rivers of the land of Kheta, the gods of the land of Kheta, the gods of the land of Tawatana,[158] Amon the Sun, Set, the gods male, the gods female, of the hills, the rivers of the land of Egypt, the great sea, the winds, the clouds.

26. These words that are on the tablet of silver of the land of Kheta, and of the land of Egypt. Whosoever shall not observe them, the thousand gods of the land of Kheta, in concert with the thousand gods of the land of Egypt shall be against his house, his family, his servants.

25. But whosoever shall observe these words that are in the tablet of silver, be he of Kheta [—] the thousand gods of the land of Kheta, in concert with the thousand gods of the land of Egypt shall give health, shall give life to his family together with himself together with his servants.

16/20. If there shall pass over one man of the land of Egypt or two, or three and they shall go to the land of Kheta then shall the King of Kheta cause them to be given up again to Ra-User-Ma, approved of the Sun, the great ruler of Egypt, but whosoever shall be given up to Ramessu-Meriamen, the great ruler of Egypt, let not his crime be set up against him, let not [—] himself, his wives, his children [—]

14/19/21. If there shall pass over a man from the land of Kheta be it one only be it two, be it three, and they come to Ra-User-Ma, approved of the Sun the great ruler of Egypt let Ramessu-Meriamen the great

[155] A catalogue of gods who will defend the treaty, omitted from the Hittite version.

[156] Hittite Sutech, a war god and the supreme Hittite god, accompanied by the names of mostly otherwise unknown Hittite nobles.

[157] Or Antarata, the consort of Sutech.

[158] A kingdom in Palestine.

ruler of Egypt seize them and cause them to be given up to the King of Kheta but whosoever shall be delivered up [—] himself his wives, his children, moreover let him not be smitten to death, moreover let him not suffer in his eyes, in his mouth, in his feet, moreover let not any crime be set up against him. That which is upon the tablet of silver upon its front side is the likeness of the figure of Set [—] of Set the great ruler of heaven, the director of the Treaty made by Kheta-Sira the great ruler of Kheta [—]

(b) Hittite Version

[prologue]

It is concluded that Ra-Amasesa-Mai-Amana, the Great King, the Pharaoh of the land of Egypt with Hattusili, the Great King, the King of the land of Hatti,[159] his brother, for the land of Egypt and the land of Hatti, in order to establish a good peace and a good fraternity forever among them. Thus speaks Ra-Amasesa, the Great King, the Pharaoh of the land of Egypt, the hero of the whole country, son of Minmuaria,[160] the Great King, the Pharaoh of the land of Egypt, the hero, son of the son of Minpahiritaria,[161] the Great King, the Pharaoh of the land of Egypt, the hero, to Hattusili, son of Mursili, the Great King, the King of the land of Hatti, the hero, son of the son of Suppiluliuma,[162] the Great King, the King of the land of Hatti, the hero. "Look, I have established a good fraternity and a good peace now forever among us, in order to establish this way forever a good peace and a good fraternity between the land of Egypt and the land of Hatti. Look, in what refers to the Great King's relationship, the King of the country of Egypt, and of the Great King, the King of the Hittite country, since eternity the gods do not allow, by reason of an eternal treaty, that enmity should exist between them. Look, Ra-Amasesa-Mai-Amana, the Great King, the King of the country of Egypt, will establish the bond that the Sun God[163] has wanted and that the God of the Tempest[164] has wanted for the country of Egypt and the country of Hatti according to the eternal bond, for not letting enmity settle between them."

1. But now Ra-Amasesa-Mai-Amana, the Great King, the King of the country of Egypt, has established this bond by treaty on a silver tablet with Hattusili, the Great King, the King of the country of Hatti, his brother, starting from this day, to settle forever among them a good peace and a good fraternity.
2. He is a brother to me and he is at peace with me; and I am a brother to him and I am forever at peace with him.
3. Look, we are united and a bond of fraternity already exists among us and of peace, and it is better than the bond of fraternity and of peace that existed between the country of Egypt and the country of Hatti.
4. Look, Ra-Amasesa-Mai-Amana, the Great King, the King of the country of Egypt, is at peace and fraternity with Hattusili, the Great King, the King of the country of Hatti.
5. Look, the children of Ra-Amasesa, the Great King, the King of the country of Egypt, they will be forever in state of peace and of fraternity with the children of Hattusili, the Great King, the King of the country of Hatti. They will remain in the line of our bond of fraternity and of peace; the country of Egypt and the

[159] "Kheta" in the Egyptian version.

[160] Seti I (1290–1279) BCE.

[161] Ramses I (1292–1290 BCE).

[162] King of the Hittites 1344–1322 BCE.

[163] Ra.

[164] The Hittites worshiped a multitude of storm gods.

country of Hatti will be forever be in a state of peace and of fraternity as it is with us.

6. Ra-Amasesa-Mai-Amana, the Great King, the King of the country of Egypt, shall never attack the country of Hatti to take possession of a part of it. And Hattusili, the Great King, the King of the country of Hatti, shall never attack the country of Egypt to take possession of a part of it.
7. Look, the order fixed for eternity that the Sun God and the God of the Tempest have created for the country of Egypt and the country of Hatti, peace and fraternity without leaving place among them to any enmity. Look, Ra-Amasesa-Mai-Amana, the Great King, the King of the country of Egypt, has established peace starting from this day. Look, the country of Egypt and the country of Hatti live forever in peace and fraternity.
8. If a foreign enemy marches against the country of Hatti and if Hattusili, the King of the country of Hatti, sends me this message: "Come to my help against him," Ra-Amasesa-Mai-Amana, the Great King, the King of the Egyptian country, has to send his troops and his chariots to kill this enemy and to give satisfaction to the country of Hatti.
9. If Hattusili, the Great King, the King of the country of Hatti, rises in anger against his citizens after they have committed a crime against him and if, for this reason, you send to Ra-Amasesa the Great King, the King of the country of Egypt, then Ra-Amasesa-Mai-Amana has to send his troops and his chariots and these should exterminate all those that he has risen in anger against.
10. If a foreigner marches against the country of Egypt and if Ra-Amasesa-Mai-Amana, the Great King, the King of the country of Egypt, your brother, sends to Hattusili, the King of the country of Hatti, his brother, the following message: "Come to my help against him," then Hattusili, King of the country of Hatti, shall send his troops and his chariots and kill my enemy.
11. If Ra-Amasesa, King of the country of Egypt, rises in anger against his citizens after they have committed a wrong against him and by reason of this he sends (a message) to Hattusili, the Great King, the King of the country of Hatti, my brother, has to send his troops and his chariots and they have to exterminate all those against, and I shall [—]
12. Look, the son of Hattusili, King of the country of Hatti, has to assure his sovereignty of the country of Hatti instead of Hattusili, his father, after the numerous years of Hattusili, King of the country of Hatti. If the children of the country of Hatti transgress against him, then Ra-Amasesa has to send to his help troops and chariots and to give him support.
13. If a great person flees from the country of Hatti and if he comes to Ra-Amasesa, the Great King, King of the country of Egypt, then Ra-Amasesa, the Great King, the King of the country of Egypt, has to take hold of him and deliver him into hands of Hattusili, the Great King, the King of the country of Hatti.
14. If a man or two men who are unknown flee, and if they come to Ra-Amasesa, to serve him, then Ra-Amasesa has to take hold of them and deliver them into the hands of Hattusili, King of the country of Hatti.
15. If a great person flees from the country of Egypt and he escapes to the country of Amurru or a city and he comes to the King of Amurru, then Benteshina, King of the country of Amurru, has to take hold of him and take him to the King of the country of Hatti; and Hattusili, the Great King, the King of the country of Hatti, shall have him to be taken to Ra-Amasesa, the Great King, the King of the country of Egypt.
16. If a man or two men who are unknown flee, and if they escape from the country of Egypt and if they do not want to serve him, then Hattusili, the Great King, the King of the country of Hatti, has to deliver them into his brother's hands and he shall not allow them to inhabit the country of Hatti.

17. If a nobleman flees from the country of Hatti, or two men, and if they do not want to serve the King of Hatti, and if they flee from the Great King's country, the King of the land of Hatti, in order not to serve him, then Ra-Amasesa has to take hold of them and order them be taken to Hattusili, the Great King, King of the land of Hatti, his brother, and he shall not allow them to reside in the country of Egypt.
18. If a nobleman or two flee from the country of Egypt and if they leave for the Land of Hatti, then Hattusili, the Great King, the King of the country of Hatti, has to take hold of them and make them be taken to Ra-Amasesa, the Great King, the King of the country of Egypt, his brother.
19. If a man flees from the country of Hatti, or two men, or three men, and if they come to Ra-Amasesa, the Great King, the King of the country of Egypt, his brother, then Ra-Amasesa, the Great King, the King of the country of Egypt, has to take hold of them and to order them to be taken to Hattusili, his brother, because they are brothers. As for their crime, it should not be imputed; their tongue and their eyes are not to be pulled out; their ears and their feet are not to be cut off; their houses with their wives and their children are not to be destroyed.
20. If a man flees from the country of Ra-Amasesa, the Great King, King of the country of Egypt, or two men, or three men, and if they come to Hattusili, the Great King, the King of the country of Hatti, my brother, then Hattusili, the Great King, King of the country of Hatti, my brother, has to take hold of them and to order them to be taken to Ra-Amasesa, the Great King, the King of the country of Egypt, because Ra-Amasesa, the Great King, King of the country of Egypt, and Hattusili are brothers. As for their crime, it should not be imputed; their tongue and their eyes are not to be pulled out; their ears and their feet are not to be cut off; their houses with their wives and their children are not to be destroyed.
21. If a man flees from the country of Hatti, or two people, and if they flee from the country of Hatti, and if they come to the country of Egypt, and if a nobleman flees from the country of Hatti or of a city and they flee from the country of Hatti to go to the country of Egypt, then Ra-Amasesa has to order them to be taken to his brother. Look, the sons of the country of Hatti and the children of the country of Egypt are at peace.
22. If some people flee from the country of Egypt to go to the country of Hatti, then Hattusili, the Great King, the King of the country of Hatti, has to order them to be taken to his brother.
23. Look, Hattusili the Great King, the King of the country of Hatti, and Ra-Amasesa, the Great King, the King of the country of Egypt, your brother, are at peace.
24. If Ra-Amasesa and the children of the country of Egypt do not observe this treaty, then the gods and the goddesses of the country of Egypt and the gods and goddesses of the country of Hatti shall exterminate the descendents of Ra-Amasesa, the Great King, the King of the country of Egypt.
25. If Ra-Amasesa and the children of the country of Egypt observe this treaty, then the gods of the oath shall protect them and their [—] They who observe the words that are in the silver tablet the great gods of the country of Egypt and the great gods of the country of Hatti shall allow them to live and prosper in their houses, their country, and with their servants.
26. They who do not observe the words that are in this silver tablet, the great gods of the country of Egypt as well as the great gods of the country of Hatti will exterminate their houses, their country, and their servants.

CHAPTER 4

Coastal Civilizations of the Eastern Mediterranean (2500–800 BCE)

The Bronze Age, quite correctly, is viewed as the great age of river valley civilizations. But we ought not to think that there was nothing going on outside the river valleys at the same time. In an unobtrusive way, other peoples were pursuing other ways of life, finding niches of opportunity, and creating their own civilizations. These bit players of the Bronze Age, inhabiting the Levant, the island of Crete, and mainland Greece, anticipated future mainstream lifestyles, uses of technology, and forms of economic activity that bridged the gap between the Bronze Age and the Iron Age and facilitated the spread of civilization out of the river valleys to encompass much larger regions and numbers of people. These cultures also help to correct the common presumption that Mesopotamia and Egypt were the only centers of Bronze Age civilization and demonstrate that, by the early Iron Age, the river valley cultures of the Bronze Age had run their course. Like the better-known river valley civilizations, these niche civilizations also had written documents, using their own systems of writing that suited their own needs. Some, such as those of the Minoans, Mycenaeans, and the city of Ebla, are preserved only on clay tablets. Other records, such as those of the Hebrews and their descendents, eventually were written on papyrus. With the exception of the Hebrews, these peoples left few surviving written documents, and one must make do either with the scraps that survive or with the appearances of these peoples, such as the Philistines and Canaanites, in the writings of other peoples, such as the Egyptians and Hebrews. The study of these documents and peoples provides historians with a more balanced perception of what was happening in the Near East and the eastern Mediterranean as a whole.

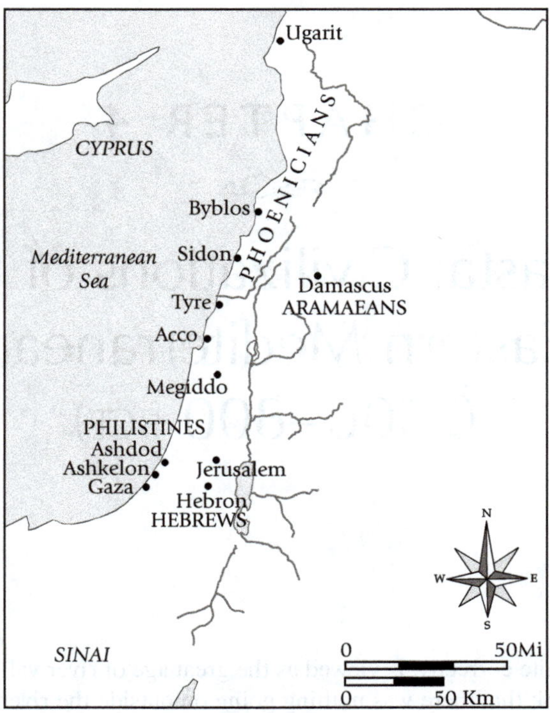

Map 4 The Peoples of the Eastern Mediterranean Coast in the Early Iron Age

30

DOCUMENTS FROM EBLA (CA. 2400 BCE)

One of the thousands of clay tablets found in the ruins of Ebla, written using Sumerian cuneiform script.

The ancient city of Ebla in Syria was not rediscovered by archaeologists until 1968. The city controlled a vast trading network that extended from the Mediterranean Sea into western Iran and marked another great civilization of the third millennium BCE, along with those of Egypt, Mesopotamia, and Crete. In the first of the following two documents, both of which were written on clay tablets in Sumerian cuneiform script ca. 2400 BCE, the superintendent of the Palace of Ebla arranges for the delivery of pack-horses, something that would be necessary for the maintenance of Ebla's extensive trade network. In the second, a successful general of Ebla reports back regarding the progress of a war against the city of Mari that had been declared because Mari blocked Ebla from commercial access to lower Mesopotamia. The campaign was so successful that the general, with or without the assent of the King of Ebla, laid claim to the throne of Mari. One wonders, however, why his recorded campaigns did not extend to the city of Mari itself.

Source: Giovanni Pettinato, *The Archives of Ebla. An Empire Inscribed in Clay* (Garden City, NY: Doubleday, 1981), 96–102.

[Ibibu, the superintendent of the Palace of Ebla writes to the ambassador of the King of Ḫamazi.]

Thus, Ibubu, the Superintendent of the Palace of the King, to the ambassador: "Listen, you are my brother and I am your brother, to you man-brother. Whatever desire issuing from your mouth I will grant and you the desire issuing from my mouth will grant. Good pack animals[1] send me, I pray: you are in fact my brother and I am your brother. Ten beams of boxwood, two boxwood wagons, I, Ibubu, have given to the messenger. Irkab-Dau, King of Ebla, is brother of Zizi, King of Ḫamazi.[2] Zizi, King of Ḫamazi, is brother of Irkab-Damu, King of Ebla." And thus Tira-il, the scribe has written and to the messenger of Zizi has given the letter.

[Enna-Dagan reports back to the King of Ebla regarding the campaign against the city of Mari.]

Thus Enna-Dagan,[3] King of Mari,[4] to the King of Ebla. I laid siege to the citi of Tibalat[5] and the city of Ilgi, and I defeated the King of Mari. In the land of Labanan I raised heaps of corpses. I laid siege to the city of Tibalat and the city of Ilwi, and I defeated the King of Mari. In the land of Angai I raised heaps of corpses. I laid siege to the towns of Raeak and Irim and Aṡaltu and Badul, and I defeated the King of Mari. Near the borders of Naḫal I raised heaps of corpses. And I defeated at Emar, and at Lalanium, and near the commercial colony of Ebla, Ištup-Šar, the commander of Mari. In Emar and Lalanium I raised heaps of corpses. And Galalabi and [—] and the commercial colony[6] I liberated. I defeated Iblul-Il, King of Mari and Ashur,[7] in Zaḫiran, and raised seven heaps of corpses. I defeated Iblul-Il, King of Mari, and the cities of Šada, Addali, and Arisum, in the territory of Burman, together with the men of Sukurrim. I raised heaps of corpses. And I defeated Šaran and Dammium together with Iblul-Il, King of Mari. I raised two heaps of corpses. Iblul-Il, King of Mari, fled toward Nerad to his house at Ḫaṡiwan, carrying with him to the city of Nema the tribute due Ebla. And I defeated Emar, raising heaps of corpses. In Ganane I defeated Iblul-Il, King of Mari, and the cities of Naḫal and Šada of the territory of Gasur. I raised seven heaps of corpses. I, Enna-Dagan, King of Mari, defeated Iblul-Il, King of Mari, and the city of Barama, for the second time, and Aburu and Tibalat in the territory of Belan. I raised heaps of corpses.

---

[1] A word that has been variously translated as "mercenaries" or "equines," that is, some kind of horse-like animal. Given that horses would not be ridden for more than a thousand years and the horse-collar would not be used for some three thousand years, this probably is a reference to some sort of pack-animal, perhaps donkeys. It is unlikely that mercenaries would have been exchanged for items made from boxwood.

[2] A city in western Iran.

[3] Enna-Dagan had been a general of Ebla who, after defeating the city of Mari, became king of Mari.

[4] The city of Mari, located on the upper Euphrates River, flourished as an important trading city in the third and early second millennium BCE. It was destroyed once by the Akkadians in the twenty-third century BCE and later by the Babylonians around 1750 BCE.

[5] The document cites this and other otherwise unknown places in upper Mesopotamia.

[6] Presumably the aforementioned "commercial colony of Ebla," another indication of Ebla's commercial expansion.

[7] Ebla and Ashur (Assyria) established early trading relations: ca. 2500 BCE the earliest known Assyrian king, Tudiya, made a commercial treaty with Ibrium, king of Ebla, whereby Assyrian traders were able to use an Eblaite trading center.

31

MYCENAEAN LINEAR B TABLETS (CA. 1200 BCE)

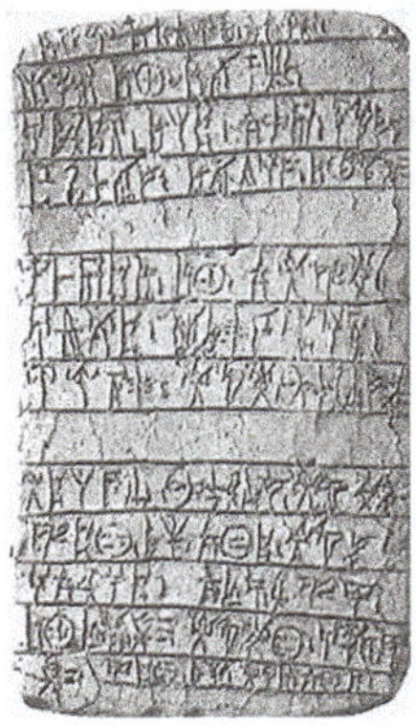

Linear B tablet An 675 from Pylos, late thirteenth century BCE, which begins with the words, "Thus the watchers are keeping guard over the coastline," and begins a series of five texts detailing military dispositions. Preserved in the National Archaeological Museum of Athens.]

The Minoan civilization of Crete developed an as yet undeciphered writing system known as "Linear A." When the Minoans were superseded by the Mycenaeans of Greece, the latter used the Minoan writing system to write their own language, which is called "Linear B." Many attempts were made to decipher Linear B, some based on existing languages such as Etruscan and even Basque. It was not until the early 1950s that Linear B was deciphered by Michael Ventris and was discovered, to the amazement of all, to be an early form of Greek. Many people found the contents of the tablets disappointing: there were no historical narratives, no legends, no poetry—mostly just inventories of people and material. As a consequence, Mycenaean Linear B tablets make for dry reading. Cited here are a few typical tablets from the southwestern Mycenaean city of Pylos; because the writing system is a syllabary, unidentified words are presented as a sequence of syllables. The last passage has been associated with troop dispositions, perhaps as a result of a threatened attack ca. 1200 BCE.

Source: John Chadwick, *The Decipherment of Linear B*, 2nd ed. (Cambridge, UK: Cambridge University Press, 1967), 158–161.

(1) (Tablet Py Ae134) Kerowos the shepherd at Asiatia is watching over the cattle of Thalamatas.

(2) (Tablet Py Ad676) At Pylos: twenty-two sons of the bath-attendants, eleven boys.

(3) (Tablet Py Eb297) The priestess holds this and claims that the deity holds the freehold, but the plot owners claim that she holds only the leases of the communal plots: 474 liters of wheat.

(4) (Tablet Py Er312) The estate of the pa-si-re-u,[8] so much seed: 1200 liters of wheat. The estate of the la-wa-ge-ta[9]: 1200 liters of wheat. The lands of the te-re-tai,[10] so much seed: 3600 liters of wheat; so many te-re-tai: three men. The deserted land of the cult association, so much seed: 720 liters of wheat.

(5) (Tablet An 675)[11] Thus the watchers are guarding the coast. Command of Maleus at O-wi-to-no: Ampelitawon, Orestas, Etewas, Kokkion. Fifty su-we-ro-wi-jo men of O-wi-to-no at Oikhalia. Command of Nedwatas: Ekhemedes, Amphi-e-ta the ma-ra-te-u, Ta-ni-ko. Ten Kuparissian ke-ki-de men at A-ru-wo-te, ten Kuparissian ke-ki-de men at Aithalewes, and with them the follower Kerkios. Aeriquhoitas, Elaphos, Ri-me-ne. Thirty men from Oikhalia to O-wi-to-no, and 20 ke-ki-de men from A-pu-ka, and with them the follower Ai-ko-ta.

[8] Antecedent of the later Greek word *basileus*, or "king." In Mycenaean times the pa-si-re-u seems to have been a local administrator.

[9] The Mycenaean Lawagetas, from words meaning "leader of the people," seems to have been second in command to the Wanax, the overall ruler, and perhaps was a military leader.

[10] The Mycenaean Telestai were other important officials, perhaps aristocrats ranking below the Wanax.

[11] Many of the places and descriptive words in this passage cannot be identified.

32

THE INVASION OF THE "SEA PEOPLES" (CA. 1180 BCE): UGARITIC CORRESPONDENCE; THE MEDINET HABU INSCRIPTION OF RAMSES III (1182–1151 BCE)

The artwork that accompanies the Medinet Habu inscription of Ramses III shows the Egyptians, led by a larger-than-life Ramses III, showering the Sea Peoples with arrows.

The end of the Near Eastern Bronze Age was marked by widespread dislocations, many of which were associated with what the Egyptian records refer to as "the Peoples of the Sea," who appear to have been a combination of Indo-Europeans newly arrived from the central Asian steppes accompanied by local peoples dislocated by political and economic disruption. Shortly after 1200 BCE, elements of the Sea Peoples first attacked and destroyed the Hittite Empire of Anatolia and a number of smaller states on the eastern Mediterranean coast. In 1174 BCE, a large coalition then moved against Egypt, where it was defeated by Pharaoh Ramses III (1182–1151 BCE). The Sea Peoples who escaped then scattered, creating more havoc throughout the Mediterranean. Correspondence preserved in the archives of the destroyed city of Ugarit between Eshuwara, King and Grand Steward of Alashiya, and Ammurapi, King of Ugarit, tells of raids by enemy ships now identified as belonging to the Sea Peoples. And the funerary temple of Ramses III at Medinet Habu not only depicts scenes of the invasion by the Sea Peoples but also preserves Ramses's victory speech and other descriptions of the Sea Peoples's attack.

Document Source: Jean Nougaryol, *Ugaritica. V: nouveaux textes accadiens, hourrites et ugaritiques des archives et bibliothèques privées d'Ugarit* (1968), nos. 22–25, pp. 83–90.

(a) Ugaritic Correspondence

[Eshuwara reports to King Ammurapi that ships coming from the territory of Ugarit have been attacking him.]

Thus says Eshuwara, Grand Steward of Alashiya[12]: "Say[13] to the King of Ugarit, 'Greetings to you and your country. As to the matters regarding the enemies from these peoples from your country and from your ships, they certainly have done this, and as to this transgression, these peoples from your county have done it.[14] But do not take offense against me about this. Now, the twenty ships that the enemies previously left in mountainous regions have not remained in place but have departed in haste, and we do not know where they can be found. It is to let you know, in order to put you on your guard, that I write to you. Know this!'"

[Eshuwara replies to Ammurapi's response, which does not survive and must have asserted that the enemy ships did not belong to him.]

Thus says the king: "To Ammurapi, King of Ugarit, say, 'Greetings to you! May the gods keep you in good health![15] Concerning that which you wrote to me, "Some ships of the enemy have been sighted at sea"—Assuming that this is true,[16] that some ships of the enemy have been spotted, then, indeed, make yourself very resolute. In fact, as far as this concerns you, where, therefore, are your soldiers and chariots stationed? Are they not stationed in your presence? No? Are they cut off by the enemy that presses upon you? Surround your cities with ramparts! Assemble there your soldiers and chariots and await the enemy there with a very firm step!'"

[Ammurapi sends a panicked letter to Eshuwara indicating that the territory of Ugarit is being overrun by the enemy. At this point, the document trail ends, suggesting that the city was destroyed soon after.]

To my father,[17] the King of Alashiya, say,[18] "Thus says your son, the King of Ugarit: 'I prostrate myself at the feet of my father; to my father, greetings! To your palaces, your wives, your soldiers, to all that is

[12] Generally thought to have been on the island of Cyprus. The kingdom still existed ca. 1050 CE, when it was visited by the Egyptian priest Wenamun (Document 33).

[13] Eshuwara addresses his own ambassador, who speaks on behalf the kingdom of Alashiya.

[14] The King of Alashiya seems to blaming the King of Ugarit for the actions of enemy ships that have based themselves in the territory of Ugarit.

[15] After receiving a letter of explanation from the King of Ugarit, the King of Alashiya now is more well disposed toward him, given that the two kings face a common threat.

[16] Eshuwara still is not totally convinced that the raiders had not been sent by Ammurapi.

[17] A form of address suggesting, if not that Eshuwara outranked Ammurapi, at least that he was older.

[18] Ammurapi addresses his own ambassador.

under the authority of the King of Alashiya, profuse, profuse greetings! My father, know that the ships of the enemy have arrived. My cities have been consumed by fire; nasty things have been done in the countryside. My father is unaware that all my solders are stationed in the country of the Hittites,[19] and that my ships are stationed in the country of the Lukka.[20] As of now, they have not returned to me and the countryside therefore is abandoned to itself. My father needs to know this! For there are seven ships of the enemy that have arrived against me and they have done bad things. Now, if there are any other ships of the enemy, inform me of it in some way[21] so that I shall know it!' "

(b) The Medinet Habu Inscription of Ramses III (1182–1151 BCE)

Year 8[22] under the majesty of Horus, mighty Bull, valiant Lion, strong-armed, Lord of Might, capturing the Asiatics, favorite of the Two Goddesses, Mighty in Strength, like his father Montu,[23] destroying the Nine Bows,[24] driving them from their land, Pharaoh of Upper and Lower Egypt, Lord of the Two Lands, Usermare-Mariamon,[25] Son of Ra, Ramses, charging into the thick of the fray, turning back the Asiatics . . . The northerners in their islands[26] were disturbed, taken away in battle at one time. Not one stood before their hands, from Kheta,[27] Carchemish,[28] Arvad,[29] and Alashiya, they were wasted. They camped in one place in Amor.[30] They desolated his people and his land like that which is not. They came with fire prepared before them, forward to Egypt. Their main support were the Peleset,[31] the Tjeker,[32] the Shekelesh,[33] the Denyen,[34] and the Weshesh.[35] These lands were united, and they laid their hands upon the land as far as the Circle of the Earth. Their hearts were confident, full of their plans.

Now, it happened through this god,[36] the lord of gods, that I was prepared and armed to trap them like wild fowl. He furnished my strength and caused my plans to prosper. I went forth, directing these marvelous things. I equipped my frontier in Zahi,[37]

[19] An empire in Anatolia; see Reading 29.

[20] Perhaps ancient Lycia, on the southwestern coast of Anatolia. The Lukka were associated with the Sea Peoples.

[21] Suggesting that there has been a disruption in communications.

[22] The inscription begins with an extended praise of Ramses and his valor.

[23] An Egyptian war god.

[24] A generic term for the foreign enemies of Egypt.

[25] Another name of Ramses.

[26] Such as the island kingdom of Alashiya.

[27] The Hittites.

[28] An important commercial city that controlled the main ford across the upper Euphrates River in western Syria. It survived the attack by the Sea Peoples.

[29] An island city off the coast of Syria; Greek Aradus; it was sacked by the Sea Peoples but later recovered.

[30] Territory west of the upper Euphrates River in Syria or Canaan; after 1200 BCE the territory was occupied by the Aramaeans.

[31] Often identified as the Philistines, who settled on the coast of Palestine, to which they gave their name.

[32] A people who also ultimately settled on the coast of Palestine, as attested in the "Report of Wen-Amon" (Reading 33).

[33] Tentatively identified as the later Siculi of Sicily.

[34] Identified variously with the Dananiyim, a people of the Hittite Empire; the Danaans, an early name for Greeks; and the Israelite tribe of Dan, located on the Palestinian coast between the Peleset and Tjeker.

[35] A people of unknown origin.

[36] The god Montu, with whom Ramses particularly identified.

[37] Djahy in western Asia, an Egyptian name for Canaan.

Source: James Henry Breasted, *Ancient Records of Egypt: Historical Documents from the Earliest Times to the Persian Conquest*, Vol. 4 (Chicago: University of Chicago Press, 1906), nos. 64–66, 75; 36–39, 44–45.

prepared before them. The chiefs, the captains of infantry, the nobles, I caused to equip the harbor-mouths, like a strong wall, with warships, galleys, and barges. They were manned completely from bow to stern with valiant warriors bearing their arms, soldiers of all the choicest of Egypt, being like lions roaring upon the mountain-tops. The charioteers were warriors, and all good officers, ready of hand. Their horses were quivering in their every limb, ready to crush the countries under their feet. I was the valiant Montu, stationed before them, that they might behold the hand-to-hand fighting of my arms. I, Pharaoh Ramses, was made a far-striding hero, conscious of his might, valiant to lead his army in the day of battle.

Those who reached my boundary, their seed is not; their heart and their soul are finished forever and ever. As for those who had assembled before them on the sea, the full flame was in their front, before the harbor-mouths, and a wall of metal upon the shore surrounded them. They were dragged, overturned, and laid low upon the beach, slain and made heaps from stern to bow of their galleys, while all their things were cast upon the water. Thus I turned back the waters to remember Egypt; when they mention my name in their land, may it consume them, while I sit upon the throne of Harakhte,[38] and the serpent-diadem is fixed upon my head, like Ra. I permit not the countries to see the boundaries of Egypt as a remembrance. As for the Nine Bows, I have taken away their land and their boundaries; they are added to mine. Their chiefs and their people come to me with praise. I carried out the plans of the All-Lord, the august, divine father, lord of the gods.

[Text over Ramses in his chariot.]
The Pharaoh, rich in might, at his going forth to the north, great in fear, the dread of the Asiatics, like Ba'al,[39] valiant in strength, ready for battle against the Asiatics, marching far in advance, smiting tens of thousands in heaps in the space of an hour.

[Texts by a scene of the naval battle.]
Lo, the northern countries, which are in their islands, are restless in their limbs; they infest the ways of the harbor-mouths. Their nostrils and their hearts cease breathing breath when his majesty goes forth like a storm-wind against them, fighting upon the strand like a warrior. His power and the terror of him penetrate into their limbs. Capsized and perishing in their places, their hearts are taken, their souls fly away, and their weapons are cast out upon the sea. His arrows pierce whomsoever he will among them, and he who is hit falls into the water. His majesty is like an enraged lion, tearing him that confronts him with his hands, fighting at close quarters on his right, valiant on his left, like Set[40]; destroying the foe, like Amon-Ra.[41] He has laid low the lands, he has crushed every land beneath his feet, the Pharaoh of Upper and Lower Egypt, the Lord of the Two Lands, Usermare-Meriamon.

[Text by the Pharaoh and his court.]
Utterance of his majesty to the king's-children, the princes, the king's butlers, and the charioteers: "Behold ye, the great might of my father, Amon-Ra. The countries which came from their isles in the midst of the sea, they advanced to Egypt, their hearts relying upon their arms. The net was made ready for them, to ensnare them. Entering stealthily into the river-mouth, they fell into it. Caught in their place, they were dispatched, and their bodies stripped. I showed you my might which was in that which my majesty wrought while I was alone. My arrow struck, and none escaped my arms or my hand. I flourished like a hawk among the fowl; my talons descended upon their heads. Amon-Ra was upon my right and upon my left, his might and his power were in my limbs, a tumult for you; commanding for me that my counsels and my designs should come to pass. Amon-Ra established the defeat of my enemies, giving to me every land in my grasp."

[38] A god who combined Ra and Horus.

[39] A Semitic storm god.

[40] An Egyptian storm god.

[41] The primary god of the Egyptian New Kingdom, with a large temple complex at Karnak at Thebes.

33

THE REPORT OF WEN-AMON (CA. 1050 BCE)

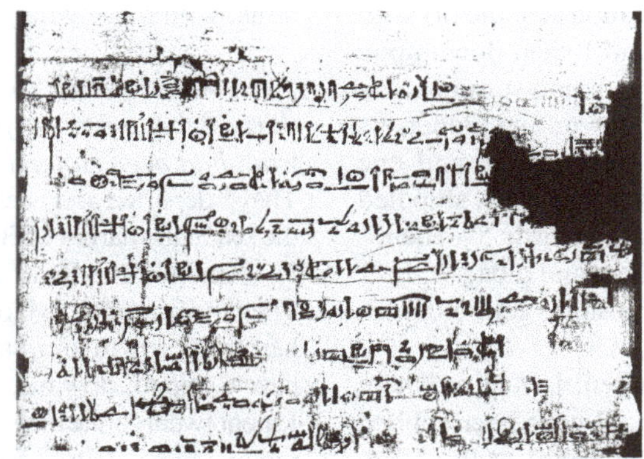

The "Report of Wen-Amon," written in Egyptian hieroglyphic script about 1000 BCE, is preserved at the Pushkin Museum in Moscow.

During its Third Intermediate Period (1077–664 BCE), Egypt split into multiple kingdoms. The once-powerful Egyptian Empire became just a memory and Egypt lost the respect of neighbors such as the Philistines and Phoenicians. Early in this period, Wen-Amon, a priest of Amon from Karnak and a representative of the Delta Pharaoh Smendes (1076–1052 BCE), was sent to Phoenicia to purchase cedar ship timber. After being robbed in Philistine territory, Wen-Amon arrived in the Phoenician city of Byblos, where he was rudely received by a local prince. Subsequently, ill winds brought him to Cyprus, where he was nearly murdered. Many specialists believe that the "Story of Wen-Amon," preserved in a single papyrus copy written in hieroglyphic script about 1000 BCE, is a work of fiction rather than the autobiographical account it purports to be, but however that may be, this account provides precious insights into the otherwise poorly known history of the peoples of the eastern Mediterranean coast during the early Iron Age.

Source: James Henry Breasted, *Ancient Records of Egypt, Historical Documents from the Earliest Times to the Persian Conquest*, Vol. IV, *The Twentieth to the Twenty-Sixth Dynasties* (Chicago: University of Chicago Press, 1906), nos. 557–591, 274–287.

Year 5, fourth month of summer, day 16, the day of departure of Wen-Amon, the Elder of the Portal of the Temple of Amon, Lord of Thrones-of-the-Two-Lands, to fetch timber for the great noble boat of Amon-Ra, King of the Gods, which is upon the river and is called Amon-user-he. On the day of my arrival at Tanis,[42] the place where Smendes[43] and Tentamon[44] are, I gave them the dispatches of Amon-Ra, King of the Gods. They had read them out before them and they said, "I will do, I will do as Amon-Ra, King of the Gods, our Lord has said."

I stayed until the fourth month of summer in Tanis. Then Smendes and Tentamon sent me off with the ship's captain Mengebet, and I went down upon the great sea of Syria in the first month summer, day 1. I arrived at Dor, a Tjeker[45] town; and Beder, its prince, had fifty loaves, one jug of wine, and one ox-haunch brought to me. Then a man of my ship fled after stealing one vessel of gold worth 5 deben,[46] four jars of silver worth 20 deben, and a bag with 11 deben of silver; total of what he stole: gold 5 deben, silver 31 deben.

That morning when I had risen, I went to where the prince was and said to him, "I have been robbed in your harbor. Now you are the prince of this land, you are the one who controls it. Search for my money! Indeed the money belongs to Amon-Ra, King of the Gods, the Lord of the lands. It belongs to Smendes; it belongs to Herihor,[47] my Lord, and to the other magnates of Egypt. It belongs to you; it belongs to Weret; it belongs to Mekmer; it belongs to Tjekerbaal,[48] the prince of Byblos!" He said to me, "Are you serious? Are you joking? Indeed I do not understand the demand you make to me. If it had been a thief belonging to my land who had gone down to your ship and had stolen your money, I would replace it for you from my storehouse, until your thief, whatever his name, had been found. But the thief who robbed you, he is yours, he belongs to your ship. Spend a few days here with me; I will search for him."

I stayed nine days moored in his harbor. Then I went to him and said to him, "Look, you have not found my money. Let me depart with the ship captains, with those who go to sea."

[Wen-Amon travels to Byblos. On the way he steals thirty deben of silver from a Tjeker ship to replace what had been stolen from him.]

They[49] departed and I celebrated in a tent on the shore of the sea in the harbor of Byblos. And made a hiding place for Amon-of-the-Road and placed possessions in it. Then the prince of Byblos sent to me saying, "Leave my harbor!" I sent to him, saying, "Where shall I go? If you have a ship to carry me, let me be taken back to Egypt." I spent twenty-nine days in his harbor, and he spent time sending to me daily to say, "Leave my harbor!"

Now while the prince was offering to his gods, the god took hold of a young man of his and put him in a trance. He said to him, "Bring the god up! Bring the envoy who is carrying him! It is Amon who sent him. It is he who made him come!" Now it was while the entranced one was entranced that night that I had found a ship headed for Egypt. I had loaded all my belongings into it and was watching for the darkness, saying, "When it descends I will load the god so that no other eye shall see him."

Then the harbor master came to me, saying, "Wait until morning, says the prince!" I said to him, "Was it not you who daily took time to come to me, saying, 'Leave my harbor'? Do you now say, 'Wait this night,' in order to let the ship that I found depart, and

---

[42] A new city in the northeastern Nile delta.

[43] Pharaoh 1076–1052 BCE, the successor of Pharaoh Ramses XI and founder of the Twenty-first dynasty, ruler of Lower Egypt only. Smendes was of Libyan descent from the people known in Egypt as the Meshwesh.

[44] Daughter of Ramses XI and wife of Smendes.

[45] The Tjeker were one of the Sea Peoples and must have settled here after being defeated in the attack on Egypt in 1174 BCE. This is the last surviving reference to them.

[46] An Egyptian unit of weight, in the New Kingdom equal to 3.2 ounces (91 grams).

[47] The High Priest of Amon at Thebes.

[48] The names, it seems, of rulers along the Mediterranean coast.

[49] The sailors.

then you will come to to say, 'Go away'?" He went and told it to the prince. Then the prince sent to the captain of the ship, saying, "Wait until morning, says the prince."

When morning came, the prince sent and brought me up, while the god rested in the tent where he was on the shore of the sea. I found him seated in his upper chamber with his back against a window, and the waves of the great sea of Syria broke behind his head. I said to him, "Blessings of Amon!" He said to me, "How long is it to this day since you came from the place where Amon is?" I said to him, "Five whole months until now." He said to me, "If you are right, where is the dispatch of Amon that was in your hand? Where is the letter of the High Priest of Amon that was in your hand?" I said to him, "I gave them to Smendes and Tentamon." Then he became very angry and said to me, "Now then, dispatches, letters you have none. Where is the ship of pinewood that Smendes gave you? Where is its Syrian crew? Did he not entrust you to this foreign ship's captain in order to have him kill you and have them throw you into the sea? From whom would one then seek the god? And you, from whom would one seek you?" So he said to me.

I said to him, "Is it not an Egyptian ship? Those who sail under Smendes are Egyptian crews. He has no Syrian crews." He said to me, "Are there not twenty ships here in my harbor that do business with Smendes? As for Sidon, that other place you passed, are there not another fifty ships there that do business with Werekter[50] and haul to this house?"

I was silent in this great moment. Then he spoke to me, saying, "On what business have you come?" I said to him, "I have come in quest of timber for the great noble boat of Amon-Ra, King of the Gods. What your father did, what the father of your father did, you too will do it." So I said to him. He said to me, "True, they did it. If you pay me for doing it, I will do it. My relations carried out this business after Pharaoh had sent six ships laden with the goods of Egypt, and they had been unloaded into their storehouses. You, what have you brought for me?"

He had the daybook of his forefathers[51] brought and had it read before me. They found entered in his book a thousand deben of silver and all sorts of things. He said to me, "If the ruler of Egypt were the Lord of what is mine and I were his servant, he would not have sent silver and gold to say, 'Carry out the business of Amon.' It was not a royal gift that they gave to my father! I, too, I am not your servant, nor am I the servant of him who sent you! If I shout aloud to the Lebanon, the sky opens and the logs lie here on the shore of the sea! Give me the sails you brought to move your ships, loaded with logs for Egypt! Give me the ropes you brought to lash the pines that I am to fell in order to make them for you [---] that I am to make for you for the sails of your ships, or the yards may be too heavy and break, and you may die in the midst of the sea. For Amon makes thunder in the sky ever since he placed Set[52] beside him! Indeed, Amon has founded all the lands. He founded them after having first founded the land of Egypt from which you have come. Thus craftsmanship came from it in order to reach the place where I am! Thus learning came from it in order to reach the place where I am! What are these foolish travels they made you do?"

I said to him, "Wrong! These are not foolish travels that I am doing. There is no ship on the river that does not belong to Amon. His is the sea and his the Lebanon of which you say, 'It is mine.' It is a growing ground for Amon-user-he, the Lord of every ship. Truly, it was Amon-Ra, King of the Gods, who said to Herihor, my master, 'Send me!' And he made me come with this great god. But look, you have let this great god spend these twenty-nine days moored in your harbor. Did you not know that he was here? Is he not he who he was? You are prepared to haggle over the Lebanon with Amon, its Lord? As to your saying, the former kings sent silver and gold, if they had owned life and health, they would not have sent

[50] A Phoenician merchant stationed in Tanis.

[51] Apparently a record of past economic transactions in which the kingdom was involved.

[52] The Egyptian storm god.

these things. It was in place of life and health that they sent these things to your fathers! But Amon-Ra, King of the gods, he is the Lord of life and health, and he was the Lord of your fathers! They passed their lifetimes offering to Amon. You too, you are the servant of Amon!"

"If you will say 'I will do' to Amon, and will carry out his business, you will live, you will prosper, you will be healthy, you will be beneficent to your whole land and your people. Do not desire what belongs to Amon-Ra, King of the Gods! Indeed, a lion loves his possessions! Have your scribe brought to me that I may send him to Smendes and Tentamon, the pillars Amon has set up for the north of his land; and they will send all that is needed. I will send him to them, saying 'Have it brought until I return to the south; then I shall refund you all your expenses.'" So I spoke to him.

He placed my letter in the hand of his messenger, and he loaded the keel, the prow-piece, and the stern-piece, together with four other hewn logs, seven in all, and sent them to Egypt. His messenger who had gone to Egypt returned to me in Syria in the first month of winter, Smendes and Tentamon having sent four jars and one kakmen-vessel of gold; five jars of silver; ten garments of royal linen; ten hrd-garments[53] of fine linen; five hundred smooth linen mats; five hundred ox-hides; five hundred ropes; twenty sacks of lentils; and thirty baskets of fish. And she[54] sent to me: five garments of fine linen; five hrd-garments of fine linen; one sack of lentils; and five baskets of fish.

The prince rejoiced. He assigned three hundred men and three hundred oxen, and he set supervisors over them to have them fell the timbers. They were felled and they lay there during the winter. In the third month of summer they dragged them to the shore of the sea. The prince came out and stood by them, and he sent to me saying, "Come!" Now when I had been brought into his presence, the shadow of his sunshade fell on me. Then Penamon, a butler of his, intervened, saying "The shadow of Pharaoh, your Lord, has fallen upon you." And he was angry with him and said, "Leave him alone."

As I stood before him, he addressed me, saying, "Look, the business my fathers did in the past, I have done it, although you did not do for me what your fathers did for mine. Look, the last of your timber has arrived and is ready. Do as I wish, and come to load it. For has it not been given to you? Do not come to look at the terror of the sea. For if you look at the terror of the sea, you will see my own! Indeed, I have not done to you what was done to the envoys of Khaemwese,[55] after they had spent seventeen years in this land. They died on the spot." And he said to his butler, "Take him to see the tomb where they lie."

I said to him, "Do not make me see it. As for Khaemwese, the envoys he sent you were men and he himself was a man. You have not here one of his envoys, although you say, 'Go and see your companions.' Should you not rejoice and have a stela made for yourself, and say on it, 'Amon-Ra, King of the Gods sent me Amon-of-the-Road, his envoy, together with Wen-Amon, his human envoy, in quest of timber for the great noble boat of Amon-Ra, King of the Gods. I felled it; I loaded it; I supplied my ships and my crews. I let them reach Egypt so as to beg for me from Amon fifty years of life over and above my allotted fate.' And if it comes to pass that in another day an envoy comes from the land of Egypt who knows writing and he reads out your name on the stela, you will receive water of the west like the gods who are there."

He said to me, "A great speech of admonition is what you have said to me." I said to him, "As to the many things you have said to me, if I reach the place where the High Priest of Amon is and he sees your accomplishment, it is your accomplishment that will draw profit to you."

I went off to the shore of the sea, to where the logs were lying. And I saw eleven ships that had come in from the sea and belonged to the Tjeker who were saying, "Arrest him! Let no ship of his leave for the land of Egypt!" Then I sat down and wept. And the secretary of the prince came out to me and said to

[53] Otherwise unknown.

[54] Tentamon.

[55] A son of the pharaoh Ramses II (1279–1212 BCE).

me, "What is it?" I said to him, "Do you not see the migrant birds going down to Egypt a second time? Look at them travelling to the cool water! Until when shall I be left here? For do you not see those who have come to arrest me?"

He went and told it to the prince. And the prince began to weep on account of the words said to him, for they were painful. He sent his secretary out to me, bringing two jugs of wine and a sheep. And he sent me Tentne, an Egyptian songstress who was with him, saying, "Sing for him! Do not let his heart be anxious." And he sent to me, saying, "Eat, drink; do not let your heart be anxious. You shall hear what I will say tomorrow."

When morning came, he had his assembly summoned. He stood in their midst and said to the Tjeker, "What have you come for?" They said to him, "We have come after the accursed ships that you are sending to Egypt with our enemy." He said to them, "I cannot arrest the envoy of Amon in my country. Let me send him off, and you go after him to arrest him."

He had me board and sent off from the harbor of the sea. And the wind drove me to the land of Alashiya.[56] Then the town's people came out against me to kill me. But I forced my way through them to where Hatiba, the princess of the town was. I met her coming from one of her houses to enter another. I saluted her and said to the people who stood around her, "Is there not one among you who understands Egyptian?" And one among them said, "I understand it." I said to him, "Tell my lady that I have heard it said as far away as Thebes, the place where Amon is, 'If wrong is done in every town, in the land of Alashiya right is done.' Now is wrong done here too every day?"

She said: "What is it you have said?" I said to her: "If the sea rages and the wind drives me to the land where you are, will you let me be received so as to kill me, although I am the envoy of Amon? Look, as for me, they would search for me until the end of time. As for this crew of the prince of Byblos, whom they seek to kill, will not their Lord find ten crews of yours and kill them also?" She had the people summoned and they were reprimanded. She said to me: "Spend the night [---]" [*The story breaks off here.*]

[56] Cyprus.

34

THE HEBREWS IN EGYPT AND THE LEGEND OF MOSES (CA. 1300 BCE): EXODUS 1:7–2:7

The story of Moses being found in a basket floating on the Nile River by the pharaoh's daughter has been a popular one in art since the Renaissance, as in this painting done ca. 1730 CE by the Italian painter Giovanni Battista Tiepolo, now in the Scottish National Gallery in Edinburgh.

In the Hebrew Bible, the Hebrews were brought to Egypt by Joseph, the son of the patriarch Isaac, perhaps during the Hyksos period (1730–1534 BCE). Subsequently, they were enslaved and forced to labor on construction projects. A popular story, similar to that about Sargon of Akkad (Reading 16; compare also Reading 73), recounted the origins of Moses, who became the most important Hebrew prophet and, according to Hebrew tradition, led the enslaved Hebrews out of Egypt ca. 1270 BCE.

Source: Hebrew Bible, Exodus 1:7–2:7; *American Revised Standard Version* (1901).

And Joseph died, and all his brethren, and all that generation. And the children of Israel were fruitful, and increased abundantly, and multiplied, and waxed exceeding mighty; and the land was filled with them. Now there arose a new pharaoh over Egypt, who knew not Joseph. And he said unto his people, "Behold, the people of the children of Israel are more and mightier than we. Come, let us deal wisely with them, lest they multiply, and it come to pass, that, when there falleth out any war, they also join themselves unto our enemies, and fight against us, and get them up out of the land." Therefore they did set over them taskmasters to afflict them with their burdens. And they built for Pharaoh store-cities, Pithom[57] and Ramesses.[58] But the more they afflicted them, the more they multiplied and the more they spread abroad. And they were grieved because of the children of Israel. And the Pharaoh of Egypt spoke to the Hebrew midwives, and he said, "When you do the office of a midwife to the Hebrew women, and see them upon the birth-stool, if it be a son, then ye shall kill him, but if it be a daughter, then she shall live." But the midwives feared God and did not as the Pharaoh of Egypt commanded them, but saved the men-children alive. And the Pharaoh of Egypt called for the midwives and said unto them, "Why have you done this thing, and have saved the men-children alive?" And the midwives said unto Pharaoh, "Because the Hebrew women are not as the Egyptian women, for they are lively, and are delivered before the midwife comes to them." And Pharaoh charged all his people, saying, "Every son that is born to the Hebrews you shall cast into the river, and every daughter you shall save alive."

And there went a man of the house of Levi,[59] and took to wife a daughter of Levi. And the woman conceived, and bore a son, and when she saw him that he was a goodly child, she hid him three months. And when she could not longer hide him, she got for him a basket[60] of bulrushes,[61] and daubed it with bitumen and with pitch. And she put the child therein, and laid it in the reeds by the river's edge. And his sister stood afar off, to know what would be done to him. And the daughter of Pharaoh came down to bathe at the river, and her maidens walked along by the riverside. She saw the basket among the reeds, and sent her handmaid to fetch it. And she opened it, and saw the child: and, behold, the babe wept. And she had compassion on him, and said, "This is one of the Hebrews' children."[62] Then said his sister to Pharaoh's daughter, "Shall I go and call thee a nurse of the Hebrew women, that she may nurse the child for thee?" And Pharaoh's daughter said to her, "Go." And the maiden went and called the child's mother. And Pharaoh's daughter said unto her, "Take this child away, and nurse it for me, and I will give thee thy wages." And the woman took the child, and nursed it. And the child grew, and she brought him unto Pharaoh's daughter, and he became her son. And she called his name Moses, and said, "Because I drew him out of the water."[63]

[57] Location unknown.

[58] Pi-Ramesses was a new Egyptian capital built near Avaris in the eastern delta during the reign of Ramses II (1279–1231 BCE).

[59] One of the twelve tribes of Israel.

[60] The same word is used for Noah's ark.

[61] That is, papyrus stalks.

[62] She presumably noticed that the child was circumcised.

[63] The name Moses actually derives from the Egyptian word *mes*, meaning "son," as seen, for example, in the Egyptian name Thutmose, meaning "Son of Thoth." Not knowing Egyptian, later Hebrews derived the name from the Hebrew word *mashah*, meaning "drawn out" (that is, drawn out of the Nile).

35

LAWS OF THE HEBREW BIBLE (CA. 1230 BCE): EXODUS 20

A whole library of early Jewish documents was discovered beginning in 1947 in a cave at Qumran on the Dead Sea. These "Dead Sea Scrolls" include fragments of a Hebrew scroll copied ca. 100 BCE and containing the book of Leviticus, the book of ancient Hebrew law.

During their time in the Sinai, the Hebrews finalized their covenant with God, who again promised to make the Hebrews his chosen people and to lead them into the Promised Land. For their part, the Hebrews agreed to obey Yahweh's laws and to worship no other god but Yahweh. The first laws were given by Yahweh to the Hebrews when Moses came down from Mount Sinai after the Exodus. They begin with the Ten Commandments and then continue with a lengthy list of regulations that has many points of contact with much earlier Near Eastern laws, as seen, for example, in the Law Codes of Ur-Nammu and Hammurabi (Readings 19 and 20). Many of the laws reflect life in a purely agricultural society.

Source: Hebrew Bible, Exodus 20; *American Revised Standard Version* (1901).

So Moses went down unto the people, and told them. And God spoke all these words, saying, "I am Yahweh thy God, who brought thee out of the land of Egypt, out of the house of bondage.

Thou shalt have no other gods before me.

Thou shalt not make unto thee a graven image, nor any likeness of anything that is in heaven above, or that is in the earth beneath, or that is in the water under the earth.

Thou shalt not bow down thyself unto them, nor serve them, for I Yahweh thy God am a jealous God, visiting the iniquity of the fathers upon the children, upon the third and upon the fourth generation of them that hate me, and showing loving kindness unto thousands of them that love me and keep my commandments.

Thou shalt not take the name of Yahweh thy God in vain, for Yahweh will not hold him guiltless that taketh his name in vain.

Remember the sabbath day, to keep it holy. Six days shalt thou labor, and do all thy work, but the seventh day is a sabbath unto Yahweh thy God; in it thou shalt not do any work.

Honor thy father and thy mother, that thy days may be long in the land that Yahweh thy God giveth thee.

Thou shalt not kill.

Thou shalt not commit adultery.

Thou shalt not steal.

Thou shalt not bear false witness against thy neighbor.

Thou shalt not covet thy neighbor's house, thou shalt not covet thy neighbor's wife, nor his man-servant, nor his maid-servant, nor his ox, nor his ass, nor anything that is thy neighbor's."

And all the people perceived the thunderings, and the lightnings, and the voice of the trumpet, and the mountain smoking, and when the people saw it, they trembled, and stood afar off. And they said unto Moses, "Speak thou with us, and we will hear, but let not God speak with us, lest we die." And Moses said unto the people, "Fear not, for God is come to prove you, and that his fear may be before you, that ye sin not." And the people stood afar off, and Moses drew near unto the thick darkness where God was. And Yahweh said unto Moses, "Thus thou shalt say unto the children of Israel, Ye yourselves have seen that I have talked with you from heaven. Ye shall not make other gods with me; gods of silver, or gods of gold, ye shall not make unto you. An altar of earth thou shalt make unto me, and shalt sacrifice thereon thy burnt-offerings, and thy peace-offerings, thy sheep, and thine oxen. In every place where I record my name I will come unto thee and I will bless thee. And if thou make me an altar of stone, thou shalt not build it of hewn stones, for if thou lift up thy tool upon it, thou hast polluted it. Neither shalt thou go up by steps unto mine altar, that thy nakedness be not uncovered thereon.

Now these are the ordinances that thou shalt set before them:

If thou buy a Hebrew servant, six years he shall serve, and in the seventh he shall go out free for nothing.

If he come in by himself, he shall go out by himself; if he be married, then his wife shall go out with him.

If his master give him a wife and she bear him sons or daughters, the wife and her children shall be her master's, and he shall go out by himself.

But if the servant shall plainly say, I love my master, my wife, and my children, I will not go out free, then his master shall bring him unto God, and shall bring him to the door, or unto the door-post, and his master shall bore his ear through with an awl, and he shall serve him for ever.

And if a man sell his daughter to be a maid-servant, she shall not go out as the men-servants do.

If she please not her master, who hath espoused her to himself, then shall he let her be redeemed, to sell her unto a foreign people he shall have no power, seeing he hath dealt deceitfully with her.

And if he espouse her unto his son, he shall deal with her after the manner of daughters.

If he take him another wife, her food, her raiment, and her duty of marriage, shall he not diminish.

And if he do not these three things unto her, then shall she go out for nothing, without paying money.

He that smiteth a man, so that he dieth, shall surely be put to death.

And if a man lie not in wait, but God deliver him into his hand,[64] then I will appoint thee a place whither he shall flee.

And if a man come presumptuously upon his neighbor, to slay him with guile,[65] thou shalt take him from mine altar, that he may die.

And he that smiteth his father, or his mother, shall be surely put to death.

And he that stealeth a man, and selleth him, or if he be found in his hand, he shall surely be put to death.

And he that curseth his father or his mother, shall surely be put to death.

And if men contend, and one smite the other with a stone, or with his fist, and he die not, but keep his bed, if he rise again, and walk abroad upon his staff, then shall he that smote him be quit, only he shall

[64] That is, unpremeditated murder.

[65] Premeditated murder.

pay for the loss of his time, and shall cause him to be thoroughly healed.

And if a man smite his servant, or his maid, with a rod, and he die under his hand, he shall surely be punished. Notwithstanding, if he continue a day or two, he shall not be punished, for he is his money.

And if men strive together, and hurt a woman with child, so that her fruit depart, and yet no harm follow, he shall be surely fined, according as the woman's husband shall lay upon him, and he shall pay as the judges determine. But if any harm follow, then thou shalt give life for life, eye for eye, tooth for tooth, hand for hand, foot for foot, burning for burning, wound for wound, stripe for stripe.

And if a man smite the eye of his servant, or the eye of his maid, and destroy it, he shall let him go free for his eye's sake. And if he smite out his man-servant's tooth, or his maid-servant's tooth, he shall let him go free for his tooth's sake.

And if an ox gore a man or a woman to death, the ox shall be surely stoned, and its flesh shall not be eaten, but the owner of the ox shall be quit.

But if the ox was wont to gore in time past, and it hath been testified to its owner, and he hath not kept it in, but it hath killed a man or a woman, the ox shall be stoned, and its owner also shall be put to death.

If there be laid on him a compensation,[66] then he shall give for the redemption of his life whatsoever is laid upon him.

Whether it have gored a son, or have gored a daughter, according to this judgment shall it be done unto him.

If the ox gore a man-servant or a maid-servant, there shall be given unto their master thirty shekels of silver, and the ox shall be stoned.

And if a man shall open a pit, or if a man shall dig a pit and not cover it, and an ox or an ass fall therein, the owner of the pit shall make it good, he shall give money unto the owner thereof, and the dead beast shall be his.

And if one man's ox hurt another's, so that it dieth, then they shall sell the live ox, and divide the price of it, and the dead also they shall divide.

Or if it be known that the ox was wont to gore in time past, and its owner hath not kept it in, he shall surely pay ox for ox, and the dead beast shall be his own.

If a man shall steal an ox, or a sheep, and kill it, or sell it, he shall pay five oxen for an ox, and four sheep for a sheep.

If the thief be found breaking in,[67] and be smitten so that he dieth, there shall be no bloodguiltiness[68] for him. If the sun be risen upon him, there shall be bloodguiltiness for him.

A thief shall make restitution. If he have nothing, then he shall be sold for his theft.

If the theft be found in his hand alive, whether it be ox, or ass, or sheep, he shall pay double.

If a man shall cause a field or vineyard to be eaten, and shall let his beast loose, and it feed in another man's field, of the best of his own field, and of the best of his own vineyard, shall he make restitution.

If fire break out, and catch in thorns, so that the shocks of grain, or the standing grain, or the field are consumed, he that kindled the fire shall surely make restitution.

If a man shall deliver unto his neighbor money or goods for safekeeping, and it be stolen out of the man's house, if the thief be found, he shall pay double.

If the thief be not found, then the master of the house shall come near unto God,[69] to see whether he have not put his hand unto his neighbor's goods.

For every matter of trespass, whether it be for ox, for ass, for sheep, for raiment, or for any manner of lost thing, whereof one saith, "This is it," the cause of both parties shall come before God. He whom God shall condemn shall pay double unto his neighbor.

If a man deliver unto his neighbor for safekeeping an ass, or an ox, or a sheep, or any beast, to keep, and it die, or be hurt, or driven away, no man seeing it,

[66] As an alternative to being stoned, the owner of the ox could be allowed to pay a compensation.

[67] At night.

[68] In most cases, a person who killed someone else acquired bloodguilt, which could be expiated in various ways, such as by making a payment to the deceased person's family.

[69] That is, to swear an oath.

the oath of Yahweh shall be between them both, whether he hath not put his hand unto his neighbor's goods, and the owner thereof shall accept it, and he shall not make restitution.

But if it be stolen from him, he shall make restitution unto the owner thereof.

If it be torn in pieces by a wild animal, let him bring it for witness; he shall not make good that which was torn.

And if a man borrow anything from his neighbor, and it be hurt, or die, the owner of it not being present, he shall surely make restitution.

If the owner of it is present, he shall not make it good. If it be a hired thing, the loss is covered by the fee paid.

And if a man entice a virgin that is not betrothed, and lie with her, he shall surely pay a dowry for her to be his wife.

If her father utterly refuse to give her unto him, he shall pay money according to the dowry of virgins.

Thou shalt not suffer a sorceress to live.

Whosoever has sexual relations with a beast shall surely be put to death.

He that sacrificeth unto any god, save unto Yahweh only, shall be utterly destroyed.

And a foreign visitor shalt thou not wrong, neither shalt thou oppress him, for ye were foreign visitors in the land of Egypt.

Ye shall not afflict any widow, or fatherless child. If thou afflict them at all, and they cry at all unto me, I will surely hear their cry, and my wrath shall wax hot, and I will kill you with the sword, and your wives shall be widows, and your children fatherless.

If thou lend money to any of my people with thee that is poor, thou shalt not be to him as a creditor, neither shall ye lay upon him interest.

If thou at all take thy neighbor's cloak as a pledge, thou shalt restore it unto him before the sun goeth down, for that is his only covering, it is his cloak for his skin, wherein shall he sleep? And it shall come to pass, when he crieth unto me, that I will hear, for I am gracious.

Thou shalt not revile God, nor curse a ruler of thy people.

Thou shalt not delay to offer of thy harvest, and of the outflow of thy presses.[70]

The first-born of thy sons shalt thou give unto me.[71]

Likewise shalt thou do with thine oxen, and with thy sheep. Seven days it shall be with its dam; on the eighth day thou shalt give it me.

And ye shall be holy men unto me, therefore ye shall not eat any flesh that is torn of beasts in the field; ye shall cast it to the dogs.

Thou shalt not take up a false report; put not thy hand with the wicked to be an unrighteous witness.

Thou shalt not follow a multitude to do evil, neither shalt thou speak in a cause to turn aside after a multitude to wrest justice, neither shalt thou favor a poor man in his cause.

If thou meet thine enemy's ox or his ass going astray, thou shalt surely bring it back to him again.

If thou see the ass of him that hateth thee lying under his burden, thou shalt forbear to leave him, thou shalt surely release it with him.

Thou shalt not wrest the justice due to thy poor in his cause.

Keep thee far from a false matter, and the innocent and righteous slay thou not, for I will not justify the wicked.

And thou shalt take no bribe, for a bribe blindeth them that have sight, and perverteth the words of the righteous.

And a foreign visitor shalt thou not oppress, for ye know the heart of a foreign visitor, seeing ye were foreign visitors in the land of Egypt.

---

[70] At Sukkot, the harvest festival, known as the Festival of the Booths after the temporary shelters farmers constructed when harvesting their crops.

[71] As priests; later in Jewish history the first-born were redeemed from priestly service by a monetary payment to someone from a priestly family.

36

THE "VICTORY HYMN" OF MERNEPTAH (1208 BCE): "THE ISRAEL STELE"

The black granite Merneptah Stele, preserved in the Cairo Museum, was engraved on the back of a stele of the pharaoh Amenhotep III (ca. 1386–1349 BCE) and tells of the pharaoh Merneptah's victory over Libyans and other peoples. The image at the top shows Merneptah, backed on one side by the mother goddess Mut and on the other by the moon god Khonsu, being given a sword by the god Amon-Ra.

The earliest attested use of the designation Israel is found on a stele erected at Thebes in the mortuary temple of the pharaoh Merneptah (1212–1202 BCE). It primarily commemorated victories in 1208 BCE over the Libyans. Its final lines also refer to a military campaign in Palestine in which Israel was defeated. The stele thus indicates that as of just before 1200 BCE, the Hebrews already were known as "Israel." At this time, Israel apparently was an insignificant place, being named after three Canaanite cities that Merneptah also had overcome.

Source: James Henry Breasted, *Ancient Records of Egypt, Historical Documents from the Earliest Times to the Persian Conquest*, Vol. III, *The Nineteenth Dynasty* (Chicago: University of Chicago Press, 1906), nos. 607–610, 259–261.

Year 5, third month of the third season,[72] third day, under the majesty of Horus, Mighty Bull, Rejoicing in Truth; Pharaoh of Upper and Lower Egypt; Binre-Meriamon,[73] Son of Ra; Merneptah-Hotephirma, magnifying might, exalting victorious sword of Horus, Mighty Bull, smiter of the Nine Bows,[74] whose name is given forever and ever.

His victories are published in all lands, to cause that every land together may see, to cause the glory of his conquests to appear; Pharaoh Merneptah, the Bull, Lord of strength, who slays his foes, beautiful upon the field of victory, when his onset occurs; he is the Sun, driving away the storm that was over Egypt, allowing Egypt to see the rays of the sun, removing the mountain of copper[75] from the neck of the people so that he might give breath to the people who were smothered. He gratified the heart of Memphis on their foes, making Tatenen[76] rejoice over his enemies. He opened the gates of the walled city that were stopped up, and caused his temples to receive their food, Pharaoh Merneptah, the unique one, who establishes the hearts of hundreds of thousands of myriads, so that breath enters into their nostrils at the sight of him. He has penetrated the land of Temeh[77] in his lifetime, and put eternal fear in the heart of the Meshwesh.[78] He has turned back Libya, who invaded Egypt, and great fear of Egypt is in their hearts. Their advanced columns they left behind them, their feet made no stand, but fled. Their archers threw down their bows, and the heart of their fleet ones was weary with marching. They loosed their water skins and threw them to the ground, their sacks were taken and thrown out.

The wretched, fallen chief of Libya fled by favor of night alone, with no plume upon his head; his two feet failed. His women were taken before his face, the grain of his supplies was plundered, and he had no water in the skin to keep him alive. The face of his brothers was hostile to slay him, one fought another among his leaders. Their camp was burned and made a roast, all his possessions were food for the troops. When he arrived in his country, he was the complaint of every one in his land. Ashamed, he bowed himself down, an evil fate removed his plume. They all spoke against him, among the inhabitants of his city: "He is in the power of the gods, the Lords of Memphis; the Lord of Egypt has cursed his name, Meryey,[79] the abomination of Memphis, from son to son of his family, forever. Binre-Meriamon is in pursuit of his children, Merneptah-Hotephirma is appointed to be his fate."

He has become a proverb for Libya. The youth say to youth, concerning his victories, "It has not been done to us before, since the time of Ra," say they. Every old man says to his son, "Alas for Libya!" They have ceased to live in the pleasant fashion of walking in the field; their going about is stopped in a single day. The Tehenu[80] are consumed in a single year. Sutekh[81] has turned his back upon their chief; their settlements are desolated with his approval. There is no work of carrying baskets in these days. Concealment is good; there is safety in the cavern. The great Lord of Egypt, possessor of might and victory! Who will fight, knowing his stride? The fool, the witless is he who receives him; he shall not know the morrow, who transgresses his boundary.

Since the time of the gods, say they, Egypt has been the only daughter of Ra; his son is he who sits upon the throne of Shu.[82] No one can make a design to invade her people, for the eye of every god is behind him who would violate her; the eye captures the rear of her foes. A great wonder has happened for

[72] That is, the month of Ipip, the eleventh month of the Egyptian year.

[73] One of the several names of Merneptah.

[74] A generic term for foreign enemies.

[75] A "mountain of copper" in Kimash (central Arabia) was a source of Egyptian copper; the term also was used, as here, as a metaphor for anything big and solid.

[76] An Egyptian creation god, god of the primordial Nile silt when the earth first rose from chaos.

[77] Libya.

[78] A Libyan coastal people who infiltrated the Nile Delta during the reign of Ramses II (1279–1212 BCE) and later.

[79] The Libyan chieftain.

[80] Libyans.

[81] Set, a god of the desert who murdered his brother Osiris.

[82] A god created by the first god Atum; he and his sister Tefnut, goddess of moisture, were the parents of Nut, goddess of the sky, and Geb, god of the earth.

Egypt, the power of which has made her invader a living prisoner. The divine pharaoh exults over his enemies in the presence of Ra. Meryey, the evil-doer, whom the god, the Lord who is in Memphis, has overthrown, has been judged in Heliopolis,[83] and the divine Ennead[84] declared him guilty of his crimes.

The All-Lord[85] has said: "On behalf of Memphis give the sword to my son, the upright of heart, the good and kindly Merneptah, the advocate of Heliopolis, who opens the towns that were closed up.[86] Let him set free multitudes who are bound in every district, let him give offerings to the temples, let him send in incense before the god, let him cause the princes to recover their possessions, let him cause the poor to enter their cities."

They say among the Lords of Heliopolis[87] regarding their son, Merneptah: "Give to him duration like Ra, let him be advocate of him who is oppressed in every country. Egypt has been assigned to him as the portion for himself forever. His strength is its people. Lo, when one dwells in the time of this hero, the breath of life comes immediately.

Meryey, the wretched, vanquished chief of Libya, came to invade the "Walls-of-the-Sovereign"[88] whose son shines in his throne, the Pharaoh Merneptah. Ptah said concerning the vanquished chief of Libya: "All his crimes shall be gathered and returned upon his head. Deliver him into the hand of Merneptah, that he may make him disgorge what he has swallowed, like a crocodile. Behold, the swift[89] is the captor of the swift; and the Pharaoh shall snare him, for Amon shall bind him in his hand and shall deliver him to his[90] ka[91] in Hermonthis,[92] to the Pharaoh Merneptah."

Great joy has come in Egypt, rejoicing comes forth from the towns of Tomeri.[93] They converse of the victories that Merneptah has achieved among the Tehenu: "How amiable is he, the victorious ruler! How magnified is the pharaoh among the gods! How fortunate is he, the commanding Lord! Sit happily down and talk, or walk far out upon the way, for there is no fear in the heart of the people. The strongholds are left to themselves, the wells are opened. The messengers skirt the battlements of the walls, shaded from the sun, until their watchmen wake. The soldiers lie sleeping, and the border scouts are in the field at their own desire. The herds of the field are left as cattle sent forth, without herdsmen, crossing the fullness of the stream. There is no uplifting of a shout in the night: "Stop! Behold, one comes, one comes with the speech of strangers!" One comes and goes with singing, and there is no lamentation of mourning people. The towns are settled again anew; as for the one that ploweth his harvest, he shall eat it. Ra has turned himself to Egypt; he was born, destined to be her protector, the Pharaoh Merneptah.

The princes are prostrate, saying: "Mercy!"
Not one raises his head among the Nine Bows.
Desolation is for Tehenu; Hatti[94] is pacified;
Plundered is Canaan with every evil;
Carried off is Ashkelon[95]; seized upon is
 Gezer[96];
Yanoam[97] is made as that which does not exist;
Isiral[98] is laid waste, its seed is not;
Hurru[99] is become a widow for Egypt!
All lands together, they are pacified.

[83] The main cult center of the gods Atum and Ra, the god of the noonday sun.

[84] The nine primary gods of Egypt, worshipped at Heliopolis.

[85] The god Atum.

[86] Presumably as a result of the Libyan raids.

[87] That is, the Ennead of Heliopolis.

[88] An epithet of the city of Memphis.

[89] A bird, similar to a swallow.

[90] That is, Merneptah's.

[91] One of the souls of the ancient Egyptians.

[92] An Egyptian city of Upper Egypt, cult center of the bull god Montu, just south of Thebes.

[93] Egypt.

[94] The Hittites, see Reading 29. Merneptah never came anywhere near the Hittite kingdom of Anatolia.

[95] One of the five cities of the Philistines, seaward of ancient Israel.

[96] A Canaanite city northwest of Jerusalem.

[97] A city in Palestine.

[98] Generally identified as Israel on the basis not only of the name, but also of its location near the other places just mentioned.

[99] Syria.

37

DEBORAH THE JUDGE DEFEATS THE CANAANITES (CA. 1050 BCE): JUDGES 4:1–5:31

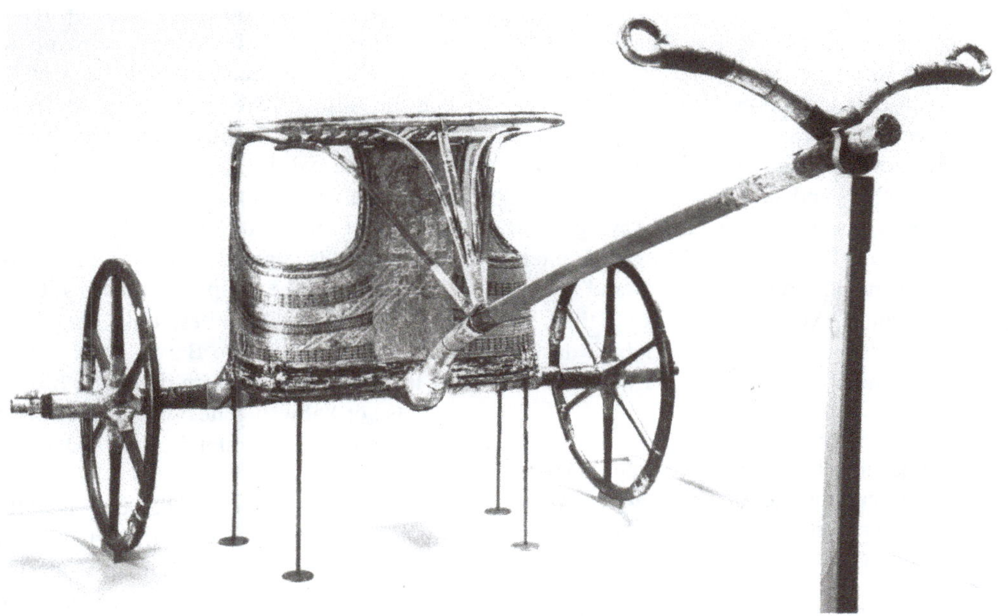

Chariots such as this one found in the tomb of the pharaoh Tutankhamon would have been used by the Canaanites in their attack on the Hebrews in the time of the judge Deborah.

After the Hebrew settlement in Canaan, perhaps ca. 1230 BCE, there was no central government. In times of emergencies, such as when there were threats to Hebrew faith in the god Yahweh or when the Hebrews were confronted with attacks by their neighbors, in particular by the Canaanites, leaders known as "judges" could arise who created temporary coalitions among the tribes for the purpose of dealing with the situation. The unsettled nature of the times gave women opportunities to hold significant leadership positions, as occurred around 1050 BCE when the judge Deborah, as reported in the Hebrew Bible, raised an army against the Canaanites.

Source: Hebrew Bible, Judges 4:1–5:31; *American Revised Standard Version* (1901).

And the children of Israel again did that which was evil in the sight of Yahweh, when Ehud was dead. And Yahweh sold them into the hand of Jabin, King of Canaan,[100] who reigned in Hazor[101]; the captain of whose host was Sisera, who dwelt in Harosheth[102] of the Gentiles.[103] And the children of Israel cried unto Yahweh, for Sisera had nine hundred chariots of iron, and for twenty years he mightily oppressed the children of Israel. Now Deborah, a prophetess, the wife of Lappidoth, judged Israel at that time. And she dwelt under the palm-tree of Deborah between Ramah and Beth-el in the hill-country of Ephraim[104]: and the children of Israel came up to her for judgment. And she sent and called Barak the son of Abinoam out of Kadesh-Naphtali,[105] and said unto him, "Hath not Yahweh, the God of Israel, commanded, saying, "Go and draw unto Mount Tabor,[106] and take with thee ten thousand men of the children of Naphtali and of the children of Zebulun.[107] And I will draw unto thee, to the river Kishon,[108] Sisera, the captain of Jabin's army, with his chariots and his multitude; and I will deliver him into thy hand." And Barak said unto her, "If thou wilt go with me, then I will go, but if thou wilt not go with me, I will not go." And she said, "I will surely go with thee; notwithstanding, the journey that thou takest shall not be for thine honor, for Yahweh will sell Sisera into the hand of a woman."

And Deborah arose, and went with Barak to Kadesh. And Barak called Zebulun and Naphtali together to Kadesh, and there went up ten thousand men at his feet, and Deborah went up with him. Now, Heber the Kenite[109] had separated himself from the Kenites, even from the children of Hobab the brother-in-law of Moses, and had pitched his tent as far as the oak in Zaanaim, which is by Kadesh. And Sisera was told that Barak the son of Abinoam had gone up to Mount Tabor. And Sisera gathered together all his chariots, even nine hundred chariots of iron, and all the people that were with him, from Harosheth of the Gentiles, unto the river Kishon. And Deborah said unto Barak, "Up!, for this is the day in which Yahweh hath delivered Sisera into thy hand. Is not Yahweh gone out before thee?" So Barak went down from Mount Tabor, and ten thousand men after him."

And Yahweh discomfited Sisera, and all his chariots, and all his host, with the edge of the sword before Barak, and Sisera alighted from his chariot, and fled away on his feet. But Barak pursued after the chariots, and after the host, unto Harosheth of the Gentiles. And all the host of Sisera fell by the edge of the sword; there was not a man left. Howbeit Sisera fled away on his feet to the tent of Jael the wife of Heber the Kenite, for there was peace between Jabin, the King of Hazor, and the house of Heber the Kenite. And Jael went out to meet Sisera, and said unto him, "Turn in, my Lord, turn in to me; fear not."

[100] Known as Ki-na-ah-na to the Egyptians, Canaan was a generic term for the eastern coast of the Mediterranean, including Lebanon and Palestine. The Philistines, who occupied a strip of seacoast, were a separate people from the Canaanites.

[101] The most important Canaanite city at the time of the Hebrew settlement in Canaan, located just north of the Sea of Galilee.

[102] An otherwise unknown Canaanite fort.

[103] Non-Hebrews.

[104] One of the twelve Hebrew tribes.

[105] The ancient Canaanite city of Kadesh, now occupied by the Hebrew tribe of Naphtali.

[106] A mountain in Lower Galilee in Israel.

[107] Another Hebrew tribe.

[108] A river in Israel that flows into the Mediterranean near the city of Haifa.

[109] A nomadic people known for metalwork.

And he turned in unto her into the tent, and she covered him with a rug. And he said unto her, "Give me, I pray thee, a little water to drink, for I am thirsty." And she opened a jar of milk, and gave him drink, and covered him. And he said unto her, "Stand in the door of the tent, and it shall be, when any man doth come and inquire of thee, and say, 'Is there any man here?' that thou shalt say, 'No.'"

Then Jael, Heber's wife, took a tent-pin, and took a hammer in her hand, and went softly unto him, and smote the pin into his temples, and it pierced through into the ground, for he was in a deep sleep. So he swooned and died. And, behold, as Barak pursued Sisera, Jael came out to meet him, and said unto him, "Come, and I will show thee the man whom thou seekest." And he came unto her, and, behold, Sisera lay dead, and the tent-pin was in his temples. So God subdued on that day Jabin, the King of Canaan, before the children of Israel. And the hand of the children of Israel prevailed more and more against Jabin the King of Canaan, until they had destroyed Jabin, King of Canaan. And the land had rest forty years.

38

KING SOLOMON CONSOLIDATES HIS AUTHORITY (CA. 950 BCE): 1 KINGS 5–10

Nothing survives of the Jewish temple built by Solomon, which was destroyed after the New Babylonians captured Jerusalem in 587 BCE. A second temple, built under Persian rule beginning in 538 BCE, was destroyed by the Romans in 70 CE. In the late seventh century CE, an Islamic shrine, the Dome of the Rock, was built on the site of the Jewish temple. All that remains of the earlier Jewish temples is a section of the massive retaining wall built ca. 19 BCE by Herod the Great, now known as the "Wailing [or Western] Wall," shown here.

During its early years it appeared that the Jewish kingdom would follow the same pattern of development as the other small Iron Age states of the Levant, such as those of the Phoenicians. King Solomon (970–930 BCE), for example, consolidated his authority not only by making alliances with foreign powers, including the Phoenicians, Egyptians, and the Queen of Sheba, but also by constructing a single Jewish center of worship in Jerusalem. The account of the reign of Solomon given in Jewish scripture also provides precious insights into the Phoenicians, who were one of the most important Hebrew trading partners.

Source: Hebrew Bible, 1 Kings 5–10; *American Revised Standard Version* (1901).

And Hiram,[110] King of Tyre, sent his servants unto Solomon; for he had heard that they had anointed him king in the room of his father, for Hiram was ever an admirer of David. And Solomon sent to Hiram, saying, "Thou knowest how that David, my father, could not build a house for the name of Yahweh his God for the wars that were about him on every side, until Yahweh put them under the soles of his feet. But now Yahweh my God hath given me rest on every side; there is neither adversary, nor evil occurrence. And, behold, I purpose to build a house for the name of Yahweh my God, as Yahweh spoke unto David my father, saying, 'Thy son, whom I will set upon thy throne in thy room, he shall build the house for my name.' Now, therefore, command thou that they cut me cedar-trees out of Lebanon[111]; and my servants shall be with thy servants; and I will give thee hire for thy servants according to all that thou shalt say: for thou knowest that there is not among us any that knoweth how to cut timber like unto the Sidonians." And it came to pass, when Hiram heard the words of Solomon, that he rejoiced greatly, and said, "Blessed be Yahweh this day, who hath given unto David a wise son over this great people." And Hiram sent to Solomon, saying, "I have heard the message that thou hast sent unto me: I will do all thy desire concerning timber of cedar, and concerning timber of fir. My servants shall bring them down from Lebanon unto the sea, and I will make them into rafts to go by sea unto the place that thou shalt appoint me, and will cause them to be broken up there, and thou shalt receive them, and thou shalt accomplish my desire, in giving food for my household."

So Hiram gave Solomon timber of cedar and timber of fir according to all his desire. And Solomon gave Hiram twenty thousand measures of wheat for food to his household, and twenty measures of pure oil. Thus gave Solomon to Hiram year by year. And Yahweh gave Solomon wisdom, as he promised him, and there was peace between Hiram and Solomon; and they two made a league together. And the king commanded, and they hewed out great stones, costly stones, to lay the foundation of the house with wrought stone. And Solomon's builders and Hiram's builders and the Gebalites[112] did fashion them, and prepared the timber and the stones to build the house.

And it came to pass in the four hundred and eightieth year after the children of Israel were come out of the land of Egypt,[113] in the fourth year of Solomon's reign over Israel, in the month Ziv, which is the second month, that he began to build the house of Yahweh. And the house that King Solomon built for Yahweh, the length thereof was threescore cubits,[114] and the breadth thereof twenty cubits, and the height thereof thirty cubits. So Solomon built the house, and finished it. And he built the walls of the house within with

[110] King of Tyre from 980 to 947 BCE. He made Tyre into the most powerful of the Phoenician trading cities.

[111] Ancient Phoenicia. For another example of Phoenicia as a source of ceremonial timber, see Reading 33.

[112] A people living inland from the Phoenician city of Sidon.

[113] The source of one of the greatest chronological problems in the Bible, this passage dates the Exodus to around 1446 BCE, but the book of Exodus itself places the Exodus during the reign of a Pharaoh Ramses, the first of whom ruled ca. 1292–1290 BCE. References to massive building projects along with the Merneptah stele (Reading 36) favor the later date.

[114] A Hebrew cubit was about 20 inches, making the temple 100 feet long, 33 1/3 feet wide, and 50 feet high.

boards of cedar: from the floor of the house unto the walls of the ceiling, he covered them on the inside with wood, and he covered the floor of the house with boards of fir. And he prepared a sanctuary in the midst of the house within, to set there the Ark of the Covenant[115] of Yahweh. So Solomon overlaid the house within with pure gold: and he drew chains of gold across before the sanctuary and he overlaid it with gold. And the whole house he overlaid with gold, until all the house was finished. In addition, the whole altar that belonged to the sanctuary he overlaid with gold. So also made he for the entrance of the temple doorposts of olive-wood, out of a fourth part of the wall, and two doors of fir-wood. The two leaves of the one door were folding, and the two leaves of the other door were folding. So was he seven years in building it.

And Solomon was building his own palace thirteen years, and he finished all his palace. For he built the palace of the forest of Lebanon; the length thereof was a hundred cubits, and the breadth thereof fifty cubits, and the height thereof thirty cubits,[116] upon four rows of cedar pillars, with cedar beams upon the pillars. He made also a palace for Pharaoh's daughter, whom he had taken to wife,[117] like unto this porch. All these were of costly stones, even of hewn stone, according to measure, sawed with saws, within and without, even from the foundation unto the coping, and so on the outside unto the great court. And the foundation was of costly stones, even great stones, stones of ten cubits, and stones of eight cubits.

And King Solomon sent and fetched Hiram[118] out of Tyre. He was the son of a widow of the tribe of Naphtali,[119] and his father was a man of Tyre, a worker in brass; and he was filled with wisdom and understanding and skill to work all works in brass. And he came to King Solomon, and wrought all his work. For he fashioned the two pillars of brass, eighteen cubits high apiece, and a line of twelve cubits compassed either of them about. And he set up the pillars at the porch of the temple. And Hiram made the ceremonial basins, shovels, and sprinkling bowls. So Hiram made an end of doing all the work that he wrought for King Solomon in the house of Yahweh.

And it came to pass at the end of twenty years, wherein Solomon had built the two houses, the house of Yahweh and the king's house, for which Hiram, the King of Tyre, had furnished Solomon with cedar-trees and fir-trees, and with gold, according to all his desire, that then King Solomon gave Hiram twenty cities in the land of Galilee. And Hiram came out from Tyre to see the cities that Solomon had given him; and they pleased him not. And he said, "What cities are these that thou hast given me, my brother?" And he called them the land of Cabul[120] unto this day. And Hiram sent to the king sixscore talents of gold. The Pharaoh of Egypt[121] had gone up, and taken Gezer,[122] and burnt it with fire, and slain the Canaanites that dwelt in the city, and given it for a portion unto his daughter, Solomon's wife. As for all the people[123] that were left of the Amorites, the Hittites, the Perizzites, the Hivites, and the Jebusites, who were not of the children of Israel, their children that were left after them in the land, whom the children of Israel were not able utterly to destroy, of them did Solomon raise a levy of bondservants unto this day.

---

[115] The chest containing the stone on which the Ten Commandments were inscribed.

[116] That is 116 2/3 feet long, 83 1/3 feet wide, and 50 feet high, more than four times as large as the temple.

[117] Indicating serious diplomatic ties to Egypt. The unnamed pharaoh may be Netjerkheperre-setepenamun Siamun (986–967), sixth pharaoh of the Twenty-first Dynasty.

[118] Not King Hiram of Tyre, but an artisan, also named Hiram. Because his mother is described here as being of the Israelite tribe of Naphtali, and in Chronicles as of the tribe of Dan, it has been suggested that there were two Phoenician bronzeworkers named Hiram.

[119] So this was a mixed marriage between a Hebrew and a Phoenician.

[120] A word meaning good-for-nothing.

[121] Probably Siamun.

[122] Gezer also had been captured by the Pharaoh Merneptah, see Reading 36.

[123] Of the entire Hebrew kingdom.

And King Solomon made a navy of ships in Ezion-geber,[124] which is beside Elath, on the shore of the Red Sea, in the land of Edom. And Hiram sent in the navy his servants, shipmen that had knowledge of the sea, with the servants of Solomon. And they came to Ophir,[125] and fetched from thence gold, four hundred and twenty talents,[126] and brought it to King Solomon.

And when the Queen of Sheba[127] heard of the fame of Solomon concerning the name of Yahweh, she came to test him with hard questions. And she came to Jerusalem with a very great train, with camels that bore spices, and very much gold, and precious stones; and when she was come to Solomon, she communed with him of all that was in her heart. And she gave the king a hundred and twenty talents of gold, and of spices very great store, and precious stones. There came no more such abundance of spices as these that the Queen of Sheba gave to King Solomon. And the navy also of Hiram, that brought gold from Ophir, brought in from Ophir great plenty of almug-trees[128] and precious stones. And King Solomon gave to the Queen of Sheba all her desire, whatsoever she asked, besides that which Solomon gave her of his royal bounty. So she turned back, and went to her own land, she and her servants.

The king had at sea a navy of Tarshish[129] with the navy of Hiram. Once every three years came the navy of Tarshish, bringing gold and silver, ivory, and apes, and peacocks. So King Solomon exceeded all the kings of the earth in riches and in wisdom. And all the earth sought the presence of Solomon, to hear his wisdom, which God had put in his heart. And they brought every man his tribute, vessels of silver, and vessels of gold, and raiment, and armor, and spices, horses, and mules, a rate year by year. And the horses that Solomon had were brought out of Egypt, and the king's merchants received them in droves, each drove at a price. And a chariot came up and went out of Egypt for six hundred shekels of silver, and a horse for a hundred and fifty; and so for all the kings of the Hittites, and for the kings of Syria, did they bring them out by their means.

[124] A seaport on the northernmost coast of the Gulf of Aqaba.

[125] A famous source of gold of unknown location; various sites ranging from Ethiopia to southern Arabia to southern India have been suggested.

[126] A talent was about fifty-six pounds.

[127] Probably to be identified with the Semitic kingdom of Saba in Yemen, which also is mentioned by the Assyrians and the Roman geographer Strabo.

[128] Perhaps juniper trees.

[129] Not Tartessus in southern Spain, as often is thought, but perhaps Tarsus near the southeastern coast of Anatolia.

CHAPTER 5

Iron Age Empires (850–500 BCE)

Just as in the Bronze Age, empires also developed in the Iron Age as one people or nation imposed its authority on another. But whereas the Bronze Age empires had been fairly short term and unstable, lacking in cohesiveness, the Iron Age empires showed an increasing ability to control larger and larger amounts of territory and to gain economic advantages from it. The Assyrians created an empire based on military might and economic exploitation that eventually included both the Mesopotamian and the Egyptian river valleys. But the Assyrians were unable to win the goodwill of their conquered peoples, and their empire eventually fell to revolt. Several successors to the Assyrians practiced empire building on a smaller scale, but it was the Persians who ultimately created the greatest and most successful Near Eastern empire by developing a system that benefited not only themselves but also their conquered peoples. The Near Eastern empires of the Assyrians, New Babylonians, and Persians continued to use stone and the traditional Mesopotamian clay tablets for writing purposes.

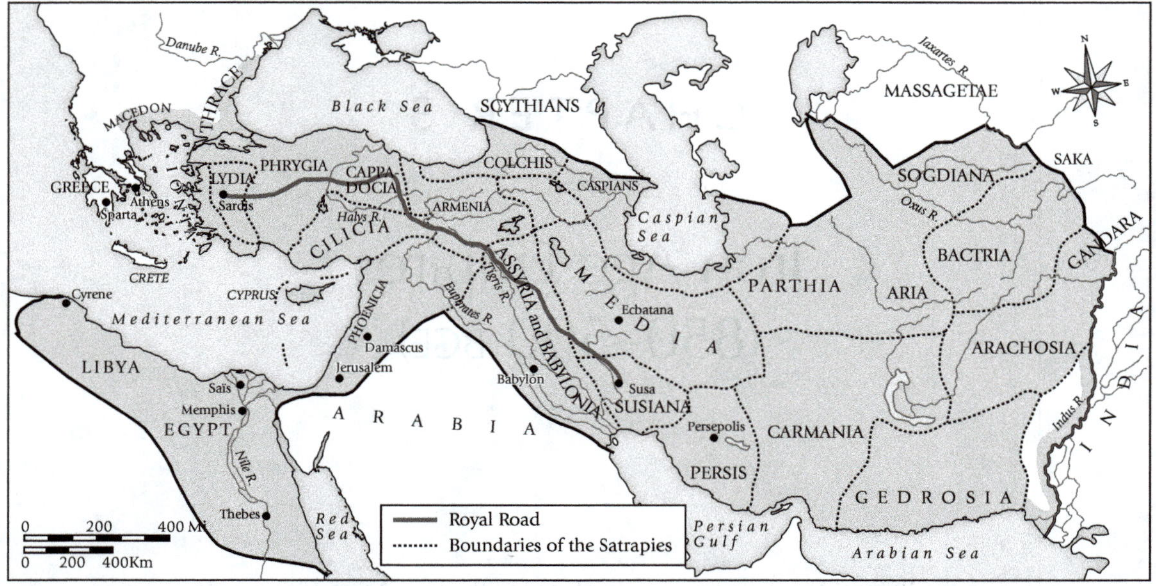

Map 5 The Satrapies of the Persian Empire

39

THE BLACK OBELISK OF SHALMANESER III (825 BCE)

A panel from the four-sided "Black Obelisk" of Shalmaneser III depicts Jehu, king of Judah, pledging loyalty to Shalmaneser. Text discussions accompany the relief illustrations. Preserved in the British Museum in London.

Assyrian kings ostentatiously advertised their achievements, in particular their military conquests, on stone monuments placed throughout the empire. King Shalmaneser III (858–824 BCE) erected two surviving monuments to his accomplishments, a monolith found at Kurkh and the "Black Obelisk" found at Kouyunjik, constructed in 825 BCE of black limestone and now in the British Museum. The four sides of the obelisk are divided into five compartments that depict tribute bring brought to the Assyrian court by Assyrian subjects and vassals. These monuments provide detailed descriptions of thirty-one campaigns, mostly pillaging and plundering expeditions, in which Shalmaneser claimed to have defeated the Aramaeans, the Babylonians, the kingdom of Urartu, and the Medes and to have made Jehu, king of Judah, into an Assyrian vassal. They illustrate the extent to which ancient Assyria was consumed by the cult of the ruler, in which a king's authority was directly related to his role as leader of the army and his ability to collect loot from subjects, vassals, and neighboring peoples. The following account comes primarily from the obelisk, with a few additions from the monolith.

Source: V. Scheil, trans., "Inscriptions of Shalmaneser II," in A. H. Sayce, ed., *Records of the Past Being English Translations of the Ancient Monuments of Egypt and Western Asia*, new series, Vol. 4 (London: Bagster, 1890), 36–79.

Assur,[1] the great Lord, the King of all the great gods; Anu,[2] King of the spirits of heaven and the spirits of earth, the god, Lord of the world; Bêl the Supreme,[3] Father of the gods, the Creator; Hea,[4] King of the deep, determiner of destinies; the King of crowns,[5] drinking in brilliance; Ramanu,[6] the crowned hero, Lord of canals; the Sun-god[7] the Judge of heaven and earth, the urger on of all; Merodach,[8] Prince of the gods, Lord of battles; Adar,[9] the terrible, Lord of the spirits of heaven and the spirits of earth, the exceeding strong god; Nergal,[10] the powerful god, king of the battle; Nebo,[11] the bearer of the high scepter, the god, the Father above; Beltis, the wife of Bêl, mother of the great gods; Istar,[12] sovereign of heaven and earth, whom the face of heroism perfectest; the great gods, determining destinies, making great my kingdom.

I am Shalmaneser, king of multitudes of men, prince and hero of Assur, the strong king, King of all the Four Zones of the Sun and of multitudes of men, the marcher over the whole world; son of Assur-Nasir-Pal,[13] the supreme hero, whom his heroism over the gods has made good and has caused all the world to kiss his feet; the noble offspring of Tiglath-Adar[14] who has laid his yoke upon all lands hostile to him, and has swept them like a whirlwind. Assur the great lord in the determination of his heart turned upon me his illustrious eyes and called me to the government of Assyria, and gave me to hold the mighty weapon that overthrows the rebellious and invested me with the sacred crown, the lordship over all lands, and strongly urged me to conquer and subjugate.

At the beginning of my reign, when on the throne of royalty mightily I had seated myself, the chariots of my host I collected. The city of Aridu,[15] the strong city of Ninni,[16] I besieged, I captured, its numerous soldiers I slew, its spoil I carried away. I erected a pyramid of heads at the entrance of his city. Their youths and maidens I delivered to the flames.

In my first year the Euphrates in its flood I crossed. To the sea of the setting sun[17] I went. My weapons on the sea I rested. Victims for my gods I took. To Mount Amanus[18] I went up. Logs of cedar-wood and pine-wood I cut. To the country of Lallar[19] I ascended.

Difficult paths and inaccessible mountains whose peaks rose to the sky like the point of an iron sword I cut with axes of bronze and copper. The chariots and troops I caused to cross. To the city of Khupushkia[20] I approached. Khupushkia with 100 towns that were dependent on it I burned with fire. Kakia, a king of the country of Nairi,[21] and the rest of his troops trembled

[1] The primary god of the Assyrians.

[2] The Sumerian god An, overall god of the heavens, see Reading 1.

[3] The Babylonian god Marduk, equivalent to the Sumerian god Enlil, the creator god, see Readings 1 and 18.

[4] Ea, or Enki; god of the sea, wisdom, and the underworld; see Reading 13.

[5] Sin, or Nanna, the moon god.

[6] "The Thunderer," another name for the storm god Adad.

[7] The sun god Samas, Babylonian Shamash.

[8] The Babylonian god Marduk; see Reading 1.

[9] A sun god.

[10] A war god and god of the dead.

[11] Or Nabu, Assyrian and Babylonian god of wisdom; the scribe of Marduk.

[12] The fertility goddess Ishtar or Inanna; see Readings 13 and 17.

[13] Assur-Nasir-Pal II (884–859 BCE).

[14] Tiglath-Adar, or Tukulti-Ninurta II (891–884 BCE).

[15] Eridu in Sumeria.

[16] The goddess Inanna, or Ishtar.

[17] The Mediterranean Sea, west of Assyria.

[18] In the Nur Mountains in south-central Turkey, the location of valuable cedar forests.

[19] In the Zagros Mountains in eastern Turkey.

[20] Modern Siirt near Lake Van.

[21] Near Lake Van in eastern Turkey.

before the splendor of my arms and fled to the strong mountains. Chasing them, I ascended the mountains. I fought a hard battle in the midst of the mountains and utterly destroyed them. I brought back from the mountains chariots, troops, and horses trained to the yoke. The terror of the glory of Assur my lord overwhelmed them; they descended and grasped my feet. Taxes and tribute I imposed upon them. From the city of Khupushkia I departed. To Sugunia the stronghold of Arame of Urartu[22] I approached. The city I besieged, I captured, their numerous soldiers I slew. Its spoil I carried away. I erected a pyramid of heads at the entrance of his city. Fourteen towns that were dependent on it I burned with fire. From Sagunia I departed. To the sea[23] of the country of Nairi I descended. I purified my weapons in the sea; I sacrificed victims to my gods. In those days an image of my person I made; I inscribed upon it the glory of Assur the great lord, my lord, and the mightiness of my empire; I erected it overlooking the sea.

In my second year to the city of Bit-Adini[24] I approached. The stronghold of Akhuni the son of Adin I approached. Under the protection of Assur and the great gods, my lords, I fought with him, I utterly defeated him. The cities of Akhuni the son of Adin I captured. In his city I shut him up. The city I besieged, I captured. I destroyed with my weapons 300 of his fighting-men. A pyramid of heads I erected at the entrance to his city. The Euphrates in its flood I crossed. The city of Dabigu,[25] a choice city of the Hittites[26] together with the cities that were dependent upon it I captured.

In my third year Akhuni the son of Adin fled from the face of my mighty weapons, and the city of Bit-Adini, his royal city, he fortified. The Euphrates I crossed. The city unto Assyria I restored. The town that is on the further side of the Euphrates, which is upon the river 'Sagurri,[27] which the kings of the Hittites call the city of Pitru,[28] I took for myself.

During the eponymy[29] of Dayan-Assur from the city of Nineveh I departed. The Euphrates in its upper part I crossed. After Akhuni the son of Adin I went. The heights on the banks of the Euphrates as his stronghold he made. The mountains I attacked, I captured. Akhuni with his gods, his chariots, his horses, his sons and his daughters I carried away. To my city Assur I brought them.

In my fifth year to the country of Kasyari[30] I ascended. The strongholds I captured. Elkhitti of the Serurians in his city I shut up. His tribute to a large amount I received.

In my sixth year the Euphrates in its upper part I crossed. The tribute of the kings of the Hittites, all of them, I received. Rimmon-idri of Damascus, Irkhulina of Hamath,[31] and the kings of the Hittites and of the sea-coasts to the forces of each other trusted, and to make war and battle against me came. By the command of Assur, the great Lord, my Lord, with them I fought. A destruction of them I made. Their chariots, their war-carriages, their war-material I took from them. 20,500 of their fighting men with arrows I slew.

In my seventh year to the head of the river, the springs of the Tigris, the place where the waters rise, I went. An image of my Royalty of large size I constructed. The laws of Assur my Lord, the records of my victories, whatsoever in the world I had done, in the midst of it I wrote; in the middle of the country I set it up.

---

22 A powerful kingdom in the area of Lake Van.

23 Lake Van.

24 An Aramaean kingdom near the Euphrates River, modern Tel-Barsip.

25 A fortress city.

26 The Neo-Hittites of Syria, not the earlier Hittites of Anatolia.

27 The Sajur River, which flows into the Euphrates River in Syria.

28 A town founded by the Assyrian king Tiglath-Pilezer I ca. 1100 BCE but later occupied by the Aramaeans.

29 Assyrian years were named after the limmus, eponymous magistrates who presided over the annual New Year's festival; a complete limmu list survives for the years 892–648 BCE.

30 In northern Mesopotamia.

31 An important city on the Orontes River in Syria.

In my eighth year did Merodach-bila-yu'sate, his foster-brother, rebel against Merodach-suma-iddin, King of Gan-Dunias.[32] Strongly had he fortified the land. To exact punishment against Merodach-suma-iddin I went. The city of the waters of the Dhurnat I took.

In my ninth campaign to the country of Kaldu[33] I descended. Their cities I captured. The tribute of the kings of the country of Kaldu I received.

In my tenth year for the eighth time the Euphrates I crossed. The cities of 'Sangara of the city of the Carchemishians[34] I captured.

In my eleventh year for the ninth time the Euphrates I crossed. Rimmon-idri of Damascus and twelve of the kings of the Hittites with one another's forces strengthened themselves. A destruction of them I made.

In my twelfth campaign for the tenth time the Euphrates I crossed. To the land of Pagar-khubuna I went. Their spoil I carried away.

In my thirteenth year to the country of Yaeti I ascended. Their spoil I carried away.

In my fourteenth year the country I assembled; the Euphrates I crossed. Twelve kings against me had come. I fought. A destruction of them I made.

In my fifteenth year among the sources of the Tigris and the Euphrates I went. An image of my Majesty in their hollows I erected.

In my sixteenth year the waters of the Zab[35] I crossed. To the country of Zimri[36] I went. Merodach-mudammik, King of the land of Zimru, to save his life the mountains ascended. His treasure, his army, and his gods to Assyria I brought. Yan'su son of Khanban to the kingdom over them I raised.[37]

[32] An Aramaean city of Syria.

[33] The Chaldeans, a Semitic people of Babylonia, later shared in the overthrow of the Assyrian Empire.

[34] Carchemish was a powerful Neo-Hittite city located on the border between Syria and Turkey.

[35] A river that originates near Lake Van and joins the Tigris River in Mesopotamia.

[36] Northeast of Assyria.

[37] The Assyrians often would set up vassal rulers in territories that they did not directly annex.

In my seventeenth year the Euphrates I crossed. To the land of Amanus I ascended. Logs of cedar I cut.

In my eighteenth year for the sixteenth time the Euphrates I crossed. Hazael of Damascus to battle came. 1,221 of his chariots, 470 of his war-carriages with his camp I took from him.

In my nineteenth campaign for the eighteenth time the Euphrates I crossed. To the land of Amanus I ascended. Logs of cedar I cut.

In my 20th year for the 20th time the Euphrates I crossed. To the land of Kahue I went down. Their cities I captured. Their spoil I carried off.

In my 21st campaign, for the 21st time the Euphrates I crossed. To the cities of Hazael of Damascus I went. Four of his fortresses I took. The tribute of the Tyrians, the Sidonians, and the Gebalites[38] I received.

In my 22nd campaign for the 22nd time the Euphrates I crossed. To the country of Tabalu[39] I went down. In those days as regards the 24 kings of the country of Tabalu their wealth I received. To conquer the mines of silver, of salt, and of stone for sculpture I went.

In my 23rd year the Euphrates I crossed. The city of Uetas, his strong city, which belonged to Lalla of the land of the Milidians[40] I captured. The kings of the country of Tabalu had set out. Their tribute I received.

In my 24th year, the lower Zab I crossed. To the land of Zimru I went down. Yan'su king of the Zimri from the face of my mighty weapons fled and to save his life ascended the mountains. His fighting men I slew. His spoil I carried away. The cities I threw down, dug up, and with fire burned. The rest of them to the mountains ascended. The peaks of the mountains I attacked, I captured. Their fighting men I slew. Their spoil and their goods I caused to be brought down. From the country of Zimru I departed. The tribute of 27 kings of the country of Par'sua[41] I received. From the country of Par'sua I

[38] Sidon, Tyre, and Gebal all were Phoenician trading cities.

[39] In Cappadocia in Anatolia.

[40] Milid, later Melitene, lay on the west bank of the Euphrates River.

[41] Persia.

departed. To the strongholds of the country of the Amadai,[42] and the countries of Arazias[43] and Kharkhar[44] I went down. Their fighting men I slew. Their spoil I carried away. The cities I threw down, dug up, and burned with fire. An image of my Majesty in the country of Kharkhara I set up. Yan'su son of Khaban with his abundant treasures, his gods, his sons, his daughters, his soldiers in large numbers I carried off. To Assyria I brought them.

In my 25th campaign the Euphrates at its flood I crossed. The tribute of the kings of the Hittites, all of them, I received. The country of Amanus I traversed. To the cities of Cati of the country of the Kahuians I descended. The city of Timur, his strong city I besieged, I captured. Their fighting men I slew. Its spoil I carried away. The cities to a countless number I threw down, dug up, and burned with fire.

In my 26th year for the seventh time the country of the Amanus I traversed. For the fourth time to the cities of Cati of the country of the Kahuians I went. The city of Tanacun, the strong city of Tulca I approached. Exceeding fear of Assur my Lord overwhelmed him and when he had come out my feet he grasped. His hostages I took. Silver, gold, iron, oxen, and sheep, as his tribute I received.

In my 27th year the chariots of my armies I mustered. Dayan-Assur, the Tartan,[45] the Commander of the wide-spreading army, to the country of Armenia I urged, I sent.[46] The river Arzane he crossed. 'Seduri of the country of the Armenians heard, and he trusted to the strength of his numerous host; and to make conflict and battle against me he came. With him I fought. A destruction of him I made. With the flower of his youth his broad fields I filled.

In my 28th year when in the city of Kalhu[47] I was stopping news had been brought me that men of the Patinians[48] had slain Lubarni their Lord and had raised 'Surri, who was not heir to the throne, to the kingdom. Dayan-Assur the Tartan, the Commander of the widespreading army at the head of my host, I urged, I sent. The Euphrates in its flood he crossed. In the city of Cinalua, his royal city, a slaughter he made. As for 'Surri the usurper, exceeding fear of Assur my Lord overwhelmed him, and to the death of his destiny he went. The men of the country of the Patinians from before the sight of my mighty weapons fled, and the children of 'Surri together with the soldiers, the rebels, whom they had taken, they delivered to me. Those soldiers on stakes I fixed. 'Sa'situr of the country of Uzza my feet grasped. To the kingdom over them I placed him. Silver, gold, lead, bronze, iron, and the horns of wild bulls to a countless number I received.

In my 29th year to the country of Cirkhi I ascended. Their cities I threw down, dug up, and burned with fire. Their country like a thunderstorm I swept. Exceeding fear over them I cast.

In my 30th year when in the city of Kalhu I was stopping, Dayan-Assur the Tartan, the Commander of the wide-spreading army at the head of my army, I urged, I sent. The river Zab he crossed. To the midst of the cities of Udaci of the country of the Mannaeans[49] he approached. Udaci of the country of the Mannaeans from before the sight of my mighty weapons fled, and the city of Zirta,[50] his royal city, he abandoned. To save his life he ascended the mountains. After him I pursued. His oxen, his sheep, his spoil, to a countless amount I brought back. His cities I threw down, dug up, and burned with fire. From the country of the Mannaeans he departed. To the cities of Sulu'sunu of the country of Kharru he approached.

[42] The first historical mention of the Medes of Iran.

[43] In Media, near ancient Ecbatana.

[44] In Iran.

[45] The Commander-in-Chief of the Assyrian army, ranking second only to the king.

[46] From this point on it appears that Dayan-Assur is leading the army, although Shalmaneser, who would have been getting up in years, still takes credit for the campaigns.

[47] An Assyrian capital city, Arabic Nimrud, the site of several significant archaeological excavations.

[48] A people living near Amanus who controlled the cedar forests.

[49] A people of northwestern Iran, later annexed by the Medes.

[50] Or Izurtu, perhaps modern Qalaichi.

The city of Mairsuru, his royal city, together with the cities that depended on it I captured. To Sulu'sunu together with his sons mercy I granted. To his country I restored him. A payment and tribute of horses I imposed. My yoke upon him I placed. To the country of Par'sua I went down. The tribute of the kings of the country of Par'sua I received. As for the rest of the country of Par'sua that did not reverence Assur, its cities I captured. Their spoil, their plunder to Assyria I brought.

In my 31st year, to the cities of the Par'sua I went. The cities of Bustu, Sala-khamanu and Cini-khamanu, fortified towns, together with 23 cities that depended upon them I captured. Their fighting-men I slew. Their spoil I carried off. To the country of Zimri I went down. Exceeding fear of Assur and Merodach overwhelmed them. Their cities they abandoned. To inaccessible mountains they ascended. Two hundred and fifty of their cities I threw down, dug up, and burned with fire.

[The epigraphs accompanying the reliefs on the Black Obelisk]
The tribute of Sûa of the country of the Guzanians: silver, gold, lead, articles of bronze, scepters for the king's hand, horses and camels with double backs, I received. The tribute of Yahua son of Khumri: silver, gold, bowls of gold, vessels of gold, goblets of gold, pitchers of gold, lead, scepters for the king's hand, and staves, I received. The tribute of the country of Muzri: camels with double backs, an ox of the river 'Saceya, horses, wild asses, elephants, and apes, I received. The tribute of Merodach-pal-itstsar of the country of the 'Sukhians: silver, gold, pitchers of gold, tusks of the wild bull, staves, antimony, garments of many colors, and linen, I received. The tribute of Garparunda of the country of the Patinians: silver, gold, lead, bronze, gums, articles of bronze, tusks of wild bulls, and ebony, I received.

[The relief captions on the Black Obelisk]
Tribute of Sûa, the Gilzânite. I received from him: silver, gold, lead, copper vessels, staves for the hand of the king, horses, two-humped camels.
Tribute of Jehu,[51] son of Omri. I received from him: silver, gold, a golden bowl, a golden beaker, golden goblets, pitchers of gold, lead, staves for the hand of the king, javelins.
Tribute of the land of Musri. I received from him: two-humped camels, a river-ox, a *sakêa*, a *sûsu*, elephants, monkeys, apes.
Tribute of Marduk-apal-usur of Suhi. I received from him: silver, gold, pitchers of gold, ivory, javelins, *bûia*, brightly colored linen garments.
Tribute of Karparunda of Hattina. I received from him: silver, gold, lead, copper, copper vessels, ivory, cypress.

[51] King of Judah, the southern Jewish kingdom.

40

THE PRISM OF SENNACHERIB (CA. 689 BCE)

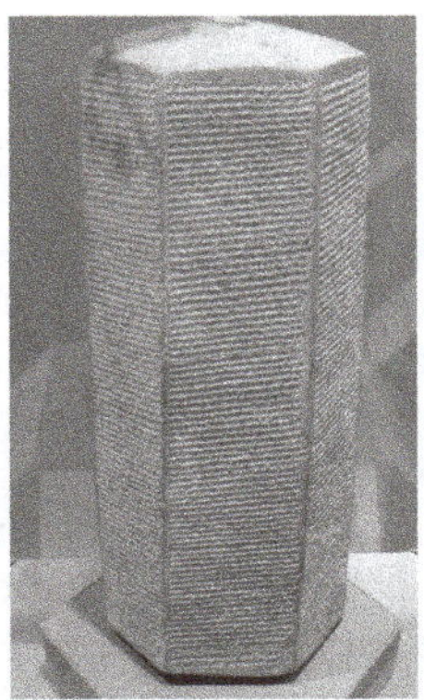

The hexagonal "Prism of Sennacherib," made from clay, is 38 centimeters (15 inches) high and 14 centimeters (5.5 inches) wide. It was illegally excavated from the mound of the ancient city of Nippur near Mosul in Iraq around 1919. It now is preserved in the Oriental Institute in Chicago. Other contemporary copies of the text are in the British Museum and in Jerusalem.

Another account of the campaigns of Assyrian kings from about 135 years later is found in the five hundred lines of Akkadian writing, known as the "Annals of Sennacherib," that are preserved on the baked clay "Prism of Sennacherib." The cuneiform text primarily documents the acquisition of loot during eight military campaigns of the Assyrian king Sennacherib III (704–681 BCE). The prism was created circa 689 BCE. It is best known for the report in the third campaign of Sennacherib's attack on the southern Hebrew kingdom of Judah in 701 BCE, which can be compared to the account of the same event in the Hebrew Bible and to the campaigns of the earlier king Shalmaneser III (Reading 39).

Source: Daniel David Luckenbill. *The Annals of Sennacherib* (Chicago: University of Chicago Press, 1924), 23–47, 128–131. http://www.utexas.edu/courses/classicalarch/readings/sennprism1.html &c.

To me, Sennacherib, the Great King, the Mighty King, King of the Universe, King of Assyria, King of the Four Quarters of the Universe, the wise ruler,[52] favorite of the great gods, guardian of the right, lover of justice, who lends support, who comes to the aid of the needy, who turns to pious deeds, perfect hero, mighty man, first among all princes, the powerful one who consumes the insubmissive, who strikes the wicked with the thunderbolt, the god Assur, the great mountain, an unrivaled kingship has entrusted, above all those who dwell in palaces, has made powerful my weapons; he has brought in submission at my feet all the black-headed people[53] from the upper sea of the setting sun[54] to the lower sea of the rising sun,[55] and mighty kings feared my warfare, leaving their abodes and flying alone, like the sudinnu, the bird of the cliffs, to some inaccessible place.

In my first campaign[56] I accomplished the defeat of Merodach-baladan, King of Babylonia, together with the army of Elam, his ally, in the plain of Kish.[57] In the midst of that battle he forsook his camp, and made his escape alone, so he saved his life. The chariots, horses, wagons, mules, that he left behind at the onset of battle, my hands seized. Into his palace, which is in Babylon, joyfully I entered. I opened his treasure-house: gold, silver, vessels of gold and silver, precious stones of every kind, goods and property without number, heavy tribute, his harem, his courtiers and officials, singers, male and female, all of his artisans, as many as there were, the servants of his palace, I brought out, I counted as spoil. In the might of Assur my Lord, 75 of his strong walled cities, of Chaldea,[58] and 420 small cities within their borders, I surrounded, I conquered, their spoil I carried off. The Arabs, Aramaeans,[59] and Chaldeans who were in Erech, Nippur, Kish, Harsagkalamma, Kutha and Sippar,[60] together with the citizens, the sinners,[61] I brought out, as booty I counted. On my return the Tu'muna Rihihu, Yadakku, Ubudu Kibre, Malahu, Gurumu, Ubulu, Damunu, Gambulu Hindaru, Ru'ua, Bukudu, Hamranu, Hagaranu, Nabatu, Li'tau, Aramaeans who were not submissive, all of them I conquered. 208,000 people, great and small, male and female, horses, mules, asses, camels, cattle and sheep, without number, a heavy booty, I carried off to Assyria.[62] In the course of my campaign, I received from Nabu-belshumate, governor of the city of Hararate,[63] gold, silver, great musukkani-trees,[64] asses, camels, cattle and sheep, as his onerous contribution. The warriors of Hirimme, wicked enemies, I cut down with the sword. Not one escaped. Their corpses I hung on stakes surrounding the city.

In my second campaign,[65] Assur my Lord, encouraged me, and against the land of the Kassites and the land of the Yasubigallai,[66] who from of old had not been submissive to the kings, my fathers, I marched. In the midst of the high mountains I rode on horseback where the terrain was difficult, and had my chariot drawn up with ropes. Where it became too steep, I clambered up on foot like the wild-ox. The cities of Bit-Kilamzah, Hardishpi, and Bit-Kubatti,[67] their strong, walled cities, I besieged, I captured. People, horses, mules, asses, cattle, and sheep, I brought out from their midst and counted as booty. And their small cities, which were numberless, I destroyed, I devastated, I turned into ruins. The houses of the steppe, the tents, wherein they dwelt, I set on fire and turned them into flames. I turned round, and made that Bit-Kilamzah into a fortress, I made its

[52] Literally, "shepherd," or "pastor."
[53] The Sumerian term for the people of Mesopotamia.
[54] The Mediterranean Sea.
[55] The Persian Gulf.
[56] 703 BCE.
[57] An ancient Sumerian city.
[58] Babylonia.
[59] From Syria.
[60] Sumerian cities.
[61] That is, the rebels.
[62] An act of deportation that was the typical Assyrian method for demoralizing conquered peoples.
[63] A fortress in Babylonia.
[64] Rosewood.
[65] 702 BCE.
[66] In the Zagros Mountains east of Assyria.
[67] Cities in the Zagros Mountains.

walls stronger than they had ever been before and settled therein people of the lands my hands had conquered.[68] The people of the land of the Kassites and the land of the Yasubigallai, who had fled before my arms, I brought down out of the mountains and settled them in Hardishpi and Bit-Kubatti. In the hands of my official, the governor of Arrapha,[69] I counted them. I had a stela made, and the might of my conquering hand, which I had established upon them, I had inscribed thereon. In the midst of the city I set it up.

The front of my yoke I turned and took the road to the land of the Elippi.[70] Before my approach Ispabara, their king, forsook his strong cities, his treasure-houses, and fled to distant parts. Over the whole of his wide land I swept like a hurricane. The cities Marubishti and Akkuddu, his royal residence-cities, together with 34 small cities of their environs, I besieged, I captured, I destroyed, I devastated, I burned with fire. The people, great and small, male and female, horses, mules, asses, camels, cattle and sheep, without number, I carried off. I brought him to naught, I diminished his land. Sisirtu and Kummahlum, strong cities, together with the small cities of their environs, the province of Bit-Barrfi in its totality, I cut off from his land and added it to the territory of Assyria. Elenzash I turned into the royal city and stronghold of that district. I changed its former name, calling its name Kar-Sennacherib. Peoples of the lands my hands had conquered I settled therein. To my official, the governor of Harhar,[71] I accounted it. Thus I extended my land. On my return, I received the heavy tribute of the distant Medes, whose name no one among the kings, my fathers, had ever heard.[72] To the yoke of my rule I made them submit.

[68] That is, deported populations.

[69] Modern Kirkuk in northeastern Iraq; originally a city of the Gutians.

[70] A kingdom on the western slopes of the Zagros Mountains in Iran.

[71] In the central western Zagros Mountains of Iran, in the territory of the Medes.

[72] The Medes in fact had been defeated by Shalmaneser III more than 130 years earlier; see Reading 39.

In my third campaign[73] I went against the Hittite-land.[74] Lule, King of Sidon, the terrifying splendor of my sovereignty overcame and far off into the midst of the sea he fled. There he died. Great Sidon, Little Sidon, Bit-Zitti, Zaribtu, Mahalliba, Ushu, Akzib, Akko,[75] his strong, walled cities, where there were fodder and drinking places for his garrisons, the terrors of the weapon of Assur, my Lord, overpowered, and they bowed in submission at my feet. Tuba'lu I seated on the royal throne over them,[76] and tribute for my majesty I imposed upon him for all time, without ceasing.

From Menachem the Shamsimurunite, Tuba'lu the Sidonite, Abdi-liti the Arvadite, Uru-milki the Gublite, Mitinti the Ashdodite, Budu-ilu the Beth-Ammonite, Kammusu-nadbi the Moabite, Malik-rammu the Edomite,[77] kings of Amurru,[78] all of them, numerous presents, as their heavy tribute, they brought before me for the fourth time, and kissed my feet. But as for Sidka, King of Ashkelon,[79] who had not submitted to my yoke, the gods of his father-house, himself, his wife, his sons, his daughters, his brothers, the seed of his father-house, I tore away and brought to Assyria. Sharru-lu-dari, son of Rukibti, their former king, I set over the people of Ashkelon and I imposed upon him the payment of tribute as presents to my majesty. He bore my yoke. In the course of my campaign, Beth-Dagon, Joppa, Banaibarka, Asuru, cities of Sidka, who had not speedily bowed in submission at my feet, I besieged, I conquered, I carried off their spoil.

The officials, nobles, and people of Ekron[80] had thrown Padi, their king, bound by oath and curse of

[73] 701 BCE.

[74] The Neo-Hittites of northern Syria, not the earlier Hittites of Anatolia.

[75] Cities in Phoenicia.

[76] As an Assyrian vassal ruler.

[77] Sidon, Arvad, Gubla (Byblos), Ashdod, Shamsimuru, and Beth-Ammon were cities in the area of Phoenicia and Canaan, whereas Ammon, Moab, and Edom were territories inland from Judaea.

[78] The Amorites of western Mesopotamia and Syria.

[79] A Philistine city south of Ashdod.

[80] A Philistine city thirty-five kilometers west of Jerusalem.

Assyria, into fetters of iron and had given him over to Hezekiah,[81] the Jew, who kept him in confinement like an enemy. Their[82] heart became afraid, and they called upon the Egyptian kings, the bowmen, chariots, and horses of the King of Meluhha,[83] a countless host, and these came to their aid. In the neighborhood of Eltekeh, their ranks being drawn up before me, they offered battle. Trusting in the aid of Assur, my Lord, I fought with them and brought about their defeat. The Egyptian charioteers and princes, together with the charioteers of the Kushite king,[84] my hands took alive in the midst of the battle. Eltekeh and Timnah I besieged, I captured and took away their spoil. I drew near to Ekron and slew the governors and nobles who had committed sin and hung their bodies on stakes around the city. The citizens who sinned and treated Assyria lightly, I counted as spoil. The rest of them, who were not carriers of sin and contempt, for whom there was no punishment, I spoke their pardon. Padi, their king, I brought out of Jerusalem, set him on the royal throne over them, and imposed upon him my kingly tribute.

As for Hezekiah, the Jew, who did not submit to my yoke, 46 of his strong, walled cities, as well as the small cities in their neighborhood, which were without number, I besieged and took by levelling with battering-rams and by bringing up siege-engines, by attacking and storming on foot, by mines, tunnels and breaches.[85] I brought away from them and counted as spoil 200,150 people, great and small, male and female, horses, mules, asses, camels, cattle and sheep, without number. Himself, like a caged bird I shut up in Jerusalem his royal city. Earthworks I threw up against him. Anyone coming out of the city-gate I turned back to his misery. The cities of his, which I had despoiled, I cut off from his land and to Mitinti, King of Ashdod, Padi, King of Ekron, and Silli-bel, King of Gaza, I gave. And thus I diminished his land. I added to the former tribute and laid upon him the giving up of his land as well as imposts-gifts for my majesty. As for Hezekiah, the terrifying splendor of my majesty overcame him, and the Urbi[86] and the mercenary troops that he had brought in to strengthen Jerusalem, his royal city, deserted him. In addition to the 30 talents of gold and 800 talents of silver, there were gems, antimony, jewels, large sandu-stones, couches of ivory, house-chairs of ivory, elephant hide, ivory, ebony, boxwood, all kinds of heavy treasures, as well as his daughters, his harem, his male and female musicians, that he had brought after me to Nineveh, my royal city. To pay tribute and to do servitude, he dispatched his messengers.

In my fourth campaign Assur, my Lord, gave me courage, and I mustered my numerous armies and gave the command to proceed against Bit-Yakin.[87] In the course of my campaign I accomplished the overthrow of Shuzubi, the Chaldean, who sat in the midst of the swamps, at Bitutu. The chills of my battle fell upon that one, and tore his heart; like a criminal he fled alone, and his place was seen no more. The front of my yoke I turned and to Bit-Yakin I took the way. That same Merodach-baladan, whose defeat I had brought about in the course of my first campaign and whose forces I had shattered, feared the roar of my mighty arms and the onset of my terrible battle and he gathered together the gods of his whole land in their shrines and loaded them into ships and fled like a bird to Nagite-rakki,[88] which is in the middle of the sea. His brothers, the seed of his father-house, whom he had left by the sea-shore, together with the rest of the people of his land, I brought out of Bit-Yakin, from the midst of the swamps and canebrakes, and counted as spoil. I turned about and ruined and devastated his cities; I made them like ruin-heaps. Upon

[81] King of the southern Hebrew kingdom of Judah ca. 715–686 BCE.

[82] The Jews.

[83] In Sumerian times the Indus River civilization, but during this period a reference to Kush, south of Egypt.

[84] Shebitku (707–690 BCE), a member of the Twenty-fifth, or Kushite, Dynasty of Egypt; see Reading 70.

[85] The Assyrian corps of military engineers was expert in the methods for capturing walled cities. For the Assyrian siege of Jerusalem, see also Reading 41.

[86] Arabs.

[87] Another name for Chaldea in southeastern Mesopotamia.

[88] In Elam, across the Persian Gulf.

his ally, the King of Elam, I poured out terror. On my return, I placed on his royal throne Assur-nadin-shum, my oldest son, offspring of my loins. I put him in charge of the wide land of Sumer and Akkad.

In my fifth campaign, the warriors of Tumurru, Sharum, Ezama, Kibshu, Halgidda, Kua, and Kana, whose abodes were set on the peak of Mt. Nipur,[89] a steep mountain, like the nests of the eagle, king of birds, were not submissive to my yoke. I had my camp pitched at the foot of Mt. Nipur and with my choice bodyguard and my relentless warriors, I, like a strong wild-ox, went before them. I surmounted gullies, mountain torrents, and waterfalls, dangerous cliffs in my sedan-chair. Where it was too steep for my chair, I advanced on foot. Like a young gazelle, I mounted the highest peaks pursuing them. Wherever my knees found a resting-place, I sat down on some mountain boulder and drank the cold water from a waterskin for my thirst. To the summits of the mountains I pursued them and brought about their overthrow. I captured their cities and carried off their spoil, I destroyed, I devastated, I burned with fire.

The front of my yoke I turned. Against Maniae, King of Ukku[90] of the land of Daie, who was not submissive, I took the road. Before my day, none of the kings who lived before me, had traveled the unblazed trails and wearisome paths that run along these rugged mountains. At the foot of Mt. Anara and Mt. Uppa, mighty mountains, I had my camp pitched, and on a house-chair I, together with my seasoned warriors, made my wearisome way through their narrow passes, and with great difficulty climbed to the highest peak of the mountains. Maniae saw the clouds of dust raised by the feet of my armies, abandoned Ukku, his royal city, and fled to distant parts. I besieged Ukku, I captured it, and took away its spoil. All kinds of goods and merchandise, the treasure of his palace, I carried away from it and counted it as booty. Furthermore, 33 cities within the bounds of his province I captured. People, asses, cattle and sheep, I carried away from them as spoil. I destroyed, I devastated, and I burned with fire.

[89] Mt. Judi in southeastern Turkey.

[90] A mountain kingdom north of Mt. Nipur.

In my sixth campaign the rest of the people of Bît-Yakin, who had run off before my powerful weapons like wild asses and had gathered together the gods of their whole land in their shrines, had crossed the great sea of the rising sun and in Nagitu of Elam had established their abodes. In Hittite ships I crossed the sea. Nagitu Nagitu-di'bina, together with the lands of Hilmu, Billatu, and Hupapanu, provinces of Elam, I conquered. The people of Bît-Yakin, together with their gods, and the people of the King of Elam, I carried off. Not a rebel escaped. I had them loaded in vessels, brought over to this side, and started on the way to Assyria. The cities that were in those provinces I destroyed, I devastated, I burned with fire. Into tells and ruins I turned them. On my return, Shuzubu, the Babylonian, who during an uprising in the land had turned to himself the rule of Sumer and Akkad, I defeated in a battle on the plain. I seized him alive with my own hands, I threw him into bonds and fetters of iron and brought him to Assyria. The King of Elam, who had gone over to his side and had aided him, I defeated. His forces I scattered and I shattered his army.

In my seventh campaign, Assur, my Lord, supported me, and I advanced against Elam. Bît-Ha'iri and Rasâ, cities on the border of Assyria that the Elamite had seized by force during the time of my father, in the course of my campaign I conquered and I despoiled. I settled my garrisons in them and restored them to the borders of Assyria. I placed them under the commandant of Dêr. 34 strong cities, together with the small cities in their areas, which were countless, I besieged, I conquered, I despoiled, I destroyed, I devastated, I burned with fire, with the smoke of their conflagration I covered the wide heavens like a hurricane. The Elamite Kudur-nahundu heard of the overthrow of his cities. Terror overwhelmed him. The people of the rest of his cities he brought into the strongholds. He himself left Madaktu, his royal city, and took his way to Haidala which is in the distant mountains. I gave the word to march against Madaktu, his royal city. In the month of rain, extreme cold set in and the heavy storms sent down rain upon rain and snow. I was afraid of the swollen mountain streams. The front of my yoke I turned and took the road to Nineveh. At that time, at the command of Assur, my Lord, Kudur-nahundu, the King of Elam, in less than three months died suddenly on a day not of his fate. After him, Umman-menanu, his younger brother, who possessed neither sense nor judgment, sat on his throne.

In my eighth campaign,[91] after Shuzubu had revolted, and the Babylonians, wicked devils, had closed the city-gates their hearts planning resistance, Shuzubu the Chaldean, a weakling, who had no knees, a slave, subject to the governor of the city of the city of Lahiri, the fugitive Arameans gathered around him, the runaway, the murderer, the bandit. Into the marshes they descended and started a rebellion. But I completely surrounded him. I pressed him to the life. Through fear and hunger he fled to Elam. When plotting and treachery were hatched against him, he fled from Elam and entered Shuanna.[92] The Babylonians placed him on the throne, for which he was not fit, and entrusted to him the government of Sumer and Akkad. They opened the treasury of the Esagila temple[93] and the gold and silver belonging to Bêl[94] and Sarpanit[95]; they brought forth the property of the temples of their gods. And to Umman-menanu, King of Elam, who had neither sense nor judgment, they sent them as a bribe saying, "Gather your army, prepare your camp, haste to Babylon, stand at our side, for you are our trust." That Elamite, whose cities I had conquered and turned into ruins on my earlier campaign against Elam, without thinking received the bribes from them, gathered his army and camp, collected his chariots and wagons, and hitched his horses and mules to them. An enormous vassal army he called to his side. The largest portion of them took the road to Akkad. Closing in on Babylon, they exchanged courtesies with Shuzubu, the Chaldean King of Babylon, and brought their army to a halt. Like the onset of locust swarms of the springtime, they steadily progressed against me to offer battle. With the dust of their feet covering the wide heavens, like a mighty storm with masses of dense clouds, they drew up in battle array before me in the city of Halulê, on the bank of the Tigris. They blocked my passage and offered battle.

As for me, I prayed victory over the mighty foe to Assur, Sin, Shamash, Bêl, Nabû, Nergal, Ishtar of Nineveh, and Ishtar of Arbela. They quickly gave ear to my prayers and came to my aid. Like a lion I raged; I put on a coat of mail. A helmet, emblem of victory, I placed upon my head. My great battle chariot, which brings the foe low, I hurriedly mounted in the anger of my heart. The mighty bow, which Assur had given me, I seized in my hands; the javelin, piercing to the life, I grasped. Against all of the armies of wicked enemies, I cried out, rumbling like a storm. I roared like Adad. At the word of Assur, the great Lord, my Lord, on flank and front I pressed upon the enemy like the onset of a raging storm. With the weapons of Assur, my Lord, and the terrible onset of my attack, I stopped their advance, I succeeded in surrounding them, I decimated the enemy host with arrow and spear. I bored through all of their bodies. Humban-undasha, the field-marshall of the King of Elam, a trustworthy man, commander of his armies, his chief support, together with his nobles who wear the golden belt-daggar and whose wrists are encircled with thick rings of shining gold like fat steers who have hobbles put on them, quickly I cut them down and defeated them. I cut their throats, and I cut off their precious lives like a string. Like the many waters of a storm, I made their gullets and entrails run down upon the wide earth.

My prancing steeds harnessed for my riding plunged into the streams of their blood as into a river. The wheels of my war chariot, which brings the wicked and evil low, were spattered with blood and filth. With the bodies of their warriors I filled the plain like grass. Their testicles I cut off and I tore out their privates like the seeds of cucumbers of Siwan.[96] I cut off their hands. The heavy rings of brightest gold that were on their wrists I took away. With sharp swords I pierced their belts and took away the belt-daggers of

[91] 691 BCE.

[92] Babylon.

[93] A temple of Marduk in Babylon.

[94] Marduk.

[95] The consort of Marduk.

[96] The third month of the Assyrian year, May-June.

gold and silver that were on their persons. The rest of his nobles, together with Nabû-shum-ishkun, son of Moerodach-baladan, who was frightened at my onslaught and had gone over to their side, my hands seized in the midst of the battle. The chariots and their horses, whose riders had been slain at the beginning of the terrible battle, and who had been left to themselves, kept running back and forth for two double-hours; I stopped their headlong flight.

That Umman-menanu, King of Elam, together with the King of Babylon and the princes of Chaldea, who had gone over to their side, the terror of my battle overturned their bodies like a bull. They abandoned their tents and to save their lives they trampled the bodies of their soldiers; they fled like young pigeons that are pursued. Their hearts were torn; they held their urine but let their dung go into their chariots. In pursuit of them, I dispatched my chariots and horses after them. Those among them who had escaped, who had fled for their lives, wherever the charioteers met them, they cut them down with the sword.

After that time, after I had completed the palace in the midst of the city of Nineveh for my royal residence, had filled it with beautiful furnishings, to the astonishment of all the people, the side-palace, which the former kings, my ancestors, had built for the care of the camp, the stabling of the horses, and general storage, because it had no terrace, because its site was too small, because its construction had not been skillfully done, so that, as the days went by, its foundation-platform had become weak, its foundation had given way and its roof had fallen in, I tore down in its entirety. A large tract of land in the meadows and environs of the city I confiscated, according to plan, and added to it. The site of the former palace I abandoned. With the ground of the meadows that I had seized from the riverflats, I filled in a terrace, I raised its top 200 tipki[97] on high. In a favorable month on an auspicious day, on the top of that terrace, following the cunning of my heart, a palace of limestone and cedar, of Hittite workmanship, also a lofty palace of Assyrian workmanship,[98] which far surpassed the former one in size and beauty, according to the plan of wise architects, I had them build for my royal residence. Mighty cedar beams, the product of Amanus, the shining mountain, I stretched over them. Door-leaves of liari-wood I covered with a sheathing of bright bronze and set up in their doors. Out of white limestone, which is found in the land of the city of Balada,[99] I had mighty statues fashioned and positioned on the right and left of the entrances. For the equipment of the black-headed people, the stabling of horses, mules, colts, riding camels, chariots, wagons, carts, quivers, bows and arrows, all kinds of battle equipment: teams of horses and mules that possessed enormous strength, and were broken to the yoke. I greatly enlarged its court of the gates. That palace, from its foundation to its coping, I constructed, I finished. A stele with my name inscribed on it I set up in it.

In the days to come among the kings, my sons, whose name Assur and Ishtar shall name for the rule of land and people, when that palace shall become old and ruined, may some future prince restore its ruins, look upon the stele with my name inscribed on it, anoint it with oil, pour out a libation upon it, and return it to its place. Then Assur and Ishtar will hear his prayers. He who destroys my inscription and my name, may Assur, the great Lord, the father of the gods, treat him as an enemy, take away the scepter and throne from him, and overthrow his rule. The month of Tammuz; eponym of Gahilu,[100] governor of Hatarikka.

[97] The thickness of a row of bricks.

[98] For Near Eastern palace construction, see also Reading 38.

[99] Near Mosul in Iraq.

[100] Limmu in 689 BCE.

41

THE ASSYRIAN SIEGE OF JERUSALEM (701 BCE): HEBREW BIBLE, 2 KINGS 18:13–19:38

In a relief from the Assyrian palace at Nineveh, Assyrian soldiers impale Hebrew captives during the siege of Lachish in 701 BCE. Preserved in the British Museum in London.

The book of 2 Kings in the Hebrew Bible contains a detailed account of the Assyrian king Sennacherib's attack on Jerusalem in 701 BCE. There are many points of contact between this report and that provided by Sennacherib himself (Reading 40), such as the Assyrian capture of a number of Galilean cities. But in other regards, the two versions place different interpretations on the Assyrian withdrawal from Jerusalem. Especially worthy of note here is the multilingual Assyrian general and his direct interactions with the Jewish negotiators and the people of Jerusalem.

Source: Hebrew Bible, 2 Kings 18:13–19:38; American Standard Version (1901).

Now in the fourteenth year of king Hezekiah did Sennacherib king of Assyria come up against all the fortified cities of Judah, and took them. And Hezekiah king of Judah sent to the king of Assyria to Lachish, saying, "I have offended; return from me: that which thou puttest on me will I bear." And the king of Assyria appointed unto Hezekiah king of Judah three hundred talents of silver and thirty talents of gold.[101]

[101] Sennacherib's account (Reading 40) cites the same amount of gold but eight hundred talents of silver.

And Hezekiah gave him all the silver that was found in the house of Jehovah, and in the treasures of the king's palace.[102] At that time did Hezekiah cut off the gold from the doors of the temple of Jehovah, and from the pillars which Hezekiah king of Judah had overlaid, and gave it to the king of Assyria. And the king of Assyria sent his field commander from Lachish[103] to king Hezekiah with a great army unto Jerusalem. And they went up and came to Jerusalem. And when they were come up, they came and stood by the conduit of the upper pool, which is in the highway of the fuller's field. And when they had called to the king, there came out to them Eliakim the son of Hilkiah, who was over the household, and Shebnah the scribe, and Joah the son of Asaph the recorder. The field commander said to them,

> Tell Hezekiah: "This is what the Great King, the King of Assyria, says: "On what are you basing this confidence of yours? You say you have strategy and military strength, but you speak only empty words. On whom are you depending, that you rebel against me? Look now, you are depending on Egypt, that splintered reed of a staff, which pierces a man's hand and wounds him if he leans on it. Such is the Pharaoh of Egypt[104] to all who depend on him. And if you say to me, "We are depending on the Lord our God," is he not the one whose high places and altars Hezekiah removed, saying to Judah and Jerusalem, "You must worship before this altar in Jerusalem?" Come now, make a bargain with my master, the King of Assyria: I will give you two thousand horses, if you can put riders on them. How can you repulse one officer of the least of my master's officials, even though you are depending on Egypt for chariots and horsemen? Furthermore, have I come to attack and destroy this place without word from the Lord? The Lord himself told me to march against this country and destroy it.[105]

Then Eliakim son of Hilkiah, and Shebna, and Joah said to the field commander, "Please speak to your servants in Aramaic, because we understand it. Do not speak to us in Hebrew in the hearing of the people on the wall."[106]

But the commander replied, "Was it only to your master and you that my master sent me to say these things, and not to the men sitting on the wall, who, like you, will have to eat their own filth and drink their own urine?" Then the commander stood and called out in Hebrew:

> Hear the word of the Great King, the King of Assyria! This is what the king says: "Do not let Hezekiah deceive you. He cannot deliver you from my hand. Do not let Hezekiah persuade you to trust in the Lord when he says, 'The Lord will surely deliver us; this city will not be given into the hand of the King of Assyria.'" Do not listen to Hezekiah. This is what the King of Assyria says: "Make peace with me and come out to me. Then every one of you will eat from his own vine and fig tree and drink water from his own cistern, until I come and take you to a land like your own, a land of grain and new wine, a land of bread and vineyards, a land of olive trees and honey. Choose life and not death!" Do not listen to Hezekiah, for he is misleading you when he says, "The Lord will deliver us." Has the god of any nation ever delivered his land from the hand of the King of Assyria? Where are the gods of Hamath[107] and Arpad[108]? Where are the gods of Sepharvaim,[109] Hena,[110] and Ivvah?[111] Have they rescued Samaria[112] from my hand? Who

[102] For the temple and royal palace of Jerusalem, see Reading 38 above.

[103] A Jewish city being besieged and about to be captured by Sennacherib.

[104] Named later in this passage as Taharqa. But Taharqa was Pharaoh from 690 to 664 BCE, not in 701 BCE, the date of this episode, so the pharaoh in question here must be Taharqa's much less distinguished predecessor, his cousin Shebitku (707–690 BCE).

[105] The general seems to be familiar with Hebrew prophets who interpreted foreign attacks as god's judgment against the sinful Hebrews.

[106] King Hezekiah's envoys clearly wanted to keep their negotiations with the Assyrians secret from the people at large.

[107] An important Canaanite city of Syria.

[108] An Aramaean city and kingdom of northwestern Syria.

[109] A city on the middle Euphrates River.

[110] A city of Syria.

[111] A city of Syria.

[112] Capital of the northern Hebrew kingdom of Israel, conquered by the Assyrians in 721 BCE.

> of all the gods of these countries has been able to save his land from me? How then can the Lord deliver Jerusalem from my hand?

But the people remained silent and said nothing in reply, because the king had commanded, "Do not answer him."

Then Eliakim son of Hilkiah the palace administrator, Shebna the secretary, and Joah son of Asaph the recorder went to Hezekiah, with their clothes torn,[113] and told him what the field commander had said. When King Hezekiah heard this, he tore his clothes and put on sackcloth and went into the temple of the Lord.

When the field commander heard that the King of Assyria had left Lachish, he withdrew and found the king fighting against Libnah.[114] Now Sennacherib received a report that Tirhakah,[115] the Kushite pharaoh of Egypt, was marching out to fight against him. So he again sent messengers to Hezekiah with this word: "Say to Hezekiah, King of Judah: "Do not let the god you depend on deceive you when he says, 'Jerusalem will not be handed over to the King of Assyria.' Surely you have heard what the kings of Assyria have done to all the countries, destroying them completely. And will you be delivered? Did the gods of the nations that were destroyed by my forefathers deliver them: the gods of Gozan,[116] Haran,[117] Rezeph[118] and the people of Eden[119] who were in the Hill of Assar[120]? Where is the King of Hamath, the King of Arpad, the King of the city of Sepharvaim, or of Hena or Ivvah?"

Hezekiah received the letter from the messengers and read it. Then he went up to the temple of the Lord and spread it out before the Lord. And Hezekiah prayed to the Lord: "O Lord, God of Israel, enthroned between the cherubim, you alone are God over all the kingdoms of the earth. You have made heaven and earth. Give ear, O Lord, and hear; open your eyes, O Lord, and see; listen to the words Sennacherib has sent to insult the living God. It is true, O Lord, that the Assyrian kings have laid waste these nations and their lands. They have thrown their gods into the fire and destroyed them, for they were not gods but only wood and stone, fashioned by men's hands. Now, O Lord our God, deliver us from his hand, so that all kingdoms on earth may know that you alone, O Lord, are God."

Then Isaiah[121] son of Amoz sent a message to Hezekiah: "This is what the Lord, the God of Israel, says: 'I have heard your prayer concerning Sennacherib King of Assyria.' This is the word that the Lord has spoken against him: 'Because you rage against me and your insolence has reached my ears, I will put my hook in your nose and my bit in your mouth, and I will make you return by the way you came.' Therefore this is what the Lord says concerning the King of Assyria: 'He will not enter this city or shoot an arrow here. He will not come before it with shield or build a siege ramp against it. By the way that he came he will return; he will not enter this city,' declares the Lord, 'I will defend this city and save it, for my sake and for the sake of David my servant.'"

That night the angel of the Lord went out and smote a hundred and eighty-five thousand men in the Assyrian camp. When the people got up the next morning, there were all the dead bodies. So Sennacherib, King of Assyria, broke camp and withdrew. He returned to Nineveh and stayed there. And it came to pass, as he was worshipping in the house of Nisroch[122] his god, that Adrammelech and Sharezer[123] his sons smote him with the sword, and they escaped into the land of Armenia. And Esarhaddon his son reigned in his stead.

---

[113] As a sign of mourning.

[114] A Jewish town, location unknown.

[115] Taharqa was Pharaoh from 690 to 664 BCE. For the Empire of Kush, see Reading 70.

[116] A region of eastern Syria where captive Israelites were exiled.

[117] A city of northwestern Mesopotamia.

[118] Perhaps Rasapha, a city west of the Euphrates River.

[119] A plain.

[120] A city of Mesopotamia.

[121] A Hebrew prophet.

[122] Otherwise unknown; word etymology would suggest something to do with an eagle.

[123] Sennacherib was murdered by his eldest son Arda-Mulissi, who had been passed over in the succession in favor of Esarhaddon (681–669 BCE).

42

JUDITH AND HOLOFERNES (CA. 587 BCE): HEBREW BIBLE, JUDITH

The beheading of the Neo-Babylonian general Holofernes by the Jew Judith has been a popular artistic motif since the Middle Ages. This manuscript illumination, perhaps from Köln, dates to circa 1360.

The book of Judith in the Hebrew Bible relates that during the invasion of Judah by the New Babylonian Empire in 587 BCE the city of Bethulia was besieged. It was in such sorry straits that the Jewish governor Uzziah decided to turn the city over to the Babylonians unless god sent help within five days. Judith, a highly respectable widow, then told the city's elders that she had a secret plan for defeating the Babylonian general Holofernes. What she did not tell them was that her plan involved seducing Holofernes. Her plan succeeded, but did not prevent the Babylonian conquest of Jerusalem soon afterward. The places and characters in the story are otherwise unknown.

Source: Judith 1–13; based on King James translation.

Judith was a widow in her house three years and four months. She also was of a goodly countenance and very beautiful to behold. Her husband Manasses had left her gold, and silver, and menservants and maidservants, and cattle, and lands, and she remained upon them. And there was none that gave her an ill word, as she feared God greatly. Now when she heard the evil words of the people against the governor, that they fainted for lack of water, for Judith had heard all the words that Uzziah had spoken unto them, and that he had sworn to deliver the city unto the Assyrians[124] after five days, then she sent her waiting woman to call Uzziah and Chabris and Charmis,[125] the ancients of the city.

And they came unto her, and she said unto them, "Hear me now, O ye governors of the inhabitants of Bethulia,[126] for your words that ye have spoken before the people this day are not right, touching this oath that ye made and pronounced between God and you, and you have promised to deliver the city to our enemies, unless within these days the Lord turn to help you. Now therefore, O brethren, let us shew an example to our brethren, because their hearts depend upon us, and because the sanctuary, and the house, and the altar, rest upon us." Then said Judith unto them, "Hear me, and I will do a thing, which shall go throughout all generations to the children of our nation. Ye shall stand this night in the gate, and I will go forth with my waiting woman: and within the days that ye have promised to deliver the city to our enemies Yahweh our God will visit Israel by mine hand. But enquire not ye of mine act, for I will not declare it unto you, until the things be finished that I do." Then said Uzziah and the princes unto her, "Go in peace, and Yahweh be before thee, to take vengeance on our enemies."

Judith called her maid, and went down into the house in which she abode in the sabbath days and in her feast days, and pulled off the sackcloth that she had on, and put off the garments of her widowhood, and washed her body all over with water, and anointed herself with precious ointment, and braided the hair of her head, and put a tiara upon it, and put on her garments of gladness, wherewith she was clad during the life of Manasses her husband. And she took sandals upon her feet, and put about her bracelets, and her chains, and her rings, and her earrings, and all her ornaments, and decked herself bravely, to allure the eyes of all men that should see her. Then she gave her maid a bottle of wine, and a cruse of oil, and filled a bag with parched grain, and lumps of figs, and with fine bread; so she folded all these things together, and laid them upon her. Thus they went forth to the gate of the city of Bethulia, and found standing there Uzziah and the ancients of the city, Chabris and Charmis. And when they saw her, that her countenance was altered, and her apparel was changed, they wondered at her beauty very greatly, and said unto her, "May God, the God of our fathers give thee favor, and accomplish thine enterprises to the glory of the children of Israel, and to the exaltation of Jerusalem." Then they worshipped God. And she said unto them, "Command the gates of the city to be opened unto me, that I may go forth to accomplish the things whereof ye have spoken with me." So they commanded the young men to open unto her, as she had spoken.

Thus they went straight forth in the valley and the first watch of the Assyrians met her, and took her, and asked her, "Of what people art thou? And whence comest thou? And whither goest thou?" And she said, "I am a woman of the Hebrews, and am fled from them: for they shall be given you to be consumed. And I am coming before Holofernes[127] the chief captain of your army, to declare words of truth, and I will shew him a way whereby he shall go and win all the hill country, without losing the body or life of any one of his men." And they brought her to the tent of Holofernes. Then the servants of Holofernes brought her into the tent, and she slept until midnight, and she arose when it was toward the morning watch, and sent to Holofernes, saying, "Let my lord now command that thine handmaid may go forth unto prayer." Then Holofernes commanded his guard that they should not stay her. Thus she abode in the camp three days, and went out in the night into the valley of Bethulia, and washed herself in a fountain of water by the camp.

And in the fourth day Holofernes made a feast for his own servants only, and called none of the officers to the banquet. Then said he to Bagoas the eunuch, who had charge over all that he had, "Go now, and persuade this Hebrew woman who is with thee, that she come unto us, and eat and drink with us. For, lo, it

---

124 The term used for the New Babylonian invaders.

125 None of these individuals are known outside of this story.

126 An otherwise unknown Jewish city.

127 An otherwise unknown New Babylonian general.

will be a shame for our person if we shall let such a woman go, not having had her company; for if we draw her not unto us, she will laugh us to scorn." Then went Bagoas from the presence of Holofernes, and came to her, and he said, "Let not this fair damsel fear to come to my lord and to be honored in his presence, and drink wine, and be merry with us, and be made this day as one of the daughters of the Assyrians who serve in the house of Nebuchadnezzar.[128]" Then said Judith unto him, "Who am I now, that I should gainsay my lord? Surely whatsoever pleaseth him I will do speedily, and it shall be my joy unto the day of my death." So she arose, and decked herself with her apparel and all her woman's attire, and her maid went and laid soft skins on the ground for her over against Holofernes, which she had received from Bagoas for her daily use, that she might sit and eat upon them.

Now when Judith came in and sat down, Holofernes' heart was ravished with her, and his mind was moved, and he desired greatly her company, for he had waited a time to deceive her, from the day that he had seen her. Then said Holofernes unto her, "Drink now, and be merry with us." So Judith said, "I will drink now, my lord, because my life is magnified in me this day more than all the days since I was born." Then she took and ate and drank before him what her maid had prepared. And Holofernes took great delight in her, and drank more wine than he had drunk at any time in one day since he was born.

Now when the evening was come, his servants made haste to depart, and Bagoas shut his tent without, and dismissed the waiters from the presence of his lord, and they went to their beds, for they were all weary because the feast had been long. And Judith was left alone in the tent and Holofernes lying alone upon his bed, for he was filled with wine. Now Judith had commanded her maid to stand without her bedchamber, and to wait for her coming forth, as she did daily, for she said she would go forth to her prayers, and she spoke to Bagoas according to the same purpose. So all went forth and none was left in the bedchamber, neither little nor great. Then Judith, standing by his bed, said in her heart, "O Yahweh, God of all power, look at this present upon the works of mine hands for the exaltation of Jerusalem. For now is the time to help thine inheritance, and to execute thine enterprises to the destruction of the enemies that are risen against us."

Then she came to the pillar of the bed, which was at Holofernes' head, and took down his scimitar from thence, and approached to his bed, and took hold of the hair of his head, and said, "Strengthen me, O Yahweh, God of Israel, this day." And she smote twice upon his neck with all her might, and she took away his head from him and tumbled his body down from the bed and pulled down the canopy from the pillars. And anon then she went forth, and gave Holofernes' head to her maid, and she put it in her bag of meat. So they two went together according to their custom unto prayer, and when they passed the camp, they compassed the valley and went up the mountain of Bethulia and came to the gates thereof.

Then said Judith afar off to the watchmen at the gate, "Open, open now the gate: God, even our God, is with us, to shew his power yet in Jerusalem, and his forces against the enemy, as he hath even done this day." Now when the men of her city heard her voice, they made haste to go down to the gate of their city and they called the elders of the city. And then they ran all together, both small and great, for it was strange unto them that she had come. So they opened the gate and received them and made a fire for a light and stood round about them. Then she said to them with a loud voice, "Praise, praise God, praise God, I say, for he hath not taken away his mercy from the house of Israel, but hath destroyed our enemies by mine hands this night."

So she took the head out of the bag, and shewed it, and said unto them, "Behold the head of Holofernes, the chief captain of the army of Assur,[129] and behold the canopy, wherein he did lie in his drunkenness, and Yahweh hath smitten him by the hand of a woman.[130] As Yahweh liveth, who hath

[128] New Babylonian king ca. 634–562 BCE who captured Jerusalem in 597 BCE and then destroyed it in 587 BCE.

[129] Actually Babylonia, not Assyria.

[130] Compare the story of Deborah, Reading 37, "Yahweh will sell Sisera into the hand of a woman."

kept me in my way that I went, my countenance hath deceived him to his destruction, and yet hath he not committed sin with me, to defile and shame me." Then all the people were wonderfully astonished, and bowed themselves and worshipped god, and said with one accord, "Blessed be thou, O our God, who hast this day brought to nought the enemies of thy people." Then said Uzziah unto her, "O daughter, blessed art thou of the most high God above all the women upon the earth; and blessed be Yahweh, who hath created the heavens and the earth, who hath directed thee to the cutting off of the head of the chief of our enemies."

43

THE CYRUS LEGEND (CA. 580 BCE)

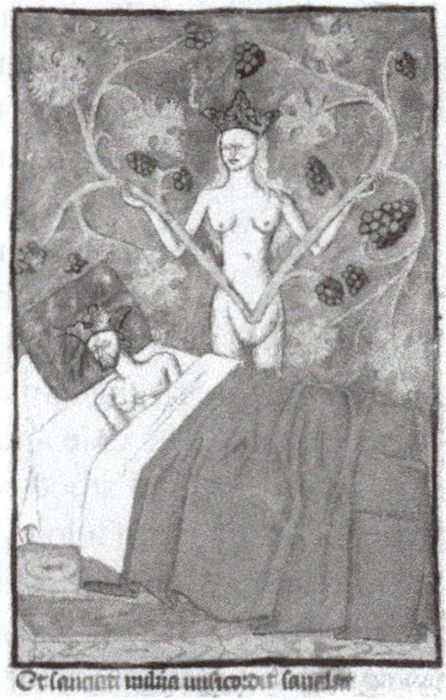

A fifteenth-century French manuscript depicts the dream of Astyages, in which a great vine grew from the womb of Mandane, the mother of Cyrus.

After the destruction of the Assyrian Empire at the end of the seventh century BCE by the Medes and Chaldeans, the Medes established a powerful kingdom that extended from Iran to central Anatolia. At this time the Persians, even though they had kings of their own, were vassals of the Medes. In the mid-sixth century, the Persian Cyrus, a descendent of the Persian royal family, led a revolt against the Medes and founded the Persian Empire. As was the case with many important persons of antiquity, legends grew up about Cyrus's origins, such as this tale related in the mid-fifth century BCE by the Greek historian Herodotus. The story is an example of a common folk tale motif of the noble child raised in disguise, much as in the legends of Romulus and Remus (Reading 73) and King Arthur.

Source: Herodotus, 1.108–119, G. C. Macaulay, *The History of Herodotus* (London/New York: Macmillan, 1890).

And when Mandane[131] was married to Cambyses,[132] in the first year Astyages saw another vision. It seemed to him that from the womb of this daughter a vine grew, and this vine overspread the whole of Asia. Having seen this vision and delivered it to the interpreters of dreams, he sent for his daughter, being then with child, to come from the land of the Persians. And when she had come he kept watch over her, desiring to destroy that which should be born of her, for the Magian[133] interpreters of dreams signified to him that the offspring of his daughter should be king in his place. Astyages then desiring to guard against this, when Cyrus was born, called Harpagus, a man who was of kin near him and whom he trusted above all the other Medes, and had made him manager of all his affairs, and to him he said, "Neglect not by any means, Harpagus, the matter that I shall lay upon thee to do, and beware lest thou set me aside, and choosing the advantage of others instead, bring thyself afterward to destruction. Take the child that Mandane bore and carry it to thy house and slay it, and afterward bury it in whatsoever manner thou thyself desirest." To this he made answer, "O king, never yet in any past time didst thou discern in me an offense against thee, and I keep watch over myself also with a view to the time that comes after, that I may not commit any error toward thee. If it is indeed thy pleasure that this should so be done, my service at least must be fitly rendered."

Thus he made answer, and when the child had been delivered to him adorned as for death, Harpagus went weeping to his wife all the words that had been spoken by Astyages. And she said to him, "Now, therefore, what is it in thy mind to do?" and he made answer, "Not according as Astyages enjoined, for not even if he shall come to be yet more out of his senses and more mad than he now is, will I agree to his will or serve him in such a murder as this. And for many reasons I will not slay the child; first because he is a kin to me, and then because Astyages is old and without male issue, and if after he is dead the power shall come through me, does not the greatest of dangers then await me? To secure me, this child must die; but one of the servants of Astyages must be the slayer of it, and not one of mine."

Thus he spoke, and straightway sent a messenger to that one of the herdsmen of Astyages who he knew fed his herds on the pastures that were most suitable for his purpose, and on the mountains most haunted by wild beasts. The name of this man was Mithridates, and he was married to one who was his fellow-slave, and the name of the woman to whom he was married was Kyno in the tongue of the Hellenes[134] and in the Median tongue Spaco, for what the Hellenes call *kyna*[135] the Medes call *spaca*. Now, it was on the skirts of the mountains that this herdsman had his cattle-pastures, from Ecbatana[136] toward the north wind and toward the Euxine Sea.[137] For here in the direction of the Saspeirians[138] the Median land is very mountainous and lofty and thickly covered with forests; but the rest of the land of Media is all level plain. So when this herdsman came, being summoned with much urgency, Harpagus said these words, "Astyages bids thee take this child and place it on the most desolate part of the mountains, so that it may perish as quickly as possible.[139] And he bade me to say that if thou do not kill it, but in any way shalt preserve it from death, he will slay thee by the most evil kind of destruction, and I have been appointed to see that the child is laid forth."

[131] Daughter of Astyages, King of the Medes ca. 585–550 BCE.
[132] King of the Persians ca. 600–559, vassal of the Medes.
[133] The Magi were the priests of the Medes.

[134] Greeks.
[135] A female dog.
[136] A capital city of the Medes.
[137] The Black Sea.
[138] A people of central Asia; see the map for Chapter 9.
[139] Compare the story of Romulus and Remus, Reading 73.

Having heard this and having taken up the child, the herdsman went back by the way he came, and arrived at his dwelling. And his wife also, as it seems, having been every day on the point of bearing a child, by a providential chance brought her child to birth just at that time, when the herdsman was gone to the city. And both were in anxiety, each for the other, the man having fear about the child-bearing of his wife, and the woman about the cause why Harpagus had sent to summon her husband, not having been wont to do so aforetime. So as soon as he returned and stood before her, the woman seeing him again beyond her hopes was the first to speak, and asked him for what purpose Harpagus had sent for him so urgently. And he said, "Wife, when I came to the city I saw and heard that which I would I had not seen, and which I should wish had never chanced to those whom we serve. For the house of Harpagus was all full of mourning, and I being astonished thereat went within, and as soon as I entered I saw laid out to view an infant child gasping for breath and screaming, which was adorned with gold ornaments and embroidered clothing. And when Harpagus saw me he bade me forthwith to take up the child and carry it away and lay it on that part of the mountains that is most haunted by wild beasts, saying that it was Astyages who laid this task upon me, and using to me many threats, if I should fail to do this. And I took it up and bore it away, supposing that it was the child of some one of the servants of the house, for never could I have supposed whence it really was; but I marvelled to see it adorned with gold and raiment, and I marvelled also because mourning was made for it openly in the house of Harpagus. And straightway as we went by the road, I learnt the whole of the matter from the servant who went with me out of the city and placed in my hands the babe, namely that it was in truth the son of Mandane the daughter of Astyages, and of Cambyses the son of Cyrus, and that Astyages bade slay it. And now here it is."

To the herdsman it seemed that, the case standing thus, his wife spoke well, and forthwith he did so. The child that he was bearing to put to death, this he delivered to his wife, and his own, which was dead, he took and placed in the chest in which he had been bearing the other. And having adorned it with all the adornment of the other child, he bore it to the most desolate part of the mountains and placed it there. And when the third day came after the child had been laid forth, the herdsman went to the city, leaving one of his underherdsmen to watch there, and when he came to the house of Harpagus he said that he was ready to display the dead body of the child; and Harpagus sent the most trusted of his spearmen, and through them he saw and buried the herdsman's child. This then had had burial, but him who was afterward called Cyrus the wife of the herdsman had received, and was bringing him up, giving him no doubt some other name, not Cyrus.

And when the boy was ten years old, it happened with regard to him as follows, and this made him known. He was playing in the village in which were stalls for oxen, he was playing there, I say, with other boys of his age in the road. And the boys in their play chose as their king this one who was called the son of the herdsman, and he set some of them to build palaces and others to be spearmen of his guard, and one of them no doubt he appointed to be the eye of the king,[140] and to one he gave the office of bearing the messages, appointing a work for each one severally. Now one of these boys who was playing with the rest, the son of Artembares a man of repute among the Medes, did not do that which Cyrus appointed him to do; therefore Cyrus bade the other boys seize him hand and foot, and when they obeyed his command he dealt with the boy very roughly, scourging him. But he, so soon as he was let go, being made much more angry because he considered that he had been treated with indignity, went down to the city and complained to his father of the treatment that he had met with from Cyrus, calling him not Cyrus, for this was not yet his name, but the son of the herdsman of Astyages. And Artembares in the anger of the moment went at once to Astyages, taking the boy with him, and he declared that he had suffered things that were unfitting and said, "O king, by

[140] The "Eyes and Ears of the King" were officials sent to spy on government officials.

thy slave, the son of a herdsman, we have been thus outraged," showing him the shoulders of his son.

And Astyages having heard and seen this, wishing to punish the boy to avenge the honor of Artembares, sent for both the herdsman and his son. And when both were present, Astyages looked at Cyrus and said, "Didst thou dare, being the son of so mean a father as this, to treat with such unseemly insult the son of this man who is first in my favor?" And he replied thus, "Master, I did so to him with right. For the boys of the village, of whom he also was one, in their play set me up as king over them, for I appeared to them most fitted for this place. Now the other boys did what I commanded them, but this one disobeyed and paid no regard, until at last he received the punishment due. If therefore for this I am worthy to suffer any evil, here I stand before thee."

While the boy thus spoke, there came upon Astyages a sense of recognition of him and the lineaments of his face seemed to him to resemble his own, and his answer appeared to be somewhat over free for his station, while the time of the laying forth seemed to agree with the age of the boy. Being struck with amazement by these things, for a time he was speechless; and having at length with difficulty recovered himself, he said, desiring to dismiss Artembares, in order that he might get the herdsman by himself alone and examine him, "Artembares, I will so order these things that thou and thy son shall have no cause to find fault"; and so he dismissed Artembares, and the servants upon the command of Astyages led Cyrus within. And when the herdsman was left alone with the king, Astyages being alone with him asked whence he had received the boy, and who it was who had delivered the boy to him. And the herdsman said that he was his own son, and that the mother was living with him still as his wife. But Astyages said that he was not well advised in desiring to be brought to extreme necessity, and as he said this he made a sign to the spearmen of his guard to seize him. So he, as he was being led away to the torture, then declared the story as it really was; and beginning from the beginning he went through the whole, telling the truth about it, and finally ended with entreaties, asking that he would grant him pardon.

So when the herdsman had made known the truth, Astyages now cared less about him, but with Harpagus he was very greatly displeased and bade his spearmen summon him. And when Harpagus came, Astyages asked him thus, "By what death, Harpagus, didst thou destroy the child whom I delivered to thee, born of my daughter?" and Harpagus, seeing that the herdsman was in the king's palace, turned not to any false way of speech, lest he should be convicted and found out, but said, "O king, so soon as I received the child, I took counsel and considered how I should do according to thy mind, and how without offense to thy command I might not be guilty of murder against thy daughter and against thyself. I did therefore thus: I called this herdsman and delivered the child to him, saying first that thou wert he who bade him slay it, and in this at least I did not lie, for thou didst so command. I delivered it, I say, to this man commanding him to place it upon a desolate mountain, and to stay by it and watch it until it should die, threatening him with all kinds of punishment if he should fail to accomplish this. And when he had done that which was ordered and the child was dead, I sent the most trusted of my eunuchs and through them I saw and buried the child. Thus, O king, it happened about this matter, and the child had this death that I say."

So Harpagus declared the truth, and Astyages concealed the anger that he kept against him for that which had come to pass, and first he related the matter over again to Harpagus according as he had been told it by the herdsman, and afterward, when it had been thus repeated by him, he ended by saying that the child was alive and that that which had come to pass was well, "for," continued he, "I was greatly troubled by that which had been done to this child, and I thought it no light thing that I had been made at variance with my daughter. Therefore consider that this is a happy change of fortune, and first send thy son to be with the boy who is newly come, and then, seeing that I intend to make a sacrifice of thanksgiving for the preservation of the boy to those gods to whom that honor belongs, be here thyself to dine with me."

When Harpagus heard this, he did reverence and thought it a great matter that his offense had turned out for his profit and moreover that he had been invited to dinner with happy augury; and so he went to his house. And having entered it straightway, he sent forth his son, for he had one only son of about thirteen years old, bidding him go to the palace of Astyages and do whatsoever the king should command; and he himself being overjoyed told his wife that which had befallen him. But Astyages, when the son of Harpagus arrived, cut his throat and divided him limb from limb, and having roasted some pieces of the flesh and boiled others he caused them to be dressed for eating and kept them ready. And when the time arrived for dinner and the other guests were present and also Harpagus, then before the other guests and before Astyages himself were placed tables covered with flesh of sheep; but before Harpagus was placed the flesh of his own son, all but the head and the hands and the feet, and these were laid aside covered up in a basket. Then when it seemed that Harpagus was satisfied with food, Astyages asked him whether he had been pleased with the banquet; and when Harpagus said that he had been very greatly pleased, they who had been commanded to do this brought to him the head of his son covered up, together with the hands and the feet. And standing near they bade Harpagus uncover and take of them that which he desired. So when Harpagus obeyed and uncovered, he saw the remains of his son, and seeing them he was not overcome with amazement but contained himself. Astyages asked him whether he perceived of what animal he had been eating the flesh, and he said that he perceived, and that whatsoever the king might do was well pleasing to him. Thus having made answer and taking up the parts of the flesh that still remained he went to his house; and after that, I suppose, he would gather all the parts together and bury them.

44

THE BEHISTUN INSCRIPTION (CA. 520 BCE)

The Behistun inscription, carved into a cliffside on Mount Behistun near Kermanshah in western Iran, describes the rise to power of the Persian king Darius I.

In order to get the news out about important events during their reigns, Persian kings had huge rock reliefs carved onto the sides of cliffs. For Darius I (522–486 BCE), the most important event of his reign was the first, his proclamation as Great King, which occurred under somewhat irregular circumstances. Although Darius was, or at least claimed to be, a direct descendent of the first

Persian king Achaemenes, he was only a distant cousin of Cyrus, the founder of the Persian Empire. It therefore was crucially important that he establish his legitimacy, and one of the means he employed to do this was the creation of this rock carving that told the story of his rise to power. It not only depicted him fully enthroned as king but also had an accompanying inscription, written in Persian, Babylonian, and Elamite. The account contained in a massive inscription carved into the side of Mount Behistun in Iran is candid about the problems that Darius had establishing his control over the empire, and, in typical near-eastern fashion, attributes his legitimacy to the support of a god, in this case Ahura Mazda, the primary god of the Zoroastrian religion. It provides in excruciating detail accounts, with exact places and dates, of the battles that Darius fought in his quest to secure the throne.

Source: L. W. King and R. C. Thompson, *The Sculptures and Inscription of Darius the Great on the Rock of Behistûn in Persia* (London: British Museum, 1907).

Column One

(1) I am Darius, the Great King, King of Kings, the King of Persia, the king of countries, the son of Hystaspes, the grandson of Arsames, the Achaemenid.

(2) King Darius says: My father is Hystaspes; the father of Hystaspes was Arsames; the father of Arsames was Ariaramnes; the father of Ariaramnes was Teispes; the father of Teispes was Achaemenes.

(3) King Darius says: That is why we are called Achaemenids; from antiquity we have been noble; from antiquity has our dynasty been royal.[141]

(4) King Darius says: Eight of my dynasty were kings before me; I am the ninth. Nine in succession we have been kings.[142]

(5) King Darius says: By the grace of Ahura Mazda am I king; Ahura Mazda has granted me the kingdom.[143]

(6) King Darius says: These are the countries that are subject unto me, and by the grace of Ahura Mazda I became king of them: Persia, Elam, Babylonia, Assyria, Arabia, Egypt, the countries by the Sea, Lydia, the Greeks, Media, Armenia, Cappadocia, Parthia, Drangiana, Aria, Chorasmia, Bactria, Sogdia, Gandara, Scythia, Sattagydia, Arachosia, and Maka; twenty-three lands in all.[144]

(7) King Darius says: These are the countries that are subject to me; by the grace of Ahura Mazda they became subject to me; they brought tribute unto me. Whatsoever commands have been laid on them by me, by night or by day, have been performed by them.

(8) King Darius says: Within these lands, whosoever was a friend, him have I surely protected; whosoever was hostile, him have I utterly destroyed. By the grace of Ahura Mazda these lands have conformed to my decrees; as it was commanded unto them by me, so was it done.

(9) King Darius says: Ahura Mazda has granted unto me this empire. Ahura Mazda brought me help, until I gained this empire; by the grace of Ahura Mazda do I hold this empire.

(10) King Darius says: The following is what was done by me after I became king. A son of Cyrus, named Cambyses, one of our dynasty, was king here before me. That Cambyses had a brother, Smerdis by name, of the same mother

[141] In order to establish his legitimacy, Darius painstakingly demonstrates his connection to the royal family.

[142] Including his distant cousins, and direct predecessors, Cyrus and Cambyses.

[143] Throughout the narrative Darius harps on the support that he received from the god Ahura Mazda.

[144] For these satrapies, see the map at the beginning of this chapter.

and the same father as Cambyses. Afterward, Cambyses slew this Smerdis. When Cambyses slew Smerdis, it was not known unto the people that Smerdis was slain. Thereupon Cambyses went to Egypt. When Cambyses had departed into Egypt, the people became hostile, and the lie multiplied in the land, even in Persia and Media, and in the other provinces.

(11) King Darius says: Afterward, there was a certain man, a Magian,[145] Gaumâta by name, who raised a rebellion in Paishiyâuvâdâ,[146] in a mountain called Arakadriš. On the fourteenth day of the month Viyaxana[147] did he rebel. He lied to the people, saying: "I am Smerdis, the son of Cyrus, the brother of Cambyses." Then were all the people in revolt, and from Cambyses they went over unto him, both Persia and Media, and the other provinces. He seized the kingdom; on the ninth day of the month Garmapada[148] he seized the kingdom. Afterward, Cambyses died of natural causes.[149]

(12) King Darius says: The kingdom of which Gaumâta, the Magian, dispossessed Cambyses, had always belonged to our dynasty. After that Gaumâta, the Magian, had dispossessed Cambyses of Persia and Media, and of the other provinces, he did according to his will. He became king.

(13) King Darius says: There was no man, either Persian or Mede or of our own dynasty, who took the kingdom from Gaumâta, the Magian. The people feared him exceedingly, for he slew many who had known the real Smerdis. For this reason did he slay them, "that they may not know that I am not Smerdis, the son of Cyrus." There was none who dared to act against Gaumâta, the Magian, until I came. Then I prayed to Ahura Mazda; Ahura Mazda brought me help. On the tenth day of the month Bâgayâdiš[150] I, with a few men, slew that Gaumâta, the Magian, and the chief men who were his followers. At the stronghold called Sikayauvatiš, in the district called Nisaia in Media, I slew him; I dispossessed him of the kingdom. By the grace of Ahura Mazda I became king; Ahura Mazda granted me the kingdom.

(14) King Darius says: The kingdom that had been wrested from our line I brought back and I reestablished it on its foundation. The temples that Gaumâta, the Magian, had destroyed, I restored to the people, and the pasture lands, and the herds and the dwelling places, and the houses that Gaumâta, the Magian, had taken away. I settled the people in their place, the people of Persia, and Media, and the other provinces. I restored that which had been taken away, as it was in the days of old. This did I by the grace of Ahura Mazda, I labored until I had established our dynasty in its place, as in the days of old; I labored, by the grace of Ahura Mazda, so that Gaumâta, the Magian, did not dispossess our house.

(15) King Darius says: This was what I did after I became king.

(16) King Darius says: After I had slain Gaumâta, the Magian, a certain man named Âššina, the son of Upadarma, raised a rebellion in Elam, and he spoke thus unto the people of Elam: "I am king in Elam." Thereupon the people of Elam became rebellious, and they went over unto that Âššina: he became king in Elam. And a certain Babylonian named Nidintu-Bêl, the son of Kîn-Zêr, raised a rebellion in Babylon: he lied to the people, saying: "I am Nebuchadnezzar, the son of Nabonidus." Then did all the province of Babylonia go over to Nidintu-Bêl, and Babylonia rose in rebellion. He seized on the kingdom of Babylonia.[151]

[145] One of the magi, the priests of the Medes.

[146] Probably on the border between Persia and Elam to the northwest.

[147] 11 March 522.

[148] 1 July 522.

[149] In Egypt in 522. Cambyses actually was said to have accidentally fallen on his sword while getting on his horse. One must wonder whether someone was holding the sword at the time.

[150] 29 September 522.

[151] 3 October 522.

(17) King Darius says: Then I sent to Elam. That Âššina was brought unto me in fetters, and I killed him.

(18) King Darius says: Then I marched against that Nidintu-Bêl, who called himself Nebuchadnezzar. The army of Nidintu-Bêl held the Tigris; there it took its stand, and on account of the waters the river was unfordable. Thereupon I floated my army on inflated skins, others I made camel-borne, for the rest I brought horses. Ahura Mazda brought me help; by the grace of Ahura Mazda we crossed the Tigris. Then did I utterly overthrow that host of Nidintu-Bêl. On the twenty-sixth day of the month Âçiyâdiya[152] we joined battle.

(19) King Darius says: After that I marched against Babylon. But before I reached Babylon, that Nidintu-Bêl, who called himself Nebuchadnezzar, came with a host and offered battle at a city called Zâzâna,[153] on the Euphrates. Then we joined battle. Ahura Mazda brought me help; by the grace of Ahura Mazda did I utterly overthrow the host of Nidintu-Bêl. The enemy fled into the water; the water carried them away. On the second day of the month Anâmaka[154] we joined battle.

Column Two

(20) King Darius says: Then did Nidintu-Bêl flee with a few horsemen into Babylon. Thereupon I marched to Babylon. By the grace of Ahura Mazda I took Babylon, and captured Nidintu-Bêl. Then I slew that Nidintu-Bêl in Babylon.

(21) King Darius says: While I was in Babylon, these provinces revolted from me: Persia, Elam, Media, Assyria, Egypt, Parthia, Margiana, Sattagydia, and Scythia.

(24) King Darius says: A certain Mede named Phraortes revolted in Media, and he said to the people: "I am Khshathrita, of the family of Cyaxares."[155] Then did the Medes who were in the palace revolt from me and go over to Phraortes. He became king in Media.

(31) King Darius says: Then I went forth from Babylon and came into Media. When I had come to Media, that Phraortes, who called himself king in Media, came against me unto a city in Media called Kunduru to offer battle. Then we joined battle. Ahura Mazda brought me help; by the grace of Ahura Mazda did my army utterly overthrow that rebel host. On the twenty-fifth day of the month Adukanaiša we fought the battle.[156]

(32) King Darius says: Thereupon that Phraortes fled thence with a few horseman to a district in Media called Rhagae. Then I sent an army in pursuit. Phraortes was taken and brought unto me. I cut off his nose, his ears, and his tongue, and I put out one eye, and he was kept in fetters at my palace entrance, and all the people beheld him. Then did I crucify him in Ecbatana[157]; and the men who were his foremost followers, those at Ecbatana within the fortress, I flayed and hung out their hides, stuffed with straw.

(34) King Darius says: This is what was done by me in Media.

(35) King Darius says: The Parthians[158] and Hyrcanians[159] revolted from me, and they declared themselves on the side of Phraortes. My father Hystaspes was in Parthia and the people forsook him; they became rebellious. Then Hystaspes marched forth with the troops that had remained faithful. At a city in Parthia called Višpauzâtiš he fought a battle with the Parthians. Ahura Mazda brought me help; by the grace of Ahura Mazda my army utterly defeated that rebel host. On the second day of the month Viyaxana[160] the battle was fought by them.

---

[152] 13 December 522.

[153] Or Susa, an ancient city of western Iran, later a capital city of the Medes and Persians.

[154] 18 December 522.

[155] The most famous king of the Medes; he assisted in the destruction of the Assyrian Empire in 612 BCE. So this was a serious revolt.

[156] 8 May 521.

[157] A capital city of the Medes and Persians; in western Iran.

[158] For the Parthians, see Reading 69.

[159] On the southern coast of the Caspian Sea.

[160] 8 March 521.

(36) King Darius says: Then did I send a Persian army unto Hystaspes from Rhagae. When that army reached Hystaspes, he marched forth with the host. At a city in Parthia called Patigrabanâ he gave battle to the rebels. Ahura Mazda brought me help; by the grace of Ahura Mazda Hystaspes utterly defeated that rebel host. On the first day of the month Garmapada[161] the battle was fought by them.

(37) King Darius says: Then was the province mine. This is what done by me in Parthia.

(40) King Darius says: A certain man named Vahyazdâta dwelt in a city called Târavâ in a district in Persia called Vautiyâ. This man rebelled for the second time in Persia, and thus he spoke unto the people: "I am Smerdis, the son of Cyrus." Then the Persian people who were in the palace fell away from allegiance. They revolted from me and went over to that Vahyazdâta. He became king in Persia.

(41) King Darius says: Then did I send out the Persian and the Median army that was with me. A Persian named Artavardiya, my servant, I made their leader. The rest of the Persian army came unto me in Media. Then went Artavardiya with the army unto Persia. When he came to Persia, at a city in Persia called Rakhâ, that Vahyazdâta, who called himself Smerdis, advanced with the army against Artavardiya to give him battle. They then fought the battle. Ahura Mazda brought me help; by the grace of Ahura Mazda my host utterly overthrew the army of Vahyazdâta. On the twelfth day of the month Thûravâhara[162] was the battle fought by them.

(42) King Darius says: Then that Vahyazdâta fled thence with a few horsemen unto Pishiyâuvâda. From that place he went forth with an army a second time against Artavardiya to give him battle. At a mountain called Parga they fought the battle. Ahura Mazda brought me help; by the grace of Ahura Mazda my host utterly overthrew the army of Vahyazdâta. On the fifth day of the month Garmapada[163] was the battle fought by them. And they seized that Vahyazdâta, and the men who were his chief followers were also seized.

(43) King Darius says: Then did I crucify that Vahyazdâta and the men who were his chief followers in a city in Persia called Uvâdaicaya.

(44) King Darius says: This is what was done by me in Persia.

(49) King Darius says: While I was in Persia and in Media, the Babylonians revolted from me a second time. A certain man named Arakha, an Armenian, son of Haldita, rebelled in Babylon. At a place called Dubâla, he lied unto the people, saying: "I am Nebuchadnezzar, the son of Nabonidus." Then did the Babylonian people revolt from me and they went over to that Arakha. He seized Babylon, he became king in Babylon.

(50) King Darius says: Then did I send an army unto Babylon. A Persian named Intaphrenes, my servant, I appointed as their leader, and thus I spoke unto them: "Go, smite that Babylonian host that does not acknowledge me." Then Intaphrenes marched with the army unto Babylon. Ahura Mazda brought me help; by the grace of Ahura Mazda Intaphrenes overthrew the Babylonians and brought over the people unto me. On the twenty-second day of the month Markâsanaš[164] they seized that Arakha who called himself Nebuchadnezzar, and the men who were his chief followers. Then I made a decree, saying: "Let that Arakha and the men who were his chief followers be crucified in Babylon!"

Column Four

(51) King Darius says: This is what was done by me in Babylon.

(52) King Darius says: This is what I have done. By the grace of Ahura Mazda have I always acted. After I became king, I fought nineteen battles in a single year and by the grace of Ahura Mazda I

[161] 11 July 521.

[162] 24 May 521.

[163] 15 July 521.

[164] 27 November 521.

overthrew nine kings and I made them captive.[165] One was named Gaumâta, the Magian; he lied, saying "I am Smerdis, the son of Cyrus." He made Persia to revolt. Another was named Âššina, the Elamite; he lied, saying: "I am the King of Elam." He made Elam to revolt. Another was named Nidintu-Bêl, the Babylonian; he lied, saying: "I am Nebuchadnezzar, the son of Nabonidus." He made Babylon to revolt. Another was named Martiya, the Persian; he lied, saying: "I am Ummanniš, the King of Elam." He made Elam to revolt. Another was Phraortes, the Mede; he lied, saying: "I am Khshathrita, of the dynasty of Cyaxares." He made Media to revolt. Another was Tritantaechmes, the Sagartian; he lied, saying: "I am king in Sagartia, of the dynasty of Cyaxares." He made Sagartia to revolt. Another was named Frâda, of Margiana; he lied, saying: "I am King of Margiana." He made Margiana to revolt. Another was Vahyazdâta, a Persian; he lied, saying: "I am Smerdis, the son of Cyrus." He made Persia to revolt. Another was Arakha, an Armenian; he lied, saying: "I am Nebuchadnezzar, the son of Nabonidus." He made Babylon to revolt.

(53) King Darius says: These nine kings did I capture in these wars.

(54) King Darius says: As to these provinces that revolted, lies made them revolt, so that they deceived the people. Then Ahura Mazda delivered them into my hand; and I did unto them according to my will.

(62) King Darius says: This is what I have done in one single year; by the grace of Ahura Mazda have I always acted. Ahura Mazda brought me help, and the other gods, all that there are.

(63) King Darius says: On this account Ahura Mazda brought me help, and all the other gods, all that there are, because I was not wicked, nor was I a liar, nor was I a tyrant, neither I nor any of my family. I have ruled according to righteousness. Neither to the weak nor to the powerful did I do wrong. Whosoever helped my house, him I favored; he who was hostile, him I destroyed.

(68) King Darius says: These are the men who were with me when I slew Gaumâta the Magian, who was called Smerdis; then these men helped me as my followers: Intaphrenes, son of Vayâspâra, a Persian; Otanes, son of Thukhra, a Persian; Gobryas, son of Mardonius, a Persian; Hydarnes, son of Bagâbigna, a Persian; Megabyzus, son of Dâtuvahya, a Persian; Ardumaniš, son of Vakauka, a Persian.

(69) King Darius says: You who may be king hereafter, protect the family of these men.

(70) King Darius says: By the grace of Ahura Mazda this is the inscription that I have made. It was in Aryan script, and it was composed on clay tablets and on parchment. Besides, a sculptured figure of myself I made. Besides, I made my lineage. And it was inscribed and was read off before me. Afterward this inscription I sent off everywhere among the provinces. The people unitedly worked upon it.

Column Five[166]

(74) King Darius says: Afterward with an army I went off to Scythia[167] after the Scythians who wear the pointed cap. These Scythians went from me. When I arrived at the river, I crossed beyond it then with all my army. Afterward, I smote the Scythians exceedingly; one of their leaders I took captive; he was led bound to me, and I killed him. Another chief of them, by name Skunkha, they seized and led to me. Then I made another their chief, as was my desire. Then the province became mine.[168]

(75) King Darius says: Those Scythians were faithless and Ahura Mazda was not worshipped by them. I worshipped Ahura Mazda; by the grace of Ahura Mazda I did unto them according to my will.

---

[165] The inscription inserts here a summary of the revolts Darius suppressed during his first year of rule.

[166] A rather brief addendum.

[167] In 519 BCE. For the Scythians, see Reading 68.

[168] This is wishful thinking; the Persians never conquered the Scythians. A subsequent invasion of Scythia in 513 BCE likewise was unsuccessful.

CHAPTER 6

Greece in the Dark and Archaic Ages (1100–500 BCE)

The origins of the ancient Greek culture of the fifth century BCE, a period generally recognized as the Golden Age of Greece, are to be found during the periods known as the Dark and Archaic Ages, which lasted from roughly 1100 to 500 BCE. During these periods, the Greeks recovered from the decline and fall of the Mycenaean civilization to create an even more complex and sophisticated civilization based on the political institution known as the polis, or city-state. The revival of Greek culture was marked not only by developments in Greek art and architecture, but also by the evolution of Greek literature, especially in the fields of poetry and philosophy.

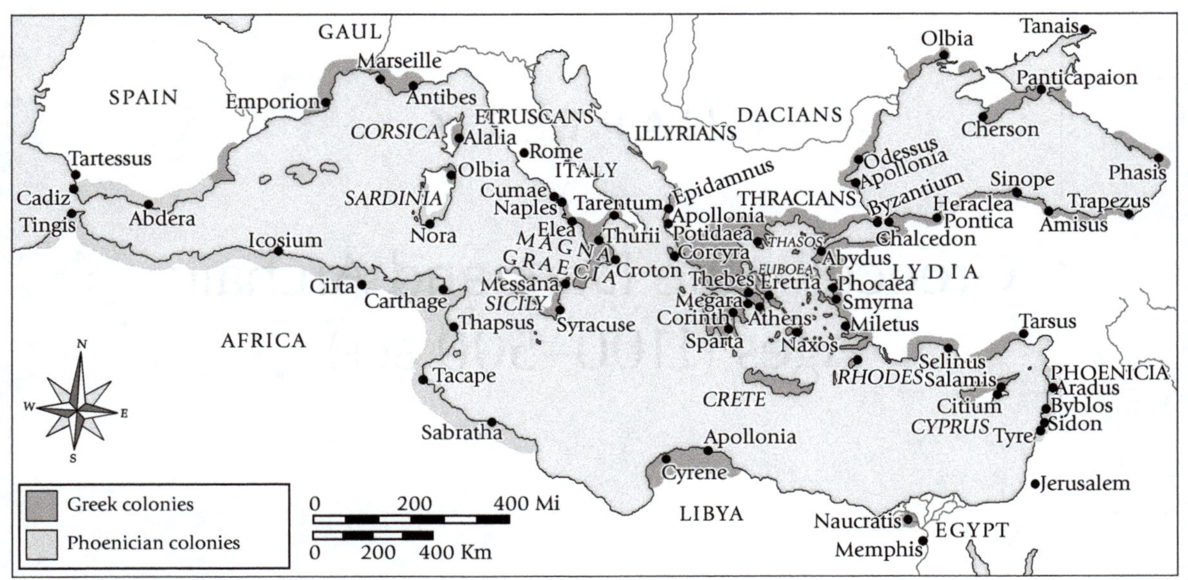

Map 6 Greek Colonization during the Archaic Age

45

THE TROJAN WAR (CA. 1185 BCE): HOMER, *ILIAD*, BOOK 6, LINES 315–494

On this Athenian black-figured amphora, now in the Vatican Museum, painted ca. 525 BCE by the Exekias painter, the Greek heroes Achilles and Ajax throw dice during some down time during the siege of Troy. The numbers "three" and "four" come from their mouths.

Homer's epic poem the Iliad, the earliest surviving work of western literature, is set at the end of the Mycenaean period, ca. 1175 BCE, and told part of the story of the Greek attack on the city of Troy, picking up when the Greek siege was already well underway and ending before the fall of the city. The poem describes the Greek hero Achilles's rage after King Agamemnon had taken away a favorite concubine, Achilles's subsequent refusal to fight, the death of Achilles's best friend Patroclus, and Achilles's resultant return to battle and his killing of the Trojan hero Hector. Homer's works were central to the development and preservation of Greek concepts of masculinity and aristocratic arētē (virtue). These concepts were especially manifested in warfare, through the actions not only of Mycenaean kings, such as Agamemnon of Mycenae, Menelaus of Sparta, Achilles of Phthia, Odysseus of Ithaca, and Ajax of Salamis, but also of Trojan nobles, such as King Priam and Priam's sons Hector and Paris. The characters manifested their human qualities, as seen in Hector's rebuking of Paris for his reluctance to fight and in his obvious love for his wife Andromache and son Astyanax.

Source: A. T. Murray, trans., *Homer. The Iliad*, Vol. 1 (Cambridge, MA: Harvard University Press, 1924).

Hector went his way to the palace of Alexander,[1] the fair palace that he himself had built with the men that were in that day the best builders in deep-soiled Troy; these had made him a chamber and hall and court hard by the palaces of Priam[2] and Hector in the citadel. There entered in Hector, dear to Zeus, and in his hand he held a spear of eleven cubits, and before him blazed the spear-point of bronze, around which ran a ring of gold. He found Paris in his chamber busied with his beauteous arms, his shield and his corselet, and handling his curved bow, and Argive[3] Helen[4] sat amid her serving-women and appointed to them their glorious handiwork.

And at sight of him Hector rebuked him with words of shame: "Strange man, thou dost not well to nurse this anger in thy heart. Thy people are perishing about the town and the steep wall in battle, and it is because of thee that the battle-cry and the war are ablaze about this city,[5] thou wouldest thyself vent wrath on any other, whomso thou shouldest haply see shrinking from hateful war. Nay, then, rouse thee, lest soon the city blaze with consuming fire." And to him did godlike Alexander make answer, saying: "Hector, seeing that thou dost chide me duly, and not beyond what is due, therefore will I tell thee, and do thou take thought and hearken unto me. Not so much by reason of wrath and indignation against the Trojans sat I in my chamber, but I was minded to yield myself to sorrow. Even now my wife sought to turn my mind with gentle words and urged me to the war, and I, mine own self, deem that it will be better so; victory shifteth from man to man. But come now, tarry a while, let me don my harness of war, or go thy way, and I will follow, and methinks I shall overtake thee."

So said he, and Hector of the flashing helm answered him not a word, but unto him spoke Helen with gentle words: "O Brother of me that am a dog, a contriver of mischief and abhorred of all, I would that on the day when first my mother gave me birth an evil storm-wind had borne me away to some mountain or to the wave of the loud-resounding sea, where the wave might have swept me away or ever these things came to pass. Howbeit, seeing the gods thus ordained these ills, would that I had been wife to a better man, that could feel the indignation of his fellows and their many revilings. But this man's understanding is not now stable, nor ever will be hereafter, of this I deem that he will even reap the fruit. But come now, enter in, and sit thee upon this chair, my brother, because above all others has trouble encompassed thy heart because of shameless me, and the folly of Alexander, on whom Zeus hath brought

[1] An alternate name for Paris, son of Priam and brother of Hector.

[2] The king of Troy.

[3] That is, a native of the city of Argos in Greece.

[4] The former wife of the Greek king Menelaus of Sparta.

[5] It was Paris's kidnaping of Helen that had led to the Trojan War.

an evil doom, that even in days to come we may be a song for men that are yet to be."

Then made answer to her great Hector of the flashing helm: "Bid me not sit, Helen, for all thou lovest me, thou wilt not persuade me. Even now my heart is impatient to bear aid to the Trojans that sorely long for me that am not with them. Nay, but rouse thou this man, and let him of himself make haste, that he may overtake me while yet I am within the city. For I shall go to my home, that I may behold my housefolk, my dear wife, and my infant son, for I know not if any more I shall return home to them again, or if even now the gods will slay me beneath the hands of the Achaeans."[6]

So saying, Hector of the flashing helmet departed, and came speedily to his well-built house. But he found not white-armed Andromache in his halls. She with her child and a fair-robed handmaiden had taken her stand upon the wall, weeping and wailing. Hector hastened from the house back over the same way along the well-built streets. When now he had come to the gate, as he passed through the great city, the Scaean gate, whereby he was minded to go forth to the plain, there came running to meet him his bounteous wife, Andromache, daughter of great-hearted Eëtion,[7] Eëtion that dwelt beneath wooded Placus, in Thebe under Placus, and was Lord over the men of Cilicia,[8] for it was his daughter that bronze-harnessed Hector had to wife. She now met him, and with her came a handmaid bearing in her bosom the tender boy, a mere babe, the well-loved son of Hector, like to a fair star. Him Hector was wont to call Scamandrius, but other men Astyanax.[9]

Then Hector smiled, as he glanced at his boy in silence, but Andromache came close to his side weeping, and clasped his hand and spoke to him, saying: "Ah, my husband, this prowess of thine will be thy doom, neither hast thou any pity for thine infant child nor for hapless me that soon shall be thy widow, for soon will the Achaeans all set upon thee and slay thee.[10] But for me it would be better to go down to the grave if I lose thee, for nevermore shall any comfort be mine, when thou hast met thy fate, but only woes. Neither father have I nor queenly mother. My father verily goodly Achilles slew, for utterly laid he waste the well-peopled city of the Cilicians, even Thebe of lofty gates. He slew Eëtion, yet he despoiled him not, for his soul had awe of that, but he burnt him in his armor, richly prepared, and heaped over him a barrow, and all about were elm-trees planted by nymphs of the mountain, daughters of Zeus who bears the aegis.[11] And the seven brothers that were mine in our halls, all these on the selfsame day entered into the house of Hades, for all were slain by swift-footed, godly Achilles, amid their kine of shambling gait and their white-fleeced sheep. And my mother, that was queen beneath wooded Placus, her brought he hither with the rest of the spoil, but thereafter set her free, when he had taken ransom past counting, and in her father's halls Artemis the archer slew her. Nay, Hector, thou art to me father and queenly mother, thou art brother, and thou art my stalwart husband. Come now, have pity, and remain here on the wall, lest thou make thy child an orphan and thy wife a widow. And for thy host, station it by the wild fig-tree, where the city may best be scaled, and the wall is open to assault. For thrice at this point came the most valiant in company with the two Ajaxes[12] and glorious Idomeneus[13] and the sons of Atreus[14] and the valiant son of

[6] Another name for the Greeks.

[7] The king of Thebe, a city near Troy. He was killed in a raid by Achilles.

[8] Not the Cilicia on the south-eastern Anatolian coast, but another, legendary, Cilicia near Troy.

[9] Because myths and legends survived in different versions, it was not uncommon for the same person to be called by different names.

[10] Andromache prophesizes Hector's death. Her own subsequent fate is discussed in Euripides's play "The Trojan Women," Reading 58.

[11] A shield carried by the gods Zeus and Athena, sometimes depicted bearing the head of the Gorgon that could turn anyone who looked on it into stone.

[12] The two Greek heroes the "Greater" and "Lesser" Ajax.

[13] King of Crete, grandson of King Minos.

[14] The son of Pelops and Hippodameia (see Reading 51) and the father of Agamemnon, king of Mycenae and/or Argos, and Menelaus, king of Sparta.

Tydeus,[15] and made essay to enter: whether it be that one well-skilled in soothsaying told them, or haply their own spirit urges and bids them there."

Then spoke to her great Hector of the flashing helm, "Woman, I too take thought of all this, but wondrously have I shame of the Trojans, and the Trojans' wives, with trailing robes, if like a coward I skulk apart from the battle. Nor doth mine own heart suffer it, seeing I have learnt to be valiant always and to fight amid the foremost Trojans, striving to win my father's great glory and mine own. For of a surety know I this in heart and soul: the day shall come when sacred Ilios[16] shall be laid low, and Priam, and the people of Priam with goodly spear of ash. Yet not so much doth the grief of the Trojans that shall be in the aftertime move me, neither Hecuba's[17] own, nor king Priam's, nor my brethren's, many and brave, who then shall fall in the dust beneath the hands of their foemen, as doth thy grief, when some brazen-coated Achaean shall lead thee away weeping and rob thee of thy day of freedom.[18] Then haply in Argos shalt thou ply the loom at another's bidding, or bear water from Messeis or Hypereia,[19] sorely against thy will, and strong necessity shall be laid upon thee. And some man shall say as he beholdeth thee weeping: 'Lo, the wife of Hector, that was pre-eminent in war above all the horse-taming Trojans, in the day when men fought about Ilios.' So shall one say, and to thee shall come fresh grief in thy lack of a man like me to ward off the day of bondage. But let me be dead, and let the heaped-up earth cover me, ere I hear thy cries as they hale thee into captivity."

So saying, glorious Hector stretched out his arms to his boy, but back into the bosom of his fair-girdled nurse shrank the child crying, affrighted at the aspect of his dear father, and seized with dread of the bronze and the crest of horse-hair, as he marked it waving dreadfully from the top of the helmet. Aloud then laughed his dear father and queenly mother, and forthwith glorious Hector took the helm from his head and laid it all-gleaming upon the ground. But he kissed his dear son, and fondled him in his arms, and spoke in prayer to Zeus and the other gods: "Zeus and ye other gods, grant that this my child may likewise prove, even as I, pre-eminent amid the Trojans, and as valiant in might, and that he rule mightily over Ilios. And some day may some man say of him as he cometh back from war, 'He is better far than his father,' and may he bear the blood-stained spoils of the foeman he hath slain, and may his mother's heart wax glad."

So saying, he laid his child in his dear wife's arms, and she took him to her fragrant bosom, smiling through her tears, and her husband was touched with pity at sight of her, and he stroked her with his hand, and spoke to her, saying: "Dear wife, in no wise, I pray thee, grieve overmuch at heart; no man beyond my fate shall send me forth to Hades; only his doom, methinks, no man hath ever escaped, be he coward or valiant, when once he hath been born. Nay, go thou to the house and busy thyself with thine own tasks, the loom and the distaff, and bid thy handmaids ply their work: but war shall be for men, for all, but most of all for me, of them that dwell in Ilios." So spoke glorious Hector and took up his helm with horse-hair crest, and his dear wife went forthwith to her house, oft turning back, and shedding great tears.

---

[15] The Greek hero Diomedes, later King of Argos.

[16] A poetic name for Troy.

[17] The wife of Priam, King of Troy.

[18] Exactly what happened; see Reading 58.

[19] The names of two springs at Argos in Greece.

46

THE "DORIAN INVASION" AND THE ORIGIN OF THE GREEK PEOPLES (CA. 1100 BCE): HERODOTUS, *HISTORIES*, BOOK 1, CHAPTERS 55–58

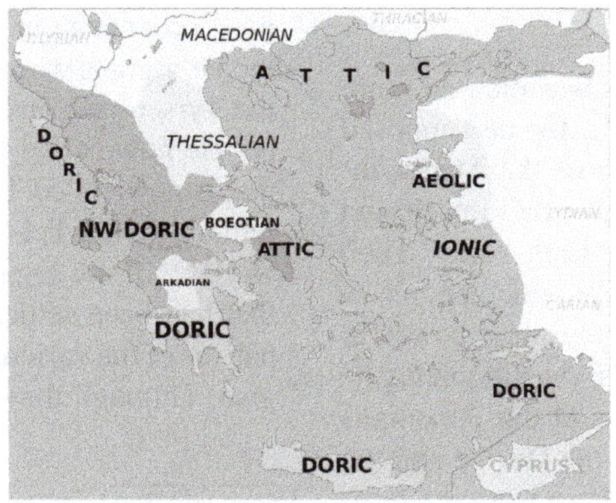

Little material evidence remains for the migration of the "Dorians" into southern Greece. Linguistic evidence, however, does attest to the movements of peoples. By the time ancient Greece entered the historical period in the eighth century BCE, speakers of originally northern Dorian dialects of Greek had moved south to inhabit the Peloponnesus, Crete, and even southern Ionia. Ionic, Aeolic, and Attic speakers, representing the earlier Mycenaean populations, had been either pushed aside or forced to migrate to Ionia.

The Greek historian Herodotus, writing in Athens around 430 BCE, gives a general account of the events termed "the Dorian Invasions," presenting them as transfers of populations. The Dorians' original home, he suggests, was in northern central Greece next to Thessaly. The Ionian people, he proposes, were descended from an original "Pelasgian" population. In his discussion of the origins of Greek peoples, Herodotus too uses the evidence of languages. Herodotus has been called "the father of history" because of his practice of assembling evidence and then analyzing it. At the same time, however, he, like Greek tragedians, placed heavy weight on fulfilling the will of the gods.

Source: George Rawlinson, Henry Rawlinson, and John Gardner Wilkinson, trans., *The History of Herodotus. A New English Version* (London: Murray, 1862).

And having made presents to the men of Delphi, Croesus[20] consulted the Oracle the third time, for from the time when he learnt the truth of the Oracle, he made abundant use of it. And consulting the Oracle he inquired whether his monarchy would endure for a long time. And the Pythian prophetess[21] answered him thus:

> But when it cometh to pass that a mule of the Medes shall be monarch
> Then by the pebbly Hermos, O Lydian delicate-footed,
> Flee and stay not, and be not ashamed to be callèd a coward.

When they came to him, Croesus was pleased more by these lines than by all the rest, for he supposed that a mule would never be ruler of the Medes instead of a man, and accordingly that he himself and his heirs would never cease from their rule.[22] Then after this he gave thought to inquire which people of the Hellenes[23] he should esteem the most powerful and gain over to himself as friends. And inquiring he found that the Lacedemonians[24] and the Athenians had the pre-eminence, the first of the Dorian and the others of the Ionian people. For these were the most eminent peoples in ancient time, the second being a Pelasgian[25] and the first a Hellenic people. The one never migrated from its place in any direction, whereas the other[26] was very exceedingly given to wanderings, for in the reign of Deucalion[27] this people dwelt in Phthiotis,[28] and in the time of Dorus[29] the son of Hellen[30] in the land lying below Ossa and Olympus, which is called Histiaiotis,[31] and when it was driven from Histiaiotis by the sons of Cadmus, it dwelt in Pindus[32] and was called Makednian,[33] and thence it moved afterward to Dryopis,[34] and from Dryopis it came finally to Peloponnesus, and began to be called Dorian.

What language however the Pelasgians used to speak I am not able with certainty to say. But if one must pronounce judging by those that still remain of the Pelasgians who dwelt in the city of Creston above the Tyrsenians, and who were once neighbors of the people now called Dorian, dwelling then in the land that is now called Thessaliotis, and also by those that remain of the Pelasgians who settled at Plakia and Skylake in the region of the Hellespont, who before that had been settlers with the Athenians, and of the natives of the various other towns that are really Pelasgian, although they have lost the name. If one must

[20] King of Lydia in the mid-sixth century BCE, Croesus often consulted the oracle of Apollo at Delphi in north-central Greece. As a result of a misunderstood oracle, he went to war with the Persian king Cyrus in 548, was defeated, and lost his kingdom.

[21] The prophetress of Apollo at the temple at Delphi.

[22] Croesus did not realize that the "mule" was the Persian king Cyrus, who had a Mede for a mother and a Persian for a father; see Reading 48.

[23] Greeks.

[24] An alternate name for Spartans.

[25] In Greek legend, an indigenous people who inhabited Greece before the arrival of the Greeks.

[26] The Dorians.

[27] For the story of Deucalion, see Reading 8.

[28] Phthiotis was a region in central Greece ruled by Achilles.

[29] The eponymous founder of the Dorian people.

[30] King of northern Greece; a son of Deucalion.

[31] A region of Thessaly in northern Greece.

[32] The Pindus mountain range between Thessaly and Epirus.

[33] The ancient homeland of the Macedonians.

[34] A region between southern Thessaly and Aetolia in northern Greece.

pronounce judging by these, the Pelasgians used to speak a barbarian language. If therefore all the Pelasgian people was such as these, then the Attic people, being Pelasgian, at the same time when it changed and became Hellenic, unlearnt also its language. For the people of Creston do not speak the same language with any of those who dwell about them, nor yet do the people of Phakia, but they speak the same language one as the other: and by this it is proved that they still keep unchanged the form of language that they brought with them when they migrated to these places.

As for the Hellenic people, it has used ever the same language, as I clearly perceive, since it first took its rise, but since the time when it parted off feeble at first from the Pelasgian people, setting forth from a small beginning it has increased to that great number of peoples that we see, and chiefly because many barbarian peoples have been added to it besides. Moreover it is true, as I think, of the Pelasgian people also, that so far as it remained barbarian it never made any great increase.

47

HUMAN SOCIETY IN THE EARLY ARCHAIC AGE (CA. 700 BCE): HESIOD, *WORKS AND DAYS*, LINES 1–736

In a miniature self-portrait on the edge of one of his pots, a potter shows himself and his assistant at work at a potter's wheel in Athens, ca. 535 BCE.

The Works and Days is a didactic (instructional) poem of some eight hundred lines addressed around 700 BCE by the poet Hesiod, a native of Askra in Boeotia in central Greece, to his brother Perses. It proposes to discuss the nature of human society, including why the Greeks were so beset by strife and conflict. It begins by summarizing the Five Ages of Humans, running from the original Golden Age to the Iron Age of Hesiod's own day, when people are forced to labor continuously in order to survive. Hesiod then proceeds to discuss the most effective means of pursuing these labors, which revolve around farming. The proper time for performing various agricultural activities is determined by an astronomical calendar. The poem has been interpreted as reflecting an agricultural crisis that resulted in many Greeks leaving Greece for settlements in Ionia during the second wave of Greek colonization, ca. 750–550 BCE.

Source: Hugh G. Evelyn-White, trans. Hesiod, *The Homeric Hymns, and Homerica*, Loeb Classical Library (London: Heinemann, 1914).

Perses, I would tell of true things. There is not one kind of Strife[35] alone, but all over the earth there are two. For one fosters evil war and battle, being cruel: her no man loves. But the other is far kinder to men. She stirs up even the shiftless to toil, for a man grows eager to work when he considers his neighbor, a rich man who hastens to plough and plant and put his house in good order, and neighbor vies with his neighbor as he hurries after wealth. This Strife is wholesome for men. And potter is angry with potter, and craftsman with craftsman, and beggar is jealous of beggar, and minstrel of minstrel. Perses, lay up these things in your heart, and do not let that Strife who delights in mischief hold your heart back from work.

Before now human peoples lived on earth remote and free from ills and hard toil and heavy sickness that bring the Fates[36] upon men, for in misery men grow old quickly. First of all the deathless gods who dwell on Olympus made a golden race[37] of mortal men who lived in the time of Cronus[38] when he was reigning in heaven. And they lived like gods without sorrow of heart, remote and free from toil and grief: miserable age rested not on them, but with legs and arms never failing they made merry with feasting beyond the reach of all evils. They dwelt in ease and peace upon their lands with many good things, rich in flocks and loved by the blessed gods.

After earth had covered this generation, they who dwell on Olympus made a second generation that was of silver[39] and less noble by far. It was like the golden race neither in body nor in spirit. A child was brought up at his good mother's side for a hundred years, an utter simpleton, playing childishly in his own home. But when they were full grown, they lived only a little time in sorrow, for they could not keep from wronging one another, nor would they sacrifice on the holy altars of the blessed ones. Then Zeus the son of Cronus was angry and destroyed them, because they would not give honor to the blessed gods who live on Olympus.

When earth had covered this generation also, Zeus the Father made a third generation of mortal

[35] Strife, personified as the goddess Eris, was driven by the obsession of Greek men with competition and was the bane of Greek existence. It beset Greek society on all levels, ranging from personal interactions to relations between Greek cities.

[36] Goddesses depicted as elderly women who control human destiny: Clotho spun the thread of life, Lachesis measured how long it would be, and Atropos cut it off at the end.

[37] The Golden Age.

[38] A Titan, known to the Romans as Saturn, who castrated his father Uranus with a sickle and became king of the gods. The time of Cronus's rule was known as the "Golden Age." Cronus, in turn, was overthrown by his own son Zeus, who imprisoned most of the Titans in Tartarus in the underworld. See Readings 5 and 6.

[39] The Silver Age.

men, a bronze race,[40] sprung from ash-trees, and it was in no way equal to the Silver Age, but was terrible and strong. They loved deeds of violence; they ate no bread, but were hard of heart. Great was their strength and unconquerable the arms that grew from their shoulders on their strong limbs. Their armor was of bronze, and their houses of bronze, and of bronze were their implements: there was no black iron. These were destroyed by their own hands and passed to the dank house of chill Hades.[41]

When earth had covered this generation also, Zeus the son of Cronus made yet another, the fourth, upon the fruitful earth, which was nobler and more righteous, a god-like race of hero-men who are called demi-gods,[42] the race before our own, throughout the boundless earth. Grim war and dread battle destroyed a part of them, some when it had brought them in ships over the great sea gulf to Troy for rich-haired Helen's sake. But to the others father Zeus the son of Cronus gave a living and an abode apart from men, and made them dwell at the ends of earth in the Islands of the Blessed[43] along the shore of deep swirling Ocean. And these equally have honor and glory.

And again far-seeing Zeus made yet another generation, the fifth, of men who are upon the bounteous earth. Thereafter, would that I were not among the men of the fifth generation, but either had died before or been born afterward. For now truly is a race of iron,[44] and men never rest from labor and sorrow by day, and from perishing by night, and the gods shall lay sore trouble upon them. The father will not agree with his children, nor the children with their father, nor guest with his host, nor comrade with comrade, nor will brother be dear to brother as aforetime. Men will dishonor their parents as they grow quickly old, and will carp at them, chiding them with bitter words, hard-hearted they, not knowing the fear of the gods. They will not repay their aged parents the cost of their nurture, for might shall be their right: and one man will sack another's city. There will be no favor for the man who keeps his oath or for the just or for the good, but rather men will praise the evil-doer and his violent dealing. Strength will be right and reverence will cease to be, and the wicked will hurt the worthy man, speaking false words against him, and will swear an oath upon them. Envy, foul-mouthed, delighting in evil, with scowling face, will go along with wretched men one and all.

But you, Perses, listen to right and do not foster violence, for violence is bad for a poor man. Even the prosperous person cannot easily bear its burden, but is weighed down under it when he has fallen into delusion. The better path is to go by on the other side toward Justice, for Justice beats Outrage when she comes at length to the end of the race. But for those who practice violence and cruel deeds far-seeing Zeus, the son of Cronus, ordains a punishment.[45] You princes, mark well this punishment, for the deathless gods are near among men and mark all those who oppress their fellows with crooked judgments, and consider not the anger of the gods.

The eye of Zeus, seeing all and understanding all, beholds these things too, if so he will, and fails not to mark what sort of justice is this that the city keeps within it. Now, therefore, may neither I myself be righteous among men, nor my son —for then it is a bad thing to be righteous —if indeed the unrighteous shall have the greater right. But I think that all-wise Zeus will not yet bring that to pass. The son of Cronus has ordained this law for men, that whoever knows the right and is ready to speak it, far-seeing Zeus gives him prosperity, but whoever deliberately lies in his witness and forswears himself, and so hurts Justice and sins beyond repair, that man's generation is left obscure thereafter. Badness can be got easily and in shoals. The road to her is smooth, and she lives very near us. But between us and Goodness the gods have placed the sweat of our brows: long and steep is

[40] The Bronze Age.

[41] The underworld.

[42] The Heroic Age, the only age not named after a metal.

[43] The "Hesperides," sometimes identified as the Canary Islands or the Azores in the Atlantic Ocean.

[44] The Iron Age, the worst of all the ages.

[45] The theme that the gods punish those who do not obey their will ran throughout Greek culture, and is seen, for example, in the *Histories* of Herodotus and in Greek tragedies.

the path that leads to her, and it is rough at the first, but when a man has reached the top, then is she easy to reach, although before that she was hard.

Work is no disgrace; it is idleness that is a disgrace. But if you work, the idle will soon envy you as you grow rich, for fame and renown attend on wealth. And whatever be your lot, work is best for you, if you turn your misguided mind away from other men's property to your work and attend to your livelihood as I bid you. An evil shame is the needy man's companion, shame that both greatly harms and prospers men: shame is with poverty, but confidence with wealth. Do not let a flaunting woman coax and cozen and deceive you: she is after your barn. The man who trusts womankind trust deceivers. There should be an only son, to feed his father's house, for so wealth will increase in the home, but if you leave a second son you should die old. Yet Zeus can easily give great wealth to a greater number. More hands mean more work and more increase.

[Then there follows advice on farming]

When the Pleiades,[46] daughters of Atlas,[47] are rising, begin your harvest, and your ploughing when they are going to set. Forty nights and days they are hidden and appear again as the year moves round, when first you sharpen your sickle. This is the law of the plains, and of those who live near the sea, and who inhabit rich country, the glens and vales far from the tossing sea: strip to sow and strip to plough and strip to reap, if you wish to get in all Demeter's[48] fruits in due season. Else, afterward, you may chance to be in want, and go begging to other men's houses, but without avail; as you have already come to me. But I will give you no more nor give you further measure. Foolish Perses! Work the work that the gods ordained for men, lest in bitter anguish of spirit you with your wife and children seek your livelihood among your neighbors, and they do not heed you. Two or three times, maybe, you will succeed, but if you trouble them further, it will not avail you, and all your talk will be in vain. Nay, I bid you find a way to pay your debts and avoid hunger.

First of all, get a house, and a woman and an ox for the plough, a slave woman and not a wife, to follow the oxen as well, and make everything ready at home. Do not put your work off until to-morrow, for a sluggish worker does not fill his barn. When the piercing power and sultry heat of the sun abate, and almighty Zeus sends the autumn rains, the wood you cut with your axe is least liable to worm. Get two ploughs ready and work on them at home, one all of a piece, and the other jointed. It is far better to do this, for if you should break one of them, you can put the oxen to the other. Get two oxen, bulls of nine years, for their strength is unspent and they are in the prime of their age: they are best for work. Let a brisk fellow of forty years[49] follow them, with a loaf of four quarters and eight slices for his dinner. No younger man will be better than he at scattering the seed and avoiding double-sowing.

As soon as the time for ploughing is proclaimed, then make haste, you and your slaves alike, in wet and in dry, to plough in the season for ploughing, and bestir yourself early in the morning so that your fields may be full. Plough in the spring, but fallow[50] and broken up in the summer will not belie your hopes. Let a slave follow a little behind with a mattock and make trouble for the birds by hiding the seed, for good management is the best for mortal men as bad management is the worst. In this way your grain-ears will bow to the ground with fullness. But if you plough the good ground at the solstice,[51] you will reap sitting, grasping a thin crop in your hand, binding the sheaves awry, dust-covered, not glad at all, so you will bring all home in a basket and not many will admire you.

Stop by the blacksmith and its crowded lounge in winter time when the cold keeps men from field work. While it is yet midsummer command your

[46] Commemorated by the star cluster of the same name, which in Hesiod's time began rising the first week in May.

[47] The son of the Titan Iapetus, Atlas held up the sky.

[48] The goddess of grain; Ceres to the Romans.

[49] Presumably a slave.

[50] Land that is not sown with crops but is given time to recover its fertility.

[51] The summer solstice, 21 June, the longest day of the year.

slaves: "It will not always be summer, build barns." Set your slaves to winnow[52] Demeter's holy grain, when strong Orion[53] first appears, on a smooth threshing-floor in an airy place. Then measure it and store it in jars. And so soon as you have safely stored all your grain indoors, I bid you put your bondman[54] out of doors and look for a servant-girl with no children, for a servant with a child to nurse is troublesome. Bring in fodder and litter so as to have enough for your oxen and mules. After that, let your men rest their poor knees and unyoke your pair of oxen.

Bring home a wife to your house when you are of the right age, while you are not far short of thirty years nor much above; this is the right age for marriage. Let your wife have been grown up four years[55] and marry her in the fifth. Marry a maiden,[56] so that you can teach her careful ways, and especially marry one who lives near you, but look well about you and see that your marriage will not be a joke to your neighbors. For a man wins nothing better than a good wife, and, again, nothing worse than a bad one, a greedy soul who roasts her man without fire and brings him to a raw old age.

Do not stand upright facing the sun when you make water,[57] but remember to do this when it has set, toward its rising. And do not make water as you go, whether on the road or off the road, and do not uncover yourself: the nights belong to the blessed gods. A scrupulous man who has a wise heart sits down or goes to the wall of an enclosed court. Do not expose yourself befouled by the fireside in your house, but avoid this. Do not beget children when you are come back from an ill-omened burial, but after a festival of the gods.

[52] To remove the chaff from the grain, but only after the harvested stalks had been allowed to dry for more than a month.

[53] A constellation named after a gigantic mythological hunter, the son of Poseidon and the Gorgon Euryale; in Greece, Orion began to rise in mid-June.

[54] That is, the plow man already mentioned. Moving him out would make room for the servant girl.

[55] After puberty, or about seventeen years old.

[56] That is, a virgin.

[57] Urinate.

48

BATTUS AND THE FOUNDING OF CYRENE (CA. 630 BCE): HERODOTUS, *HISTORIES*, BOOK 4, SECTIONS 145–159

A Laconian (Spartan) black-figured kylix (wide drinking cup) dated to 560–550 BCE depicts King Arcesilaus I (ca. 600–580 BCE) of the Greek trading colony of Cyrene in Libya, the son of Battus, sitting on the deck of a merchant chip and overseeing the weighing of silphium, the main product of Cyrene, which is put but below deck. Silphium was used as a condiment and for medicinal purposes, for coughs, and as a contraceptive.

During the first wave of Greek colonization, ca. 750–550 BCE, Greek cities sent colonists out to found new cities on the shores of the Mediterranean and Black seas. Hundreds of independent new cities thus were created, all replications of the cities back on mainland Greece. The process by which colonies were established is depicted in the historian Herodotus's account, written in Athens in the mid-fifth century BCE, of the founding of the city of Cyrene on the coast of Libya in the 630s BCE.

Source: George Rawlinson, Henry Rawlinson, and John Gardner Wilkinson, trans., *The History of Herodotus. A New English Version* (London: Murray, 1862).

About this very time another great expedition was undertaken against Libya. Grinus, the son of Aesanius, a descendent of Theras and king of the island of Thera,[58] went to Delphi to offer a hecatomb[59] on behalf of his native city. He was accompanied by a large number of the citizens, and among the rest by Battus, the son of Polymnestus. On Grinus consulting the Oracle about sundry matters, the Pythoness[60] gave him for answer that he should found a city in Libya. Grinus replied to this, "I am too far advanced in years for such a work. Bid one of these youngsters undertake it." As he spoke, he pointed toward Battus. When the embassy returned to Thera, small account was taken of the oracle by the Theraeans, as they were quite ignorant where Libya was, and were not so venturesome as to send out a colony in the dark.

Seven years passed from the utterance of the oracle, and not a drop of rain fell in Thera: all the trees in the island, except one, were killed with the drought. The Theraeans upon this sent to Delphi, and were reminded reproachfully that they had never colonized Libya. They of Thera resolved that men should be sent to join the colony and Battus was chosen to be king and leader of the colony. The Theraeans sent out Battus with two penteconters, and with these he proceeded to Libya, but, not knowing what else to do, the men returned and arrived off Thera. The Theraeans received them with showers of missiles and ordered them to sail back from whence they came. Thus compelled to return, they settled on an island near the Libyan coast, which was called Plataea.

In this place they continued two years, but at the end of that time, as ill luck followed them, they left the island to the care of one of their number, and went to Delphi, where they made complaint at the shrine to the effect that, notwithstanding they had colonized Libya, they prospered as poorly as before. The Pythoness in reply told them that if they and Battus would make a settlement at Cyrene[61] in Libya, things would go better with them. Battus and his friends, when they heard this, sailed back to Plataea: it was plain the god would not hold them acquitted of the colony until they were absolutely in Libya. So, taking with them the man whom they had left upon the island, they made a settlement on the mainland directly opposite Plataea, fixing themselves at a place called Aziris,[62] which is closed in on both sides by the most beautiful hills, and on one side is washed by a river.

Here they remained six years, at the end of which time the Libyans induced them to move, promising that they would lead them to a better situation. So the Greeks left Aziris and were conducted by the Libyans toward the west, their journey being so arranged, by the calculation of their guides, that they passed in the night the most beautiful district of that whole country, which is the region called Irasa. The Libyans brought them to a spring, which goes by the name of Apollo's fountain,[63] and told them, "Here,

[58] Modern Santorini; the Minoan colony on Thera was destroyed by a volcanic eruption ca. 1500 BCE.

[59] A sacrifice of a hundred oxen.

[60] The priestess at the temple of Apollo at Delphi. The oracle often was consulted about the foundation of colonies.

[61] On the Mediterranean coast just west of Egypt.

[62] In eastern Cyrenaica.

[63] A fountain that provided water for the city of Cyrene.

Greeks, is the proper place for you to settle, for here the sky leaks."

During the lifetime of Battus, the founder of the colony, who reigned forty years, and during that of his son Arcesilaus, who reigned sixteen, the Cyrenaeans continued at the same level, neither more nor fewer in number than they were at the first. But in the reign of the third king, Battus, surnamed the Happy, the advice of the Pythoness brought Greeks from every quarter into Libya, to join the settlement. The Cyrenaeans had offered to all comers a share in their lands, for the Oracle had spoken as follows:

> He that is backward to share in the pleasant Libyan acres,
> Sooner or later, I warn him, will feel regret at his folly.

49

PERSONAL POETRY (CA. 600 BCE): SAPPHO OF LESBOS

An Athenian red-figured kalathos (bowl) of around 470 BCE depicts the poet Alcaeus, holding a lyre, and Sappho. The two were reputed to have been lovers.

In the early seventh century BCE, Greeks began to write lyric poetry, which gets its name because it was sung to playing on a lyre, as a means of self-centered personal expression that stressed the value of the individual. One finds, for example, descriptions of heterosexual and homosexual love that look surprisingly modern. One of the most famous lyric poets was Sappho of Lesbos, who wrote ca. 600 BCE. Soon after 600 she was exiled to Sicily for unknown reasons. Only a few examples of her poetry still survive, mostly embedded in the works of other authors.

Source: Ambrose Philips, trans., in William Hyde Appleton, ed., *Greek Poets in English Verse* (Cambridge, MA: Riverside Press, 1893).

"Ode to a Loved One"

Blest as the immortal gods is he,
The youth who fondly sits by thee,
And hears and sees thee, all the while,
Softly speaks and sweetly smiles.

'Twas this deprived my soul of rest,
And raised such tumults in my breast,
For, while I gazed, in transport tossed,
My breath was gone, my voice was lost,

My bosom glowed; the subtle flame
Ran quick through all my vital frame;
Over my dim eyes a darkness hung;
My ears with hollow murmurs rung;

In dewy damps my limbs were chilled;
My blood with gentle horrors thrilled:
My feeble pulse forgot to play;
I fainted, sank, and died away.

"The Moon"

The stars about the lovely moon
Fade back and vanish very soon,
When, round and full, her silver face
Swims into sight, and lights all space

"Hymn to Aphrodite"

Throned in splendor, immortal Aphrodite!
Child of Zeus, Enchantress, I implore thee
Slay me not in this distress and anguish,
Lady of beauty.

Hither come as once before thou camest,
When from afar thou heard'st my voice
lamenting,
Heard'st and camest, leaving thy glorious father's
Palace golden,
Yoking thy chariot. Fair the doves that bore thee,
Swift to the darksome earth their course
directing,
Waving their thick wings from the highest
heaven
Down through the ether.

Quickly they came. Then thou, O blessed
goddess,
All in smiling wreathed thy face immortal,
Bade me tell thee the cause of all my suffering,
Why now I called thee;

What for my maddened heart I most was
longing.
"Whom," thou criest, "dost wish that sweet
Persuasion
Now win over and lead to thy love, my Sappho?
Who is it wrongs thee?

For, although now he flies, he soon shall follow,
Soon shall be giving gifts who now rejects them.
Even though now he love not, soon shall he
love thee
Even though thou wouldst not."

Come then now, dear goddess, and release me
From my anguish. All my heart's desiring
Grant thou now. Now too again as aforetime,
Be thou my ally.

"Song of the Rose"

If Zeus chose us a King of the Flowers in
his mirth,
He would call to the rose, and would royally
crown it,

For the rose, ho, the rose! is the grace of the earth,
Is the light of the plants that are growing upon it!
For the rose, ho, the rose! is the eye of the flowers,
Is the blush of the meadows that feel themselves fair,
Is the lightning of beauty that strikes through the bowers
On pale lovers that sit in the glow unaware.
Ho, the rose breathes of love! ho, the rose lifts the cup
To the red lips of Cypris[64] invoked for a guest!
Ho, the rose having curled its sweet leaves for the world
Takes delight in the motion its petals keep up,
As they laugh to the wind as it laughs from the west.

"To Evening"

O Hesperus![65] Thou bringest all things home;
All that the garish day hath scattered wide;
The sheep, the goat, back to the welcome fold;
Thou bring'st the child, too, to his mother's side.

50

THE PRE-SOCRATIC PHILOSOPHERS (CA. 530 BCE): PORPHYRY, *THE LIFE OF PYTHAGORAS*

A Roman copy of a Greek bust of Pythagoras now in the Capitoline Museum in Rome.

[64]Another name for the love goddess Aphrodite, who came from Cyprus.
[65]The evening star; the planet Venus.

The Archaic Age also saw the rise of Greek scientific thought known as "philosophia" ("love of wisdom," or philosophy), influenced by contact with the astronomical and mathematical thought of the much more ancient civilization of Babylonia. Ionian pre-Socratic philosophers (who lived before the famous philosopher Socrates of Athens), several of whom came from Miletus, a major point of commercial contact with the Near East, speculated on issues such as cosmogony (the creation and composition of matter and the universe) and the nature of the gods. Rather than attributing the origin of the universe and the world to the activities of gods, as in mythology, philosophers looked for rational explanations that usually did not involve gods directly at all. Pythagoras of Samos, who, like many Ionians fled the Persians and migrated to Croton in southern Italy ca. 530 BCE, understood the universe in terms of mathematical harmony. He not only invented the Pythagorean Theorem, used for calculating the lengths of the sides of triangles, but also believed in reincarnation. The extracts presented here are from the "Life of Pythagoras" written in the late third century CE by the Neoplatonic philosopher Porphyry of Tyre, who, like Pythagoras, was a committed vegetarian.

Source: Kenneth Sylvan Guthrie, trans., *Pythagoras: Source Book and Library* (Alpine, NJ: Platonist Press, 1920).

Many think that Pythagoras was the son of Mnesarchus, but they differ as to the latter's origin, some thinking him a Samian,[66] while Neanthes, in the fifth book of his *Fables*, states he was a Syrian, from the city of Tyre.[67] It is said that he learned the mathematical sciences from the Egyptians, Chaldeans,[68] and Phoenicians, for of old the Egyptians excelled in geometry, the Phoenicians in numbers and proportions, and the Chaldeans in astronomical theorems, divine rites, and worship of the gods. Other secrets concerning the course of life he received and learned from the Magi.[69] Pythagoras used the greatest purity, and was shocked at all bloodshed and killing, so that he not only abstained from animal food, but never in any way approached butchers or hunters. He opened in his own country a school, which even now is called Pythagoras's Semicircles, in which the Samians meet to deliberate about matters of common interest. Outside the city he made a cave adapted to the study of his philosophy, in which he abode day and night, discoursing with a few of his associates. He was now forty years old, says Aristoxenus.[70]

When the Samians were oppressed with the tyranny of Polycrates,[71] Pythagoras saw that life in such a state was unsuitable for a philosopher, and so planned to travel to Italy. When he reached Italy he stopped at Croton.[72] His presence was that of a free man, tall, graceful in speech and gesture, and in all things else. The arrival of this great traveler, endowed with all the advantages of nature, and prosperously guided by fortune, produced on the Crotonians so great an impression that he won the esteem of the elder magistrates by his many and excellent discourses. They ordered him to exhort the young men, and then the boys who flocked out of the school to hear him, and lastly the women, who came together on purpose. Through this he achieved great reputation, he drew great audiences from the city, not only of men, but also of women, among whom was an especially illustrious person named Theano.[73] He also drew audiences from among the neighboring barbarians,[74] among whom were magnates and kings. What he told his audiences cannot be said

[66] That is, from the island of Samos in the eastern Aegean Sea.

[67] In Phoenicia.

[68] Or New Babylonians, known for their expertise in astronomy.

[69] The Zoroastrian priests of the Persians

[70] A Greek philosopher and pupil of Aristotle.

[71] The tyrant of Samos ca. 538 to 522 BCE.

[72] A Greek colony from Achaea in Calabria on the southern coast of Italy.

[73] A philosopher of Croton, said by some to have been Pythagoras's wife.

[74] The native peoples of Italy.

with certainty, for he enjoined silence upon his hearers. But the following is a matter of general information. He taught that the soul was immortal and that after death it transmigrated into other animated bodies. After certain specified periods, the same events occur again, so that nothing was entirely new. He taught that all animated beings were kin, and should be considered as belonging to one great family. Pythagoras was the first one to introduce these teachings into Greece.

His speech was so persuasive that he made more than two thousand adherents. Out of desire to live with him, they built a large auditorium, to which both women and boys were admitted. His ordinances and laws were received by them as divine precepts, and without them they would do nothing. Indeed, they ranked him among the divinities. They held all property in common. During his travels in Italy and Sicily he founded various cities. By his disciples he infused into them an aspiration for liberty, thus restoring to freedom Croton, Sybaris, Catana, Rhegium, Himera, Agrigentum, Tauromenium, and others,[75] on whom he imposed laws through Charondas the Catanean,[76] and Zaleucus the Locrian,[77] which resulted in a long era of good government, emulated by all their neighbors. Simichus the tyrant of the Centorupini,[78] on hearing Pythagoras's discourse, abdicated his rule and divided his property between his sister and the citizens. Some Lucanians, Messapians, Picentinians,[79] and Romans came to him.

Pythagoras continuously harped on the maxim, "We ought, to the best of our ability avoid, and even extirpate from the body with fire and sword, sickness; from the soul, ignorance; from the belly, luxury; from a city, sedition; from a family, discord; and from all things excess." He reminded his associates of the lives lived by their souls before it was bound to the body, and by irrefutable arguments demonstrated that he had been Euphorbus,[80] the son of Panthous. Verified predictions of earthquakes are handed down, also that he immediately chased a pestilence, suppressed violent winds and hail, and calmed storms both on rivers and on seas for the comfort and safe passage of his friends.

His friends he loved exceedingly, being the first to declare that the goods of friends are common, and that a friend was another self. While they were in good health he always conversed with them; if they were sick, he nursed them; if they were afflicted in mind, he solaced them, some by incantations and magic charms, others by music. His utterances were of two kinds, plain or symbolic. His teaching was twofold: of his disciples some were called Students, and others Hearers. The Students learned the fuller and more exactly elaborate reasons of science, whereas the Hearers heard only the chief heads of learning, without more detailed explanations.

He cultivated philosophy, the scope of which is to free the mind implanted within us from the impediments and fetters within which it is confined, without whose freedom none can learn anything sound or true, or perceive the unsoundedness in the operation of sense. Pythagoras thought that the mind alone sees and hears, whereas all the rest are blind and deaf. That is the reason he made so much use of mathematical disciplines and speculations, which are intermediate between the physical and the incorporeal realm. Like bodies, mathematical disciplines have a threefold dimension and yet they share the impassibility of incorporeals. As degrees of preparation for the contemplation of the really existent things, by an artificial reason they divert the eyes of the mind from corporeal things, whose manner and state never remain in the same condition, to a desire for true[81] food. By means of these mathematical sciences therefore, Pythagoras rendered men truly happy, by this artistic introduction of truly consistent things. The Pythagoreans specialized in the study of numbers to explain their teachings symbolically, as

[75] Cities in southern Italy and Sicily that previously had been governed by tyrants or by other cities.

[76] From Catania in Sicily.

[77] From Locri in southern Italy.

[78] A people of Sicily.

[79] Peoples of Italy.

[80] A Trojan who was killed by the Greek hero Menelaus during the Trojan War.

[81] That is, spiritual.

do geometricians, inasmuch as the primary forms and principles are hard to understand and express, otherwise, in plain discourse.

Pythagoras and his associates were long held in such admiration in Italy, so that many cities invited them to undertake their administration. At last, however, they incurred envy, and a conspiracy was formed against them as follows. Cylon, a Crotonian, who in origin, nobility, and wealth was the most pre-eminent, was of a severe, violent, and tyrannical disposition, and did not scruple to use the multitude of his followers to achieve his ends. As he esteemed himself worthy of whatever was best, he considered it his right to be admitted to Pythagorean fellowship. He therefore went to Pythagoras extolled himself, and desired his conversation. Pythagoras, however, who was accustomed to read in human bodies' nature and manners the disposition of the man, bade him depart and go about his business. Cylon, being of a rough and violent disposition, took it as a great affront, and became furious. He therefore assembled his friends, began to accuse Pythagoras, and conspired against him and his disciples. Pythagoras then went to Delos[82] to visit the Syrian Pherecydes,[83] formerly his teacher, who was dangerously sick, to nurse him. Pythagoras's friends then gathered together in the house of Milo[84] the wrestler, and were all stoned and burned when Cylon's followers set the house on fire. Only two escaped. Pythagoras fled to the temple of the Muses, in Metapontum.[85] There he abode forty days, and starving, died.

[82] A small island in the south-central Aegean Sea.

[83] A philosopher from the island of Syros who was among the first to teach of the transmigration of souls, the belief popularized by Pythagoras.

[84] The winner of the Olympic wrestling matches six times and of the "grand slam" of victories at all four of the pan-Hellenic games five times in a row.

[85] A Greek colony from Achaea on the Gulf of Tarentum on the southern coast of Italy.

51

GREEK ARĒTĒ (CA. 476 BCE): PINDAR, "OLYMPIAN ODE" 1

An Athenian black-figured amphora depicts two bareback riders in the Olympic horse race. Preserved in the Tampa Museum of Art.

The last and greatest of the Greek lyric poets was Pindar of Thebes, who was born around 522 BCE. In the first half of the fifth century BCE, he composed choral lyric, in an archaic style, on the topic of "arētē,"or excellence and dealing with the uncertainties and the glories of life. His "Victory odes," accompanied by music and dance, praised the achievements of distinguished winners at the Panhellenic games, whose victories had been aided by the gods. The odes are full of obscure and convoluted grammar, language, and mythological allusions that attest to their Greek cultural background. No one who was not Greek could possibly understand them. One of these odes honored Hiero I, the tyrant of Syracuse from 478 to 467 BCE, whose horse won the horse race at the Olympic Games at Olympia in 476 BCE.

Source: Ernest Myers, trans., *The Extant Odes of Pindar Translated into English* (London: Macmillan, 1874).

Best is Water of all, and Gold as a flaming fire in the night shineth eminent amid lordly wealth, but if you desire prizes in the games, O my soul, to tell, then, as for no bright star more quickening than the sun must thou search in the void firmament by day, so neither shall we find any games greater than the Olympic whereof to utter our voice. For hence cometh the glorious hymn and entereth into the minds of the skilled in song, so that they celebrate the son[86] of Cronus, when to the rich and happy hearth of Hiero[87] they are come, for he wieldeth the scepter of justice in Sicily of many flocks, culling the choice fruits of all kinds of arētē (excellence), and with the flower of music is he made splendid, even such strains as we sing blithely at the table of a friend.

Take from the peg the Dorian lute, if in any wise the glory of Pherenikus[88] at Pisa[89] hath swayed thy soul unto glad thoughts, when by the banks of Alpheus[90] he ran, and gave his body ungoaded in the course, and brought victory to his master, the Syracusans' king, who delighteth in horses.

Bright is his fame in Lydian Pelops' colony,[91] inhabited by a goodly people, whose founder mighty earth-enfolding[92] Poseidon loved, what time from the vessel of purifying Clotho[93] took him with the bright ivory furnishment of his shoulder.[94] Verily many things are wondrous, and haply tales decked out with cunning fables beyond the truth make false men's speech concerning them. For Charis,[95] who maketh all sweet things for mortal men, by lending honor unto such maketh oft the unbelievable thing to be believed; but the days that follow after are the wisest witnesses.[96] It is fitting for a man that concerning gods he speaks honorably, for the reproach is less. Of thee, son of Tantalus,[97] I will speak contrariwise to them who have gone before me, and I will tell how when thy father had bidden thee to that most seemly feast at his beloved Sipylos,[98] repaying to the gods their banquet, then did he of the Bright Trident,[99] his heart vanquished by love, snatch thee and bear thee behind his golden steeds to the house of august Zeus in the highest, whither again on a like errand came Ganymede[100] in the after time.

But when thou hadst vanished, and the men who sought thee long brought thee not to thy mother, someone of the envious neighbors said secretly that over water heated to boiling they had hewn asunder with a knife thy limbs, and at the tables had shared among them and eaten sodden fragments of thy flesh.[101] But to me it is impossible to call one of the

[86] Greek Zeus, Roman Jupiter.

[87] Tyrant of Syracuse from 478 to 467 BCE.

[88] The name of Hiero's horse.

[89] A city in the northwestern Peloponessus that controlled Olympia, where the Olympic Games were held.

[90] A river in the Peloponessus.

[91] The Peloponessus, named after Pelops, the son of Tantalus.

[92] Along with being god of the sea, Poseidon also was the god of earthquakes.

[93] One of the three Fates, along with Lachesis and Atropos.

[94] In his youth, Pelops was dismembered by his father Tantalus, cooked into a stew, and served to the gods. Only the goddess Demeter took a bite, from his shoulder. When Pelops was reassembled, a piece of ivory was inserted to replace the missing piece.

[95] One of the Charites, or Graces, the goddesses of charm.

[96] Later in the poem Pindar claims that the stew story is false, for Hiero claims descent himself from Tantalus and Pelops.

[97] That is, Pelops.

[98] A mountain in Lydia, the homeland of Pelops.

[99] Poseidon, god of the sea, represented in iconography by a trident.

[100] A Trojan hero who was abducted by Zeus in the form of an eagle. He was granted immortality and served as cupbearer of the gods.

[101] Compare the story of Harpagus in Reading 43.

blessed gods cannibal; I keep aloof; in telling ill tales is often little gain.

Now if any man ever had honor of the guardians of Olympus, Tantalus was that man; but his high fortune he could not digest, and his excess of fortune won him an overwhelming woe, in that the Father[102] hath hung above him a mighty stone that he would gladly ward from his head, and therewithal he is fallen from joy.[103]

This hopeless life of endless misery he endureth with other three, for that he stole from the immortals and gave to his fellows at a feast the nectar and ambrosia, whereby the gods had made him incorruptible. But if a man thinketh that in doing nothing he shall be hidden from god, he erreth.

Therefore also the immortals sent back again his son to be once more counted with the short-lived race of men. And he when toward the bloom of his sweet youth the down began to shade his darkening cheek, he took counsel with himself speedily to take to him for his wife the noble Hippodameia[104] from her Pisan father's hand. And he came and stood upon the margin of the hoary sea, alone in the darkness of the night, and called aloud to the deep-voiced Wielder of the Trident, and he appeared unto him nigh at his foot. Then he said unto him, "Lo now, O Poseidon, if the kind gifts of the Cyprian goddess[105] are anywise pleasant in thine eyes, restrain Oenomäus' bronze spear, and send me unto Elis[106] upon a chariot exceeding swift, and give the victory to my hands.[107] Thirteen lovers already hath Oenomäus slain, and still delayeth to give his daughter in marriage. Now a great peril alloweth not of a coward: and forasmuch as men must die, wherefore should one sit vainly in the dark through a dull and nameless age, and without lot in noble deeds? Not so, but I will dare this strife: do thou give the issue I desire."

Thus spoke he, nor were his words in vain, for the god made him a glorious gift of a golden car and winged untiring steeds. So he overcame Oenomäus and won the maiden for his bride. And he begat six sons, chieftains, whose thoughts were ever of brave deeds, and now hath he his part in honor of blood-offerings at his grave beside Alpheus' stream, and hath a frequented tomb, whereto many strangers resort, and from far off he beholdeth the glory of the Olympian games in the courses called of Pelops, where there is striving of swift feet and of strong bodies brave to labor, and he that overcometh hath for the sake of those games a sweet tranquillity throughout his life for evermore.

Now the good that cometh of today is ever sovereign unto every man. My part it is to crown Hiero with an equestrian strain in Aeolian mood,[108] and sure am I that no host among men that now are shall I ever glorify in sounding labyrinths[109] of song more learned in the learning of honor and withal with more might to work thereto. A god hath guard over thy hopes, O Hiero, and taketh care for them with a peculiar care, and if he fail thee not, I trust that I shall again proclaim in song a sweeter glory yet, and find thereto in words a ready way, when to the fair-shining hill of Cronus I am come. Her strongest-winged dart my Muse hath yet in store. Of many kinds is the greatness of men, but the highest is to be achieved by kings. Look not thou for more than this. May it be thine to walk loftily all thy life, and mine to be the friend of winners in the games, winning honor for my art[110] among Hellenes[111] everywhere.

---

[102] Zeus.

[103] Tantalus, a native of Phrygia in Anatolia, was said to have stolen the ambrosia and nectar of the gods from a banquet to which he had been invited and as a consequence was imprisoned forever in Tartarus, the lowest level of the underworld.

[104] Daughter of Oenomäus, King of Pisa in the western Peloponnesus.

[105] Aphrodite.

[106] The area of Greece around Olympia.

[107] A suitor had to defeat Oenomäus in a chariot race in order to win the hand of the latter's daughter Hippodamaia: all past suitors had been killed for losing the race.

[108] A minor musical key.

[109] Complex passages, as in the labyrinth built at Knossos on Crete to imprison the Minotaur.

[110] Pindar's own form of arētē lay in writing poetry.

[111] Greeks.

52

GREEK TYRANTS: THE SWORD OF DAMOCLES (CA. 360 BCE): CICERO, *TUSCULAN DISPUTATIONS* 5.61, AND SIDONIUS APOLLINARIS, *LETTERS* 2.13

An Athenian vase painting of ca. 470 BCE depicts a tyrant's worst fear. Here, the Athenian tyrant Hipparchus, the son of the tyrant Peisistratus, is assassinated in 514 by Harmodius and Aristogeiton. The murder occurred not for political reasons but as a result of a lovers' quarrel. From the Martin von Wagner Museum, University of Würzburg.

During the Greek Archaic Age (776–500 BCE), newly monied people demanded greater rights from the governing aristocrats. In cities where the aristocrats resisted making any changes at all, it was only a matter of time until there was an overthrow of the state. Disadvantaged groups, including rich merchants, ruined farmers, and the urban poor, would sponsor an illegal ruler called a tyrant, and the period 650–500 BCE is known as the Age of Tyrants because so many Greek cities used this means of dealing with intransigent aristocrats. Not all tyrants were bad, as the modern sense of their name would suggest. There were good tyrants, bad tyrants, and mediocre tyrants. Because tyrants were unconstitutional rulers, they always feared assassination, a theme reprised by John Wilkes Booth, who supposedly declared "Sic semper tyrannis" ("And thus always to tyrants") when he assassinated Abraham Lincoln in 1865. A popular story about the tyrant Dionysius II of Syracuse (367–357, 346–344 BCE) underlined the anxious life of a tyrant. Dionysius himself escaped assassination and died in poverty in exile in Corinth. The tale was told by the Roman orator Cicero in the first century BCE and then again in Gaul five hundred years later in the letters of the Prefect of Rome, later bishop of Clermont, Sidonius Apollinaris, attesting to its longevity and continued relevance.

(a) Cicero, *Tusculan Disputations* 5.61

Indeed this tyrant [Dionysius II of Syracuse] himself gave his judgment as to how fortunate he was. For when one of his flatterers, Damocles, mentioned in conversation the wealth of Dionysius, the majesty of his rule, the abundance of his possessions, the magnificence of the royal palace and denied that there had ever been anyone more fortunate, he said, "So, Damocles, because this life delights you, do you wish to taste it yourself and make trial of my fortune?" When Damocles said that he desired this, Dionysius gave orders that the man be placed on a golden couch covered with a most beautiful woven rug, embroidered with splendid works; he adorned many sideboards with chased silver and gold; then he gave orders that chosen boys of outstanding beauty should stand by his table and that they, watching for a sign from Damocles, should attentively wait on him. There were unguents and garlands, perfumes were burning, tables were piled up with the most select foods. Damocles seemed to himself fortunate. In the middle of this luxury Dionysius ordered that a shining sword, fastened from the ceiling by a horsehair, be let down so that it hung over the neck of that fortunate man. And so he looked neither at those handsome waiters nor the wonderful silver work, nor did he stretch his hand to the table. Now the very wreaths slipped off. Finally he begged the tyrant that he should be allowed to depart because he no longer wanted to be fortunate.

(b) Sidonius Apollinaris, *Letter* 2.13

Source: O. M. Dalton, trans., *The Letters of Sidonius*, two vols. (Oxford: Clarendon, 1915).

A prominent, noble man of high culture, whose talents raised him to Quaestor's[112] rank, a man of great influence among the nobility, I mean Fulgentius,[113] used to say that whenever the thrice-loathed burden of a crown set Maximus[114] longing for his ancient ease, he would often hear him exclaim, "Happy thou, O Damocles, whose royal duress did not outlast a single banquet!" History tells us that Damocles was a Sicilian of Syracuse, and an acquaintance of the tyrant Dionysius. One day, when he was extolling to the skies the privileges of his patron's life without any comprehension of its drawbacks, Dionysius said to him, "Would you like to see for yourself, at this very board, what the blessings and the curses of royalty are like?" "I should think I would," replied the other. Instantly the dazzled and delighted creature was stripped of his commoner's garb and made resplendent with robes of Tyrian and Tarentine dye.[115] They set him on a gold couch with coverings of silk, a figure glittering with gems and pearls. But just as a Sardanapalian[116] feast was about to begin, and bread of fine Leontine[117] wheat was handed round; just as rare viands were brought in on plate of yet greater rarity; just as the Falernian[118] foamed in great gem-like cups and unguents tempered the ice-cold crystal; just as the whole room breathed cinnamon and frankincense and exotic perfumes floated to every nostril; just as the garlands were drying on heads drenched with nard,[119] behold a bare sword, swinging from the ceiling right over his purple-mantled shoulders, as if every instant it must fall and pierce his throat. The menace of that heavy blade on that horsehair thread curbed his greed and made him reflect on Tantalus[120]; the awful thought oppressed him that all he swallowed might be rendered through gaping wounds. He wept, he prayed, he sighed in every key, and when at last he was let go, he was off like a flash, flying the wealth and the delights of kings as fast as most men follow after them. A horror of high estate brought him back with longing to the mean, nicely cautioned never again to think or call the mortal happy who lives ringed round with army and guards, or broods heavy over his spoils while the steel presses no less heavily upon him than he himself upon his gold.

112 At this time, the "Quaestor of the Sacred Palace" was the imperial official in charge of legal matters.

113 A old and good friend of Sidonius.

114 The short lived emperor Petronius Maximus (455). He attempted to flee Rome disguised as a slave when the city was sacked by the Vandals but was apprehended by the mob and dismembered.

115 The Phoenician city of Tyre produced a legendary purple dye; Tarentum on the southern coast of Italy also produced a purple dye.

116 Sardanapalus was the legendary last king of Assyria whose decadent pleasure-seeking lifestyle led to the fall of the Assyrian Empire.

117 Leontini was a Greek colony near Syracuse in Sicily that controlled a fertile plain.

118 A famous wine produced south of Rome on the border between Latium and Campania.

119 An oil from the spikenard plant used as a perfume.

120 For Tantalus of Greek mythology, see Reading 51.

CHAPTER 7

Sparta, Athens, and the Classical Age (500–387 BCE)

By the end of the Archaic Age, circa 500 BCE, the Greeks were on their way to becoming the greatest economic and even cultural force in the Mediterranean world. But politically they continued to be disunited and spent much of their time squabbling with each other. Until this point, the Greeks had confronted no serious foreign threats and had been able to develop socially and politically without outside interference. But the Classical Age of Greek history (500–323 BCE) brought the Greeks first into conflict with the greatest power in the world, the Persian Empire, and then into destructive conflict with each other, all while they were reaching a point of their own civilization. In particular, the Classical Age generally is viewed as representing the height of Greek literature, as particularly manifested in the fields of drama, philosophy, and history. Many literary works of great sophistication and cultural significance survive from this period.

Map 7 Ancient Greece during the Classical Age

53

SPARTAN EDUCATION (CA. 750 BCE): PLUTARCH, *LIFE OF LYCURGUS*

In this sketch by Edgar Degas (ca. 1860–1880), with Mt. Taÿgetus in the background, Spartan girls, wearing characteristic slit tunics, challenge Spartan boys during their physical training. The whole Spartan population had to be well trained to defend the Spartan way of life.

According to Spartan tradition, about 700 BCE the Spartan lawgiver Lycurgus devised a constitution called the "Great Rhetra" that established the uniquely Spartan system of life known as the "Good Rule." The Rhetra was intended to create unity by eliminating the political importance of the family by making all male citizens equal and by focusing everyone's loyalty on the polis, or city-state. The Spartan commitment to simplicity was reflected in Spartan speech, which was in terse, pithy, ironic sentences, a speaking style that came to be known as "laconic" (from Laconia, the Spartan home territory). The second-century CE Greek writer Plutarch composed a series of biographies of famous Romans and Greeks. His life of Lycurgus described the upbringing and role of Spartan women, which was quite different from that of women in other Greek cities.

Source: John Dryden, *Plutarch: The Lives of the Noble Greeks and Romans*, revised by A. H. Clough, Vol. 1 (Boston: Little, Brown, 1910).

In order to accomplish the good education of their youth (which, as I said before, he thought the most important and noblest work of a lawgiver[1]), he went so far as to take into consideration their very conception and birth, by regulating their marriages. For Aristotle[2] is wrong in saying, that, after he had tried all ways to reduce the women to more modesty and sobriety, he was at last forced to leave them as they were, because that in the absence of their husbands, who spent the best part of their lives in the wars, their wives, whom they were obliged to leave absolute mistresses at home, took great liberties and assumed the superiority, and were treated with overmuch respect and called by the title of lady or queen. The truth is that in their case he also took all possible care. He ordered the maidens to exercise themselves with wrestling, running, throwing the quoit,[3] and casting the dart, to the end that the fruit they conceived might, in strong and healthy bodies, take firmer root and find better growth, and withal that they, with this greater vigor, might be the more able to undergo the pains of child-bearing. And so that he might take away their overgreat tenderness and fear of exposure to the air, and all acquired womanishness, he ordered that the young women should go naked in the processions, as well as the young men, and dance, too, in that condition, at certain solemn feasts, singing certain songs, while the young men stood around, seeing and hearing them. On these occasions the women now and then made, by jests, a befitting reflection upon those who had misbehaved themselves in the wars, and again sang encomiums upon those who had done any gallant action, and by these means inspired the younger sort with an emulation of their glory. Those that were thus commended went away proud, elated, and gratified with their honor among the maidens, and those who were disparaged were as sensibly touched with it as if they had been formally reprimanded; and so much the more, because the kings and the elders, as well as the rest of the city, saw and heard all that passed.

Nor was there anything shameful in this nakedness of the young women. Modesty attended them and all wantonness was excluded. It taught them simplicity and a care for good health, and gave them some taste of higher feelings, admitted as they thus were to the field of noble action and glory. Hence it was natural for them to think and speak as Gorgo, for example, the wife of Leonidas,[4] is said to have done, when some foreign lady, as it would seem, told her that the women of Lacedaemon were the only women in the world who could rule men; "With good reason," she said, "for we are the only women who give birth to men."

These public processions of the maidens, and their appearing naked in their exercises and dances, were incitements to marriage, operating upon the young with the rigor and certainty, as Plato[5] says, of love, if not of mathematics. But besides all this, to promote marriage yet more effectually, those who continued bachelors were in a degree disfranchised by law; for they were excluded from the sight of those public processions in which the young men and maidens danced naked. In winter-time, the officers compelled them to march naked themselves round the marketplace, singing as they went a song to their own disgrace, that they justly suffered this punishment for disobeying the laws. Moreover, they were denied that respect and observance that the younger men paid their elders, and no man, for example, found fault with what was said to Dercyllidas,[6] although so eminent a commander, upon whose approach one day, a young man, instead of rising,

[1] The lawgivers of Greek cities wrote down laws that hitherto had been known only to aristocratic "law rememberers"; for the lawgiver Draco of Athens, see Reading 54.

[2] An Athenian philosopher of the mid-fourth century BCE whose work the *Politics* attempted to describe the functioning of human society; see Reading 65.

[3] A game in which rings were thrown so as to land over a metal spike or wooden post.

[4] The Spartan king who died at the Battle of Thermopylae in 480 BCE.

[5] A famous Athenian philosopher of the early fourth century BCE.

[6] A bachelor, thus without any children.

retained his seat, remarking, "No child of yours will make room for me."

In their marriages, the husband carried off his bride as if by kidnaping, nor were their brides ever small and of tender years,[7] but in their full bloom and ripeness. After this, she who superintended the wedding comes and clips the hair of the bride close round her head, dresses her up in man's clothes, and leaves her upon a mattress in the dark. Afterward comes the bridegroom, in his everyday clothes, sober and composed, as having supped at the common table, and, entering privately into the room where the bride lies, unties her virgin zone and takes her to himself. After staying some time together, he returns composedly to his own apartment, to sleep as usual with the other young men. And so he continues to do, spending his days, and, indeed, his nights, with them, visiting his bride in fear and shame, and with circumspection, when he thought he should not be observed. She, also, on her part, uses her wit to help and find favorable opportunities for their meeting, when company is out of the way. In this manner they lived a long time, insomuch that they sometimes had children by their wives before ever they saw their faces by daylight. Their interviews, being thus difficult and rare, served not only for continual exercise of their self-control, but brought them together with their bodies healthy and vigorous, and their affections fresh and lively, unsated and undulled by easy access and long continuance with each other, whereas their partings were always early enough to leave behind unextinguished in each of them some remaining fire of longing and mutual delight.

After guarding marriage with this modesty and reserve, Lycurgus was equally careful to banish empty and womanish jealousy. For this object, excluding all licentious disorders, he made it, nevertheless, honorable for men to give the use of their wives to those whom they should think fit, so that they might have children by them, ridiculing those in whose opinion such favors are so unfit for participation as to fight and shed blood and go to war about it. Lycurgus allowed a man who was advanced in years and had a young wife to recommend some virtuous and approved young man so that she might have a child by him, who might inherit the good qualities of the father and be a son to himself. On the other side, an honest man who had love for a married woman upon account of her modesty and the well-favoredness of her children, might, without formality, beg her company of her husband, so that he might raise, as it were, from this plot of good ground worthy and well-allied children for himself.

And indeed, Lycurgus was of a persuasion that children were not so much the property of their parents as of the whole commonwealth, and, therefore, would not have his citizens begot by the first-comers, but by the best men that could be found. The laws of other nations seemed to him very absurd and inconsistent, where people would be so solicitous for their dogs and horses as to exert interest and to pay money to procure fine breeding, and yet kept their wives shut up, to be made mothers only by themselves, who might be foolish, infirm, or diseased; as if it were not apparent that children of a bad breed would prove their bad qualities first upon those who kept and were rearing them, and well-born children, in like manner, their good qualities. These regulations, founded on natural and social grounds, were certainly so far from that scandalous liberty that was afterward charged upon their women, that they knew not what adultery meant. It is told, for instance, of Geradas, a very ancient Spartan, that, being asked by a stranger what punishment their law had appointed for adulterers, he answered, "There are no adulterers in our country." "But," replied the stranger, "suppose there were?" "Then," answered he, "the offender would have to give the plaintiff a bull with a neck so long as that he might drink from the top of Taÿgetus of the Eurotas river below it." The man, surprised at this, said, "Why, 'tis impossible to find such a bull." Geradas smilingly replied, "'Tis as possible as to find an adulterer in Sparta." So much I had to say of their marriages.

Nor was it in the power of the father to dispose of the child as he thought fit; he was obliged to carry it before certain judges at a place called Lesche. These

[7] Unlike other Greeks, where child brides were common.

judges were some of the elders of the *phylē*[8] to which the child belonged. It was their business to view the infant carefully, and, if they found it stout and well made, they gave order for its rearing, and allotted to it one of the nine thousand shares of land[9] for its maintenance. But if they found it puny and ill-shaped, they ordered it to be taken to what was called the Apothetae, a sort of chasm under Taÿgetus, thinking it neither for the good of the child itself, nor for the public interest, that it should be brought up, if it did not, from the very outset, appear made to be healthy and vigorous. Upon the same account, the women did not bathe the new-born children with water, as is the custom in all other countries, but with wine, to prove the temper and complexion of their bodies, from a notion they had that epileptic and weakly children faint and waste away upon their being thus bathed while, on the contrary, those of a strong and vigorous habit acquire firmness and get a temper by it, like steel. There was much care and art, too, used by the nurses. They had no swaddling bands; the children grew up free and unconstrained in limb and form, and not dainty and fanciful about their food; not afraid in the dark, or of being left alone; and without peevishness, or ill-humor, or crying. Upon this account Spartan nurses often were hired by people of other countries; it is recorded that she who suckled Alcibiades[10] was a Spartan.

Lycurgus would not have masters bought out of the market for his young Spartans, nor such as should sell their pains,[11] nor was it lawful, indeed, for the father himself to raise children after his own fancy. As soon as boys were seven years old they were to be enrolled in certain companies and classes, where they all lived under the same order and discipline, doing their exercises and taking their play together. Of these, he who showed the most conduct and courage was made captain. The boys had their eyes always upon him, obeyed his orders, and underwent patiently whatsoever punishment he inflicted, so that the whole course of their education was one continued exercise of a ready and perfect obedience. The old men, too, were spectators of their performances, and often raised quarrels and disputes among them, to have a good opportunity of finding out their different characters, and of seeing which would be valiant, which a coward, when they should come to more dangerous encounters. Reading and writing they gave them, just enough to serve their turn. Their chief care was to make them good subjects, and to teach them to endure pain and conquer in battle. To this end, as they grew in years, their discipline was proportionately increased. Their heads were close-clipped, they were accustomed to go barefoot, and for the most part to play naked.

After they were twelve years old, they no longer were allowed to wear any undergarments. They had one coat to serve them a year; their bodies were hard and dry, with but little acquaintance of baths and perfumes; these human indulgences they were allowed only on some few particular days in the year. They lodged together in little bands upon beds made of the rushes that grew by the banks of the river Eurotas, which they were to break off with their hands without a knife; if it were winter, they mingled some thistle-down with their rushes, which it was thought had the property of giving warmth. By the time they were come to this age there was not any of the more hopeful boys who had not a lover to bear him company. The old men, too, had an eye upon them, coming often to the grounds to hear and see them contend either in wit or strength with one another, and this as seriously and with as much concern as if they were their fathers, their guardians, or their magistrates, so that there scarcely was any time or place without someone present to put them in mind of their duty, and punish them if they had neglected it.

---

[8] The Dorian Greeks were divided into three *phylai* (peoples), often in older works called "tribes," each of which was subdivided into smaller kinship groups: phratries (clans), *genai* (extended families), and *oikoi* (households). See Reading 46.

[9] Full Spartan citizens were allotted landholdings that supported them while they performed their military services.

[10] A famous Athenian general during the Peloponnesian War.

[11] That is, the Spartans had no child-care workers.

Besides all this, there was always one of the best and most honest men in the city appointed to undertake the charge and governance of them. He again arranged them into their several bands, and set over each of them for their captain the most temperate and boldest of those, whom they called *Irens*, who usually were twenty years old, two years out of boyhood. The oldest of the boys were *Mell-Irens*, that is, those who shortly would be men. This young man, therefore, was their captain when they fought and their master at home. He used them for the offices of the house, sending the eldest of them to fetch wood, and the weaker and less able to gather salads and herbs, and these they must either go without or steal, which they did by creeping into the gardens or conveying themselves cunningly and closely into the eating-houses. If they were caught in the act, they were whipped without mercy for thieving so ill and awkwardly. They stole, too, all other meat they could lay their hands on, looking out and watching all opportunities, when people were asleep or more careless than usual. If they were caught, they were not only punished with whipping, but hunger, too, being reduced to their ordinary allowance, which was but very slender, and so contrived on purpose, so that they might set about to help themselves and be forced to exercise their energy and craftiness.

This was the principal design of their hard fare. There also was another not inconsiderable intent, that they might grow taller, for the vital spirits, not being overburdened and oppressed by too great a quantity of nourishment, which necessarily discharges itself into thickness and breadth, do, by their natural lightness, rise, and the body, giving and yielding because it is pliant, grows in height. The same thing seems, also, to conduce to beauty of shape; a dry and lean habit is a better subject for nature's configuration, which the gross and over-fed are too heavy to submit to properly. Just as we find that women who take laxatives while they are with child bear leaner and smaller but better-shaped and prettier children, the material they come of having been more pliable and easily molded. The reason, however, I leave others to determine.

To return from whence we have digressed. So seriously did the Lacedaemonian children go about their stealing, that a youth, having stolen a young fox and hid it under his coat, suffered it to tear out his very bowels with its teeth and claws and died upon the place, rather than let it be seen. What is practised to this very day in Lacedaemon is enough to gain credit to this story, for I myself have seen several of the youths endure whipping to death at the foot of the altar of Diana surnamed Orthia.

The *Iren*, or under-master, used to stay a little with them after supper, and one of them he bade to sing a song, to another he put a question that required an advised and deliberate answer, for example, Who was the best man in the city? What he thought of such an action of such a man? They trained them thus early to pass a right judgment upon persons and things, and to inform themselves of the abilities or defects of their countrymen. If they had not an answer ready to the question, Who was a good or who an ill-reputed citizen, they were looked upon as of a dull and careless disposition, and to have little or no sense of virtue and honor; besides this, they were to give a good reason for what they said, and in as few words and as comprehensive as might be. He that failed of this, or answered not to the purpose, had his thumb bit by the master. Sometimes the Iren did this in the presence of the old men and magistrates, that they might see whether he punished them justly and in due measure or not, and when he did amiss, they would not reprove him before the boys, but, when they were gone, he was called to an account and underwent correction, if he had run far into either of the extremes of indulgence or severity.

Their lovers and favorers, too, had a share in the young boy's honor or disgrace, and there goes a story that one of them was fined by the magistrate because the lad whom he loved cried out effeminately as he was fighting. And although this sort of love was so approved among them that the most virtuous matrons would make professions of it to young girls, yet rivalry did not exist, and if several men's fancies met in one person, it was rather the beginning of an intimate friendship, while they all jointly conspired to render the object of their affection as accomplished as possible.

They taught them, also, to speak with a natural and graceful raillery, and to comprehend much matter of thought in few words. For Lycurgus, who ordered, as we saw, that a great piece of money should be but of an inconsiderable value, on the contrary would allow no discourse to be current that did not contain in few words a great deal of useful and curious sense. Children in Sparta, by a habit of long silence, came to give just and sententious answers; for, indeed, as loose and incontinent livers are seldom fathers of many children, so loose and incontinent talkers seldom originate many sensible words. King Agis, when some Athenian laughed at their short swords, and said that the jugglers on the stage swallowed them with ease, answered him, "We find them long enough to reach our enemies with"; and as their swords were short and sharp, so, it seems to me, were their sayings.

They reach the point and arrest the attention of the hearers better than any. Lycurgus himself seems to have been short and sententious, if we may trust the anecdotes of him; as appears by his answer to one who by all means would set up a democracy in Lacedaemon. "Begin, friend," said he, "and set it up in your family." Another asked him why he allowed of such mean and trivial sacrifices to the gods. He replied, "That we may always have something to offer to them." Being asked what sort of martial exercises or combats he approved of, he answered, "All sorts, except that in which you stretch out your hands."[12] Similar answers, addressed to his countrymen by letter, are ascribed to him; as, being consulted how they might best oppose an invasion of their enemies, he returned this answer, "By continuing poor, and not coveting each man to be greater than his fellow." Being consulted again whether it were requisite to enclose the city with a wall, he sent them word, "The city is well fortified that hath a wall of men instead of brick."

[12] A sign of surrender.

54

THE CONSTITUTIONS OF ATHENS (800–507 BCE): ARISTOTLE, *THE ATHENIAN CONSTITUTION*

One of two surviving copies of Aristotle's "Athenian Constitution," dating to ca. 100 CE, written on papyrus and preserved in the British Library in London.

The Athenian philosopher Aristotle, who worked in the mid-fourth century CE, proposed to study how human society functioned by collecting 170 constitutions of a multitude of cities and peoples, including that of the city of Carthage (see Reading 71). The result was his famous work the *Politics* (see Reading 65). A separate study, "The Athenian Constitution," was lost to history until it was discovered at Oxyrhyncus in Egypt in 1879 preserved on two leaves of a papyrus codex originally written around 100 CE. A second, longer, version was discovered in 1890. The first section describes the evolution of the Athenian constitution up to the year 403 BCE, including the aristocratic, oligarchic, and democratic constitutions, and the second part discusses Athenian institutions.

Source: Fredrick G. Kenyon, trans., *Aristotle, The Athenian Constitution* (London: Bell, 1914).

[The Ancient Aristocratic Constitution: ca. 800 BCE] Now the ancient constitution,[13] as it existed before the time of Draco,[14] was organized as follows. The magistrates were elected according to qualifications of birth and wealth. At first they governed for life, but subsequently for terms of ten years. The first

[13] That is, the aristocratic constitution.

[14] A lawgiver, like Lycurgus of Sparta, who in 621 BCE issued the first written constitution and law code of Athens. The laws were known for their harshness; hence, the modern word "draconian" to refer to a particularly severe measure.

magistrates, both in date and in importance, were the King, the Polemarch,[15] and the Archon.[16] The earliest of these offices was that of the King, which existed from ancestral antiquity. To this was added, secondly, the office of Polemarch, on account of some of the kings proving feeble in war, for it was on this account that Ion[17] was invited to accept the post on an occasion of pressing need. The last of the three offices was that of the Archon, which most authorities state to have come into existence in the time of Medon.[18] Others assign it to the time of Acastus,[19] and adduce as proof the fact that the nine Archons swear to execute their oaths "as in the days of Acastus," which seems to suggest that it was in his time that the descendents of Codrus[20] retired from the kingship in return for the prerogatives conferred upon the Archon. Whichever way it be, the difference in date is small. That it was the last of these magistracies to be created is shown by the fact that the Archon has no part in the ancestral sacrifices, as the King and the Polemarch have, but exclusively in those of later origin. So it is only at a comparatively late date that the office of Archon has become of great importance, through the dignity conferred by these later additions. The Thesmothetes[21] were appointed many years afterward, when these offices already had become annual, with the object that they might publicly record all legal decisions, and act as guardians of them with a view to determining the issues between litigants. Accordingly their office, alone of those that have been mentioned, was never of more than annual duration.

The Thesmothetes had power to decide cases finally on their own authority, not, as now, merely to hold a preliminary hearing. Such then was the arrangement of the magistracies. The Council of the Areopagus[22] had as its constitutionally assigned duty the protection of the laws but in point of fact it administered the greater and most important part of the government of the state, and inflicted personal punishments and fines summarily upon all who misbehaved themselves. This was the natural consequence of the facts that the Archons were elected under qualifications of birth and wealth,[23] and that the Areopagus was composed of those who had served as Archons, for which latter reason the membership of the Areopagus is the only office that has continued to be a life-magistracy to the present day.

[The Constitution of Draco: 621 BCE]

Such was, in outline, the first constitution, but not very long after the archonship of Aristaichmus,[24] Draco enacted his ordinances. Now his constitution had the following form. The franchise[25] was given to all who could furnish themselves with a military equipment. The nine Archons and the Treasurers were elected by this body from persons possessing an unencumbered property of not less than ten minas,[26] the less important officials from those who could furnish themselves with a military equipment, and the *Strategoi*[27] and *Hipparchoi*[28] from those who

[15] The chief general.

[16] A chief magistrate in Greek cities.

[17] The first Athenian Polemarch.

[18] The son of Codrus, the first king of Athens.

[19] Another son of Codrus who succeeded his brother, Medon.

[20] The last of the legendary kings of Athens, ca. 1089–1068 BCE.

[21] The six guardians of the laws in ancient Athens.

[22] A council of elders composed of ex-archons that was the primary governing body of Athens under the aristocracy.

[23] Only aristocrats met the birth qualification, and there was no way for someone not born an aristocrat to become one.

[24] 621 BCE. Athenian years were dated by the holders of one of the archonships, in the same way that the Romans dated years by the names of their consuls.

[25] Full citizenship, with the right to vote, hold office, and be a member of the Council.

[26] A unit of weight; there were sixty minas in a talent (about fifty-six pounds), and sixty shekels in a mina. This reform opened up to wealthy nonaristocrats the opportunity to hold office.

[27] Generals.

[28] Commanders of the cavalry.

could show an unencumbered property of not less than a hundred minas, and had children born in lawful wedlock over ten years of age. There was also to be a Council, consisting of four hundred and one members, elected by lot from among those who possessed the franchise. Both for this and for the other magistracies the lot was cast among those who were over thirty years of age, and no one might hold office twice until every one else had had his turn, after which they were to cast the lot afresh. If any member of the Council failed to attend when there was a sitting of the Council or of the Assembly, he paid a fine, to the amount of three drachmas if he was a *Pentacosiomedimnos*,[29] two if he was one of the *Hippeis*,[30] and one if he was a *Zeugitēs*.[31] The Council of Areopagus was guardian of the laws, and kept watch over the magistrates to see that they executed their offices in accordance with the laws. Any person who felt himself wronged might lay an accusation before the Council of Areopagus, on declaring what law was broken by the wrong done to him.

[The Oligarchic Constitution of Solon: 596/594 BCE]
Next Solon[32] drew up a constitution[33] and enacted new laws; and the ordinances of Draco ceased to be used, with the exception of those relating to murder. He divided the population according to property into four classes, just as it had been divided before, namely, *Pentacosiomedimnoi*, *Hippeis*, *Zeugitai*, and Thetes. The various magistracies, namely, the nine Archons, the Treasurers, the Commissioners for Public Contracts [*Poletai*], the Eleven, and the Exchequer Clerks [*Colacretai*], he assigned to the *Pentacosiomedimnoi*, the *Hippeis*, and the *Zeugitai*, giving offices to each class in proportion to the value of their rateable property. To those who ranked among the Thetes he gave nothing but a place in the Assembly and in the juries. A man had to rank as a *Pentacosiomedimnos* if he made, from his own land, five hundred measures, whether liquid or solid. Those ranked as *Hippeis* who made three hundred measures, or, as some say, those who were able to maintain a horse. Those ranked as *Zeugitai* who made two hundred measures, liquid or solid; and the rest ranked as Thetes, and were not eligible for any office.

The elections to the various offices Solon enacted should be by lot, out of candidates selected by each of the *phylai*.[34] Each *phylē* selected ten candidates for the nine archonships, and among these the lot was cast. Such was Solon's legislation with respect to the nine Archons; whereas in early times the Council of Areopagus summoned suitable persons according to its own judgement and appointed them for the year to the several offices. There were four *phylai*, as before. Each *phylē* was divided into three *trittyes*.[35] Solon also appointed a Council of Four Hundred, a hundred from each *phylē*. He assigned to the Council of the Areopagus the duty of superintending the laws, acting as before as the guardian of the constitution in general. It kept watch over the affairs of the state in most of the more important matters, and corrected offenders, with full powers to inflict either fines or personal punishment. It also tried those who conspired for the overthrow of the state.

Such, then, was Solon's legislation concerning the magistracies. There are three points in the constitution of Solon that appear to be its most democratic

[29] "500 bushel men," an indication of their annual income in measures of grain or olive oil.

[30] Originally, those rich enough to own a horse; sometimes also called "Knights."

[31] "Yoke men," referring to their being yoked together in the line of battle.

[32] An aristocrat appointed to create an oligarchic constitution.

[33] The oligarchic constitution of Solon formalized the collection between wealth and the opportunity to hold office and reduced the power of the aristocratic Areopagus.

[34] The Ionian Greeks were divided into four *phylai* (peoples) to which all citizens of a city belonged; each was subdivided into smaller kinship groups: phratries (clans), *genai* (extended families), and *oikoi* (households). See Reading 46.

[35] "Thirds."

features: first and most important, the prohibition of loans on the security of the debtor's person; secondly, the right of every person who so willed to claim redress on behalf of anyone to whom wrong was being done; thirdly, the institution of the appeal to the jury-courts, and it is to this last, they say, that the masses have owed their strength most of all, because when the democracy is master of the voting-power it is master of the constitution.

[The Democratic Constitution of Cleisthenes: 507 BCE]
The people had good reason to place confidence in Cleisthenes.[36] Accordingly, now that he was the popular leader, three years after the expulsion of the tyrants,[37] in the archonship of Isagoras,[38] his first step was to distribute the whole population into ten *phylai* in place of the existing four, with the object of intermixing the members of the different *phylai*, and so securing that more persons might have a share in the franchise. Next he made the Council to consist of five hundred members instead of four hundred, each *phylē* now contributing fifty, whereas formerly each had sent a hundred. Further, he divided the country into thirty groups of demes,[39] ten from the districts about the city, ten from the coast, and ten from the interior. These he called *trittyes*; and he assigned three of them by lot to each *phylē*, in such a way that each should have one portion in each of these three localities.[40] All who lived in any given deme he declared fellow-demesmen, to the end that the new citizens might not be exposed by the habitual use of family names, but that men might be officially described by the names of their demes. Accordingly it is by the names of their demes that the Athenians speak of one another.

By these reforms the constitution became much more democratic than that of Solon. The laws of Solon had been obliterated by disuse during the period of the tyranny, while Cleisthenes substituted new ones with the object of securing the goodwill of the masses. Among these was the law concerning ostracism.[41] Next they began to elect the generals by *phylai*, one from each *phylē*, whereas the Polemarch remained the commander of the whole army. Then, eleven years later, they won the Battle of Marathon,[42] and two years after this victory, when the people had now gained self-confidence, they for the first time made use of the law of ostracism. This had originally been passed as a precaution against men in high office, because Peisistratus[43] took advantage of his position as a popular leader and general to make himself tyrant. Then in the very next year, in the archonship of Telesinus, they for the first time since the tyranny elected, *phylē* by *phylē*, the nine Archons by lot out of the five hundred candidates selected by the demes, all the earlier ones having been elected by vote. For three years they continued to ostracize the friends of the tyrants, on whose account the law had been passed, but in the following year they began to remove others as well, including anyone who seemed to be more powerful than was expedient. Two years later, the mines of Maroneia[44] were discovered, and the state made a profit of a hundred talents from the working of them. Some persons advised the people to make a distribution of the money among themselves, but this was prevented by Themistocles.[45] He

[36] An Athenian aristocrat who attempted to lessen aristocratic influence even further and create a more democratic constitution.

[37] Between 546 and 510 BCE Athens was governed by the tyrant Peisistratus and his two sons, Hipparchus and Hippias. For Greek tyrants, see Reading 52.

[38] 507 BCE.

[39] Subdivisions of the territory of Athens, including, at this time, the city itself.

[40] As a result, whereas Solon's *trittyes* were based on family membership, Cleisthenes's were based on geographical residence.

[41] Every year Athenian citizens voted to see whether there would be an ostracism election. If there was, anyone receiving more than six thousand votes was required to go into exile for ten years.

[42] In 490 BCE.

[43] Tyrant of Athens from 546 until 527 BCE.

[44] Ca. 483 BCE, significant silver mines were discovered at Athens at Laurion; Maroneia was in the same area.

[45] An important Athenian politician who regularly advocated for the importance of sea power.

received the money and with it he had a hundred triremes[46] built, and it was with these ships that they fought the battle of Salamis[47] against the barbarians. Three years later,[48] all the ostracized persons were recalled, on account of the advance of the army of Xerxes.[49]

55

THE BATTLE OF SALAMIS (480 BCE): HERODOTUS, *HISTORIES*, BOOK 8

Only a single surviving artifact, the so-called Lenormant relief, from Athens ca. 410 BCE, shows the position of the rowers in an Athenian trireme.

The Battle of Salamis in 480 BCE was the pivotal battle of the Persian Wars. In 480 BCE, the Persian king Xerxes crossed from Asia to Europe and defeated the Greeks at the Battle of

[46] Warships with three banks of oars powered by about two hundred citizen rowers.

[47] In 480 BCE.

[48] That is, three years after the discovery of the mines.

[49] Persian king from 486 until 465 BCE.

Thermopylae in northern Greece. The Persians also fought the Greeks to a draw at the naval Battle of Artemesium, off the northern coast of the island of Euboea, where both sides lost a roughly equal number of warships. This was a war of attrition that the heavily outnumbered Greeks could not hope to win. The Persians then advanced south, and all the cities of central Greece capitulated. The Greek opposition withdrew to a line of defense across the Isthmus of Corinth, leaving Athens undefended. Athens was captured without a fight and burned in retaliation for the burning of the Persian capital of Asia at Sardis in 498 BCE. The Greeks then debated their next step. The Peloponnesians favored withdrawing the Greek fleet to defend the Peloponnesus, but the Athenian general Themistocles, by threatening to withdraw the Athenian fleet and population and flee to Sicily, convinced the Greeks to resist the Persian fleet at Salamis. The historian Herodotus, writing in Athens around 440 BCE, provides a patriotic description of the course of the battle, which also attested to the personal role of the Persian king Xerxes and the heroic acts of Artemisia, Queen of Halicarnassus. After the Greek victory, it was popularly believed that the oracle of Apollo at Delphi saying that the Athenians should "trust to their wooden walls" when the Persians attacked was a reference to the Athenian wooden warships.

Source: George Rawlinson, Henry Rawlinson, and John Gardner Wilkinson, trans., *The History of Herodotus. A New English Version* (London: Murray, 1862).

When the captains from the various nations were come together at Salamis, a council of war was summoned; and Eurybiades[50] proposed that anyone who liked to advise, should say which place seemed to him the fittest, among those still in the possession of the Greeks, to be the scene of a naval combat. Attica, he said, was not to be thought of now; but he desired their counsel as to the remainder. The speakers mostly advised that the fleet should sail away to the Isthmus, and there give battle in defense of the Peloponnese. They urged as a reason for this that if they were worsted in a sea-fight at Salamis they would be shut up in an island where they could get no help; but if they were beaten near the Isthmus, they could escape to their homes. As the captains from the Peloponnese were advising this, there came an Athenian to the camp, who brought word that the barbarians[51] had entered Attica, and were ravaging and burning everything. The Persians found the city forsaken. Xerxes, thus was completely master of Athens.

Meanwhile, at Salamis, the Greeks no sooner heard what had befallen the Athenian citadel than they fell into such alarm that some of the captains did not even wait for the council to come to a vote, but embarked hastily on board their vessels, and hoisted sail as if to take flight immediately. The rest came to a vote that the fleet should give battle at the Isthmus. Themistocles, as he entered his own vessel, was met by Mnesiphilus, an Athenian, who exclaimed, "If these men sail away from Salamis, thou wilt have no fight at all for the one fatherland, for they all will scatter themselves to their own homes, and neither Eurybiades nor anyone else will be able to hinder them. Thus will Greece be brought to ruin." Themistocles, without answering a word, went straight to the vessel of Eurybiades. He persuaded Eurybiades, by his importunity, to again collect the captains to council. He addressed him as follows:

> With thee it rests, O Eurybiades!, to save Greece, if thou wilt only hearken unto me, and give the enemy battle here, rather than yield to the advice of those among us, who would have the fleet withdrawn to

[50] A Spartan commander placed in overall command of the Greek naval forces because the Spartans refused to serve under an Athenian.

[51] The typical Greek disparaging term for any non-Greeks, including the highly civilized Persians.

> the Isthmus. If thou wilt stay here and behave like a brave man, all will be well—if not, thou wilt bring Greece to ruin. For the whole fortune of the war depends on our ships. Be thou persuaded by my words. If not, we will take our families on board, and go, just as we are, to Siris, in Italy, which is ours from of old, and which the prophecies declare we are to colonize some day or other.[52] You then, when you have lost allies like us, will hereafter call to mind what I now have said.

At these words of Themistocles, Eurybiades changed his determination; principally, as I believe, because he feared that if he withdrew the fleet to the Isthmus, the Athenians would sail away, and knew that without the Athenians, the rest of their ships could be no match for the fleet of the enemy. He therefore decided to remain, and give battle at Salamis. And now, the different chiefs, on learning the decision of Eurybiades, at once made ready for the fight.

Reinforced by the contingents of various states, the barbarians[53] reached Athens, where they were visited by Xerxes, who had conceived a desire to go aboard and learn the wishes of the fleet. So he came and sat in a seat of honor; and the sovereigns of the nations, and the captains of the ships, were sent for, to appear before him. Xerxes, to try them, sent Mardonius[54] and questioned each, whether a sea-fight should be risked or no. All gave the same answer, advising to engage the Greeks, except only Artemisia,[55] who spoke as follows:

> Say to the king, Mardonius, that these are my words to him: I was not the least brave of those who fought at Euboea, nor were my achievements there among the meanest; it is my right, therefore, O my lord, to tell thee plainly what I think to be most for thy advantage now. This then is my advice. Spare thy ships, and do not risk a battle, for these people are as much superior to thy people in seamanship, as men to women.[56] What so great need is there for thee to incur hazard at sea? Art thou not master of Athens, for which thou didst undertake thy expedition? Is not Greece subject to thee? Keep thy fleet near the land, then thou wilt easily accomplish all for which thou art come hither. The Greeks cannot hold out against thee very long; thou wilt soon part them asunder, and scatter them to their several homes. On the other hand, if thou art hasty to fight, I tremble lest the defeat of thy sea force bring harm likewise to thy land army.

Xerxes, when the words of the several speakers were reported to him, was pleased beyond all others with the reply of Artemisia, and whereas, even before this, he had always esteemed her much, he now praised her more than ever. Nevertheless, he gave orders that the advice of the greater number should be followed. Orders were now given to stand out to sea. The ships proceeded toward Salamis and took up the stations to which they were directed, without let or hindrance from the enemy. The day, however, was too far spent for them to begin the battle, for night already approached, so they prepared to engage upon the morrow.

The Greeks now made ready for the coming fight. At the dawn of day, the Greeks put to sea with all their fleet. The fleet had scarce left the land when they were attacked by the barbarians. At once most of the Greeks began to back water, and were about touching the shore, when Ameinias of Pallene, one of the Athenian captains, darted forth in front of the line, and charged a ship of the enemy, whereupon the rest of the fleet came up to help Ameinias and engaged with the Persians. It also is reported that a phantom in the form of a woman appeared to the Greeks, and, in a voice that was heard from end to end of the fleet, cheered them on to the fight, first, however, rebuking them, and saying, "Strange men, how long are ye going to back water?" Far the greater

[52] Themistocles thus threatened to take the two hundred Athenian warships to Italy, thus making it totally impossible for the Greek navy to resist the Persian navy.

[53] That is, the Persian navy.

[54] The primary general of Xerxes.

[55] The queen of Halicarnassus in Ionia. The five ships that she commanded at the Battle of Salamis were reputed to be the best in the Persian navy after the ships of Phoenician Sidon.

[56] An ironic statement, given Artemisia's own superiority to most of the male captains in the Persian fleet.

number of the Persian ships engaged in this battle were disabled, either by the Athenians or by the Aeginetans.[57] For as the Greeks fought in order and kept their line, whereas the barbarians were in confusion and had no plan in anything that they did, the issue of the battle could scarce be other than it was. Yet the Persians fought far more bravely here than at Euboea, and indeed surpassed themselves; each did his utmost through fear of Xerxes, for each thought that the king's eye was upon himself.

What part the several nations, whether Greek or barbarian, took in the combat, I am not able to say for certain. Artemisia, however, I know, distinguished herself in such a way as raised her even higher than she stood before in the esteem of the king. For after confusion had spread throughout the whole of the king's fleet, and her ship was closely pursued by an Athenian trireme, she, having no way to flee, because in front of her were a number of friendly vessels, and she was nearest of all the Persians to the enemy, resolved on a measure that in fact proved her safety. Pressed by the Athenian pursuer,[58] she bore straight against one of the ships of her own party and sank it, and thereby she had the good fortune to procure herself a double advantage. For the commander of the Athenian trireme thought immediately that her vessel was a Greek, or else had deserted from the Persians, and was now fighting on the Greek side; he therefore gave up the chase.

Thus in the first place she saved her life by the action, while further, it fell out that in the very act of doing the king an injury she raised herself to a greater height than ever in his esteem. For as Xerxes beheld the fight, bystanders observed to him, "Seest thou, master, how well Artemisia fights, and how she has just sunk a ship of the enemy?" Then Xerxes asked if it were really Artemisia's doing; and they answered, "Certainly; for they knew her standard." Xerxes in reply observed, "My men have behaved like women, my women like men!"

There perished a vast number of men of high repute, Persians, Medes, and allies. Of the Greeks there died only a few, for, as they were able to swim, all those that were not slain outright by the enemy escaped from the sinking vessels and swam across to Salamis. But on the side of the barbarians more perished by drowning than in any other way, because they did not know how to swim. The great destruction took place when the ships that had been first engaged began to flee, for they who were stationed in the rear, anxious to display their valor before the eyes of the king, made every effort to force their way to the front, and thus became entangled with such of their own vessels as were retreating.

The Greeks who gained the greatest glory of all in the sea-fight off Salamis were the Aeginetans, and after them the Athenians. The individuals of most distinction were Polycritus the Aeginetan, and two Athenians, Eumenes of Anagyrus and Ameinias of Pallene, the latter of whom had pressed Artemisia so hard. And assuredly, if he had known that the vessel carried Artemisia on board, he would never have given over the chase until he had either succeeded in taking her or else been taken himself. For the Athenian captains had received special orders touching the queen, and moreover a reward of ten thousand drachmas had been proclaimed for anyone who should make her prisoner because there was great indignation felt that a woman should appear in arms against Athens.[59] However, as I said before, she escaped, and so did some others whose ships survived the engagement; and these were all now assembled at the port of Phalerum.[60]

As soon as the sea-fight was ended, the Greeks drew together to Salamis all the wrecks that were to be found in that quarter, and prepared themselves for another engagement, supposing that the king would renew the fight with the vessels that still remained to him. Xerxes, when he saw the extent of his loss, began to be afraid lest the Greeks might decide to sail straight to the Hellespont and break down the bridges there, in which case he would be blocked up in Europe, and run great risk of perishing. He therefore made up his mind to flee.

[57] Aegina was an island city south of Athens.

[58] Ameinias of Pallene, a deme of Athens.

[59] Greek men felt extremely threatened by talented and able women.

[60] The port of Athens, given that Athens was not located directly on the seacoast.

56

PERICLES'S FUNERAL ORATION AND THE PLAGUE IN ATHENS (431–430 BCE): THUCYDIDES, *HISTORIES*, BOOK 2.34–54

A Roman copy of a Greek portrait bust of ca. 430 BCE of the Athenian leader Pericles, now in the British Museum.

In the first phase of the Peloponnesian War (431–421 BCE), the strategy of the Spartans, on the one hand, who had uncontested superiority on land, was to invade Attica each year and destroy the crops and olive trees. On the other hand, the policy of the Athenian leader Pericles was to withdraw the Athenian population behind their walls and refuse to fight until the Spartans withdrew their forces in the fall. Pericles hoped simply to hold out by supplying the city by sea, keeping control over the empire, and using Athens's control of the sea to raid the Peloponnesus. In the winter of 431/430 BCE, after the campaigning season was over, Pericles presented the traditional funeral eulogy in honor of the Athenians who had fallen in battle the previous year. He took the opportunity to glorify Athens, Athenian government, and his own policies. What Pericles did not anticipate, however, was that in the second year of the war the unsanitary conditions resulting from so many people crowded into the city would result in a terrible plague that killed thousands of people. The plague also struck in 429, when Pericles himself died of it, and 427 BCE. Suggestions of the nature of the plague have included typhus, typhoid fever, and Ebola. A graphic description of how the plague progressed was given by the Athenian historian Thucydides, himself a failed general, in his "Histories" of the Peloponnesian War. Thucydides is seen as the creator of "scientific history," which attributes historical events not to the will of the gods but to the actions of human beings engaged in struggles for power.

Source: Benjamin Jowett, trans., *Thucydides* (Cambridge, UK: Clarendon, 1881), 115–129.

During the same winter,[61] in accordance with an ancestral custom, the funeral of those who first fell in this war was celebrated by the Athenians at the public charge. The ceremony is as follows: Three days before the celebration they erect a tent in which the bones of the dead are laid out, and every one brings to his own dead any offering which he pleases. At the time of the funeral the bones are placed in chests of cypress wood, which are conveyed on wagons; there is one chest for each tribe. They also carry a single empty litter decked with a pall for all whose bodies are missing, and cannot be recovered after the battle. The procession is accompanied by anyone who chooses, whether citizen or stranger, and the female relatives of the deceased are present at the place of interment and make lamentation. The public sepulcher is situated in the most beautiful spot outside the walls; there they always bury those who fall in war; only after the battle of Marathon the dead, in recognition of their pre-eminent valor, were interred on the Held. When the remains have been laid in the earth, some man of known ability and high reputation, chosen by the city, delivers a suitable oration over them; after which the people depart. Such is the manner of interment; and the ceremony was repeated from time to time throughout the war. Over those who were the first buried Pericles was chosen to speak. At the fitting moment he advanced from the sepulcher to a lofty platform, which had been erected in order that he might be heard as far as possible by the multitude, and spoke as follows:

"Most of those who have spoken here before me have commended the lawgiver who added this oration to our other funeral customs; it seemed to them a worthy thing that such an honor should be given at their burial to the dead who have fallen on the field of battle. But I should have preferred that, when men's deeds have been brave, they should be honored in deed only, and with such an honor as this public funeral, which you are now witnessing. Then the reputation of many would not have been imperilled on the eloquence or want of eloquence of one, and their virtues believed or not as he spoke well or ill. For it is difficult to say neither too little nor too much; and even moderation is apt not to give the impression of truthfulness. The friend of the dead who knows the facts is likely to think that the words of the speaker fall short of his knowledge and of his wishes; another who is not so well informed, when he hears of anything which surpasses his own powers, will be envious and will suspect exaggeration. Mankind are tolerant of the praises of others so long as each hearer thinks that he can do as well or nearly as well himself, but, when the deed is beyond him, jealousy is aroused and he begins to be incredulous. However, since our ancestors have set the seal of their approval upon the practice, I must obey, and to the utmost of my power shall endeavor to satisfy the wishes and beliefs of all who hear me.

I will speak first of our ancestors, for it is right and becoming that now, when we are lamenting the dead, a tribute should be paid to their memory. There has never been a time when they did not inhabit this land, which by their valor they have handed down from generation to generation, and we have received from them a free state. But if they were worthy of praise, still more were our fathers, who added to their inheritance, and after many a struggle transmitted to us their sons this great empire. And we ourselves assembled here today, who are still most of us

[61] In 431 BCE.

in the vigor of life, have chiefly done the work of improvement, and have richly endowed our city with all things, so that she is sufficient for herself both in peace and war. Of the military exploits by which our various possessions were acquired, or of the energy with which we or our fathers drove back the tide of war, Hellenic or barbarian, I will not speak; for the tale would be long and is familiar to you. But before I praise the dead, I should like to point out by what principles of action we rose to power, and under what institutions and through what manner of life our empire became great. For I conceive that such thoughts are not unsuited to the occasion, and that this numerous assembly of citizens and strangers may profitably listen to them.

Our form of government does not enter into rivalry with the institutions of others. We do not copy our neighbors, but are an example to them. It is true that we are called a democracy, for the administration is in the hands of the many and not of the few. But while the law secures equal justice to all alike in their private disputes, the claim of excellence is also recognized; and when a citizen is in any way distinguished, he is preferred to the public service, not as a matter of privilege, but as the reward of merit. Neither is poverty a bar, but a man may benefit his country whatever be the obscurity of his condition. There is no exclusiveness in our public life, and in our private intercourse we are not suspicious of one another, nor angry with our neighbor if he does what he likes; we do not put on sour looks at him which, though harmless, are not pleasant. While we are thus unconstrained in our private intercourse, a spirit of reverence pervades our public acts; we are prevented from doing wrong by respect for authority and for the laws, having an especial regard to those which are ordained for the protection of the injured as well as to those unwritten laws which bring upon the transgressor of them the reprobation of the general sentiment.

And we have not forgotten to provide for our weary spirits many relaxations from toil; we have regular games and sacrifices throughout the year; at home the style of our life is refined; and the delight which we daily feel in all these things helps to banish melancholy. Because of the greatness of our city the fruits of the whole earth flow in upon us; so that we enjoy the goods of other countries as freely as of our own.

Then, again, our military training is in many respects superior to that of our adversaries. Our city is thrown open to the world, and we never expel a foreigner or prevent him from seeing or learning anything of which the secret if revealed to an enemy might profit him. We rely not upon management or trickery, but upon our own hearts and hands. And in the matter of education, whereas they from early youth are always undergoing laborious exercises which are to make them brave, we live at ease, and yet are equally ready to face the perils which they face. And here is the proof. The Lacedaemonians come into Attica not by themselves, but with their whole confederacy following; we go alone into a neighbor's country; and although our opponents are fighting for their homes and we on a foreign soil, we have seldom any difficulty in overcoming them. Our enemies have never yet felt our united strength; the care of a navy divides our attention, and on land we are obliged to send our own citizens everywhere. But they, if they meet and defeat a part of our army, are as proud as if they had routed us all, and when defeated they pretend to have been vanquished by us all.

If then we prefer to meet danger with a light heart but without laborious training, and with a courage which is gained by habit and not enforced by law, are we not greatly the gainers? Since we do not anticipate the pain, although, when the hour comes, we can be as brave as those who never allow themselves to rest; and thus too our city is equally admirable in peace and in war.

For we are lovers of the beautiful, yet with economy, and we cultivate the mind without loss of manliness. Wealth we employ, not for talk and ostentation, but when there is a real use for it. To avow poverty with us is no disgrace; the true disgrace is in doing nothing to avoid it. An Athenian citizen does not neglect the status because he takes care of his own household; and even those of us who are engaged in business have a very fair idea of politics. We alone regard a man who takes no interest in public affairs, not as a harmless, but as a useless character; and if few of us are originators, we are all sound judges of a policy. The great impediment to action is, in our opinion, not discussion, but the want of that knowledge which is gained by discussion preparatory to action, For we have a peculiar power of thinking before we act and of acting too, whereas other men are courageous from ignorance but hesitate upon reflection. And they are surely to be esteemed the bravest spirits who, having the clearest sense both of the pains and pleasures of life, do not on that account shrink from danger. In doing good, again, we are unlike others; we make our friends by conferring, not by receiving favors. Now he who confers a favor is the firmer friend, because he would fain by kindness keep alive the memory of an obligation; but the recipient is colder in his feelings, because he knows that in requiting another's generosity he will not be winning gratitude but only paying a debt. We alone do good to our neighbors not upon a calculation of interest, but in the confidence of freedom and in a frank and fearless spirit.

To sum up: I say that Athens is the school of Hellas, and that the individual Athenian in his own person seems to have the power of adapting himself to the most varied florins of action with the utmost versatility and grace. This is no passing and idle word, but truth and fact; and the assertion is verified by the position to which these qualities have raised the state. For in the hour of trial Athens alone among her contemporaries is superior to the report of her. No enemy who comes against her is indignant at the reverses which he sustains at the hands of such a city; no subject complains that his masters are unworthy of him. And we shall assuredly not be without witnesses; there are mighty monuments of our power which will make us the wonder of this and of succeeding ages; we shall not need the praises of Homer or of any other panegyrist whose poetry may please for the moment, although his representation of the facts will not bear the light of day. For we have compelled every land and every sea to open a path for our valor, and have everywhere planted eternal memorials of our friendship and of our enmity. Such is the city for whose sake these men nobly fought and died; they could not bear the thought that she might be taken from them; and every one of us who survive should gladly toil on her behalf.

I have dwelt upon the greatness of Athens because I want to show you that we are contending for a higher prize than those who enjoy none of these privileges, and to establish by manifest proof the merit of these men whom I am now commemorating. Their loftiest praise has been already spoken. For in magnifying the city I have magnified them, and men like them whose virtues made her glorious. And of how few Hellenes can it be said as of them, that their deeds when weighed in the balance have been found equal to their fame! It seems to me that a death such as theirs has been gives the true measure of a man's worth; it may be the first revelation of his virtues, but is at any rate their final seal. For even those who come short in other ways may justly plead the velour with which they have fought for their country; they have blotted out the evil with the good, and have benefited the state more by their public services than they have injured her by their private actions. None of these men were enervated by wealth or hesitated to resign the pleasures of life; none of them put off the evil day in the hope, natural to poverty, that a man, though poor, may one day become rich. But, deeming that the punishment of their enemies was sweeter than any of these things, and that they could fall in no nobler cause, they determined at the hazard of their lives to be honorably avenged, and to leave the rest. They resigned to hope their unknown chance of happiness; but in the face of death they resolved to rely upon themselves alone. And when the moment came they were minded to resist and suffer, rather than to fly and save their lives; they ran away from the word of dishonor, but on the battlefield their feet stood fast, and in an instant, at the height of their fortune, they passed away from the scene, not of their fear, but of their glory.

Such was the end of these men; they were worthy of Athens, and the living need not desire to have a more heroic spirit, although they may pray for a less fatal issue. The value of such a spirit is not to be expressed in words. Anyone can discourse to you for ever about the advantages of a brave defense which you know already. But instead of listening to him I would have you day by day fix your eyes upon the greatness of Athens, until you become filled with the love of her; and when you are impressed by the spectacle of her glory, reflect that this empire has been acquired by men who knew their duty and had the courage to do it, who in the hour of conflict had the fear of dishonor always present to them, and who, if ever they failed in an enterprise, would not allow their virtues to be lost to their country, but freely gave their lives to her as the fairest offering which they could present at her feast. The sacrifice which they collectively made was individually repaid to them; for they received again each one for himself a praise which grows not old, and the noblest of all sepulchers—speak not of that in which their remains are laid, but of that in which their glory survives, and is proclaimed always and on every fitting occasion both in word and deed. For the whole earth is the sepulcher of famous men; not only are they commemorated by columns and inscriptions in their own country, but in foreign lands there dwells also an unwritten memorial of them, graven not on stone but in the hearts of men. Make them your examples, and esteeming courage to be freedom and freedom to be happiness, do not weigh too nicely the perils of war. The unfortunate who has no hope of a change for the better has less reason to throw away his life than the prosperous who, if he survive, is always liable to a change for the worse, and to whom any accidental fall makes the most serious difference. To a man of spirit, cowardice and disaster coming together are far more bitter than death striking him unperceived at a time when he is full of courage and animated by the general hope.

Wherefore I do not now commiserate the parents of the dead who stand here; I would rather comfort them. You know that your life has been passed amid manifold vicissitudes; and that they may be deemed fortunate who have gained most honor, whether an honorable death like theirs, or an honorable sorrow like yours, and whose days have been so ordered that the term of their happiness is likewise the term of their life. I know how hard it is to make you feel this, when the good fortune of others will too often remind you of the gladness which once lightened your hearts. And sorrow is felt at the want of those blessings, not which a man never knew, but which were a part of his life before they were taken from him. Some of you are of an age at which they may hope to have other children, and they ought to bear their sorrow better; not only will the children who may hereafter be born make them forget their own lost ones, but the city will be doubly a gainer. She will not be left desolate, and she will be safer. For a man's counsel cannot have equal weight or worth, when he alone has no children to risk in the general danger. To those of you who have passed their prime, I say, 'Congratulate yourselves that you have been happy during the greater part of your days; remember that your life of sorrow will not last long, and be comforted by the glory of those who are gone. For the love of honor alone is ever young, and not riches, as some say, but honor is the delight of men when they are old and useless.'

To you who are the sons and brothers of the departed, I see that the struggle to emulate them will be an arduous one. For all men praise the dead, and, however pre-eminent your virtue may be, hardly will you be thought, I do not say to equal, but even to approach them. The living have their rivals and detractors, but when a man is out of the way, the honor and good-will which he receives is unalloyed. And, if I am to speak of womanly virtues to those of you who will henceforth be widows, let me sum them up in one short admonition: To a woman not to show more weakness than is natural to her sex is a great glory, and not to be talked about for good or for evil among men.

I have paid the required tribute, in obedience to the law, making use of such fitting words as I had. The tribute of deeds has been paid in part; for the dead have been honorably interred, and it remains only that their children should be maintained at the public charge until they are grown up: this is the solid prize with which, as with a garland, Athens crowns her sons living and dead, after a struggle like theirs. For where the rewards of virtue are greatest, there the noblest citizens are enlisted in the service of the state. And now, when you have duly lamented, every one his own dead, you may depart." Such was the order of the funeral celebrated in this winter, with the end of which ended the first year of the Peloponnesian War.

As soon as summer returned,[62] the Peloponnesian army, comprising as before two-thirds of the force of each confederate state, under the command of the Lacedaemonian[63] king Archidamus,[64] the son of Zeuxidamus, invaded Attica, where they established themselves and ravaged the country. They had not been there many days when the plague broke out at Athens for the first time. A similar disorder is said to have previously smitten many places, particularly Lemnos,[65] but there is no record of such a pestilence occurring elsewhere, or of so great a destruction of human life. For a while physicians, in ignorance of the nature of the disease, sought to apply remedies; but it was in vain, and they themselves were among the first victims, because they oftenest came into contact with it. No human art was of any avail, and as to supplications in temples, enquiries of oracles, and the like, they were utterly useless, and at last men were overpowered by the calamity and gave them all up.

The disease is said to have begun south of Egypt in Aethiopia; thence it descended into Egypt and Libya, and after spreading over the greater part of the Persian empire, suddenly fell upon Athens.[66] It first attacked the inhabitants of the Piraeus,[67] and it was supposed that the Peloponnesians had poisoned the cisterns, no conduits having as yet been made there. It afterward reached the upper city, and then the mortality became far greater. As to its probable origin or the causes that might or could have produced such a disturbance of nature, every man, whether a physician or not, will give his own opinion. But I shall describe its actual course, and the symptoms by which anyone who knows them beforehand may recognize the disorder should it ever reappear. For I was myself attacked, and witnessed the sufferings of others.

The season was admitted to have been remarkably free from ordinary sickness; and if anybody was already ill of any other disease, it was absorbed in this. Many who were in perfect health, all in a moment, and without any apparent reason, were seized with violent heats in the head and with redness and inflammation of the eyes. Internally the throat and the tongue were quickly suffused with blood, and the breath became unnatural and fetid. There followed sneezing and hoarseness; in a short time the disorder, accompanied by a violent cough, reached the chest. Then, fastening lower down, it would move the stomach and bring on all the vomits of bile to which physicians have ever given names, and they were very distressing. An ineffectual retching producing violent convulsions attacked most of the sufferers; some as soon as the previous symptoms had abated, others not until long afterward. The body externally was not so very hot to the touch, nor yet pale; it was of a livid color inclining to red, and breaking out in pustules and ulcers. But the internal fever was intense; the sufferers could not bear to have on them even the finest linen garment; they insisted on being naked, and there was nothing that they longed for more eagerly than to throw themselves into cold water. And many of those who had no one to look after them actually plunged into the cisterns, for they were tormented by unceasing thirst, which was not in the least assuaged whether they drank little or much. They could not sleep and a restlessness that was intolerable never left them.

While the disease was at its height the body, instead of wasting away, held out amid these sufferings in a marvelous manner, and either they died on the seventh or ninth day, not of weakness, for their strength was not exhausted, but of internal fever, which was the end of most. If they survived, then the disease descended into the bowels and there produced violent ulceration; severe diarrhea at the same time set in, and at a later stage caused exhaustion, which finally with few exceptions carried them off. For the disorder that had originally settled in the head passed gradually through the whole body, and,

[62] In 430 BC, the second year of the Peloponnesian War.

[63] From Lacedaemon, the original Spartan homeland in the Peloponnesus.

[64] Archidamus (476–427 BCE) gave his name to the "Archidamian War" (431–421 BCE), the first phase of the Peloponnesian War.

[65] A large island in the northeastern Aegean Sea.

[66] The plague's trajectory suggests that it was spread via commerce.

[67] A fortified port and naval base for the city of Athens.

if a person got over the worst, often would seize the extremities and leave its mark, attacking the genitals and the fingers and the toes. Some escaped with the loss of these, some with the loss of their eyes. Some again had no sooner recovered than they were seized with a forgetfulness of all things and knew neither themselves nor their friends.

The malady took a form not to be described, and the fury with which it fastened upon each sufferer was too much for human nature to endure. There was one circumstance in particular that distinguished it from ordinary diseases. The birds and animals that feed on human flesh, although so many bodies were lying unburied, either never came near them, or died if they touched them. This was proved by a remarkable disappearance of the birds of prey, who were not to be seen either about the bodies or anywhere else, whereas in the case of the dogs the fact was even more obvious, because they live with man.

Such was the general nature of the disease: I omit many strange peculiarities that characterized individual cases. None of the ordinary sicknesses attacked anyone while it lasted, or, if they did, they ended in the plague. Some of the sufferers died from want of care, others equally who were receiving the greatest attention. No single remedy could be deemed a specific, for that which did good to one did harm to another. No constitution was of itself strong enough to resist or weak enough to escape the attacks; the disease carried off all alike and defied every mode of treatment. Most appalling was the despondency that seized upon anyone who felt himself sickening; for he instantly abandoned his mind to despair and, instead of holding out, absolutely threw away his chance of life. Appalling too was the rapidity with which men caught the infection, dying like sheep if they attended on one another, and this was the principal cause of mortality. When they were afraid to visit one another, the sufferers died in their solitude, so that many houses were empty because there had been no one left to take care of the sick, or if they ventured to assist, they perished, especially those who aspired to heroism. For they went to see their friends without thought of themselves and were ashamed to leave them, even at a time when the very relations of the dying were at last growing weary and ceased to make lamentations, overwhelmed by the vastness of the calamity. But whatever instances there may have been of such devotion, more often the sick and the dying were tended by the pitying care of those who had recovered, because they knew the course of the disease and were themselves free from apprehension.[68] For no one was ever attacked a second time, or not with a fatal result. All men congratulated them, and they themselves, in the excess of their joy at the moment, had an innocent fancy that they could not die of any other sickness.

The crowding of the people out of the country into the city aggravated the misery, and the newly arrived suffered most. For, having no houses of their own, but inhabiting in the height of summer stifling huts, the mortality among them was dreadful, and they perished in wild disorder. The dead lay as they had died, one upon another, while others hardly alive wallowed in the streets and crawled about every fountain craving for water. The temples in which they lodged were full of the corpses of those who died in them, for the violence of the calamity was such that men, not knowing where to turn, grew reckless of all law, human and divine. The customs that hitherto had been observed at funerals were universally violated, and they buried their dead each one as best he could. Many, having no proper appliances, because the deaths in their household had been so frequent, made no scruple of using the burial-place of others. When one man had raised a funeral pyre, others would come, and throwing on their dead first, set fire to it; or when some other corpse was already burning, before they could be stopped would throw their own dead upon it and depart.

There were other and worse forms of lawlessness that the plague introduced at Athens. Men who had hitherto concealed their indulgence in pleasure now grew bolder. For, seeing the sudden change, how the rich died in a moment, and those who had nothing immediately inherited their property, they reflected that life and riches were alike transitory, and they resolved to enjoy themselves while they could, and to

[68] Because they had gained immunity.

think only of pleasure. Who would be willing to sacrifice himself to the law of honor when he knew not whether he would ever live to be held in honor? The pleasure of the moment and any sort of thing that conduced to it took the place both of honor and of expediency. Already a far heavier sentence had been passed and was hanging over a man's head; before that fell, why should he not take a little pleasure?

Such was the grievous calamity that now afflicted the Athenians; within the walls their people were dying, and without, their country was being ravaged. All the time during which the Peloponnesians[69] remained in the country and the armament of the Athenians continued at sea the plague was raging both among the troops and in the city. The fear that it inspired was said to have induced the enemy to leave Attica sooner than they intended, for they heard from deserters that the disease was in the city, and they likewise saw the burning of the dead. Still, in this invasion the whole country was ravaged by them, and they remained about forty days, which was the longest stay they ever made.

[69] The Spartan army.

57

AN ASSESSMENT OF ATHENIAN DEMOCRACY (CA. 425 BCE): THE "OLD OLIGARCH"

Athens's economic imperialism was manifested in its coinage, which served as currency in all the markets controlled by the Athenians. A "Coinage Decree" of ca. 447 even imposed Athenian coinage, weights, and measures on all Athenian allies. The primary Athenian coin was the large silver tetradrachm, or four-drachm piece. It bore the head of Athena on the obverse and Athena's owl and an olive sprig on the reverse. The legend AΘE ("Athe") identified Athens as the issuing city. These coins were intended for large-scale transactions as opposed to small purchases in the agora (marketplace). One tetradrachm was about four days' salary for a mercenary soldier.

The Athenian democracy (see Reading 54) was not uniformly popular among the citizens of Athens. A rather negative and personal portrayal was presented by an anonymous author known as "The Old Oligarch," who, in a curmudgeonly manner, suggests that neither the aristocrats, whom the author calls "the good people," nor the masses of the unprivileged were really qualified to lead the government because both groups only sought to advance their private interests. The text acknowledges the benefits of naval power and may have been written by a wealthy merchant who had profited from democratic policies even if he did not agree with them. The text is preserved among the works of the early fourth century BCE Athenian historian Xenophon and usually is dated to around 425 BCE.

Source: E. C. Marchant and G. W. Bowersock, eds., *Pseudo-Xenophon. Constitution of the Athenians. In Xenophon VII. Scripta minora*, Loeb Classical Library (Cambridge, MA: Harvard University Press, 1968), 459–507.

And as for the fact that the Athenians have chosen the kind of constitution that they have, I do not think well of their doing this inasmuch as in making their choice they have chosen to let the worst people be better off than the good.[70] Therefore, on this account I do not think well of their constitution. But because they have decided to have it so, I intend to point out how well they preserve their constitution and accomplish those other things for which the rest of the Greeks criticize them.

First I want to say this: there the poor and the people generally are right to have more than the highborn and wealthy for the reason that it is the people who man the ships and impart strength to the city; the steersmen, the boatswains, the sub-boatswains, the look-out officers, and the shipwrights: these are the ones who impart strength to the city far more than the hoplites, the highborn, and the good men. This being the case, it seems right for everyone to have a share in the magistracies, both allotted[71] and elective, and for anyone to be able to speak his mind if he wants to. Then there are those magistracies that bring safety or danger to the people as a whole depending on whether or not they are well managed: of these the people claim no share (they do not think they should have an allotted share in the generalships or cavalry commands).[72] For these people realize that there is more to be gained from their not holding these magistracies but leaving them instead in the hands of the most influential men. However, such magistracies as are salaried and domestically profitable the people are keen to hold.

Then there is a point that some find extraordinary, that the Athenians everywhere assign more to the worst persons, to the poor, and to the popular types than to the good men: in this very point they will be found manifestly preserving their democracy. For the poor, the popular, and the base, insofar as they are well off and the likes of them are numerous, will increase the democracy; but if the wealthy, good men are well off, the men of the people create a strong opposition to themselves. And everywhere on earth the best element is opposed to democracy. For among the best people there is minimal wantonness and injustice but a maximum of scrupulous care for what is good, whereas among the people there is a maximum of ignorance, disorder, and wickedness, for poverty inclines them to disgraceful actions, and because of a lack of money some men are uneducated and ignorant.

Someone might say that they ought not to let everyone speak on equal terms and serve on the Council,[73] but rather just the cleverest and finest. Yet the Athenians' policy is also excellent in this very point of allowing even the worst people to speak. For if the good men were to speak and make policy, it would be splendid for the likes of themselves but not so for the men of the people. But, as things are, any wretch who wants to can stand up and obtain what is good for him and the likes of himself. Someone might say, "What

[70] The "aristoi," that is, the "best people," as they called themselves.

[71] That is, chosen by lot.

[72] Generals were elected because it was thought that generals needed military skills; although the rich usually were elected, there was no regulation preventing a poor man from being chosen.

[73] The Council of 500, introduced by Cleisthenes (see Reading 54).

good would such a man propose for himself and the people?" But they know that this man's ignorance, baseness, and favor are more profitable than the good man's virtue, wisdom, and ill will. A city would not be the best on the basis of such a way of life, but the democracy would be best preserved that way. For the people do not want a good government under which they themselves are slaves; they want to be free and to rule. Bad government is of little concern to them. What you consider bad government is the very source of the people's strength and freedom. If it is good government you seek, you will first observe the cleverest men establishing the laws in their own interest. Then the good men will punish the bad; they will make policy for the city and not allow madmen to participate or to speak their minds or to meet in assembly. As a result of these excellent measures the people would swiftly fall into slavery.

In regard to the allies,[74] the Athenians sail out and lay information, as they are said to do; they hate the aristocrats inasmuch as they realize that the ruler is necessarily hated by the ruled and that if the rich and aristocratic men in the cities are strong, the rule of the people at Athens will last for a very short time. This is why they[75] disfranchise the aristocrats, take away their money, expel and kill them, whereas they promote the interests of the lower class. The Athenian aristocrats protect their opposite numbers in the allied cities, because they realize that it will be to their advantage always to protect the finer people in the cities. Someone might say that the Athenians' strength consists in the allies' ability to pay tribute-money, but the rabble thinks it more advantageous for each one of the Athenians to possess the resources of the allies and for the allies themselves to possess only enough for survival and to work without being able to plot defection.

Furthermore, as a result of their possessions abroad and the tenure of magistracies that take them abroad, both they[76] and their associates have imperceptibly learned to row, for of necessity a man who is often at sea takes up an oar, as does his slave, and they learn naval terminology. Both through experience of voyages and through practice they become fine steersmen. Some are trained by service as steersmen on an ordinary vessel, others on a freighter, others, after such experience, on triremes.[77] Many are able to row as soon as they board their ships, because they have been practicing beforehand throughout their whole lives. But the Athenian infantry, which has the reputation of being very weak, has been deliberately so constituted: they consider that they are weaker and fewer than their enemies,[78] but they are stronger, even on land than such of their allies as pay the tribute, and they think their infantry sufficient if they are more powerful than their allies.

Moreover, the rulers of the sea can do just what rulers of the land sometimes can do, ravage the territory of the stronger. For wherever there is no enemy (or wherever enemies are few), it is possible to put in along the coast and, if there is an attack, to go back on board one's ship and sail away; one who does this is less badly off than one who comes to help with infantry. Further, the rulers of the sea can sail away from their own land to anywhere at all, whereas a land power can take a journey of only a few days from its own territory. Progress is slow, and going on foot one cannot carry provisions sufficient for a long time, whereas imports reach the rulers of the sea.

Wealth they alone of the Greeks and non-Greeks are capable of possessing. If some city is rich in ship-timber, where will it distribute it without the consent of the rulers of the sea? Again if some city is rich in iron, copper, or flax, where will it distribute without the consent of the rulers of the sea? Moreover, it is from these very things that I have my ships: timber from one place, iron from another, copper from another, flax from another, wax from another. In addition, they will forbid export to wherever any of our enemies are, on pain of being unable to use the

[74] The cities coerced into being part of the Athenian Empire.

[75] The Athenian poor.

[76] The Athenian poor.

[77] Athenian warships with three banks of oars.

[78] The Spartans.

sea. And I, without doing anything, have all this from the land because of the sea.

But there is one thing the Athenians lack. If they were thalassocrats[79] living on an island, it would be possible for them to inflict harm, if they wished, but as long as they ruled the sea, to suffer none, neither the ravaging of their land nor the taking on of enemies. As it is, they place their property on islands while trusting in the naval empire and they allow their land to be ravaged, for they realize that if they concern themselves with this, they will be deprived of other greater goods.

Further, for oligarchic[80] cities it is necessary to keep to alliances and oaths. If they do not abide by agreements or if injustice is done, there are the names of the few who made the agreement. But whatever agreements the populace makes can be repudiated by referring the blame to the one who spoke or took the vote, while the others declare that they were absent or did not approve of the agreement made in the full assembly. If it seems advisable for their decisions not to be effective, they invent myriad excuses for not doing what they do not want to do. And if there are any bad results from the people's plans, they charge that a few persons, working against them, ruined their plans; but if there is a good result, they take the credit for themselves.

They do not permit the people to be ill spoken of in comedy,[81] so that they may not have a bad reputation; but if anyone wants to attack private persons, they bid him do so, knowing perfectly well that the person so treated usually is a person of either wealth, high birth, or influence.[82] Some few poor and plebeian types are indeed abused in comedy but only if they have been meddling in others' affairs and trying to rise above their class, so that the people feel no vexation at seeing such persons abused in comedy.

It is my opinion that the people at Athens know which citizens are good and which bad, but that in spite of this knowledge they cultivate those who are complaisant and useful to themselves, even if bad; and they tend to hate the good. For they do not think that the good are naturally virtuous for the people's benefit, but for their hurt. On the other hand, some persons are not by nature democratic although they are truly on the people's side. I pardon the people themselves for their democracy. One must forgive everyone for looking after his own interests. But whoever is not a man of the people and yet prefers to live in a democratic city rather than in an oligarchic one has readied himself to do wrong and has realized that it is easier for an evil man to escape notice in a democratic city than in an oligarchic.

As for the constitution of the Athenians I do not praise its form; but because they have decided to have a democracy, I think they have preserved the democracy well by the means that I have indicated.

[79] A "thalassocracy," a Greek word meaning "rule by sea," was a state that based its power on its navy.

[80] For oligarchy, that is, rule by the well-to-do, see Reading 54.

[81] In Athenian comedy it was permitted to refer to contemporary political events in a humorous manner, but even then an author had to be careful not to offend the wrong people; see Reading 59. Alluding to contemporary events in tragedies could be even more dangerous; see Reading 58.

[82] The comedies of Aristophanes, for example, regularly lampooned individuals, such as Socrates, who were thought to threaten the dynamics of Athenian life.

58

ATHENIAN ANTI-WAR SENTIMENT AND PERCEPTIONS OF WOMEN (415 BCE): EURIPIDES, *TROJAN WOMEN*

A fresco from the "House of the Menander" in Pompeii (79 CE) depicts the treatment of Trojan woman after the fall of Troy. Ajax tears Cassandra away from the Palladium, the ancient wooden statue of Athena that fell from heaven and was kept at the Temple of Athena in Troy, and other Trojan women are carried off into slavery in the background. Cassandra's father Priam, the king of Troy, sadly looks on. This sacrilege brought the wrath of the gods on the Greeks. The Palladium later was said to have been brought from Troy to Italy by Aeneas and eventually kept in the Temple of Vesta in Rome.

Although it was common, and indeed expected, that Athenian comedies would discuss contemporary events, doing so in tragedy, because of its much more serious nature and devastating endings, was forbidden. Indeed, shortly after 494 the poet Phrynicus was fined for presenting a tragedy entitled "The Taking of Miletus," which reminded the Athenians of their disastrous involvement in the Ionian revolt against the Persians in 498. Tragedians, therefore, had to be more circumspect about references to current events. Thus, the Athenian playwright Euripides's drama "The Trojan Women," presented in 415 BCE, approached the topic of the horrors of war by discussing the fate of the Trojan women after the capture of Troy by the Greeks. The four women in the play—Hecuba, Cassandra, Andromache, and Helen—would have been familiar to the audience as the four women who appeared in the last book of Homer's Iliad. Although no mention was made of current events, no one in the audience would have missed the implied connection to the possible fate of the city of Athens in the Peloponnesian War (431–404 BCE) and a more specific allusion to the Athenian punishment of the island city of Melos only the year before for trying to secede from the Athenian Empire. The Athenians captured the city with the assistance of Melian traitors and made good their threats, killing all the men and selling the women and children into slavery. Euripides won only the second prize for his efforts.

Source: E. P. Coleridge, trans., *The Plays of Euripides, Translated into English Prose*, Vol. I (London: Bell, 1906).

SCENE: In front of Agamemnon's tent near Troy, a tall woman with white hair is lying on the ground asleep. In the background is a battlefield behind which stand the partially destroyed walls of Troy. At one side are dead bodies of armed men and on the other side are tents holding the captive women of Troy. Just before sunrise, the god Poseidon is dimly seen before the walls.

POSEIDON, GOD OF THE SEA: I am leaving Ilium,[83] that famous town, and the altars that I love, for when dreary desolation seizes on a town, the worship of the gods decays and loses respect. Scamander's[84] banks reecho long and loud the screams of captive maids, as by lot they receive their masters. Arcadia[85] taketh some, and some the folk of Thessaly[86]; others are assigned to Theseus' sons, the Athenian chiefs. And such of the Trojan women as are not yet portioned out are in these tents, set apart for the leaders of the host, and with them Spartan Helen,[87] daughter of Tyndareus,[88] justly counted among the captives. And wouldst thou see that queen of misery, Hecuba;[89] thou canst, for there she lies before the gates, weeping many a bitter tear for many a tribulation. For at Achilles' tomb, although she knows this not, her daughter Polyxena has died most piteously. Likewise is Priam[90] dead, and her children too: Cassandra,[91] whom the god Apollo left to be a virgin, frenzied maid,[92] hath Agamemnon,[93] in contempt of

[83] A poetic name for Troy, going back to Hittite sources.
[84] The river that ran near Troy.
[85] A region of central Greece.
[86] A region of northern Greece.
[87] The wife of Menelaus of Sparta; she either ran off with or was kidnaped by Paris of Troy and thus caused the Trojan War.
[88] Stepfather of Helen of Troy, whose actual father was the god Zeus.
[89] The wife of king Priam of Troy and mother of nineteen children, including Hector, Paris, Cassandra, and Polyxena.
[90] King of Troy and husband of Hecuba.
[91] Daughter of Priam.
[92] In an effort to seduce her, the god Apollo gave Cassandra the power of prophecy, but when she refused his advances he cursed her so that her true prophesies never would be believed. Prophetresses were thought to have been driven mad by Apollo when they gave their prophecies; see also Reading 88.
[93] King of Mycenae and Argos and leader of the Greek army.

the god's ordinance and of piety, forced to a dishonored wedlock. Farewell, O city prosperous once! Farewell, ye ramparts of hewn stone! Had not Pallas,[94] daughter of Zeus, decreed thy ruin, thou would be standing firmly still.

[Enter the Goddess Athena, Daughter of Zeus]

Athena: Dost not know the insult done to me and to the shrine I love?

Poseidon: Surely, in the hour that Ajax[95] tore Cassandra thence.

Athena: Yea, and the Achaeans[96] did naught, said naught to him.[97]

Poseidon: And yet 'twas by thy mighty aid they sacked Ilium.

Athena: For which cause I would join with thee to work their bane.

Poseidon: My powers are ready at thy will. What is thy intent?

Athena: When they have set sail from Ilium for their homes. On them will Zeus also send his rain and fearful hail, and inky tempests from the sky; yea, and he promises to grant me his lightning-bolts to hurl on the Achaeans and fire their ships. And do thou, for thy part, make the Aegean strait to roar with mighty billows and whirlpools, and fill Euboea's hollow bay with corpses, that Achaeans may learn henceforth to reverence my temples and regard all other deities.[98]

[Exit]

Hecuba (awakening, to herself): Lift thy head, unhappy lady, from the ground, thy neck upraise. This is Troy no more, no longer am I queen in Ilium. Although fortune change, endure thy lot; sail with the stream, and follow fortune's tack, steer not thy vessel of life against the tide, because chance must guide thy course. Ah me! Ah me! What else but tears is now my hapless lot, whose country, children, husband, all are lost? Oh that I should sit here over against the tent of Agamemnon. Forth from my home to slavery they hale my aged frame, while from my head in piteous manner the hair is shorn for grief. Ah! Hapless wives of those mail-clad sons of Troy! Ah! Poor maidens, luckless brides, come weep, for Ilium is now but a ruin.

[Enter CHORUS OF CAPTIVE TROJAN WOMEN]

Semi-Chorus: O Hecuba why these cries, these piercing shrieks? What mean thy words? For I heard thy piteous wail echo through the building, and a pang of terror shoots through each captive Trojan's breast, as pent within these walls they mourn their slavish lot.

Hecuba: My child, even now the hands of Argive[99] rowers are busy at their ships.

Semi-Chorus: Ah, woe is me! what is their intent? Will they really bear me hence in sorrow from my country in their fleet?

Hecuba: I know not, although I guess our doom.

Semi-Chorus: O misery! Woe to us Trojan women, soon to hear the order given, "Come forth from the house; the Argives are preparing to return." Hath a herald from the Danaans[100] already come? To whom am I, poor captive, given as a slave?

Hecuba: Thou art not far from being allotted now.

Semi-Chorus II: Oh woe! What Argive or Phthiotian[101] chief will bear me far from Troy? Alas!

Hecuba: Ah me! Ah me! Whose slave shall I become in my old age? In what far clime? The wretched copy of a corpse, set to keep the gate or tend their children, I who once held royal rank in Troy.

---

[94] Another name for Athena.

[95] Not the Ajax who was one of the primary Greek heroes and known as "Telamonian Ajax" or "Greater Ajax," but a second Ajax, "Lesser Ajax."

[96] Another name for the Greeks.

[97] In fact the Greeks, and in particular Odysseus, did rebuke Ajax for his sacrilegious violation of Cassandra in Athena's temple, where she had taken refuge.

[98] Many of the Greeks had difficulties returning home, especially Odysseus, who wandered the Mediterranean for ten years.

[99] From Argos in the northeastern Peloponnesus.

[100] A poetic name for Greeks.

[101] Phthiotis, or Phthia, was a region in central Greece ruled by Achilles.

[Enter the Greek Herald TALTHYBIUS]

Talthybius: The lot has decided your fates already, if that was what you feared.

Hecuba: Then tell me, whose prize is my daughter, hapless Cassandra?

Talthybius: King Agamemnon hath chosen her out for himself.

Hecuba: To be the slave-girl of his Spartan wife? Ah me!

Talthybius: Nay, to share with him his stealthy love.

Hecuba: What! Phoebus'[102] virgin-priestess, to whom the god with golden locks granted the boon of maidenhood?

Talthybius: The dart of love hath pierced his heart, love for the frenzied maid.

Hecuba: What have ye done to my child whom late ye took from me?

Talthybius: Do you mean Polyxena, or whom do you inquire about?

Hecuba: To whom hath the lot assigned her?

Talthybius: To minister at Achilles' tomb hath been appointed her.

Hecuba: Woe is me! I the mother of a dead man's slave! What custom, what ordinance is this among Hellenes, good sir?

Talthybius: Count thy daughter happy: 'tis well with her.

Hecuba: What wild words are these? Say, is she still alive?

Talthybius: Her fate is one that sets her free from trouble.[103]

Hecuba: And what of mail-clad Hector's wife, sad Andromache? Declare her fate.

Talthybius: She too was a chosen prize; Achilles' son did take her.

Hecuba: As for me whose hair is white with age, who need to hold a staff to be to me a third foot, whose servant am I to be?

Talthybius: Odysseus, King of Ithaca, hath taken thee to be his slave.

Hecuba: O god! Now smite the close-shorn head! Tear your cheeks with your nails. God help me! I have fallen as a slave to a treacherous foe I hate, a monster of lawlessness, one that by his double tongue hath turned against us all that once was friendly in his camp, changing this for that and that for this again. Oh weep for me, ye Trojan women! Undone! Undone and lost! Ah woe, a victim to a most unhappy lot!

[Enter CASSANDRA Carrying Torches]

Cassandra: Bring the light, uplift and show its flame! I am doing the god's service, see! Blest am I, the maiden soon to wed a princely lord in Argos. Hail Hymen, king of marriage! Because thou, my mother, art ever busied with tears and lamentations in thy mourning for my father's death and for our country dear, I at my own nuptials am making this torch to blaze and show its light, in thy honor, O Hymen, king of marriage.

Hecuba: Ah, my child! how little did I ever dream that such would be thy marriage, a captive, and of Argos too!

Cassandra: O mother, rejoice in my royal match. Lead me to my lord Agamemnon, that famous king of the Achaeans, he will find in me a bride more fraught with woe to him than Helen. For I will slay him and lay waste his home to avenge my father's and my brethren's death. Wherefore, mother mine, thou shouldst not pity thy country or my betrothal, for this my marriage will destroy those whom thou and I most hate.[104]

Talthybius: Had not Apollo turned thy wits astray, thou wouldst not have sent my chiefs on their way with such ominous predictions. Follow me now to the ships to grace the wedding of our chief.

Cassandra: Fare thee well, mother mine! Dry thy tears, O country dear! After yet a little while my brothers sleeping in the tomb and my own father true shall welcome me; yet shall victory crown my

---

[102] An epithet of the god Apollo.

[103] Hecuba does not yet realize that this obscure reply means that Polyxena is dead.

[104] After Agamemnon returned home, he and Cassandra were murdered by his wife Clytemnestra and her lover Aegisthus.

advent amongst the dead, when I have overthrown the home of our destroyers, the house of the sons of Atreus.[105]

[Exit TALTHYBIUS and CASSANDRA]

Hecuba: Ah, woe is me! And this is what I bear and am to bear for one weak woman's wooing![106] O my daughter, O Cassandra! How cruel the lot that ends thy virgin days! And thou, Polyxena! My child of sorrow, where, oh!, where art thou? None of all the many sons and daughters I have borne comes to aid a wretched mother. Why then raise me up? What hope is left us? Of all the prosperous crowd, count none a happy man before he die.[107]

[Enter ANDROMACHE with ASTYANAX]

Hecuba: Whither art thou borne, unhappy wife, mounted on that car, side by side with Hector's bronze arms and Phrygian[108] spoils of war, with which Achilles' son will deck the shrines of Phthia on his return from Troy?

Andromache: My Achaean masters drag me hence.

Hecuba: Woe is thee!

Andromache: Come, my husband, come to me!

Hecuba: Ah hapless wife! Thou callest on my son who lieth in the tomb.

Andromache: Thy wife's defender, come!

Hecuba: O my country, O unhappy land, I weep for thee now left behind; now dost thou behold thy piteous end.

Chorus: What sweet relief to sufferers 'tis to weep, to mourn, lament, and chant the dirge that tells of grief!

Andromache: Thy daughter Polyxena is dead, slain at Achilles' tomb, an offering to his lifeless corpse.

Hecuba: O woe is me!

Andromache: I saw her with mine eyes, and covered her corpse with a mantle. Her death was a happier fate than this my life.

Hecuba: Death and life are not the same, my child; the one is annihilation, the other keeps a place for hope.

Andromache: 'Tis all one, I say, ne'er to have been born and to be dead, and better far is death than life with misery. For the dead feel no sorrow any more and know no grief, but he who has known prosperity and has fallen on evil days feels his spirit straying from the scene of former joys.

[Enter TALTHYBIUS]

Talthybius: Oh hate me not, thou that first were Hector's wife, the bravest of the Phrygians! For my tongue would fain not tell that which the Danaans and sons of Pelops[109] both command. 'Tis decreed thy son is—how can I tell my news? I know no words to break the sorrow lightly to thee.

Andromache: I thank thee for thy consideration, unless indeed thou hast good news to tell.

Talthybius: They mean to slay thy son[110]; there is my hateful message to thee.

Andromache: O god! This is worse tidings than my forced marriage.

Talthybius: So spoke Odysseus. He said they should not rear so brave a father's son. From Troy's battlements he must be thrown.

Andromache: My child! My own sweet babe and priceless treasure! Thy death the foe demands, and thou must leave thy wretched mother. Hector will not rise to bring thee salvation. One awful headlong leap from the dizzy height and thou wilt dash out thy life with none to pity thee. In vain it seems these breasts did suckle thee, wrapped in thy swaddling-clothes. Kiss thy mother now for the last time, twine thy arms about my neck and join thy lips to mine!

---

[105] The son of Pelops and Hippodameia (see Reading 51) and the father of Agamemnon, king of Mycenae and/or Argos, and Menelaus, king of Sparta.

[106] That is, Paris's wooing of Helen.

[107] A Greek commonplace.

[108] The Trojans also were known as Phrygians.

[109] Ironically, a native of Phrygia or Lydia near Troy who became king of Pisa in the northwestern Peloponnesus. His son Atreus was the father of Agamemnon and Menelaus.

[110] Astyanax; see Reading 45.

Talthybius: Come, child, leave fond embracing of thy woeful mother, and mount thy ancestral towers, there to draw thy parting breath.

[Exit ANDROMACHE and TALTHYBIUS with ASTYANAX]

Hecuba: O child, son of my hapless boy, an unjust fate robs me and thy mother of thy life. Woe for my city! Woe for thee! What is wanting now to our utter and immediate ruin?

[Enter TALTHYBIUS and attendants, bearing the corpse of ASTYANAX on HECTOR's shield]

Talthybius: Hecuba, one ship alone delays its plashing oars, for Neoptolemus is already out at sea and with him goes Andromache, who drew many a tear from me, wailing her country and crying her farewell to Hector's tomb. And she craved her master leave to bury this poor dead child of Hector. But now will I go to dig a grave for him, that our united efforts shortening our task may speed our ship toward home.

[Exit TALTHYBIUS]

Hecuba: O ye Achaeans, more reason have ye to boast of your prowess than your wisdom. Why have ye in terror of this child been guilty of murder never matched before?

Chorus: Wail for the dead.

Hecuba: Woe is me!

Chorus: Alas! For thy unending sorrow.

Hecuba: Go, bury now in his poor tomb the dead, wreathed all duly as befits a corpse. And yet I deem it makes but little difference to the dead, although they get a gorgeous funeral, for this is but a cause of idle pride to the living.

[The corpse is carried off to burial]

Talthybius: Ye captains, whose allotted task it is to fire this town of Priam, to you I speak. No longer keep the firebrand idle in your hands, but launch the flame, that when we have destroyed the city of Ilium we may set forth in gladness on our homeward voyage from Troy. And thou, unhappy grey haired woman, follow, yonder come servants from Odysseus to fetch thee, for to him thou art assigned by lot to be a slave far from thy country.

Hecuba: Woe! Thrice woe upon me! Ilium is ablaze, the homes of Pergamos[111] and its towering walls are now one sheet of flame.

Chorus: As the smoke soars on wings to heaven, so sinks our city to the ground before the spear. With furious haste both fire and foeman's spear devour each house.

Hecuba: I am being dragged and hurried away.

Chorus: O the sorrow of that cry!

Hecuba: From my own dear country, to dwell beneath a master's roof. Woe is me! O Priam, Priam, unburied, left without a friend, naught dost thou know of my cruel fate.

Chorus: Woe for our unhappy town! And yet to the Achaean fleet advance.

Hecuba: Woe for thee, O land that nursed my little babes!

Chorus: Ah! Woe!

[111] Another name for Troy, later applied to the kingdom of Pergamum in western Anatolia.

59

ATHENIAN ANTI-WAR SENTIMENT AND PERCEPTIONS OF WOMEN (411 BCE): ARISTOPHANES, *LYSISTRATA*

In most cases, ancient Greek women had little opportunity for self-expression, being generally relegated to domestic duties. One exception to this was the Heraean Games, where a women's footrace took place at Olympia on the same racetrack as used for the men's Olympic Games. The winner received an olive crown and part of a cow.

In 411 BCE, in the middle of the Peloponnesian War, the Athenian comic poet Aristophanes authored the *Lysistrata,* in which the women of Athens, Sparta, and other Greek cities, led by the Athenian *Lysistrata,* crafted a plan for ending the war: they all would refuse to have sex with their husbands until the men stopped fighting. It would not have been safe to express an unpatriotic desire about ending the war openly in the Assembly or in more serious literature, but in a comedy, this inflammatory topic could be brought up. The play also betrays many of the stereotypes that Greek men had about Greek women.

Source: Aristophanes, *Lysistrata*, in *The Eleven Comedies*, Vol. 1 (London: Athenian Society, 1912), 254ff; unknown translator rumored to be Oscar Wilde.

SCENE: At the base of the Orchestra are two buildings, the house of Lysistrata, and the entrance to the Acropolis; a winding and narrow path leads up to the latter. Between the two buildings is the opening of the Cave of Pan on the northern slope of the Acropolis. Lysistrata is pacing up and down in front of her house.

Lysistrata: Ah! If only they had been invited to a Bacchic revelling,[112] or a feast of Pan[113] or Aphrodite or Genetyllis,[114] why, the streets would have been impassable for the thronging tambourines! Now there's never a woman here. Ah! Except my neighbor Cleonice, whom I see approaching yonder. Good day, Cleonice.

Cleonice: Good day, Lysistrata; but pray, why this dark, forbidding face, my dear? Believe me, you don't look a bit pretty with those black, lowering brows.

Lysistrata: Oh, Cleonice, my heart is on fire; I blush for our sex. Men will have it we are tricky and sly.

Cleonice: And they are quite right, upon my word!

Lysistrata: Yet, look you, when the women are summoned to meet for a matter of the greatest importance, they lie in bed instead of coming.

Cleonice: Oh! They will come, my dear; but it's not easy, you know, for women to leave the house. One is busy pottering about her husband; another is getting the servant up; a third is putting her child asleep or washing the brat or feeding it.

Lysistrata: But I tell you, the business that calls them here is far and away more urgent.

Cleonice: And why do you summon us, dear Lysistrata? What is it all about?

Lysistrata: About a big thing.

Cleonice (taking this in a different sense; with great interest): And is it thick too?

Lysistrata: Yes, very thick.

Cleonice: And we are not all here on the spot! Imagine!

Lysistrata (wearily): Oh! If it were what you suppose, there would be never an absentee. No, no, it concerns a thing I have turned about and about this way and that so many sleepless nights. It means just this: Greece saved by the women!

Cleonice: By the women! Why, its salvation hangs on a poor thread then!

Lysistrata: Our country's fortunes depend on us. If the Boeotian[115] and Peloponnesian[116] women join us, Greece is saved.

Cleonice: But how should women perform so wise and glorious an achievement, we women who dwell in the retirement of the household, clad in diaphanous garments of yellow silk and long flowing gowns, decked out with flowers and shod with dainty little slippers?

Lysistrata: Ah, but those are the very sheet-anchors[117] of our salvation, those yellow tunics, those scents and slippers, those cosmetics and transparent robes.

[112] A celebration in honor of the wine god Dionysus attended only by women; see Reading 79.

[113] A fertility god, associated with sexuality, with the hindquarters, legs, and horns of a goat.

[114] The goddess of birth.

[115] Boeotia was in central Greece; its major city was Thebes.

[116] The Peloponnesus was the southernmost part of Greece; its major cities were Sparta and Argos.

[117] Emergency anchors made of anything that would float.

Cleonice: How so, pray?

Lysistrata: There is not a man who will wield a lance against another.

Cleonice: Quick, I will get me a yellow tunic from the dyer's.

Lysistrata: . . . or want a shield.

Cleonice: I'll run and put on a flowing gown.

Lysistrata: . . . or draw a sword.

Cleonice: I'll haste and buy a pair of slippers this instant.

Lysistrata: Now tell me, would not the women have done best to come?

(Myrrhine, another Athenian, enters, followed by other women.)

Myrrhine: Are we late, Lysistrata? Tell us, pray; what, not a word?

Lysistrata: I cannot say much for you, Myrrhine! You have not bestirred yourself overmuch for an affair of such urgency.

Myrrhine: I could not find my girdle in the dark. However, if the matter is so pressing, here we are; so speak.

Cleonice: No, let's wait a moment more, until the women of Boeotia arrive and those from the Peloponnese.

Lysistrata: Yes, that is best. . . Ah! here comes Lampito.

(Lampito, a husky Spartan damsel, enters with three others, two from Boeotia and one from Corinth.)

Good day, Lampito, dear friend from Lacedaemon.[118] How well and handsome you look! what a rosy complexion! And how strong you seem. Why, you could strangle a bull surely!

Lampito: Yes, indeed, I really think I could. It is because I do gymnastics and practice the bottom-kicking dance.

Cleonice (opening Lampito's robe): And what superb breasts!

Lysistrata: And this young woman, where is she from?

Lampito: She is a noble lady from Boeotia.

Lysistrata: Ah! My pretty Boeotian friend, you are as blooming as a garden.

[118] The territory surrounding Sparta.

Cleonice (making another inspection): Yes, on my word! And her "garden" is so thoroughly weeded too!

Lysistrata (pointing to the Corinthian): And who is this?

Lampito: 'Tis an honest woman, by my faith! She comes from Corinth.

Cleonice: Oh! Honest, no doubt then, as honesty goes at Corinth.[119]

Lampito: But who has called together this council of women, pray?

Lysistrata: I have.

Lampito: Well then, tell us what you want of us.

Cleonice: Yes, please tell us! What is this very important business you wish to inform us about?

Lysistrata: I will tell you. But first answer me one question.

Cleonice: Anything you wish.

Lysistrata: Don't you feel sad and sorry because the fathers of your children are far away from you with the army? For I'll wager there is not one of you whose husband is not abroad at this moment.

Cleonice: Mine has been the last five months in Thrace,[120] looking after Eucrates.[121]

Myrrhine: It's seven long months since mine left for Pylos.[122]

Lampito: As for mine, if he ever does return from service, he's no sooner home than he takes down his shield again and flies back to the wars.

Lysistrata: And not so much as the shadow of a lover! Since the day the Milesians betrayed us,[123] I have

[119] A clever way of suggesting that there was not much honesty at Corinth.

[120] A mountainous area northeast of Greece; modern Bulgaria.

[121] An Athenian general in Thrace in 412 BCE; brother of Nicias, who had negotiated the truce with Sparta in 421.

[122] After an Athenian defeat of the Spartans in 425 BCE, Athens gained control of the site of the Mycenaean city Pylos, located on the southwestern coast of the Peloponnesus. The place became an Athenian strongpoint and required constant reinforcements.

[123] In 412 BCE, after the Athenian defeat at Syracuse in Sicily, the Ionian city of Miletus revolted against Athens and became a base for the Spartans.

never once seen an eight-inch gadget,[124] even to be a leather consolation to us poor widows. Now tell me, if I have discovered a means of ending the war, will you all second me?

Cleonice: Yes verily, by all the goddesses, I swear I will, even if I have to put my gown in pawn.

Myrrhine: And so will I, even if I must be split in two like a flat-fish, and have half myself removed.

Lampito: And I too; why to secure peace, I would climb to the top of Mount Taÿgetus.[125]

Lysistrata: Then I will out with it at last, my mighty secret! Oh! sister women, if we would compel our husbands to make peace, we must refrain.

Cleonice: Refrain from what? Tell us, tell us!

Lysistrata: We must refrain from the male altogether. Nay, why do you turn your backs on me? Where are you going? So, you bite your lips, and shake your heads, eh? Why these pale, sad looks? Why these tears? Come, will you do it, yes or no? Do you hesitate?

Cleonice: I will not do it, let the war go on. Anything, anything but that! Bid me go through the fire, if you will, but to rob us of the sweetest thing in all the world, Lysistrata darling!

Lysistrata (to Myrrhine): And you?

Myrrhine: Yes, I agree with the others; I too would sooner go through the fire.

Lysistrata: But you, my dear, you from hardy Sparta, if you join me, all may yet be well; help me, second me, I beg you.

Lampito: 'Tis a hard thing, by the two goddesses[126] it is! For a woman to sleep alone without ever a strong male in her bed. But there, peace must come first.

Lysistrata: Oh, my darling, my dearest, best friend, you are the only one deserving the name of woman!

Cleonice: But if, may the gods forbid, we do refrain altogether from what you say, should we get peace any sooner?

Lysistrata: Of course we should, by the two goddesses! We need only sit indoors with painted cheeks, and meet our mates lightly clad in transparent gowns of Amorgos silk, and perfectly depilated. They will get their tools up and be wild to lie with us. That will be the time to refuse, and they will hasten to make peace, I am convinced of that!

Cleonice: But, oh dear, suppose our husbands drag us into our bedchamber?

Lysistrata: Hold on to the door posts.

Cleonice: But if they beat us?[127]

Lysistrata: Then yield to their wishes, but with a bad grace; there will be no pleasure in it for them. Besides, there are a thousand ways of tormenting them. Never fear, they'll soon tire of the game; there's no satisfaction for a man, unless the woman shares it.

Cleonice: Very well, if you must have it so, we agree.

Lampito: For ourselves, no doubt we shall persuade our husbands to conclude a fair and honest peace; but there is the Athenian populace, how are we to cure these folk of their warlike frenzy?

Lysistrata: Have no fear; we undertake to make our own people listen to reason.

Lampito: That's impossible, as long as they have their trusty ships and the vast treasures stored in the temple of Athena.

Lysistrata: Ah! But we have seen to that; this very day the Acropolis will be in our hands. That is the task assigned to the older women. While we are here in council, they are going, under pretence of offering sacrifice, to seize the citadel.

Lampito: Well said indeed! Everything is going for the best.

Lysistrata: Come, quick, Lampito, and let us bind ourselves by an inviolable oath.

Lampito: Recite the terms; we will swear to them.

Lysistrata: With pleasure. Where is our Scythian policewoman?[128] Lay this shield on the earth before us, its hollow upwards. In Aeschylus, they sacrifice a sheep, and swear over a shield; we will do the same.

Cleonice: No, Lysistrata, one cannot swear peace over a shield, surely.

[124] A dildo.

[125] A mountain near Sparta.

[126] Demeter and her daughter Persephone.

[127] Spousal abuse was a regular part of ancient Greek domestic life.

[128] After the Battle of Salamis in 480 BCE, the Athenians bought 300 Scythian archers to serve as a local police force. In other comedies, Aristophanes also makes jokes about the Scythians' inability to pronounce Greek. For Scythians, see Reading 68.

Lysistrata: Then listen to me. Let's set a great black bowl on the ground; let's sacrifice a skin of Thasian[129] wine into it, and take oath not to add one single drop of water.[130]

Lampito: Ah! That's an oath pleases me more than I can say.

Lysistrata: Set the bowl down on the ground, and lay your hands on the victim. Almighty goddess, Peitho,[131] and thou, bowl, boon comrade of joy and merriment, receive this our sacrifice, and be propitious to us poor women!

Cleonice (as Lysistrata pours the wine into the bowl): Oh! The fine red blood! How well it flows!

Lysistrata: Come, then, Lampito, and all of you, put your hands to the bowl, and you, too, Cleonice. You must all swear, and pledge yourselves by the same promises: I will have naught to do whether with lover or husband . . .

Cleonice (faintly): I will have naught to do whether with lover or husband . . .

Lysistrata: Albeit he come to me with an erection . . .

Cleonice (her voice quavering): Albeit he come to me with an erection . . . (*in despair*) Oh! Lysistrata, I cannot bear it!

Lysistrata (ignoring this outburst): I will live at home unbulled . . .

Cleonice: I will live at home unbulled . . .

Lysistrata: Beautifully dressed and wearing a saffron-coloured gown

Cleonice: Beautifully dressed and wearing a saffron-coloured gown . . .

Lysistrata: To the end I may inspire my husband with the most ardent longings.

Cleonice: To the end I may inspire my husband with the most ardent longings.

Lysistrata: Never will I give myself voluntarily . . .

Cleonice: Never will I give myself voluntarily . . .

Lysistrata: I will be cold as ice, and never stir a limb . . .

Cleonice: I will be cold as ice, and never stir a limb . . .

Lysistrata: I will neither extend my Persian slippers toward the ceiling . . .

Cleonice: I will neither extend my Persian slippers toward the ceiling . . .

Lysistrata: Nor will I crouch like the lions engraved on a knife-handle.

Cleonice: Nor will I crouch like the lions engraved on a knife-handle.

Lysistrata: And if I keep my oath, may I be suffered to drink of this wine.

Cleonice (more courageously): And if I keep my oath, may I be permitted to drink this wine.

Lysistrata: But if I break it, let my bowl be filled with water.

Cleonice: But if I break it, let my bowl be filled with water.

Lysistrata: Will you all take this oath?

All: We do.

Lysistrata: Then I'll now consume this remnant. (*She drinks.*)

Cleonice (reaching for the cup): Enough, enough, my dear; now let us all drink in turn to cement our friendship. (*They pass the cup around and all drink. A great commotion is heard off stage.*)

Lampito: Listen! what do those cries mean?

Lysistrata: It's what I was telling you; the women have just occupied the Acropolis. So now, Lampito, you return to Sparta to organize the plot, while your comrades here remain as hostages.[132] For ourselves, let us go and join the rest in the citadel, and let us push the bolts well home.

Cleonice: But don't you think the men will march up against us?

Lysistrata: I laugh at them. Neither threats nor flames shall force our doors; they shall open only on the conditions I have named.

Cleonice: Yes, yes, by Aphrodite; otherwise we should be called cowardly and wretched women. (*She follows Lysistrata out.*)

[129] Thasos was a large island in the northern Aegean Sea.

[130] Ancient Greeks and Romans generally drank wine liberally mixed with water.

[131] The goddess of persuasion and seduction.

[132] As a sign of good faith it was customary in international agreements to exchange hostages who would be honored guests.

60

THE DEATH OF SOCRATES (399 BCE): PLATO, *PHAEDO* 15.115A–118A

A second-century CE Roman marble copy of a portrait bust meant to represent Socrates, made from a Greek original dating to the fourth century CE, now in the Alte Museum in Berlin.

The Athenian teacher Socrates, the most famous user of sophistic rhetoric (although not a sophist himself because he accepted no fees and made no promises), taught in Athens during the Peloponnesian War. He left no writings of his own, so his teachings have come down to us secondhand through the writings of his pupil, the Athenian philosopher Plato. Socrates's teaching involved attempts to understand universal moral concepts that all humans comprehend. In order to understand these concepts and the human interactions that they affect, Socrates asked questions such as, "What is justice?" His question-and-answer way of attempting to gain insight into these questions is still known as the Socratic method. Socrates rather simplistically assumed that if one could define concepts such as "virtue," then one would necessarily be virtuous and that lack of virtue was simply the result of ignorance. In 399 BCE, Socrates was charged with corrupting the youth and atheism, that is, teaching that the gods did not exist. What probably really troubled the Athenians, however, was Socrates's penchant for teaching people to question their beliefs about such matters as the proper role of government. In the uneasy times after the end of the Peloponnesian War, these were touchy issues. At his trial before the Council of 500 (see Readings 54 and 57), Socrates insulted the jury by using the occasion to present his teachings. He was convicted by a vote of 280 to 220, and the death sentence was imposed by an even greater vote, probably in the hope, even of his supporters, that he would follow the usual course of action by those sentenced to death and go into exile. Socrates refused even to make an appeal for leniency, which might well have been granted, stating that Athens could kill his physical body but never his soul. On the appointed day, with his friends and pupils around him, Socrates carried out his own execution by drinking hemlock, and a fatal numbness crept up from his legs to his vital organs. Plato's dialogue "The Phaedo," told from the perspective of Phaedo of Elis, one of Socrates's students, tells of Socrates's suicide.

Source: Benjamin Jowett, *The Apology, Phaedo, and Crito of Plato* (New York: Collier, 1909).

When he had finished speaking, Crito[133] said: "And have you any commands for us, Socrates, anything to say about your children, or any other matter in which we can serve you?"

"Nothing particular," he said, "Only, as I have always told you, I would have you look to yourselves; that is a service that you may always be doing to me and mine as well as to yourselves. And you need not make professions, for if you take no thought for yourselves, and walk not according to the precepts that I have given you, not now for the first time, the warmth of your professions will be of no avail."

"We will do our best," said Crito, "But in what way would you have us bury you?"

"In any way that you like, only you must get hold of me, and take care that I do not walk away from you." Then he turned to us, and added with a smile, "I cannot make Crito believe that I am the same Socrates who has been talking and conducting the argument; he fancies that I am the other Socrates whom he will soon see, a dead body, and he asks, 'How shall he bury me?' And although I have spoken many words in the endeavor to show that when I have drunk the poison I shall leave you and go to the joys of the blessed, these words of mine, with which I comforted you and myself, have had, as I perceive, no effect upon Crito. And therefore I want you to be surety[134] for me now, as he was surety for me at the trial, but let the promise be of another sort, for he was my surety to the judges that I would remain, but you must be my surety to him that I shall not remain, but go away and depart; and then he will suffer less at my death, and not be grieved when he sees my body being burned or buried. I would not have him sorrow at my hard lot, or say at the burial, 'Thus we lay out Socrates,' or, 'Thus we follow him to the grave or bury him,' for false words are not only evil in themselves, but they infect the soul with evil. Be of good cheer then, my dear Crito, and say that you are burying my body only, and do with that as is usual, and as you think best."

When he had spoken these words, he arose and went into the bath-chamber with Crito, who bid us wait, and we waited, talking and thinking of the subject of discourse, and also of the greatness of our sorrow. He was like a father of whom we were being bereaved, and we were about to pass the rest of our lives as orphans. When he had taken the bath his children were brought to him (he had two young sons and an elder one) and the women of his family also came, and he talked to them and gave them a few directions in the presence of Crito. He then dismissed them and returned to us.

Now the hour of sunset was near, for a good deal of time had passed while he was within. When he came out, he sat down with us again after his bath,

133 An old, wealthy friend of Socrates who offered to finance Socrates's escape from prison.

134 A person who guarantees that another person will fulfil their obligations.

but not much was said. Soon the jailer, who was the servant of The Eleven,[135] entered and stood by him, saying, "To you, Socrates, whom I know to be the noblest and gentlest and best of all who ever came to this place, I will not impute the angry feelings of other men, who rage and swear at me when, in obedience to the authorities, I bid them drink the poison, indeed, I am sure that you will not be angry with me, for others, as you are aware, and not I, are the guilty cause. And so fare you well, and try to bear lightly what must needs be. You know my errand." Then bursting into tears he turned away and went out.

Socrates looked at him and said, "I return your good wishes, and will do as you bid." Then, turning to us, he said, "How charming the man is. Ever since I have been in prison he has always been coming to see me, and at times he would talk to me, and was as good as could be to me, and now see how generously he sorrows for me. But we must do as he says. Crito, let the cup be brought, if the poison[136] is prepared; if not, let the attendant prepare some."

"Yet," said Crito, "the sun is still upon the hilltops, and many a one has taken the draught late, and after the announcement has been made to him. He has eaten and drunk, and indulged in sensual delights; do not hasten then, there is still time."

Socrates said, "Yes, Crito, and they of whom you speak are right in doing thus, for they think that they will gain by the delay. But I am right in not doing thus, for I do not think that I should gain anything by drinking the poison a little later, that I should be sparing and saving a life that is already gone. I could only laugh at myself for this. Please then do as I say, do not refuse me."

Crito, when he heard this, made a sign to the servant and the servant went in and remained for some time, and then returned with the jailer carrying a cup of poison. Socrates said, "You, my good friend, who are experienced in these matters, shall give me directions how I am to proceed." The man answered, "You have only to walk about until your legs are heavy, and then to lie down, and the poison will act." At the same time he handed the cup to Socrates, who in the easiest and gentlest manner, without the least fear or change of color or feature, looking at the man with all his eyes, as his manner was, took the cup and said, "What do you say about making a libation[137] out of this cup to any god? May I, or not?" The man answered, "We only prepare, Socrates, just so much as we deem enough." "I understand," he said, "Yet I may and must pray to the gods to prosper my journey from this to that other world, may this, then, which is my prayer, be granted to me."

Then holding the cup to his lips, quite readily and cheerfully he drank off the poison. And hitherto most of us had been able to control our sorrow; but now when we saw him drinking, and saw too that he had finished the draught, we could no longer forbear, and in spite of myself my own tears were flowing fast, so that I covered my face and wept over myself, for certainly I was not weeping over him, but at the thought of my own calamity in having lost such a companion. Nor was I the first, for Crito, when he found himself unable to restrain his tears, had got up and moved away, and I followed, and at that moment, Apollodorus, who had been weeping all the time, broke out into a loud cry that made cowards of us all. Socrates alone retained his calmness. "What is this strange outcry?", he said, "I sent away the women mainly in order that they might not offend in this way, for I have heard that a man should die in peace. Be quiet, then, and have patience."

When we heard that, we were ashamed, and refrained our tears, and he walked about until, as he said, his legs began to fail, and then he lay on his back, according to the directions, and the man who gave him the poison now and then looked at his feet and legs, and after a while he pressed his foot hard and asked him if he could feel; and he said, "No,";

---

135 Athenian officials who kept order in the agora (marketplace) and supervised the prisons.

136 The poison used was hemlock, technically called *Conium maculatum*. It is an alkaloid poison that causes death by disrupting the central nervous system and paralyzing the respiratory muscles.

137 That is, to pour some of the liquid out as an offering.

and then his leg, and so upwards and upwards, and showed us that he was cold and stiff. And he felt them himself, and said, "When the poison reaches the heart, that will be the end." He was beginning to grow cold about the groin, when he uncovered his face, for he had covered himself up, and said (they were his last words), he said: "Crito, I owe a rooster to Asclepius.[138] Will you remember to pay the debt?" "The debt shall be paid," said Crito, "Is there anything else?" There was no answer to this question, but in a minute or two a movement was heard, and the attendants uncovered him. His eyes were set, and Crito closed his eyes and mouth.

Such was the end of our friend, whom I may truly call the wisest, and justest, and best of all the men whom I ever have known.

[138] The god of healing.

CHAPTER 8

Alexander the Great and the Hellenistic Age (387–31 BCE)

During the Classical Age (500–323 BCE), the Greeks had the opportunity to become the preeminent military and political power of the Mediterranean world, but their inability to get along eventually weakened them and left them open to attack from outside. Unity finally was imposed on Greece by the kingdom of Macedon to the north. Soon thereafter, the Macedonian king Alexander the Great defeated the Persians and created the largest empire yet known. Alexander's conquests opened Greece up to much greater interaction with the eastern world and created the Hellenistic Age (323–31 BCE) of Greek history.

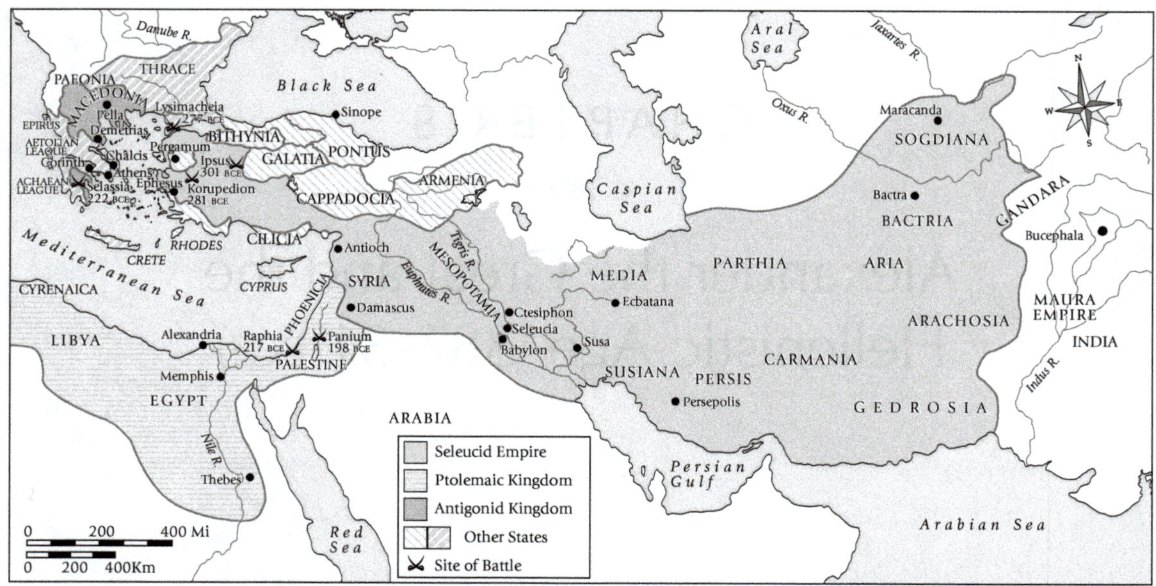

Map 8 The Successors of Alexander the Great

61

THE "SACRED BAND" OF THEBES (375–338 BCE): PLUTARCH, *LIFE OF PELOPIDAS*

In 1818, a British tourist out horseback riding near the village of Chaeronea tripped over a rock that was revealed to be a massive stone lion. The so-called "Lion of Thebes" was erected, it is thought, in honor of the Battle of Chaeronea (338 BCE), where Philip II of Macedon had defeated Thebes and other Greek cities. In subsequent excavations, 254 skeletons were found, laid in seven rows. Given that the Theban Sacred Band included 300 men, it has been surmised that the bodies belong to them.

In the early decades of the fourth century BCE, the army of Thebes in central Greece was based on a professional core of 150 superbly trained male couples, each consisting of an older and a younger man, known as the "Sacred Band." In 375 BCE, the Sacred Band became the first Greek army unit to defeat a larger army of Spartans. This destroyed the stereotype of Spartan invincibility and marked the rise of Thebes as a new Greek power after the Athenians and Spartans had so grievously weakened themselves during the Peloponnesian War and its aftermath leading up to the King's Peace in 387. The Sacred Band is discussed most extensively in the "Life of Pelopidas," a famous Theban general, authored by the second-century CE Greek biographer Plutarch.

Source: John Dryden, *Plutarch: The Lives of the Noble Greeks and Romans*, revised by A. H. Clough, Vol. 1 (Boston: Little, Brown, 1910).

The Thebans, meantime, singly had many skirmishes with the Spartans in Boeotia, and fought some battles, not great indeed, but important as training and instructing them. They thus had their minds raised and their bodies inured to labor, and they gained both experience and courage by these frequent encounters, so much so that we have it related that Antalcidas,[1] the Spartan, said to Agesilaus,[2] returning wounded from Boeotia, "Indeed, the Thebans have paid you handsomely for instructing them in the art of war, against their wills."[3] In real truth, however, Agesilaus was not their master in this, but rather those Thebans that prudently and opportunely, as men do young dogs, set them on their enemies, and brought them safely off after they had tasted the sweets of victory and resolution.

Of all those leaders, Pelopidas deserves the most honor, insofar as after they had once chosen him general, he was every year in command as long as he lived, either as captain of the Sacred Band, or, what was most frequent, as chief captain of Boeotia.[4] About Plataea and Thespiae[5] the Spartans were routed and put to flight, and Phoebidas, who had surprised the Cadmea, slain;[6] and at Tanagra a considerable force was worsted, and the leader Panthoides killed.[7] But these encounters, although they raised the victors' spirits, did not thoroughly dishearten the unsuccessful.[8] for there was no set battle, or regular fighting, but mere incursions on advantage, in which, according to occasion, they charged, retired again, or pursued. But the Battle of Tegyrae,[9] which seemed a prelude to Leuctra,[10] won Pelopidas great reputation, for none of the other commanders could claim any hand in the design, nor the enemies any show of victory. The city of the Orchomenians[11] siding with the Spartans, and having received two companies for its guard, he kept a constant eye upon, and watched his opportunity. Hearing that the garrison had moved into Locris,[12] and hoping to find Orchomenus defenseless, he marched with his Sacred Band and some few horsemen. But when he approached the city and found that a reinforcement of the garrison was on its march from Sparta, he made a circuit round the foot of the mountains and retreated with his little army through Tegyrae, that being the only way he could pass.

As the Thebans were retreating from Orchomenus toward Tegyrae, the Spartans, at the same time marching from Locris, met them. As soon as they came in view, advancing through the straits, someone told Pelopidas, "We are fallen into our enemy's hands." He replied, "And why not they into ours?," and immediately commanded his horse to come up

[1] A Spartan diplomat who negotiated the "King's Peace" in 387 BCE, also known as the "Peace of Antalcidas."

[2] An experienced and able king of Sparta from ca. 400 to 360 BCE.

[3] Because Agesilaus had campaigned in Boeotia and thus "instructed" the Thebans in warfare.

[4] A region of east central Greece.

[5] Cities in Boeotia.

[6] In 378 BCE, the Spartan harmost (military governor) of Thespiae Phoebidas, who had captured the Cadmea (the acropolis of Thebes) in 382, was defeated and killed by the Thebans, including the Sacred Band, in a skirmish near Thespiae.

[7] The Spartan harmost of Tanagra, where Panthoides was killed in another skirmish.

[8] The Spartans.

[9] A battle in 375 BCE where a numerically inferior Theban army under Pelopidas defeated a larger Spartan army, the first time this ever had happened.

[10] A massive defeat of the Spartan army by the Theban general Epaminondas in 371 BCE.

[11] Orchomenus was an ancient city of Boeotia, going back to Mycenaean times.

[12] An area of the eastern coast of central Greece.

from the rear and charge, while he himself drew his infantry, being three hundred in number, into a close body, hoping by that means, at whatsoever point he made the attack, to break his way through his more numerous enemies. The Spartans had two companies (the company consisting, as Ephorus[13] states, of five hundred; Callisthenes[14] says seven hundred; others, as Polybius,[15] nine hundred), and their leaders, Gorgoleon and Theopompus, confident of success, advanced upon the Thebans. The charge was made with much fury, chiefly where the commanders were posted, that the Spartan captains who engaged Pelopidas were first killed and those immediately around them suffered severely. The whole army was thus disheartened, and opened a lane for the Thebans as if they desired to pass through and escape. But when Pelopidas entered, and turning against those that stood their ground, still went with a bloody slaughter, an open flight ensued among the Spartans.

They returned home extremely encouraged with their achievements. For in all the great wars there had ever been against Greeks or barbarians, the Spartans were never before beaten by a smaller company than their own; nor, indeed, in a set battle, when their number was equal. Hence their courage was thought irresistible, and their high repute before the battle made a conquest already of enemies, who thought themselves no match for the men of Sparta even on equal terms. But this battle first taught the other Greeks that when the youth are ashamed of baseness, and ready to venture in a good cause, when they flee disgrace more than danger, there, wherever it be, are found the bravest and most formidable opponents.

Gorgidas, according to some, first formed the Sacred Band of three hundred chosen men, to whom, as being a guard for the citadel, the state allowed provision, and all things necessary for exercise, and hence they were called the city band, as citadels of old were usually called cities. Others say that it was composed of young men attached to each other by personal affection, and a pleasant saying of Pammenes is current, that Homer's Nestor[16] was not well skilled in ordering an army when he advised the Greeks to rank *phylē*[17] with *phylē*, and family with family, together, so that, "So *phylē* might aid *phylē*, and kinsmen aid kinsmen," but that he should have joined lovers and their beloved. For men of the same *phylē* or family little value one another when dangers press; but a band cemented by friendship grounded upon love is never to be broken, and invincible; because the lovers, ashamed to be base in sight of their beloved, and the beloved before their lovers, willingly rush into danger for the relief of one another. Nor can that be wondered at because they have more regard for their absent lovers than for others present, as in the instance of the man who, when his enemy was going to kill him, earnestly requested him to run him through the breast, that his lover might not blush to see him wounded in the back. It is a tradition likewise that Iolaus, who assisted Hercules in his labors and fought at his side, was beloved of him; and Aristotle observes that, even in his time, lovers plighted their faith at Iolaus's tomb. It is likely, therefore, that this band was called sacred on this account, for Plato calls a lover a divine friend. It is stated that it was never beaten until the Battle at Chaeronea, and when Philip,[18] after the fight, took a view of the slain, and came to the place where the three hundred that fought his phalanx lay dead together, he wondered, and understanding that it was the band of lovers, he shed tears and said, "Perish any man who suspects that these men either did or suffered anything that was base."

It was not the disaster of Laius,[19] as the poets imagine, that first gave rise to this form of attachment among the Thebans, but their lawgivers, designing to soften while they were young their natural fierceness,

[13] A Greek historian of the mid-fourth century BCE.

[14] A Greek historian who accompanied Alexander the Great (336–323) on his campaigns in Asia; he eventually was executed for treason.

[15] A Greek historian who wrote during the second century BCE.

[16] The king of Pylos in the southwestern Peloponnesus.

[17] A large subgroup of Greeks: the Dorians had three and the Ionians four.

[18] At the Battle of Chareonea in 338 BCE, the Macedonian king Philip II defeated the Thebans and killed the entire Sacred Band.

[19] A legendary king of Thebes who assaulted and kidnaped Chrysippus, the son of Pelops, king of Pisa.

brought, for example, the flute into great esteem, both in serious and sportive occasions, and gave great encouragement to these friendships in the palaestra,[20] to temper the manners and characters of the youth. With a view to this they did well, again, to make Harmony, the daughter of Mars and Venus, their tutelar deity, because, where force and courage is joined with gracefulness and winning behavior, a harmony ensues that combines all the elements of society in perfect consonance and order.

Gorgidas distributed this Sacred Band all through the front ranks of the infantry, and thus made their gallantry less conspicuous. Not being united in one body, but mingled with so many others of inferior resolution, they had no fair opportunity of showing what they could do. But Pelopidas, having sufficiently tried their bravery at Tegyrae, where they had fought alone and around his own person, never afterward divided them, but, keeping them entire, and as one man, gave them the first duty in the greatest battles. For as horses ran brisker in a chariot than singly, not so that their joint force divides the air with greater ease but because being matched one against the other emulation kindles and inflames their courage, thus he thought brave men, provoking one another to noble actions, would prove most serviceable, and most resolute, where all were united together.

62

THE YOUNG ALEXANDER THE GREAT (CA. 350–334 BCE): PLUTARCH, *LIFE OF ALEXANDER*

A silver tetradrachm (four-drachm coin) of Alexander the Great depicts him wearing the lion skin of Hercules, son of Zeus. This portrayal would have been consistent with his claim that he himself was the son not of Philip II of Macedon but of the god Zeus.

[20] The exercise ground, where men worked out in the nude.

It was believed that during his youth, Alexander the Great demonstrated many of the qualities and character attributes that would result in his creating the largest empire the world yet had known. When, at the age of only twenty-three, he invaded the mighty and massive Persian Empire, which could raise an army of a quarter of a million soldiers and commanded resources of more than 200,000 talents of silver, his prospects looked bleak. The second-century CE Greek biographer Plutarch reported a famous story depicting Alexander's character that took place when he was only about ten years old.

Source: John Dryden, *Plutarch: The Lives of the Noble Greeks and Romans*, revised by A. H. Clough, Vol. 1 (Boston: Little, Brown, 1910).

Philonicus the Thessalian brought the horse Bucephalus to Philip, offering to sell him for thirteen talents,[21] but when they went into the field to try him, they found him so very vicious and unmanageable, that he reared up when they endeavored to mount him, and would not so much as endure the voice of any of Philip's attendants. Upon which, as they were leading him away as wholly useless and untractable, Alexander, who stood by, said, "What an excellent horse do they lose for want of address and boldness to manage him!" Philip at first took no notice of what he said; but when he heard him repeat the same thing several times, and saw he was much vexed to see the horse sent away, "Do you reproach," said he to him, "those who are older than yourself, as if you knew more, and were better able to manage him than they?" "I could manage this horse," replied he, "better than others do." "And if you do not," said Philip, "what will you forfeit for your rashness?" "I will pay," answered Alexander, "the whole price of the horse." At this the whole company fell to laughing. As soon as the wager was settled among them, Alexander immediately ran to the horse, and taking hold of the bridle, turned him directly toward the sun, having, it seems, observed that he was disturbed at and afraid of the motion of his own shadow. Then, letting him go forward a little, still keeping the reins in his hands, and stroking him gently when he found him begin to grow eager and fiery, he let fall his upper garment softly, and with one nimble leap securely mounted him, and when he was seated, by little and little drew in the bridle, and curbed him without either striking or spurring him. Presently, when he found him free from all rebelliousness, and only impatient for the course, he let him go at full speed, inciting him now with a commanding voice, and urging him also with his heel. Philip and his friends looked on at first in silence and anxiety for the result, until seeing him turn at the end of his career, and come back rejoicing and triumphing for what he had performed, they all burst out into acclamations of applause, and his father shedding tears, it is said, for joy, kissed him as he came down from his horse, and in his transport said, "O my son, look thee out a kingdom equal to and worthy of thyself, for Macedonia is too little for thee."

Philip sent for Aristotle, the most learned and most celebrated philosopher of his time, and rewarded him with a munificence proportional to and becoming the care he took to instruct his son. It would appear that Alexander received from him not only his doctrines of Morals and of Politics, but also something of those more abstruse and profound theories that these philosophers, by the very names they gave them, professed to reserve for oral communication to the initiated, and did not allow many to become acquainted with. Doubtless also it was to Aristotle that he owed the inclination he had, not to the theory only, but likewise to the practice of the art of medicine.

Alexander was but twenty years old when his father was murdered, and succeeded to a kingdom beset on all sides with great dangers and rancorous enemies. For not only the barbarous nations that bordered on Macedonia were impatient of being governed by any but their own native princes, but Philip

[21] Of silver. A talent was about fifty-six pounds.

likewise, although he had been victorious over the Greeks, yet, as the time had not been sufficient for him to complete his conquest and accustom them to his sway, had simply left all things in a general disorder and confusion. It seemed to the Macedonians a very critical time; and some would have persuaded Alexander to give up all thought of retaining the Greeks in subjection by force of arms, and rather to apply himself to win back by gentle means the allegiance of the *phylai*[22] who were designing revolt, and try the effect of indulgence in arresting the first motions toward revolution. But he rejected this counsel as weak and timorous, and looked upon it to be more prudent to secure himself by resolution and magnanimity, than, by seeming to submit to anyone, to encourage all to trample on him. In pursuit of this opinion, he reduced the barbarians to tranquility, and put an end to all fear of war from them. He made a rapid expedition into their country as far as the river Danube, where he gave Syrmus, King of the Triballians,[23] an entire overthrow. And hearing the Thebans were in revolt, and the Athenians in correspondence with them, he immediately marched through the pass of Thermopylae, saying to Demosthenes,[24] who had called him a child while he was in Illyria and in the country of the Triballians and a youth when he was in Thessaly, that he would appear a man before the walls of Athens.

When he came to Thebes, to show how willing he was to accept of their repentance for what was past, he only demanded of them Phoenix and Prothytes, the authors of the rebellion, and proclaimed a general pardon to those who would come over to him. But when the Thebans merely retorted by demanding Philotas and Antipater[25] to be delivered into their hands, and by a proclamation on their part invited all who would assert the liberty of Greece to come over to them, he presently applied himself to make them feel the last extremities of war. The Thebans indeed defended themselves with a zeal and courage beyond their strength, being much outnumbered by their enemies. But when the Macedonian garrison sallied out upon them from the citadel,[26] they were so hemmed in on all sides that the greater part of them fell in the battle. The city itself was taken by storm, and sacked and razed. Alexander's hope was that so severe an example might terrify the rest of Greece into obedience,[27] so that, except the priests, and some few who had heretofore been the friends and connections of the Macedonians, the family of the poet Pindar, and those who were known to have opposed the public vote for the war, all the rest, to the number of thirty thousand, were publicly sold for slaves. It also is computed that upwards of six thousand were put to the sword.

After this he received the Athenians into favor, although they had shown themselves so much concerned at the calamity of Thebes that out of sorrow they omitted the celebration of the Mysteries,[28] and entertained those who escaped with all possible humanity. Whether it were, like the lion, that his passion was now satisfied, or that, after an example of extreme cruelty, he had a mind to appear merciful, it happened well for the Athenians; for he not only forgave them all past offenses, but bade them look to their affairs with vigilance, remembering that if he should miscarry, they were likely to be the arbiters of Greece.

Soon after, the Greeks, being assembled at the Isthmus,[29] declared their resolution of joining with Alexander in the war against the Persians, and proclaimed him their general.[30] While he stayed here, many public ministers and philosophers came from all

[22] The different Macedonian peoples.

[23] A Thracian people of the central Balkans.

[24] An Athenian orator who in his "Philippic" speeches had advised the Athenians to resist the expansion of Alexander's father Philip II, King of Macedon.

[25] Two of Alexander's leading generals.

[26] The acropolis of Thebes, known as the "Cadmea"; see Reading 61.

[27] In this, Alexander was successful.

[28] The Eleusinian Mysteries, an annual festival in honor of the harvest goddess Demeter and her daughter Persephone.

[29] The Isthmus of Corinth, which separates the Peloponnesus from the rest of Greece.

[30] Marking the reestablishment of the Hellenic League, an alliance of Macedonia with Greek city-states initially established by Alexander's father, Philip II.

parts to visit him and congratulated him on his election, but contrary to his expectation, Diogenes of Sinope,[31] who then was living at Corinth, thought so little of him, that instead of coming to compliment him, he never so much as stirred out of the suburb called the Cranium, where Alexander found him lying in the sun. When he saw so much company near him, he raised himself a little, and condescended to look upon Alexander; and when he kindly asked him whether he wanted anything, "Yes," said he, "I would have you stand from between me and the sun." Alexander was so struck at this answer, and surprised at the greatness of the man, who had taken so little notice of him, that as he went away he told his followers, who were laughing at the moroseness of the philosopher, that if he were not Alexander, he would choose to be Diogenes.

Soon after, the Greeks, being assembled at the Isthmus, declared their resolution of joining with Alexander in the war against the Persians, and proclaimed him their general. His army, by their computation who make the smallest amount, consisted of thirty thousand foot and four thousand horse; and those who make the most of it, speak but of forty-three thousand foot and three thousand horse. Aristobulus[32] says he had not a fund of above seventy talents for their pay, nor had he more than thirty days' provision, if we may believe Duris; Onesicritus[33] tells us he was two hundred talents in debt.[34]

[31] A famous Cynic philosopher; the Cynics advocated the abandonment of all human conventions.

[32] A friend of Alexander's father, Philip II, who accompanied Alexander on his expeditions.

[33] A Greek historian who accompanied Alexander on his expeditions.

[34] Compared with the 200,000 talents of silver and huge amount of gold that the Persians had in their treasury.

63

ALEXANDER'S EXPEDITION INTO INDIA (326–324 BCE): PLUTARCH, *LIFE OF ALEXANDER*

A very rare silver decadrachm (ten-drachm coin) issued at Babylon ca. 325 BCE depicts on the obverse Alexander the Great on his horse Bucephalus attacking a war elephant in India and on the reverse Alexander holding the thunderbolt of Zeus and being crowned by the goddess victory. The coin was issued in commemoration of Alexander's campaigns in India, which were still underway at the time it was struck.

In his "Life of Alexander," the second-century CE Greek biographer Plutarch relates that at the end of 326, Alexander invaded India. In the next year, at the hard-fought Battle of the Hydaspes River (modern Jhelum), the Macedonians were confronted by the war elephants of the Indian king Porus. Alexander again emerged victorious and proposed next to attack the powerful Nanda Empire of the Ganges River valley. But the Macedonian army soldiers were getting their fill of war. Finally, at the Hyphasis River (modern Beas), the army mutinied and refused to take one step farther east. After sulking in his tent for three days, Alexander finally agreed to turn back, but to avoid the appearance of a retreat, the Macedonians returned along the Indus River valley, fighting every inch of the way as the Indians defended themselves desperately, village by village. After reaching the Indian Ocean in 325, Alexander made a foolish and harrowing trek across the Gedrosian Desert of southern Iran to get back to Persepolis. Many never made it back at all.

Source: John Dryden, *Plutarch: The Lives of the Noble Greeks and Romans*, revised by A. H. Clough, Vol. 1 (Boston: Little, Brown, 1910).

Alexander, now intent upon his expedition into India, took notice that his soldiers were so charged with booty that it hindered their marching. Therefore, at break of day, as soon as the baggage wagons were laden first he set fire to his own, and to those of his friends, and then commanded those to be burnt that belonged to the rest of the army. An act that in the deliberation of it had seemed more dangerous and difficult than it proved in the execution, with which few were dissatisfied for most of the soldiers, as if they had been inspired, uttering loud outcries and warlike shoutings, supplied one another with what was absolutely necessary, and burnt and destroyed all that was superfluous, the sight of which redoubled Alexander's zeal and eagerness for his design. And, indeed, he was now grown very severe and inexorable in punishing those who committed any fault. For he put Menander, one of his friends, to death for deserting a fortress where he had placed him in garrison,[35] and shot Orsodates, one of the barbarians who revolted from him, with his own hand.

The extent of King Taxiles'[36] dominions in India was thought to be as large as Egypt, abounding in good pastures, and producing beautiful fruits. The king himself had the reputation of a wise man, and at his first interview with Alexander he spoke to him in these terms: "To what purpose," said he, "should we make war upon one another, if the design of your coming into these parts be not to rob us of our water or our necessary food, which are the only things that wise men are indispensably obliged to fight for? As for other riches and possessions, as they are accounted in the eye of the world, if I am better provided of them than you, I am ready to let you share with me; but if fortune has been more liberal to you than me, I have no objection to be obliged to you." This discourse pleased Alexander so much that, embracing him, "Do you think," said he to him, "your kind words and courteous behavior will bring you off in this interview without a contest? No, you shall not escape so. I shall contend and do battle with you so far, that however obliging you are, you shall not have the better of me." Then receiving some presents from him, he returned him others of greater value, and to complete his bounty gave him in money ready coined one thousand talents,[37] at which his old friends were much displeased, but it gained him the hearts of many of the barbarians.

The best soldiers of the Indians, now entering into the pay of several of the cities, undertook to defend them, and did it so bravely, that they put Alexander to a great deal of trouble, until at last, after a capitulation, upon the surrender of the place, he fell upon them as they were marching away, and put them all to the sword. This one breach of his word remains as a blemish upon his achievements in war, which he otherwise had performed throughout with that justice and honor that became a king. Nor was he less incommoded by the Indian philosophers, who inveighed against those princes who joined his party, and solicited the free nations to oppose him. He took several of these also and caused them to be hanged.

Alexander, in his own letters, has given us an account of his war with Porus.[38] He says that the two armies were separated by the Hydaspes River,[39] on whose opposite bank Porus continually kept his

[35] In an isolated area of Bactria or Sogdiana near India.

[36] An Indian king, favored by Alexander, who ruled between the Indus and Hydaspes rivers in the Punjab in northwestern India.

[37] A talent was about fifty-six pounds.

[38] The Indian king of the territory east of the Hydaspes River in the Punjab.

[39] Modern Jhelum River.

elephants in order of battle, with their heads toward their enemies, to guard the passage, whereas he, on the other hand, made every day a great noise and clamor in his camp, to dissipate the apprehensions of the barbarians. One stormy dark night he passed the river, at a distance from the place where the enemy lay, onto a little island, with part of his foot and the best of his horse. Here there fell a most violent storm of rain, accompanied with lightning and whirlwinds, and seeing some of his men burnt and dying with the lightning, he nevertheless quitted the island and made over to the other side. The Hydaspes, he says, now after the storm, was so swollen and grown so rapid as to have made a breach in the bank, and a part of the river was now pouring in here, so that when he came across it was with difficulty he got a footing on the land, which was slippery and unsteady, and exposed to the force of the currents on both sides. This is the occasion when he is related to have said, "O ye Athenians, will ye believe what dangers I incur to merit your praise?" This, however, is Onesicritus's[40] story.

Alexander says that the men left their boats here and crossed the gap in their armor, up to the breast in water, and that then he advanced with his horse about twenty furlongs[41] before his foot, concluding that if the enemy charged him with their cavalry he would be too strong for them; if with their foot, his own would come up time enough to his assistance. Nor did he judge wrongly, for being charged by a thousand horse and sixty armed chariots, which advanced before their main body, he took all the chariots and killed four hundred horse upon the place. Porus, by this time, guessing that Alexander himself had crossed over, came on with his whole army, except a party that he left behind to hold the rest of the Macedonians in play if they should attempt to pass the river. But Alexander, apprehending the multitude of the enemy, and to avoid the shock of their elephants, divided his forces and attacked their left wing himself and commanded Coenus[42] to fall upon the right, which was performed with good success. For by this means both wings being broken, the enemies fell back in their retreat upon the center, and crowded in upon their elephants. There rallying, they fought a hand-to-hand battle, and it was the eighth hour of the day before they were entirely defeated. This description the conqueror himself has left us in his own epistles.

Almost all the historians agree in relating that Porus was four cubits and a span high,[43] and that when he was upon his elephant, which was of the largest size, his stature and bulk were so consistent that he appeared to be proportionately mounted, as a horseman on his horse. This elephant, during the whole battle, gave many singular proofs of sagacity and of particular care of the king, whom as long as he was strong and in a condition to fight, he defended with great courage, repelling those who set upon him; and as soon as he perceived him overpowered with his numerous wounds and the multitude of darts that were thrown at him, to prevent his falling off, he softly knelt down and began to draw out the darts with his proboscis. When Porus was taken prisoner, and Alexander asked him how he expected to be used, he answered, "As a king." For that expression, he said, when the same question was put to him a second time, comprehended everything. And Alexander, accordingly, not only suffered him to govern his own kingdom as satrap under himself, but gave him also the additional territory of various independent *phylai* that he subdued, a district that, it is said, contained fifteen nations and five thousand considerable towns, besides abundance of villages. To another government, three times as large as this, he appointed Philip, one of his friends.

Some little time after the battle with Porus, Bucephalus[44] died, as most of the authorities state, under cure of his wounds, or, as Onesicritus says, of fatigue and age, being thirty years old. Alexander was no less concerned at his death than if he had lost

[40] A Greek historian who accompanied Alexander on his expeditions.

[41] A furlong equals 660 feet.

[42] One of Alexander's most able generals.

[43] The cubit was the length of a forearm, about eighteen inches, and the span was the width of a hand or half a cubit, about nine inches, making Porus six feet, nine inches tall.

[44] For Alexander's horse Bucephalus, see Reading 62.

an old companion or an intimate friend, and built a city, which he named Bucephalia, in memory of him, on the bank of the river Hydaspes. He also, we are told, built another city, and called it after the name of a favorite dog, Peritas, which he had brought up himself. So Sotion assures us he was informed by Potamon of Lesbos.

This last combat with Porus took the edge off the Macedonians' courage, and stayed their further progress into India. For having found it hard enough to defeat an enemy who brought but twenty thousand foot and two thousand horse into the field, they thought they had reason to oppose Alexander's design of leading them on to pass the Ganges, too, which they were told was thirty-two furlongs broad and a hundred fathoms deep,[45] and the banks on the further side covered with multitudes of enemies.[46] For they were told the kings of the Gandaritans and Praesians[47] expected them there with eighty thousand horse, two hundred thousand foot, eight thousand armed chariots, and six thousand fighting elephants. Nor was this a mere vain report, spread to discourage them. For Sandrocottus,[48] who not long after reigned in those parts, made a present of five hundred elephants at once to Seleucus,[49] and with an army of six hundred thousand men subdued all India.

Alexander at first was so grieved and enraged at his men's reluctance that he shut himself up in his tent and threw himself upon the ground, declaring, if they would not pass the Ganges, he owed them no thanks for anything they had hitherto done, and that to retreat now was plainly to confess himself vanquished. But at last the reasonable persuasions of his friends and the cries and lamentations of his soldiers, who in a suppliant manner crowded about the entrance of his tent, prevailed with him to think of returning. Yet he could not refrain from leaving behind him various deceptive memorials of his expedition, to impose upon aftertimes, and to exaggerate his glory with posterity, such as arms larger than were really worn, and mangers for horses, with bits and bridles above the usual size, which he set up, and distributed in several places. He erected altars, also, to the gods, which the kings of the Praesians even in our time do honor to when they pass the river, and offer sacrifice upon them after the Grecian manner. Sandrocottus, then a boy, saw Alexander there, and is said often afterward to have been heard to say, that he missed but little of making himself master of those countries; their king, who then reigned, was so hated and despised for the viciousness of his life and the meanness of his extraction.

Alexander now was eager to see the ocean.[50] To which purpose he caused a great many tow-boats and rafts to be built, in which he travelled gently down the rivers[51] at his leisure, yet so that his navigation was neither unprofitable nor inactive. For by several descents upon the bank, he made himself master of the fortified towns, and consequently of the country on both sides. But at a siege of a town of the Mallians, who have the repute of being the bravest people of India, he ran in great danger of his life. For having beaten off the defendants with showers of arrows, he was the first man that mounted the wall by a scaling-ladder, which, as soon as he was up, broke and left him almost alone, exposed to the darts that the barbarians threw at him in great numbers from below. In this distress, turning himself as well as he could, he leaped down in the midst of his enemies, and had the good fortune to light upon his feet. The brightness and clattering of his armor when he came to the ground made the barbarians think they saw rays of light, or some bright phantom playing before his body, which frightened them so at first that they

[45] A furlong equals 660 feet, making the Ganges four miles wide; a fathom is 6 feet.

[46] The Nanda Empire.

[47] Gandhara lay on the Indus River in northwestern India; the Praesians (a word meaning "easterners") came from the same region.

[48] Known in India as Chandragupta, the creator of the Mauryan Empire after Alexander left India.

[49] The general who after Alexander's death gained control of the eastern part of the empire (see Reading 64). In 305 CE he granted his holdings in India to Sandrocottus for the war elephants.

[50] The Indian Ocean.

[51] The Indus and its tributaries.

ran away and dispersed. until seeing him seconded but by two of his guards, they fell upon him hand-to-hand, and some, while he bravely defended himself, tried to wound him through his armor with their swords and spears. And one who stood further off drew a bow with such strength that the arrow, finding its way through his cuirass, stuck in his ribs under the breast. This stroke was so violent that it made him give back, and set one knee to the ground, upon which the man ran up with his drawn scimitar, thinking to dispatch him, and had done it, if Peucestes and Limnaeus had not interposed, who were both wounded, Limnaeus mortally, but Peucestes stood his ground, while Alexander killed the barbarians. But this did not free him from danger, for, besides many other wounds, at last he received so weighty a stroke of a club upon his neck that he was forced to lean his body against the wall, still, however, facing the enemy.

At this extremity, the Macedonians made their way in and gathered round him. They took him up, just as he was fainting away, having lost all sense of what was done near him, and conveyed him to his tent, upon which it was presently reported all over the camp that he was dead. But when they had with great difficulty and pains sawed off the shaft of the arrow, which was of wood, and so with much trouble got off his cuirass, they came to cut the head of it, which was three fingers broad and four long, and stuck fast in the bone. During the operation he was taken with almost mortal swoonings, but when it was out he came to himself again. Yet although all danger was past, he continued very weak, and confined himself a great while to a regular diet and the method of his cure, until one day hearing the Macedonians clamoring outside in their eagerness to see him, he took his cloak and went out. And having sacrificed to the gods, without more delay he went on board again, and as he coasted along subdued a great deal of the country on both sides, and several considerable cities.

In this voyage he took ten of the Indian philosophers prisoners who had been most active in persuading Sabbas[52] to revolt, and had caused the Macedonians a great deal of trouble. These men, called Gymnosophists,[53] were reputed to be extremely ready and succinct in their answers, which he made trial of, by putting difficult questions to them, letting them know that those whose answers were not pertinent should be put to death, on which he made the eldest of them judge. The first being asked which he thought the most numerous, the dead or the living, answered, "The living because those who are dead are not at all." Of the second, he desired to know whether the earth or the sea produced the largest beasts; who told him, "The earth, for the sea is but a part of it." His question to the third was, which is the cunningest of beasts? "That," said he, "which men have not yet found out." He bade the fourth tell him what argument he used to Sabbas to persuade him to revolt. "No other," said he, "than that he should either live or die nobly." Of the fifth he asked, which was the eldest, night or day? The philosopher replied, "Day was eldest, by one day at least." But perceiving Alexander not well satisfied with that account, he added, that he ought not to wonder if strange questions had as strange answers made to them. Then he went on and inquired of the next, what a man should do to be exceedingly beloved. "He must be very powerful," said he, "without making himself too much feared." The answer of the seventh to his question, how a man might become a god, was, "By doing that which was impossible for men to do." The eighth told him, "Life is stronger than death, because it supports so many miseries." And the last being asked, how long he thought it decent for a man to live, said, "Till death appeared more desirable than life." Then Alexander turned to him whom he had made judge, and commanded him to give sentence. "All that I can determine," said he, "is, that they have every one answered worse than another." "Nay," said the king, "then you shall die first, for giving such a sentence." "Not so, O king," replied the gymnosophist, "unless you said falsely that he should die first who made the worst answer." In conclusion he gave them presents and dismissed them.

[52] An Indian prince.

[53] From "gymnos," or "naked," because they were unclothed.

But to those who were in greatest reputation among them, and lived a private quiet life, he sent Onesicritus, one of Diogenes[54] the Cynic's disciples, desiring them to come to him. Calanus,[55] it is said, very arrogantly and roughly commanded him to strip himself and hear what he said naked, otherwise he would not speak a word to him, although he came from Jupiter himself. But Dandamis[56] received him with more civility, and hearing him discourse of Socrates,[57] Pythagoras,[58] and Diogenes, told him he thought them men of great parts and to have erred in nothing so much as in having too great respect for the laws and customs of their country. Others say Dandamis only asked him the reason why Alexander undertook so long a journey to come into those parts. Taxiles, however, persuaded Calanus to wait upon Alexander. His proper name was Sphines, but because he was accustomed to say Cale, which in the Indian tongue is a form of salutation to those he met with anywhere, the Greeks called him Calanus. He is said to have shown Alexander an instructive emblem of government, which was this. He threw a dry shrivelled hide upon the ground, and trod upon the edges of it. The skin when it was pressed in one place still rose up in another, whereever he trod round about it, until he set his foot in the middle, which made all the parts lie even and quiet. The meaning of this similitude being that he ought to reside most in the middle of his empire, and not spend too much time on the borders of it.

Alexander's voyage down the rivers took up seven months' time, and when he came to the sea, he sailed to an island that he himself called Scillustis, others Psiltucis, where going ashore, he sacrificed, and made what observations he could as to the nature of the sea and the sea-coast. Then having besought the gods that no other man might ever go beyond the bounds of this expedition, he ordered his fleet, of which he made Nearchus[59] admiral and Onesicritus pilot, to sail round about, keeping the Indian shore on the right hand, and returned himself by land through the country of the Orites,[60] where he was reduced to great straits for want of provisions, and lost a vast number of his men, so that of an army of one hundred and twenty thousand foot and fifteen thousand horse, he scarcely brought back above a fourth part out of India, they were so diminished by disease, ill diet, and the scorching heats, but most by famine. For their march was through an uncultivated country whose inhabitants fared hardly, possessing only a few sheep, and those of a wretched kind, whose flesh was rank and unsavory on account of their continual feeding upon sea-fish.

[54] The founder of the philosophical school of the Cynics; see Reading 62.

[55] One of the Gymnosophists.

[56] Another of the Gymnosophists.

[57] See Reading 60.

[58] See Reading 50.

[59] Later the author of an ethnographic study of India.

[60] The Gedrosian Desert, in southern Iran.

64

THE WARS OF THE SUCCESSORS (323–301 BCE): JUSTIN, *PHILIPPIC HISTORIES*, BOOK 13

A silver tetradrachm (four-drachm coin) issued ca. 311–305 BCE by Alexander's general Seleucus, who became satrap of Babylonia in the division of Alexander's empire after his death. Seleucus showed his respect for local culture not only by not divorcing his Persian wife but also by portraying on the obverse of this coin an image of the eastern god Ba'al of Tarsus seated and holding a scepter and on the reverse a lion walking left with an anchor, a Seleucid symbol, above.

After the death of Alexander the Great in 323 BCE, some generals, especially Perdiccas, Eumenes, and Polyperchon, wished to hold the empire together in the name of Alexander's infant son. But most other generals looked to their own advantage. The generals therefore parceled out sections of the empire among themselves. These included Perdiccas, Craterus, Antipater, the guardian of Alexander's infant son Alexander IV; and Polyperchon, governor of Greece and Macedonia; as well as Eumenes; Antigonus the One-Eyed; Lysimachus; Ptolemy;

and Seleucus, who in the initial division, respectively, received Cappadocia and Paphlagonia, "Greater Phrygia," Thrace, Egypt, and "The Command of the Camp." Conflicts immediately ensued as these generals attempted to expand their holdings, and there was a rapid shakeout as many soon fell by the wayside. Alliances changed quickly as the generals ganged up on anyone who appeared to be getting too powerful. Soon only a handful were left. Just when it looked like Antigonus the One-Eyed and his son Demetrius "The Besieger of Cities" were on the verge of reconstituting Alexander's Empire, they were defeated in 301 BCE at the Battle of Ipsus in 301 by a coalition including Ptolemy, Lysimachus, and Seleucus. It was not until 281 BCE, when the eighty-year-old Seleucus defeated Lysimichus at the Battle of Couropedium, that the Wars of the Successors finally came to an end. The story of these conflicts was related in the "Philippic Histories" of the Augustan writer Pompeius Trogus. His work does not survive, but an epitome made circa the second or third century CE by Marcus Junianus Justinus, or simply Justin, does.

Source: John Selby Watson, trans., *Marcus Junius Justinus, Epitome of the Philippic History of Pompeius Trogus* (London: Bohn, 1853).

When this allotment,[61] like a gift from the Fates,[62] was made to each, it was to many of them a great occasion for improving their fortunes, for not long after, as if they had divided kingdoms, not governments, among themselves, they became princes instead of prefects,[63] and not only secured great power to themselves but also bequeathed it to their descendents. Afterward a war arose between Antigonus[64] and Perdiccas.[65] Craterus and Antipater,[66] who, having made peace with the Athenians, had appointed Polyperchon to govern Greece and Macedonia, lent their aid to Antigonus. Perdiccas, as the aspect of affairs was unfavorable, called Arridaeus[67] and Alexander the Great's son,[68] then in Cappadocia,[69] the charge of both of whom had been committed to him, to a consultation concerning the management of the war. It seemed more to the purpose to begin with Egypt, lest, while they were gone into Macedonia, Asia should be seized by Ptolemy.[70] Ptolemy, by his wise exertions in Egypt, was acquiring great power. He had secured the favor of the Egyptians by his extraordinary prudence. He had attached the neighboring princes by acts of kindness and courtesy. He had extended the boundaries of his kingdom by getting possession of the city Cyrene,[71] and was grown so great that he did not fear his enemies so much as he was feared by them.

[61] The division of Alexander's empire made in Babylon after his death in 323 BCE.

[62] Goddesses depicted as elderly women who control human destiny: Clotho spun the thread of life, Lachesis measured how long it would be, and Atropos cut it off at the end.

[63] That is, governors.

[64] Nicknamed "Monopthalmos," "The One-Eyed." He received "Greater Phrygia" in central Anatolia in the original division of territories but went on to reconquer nearly the entire empire.

[65] After Alexander's death he was appointed guardian of Alexander's young son Alexander IV and, as "Regent of the Empire," for a brief time was the effective ruler of the empire.

[66] Craterus and Antipater also were guardians of Alexander IV and wanted to maintain the integrity of the empire.

[67] Philip III (323–317), Alexander's incapable brother who succeeded him as King of Macedon.

[68] Alexander IV only would have been a few years old at the time.

[69] A mountainous region of northern Anatolia that remained under the control of a Persian dynasty until it was incorporated into the Roman Empire in 17 CE.

[70] One of the main instigators of the division of Alexander's empire; he received the rich satrapy of Egypt.

[71] For Cyrene, see Reading 48.

Ptolemy, having increased his strength from the forces of this city, made preparations for war against the coming of Perdiccas. But the hatred that Perdiccas had incurred by his arrogance did him more injury than the power of the enemy. For his allies, detesting his overbearingness went over in troops to Antipater. Neoptolemus,[72] too, who had been left to support Eumenes,[73] intended not only to desert to Antipater but also to betray the force of his party. Eumenes, understanding his design, thought it a matter of necessity to engage the traitor in the field. Neoptolemus, being worsted, fled to Antipater and Polyperchon, and persuaded them to surprise Eumenes, by marching without intermission, while he was full of joy for his victory, and freed from apprehension by Neoptolemus' flight. But this project did not escape Eumenes. The plot was in consequence turned upon the contrivers of it, and they who expected to attack him unguarded were attacked themselves when they were on their march and wearied with watching through the previous night. In this battle, Polyperchon was killed. Neoptolemus, too, engaging hand to hand with Eumenes, and maintaining a long struggle with him, in which both were wounded more than once, was at last overpowered and fell.

Eumenes, therefore, being victorious in two successive battles, supported in some degree the spirits of his party, which had been cast down by the desertion of their allies. At last, however, Perdiccas having been killed,[74] Eumenes was declared an enemy by the army, and the conduct of the war against him was committed to Antigonus. When Eumenes found that Perdiccas was slain, that he himself was declared an enemy by the Macedonians, and that the conduct of the war against him was committed to Antigonus, he at once made known the state of affairs to his troops, lest report should either exaggerate matters, or alarm the minds of the men with the unexpected nature of the events. When he returned to his camp, letters were found scattered through it in which great rewards were offered to any that should bring the head of Eumenes to Antigonus.

In the meantime Antigonus came up with his army, and having pitched his camp, offered battle on the following day. Nor did Eumenes delay to engage with him, but, being defeated, he fled to a fortress, where, when he saw that he must submit to the hazard of a siege, he dismissed the greater part of his army, lest he should either be delivered to the enemy by consent of the multitude, or the sufferings of the siege should be aggravated by too great a number. He then sent a deputation to Antipater, who was the only general that seemed a match for the power of Antigonus, to entreat his aid; and Antigonus, hearing that succor was dispatched by Antipater to Eumenes, gave up the siege. Eumenes was thus for a time, indeed, relieved from fear of death, but, as so great a portion of his army had been sent away, he had no great hope of ultimate safety. After taking everything into consideration, therefore, he thought it best to apply to the Argyraspides[75] of Alexander the Great, a body of men that had never yet been conquered.

At length, when it was announced that Antigonus was approaching with his army, he obliged the Argyraspides to march into the field, where, slighting the orders of their general, they were defeated by the bravery of the enemy. In this battle they lost, with their wives and children, not only their glory from so many wars but also the booty obtained in their long service. Immediately after, without the knowledge of their leaders, they sent deputies to Antigonus, requesting that "he would order what was theirs to be restored to them." Antigonus promised that he would restore what they asked if they would deliver up Eumenes to him, saying that his single victory was so far more glorious to Antigonus than so many other victories had been to Alexander, and that whereas Alexander subdued the east, Antigonus had defeated those by whom the east had been subdued.

[72] A Macedonian general who had been assigned the satrapy of Armenia.

[73] A supporter of Perdiccas, he received the territories of Paphlagonia and Cappadocia, which had not yet been conquered.

[74] Assassinated in 321 BCE.

[75] The "Silver Shields," an elite body of Alexander's troops.

Perdiccas and his brother, with Eumenes and Polyperchon, and other leaders of the opposite party, having been killed,[76] the contention among the successors of Alexander seemed to be at an end, when, on a sudden, a dispute arose among the conquerors themselves, for Ptolemy, Cassander,[77] and Lysimachus,[78] demanding that the money taken among the spoil, and the provinces, should be divided. Antigonus said that he would admit no partners in the advantages of a war of which he alone had undergone the perils. And that he might seem to engage in an honorable contest with his confederates, he gave out that his object was to avenge the death of Olympias,[79] who had been murdered by Cassander, and to release the son of Alexander, his king, with his mother,[80] from their confinement at Amphipolis.[81] On hearing this news, Ptolemy and Cassander, forming an alliance with Lysimachus and Seleucus,[82] made vigorous preparations for war by land and sea. Ptolemy had possession of Egypt, with the greater part of Africa, Cyprus, and Phoenicia. Macedonia and Greece were subject to Cassander. Antigonus had taken possession of Asia and the eastern countries. Demetrius, the son of Antigonus, was defeated in the first engagement by Ptolemy, at Gamala.[83]

Ptolemy meanwhile engaged a second time with Demetrius at sea,[84] and, having lost his fleet, and left the victory to the enemy, fled back to Egypt. Antigonus, being elated with this victory, gave orders that he himself, as well as his son Demetrius, should be styled "basileus" ("king") by the people.[85] Ptolemy also, so that he might not appear of less authority among his subjects, was called "king" by his army. Cassander and Lysimachus, too, when they heard of these proceedings, assumed regal dignity themselves. They all abstained, however, from taking the insignia of royalty,[86] as long as any sons of their king[87] survived. Such forbearance was there in them, that, although they had the power, they yet contentedly remained without the distinction of kings as long as Alexander had a proper heir. But Ptolemy and Cassander, and the other leaders of the opposite faction, perceiving that they were individually weakened by Antigonus,[88] whereas each regarded the war, not as the common concern of all, but as merely affecting himself, and all were unwilling to give assistance to one another, as if victory would be only for one, and not for all of them, appointed, after encouraging each other by letters, a time and place for a conference, and prepared for the contest with united strength. Cassander, being unable to join in it, because of a war near home, dispatched Lysimachus to the support of his allies with a large force.

Before the war with Antigonus was commenced by Ptolemy and his allies, Seleucus, on a sudden, leaving Greater Asia, came forward as a fresh enemy to Antigonus. The merit of Seleucus was well known, and his birth had been attended with extraordinary circumstances. His mother Laodice, being married to Antiochus, a man of eminence among Philip's generals, seemed to herself, in a dream, to have conceived from a union with Apollo and, after becoming pregnant, to have received from him, as a reward for her compliance, a ring, on the stone of which was engraved an anchor and which she was advised to give to the child that she should bring forth. A ring similarly engraved was found the next day in the bed, and the figure of an anchor, which was visible on the thigh of Seleucus when he

[76] Eumenes was executed by Antigonus in 316 BCE, but Polyperchon survived until 304 BCE or later.

[77] The son of Antipater; in 317 BCE he became King of Macedon.

[78] The satrap of Thrace, northeast of Greece in the Balkans.

[79] The mother of Alexander the Great.

[80] Roxanne, Alexander's first wife.

[81] One of the capital cities of Macedonia, on the northern coast of the Aegean Sea.

[82] The satrap of Babylonia, who had been accumulating additional territory in the eastern regions of the empire.

[83] The Battle of Gaza, in 312 BCE.

[84] The Battle of Myus, a city in Caria in southern Anatolia.

[85] The first time that any of the successors referred to themselves as "king." Others soon followed.

[86] Such as wearing the royal diadem.

[87] The child Alexander IV.

[88] In 301 BCE.

was born, made this dream extremely remarkable.[89] After the division of the Macedonian empire among the followers of Alexander, he carried on several wars in the east. He first took Babylon,[90] and then, his strength being increased by this success, subdued the Bactrians. After settling his affairs in the east, Seleucus proceeded to join in the war against Antigonus. As soon as the forces of all the confederates were united, a battle was fought, in which Antigonus was slain, and his son Demetrius put to flight.[91] But the allied generals, after thus terminating the war with the enemy, turned their arms again upon each other, and, as they could not agree about the spoil, they were divided into two parties. Seleucus joined Demetrius, and Ptolemy joined Lysimachus. Thus new wars arose.

65

THE SUBORDINATION OF WOMEN AND SLAVES (CA. 325 BCE): ARISTOTLE, *POLITICS*, BOOK 1

A Roman marble copy of a Greek original bronze bust of Aristotle made by Lysippus ca. 330 BCE.

[89] The anchor then became a Seleucid insignia and often appeared on their coins.

[90] In the Babylonian War, 312–311 BCE, Seleucus drove Antigonus out of Babylonia, thus ending the possibility of a reunification of Alexander's empire.

[91] The Battle of Ipsus in 301 BCE.

The first great practical, as opposed to theoretical, philosopher was Aristotle, a native of northern Greece. After studying medicine with his father and philosophy with Plato in Athens, he was employed by Philip II of Macedon as the tutor of Alexander the Great. He returned to Athens in 335 BCE and founded his own school, called the Lyceum. In his work the *Politics*, Aristotle formulated his concept of an ideal society that was not based on pure hypothesis, like Plato's, but on a collection of the constitutions of a multitude of actual human governments. Aristotle believed that virtuous people could govern themselves. He introduced the concept of "natural slavery," suggesting that people were suited by nature to be slaves if, like beasts, all that could be expected from them was labor. But he also argued that people who were not naturally suited to be slaves should not be enslaved. Aristotle viewed women as being subordinate to men but ranking higher than slaves.

Source: Benjamin Jowett, trans., *The Politics of Aristotle* (London: Colonial Press, 1900).

Every state is a community of some kind, and every community is established with a view to some good, for people always act in order to obtain that which they think is good. But, if all communities aim at some good, the state or political community, which is the highest of all, and which embraces all the rest, aims at good in a greater degree than any other, and at the highest good.

Some people think that the qualifications of a statesman, king, householder, and master are the same, and that they differ, not in kind, but only in the number of their subjects. For example, the ruler over a few is called a master; over more, the manager of a household; over a still larger number, a statesman or king, as if there were no difference between a great household and a small state. The distinction that is made between the king and the statesman is as follows: when the government is personal, the ruler is a king; when, according to the rules of the political science, the citizens rule and are ruled in turn, then he is called a statesman.

But all this is a mistake, for governments differ in kind, as will be evident to anyone who considers the matter according to the method that hitherto has guided us. As in other departments of science, so in politics, the compound should always be resolved into the simple elements or least the parts of the whole. We therefore must look at the elements of which the state is composed in order that we may see how the different kinds of rule differ from one another, and whether any scientific result can be attained about each one of them.

He who thus considers things in their first growth and origin, whether a state or anything else, will obtain the clearest view of them. In the first place there must be a union of those who cannot exist without each other, namely, of male and female, that the race may continue (and this is a union that is formed, not of deliberate purpose, but because, in common with other animals and with plants, people have a natural desire to leave behind them an image of themselves), and a concept of natural ruler and subject, that both may be preserved. For whoever can foresee by the exercise of mind is by nature intended to be lord and master, and whoever can with their body give effect to such foresight is a subject, and by nature a slave; hence master and slave have the same interest. Now nature has distinguished between the female and the slave. For the female is not niggardly, like the smith who fashions the Delphian knife[92] for many uses. She makes each thing for a single use, and every instrument is best made when intended for one and not for many uses. But among barbarians no distinction is made between women and slaves, because there is no natural ruler among them: they are a community of slaves, male and female. Therefore

[92] A double-edged knife that can be used for several purposes, much like the Delphic oracles could have several meanings.

the poets say, "It is right that Hellenes[93] should rule over barbarians," as if they thought that the barbarian and the slave were by nature one.

Out of these two relationships between man and woman, master and slave, the first thing to arise is the family, and Hesiod is right when he says, "First house and wife and an ox for the plough,"[94] for the ox is the poor man's slave. The family is the association established by nature for the supply of men's everyday wants, and the members of it are called by Charondas[95] "companions of the cupboard," and by Epimenides[96] the Cretan, "companions of the manger." But when several families are united, and the association aims at something more than the supply of daily needs, the first society to be formed is the village. And the most natural form of the village appears to be that of a colony from the family, composed of the children and grandchildren, who are said to be suckled "with the same milk." And this is the reason why Hellenic states were originally governed by kings; because the Hellenes were under royal rule before they came together, as the barbarians still are.

Every family is ruled by the eldest, and therefore in the colonies of the family the kingly form of government prevailed because they were of the same blood. As Homer says, "Each one gives law to his children and to his wives." For they lived dispersedly, as was the manner in ancient times. Wherefore men say that the gods have a king, because they themselves either are or were in ancient times under the rule of a king. For they imagine, not only the forms of the gods, but their ways of life to be like their own.

When several villages are united in a single complete community, large enough to be nearly or quite self-sufficing, the state comes into existence, originating in the bare needs of life, and continuing in existence for the sake of a good life. And therefore, if the earlier forms of society are natural, so is the state, for it is the end result of them, and the nature of a thing is its end result. For what each thing is when fully developed, we call its nature, whether we are speaking of a man, a horse, or a family. Besides, the final cause[97] and end of a thing is the best, and to be self-sufficing is the end and the best. Hence it is evident that the state is a creation of nature, and that man is by nature a political[98] animal.

Seeing then that the state is made up of households, before speaking of the state we must speak of the management of the household. The parts of household management correspond to the persons who compose the household, and a complete household consists of slaves and freemen. Now we should begin by examining everything in its fewest possible elements, and the first and fewest possible parts of a family are master and slave, husband and wife, father and children. We have therefore to consider what each of these three relations is and ought to be: I mean the relation of master and servant, the marriage relation (the conjunction of man and wife has no name of its own), and thirdly, the procreative relation (this also has no proper name). Let us first speak of master and slave, looking to the needs of practical life and also seeking to attain some better theory of their relation than exists at present. For some are of opinion that the rule of a master is a science, and that the management of a household, and the mastership of slaves, and the political and royal rule, as I was saying at the outset, are all the same. Others affirm that the rule of a master over slaves is contrary to nature and that the distinction between slave and freeman exists by law only, and not by nature; and being an interference with nature is therefore unjust.

The master is only the master of the slave, he does not belong to him, whereas the slave is not only the slave of his master, but wholly belongs to him. Hence

[93] Greeks.

[94] See Reading 47. Aristotle has misquoted Hesiod, who recommended getting a slave woman, not a wife.

[95] A famous sixth-century BCE lawgiver of Catania in Sicily.

[96] A legendary philosopher of Knossos in Crete in the seventh century BCE who fell asleep for fifty-seven years and awoke with the gift of prophecy.

[97] Aristotle identified four "causes" of change, called the final, formal, material, and efficient.

[98] From "polis," or "city-state," referring to life in a city.

we see what is the nature and office of a slave; he who is by nature not his own but another's man is by nature a slave; and he may be said to be another's man who, being a human being, is also a possession. And a possession may be defined as an instrument of action, separable from the possessor.

But is there anyone thus intended by nature to be a slave, and for whom such a condition is expedient and right, or rather is not all slavery a violation of nature? There is no difficulty in answering this question, on grounds both of reason and of fact. For that some should rule and others be ruled is a thing not only necessary, but expedient. From the hour of their birth, some are marked out for subjection, others for rule. And there are many kinds both of rulers and subjects, and that rule is the better which is exercised over better subjects, for example, to rule over men is better than to rule over wild beasts. The male is by nature superior and the female inferior; the one rules and the other is ruled. This principle, of necessity, extends to all mankind. Where then there is such a difference as that between soul and body, or between men and animals (as in the case of those whose business is to use their body, and who can do nothing better), the lower sort are by nature slaves, and it is better for them as for all inferiors that they should be under the rule of a master. For he who can be, and therefore is, another's and he who participates in rational principle enough to apprehend, but not to have, such a principle, is a slave by nature. Whereas the lower animals cannot even apprehend a principle, they obey their instincts.

And indeed the use made of slaves and of tame animals is not very different, for both with their bodies minister to the needs of life. Nature would like to distinguish between the bodies of freemen and slaves, making the one strong for servile labor and the other upright, and, although useless for such services, useful for political life in the arts both of war and peace. But the opposite often happens, that some have the souls and others have the bodies of freemen. And doubtless if men differed from one another in the mere forms of their bodies as much as the statues of the gods do from men, all would acknowledge that the inferior class should be slaves of the superior. And if this is true of the body, how much more just that a similar distinction should exist in the soul? But the beauty of the body is seen, whereas the beauty of the soul is not seen. It is clear, then, that some men are by nature free, and others slaves, and that for these latter slavery is both expedient and right.

66

STOICISM (300 BCE): EPICTETUS, *THE ENCHIRIDION*

A marble Roman copy of the first century CE of a portrait bust of the Stoic philosopher Zeno of Citium, the creator of Stoicism, from a Greek original of the fourth century BCE, now in the Alte Museum in Berlin.

The Stoic philosophy was introduced by Zeno, a native of Citium on Cyprus who settled in Athens about 300 BCE. His teachings were centered on a physical universe that was highly structured into a pattern that was established by a rational governing force called the "logos." The universe was like a finely tuned machine and each person represented one part of the machine. It was everyone's duty to perform the role that they had been assigned by god. The Stoic creed was, "Lead me, O Zeus, wherever you will, and I will follow willingly, and if I do not, you will drag me." The only choice a Stoic had was either to accept the inevitable, which already had been determined by the logos, or to fight against it and inevitably be destroyed. The importance given to the performance of duty made Stoicism well suited for individuals committed to public service. Reflecting earlier views, the tenets of Stoic philosophy were set forth in the early second century CE in the Enchiridion ("Manual") of Epictetus, an ex-slave from Hierapolis in Anatolia who taught in Rome and Greece. For Epictetus, Stoicism was not just a theoretical model but was meant to be put into practice in real life.

Source: Elizabeth Carter, trans., *The Works of Epictetus, Translated from the Original Greek* (London: Richardson, 1758), reprinted in W. H. D. Rouse, ed., *The Moral Discourses of Epictetus*, (London–Toronto: Dent, 1910).

Some things are in our control and others not. Things in our control are opinion, pursuit, desire, aversion, and, in a word, whatever are our own actions. Things not in our control are body, property, reputation, command, and, in one word, whatever are not our own actions. The things in our control are by nature free, unrestrained, unhindered; but those not in our control are weak, slavish, restrained, belonging to others. Remember, then, that if you suppose that things that are slavish by nature are also free, and that what belongs to others is your own, then you will be hindered. You will lament, you will be disturbed, and you will find fault both with gods and men. But if you suppose that only to be your own which is your own, and what belongs to others such as it really is, then no one will ever compel you or restrain you. Further, you will find fault with no one or accuse no one. You will do nothing against your will. No one will hurt you, you will have no enemies, and you not be harmed.

Aiming therefore at such great things, remember that you must not allow yourself to be carried, even with a slight tendency, toward the attainment of lesser things. Instead, you must entirely quit some things and for the present postpone the rest. But if you would both have these great things, along with power and riches, then you will not gain even the latter, because you aim at the former too: but you will absolutely fail of the former, by which alone happiness and freedom are achieved.

Work, therefore to be able to say to every harsh appearance, "You are but an appearance, and not absolutely the thing you appear to be." And then examine it by those rules that you have, and first, and chiefly, by this: whether it concerns the things that are in our own control or those that are not, and if it concerns anything not in our control, be prepared to say that it is nothing to you.

Remember that following desire promises the attainment of that of which you are desirous; and aversion promises the avoiding that to which you are averse. He, however, who fails to obtain the object of his desire is disappointed, and he who incurs the object of his aversion wretched. If, then, you confine your aversion to those objects only that are contrary to the natural use of your faculties, which you have in your own control, you will never incur anything to which you are averse. But if you are averse to sickness, or death, or poverty, you will be wretched. Remove aversion, then, from all things that are not in our control, and transfer it to things contrary to the nature of what is in our control. But, for the present, totally suppress desire: for, if you desire any of the things that are not in your own control, you must necessarily be disappointed; and of those that are, and which it would be laudable to desire, nothing is yet in your possession. Use only the appropriate actions of pursuit and avoidance, and even these lightly, and with gentleness and reservation.

With regard to whatever objects give you delight, are useful, or are deeply loved, remember to tell yourself of what general nature they are, beginning from the most insignificant things. If, for example, you are fond of a specific ceramic cup, remind yourself that it is only ceramic cups in general of which you are fond. Then, if it breaks, you will not be disturbed. If you kiss your child, or your wife, say that you only kiss things that are human, and thus you will not be disturbed if either of them dies.

When you are going about any action, remind yourself what nature the action is. If you are going to bathe, picture to yourself the things that usually happen in the bath: some people splash the water, some push, some use abusive language, and others steal. Thus you will more safely go about this action if you say to yourself, "I will now go bathe, and keep my own mind in a state conformable to nature." And in the same manner with regard to every other action. For thus, if any hindrance arises in bathing, you will have it ready to say, "It was not only to bathe that I desired, but to keep my mind in a state conformable to nature, and I will not keep it if I am bothered by things that happen.

Men are disturbed, not by things, but by the principles and notions that they form concerning things. Death, for instance, is not terrible, else it would have appeared so to Socrates.[99] But the terror consists in our notion of death that it is terrible. When therefore

[99] For Socrates's view on death, see Reading 60.

we are hindered, or disturbed, or grieved, let us never attribute it to others, but to ourselves, that is, to our own principles. An uninstructed person will lay the fault of his own bad condition upon others. Someone just starting instruction will lay the fault on himself. Someone who is perfectly instructed will place blame neither on others nor on himself.

Do not be prideful with any excellence that is not your own. If a horse should be prideful and say, "I am handsome," it would be supportable. But when you are prideful, and say, "I have a handsome horse," know that you are proud of what is, in fact, only the good of the horse. What, then, is your own? Only your reaction to the appearances of things. Thus, when you behave conformably to nature in reaction to how things appear, you will be proud with reason, for you will take pride in some good of your own

Do not demand that things happen as you wish, but wish that they happen as they do happen, and you will go on well.

If you want to improve, reject such reasonings as these: "If I neglect my affairs, I will have no income; if I do not correct my servant, he will be bad." For it is better to die with hunger, exempt from grief and fear, than to live in affluence with perturbation; and it is better your servant should be bad, than you unhappy.

Begin therefore from little things. Is a little oil spilt? A little wine stolen? Say to yourself, "This is the price paid for apathy, for tranquillity, and nothing is to be had for nothing." When you call your servant, it is possible that he may not come; or, if he does, he may not do what you want. But he is by no means of such importance that it should be in his power to give you any disturbance.

If you want to improve, be content to be thought foolish and stupid with regard to external things. Do not wish to be thought to know anything, and even if you appear to be somebody important to others, distrust yourself. For it is difficult to both keep your faculty of choice in a state conformable to nature, and at the same time acquire external things. But while you are careful about the one, you must of necessity neglect the other.

Remember that you are an actor in a drama, of such a kind as the author[100] pleases to make it. If short, of a short one; if long, of a long one. If it is his pleasure you should act a poor man, a cripple, a governor, or a private person, see that you act it naturally. For this is your business, to act well the character assigned you; to choose it is another's.

Remember that he who gives ill language or a blow does not cause insults, but rather the principle that represents these things as insulting. When, therefore, anyone provokes you, be assured that it is your own opinion that provokes you. Try, therefore, in the first place, not to be hurried away with the appearance. For if you once gain time and respite, you will more easily command yourself.

If you ever happen to turn your attention to externals, so as to wish to please anyone, be assured that you have ruined your scheme of life. Be contented, then, in everything with being a philosopher, and, if you wish to be thought so likewise by anyone, appear so to yourself, and it will suffice you.

Is anyone preferred before you at an entertainment, or in a compliment, or in being admitted to a consultation? If these things are good, you ought to be glad that he has gotten them, and if they are evil, do not be grieved that you have not gotten them. And remember that you cannot, without using the same means that others do to acquire things not in our own control, expect to be thought worthy of an equal share of them. For how can he who does not frequent the door of any great man, does not attend him, does not praise him, have an equal share with him who does? You are unjust, then, and insatiable, if you are unwilling to pay the price for which these things are sold, and would have them for nothing. For how much is lettuce sold? A denarius, for instance. If another, then, paying denarius, takes the lettuce, and you, not paying it, go without them, do not imagine that he has gained any advantage over you. For as he has the lettuce, so you have the denarius that you did not give. So, in the present case, you have not been

[100] That is the "logos," which set the entire universe on its preordained course.

invited to such a person's entertainment, because you have not paid him the price for which a supper is sold. It is sold for praise; it is sold for attendance. Give him then the value, if it is for your advantage. But if you would, at the same time, not pay the one and yet receive the other, you are insatiable, and a blockhead. Have you nothing, then, instead of the supper? Yes, indeed, you have: the not praising him, whom you do not like to praise; the not bearing with his behavior at coming in.

Duties universally are measured by relations. Is anyone a father? If so, it is implied that the children should take care of him, submit to him in everything, patiently listen to his reproaches, his correction. But he is a bad father. Are you naturally entitled, then, to a good father? No, only to a father. Is a brother unjust? Well, keep your own situation toward him. Consider not what he does, but what you are to do to keep your own faculty of choice in a state conformable to nature. For another will not hurt you unless you please. You will then be hurt when you think you are hurt. In this manner, therefore, you will find, from the idea of a neighbor, a citizen, a general, the corresponding duties if you accustom yourself to contemplate the several relations.

Upon all occasions we ought to have these maxims ready at hand: "Conduct me, Jove, and you, O Destiny, wherever your decrees have fixed my station, and I follow cheerfully, and, if I do not, wicked and wretched, I must follow still"[101]; or

"Whoever yields properly to Fate is deemed wise among men, and knows the laws of heaven."[102]

[101] A saying attributed to Cleanthes, a Stoic philosopher who followed Zeno as the head of the Stoic school in Athens.

[102] A saying attributed to the Greek tragedian Euripides.

67

REVOLT OF THE MACCABEES (167 BCE): *THE BOOK OF MACCABEES*

A silver tetradrachm (four-drachm coin) of the Seleucid king Antiochus IV Epiphanes depicts the head of Antiochus on the obverse wearing a diadem (a piece of cloth tied around the head) signifying royal status. The reverse portrays Zeus seated and holding a scepter in his left hand and the goddess Nikē (Victory) in his right. The legend reads, "King Antiochus Epiphanes ['God Manifest'], Bearer of Victory."

After the Seleucid king Antiochus IV Epiphanes (175–164 BCE), the son of Antiochus III (222–187 BCE), came to power in the Seleucid Empire, he attempted to unify the empire by enforcing the adoption of Greek customs on the Jews of Palestine. This offended many of the Jews in the kingdom. In 167 BCE, one of them, Mattathias, resisted and raised a rebellion. Mattathias was succeeded as leader of the rebellion by his son Judas Maccabaeus, who gave it its name. A full account of the Maccabean revolt is preserved in the biblical Book of Maccabees.

Source: "First Book of Maccabees," *New Revised Standard Version*.

After Alexander[103] son of Philip, the Macedonian, who came from the land of Kittim,[104] had defeated King Darius of the Persians and the Medes, he succeeded him as king. He fought many battles, conquered strongholds, and put to death the kings of the earth. He advanced to the ends of the earth and plundered many nations. When the earth became quiet before him, he was exalted, and his heart was lifted up. He gathered a very strong army and ruled over countries, nations, and princes, and they became tributary to him. After this he fell sick and perceived that he was dying. So he summoned his most honored officers, who had been brought up with him from youth, and divided his kingdom among them while he was still alive.[105] And after Alexander had reigned twelve years,[106] he died. Then his officers began to rule, each in his own place. They all put on crowns after his death, and so did their descendents after them for many years, and they caused many evils on the earth. From them came forth a sinful root, Antiochus Epiphanes, son of King Antiochus.[107] He had been a hostage in Rome. He began to reign in the one hundred thirty-seventh year of the kingdom of the Greeks.[108]

In those days certain renegades came out from Israel and misled many, saying, "Let us go and make a covenant with the Gentiles[109] around us, for since we separated from them many disasters have come upon us." This proposal pleased them, and some of the people eagerly went to the king, who authorized them to observe the ordinances of the Gentiles. So they built a gymnasium[110] in Jerusalem, according to Gentile custom, removed the marks of circumcision,[111] and abandoned the holy covenant. They joined with the Gentiles and sold themselves to do evil.

When Antiochus saw that his kingdom was established, he determined to become king of the land of Egypt, in order that he might reign over both kingdoms. So he invaded Egypt with a strong force, with chariots and elephants and cavalry and a large fleet.[112] He engaged King Ptolemy[113] of Egypt in battle, and Ptolemy turned and fled before him, and many were wounded and fell. He captured the fortified cities in the land of Egypt, and he plundered the land of Egypt. After subduing Egypt,[114] Antiochus returned in the one hundred forty-third year.[115] He went up against Israel and came to Jerusalem with a strong force. He arrogantly entered the sanctuary[116] and took the golden altar, the lampstand for the light, and all its utensils. He took also the table for the Bread of the Presence,[117] the cups for drink offerings, the bowls, the golden censers, the curtain, the crowns, and the gold decoration on the front of the temple; he stripped it all off. He took the silver and the gold, and the costly vessels; he took also the hidden treasures that he found. Taking them all, he went into his own land.[118]

---

[103] For Alexander, see also Readings 62 and 63.

[104] Specifically Cyprus, but, in this case, used to refer generically to "the west."

[105] An error. Alexander failed to indicate the disposition of his empire, which led to a long period of conflicts among his generals; see Reading 64.

[106] Alexander actually reigned from 336 until 323 BCE.

[107] The Seleucid king Antiochus I (281–261 BCE).

[108] That is, the Seleucid Empire, begun by Seleucus I in 311 BCE.

[109] Non-Jews.

[110] A Greek exercise ground, where participants exercised in the nude.

[111] Permanent restoration of the foreskin was accomplished by epispasm, or decircumcision, which involved slicing the skin of the penis circumferentially to loosen it, extending it over the glans, and then tying it off until it had reattached itself. A temporary process, infibulation, involved pulling the skin of the penis over the glans and then tying it off or pinning it with a fibula.

[112] In 168 BCE.

[113] In 170 BCE Antiochus invaded Egypt and defeated King Ptolemy VI (180–145 BCE); in 168 he invaded Egypt again and defeated both Ptolemy VI and his younger brother, Ptolemy VIII (169–116).

[114] Not exactly. Antiochus was forced by the Romans to evacuate Egypt.

[115] Of the Seleucid Empire, 168 BCE.

[116] Of the Jewish temple in Jerusalem.

[117] Loaves of bread always kept as an offering to God on a special table in the Jewish temple in Jerusalem.

[118] Antiochus needed the money to pay off the war indemnity imposed by the Romans on his father by the Treaty of Apamea in 188 BCE.

Then the king wrote to his whole kingdom that all should be one people, and that all should give up their particular customs. All the Gentiles accepted the command of the king. Many even from Israel gladly adopted his religion; they sacrificed to idols and profaned the sabbath. And the king sent letters by messengers to Jerusalem and the towns of Judah; he directed them to follow customs strange to the land, to forbid burnt offerings and sacrifices and drink offerings in the sanctuary, to profane sabbaths[119] and festivals, to defile the sanctuary and the priests, to build altars and sacred precincts and shrines for idols, to sacrifice swine and other unclean animals, and to leave their sons uncircumcised. They were to make themselves abominable by everything unclean and profane, so that they would forget the law and change all the ordinances. He added, "And whoever does not obey the command of the king shall die."

In those days Mattathias son of John son of Simeon, a priest of the family of Joarib, moved from Jerusalem and settled in Modein.[120] He had five sons, John surnamed Gaddi, Simon called Thassi, Judas called Maccabeus,[121] Eleazar called Avaran, and Jonathan called Apphus. He saw the blasphemies being committed in Judah and Jerusalem. Then Mattathias and his sons tore their clothes, put on sackcloth, and mourned greatly. The king's officers who were enforcing the apostasy[122] came to the town of Modein to make them offer sacrifice. Many from Israel came to them, and Mattathias and his sons were assembled. Then the king's officers spoke to Mattathias as follows: "You are a leader, honored and great in this town, and supported by sons and brothers. Now be the first to come and do what the king commands, as all the Gentiles and the people of Judah and those that are left in Jerusalem have done. Then you and your sons will be numbered among the friends of the king, and you and your sons will be honored with silver and gold and many gifts."

But Mattathias answered and said in a loud voice, "Even if all the nations that live under the rule of the king obey him, and have chosen to obey his commandments, everyone of them abandoning the religion of their ancestors, I and my sons and my brothers will continue to live by the covenant of our ancestors. Far be it from us to desert the law and the ordinances. We will not obey the king's words by turning aside from our religion to the right hand or to the left." When he had finished speaking these words, a Jew came forward in the sight of all to offer sacrifice on the altar in Modein, according to the king's command. When Mattathias saw it, he burned with zeal and his heart was stirred. He gave vent to righteous anger; he ran and killed him on the altar. At the same time he killed the king's officer who was forcing them to sacrifice, and he tore down the altar. Then Mattathias cried out in the town with a loud voice, saying: "Let every one who is zealous for the law and supports the covenant come out with me!" Then he and his sons fled to the hills and left all that they had in the town.

At that time many who were seeking righteousness and justice went down to the wilderness to live there, they, their sons, their wives, and their livestock, because troubles pressed heavily upon them. And it was reported to the king's officers, and to the troops in Jerusalem the city of David, that those who had rejected the king's command had gone down to the hiding places in the wilderness. Many pursued them, and overtook them; they encamped opposite them and prepared for battle against them on the sabbath day. The troops said to them, "Enough of this! Come out and do what the king commands, and you will live." But the Jews replied, "We will not come out, nor will we do what the king commands and so profane the sabbath day." Then the enemy quickly attacked them. But they did not answer them or hurl a stone at them or block up their hiding places, for they said, "Let us all die in our innocence; heaven and earth testify for us that you are killing us unjustly."

119 Saturday, the Jewish day of worship.

120 A town in Judaea near Jerusalem.

121 A word meaning "the hammer."

122 To abandon one religion and adopt another one.

So they attacked them on the sabbath, and they died, with their wives and children and livestock, to the number of a thousand persons.

When Mattathias and his friends learned of it, they mourned for them deeply. And all said to their neighbors: "If we all do as our kindred have done and refuse to fight with the Gentiles for our lives and for our ordinances, they will quickly destroy us from the earth." So they made this decision that day: "Let us fight against anyone who comes to attack us on the sabbath day; let us not all die as our kindred died in their hiding places." Then there united with them a company of Hasideans,[123] mighty warriors of Israel, all who offered themselves willingly for the law. And all who became fugitives to escape their troubles joined them and reinforced them. They organized an army, and struck down sinners in their anger and renegades in their wrath; the survivors fled to the Gentiles for safety. And Mattathias and his friends went around and tore down the altars. They forcibly circumcised all the uncircumcised boys that they found within the borders of Israel. They hunted down the arrogant, and the work prospered in their hands. They rescued the law out of the hands of the Gentiles and kings, and they never let the sinner gain the upper hand.

[123] A Jewish religious sect.

CHAPTER 9

Civilization Beyond the Near East, Greece, and Rome (2300–31 BCE)

By 31 BCE, at the end of the Hellenistic Age, the western Mediterranean city of Rome in Italy had risen to become the strongest, indeed the only, power in the Mediterranean world. But before embarking on an account of Rome's rise to power, one might step back and consider the other peoples who existed on the periphery of the Near Eastern, and, in particular, the Greek and Roman, worlds. The characteristics and significance of these peoples all too often have been unappreciated, both then and now. In the modern day, these peoples can be submerged or marginalized as a consequence of the natural focus on the two civilizations that had such a tremendous impact on the future development of western history and culture. And in Greek and Roman antiquity, views of the peoples who lived beyond the known world became more and more fanciful the farther away one got. Indeed, in the mid-fifth century BCE, the Greek historian Herodotus expressed the view that "the extreme regions of the earth, which surround and shut up within themselves all other countries, produce the things that are the rarest." But in many ways, cultures besides Greece and Rome, some of them far from the Mediterranean world, also influenced the future, not only because of their own impact on the Greek and Roman world but also because we always must remind ourselves that the Greeks and Romans were not the only civilizations of antiquity. The following examples consider the peoples on the fringes of the Greek and Roman worlds, during the Hellenistic Period and before. All of them, with the exception of the "Stele of Piye," were written by Greeks and Romans, not by the peoples who are being discussed, so the reader must bear in mind that descriptions written by other peoples may not, and probably do not, reflect the perceptions that these peoples actually had of themselves.

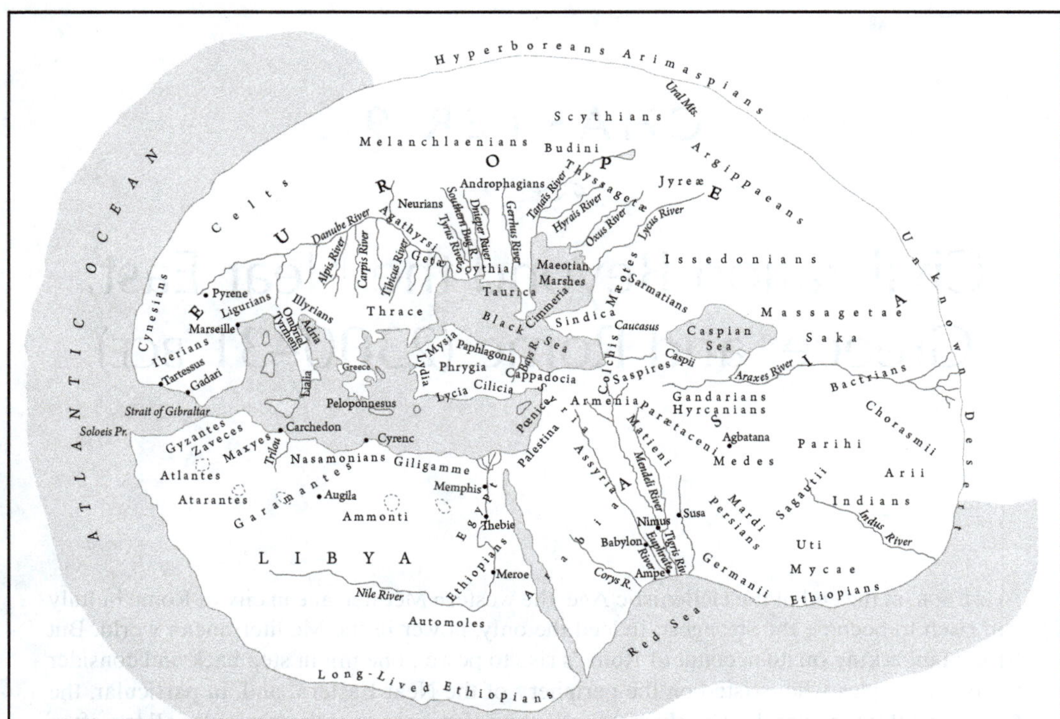

Map 9 A visual presentation of the world as described by the Greek historian Herodotus about 440 BCE. Herodotus rejected the prevalent ideas that Libya (Africa), Europe, and Asia were all the same size and that a single ocean encircled the whole world.

68

THE SCYTHIANS (513 BCE): HERODOTUS, *THE HISTORIES*, BOOK 4

An Attic red-figured plate dated to ca. 510 BCE and now in the British Museum depicts a Scythian archer running left and pulling an arrow out of a quiver.

In the course of his discussion of the attack on the Scythians in 513 BCE by the Persian king Darius, the Greek historian Herodotus, writing about 440 BCE, added a lengthy digression about Scythian customs, reflecting a contemporary Greek fascination with the curious practices of peoples they referred to as "barbarians."

Source: George Rawlinson, Henry Rawlinson, and John Gardner Wilkinson, trans., *The History of Herodotus. A New English Version* (London: Murray, 1862).

The Scythians are provided with the most important necessaries. Their manners and customs come now to be described. They worship only the following gods, namely, Hestia,[1] whom they reverence beyond all the rest, Zeus, and Earth, whom they consider to be the wife of Zeus; and after these Apollo, Heavenly Aphrodite, Hercules, and Ares. These gods are worshipped by the whole nation; the Royal Scythians[2]

[1] The goddess of the hearth, Roman Vesta.

[2] The Scythian royal family.

offer sacrifice likewise to Poseidon. In the Scythian tongue Hestia is called Tabiti, Zeus (very properly, in my judgment) Papaeus, Earth Apia, Apollo Goetosyrus, Celestial Venus Argimpasa, and Neptune Thagimasadas. They use no images, altars, or temples, except in the worship of Ares, but in his worship they do use them.

The manner of their sacrifices is everywhere and in every case the same. The victim[3] stands with its two fore-feet bound together by a cord, and the person who is about to offer, taking his station behind the victim, gives the rope a pull, and thereby throws the animal down. As it falls he invokes the god to whom he is offering, after which he puts a noose round the animal's neck, and, inserting a small stick, twists it round, and so strangles him. No fire is lighted, there is no consecration, and no pouring out of drink-offerings, but as soon as the beast is strangled the sacrificer skins it and then sets to work to boil the flesh.

As Scythia, moreover, is utterly barren of firewood, a plan has had to be contrived for boiling the flesh, which is the following. After flaying the beasts, they take out all the bones, and, if they possess such gear, put the flesh into boilers made in the country, which are very like the cauldrons of the Lesbians, except that they are of a much larger size. Then placing the bones of the animals beneath the cauldron, they set them alight, and so boil the meat. If they do not happen to possess a cauldron, they make the animal's paunch hold the flesh, and pouring in at the same time a little water, lay the bones under and light them. The bones burn beautifully, and the paunch easily contains all the flesh when it is stript from the bones, so that by this plan an ox is made to boil itself, and other victims also to do the like. When the meat is all cooked, the sacrificer makes an offering of a portion of the flesh and of the entrails by casting them on the ground before him. They sacrifice all sorts of cattle, but most commonly horses.

Such are the victims offered to the other gods, and such is the mode in which they are sacrificed, but the rites paid to Ares are different. In every district, at the seat of government, there stands a temple of this god, whereof the following is a description. It is a vast pile of brushwood, in length and breadth three furlongs[4]; in height somewhat less. It has a square platform upon the top, three sides of which are precipitous, whereas the fourth slopes so that people may walk up it. Each year a hundred and fifty wagon-loads of brushwood are added to the pile, which sinks continually by reason of the rains. An antique iron sword is planted on the top of every such mound, and serves as the image of Ares. Yearly sacrifices of cattle and of horses are made to it, and more victims are offered thus than to all the rest of their gods. When prisoners are taken in war, out of every hundred men they sacrifice one, not however with the same rites as the cattle, but with different ones. Libations of wine are first poured upon their heads after which they are slaughtered over a vessel. The vessel then is carried up to the top of the pile, and the blood poured upon the scimitar. While this takes place at the top of the mound, below, by the side of the temple, the right hands and arms of the slaughtered prisoners are cut off and tossed on high into the air. Then the other victims are slain and those who have offered the sacrifice depart, leaving the hands and arms where they may chance to have fallen, and the bodies also, separate. Such are the observances of the Scythians with respect to sacrifice. They never use swine for the purpose, nor indeed is it their custom to breed them in any part of their country.

In what concerns war, their customs are the following. The Scythian soldier drinks the blood of the first man he overthrows in battle. Whatever number he slays, he cuts off all their heads, and carries them to the king because he is thus entitled to a share of the booty, wherefore he forfeits all claim if he does not produce a head. In order to strip the skull of its covering, he makes a cut round the head above the ears, and, laying hold of the scalp, shakes the skull out; then with the rib of an ox he scrapes the scalp clean of flesh, and softening it by rubbing between the hands, uses it thenceforth as a napkin. The Scythian is proud of these scalps, and hangs them from his

[3] A four-footed animal such as a cow, bull, or horse.

[4] A furlong equals 660 feet.

bridle-rein; the greater the number of such napkins that a man can show, the more highly is he esteemed among them. Many make themselves cloaks, like the capotes[5] of our peasants, by sewing a quantity of these scalps together. Others flay the right arms of their dead enemies, and make of the skin, which stripped off with the nails hanging to it, a covering for their quivers. Now the skin of a man is thick and glossy, and would in whiteness surpass almost all other hides. Some even flay the entire body of their enemy, and stretching it upon a frame carry it about with them wherever they ride. Such are the Scythian customs with respect to scalps and skins.

The skulls of their enemies, not indeed of all, but of those whom they most detest, they treat as follows. Having sawn off the portion below the eyebrows, and cleaned out the inside, they cover the outside with leather. When a man is poor, this is all that he does, but if he is rich, he also lines the inside with gold. In either case the skull is used as a drinking-cup. They do the same with the skulls of their own kith and kin if they have been at feud with them and have vanquished them in the presence of the king. When strangers whom they deem of any account come to visit them, these skulls are handed round and the host tells how that these were his relations who made war upon him, and how that he got the better of them; all this being looked upon as proof of bravery.

Once a year the governor of each district, at a set place in his own province, mingles a bowl of wine from which all Scythians who have slain foes have a right to drink, whereas those who have slain no enemy are not allowed to taste of the bowl but sit aloof in disgrace. No greater shame than this can happen to them. Such as have slain a very large number of foes, have two cups instead of one and drink from both.

Scythia has an abundance of soothsayers, who foretell the future by means of a number of willow wands. A large bundle of these wands is brought and laid on the ground. The soothsayer unties the bundle, and places each wand by itself, at the same time uttering his prophecy. Then, while he still is speaking, he gathers the rods together again, and makes them up once more into a bundle. This mode of divination is of home growth in Scythia. The Enarees, or woman-like men, have another method, which they say Aphrodite taught them. It is done with the inner bark of the linden-tree. They take a piece of this bark, and, splitting it into three strips, keep twining the strips about their fingers, and untwining them, while they prophesy.

Whenever the Scythian king falls sick he sends for the three soothsayers of most renown at the time, who come and make trial of their art in the mode above described. Generally, they say that the king is ill because such and such a person, mentioning his name, has sworn falsely by the royal hearth. This is the usual oath among the Scythians, when they wish to swear with very great solemnity. Then the man accused of having foresworn himself is arrested and brought before the king. The soothsayers tell him that by their art it is clear he has sworn a false oath by the royal hearth, and so caused the illness of the king. He denies the charge, protests that he has sworn no false oath, and loudly complains of the wrong done to him. Upon this the king sends for six new soothsayers, who try the matter by soothsaying. If they too find the man guilty of the offense, straightway he is beheaded by those who first accused him and his goods are divided among them: if, on the contrary, they acquit him, other soothsayers, and again others, are sent for, to try the case. Should the greater number decide in favor of the man's innocence, then they who first accused him forfeit their lives.

The mode of their execution of soothsayers is the following: a wagon is loaded with brushwood and oxen are harnessed to it. The soothsayers, with their feet tied together, their hands bound behind their backs, and their mouths gagged, are thrust into the midst of the brushwood. Finally the wood is set alight, and the oxen, being startled, are made to rush off with the wagon. It often happens that the oxen and the soothsayers are both consumed together, but sometimes the pole of the wagon is burnt through, and the oxen escape with a scorching. Lying diviners are burnt in the way described for other causes besides the one

[5] A long hooded coat.

here spoken of. When the king puts one of them to death, he takes care not to let any of his sons survive: all the male offspring are slain with the father, only the females being allowed to live.

Oaths among the Scythians are accompanied with the following ceremonies: a large earthen bowl is filled with wine, and the parties to the oath, wounding themselves slightly with a knife or an awl, drop some of their blood into the wine; then they plunge into the mixture a scimitar, some arrows, a battle-axe, and a javelin, all the while repeating prayers. Lastly the two contracting parties drink each a draught from the bowl, as do also the chief men among their followers.

69

THE PARTHIANS (CA. 250–100 BCE): JUSTIN, *PHILIPPIC HISTORIES*, BOOK 41

A spiral-haired Parthian of the first century CE depicted wearing a belted, decorated tunic with a dagger at his side and perhaps engaged in worship. From the ancient province of Khwuzestan in western Iran. Preserved in the Metropolitan Museum in New York.

The Parthians were a steppe people said to have been related to the Scythians. According to legend, the Parthians originated with the Scythian Arsaces, the leader of a people known as the Parni who lived on the lower Oxus (Amu Darya) River on the southern Eurasian steppe. In 238 BCE they invaded and occupied the Seleucid satrapy of Parthia in northeastern Iran, from which they took their name. Arsaces founded the Arsacid Dynasty of Parthian kings. The

Parthians, being located intermediate between the western Mediterranean world and the world of the Far East, served as important conduits for commerce and culture between west and east. In the west they interacted first with the Seleucid Empire and then with the Romans before being overthrown by the Sasanid Persians in the 220s CE. This account of Parthian history comes from the "*Philippic Histories*" of the Augustan writer Pompeius Trogus, which were summarized circa the second or third century CE by Marcus Junianus Justinus, or simply Justin.

Source: John Selby Watson, *Marcus Junius Justinus, Epitome of the Philippic History of Pompeius Trogus* (London: Bohn, 1853).

The Parthians originally were exiles from Scythia.[6] This is apparent from their very name, for in the Scythian language exiles are called Parthi. During the time of the Assyrians[7] and Medes,[8] they were the most obscure of all the people of the east. Subsequently, too, when the empire of the east was transferred from the Medes to the Persians, they were but as a herd without a name, and fell under the power of the stronger.[9] At last they became subject to the Macedonians,[10] when they conquered the east; so that it must seem wonderful to every one, that they should have reached such a height of good fortune as to rule over those nations under whose sway they had been merely slaves. Being assailed by the Romans, also, in three wars,[11] under the conduct of the greatest generals, and at the most flourishing period of the Republic, they alone, of all nations, were not only a match for them, but came off victorious. It may, however, have been a greater glory to them, indeed, to have been able to rise amid the Assyrian, Median, and Persian empires, so celebrated of old, and the most powerful dominion of Bactria, peopled with a thousand cities, than to have been victorious in war against a people that came from a distance, especially when they were continually harassed by severe wars with the Scythians and other neighboring nations, and pressed with various other formidable contests.

The Parthians, being forced to quit Scythia by discord at home, gradually settled in the deserts between Hyrcania,[12] the Dahae, the Arci, the Sparni, and the Marsiani.[13] They then advanced their borders, although their neighbors, who at first made no opposition, at length endeavored to prevent them, to such an extent, that they not only got possession of the vast level plains, but also of steep hills, and heights of the mountains; and hence it is that an excess of heat or cold prevails in most parts of the Parthian territories, because the snow is troublesome on the higher grounds and the heat in the plains.

The government of the nation, after their revolt from the Macedonian power,[14] was in the hands of kings. Next to the royal authority is the order of the people, from which they take generals in war and magistrates in peace. Their language is something between those of the Scythians and Medes, being a compound of both. Their dress was formerly of a fashion peculiar to themselves; afterward, when their power had increased, it was like that of the Medes, light and full flowing. The fashion of their arms is that of their own country and of Scythia. They have an army, not like other nations, of free men, but chiefly consisting of slaves, the numbers of whom daily increase, the power of manumission being allowed to none, and all their offspring, in consequence, being born slaves. These bondmen they bring up as

[6] See Reading 68.

[7] See Readings 39 and 40.

[8] See Reading 43.

[9] "Parthia" was one of the satrapies of the Persian Empire; see Reading 44.

[10] During the campaigns of Alexander the Great.

[11] Perhaps campaigns undertaken by Crassus (54–53 BCE), Ventidius (40 BCE), and Mark Antony (37 BCE).

[12] On the southern coast of the Caspian Sea.

[13] For some of these peoples, see the map at the beginning of this chapter.

[14] The Seleucid Empire.

carefully as their own children, and teach them, with great pains, the arts of riding and shooting with the bow. As anyone is eminent in wealth, so he furnishes the king with a proportionate number of horsemen for war. Indeed when fifty thousand cavalry encountered Antony,[15] as he was making war upon Parthia, only four hundred of them were free men.

Of engaging with the enemy in close fighting and of taking cities by siege, they know nothing. They fight on horseback, either galloping forward or turning their backs. Often, too, they counterfeit flight so that they may throw their pursuers off their guard against being wounded by their arrows. The signal for battle among them is given, not by trumpet but by drum. Nor are they able to fight long, but they would be irresistible if their vigor and perseverance were equal to the fury of their onset. In general, they retire before the enemy in the very heat of the engagement, and, soon after their retreat, return to the battle afresh, so that, when you feel most certain that you have conquered them, you have still to meet the greatest danger from them. Their armor, and that of their horses, is formed of plates, lapping over one another like the feathers of a bird, and covers both man and horse entirely. Of gold and silver, except for adorning their arms, they make no use.

Each man has several wives for the sake of gratifying desire with different objects. They punish no crime more severely than adultery, and accordingly they not only exclude their women from entertainments but also forbid them the very sight of men. They eat no flesh but that which they take in hunting. They ride on horseback on all occasions; on horses they go to war, and to feasts; on horses they discharge public and private duties; on horses they go abroad, meet together, traffic, and converse. Indeed the difference between slaves and freemen is, that slaves go on foot, but freemen only on horseback. Their general mode of burial is dilaniation[16] by birds or dogs; the bare bones they at last bury in the ground. In their superstitions and worship of the gods the principal veneration is paid to rivers. The disposition of the people is proud, quarrelsome, faithless, and insolent, for they think that a certain roughness of behavior is becoming to men and gentleness only to women. They are always restless and ready for any commotion, at home or abroad. They are taciturn by nature, more ready to act than speak, and consequently they shroud both their successes and miscarriages in silence. They obey their princes, not from humility, but from fear. They are libidinous, but frugal in diet. To their word or promise they have no regard, except as far as suits their interest.

After the death of Alexander the Great, when the kingdoms of the east were divided among his successors, the government of Parthia was committed to Stasanor, a foreign ally, because none of the Macedonians would deign to accept it.[17] Subsequently, when the Macedonians were divided into parties by civil discord, the Parthians, with the other people of Upper Asia, followed Eumenes, and, when he was defeated, went over to Antigonus.[18] After his death they were under the rule of Seleucus Nicator,[19] and then under Antiochus[20] and his successors, from whose great-grandson Seleucus[21] they first revolted, at the time of the First Punic war, when Lucius Manlius Vulso and Marcus Attilius Regulus were Consuls.[22] For their revolt, the dispute between the two brothers, Seleucus and Antiochus,[23] procured them impunity, for while they sought to wrest the throne from one another they neglected to pursue the revolters.

At the same period, also, Theodotus, governor of the thousand cities of Bactria, revolted,[24] and assumed

[15] The Roman Triumvir Mark Antony, who invaded Parthia in 37 BCE.

[16] Tearing into pieces.

[17] According to Justin himself, at the "Partition of Babylon" in 323 BCE, Stasanor was granted the administration of the Dranci and Arci, and Nicanor was granted the Parthians.

[18] For these conflicts, see Reading 64.

[19] Seleucus I (311–281 BCE), who founded the Seleucid Empire.

[20] Antiochus I "The Great" (281–261 BCE), son of Seleucus I.

[21] Seleucus II (246–225 BCE).

[22] 256 BCE; rather earlier than the reign of Seleucus II.

[23] Antiochus Hierax (246–226 BCE), a brother and rival of Seleucus II.

[24] In 250 BCE.

the title of king; and all the other people of the east, influenced by his example, fell away from the Macedonians. One Arsaces, a man of uncertain origin, but of undisputed bravery, happened to arise at this time; and he, who was accustomed to live by plunder and depredations, hearing a report that Seleucus was overcome by the Gauls in Asia, and being consequently freed from dread of that prince, invaded Parthia with a band of marauders, overthrew Andragorus, Seleucus' lieutenant,[25] and, after putting him to death,[26] took upon himself the government of the country. Not long after, too, he made himself master of Hyrcania,[27] and thus, invested with authority over two nations, raised a large army, through fear of Seleucus and Theodotus, King of the Bactrians. But being soon relieved of his fears by the death of Theodotus, he made peace and an alliance with his son, who was also named Theodotus, and not long after, engaging with king Seleucus, who came to take vengeance on the revolters, he obtained a victory,[28] and the Parthians observe the day on which it was gained with great solemnity, as the date of the commencement of their liberty.

Seleucus being then recalled into Asia by new disturbances, and respite being thus given to Arsaces, he settled the Parthian government, levied soldiers, built fortresses, and strengthened his towns. He founded a city also, called Dara, in Mount Zapaortenon, of which the situation is such, that no place can be more secure or more pleasant, for it is so encircled with steep rocks that the strength of its position needs no defenders, and such is the fertility of the adjacent soil, that it is stored with its own produce. Such too is the plenty of springs and wood, that it is amply supplied with streams of water and abounds with all the pleasures of hunting. Thus Arsaces, having at once acquired and established a kingdom, and having become no less memorable among the Parthians than Cyrus[29] among the Persians, Alexander[30] among the Macedonians, or Romulus[31] among the Romans, died at a mature old age, and the Parthians paid this honor to his memory, that they called all their kings thenceforward by the name of Arsaces.[32] His son and successor on the throne, whose name also was Arsaces,[33] fought with the greatest bravery against Antiochus, the son of Seleucus, who was at the head of a hundred thousand foot and twenty thousand horse, and was at last taken into alliance with him.

The third king of the Parthians was Priapatius,[34] but he was also called Arsaces, for, as has just been observed, they distinguished all their kings by that name, as the Romans use the titles of Caesar and Augustus. He, after reigning fifteen years, died, leaving two sons, Mithridates and Phraates. The elder, Phraates,[35] being, according to the custom of the nation, heir to the crown, subdued the Mardi, a strong people, by force of arms, and died not long after, leaving several sons, whom he set aside, and left the throne, in preference, to his brother Mithridates,[36] a man of extraordinary ability, thinking that more was due to the name of king than to that of father, and that he ought to consult the interests of his country rather than those of his children.

Almost at the same time that Mithridates ascended the throne among the Parthians, Eucratides[37] began to reign among the Bactrians, both of them being great men. But the fortune of the Parthians, being the more successful, raised them, under this prince, to the highest degree of power, whereas the Bactrians, harassed with various wars, lost not only their dominions, but their liberty, for having suffered from contentions with the Sogdianians, the Drangians, and the Indians, they were at last overcome, as if exhausted, by the weaker Parthians. Eucratides, however, carried on several wars with great spirit, and although much reduced by his losses in them, yet,

---

[25] A satrap of Seleucus II who had revolted in the mid-240s.

[26] In 238 BCE.

[27] On the southern coast of the Caspian Sea.

[28] Ca. 235 BCE.

[29] See Reading 43.

[30] See Readings 62 and 63.

[31] See Reading 73.

[32] The royal family of the Parthians was called the Arsacids.

[33] Arsaces II, King of Parthia from 211 to 185 BCE.

[34] King of Parthia from 185 to 170 BCE.

[35] Phraates I, King of Parthia from 168 to 165 BCE.

[36] Mithridates I, King of Parthia from 165 to 132 BCE.

[37] King of Bactria ca. 170–145 BCE.

when he was besieged by Demetrius,[38] King of the Indians, with a garrison of only three hundred soldiers, he repulsed, by continual sallies, a force of sixty thousand enemies. Having accordingly escaped, after a five months' siege, he reduced India under his power. But as he was returning from the country, he was killed on his march by his son, with whom he had shared his throne, and who was so far from concealing the murder, that, as if he had killed an enemy, and not his father, he drove his chariot through his blood, and ordered his body to be cast out unburied.

During the course of these proceedings among the Bactrians, a war arose between the Parthians and Medes, and after fortune on each side had been some time fluctuating, victory at length fell to the Parthians when Mithridates, enforced with this addition to his power, appointed Bacasis over Media, while he himself marched into Hyrcania. On his return from thence, he went to war with the king of the Elymaeans,[39] and having conquered him, added this nation also to his dominions, and extended the Parthian empire, by reducing many other peoples under his yoke, from Mount Caucasus to the river Euphrates. Being then taken ill, he died in an honorable old age, and not inferior in merit to his great-grandfather Arsaces.

[38] Several Greek kings of this name are attested; this one may be Demetrius II, who may have reigned ca. 175–150 BCE.

[39] Elymais was in southern Persia on the northwestern shore of the Persian Gulf.

70

THE EMPIRE OF KUSH (731 BCE): "THE VICTORY STELA OF PIYE"

The "Victory Stela" of Piye, also known as Piankhi, a six-foot-tall slab of granite now in the Cairo Museum, was discovered in 1862 at the temple of Amon at Gebel Barkal in modern Sudan. The scene at the top shows Piye standing before the seated god Amon and receiving the submission of Namlot, ruler of Khmunu (Hermopolis), three Libyan kings, and several princes who crouch subserviently on the ground.

Ca. 731 BCE, Tefnakhte, a Libyan prince based in the Egyptian nome of Saïs, began to expand south, seizing Memphis and continuing upstream. He was opposed by the Kushite pharaoh Piye (753–722 BCE), the founder of Egypt's Twenty-sixth Dynasty, who captured Hermopolis and Memphis and received Tefnakhte's submission. After his remarkably lenient treatment of the rebels, Piye then withdrew to his capital city of Napata in Kush. Piye's exploits were recounted in a lengthy 159-line account written in hieroglyphic script inscribed on the "Victory Stela" of Piye.

Source: James Henry Breasted, "The Piankhi Stela," in *Ancient Records of Egypt*, Vol. 4 (Chicago: University of Chicago Press, 1906), nos. 817–852, 419–430.

Year 21, first month of the first season, under the majesty of the Pharaoh of Upper and Lower Egypt, Meriamon-Piankhi,[40] living forever. The command that my majesty speaks, "Hear of what I did, more than the ancestors. I, beloved of the gods, achieving with his hands, Meriamon-Piankhi, am a pharaoh, divine emanation, living image of Atum,[41] who came forth from the womb, adorned as a ruler, of whom those greater than he were afraid, whose father knew and whose mother recognized that he would rule in the egg, the Good God."

One came to say to His Majesty, "A chief of the west,[42] the great prince of Neter, Tefnakhte[43] is in the nome of Xois,[44] in Hapi, in Ayan, in Pernub, and in Memphis[45]. He has seized the whole west from the back-lands to Ithtowe, coming southward with a numerous army, while the Two Lands[46] are united behind him, and the princes and rulers of walled towns are as dogs at his heels. No stronghold has closed its doors in the nomes of the south, and every city of the west has opened the doors for fear of him. He turned to the east, they opened to him likewise. Behold, he besieges Heracleopolis,[47] he has completely invested it, not letting comers-out come out, and not letting goers-in go in, fighting every day.

Then His Majesty heard with courageous heart, laughing, and joyous of heart. The princes and commanders of the army who were in their cities sent to His Majesty daily, saying, "Wilt thou be silent, even to forgetting the Southland?[48] While Tefnakhte advances his conquest and finds none to repel his arm. Namlot, prince of Hatweret, has overthrown the wall of Nefrus, he has demolished his own city, for fear of him who might take it from him, in order to besiege another city. Behold, he goes to follow at the heels of Tefnakhte, having cast off allegiance to His Majesty."

Then His Majesty sent to the princes and commanders of the army who were in Egypt the commander Purem, and the commander Lemersekeny, and every commander of His Majesty who was in Egypt, saying, "Hasten into battle line, engage in battle. Let not the peasants go forth to the field, let not the plowmen plow, beset the frontier of the Hare nome[49] fight against it daily. Force battle upon him. Hasten to them; these princes whom he has brought for his support: Libyans and favorite soldiers, force battle upon them. Say, 'Yoke the war horses, the best of thy stable; draw up the line of battle! Thou knowest that Amon is the god who has sent us.'"

Then they threw themselves upon their bellies before His Majesty, saying, "It is thy name that endues us with might, and thy counsel is the mooring-post of thy army. Thy bread is in our bellies on every march, thy beer quenches our thirst. It is thy valor that giveth us might, and there is strength at the remembrance of thy name; for no army prevails whose commander is a coward. Who is thy equal therein? Thou art a victorious pharaoh, achieving with his hands, chief of the work of war."

They sailed down-stream, they arrived at Thebes, they did according to all that His Majesty had said. They sailed down-stream upon the river, they found many ships coming up-streams bearing soldiers, sailors, and commanders, every valiant man of the Northland, equipped with weapons of war, to fight against the army of His Majesty. Then there was made a great slaughter among them, whose number was unknown. Their troops and their ships were captured, and brought as living captives to the place where His Majesty was. They then went to the nome of Heracleopolis, demanding battle. Prince Namlot and Prince Yewepet, Chief of the Meshwesh,[50]

[40] An alternate name for Piye.

[41] See Reading 4.

[42] Libya.

[43] From the nome of Saïs in Lower Egypt; founder of the short-lived Twenty-fourth Dynasty. Although the account of the stele of Piye would lead the reader to believe that Tefnakhte had been fully defeated, he in fact remained independent and reclaimed his royal title after Piye departed. A stele of Tefnakhte also survives.

[44] The sixth nome of Lower Egypt.

[45] All places in Lower Egypt, the area of the Nile delta.

[46] Upper and Lower Egypt.

[47] Capital of the twentieth nome of Upper Egypt.

[48] The southern part of Upper Egypt.

[49] The fifteenth nome, with its capital at Khmunu (Greek Hermopolis).

[50] Libyans.

Sheshonq of Per-Osiris, Lord of Ded, Great Chief of the Meshwesh, Zeamonefonekh of Per-Benebded together with his eldest son, who was commander of the army of Per-Thutuprehui. Every prince, the rulers of the walled towns in the west, in the east, the islands in the midst, were united of one mind as followers of the great chief of the west, ruler of the walled towns of the Northland, prophet of Neit, mistress of Saïs, sem priest of Ptah, Tefnakhte. They went forth against them; then they made a great slaughter among them, greater than anything. Their ships were captured upon the river. When the land brightened early in the morning, the army of His Majesty crossed over against them. Army mingled with army; they slew a multitude of people among them; horses of unknown number; a rout ensued among the remnant. They fled to the Northland, from the blow, great and evil beyond everything.

Prince Namlot fled up-stream southward, when it was told him, "Hermopolis is in the midst of the foe from the army of His Majesty, who capture its people and its cattle." Then he entered into Hermopolis, while the army of His Majesty was upon the river, in the harbor of the Hare nome. Then they heard of it, and they surrounded the Hare nome on its four sides, not letting comers-out come out, and not letting goers-in go in.

Then His Majesty was enraged thereat like a panther, saying, "Have they allowed a remnant of the army of the Northland to remain? Allowing him that went forth of them to go forth, to tell of his campaign? Not causing their death, in order to destroy the last of them? I swear, as Ra loves me! I will myself go northward, that I may destroy that which he has done, that I may make him turn back from fighting, forever."

Then the army that was there in Egypt heard of the wrath that His Majesty felt toward them. Then they fought against Per-Mezed of the Oxyrhynchite nome,[51] they took it like a flood of water, and they sent to His Majesty, but his heart was not satisfied therewith. Then they fought against Tetehen, great in might. They found it filled with soldiers, with every valiant man of the Northland. Then the battering-ram was employed against it, its wall was overthrown, and a great slaughter was made among them of unknown number; also the son of the chief of Me, Tefnakhte. Then they sent to His Majesty concerning it, but his heart was not satisfied therewith. Then they fought against Hatbenu, its interior was breached, the army of His Majesty entered into it. Then they sent to His Majesty, but his heart was not satisfied therewith.

First month of the first season, ninth day; His Majesty went northward to Thebes, and completed the Feast of Amon at the festival of Opet.[52] His Majesty sailed northward to the city of the Hare nome. His Majesty came forth from the cabin of the ship, the horses were yoked up, the chariot was mounted. The terror of His Majesty reached to the end of the Asiatics, every heart was heavy with the fear of him. Then His Majesty went forth, enraged at his soldiers like a panther, saying, "Is the steadfastness of your fighting this slackness in my affairs? Has the year reached its end, when the fear of me has been inspired in the Northland? A great and evil blow shall smite them."

He set up for himself the camp on the southwest of Hermopolis and besieged it daily. Days passed and Hermopolis was foul to the nose without her usual fragrance. Then Hermopolis threw herself upon her belly, and pled before the pharaoh. Messengers came forth and descended bearing everything beautiful to behold: gold, every splendid costly stone, clothing in a chest, and the diadem that was upon his head, the uraeus that inspired the fear of him. Then they sent his wife, the prince's wife, and prince's daughter, Nestent, to plead with the pharaoh's wives, pharaoh's concubines, pharaoh's daughters, and pharaoh's sisters, to throw herself upon her belly in the harem, before the pharaoh's wives, saying, "We come to you, O pharaoh's wives, pharaoh's daughters, and pharaoh's sisters, that ye may appease Horus, lord of the palace, whose fame is great and his triumph mighty.

The prince threw himself upon his belly before His Majesty, saying, "Be appeased, Horus, Lord of the Palace, it is thy might that has done it. I am one

[51] The nineteenth nome of Upper Egypt.

[52] An annual festival held in Thebes in honor of the gods Amon and Mut and their child Khonsu.

of the pharaoh's slaves, paying impost into the treasury." Then he presented much silver, gold, lapis lazuli, malachite, bronze, and all costly stones. Then he filled the treasury with this tribute; he brought a horse in the right hand and a sistrum[53] in the left hand, of gold and lapis lazuli.

Then His Majesty appeared in splendor in his palace, proceeded to the house of Thoth,[54] lord of Hermopolis, and he slew bulls, calves, and fowl for his father Thoth, lord of Hermopolis. His Majesty proceeded to the house of Prince Namlot, he entered every chamber of the prince's house, his treasury and his magazines. He caused that there be brought to him the prince's wives and prince's daughters; they saluted His Majesty in the fashion of women, but His Majesty turned not his face to them. Then his possessions were assigned to the treasury, and his granary to the divine offerings of Amon in Karnak.[55]

The ruler of Heracleopolis, Pefnefdibast, came, bearing tribute to the palace: gold, silver, every costly stone, and horses of the choicest of the stable. He threw himself upon his belly before His Majesty; he said: "Hail to thee, Horus, mighty Pharaoh, Bull subduer of Bulls! The Nether World had seized me, and I was submerged in darkness, upon which the light now has shone. I found not a friend in the evil day, who was steadfast in the day of battle; but thou, O mighty Pharaoh, thou hast expelled the darkness from me. I will labor together with thy subjects, and Heracleopolis shall pay taxes into thy treasury, thou likeness of Harakhte,[56] chief of the imperishable stars. As he was, so art thou Pharaoh; as he perishes not so thou shalt not perish, O Pharaoh of Upper and Lower Egypt, Piankhi, living forever."

His Majesty sailed north to the opening of the canal beside Illahun; he found Per-Sekhemkhperre with its valiant wall raised and its stronghold closed, filled with every valiant man of the Northland. Then His Majesty sent to them, saying: "Ye living in death! If an hour passes without opening to me, behold, ye are of the number of the fallen." Then they came out, with the son of the chief of Me, Tefnakhte. The army of His Majesty entered into it, without slaying one of all the people. His treasuries were assigned to the Treasury, and his granaries to the divine offerings of his father, Amon-Ra, lord of Thebes.

His Majesty sailed north to Memphis; then he sent to them, saying, "Shut not up, fight not, thou abode of Shu in the beginning. I would offer an oblation to Ptah and to the gods dwelling in Memphis. The people of Memphis shall be safe and sound; not even a child shall weep. Look ye to nomes of the south; not a single one has been slain therein, except the enemies who blasphemed against the god, who were dispatched as rebels."

Then they closed their stronghold; they sent forth an army against some of the soldiers of His Majesty. Lo, that chief of Saïs[57] arrived at Memphis in the night, charging his infantry and his sailors, all the best of his army, a total of 8000 men, charging them very earnestly: "Behold, Memphis is filled with troops of all the best of the Northland, with barley and spelt and all kinds of grain, the granaries are running over. I will go, and I will give something to the chiefs of the north, and in a few days I will return." He mounted upon a horse, he went north in fear of His Majesty.

When day broke, at early morning, His Majesty reached Memphis. When he landed on the north of it, he found that the water had approached to the walls, the ships mooring at the walls of Memphis. Then His Majesty saw it was strong, and that the wall was raised by a new rampart, and battlements manned with mighty men. There was found no way of attacking it. Every man told his opinion among the army of His Majesty, according to every rule of war. Every man said; "Let us besiege it; lo, its troops are numerous." Others said, "Let a causeway be made against it, let us elevate the ground to its walls."

Then His Majesty was enraged against it like a panther. Then he sent forth his fleet and his army to assault the harbor of Memphis; they brought to him

[53] A sacred rattle

[54] The god of wisdom.

[55] An extensive temple complex on the Nile in Upper Egypt.

[56] A god who combined Ra and Horus.

[57] Tefnakhte.

every ferry-boat, every cargo-boat, every transport, and the ships, as many as there were, which had moored in the harbor of Memphis. His Majesty himself came to line up the ships, as many as there were. His Majesty commanded his army, "Forward against it! Mount the walls! Penetrate the houses over the river. If one of you gets through upon the wall, let him not halt before it, so the enemy may not repulse you." Then Memphis was taken, a multitude of people were slain therein, and brought as living captives to the place where His Majesty was. His Majesty proceeded to the house of Ptah, his purification was performed in the Dewat-chamber.

Then all the nomes that were in the district of Memphis, heard: Herypedemy, Peniney we, the Tower of Beyew, the Oasis of Bit. They opened the strongholds and fled away; none knew the place whither they had gone. Prince Yewepet came, and the chief of the Meshwesh, Akenesh, and the hereditary prince, Pediese, together with all the princes of the Northland, bearing their tribute, to behold the beauty of His Majesty. Then the treasuries and granaries of Memphis were assigned to the divine offerings of Amon.

His Majesty proceeded to Heliopolis.[58] He came, proceeding to the house of Ra, and entered into the temple with great praise. The chief ritual priest praised the god, that rebels might be repelled from the pharaoh. The pharaoh himself stood alone, he broke through the bolts, opened the double doors, and beheld his father, Ra.

Then came those rulers and princes of the Northland, all the chiefs who wore the feather, every vizier, all chiefs, and every prince's confidant, from the west, from the east, and from the islands in the midst, to see the beauty of His Majesty. Said these rulers and princes to His Majesty, "Dismiss us to our cities, that we may open our treasuries, that we may choose as much as thy heart desires, that we may bring the best of our stables, the first of our horses." Then His Majesty did so.

Then the chief of the Meshwesh, Tefnakhte, heard of it and caused a messenger to come to the place where His Majesty was, with flattery, saying, "Be thou appeased! I have not beheld thy face for shame; I cannot stand before thy flame, I tremble at thy might. Lo, thou art Nubti,[59] presiding over the Southland, Montu,[60] the Bull of mighty arm. To whatsoever city thou hast turned thy face, thou hast not found your servant[61] there, until I reached the islands of the sea, trembling before thy might. Is not the heart of thy majesty appeased, with these things that thou hast done to me? For I am verily a wretched man. By thy ka, the terror of thee is in my body, and the fear of thee in my bones. I have not sat in the beer-hall, nor has the harp been played for me. Cleanse thy servant of his fault, let my possessions be received into the Treasury, of gold and every costly stone, and the best of the horses, even payment for everything. Let me go forth to the temple, that I may cleanse myself with a divine oath." Tefnakhte presented the pharaoh with silver and gold, clothing, and every splendid, costly stone. He went forth to the temple, he worshiped the god, he cleansed himself with a divine oath, saying, "I will not transgress the command of the Pharaoh, I will not overstep that which the Pharaoh saith. I will not do a hostile act against a prince without thy knowledge. I will do according to that which the Pharaoh says, and I will not transgress that which he has commanded." Then His Majesty was satisfied therewith.

Then the ships were laden with silver, gold, copper, clothing, and everything of the Northland, every product of Syria, and all sweet woods of God's Land. His Majesty sailed up-stream, with glad heart, the shores on his either side were jubilating in the presence of His Majesty; singing and jubilating as they said, "O mighty, mighty Ruler, Piankhi, O mighty Ruler, thou comest having gained the dominion of the Northland. Thou makest bulls into women. Happy the heart of the mother who bore thee, and the man who begat thee. Those who are in the valley give to her praise, the cow that hath borne a bull, Thou art unto eternity, thy might endureth, O Ruler, beloved of Thebes."

[58] The main cult center of the gods Atum and Ra.

[59] Another name for the god Set.

[60] A war god.

[61] Tefnakhte.

71

THE CONSTITUTION OF CARTHAGE (CA. 340 BCE): ARISTOTLE, *POLITICS*, BOOK 2, CHAPTER 11

A reconstructed plan in the Bardo Museum in Tunis, Tunisia, depicts the city of Carthage in antiquity. The outer merchant harbor and inner war harbor are in the foreground and the Byrsa, the high fortified strong point, is at the back.

Even though the Carthaginians would have been considered "barbarians" by Greek standards, in his book the *Politics*, the late-fourth-century philosopher Aristotle nevertheless thought them civilized enough to include their constitution in his catalogue of model forms of government, illustrating well the ambivalence that even the most chauvinistic of ancient peoples felt toward other peoples.

Source: Benjamin Jowett, trans., *The Politics of Aristotle* (London: Colonial Press, 1900), 49–51.

The Carthaginians also are considered to have an excellent form of government, which differs from that of any other state in several respects, although it is in some ways very like the Spartan. Indeed, all three states, the Spartan,[62] the Cretan, and the Carthaginian, nearly resemble one another, and are very different from any others. Many of the Carthaginian institutions are excellent. The superiority of their constitution is proved by the fact that the common people remain loyal to the constitution. The Carthaginians never have had any rebellion worth speaking of, and never have been under the rule of a tyrant. Among the points in which the Carthaginian constitution resembles the Spartan are the following: the common tables of the clubs answer to the Spartan *phiditia*, and their magistracy of the Hundred-Four[63] to the Ephors; but, whereas the Ephors are any chance persons, the magistrates of the Carthaginians are elected according to merit: this is an improvement. They have also their kings and their Gerousia, or council of elders, who correspond to the kings and elders of Sparta. Their kings,[64] unlike the Spartan, are not always of the same family, nor that an ordinary one, but if there is some distinguished family they are selected[65] out of it and not appointed by seniority: this is far better. Such officers have great power, and therefore, if they are persons of little worth, they do a great deal of harm, and they already have done harm at Sparta.

Most of the defects or deviations from the perfect state, for which the Carthaginian constitution would be censured, apply equally to all the forms of government that we have mentioned. But of the deflections from aristocracy and constitutional government, some incline more to democracy and some to oligarchy. The kings and elders, if unanimous, may determine whether they will or will not bring a matter before the people, but when they are not unanimous, the people decide on such matters as well.[66] And whatever the kings and elders bring before the people is not only heard but also determined by them, and anyone who likes may oppose it; now this is not permitted in Sparta and Crete. That the magistrates of five who have under them many important matters should be co-opted,[67] that they should choose the supreme council of One Hundred and Four and should hold office longer than other magistrates (for they are virtually rulers both before and after they hold office), these are oligarchical features, their being without salary and not elected by lot, and any similar points, such as the practice of having all suits tried by the magistrates, and not some by one class of judges or jurors and some by another, as at Sparta, are characteristic of aristocracy.

The Carthaginian constitution deviates from aristocracy and inclines to oligarchy, chiefly on a point where popular opinion is on their side. For men in general think that magistrates should be chosen not only for their merit, but for their wealth: a man, they say, who is poor cannot rule well, for he has not the leisure. If, then, election of magistrates for their wealth be characteristic of oligarchy, and election for merit of aristocracy, there will be a third form under which the constitution of Carthage is comprehended, for the Carthaginians choose their magistrates, and particularly the highest of them, their kings and generals, with an eye both to merit and to wealth. But we must acknowledge that, in thus

[62] See Reading 53.

[63] The Council of 104 oversaw the Carthaginian government.

[64] In the fifth century, single kings were replaced by two Suffets, who also were called kings.

[65] By the Gerousia.

[66] In a popular assembly.

[67] From among the wealthy, not elected.

deviating from aristocracy, the legislator has committed an error. Nothing is more absolutely necessary than to provide that the highest class, not only when in office but also when out of office, should have leisure and not disgrace themselves in any way, and to this their attention should be first directed. Even if you must have regard to wealth, in order to secure leisure, yet it is surely a bad thing that the greatest offices, such as those of kings and generals, should be bought. The law that allows this abuse makes wealth of more account than virtue, and the whole state becomes avaricious.

For, whenever the chiefs of the state deem anything honorable, the other citizens are sure to follow their example, and, where virtue has not the first place, their aristocracy cannot be firmly established. Those who have been at the expense of purchasing their places will be in the habit of repaying themselves, and it is absurd to suppose that a poor and honest man will be wanting to make gains, and that a lower stamp of man who has incurred a great expense will not. Wherefore they should rule who are able to rule best. And even if the legislator does not care to protect the good from poverty, he should at any rate secure leisure for them when in office. It would seem also to be a bad principle that the same person should hold many offices, which is a favorite practice among the Carthaginians, for one business is better done by one man.

The government of the Carthaginians is oligarchical, but they successfully escape the evils of oligarchy by enriching one portion of the people after another by sending them to their colonies. This is their panacea and the means by which they give stability to the state. Accident favors them, but the legislator should be able to provide against revolution without trusting to accidents. As things are, if any misfortune occurred, and the bulk of the subjects revolted, there would be no way of restoring peace by legal methods.

72

THE EXPANSION OF THE CELTS INTO GREECE AND ANATOLIA (279–277 BCE): JUSTIN, *PHILIPPIC HISTORIES*, BOOKS 24–28

A golden torque, or neck ring, worn by Celtic warriors as a magical amulet that supposedly protected them in battle. The torque was forged as a single piece around the neck and was most easily removed by decapitation, which Celtic warriors practiced after they had killed an enemy in battle. The use of decapitation also was adopted by the Roman army.

As of the sixth century BCE, Celts, also known to the Greeks and Romans as Gauls, occupied the inland regions of western Europe, that is, Spain, Gaul, northern Italy, Britain, and the areas along the Danube River. Although they were politically disunified, they shared the same complex culture and civilization. In the early third century BCE, not long after the dismemberment of the Empire of Alexander, groups of Celts began to move south into Greece. Some reached as far as Anatolia.

Source: John Selby Watson, *Marcus Junius Justinus, Epitome of the Philippic History of Pompeius Trogus* (London: Bohn, 1853).

The Gauls, when the land that had produced them was unable, because of their excessive increase of population, to contain them, sent out three hundred thousand men as a sacred spring,[68] to seek new settlements. Of these adventurers part settled in Italy,[69] and took and burnt the city of Rome, and part penetrated into the remotest parts of Illyricum under the direction of a flight of birds, for the Gauls are skilled in augury beyond other nations. Making their way amid great slaughter of the barbarous *phylē*'s,[70] they fixed their abode in Pannonia.[71] They were a savage, bold, and warlike nation, and were the first after Hercules, to whom that undertaking procured great admiration for his valor, and a belief in his immortality, to pass the unconquered heights of the Alps, and places uninhabitable from excess of cold. After having subdued the Pannonians, they carried on various wars with their neighbors for many years. Success encouraging them, they betook themselves, in separate bands, some to Greece, and some to Macedonia,[72] laying waste all before them with the sword. Such indeed was the terror of the Gallic name, that even kings, before they were attacked, purchased peace from them with large sums of money.

Ptolemy[73] alone, the King of Macedonia, heard of the approach of the Gauls without alarm, and, hurried on by the madness that distracted him for his unnatural crimes, went out to meet them with a few undisciplined troops, as if wars could be dispatched with as little difficulty as murders.[74] An embassy from the Dardanians,[75] offering him twenty thousand armed men for his assistance, he spurned, adding insulting language, and saying that "the Macedonians would be in a sad condition if, after having subdued the whole east without assistance, they now required aid from the Dardanians to defend their country; and that he had for soldiers the sons of those who had served under Alexander the Great,[76] and had been victorious throughout the world." This answer being repeated to the Dardanian prince, he observed that the famous kingdom of Macedonia would soon fall as a sacrifice to the rashness of a raw youth.

The Gauls, under the command of Belgius,[77] sent deputies to Ptolemy to sound out the disposition of the Macedonians, offering him peace if he wanted to purchase it, but Ptolemy bragged to his courtiers that the Gauls sued for peace from fear of war. Nor was his manner less boastful before the ambassadors than before his own adherents, saying that he would grant peace only on condition that they would give their chiefs as hostages and deliver up their arms; for he would put no trust in them until they were disarmed. When the deputies brought back this answer, the Gauls laughed and exclaimed throughout their camp that Ptolemy would soon see whether they had offered peace from regard for themselves or for him. Some days after a battle was fought, and the Macedonians were defeated and cut to pieces. Ptolemy, after receiving several wounds, was captured and his head, cut off and stuck on a lance, was carried round the whole army to strike terror into the enemy.[78] Flight saved a few of the Macedonians; the rest were either taken or slain.

When the news of this event was spread through all Macedonia, the gates of the cities were shut and all places were filled with mourning. Sometimes the Macedonians lamented their bereavement, from the loss of their children; sometimes they were seized with dread, lest their cities should be destroyed; and

---

[68] When some ancient groups of people became too large, they would declare a "Sacred Spring," in which all of the children born in a certain year would be sent away to find new homes after they had reached the age of about twenty.

[69] During the fifth century BCE, groups of Gallic Celts seized the Po River valley in northern Italy from the Etruscans.

[70] Peoples.

[71] Modern Hungary.

[72] In 279 BCE.

[73] Ptolemy Keraunos ("The Thunderbolt"), the eldest son of Ptolemy I of Egypt, who briefly seized control of Macedonia in 281.

[74] Among others, Ptolemy had murdered Seleucus I (see Reading 64) in 281 BCE.

[75] Dardania was a region northeast of Macedonia.

[76] See Readings 62 and 63.

[77] A Gallic leader sometimes thought to be connected to the Belgae ("Belgians"), a Celtic people of northern Gaul.

[78] The Celts had a reputation as head hunters.

at other times they called on the names of their kings, Alexander and Philip,[79] as deities, to protect them; saying that under them they were not only secure, but conquerors of the world, and begging that they would guard their country, whose fame they had raised to heaven by the glory of their exploits, and give assistance to the afflicted, whom the insanity and rashness of Ptolemy had ruined. While all were thus in despair, Sosthenes,[80] one of the Macedonian chiefs, thinking that nothing would be effected by prayers, assembled such as were of age for war, repulsed the Gauls in the midst of their exultation at their victory, and saved Macedonia from devastation. For these great services, he, although of humble extraction, was chosen before many nobles that aspired to the throne of Macedonia. Although he was saluted as king by the army, he made the soldiers take an oath to him, not as king, but as general.

In the meantime Brennus,[81] under whose command a part of the Gauls had made an attack into Greece,[82] having heard of the success of their countrymen, who, under the leadership of Belgius, had defeated the Macedonians, and being indignant that so rich a booty, consisting of the spoils of the east, had been so lightly abandoned, assembled an army of a hundred and fifty thousand foot and fifteen thousand horse,[83] and suddenly invaded Macedonia. As he was laying waste the fields and villages, Sosthenes met him with his army of Macedonians in full array, but being few in number, and in some consternation, they were easily overcome by the more numerous and powerful Gauls. The defeated Macedonians retired within the walls of their cities and the victorious Brennus, meeting with no opposition, ravaged the lands throughout the whole of Macedonia. Soon after, as if the spoils of mortals were too mean for him, he turned his thoughts to the temples of the immortal gods, saying, with a profane jest, that the gods, being rich, ought to be liberal to men. He suddenly, therefore, directed his march toward Delphi,[84] regarding plunder more than religion and caring for gold more than for the wrath of the deities, "Who," he said, "stood in no need of riches, as being accustomed rather to bestow them on mortals."

The temple of Apollo at Delphi is situated on Mount Parnassus, on a rock steep on all sides. A concourse of people, who, collecting from the parts around on account of veneration for the majesty of the god had settled on the rock, formed a city there. Thus, not walls, but precipices, not defenses formed by the hand, but by nature, protect the temple and the city, so that it is utterly uncertain whether the strength of the place, or the influence of the deity residing in it, attracts more admiration. The central part of the rock falls back in the shape of an amphitheater, and, in consequence, if ever shouts are raised or if the noise of trumpets is mingled with them the sound, from the rocks echoing and re-echoing to one another, is heard many times repeated, and louder than it was made at first. The effect on those who are ignorant of its cause and are struck with wonder at it produces a greater awe of the power of the god. In the winding of the rock, about half way up the hill, there is a small plain and in it a deep fissure in the ground that is open for giving oracles, for a cold exhalation, driven upwards by some force, as it were by a wind, produces in the minds of the priestesses a certain madness and compels them, filled with the influence of the god, to give answers to such as consult them.[85] Hence many rich presents of kings and nations are to be seen there, which, by their magnificence, testify the grateful feelings of those that have

[79] Alexander the Great and his father, Philip II.

[80] Macedonian general who ruled as a king from 279 to 278 BCE.

[81] A Gallic leader of the same name as the Brennus who sacked Rome in 390 BCE (see Reading 77).

[82] In 279 BCE.

[83] A gross exaggeration.

[84] On the northern coast of the Gulf of Corinth, the site of a richly endowed oracle and shrine of Apollo.

[85] The priestesses of Apollo served as oracles and responded to questions posed to them, as by the Theraeans (Reading 48), by King Croesus of Lydia (Reading 46), by the Athenians prior to the second Persian invasion of Greece (Reading 55), by Romulus when he founded Rome (Reading 73), and by the Romans during the Second Punic War (Reading 78).

paid their vows, and their belief in the oracles given by the deity.

Brennus, when he came within sight of the temple, deliberated for some time as to whether he should at once make an attempt upon it or should allow his soldiers, wearied with their march, a night to refresh themselves. The captains of the Aeniani and Thessalori,[86] who had joined him for a share in the booty, advised that no delay should be made, while the enemy were unprovided for defense and the alarm at their coming still fresh, that in the interval of a night, the courage of the enemy would perhaps revive and assistance come to them, and that the approaches, which now were open, might be blocked up. But the common soldiers, when, after a long endurance of scarcity, they found a country abounding with wine and other provisions, had dispersed themselves over the fields, rejoicing as much at the plenty as if they had gained a victory, and leaving their standards deserted wandered about to seize on everything like conquerors. This conduct gave some respite to the Delphians.

At the first report that the Gauls were approaching, the country people are said to have been prohibited by the Oracle from carrying away their grain and wine from their houses. The salutariness of this prohibition was not understood, until, because this abundance of wine and other provisions had been thrown in the way of the Gauls as a stop to their progress, reinforcements from their neighbors had time to collect. The Delphians, accordingly, supported by the strength of their allies, secured their city before the Gauls, who clung to the wine-skins on which they had seized, could be recalled to their standards. Brennus had sixty-five thousand infantry, selected from his whole army; of the Delphians there were not more than four thousand, in utter contempt of whom Brennus, to rouse the courage of his men, pointed to the vast quantity of spoil before them, declaring that the statues and four-horse chariots, of which a great number were visible at a distance, were made of solid gold, and would provide greater prices when they came to be weighed than they were in appearance.

The Gauls, animated by these assertions, and disordered at the same time on account of the wine that they had drunk the day before, rushed to battle without any fear of danger. The Delphians, on the other hand, placing more confidence in the god than in their own strength, resisted the enemy with contempt, and, from the top of the hill, repelled the Gauls as they climbed up, partly with pieces of rock and partly with their weapons. Amid this contest between the two, the priests of all the temples as well as the priestesses themselves, with their hair loose and with their decorations and fillets, rushed, trembling and frantic, into the front ranks of the combatants, exclaiming that the god had come, that they had seen him leap down into his temple through the opening roof, that, while they were all humbly imploring aid of the deity, a youth of extraordinary beauty, far above that of mortals, and two armed virgins, coming from the neighboring temples of Diana and Minerva,[87] met them; that they had not only perceived them with their eyes but also had heard also the sound of a bow and the rattling of arms, and they therefore conjured them with the strongest entreaties not to delay, when the gods were leading them on, to spread slaughter among the enemy, and to share the victory with the powers of heaven. Incited by these exhortations, they all rushed eagerly to the field of battle, where they themselves also soon perceived the presence of the divinity, for a part of the mountain, broken off by an earthquake, overwhelmed a host of the Gauls and some of the densest bodies of the enemy were scattered abroad, not without wounds, and fell to the earth. A tempest then followed, which destroyed, with hail and cold, those that were suffering from bodily injuries.

General Brennus himself, unable to endure the pain of his wounds, ended his life with his dagger. The other general, after punishing the advisers of the war, made off from Greece with all haste, accompanied with ten thousand wounded men. But neither

[86] Peoples of central Greece who had joined up with the Gauls.

[87] Greek Artemis and Athena.

was fortune more favorable to those who fled, for in their terror they passed no night under shelter and no day without hardship and danger. Continual rains, snow congealed by the frost, famine, fatigue, and, what was the greatest evil, the constant want of sleep, consumed the wretched remains of the unfortunate army. The nations and people too, through whom they marched, pursued their stragglers in order to despoil them. Hence it happened that, of so great an army that, little before, presuming on its strength contended even against the gods, not a man was left to be a memorial of its destruction.

After peace was made between the two kings, Antigonus[88] and Antiochus,[89] a new enemy suddenly started up against Antigonus as he was returning to Macedonia. The Gauls who had been left behind to defend the borders of their country by their general Brennus when he marched into Greece, armed fifteen thousand foot and three thousand horse and having routed the forces of the Getae and Triballi,[90] and preparing to invade Macedonia, sent ambassadors to Antigonus to offer him peace if he would pay for it, and to play the part of spies, at the same time, in his camp. Antigonus, with royal munificence, invited them to a banquet, and entertained them with a sumptuous display of luxuries. The Gauls were so struck with the vast quantity of gold and silver set before them, and so tempted with the richness of such a spoil, that they returned more inclined to war than they had come. The king also ordered his elephants to be shown them, as monsters unknown to those barbarians, and his ships laden with stores to be displayed, little thinking that he was thus exciting the desire to seize his treasures among those whom he sought to strike with terror by the ostentation of his strength.[91] The ambassadors, returning to their countrymen, and exaggerating every thing excessively, set forth at once the wealth and unsuspiciousness of the king; saying that his camp was filled with gold and silver, but secured neither by rampart nor trench, and that the Macedonians, as if they had sufficient protection in their wealth, neglected all military duties, apparently thinking that, as they had plenty of gold, they had no use for steel.

By this statement, the desires of a covetous people were sufficiently stimulated to take possession of such spoil. The example of Belgius, too, had its influence with them, who, a little before, had cut to pieces the army of the Macedonians and their king. Being all of one mind, therefore, they attacked the king's camp by night, but he, foreseeing the storm that threatened him, had given notice to his soldiers to remove all their baggage and to conceal themselves noiselessly in a neighboring wood, and the camp was only saved because it was deserted. The Gauls, when they found the camp destitute not only of defenders but also of sentinels, suspecting that there was not a flight but some stratagem on the part of the enemy, were for some time afraid to enter the gates.[92] At last, leaving the defenses entire and untouched, and more like men come to explore than to plunder, they took possession of the camp, and then, carrying off what they found, they directed their course toward the coast. Here, as they were incautiously plundering the vessels and fearing no attack, they were cut down by the sailors and a part of the army that had fled thither with their wives and children.[93] Such was the slaughter among them that the report of this victory procured Antigonus peace, not only from the Gauls, but from his other barbarous neighbors.[94]

The nation of the Gaul was at that time so prolific that they filled all Asia as with one swarm. The kings of the east carried on no wars without a mercenary

[88] Antigonus Gonatas (277–239 BCE), son of Demetrius Poliorcetes, the son of Antigonus I "the One-Eyed"; he still lacked a kingdom.

[89] Antiochus I (281–261 BCE), son of Seleucus I and ruler of the Seleucid Empire.

[90] Peoples of Thrace, north of Greece and Macedonia.

[91] The rest of the story suggests that Antigonus, an experienced general, was in fact trying to lure the Gauls into an ambush.

[92] For a similar situation during the sack of Rome by the Gauls in 390 BCE, see Reading 77.

[93] The Gauls in fact were destroyed by Antigonus and his army in a successful ambush.

[94] The Battle of Lysimacheia in 277 BCE. Antigonus's victory gained for him the throne of Macedonia.

army of Gauls, nor, if they were driven from their thrones, did they seek protection with any other people than the Gauls. Such indeed was the terror of the Gallic name, and the unvaried good fortune of their arms, that princes thought they could neither maintain their power in security, nor recover it if lost, without the assistance of Gallic valor. Hence, being called by the king of Bithynia to his aid, and having gained him the victory over his enemies, they shared his kingdom with him and called their part of it Gallograecia.[95]

[95] That is, "Gallic Greece." In 278 BCE Nicomedes, King of Bithynia, invited several bands of Gauls into Anatolia as mercenaries. They remained and established their own kingdoms in central Anatolia in what came to be called Galatia.

CHAPTER 10

The Rise of Rome and the Roman Republic (753–120 BCE)

During the course of the Iron Age, the centers of new cultural and political development continued to move ever farther to the west. The third and final great center of cultural development in the ancient world, after the Near East and Greece, was Rome. After its foundation as a small farming village on the Tiber River in the mid-eighth century BCE, Rome assimilated both population and culture from its neighbors, creating a truly multicultural society. Then, over the course of the Roman Republic, Rome expanded to become the greatest power of the ancient Mediterranean world. In spite of its increasingly important position in the Mediterranean world, Rome was rather slow to create its own literary heritage. Thus, for the period before the first century BCE, not many primary sources were created or survive, and literary coverage for the crucial early period of Roman history must be drawn largely from later sources.

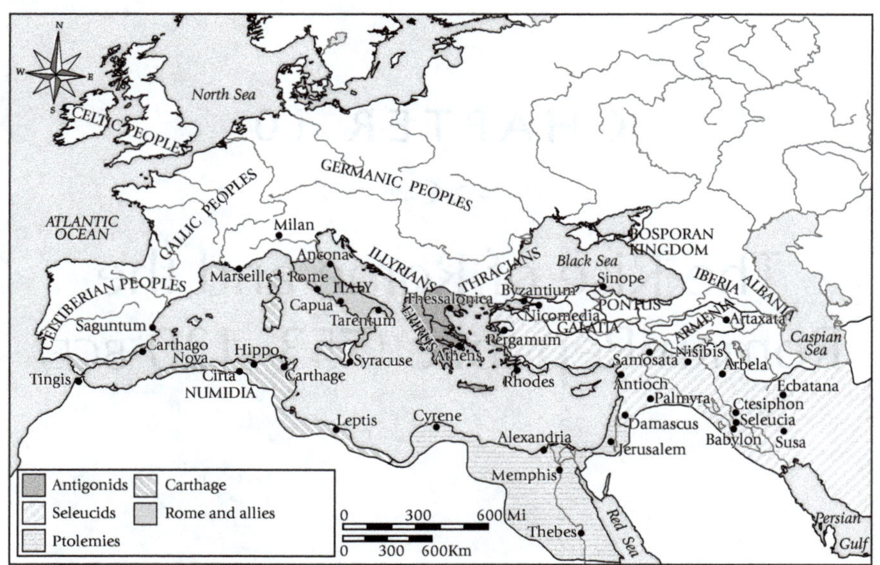

Map 10 The Roman Republic, Carthage, and the Hellenistic Kingdoms as of 264 BCE

73

THE FOUNDING OF ROME (753 BCE): PLUTARCH, *LIFE OF ROMULUS*

A small copper coin issued ca. 330–335 CE under the emperor Constantine I (306–337) depicts on the obverse a helmeted bust of the goddess Roma with the legend "The City of Rome" and on the reverse a scene from the legends surrounding the foundation of Rome, the infants Romulus and Remus being suckled by a wolf.

By the time that Roman history began to be written down ca. 200 BCE, stories of Rome's past existed in many different versions. The most popular version of the founding of Rome involved the twins Romulus and Remus, descended in legend from the hero Aeneas of Troy, who himself was the son of the goddess Venus. The story included several curious elements that had to be incorporated because they were integral parts of the legend. It is up to modern historians to attempt to disentangle the historical kernels of truth from the legendary accretions. The foundation of Rome by Romulus inaugurated the period of "Rome of the Kings" (753–509 BCE). This account comes from the "Parallel Lives" authored by the Greek biographer Plutarch in the mid-second century CE. Plutarch's account makes it clear that there were different versions of the details of the story in circulation.

Source: John Dryden, *The Lives of the Noble Greeks and Romans*, revised by A. H. Clough, Vol. 1 (Boston: Little, Brown, 1910).

The story that has the widest credence and the greatest number of vouchers was first published among the Greeks, in its principal details, by Diocles of Peparethus,[1] and Fabius Pictor[2] follows him in most points. Here again there are variations in the story, but its general outline is as follows. The descendents of Aeneas[3] reigned as kings in Alba, and the succession devolved at length upon two brothers, Numitor and Amulius. Amulius divided the whole inheritance into two parts, setting the treasures and gold that had been brought from Troy over against the kingdom, and Numitor chose the kingdom. Amulius, then, in possession of the treasure and made more powerful by it than Numitor, easily took the kingdom away from his brother. Fearing lest that brother's daughter should have children, he made her a priestess of Vesta, bound to live unwedded and a virgin all her days. Her name is variously given as Ilia, or Rhea, or Silvia.

Not long after this, she was discovered to be with child, contrary to the established law for the Vestals. She did not, however, suffer the capital punishment that was her due,[4] because the king's daughter, Antho, interceded successfully in her behalf, but she was kept in solitary confinement, that she might not be delivered without the knowledge of Amulius. Delivered she was of two boys, and their size and beauty were more than human. Wherefore Amulius was all the more afraid, and ordered a servant to take the boys and cast them away. This servant's name was Faustulus, according to some, but others give this name to the man who took the boys up. Obeying the king's orders, the servant put the babes into a basket and went down toward the river, intending to cast them in, but when he saw that the stream was much swollen and violent, he was afraid to go close up to it, and setting his burden now near the bank, went his way. Then the overflow of the swollen river took and bore up the basket, floating it gently along, and carried it down to a fairly smooth spot.

Now there was a wild fig-tree hard by, which they called Ruminalis, either from Romulus, as is generally thought, or because cud-chewing, or ruminating, animals spent the noon-tide there for the sake of the shade, or best of all, from the suckling of the babes there, for the ancient Romans called the breast "ruma." Here, then, the babes lay, and the she-wolf of story here gave them suck, and a woodpecker came to help in feeding them and to watch over them. Now these creatures are considered sacred to Mars and this was the chief reason why Rhea Silvia was believed when she declared that Mars was the father of her babes. And yet it is said that she was deceived into doing this, and really lost her virginity to Amulius himself, who came to her in armor.[5] But some say that the name of the children's nurse, by its ambiguity, deflected the story into the fabulous. For the Latins not only called she-wolves "lupae," but also prostitutes.

As for the babes, they were taken up and reared by Faustulus, a swineherd of Amulius, and no man knew of it, or, as some say with a closer approach to probability, Numitor did know of it, and secretly aided the foster-parents in their task. They applied themselves to generous occasions and pursuits, not esteeming sloth and idleness generous, but rather bodily exercise, hunting, running, driving off robbers, capturing thieves, and rescuing the oppressed from violence. For these things, indeed, they were famous far and near.

When a quarrel arose between the herdsmen of Numitor and Amulius, and some of the latter's cattle were driven off, the brothers would not suffer it, but fell upon the robbers, put them to flight, and intercepted most of the booty. To the displeasure of Numitor they gave little heed, but collected and took into their company many needy men and many slaves, exhibiting thus the beginnings of seditious boldness and temper.

[1] A Greek author of ca. 400 BCE, the earliest known historian to write about the foundation of Rome.

[2] The first Roman writer of history, who wrote in Greek ca. 200 BCE.

[3] A Trojan hero who escaped Troy during its sack by the Greeks and traveled around the Mediterranean, eventually settling at Alba Longa not far from the future site of Rome; see Reading 88.

[4] Vestal Virgins who violated their vows of chastity normally were buried alive.

[5] That is, dressed like Mars.

But once when Romulus was busily engaged in some sacrifice, being fond of sacrifices and of divination, the herdsmen of Numitor fell in with Remus as he was walking with a few companions, and a battle ensued. After blows and wounds given and received on both sides, the herdsmen of Numitor prevailed and took Remus prisoner. When Numitor came home,[6] after getting Remus into his hands, he was amazed at the young man's complete superiority in stature and strength of body. Perceiving by his countenance that the boldness and vigor of his soul were unsubdued and unharmed by his present circumstances, and hearing that his acts and deeds corresponded with his looks, but chiefly, as it would seem, because a divinity was aiding and assisting in the inauguration of great events, he grasped the truth by a happy conjecture. He asked him who he was and what were the circumstances of his birth, while his gentle voice and kindly look inspired the youth with confidence and hope.

Then Remus boldly said: "Indeed, I will hide nothing from thee; for thou seemest to be more like a king than Amulius; thou hearest and weighest before punishing, but he surrenders men without a trial. Formerly, my twin brother and I believed ourselves children of Faustulus and Larentia, servants of the king, but since being accused and slandered before thee and brought in peril of our lives, we hear great things concerning ourselves. Whether they are true or not, our present danger is likely to decide. Our birth is said to have been secret, and our nursing and nurture as infants stranger still. We were cast out to birds of prey and wild beasts, only to be nourished by them, by the breasts of a she-wolf and the morsels of a woodpecker, as we lay in a little basket by the side of the great river. The basket still exists and is kept safe, and its bronze girdles are engraved with letters now almost effaced, which may perhaps hereafter prove unavailing tokens of recognition for our parents, when we are dead and gone."

Then Numitor, hearing these words and conjecturing the time that had elapsed from the young man's looks, welcomed the hope that flattered him, and thought how he might talk with his daughter concerning these matters in a secret interview, for she still was kept in the closest custody.[7] Meanwhile, Faustulus, on hearing that Remus had been seized and delivered up to Numitor, called upon Romulus to go to his aid, and then told him clearly the particulars of their birth. Faustulus took the basket and went to see Numitor. Naturally enough, the guards at the king's gate were suspicious of him, and when he was scrutinized by them and made confused replies to their questions, he was found to be concealing the basket in his cloak. Now by chance there was among the guards one of those who had taken the boys to cast them into the river and were concerned in their exposure. This man, now seeing the basket, and recognizing it by its make and inscription, conceived a suspicion of the truth, and without any delay told the matter to the king and brought Faustulus before him to be examined. In these dire and pressing straits, Faustulus admitted that the boys were alive and well.

Romulus was now close at hand, and many of the citizens who hated and feared Amulius were running forth to join him. He also was leading a large force with him, divided into companies of a hundred men, each company headed by a man who bore aloft a handful of hay and shrubs tied round a pole (the Latin word for handful is "manipulus," and hence in their armies they still call the men in such companies "maniples"). And when Remus incited the citizens within the city to revolt, and at the same time Romulus attacked from without, the tyrant,[8] without taking a single step or making any plan for his own safety, from sheer perplexity and confusion, was seized and put to death.

Amulius now being dead and matters settled in the city, the brothers were neither willing to live in Alba, unless as its rulers, nor to be its rulers while their grandfather[9] was still alive. Having therefore restored the government to him and paid fitting honors to their mother, they resolved to dwell by themselves, and to found a city in the region where, at the first, they were

[6] In Alba Longa, where he still lived despite having been deposed as king.

[7] By Numitor's brother, King Amulius.

[8] Amulius is called a "tyrant" because he was an illegal ruler; see Reading 52.

[9] Numitor.

nourished and sustained. But perhaps it was necessary, now that many slaves and fugitives were gathered about them, either to disperse these and have no following at all, or else to dwell apart with them. For that the residents of Alba would not consent to give the fugitives the privilege of intermarriage with them, nor even receive them as fellow-citizens, is clear, in the first place, from the kidnaping of the Sabine women, which was not a deed of wanton daring but one of necessity, owing to the lack of marriages by consent, for they certainly honored the women, after they had carried them off, beyond measure.[10] And in the second place, when their city was first founded, they made a sanctuary of refuge for all fugitives, which they called the sanctuary of the God of Asylum. There they received all who came, delivering none up, neither slave to masters, nor debtor to creditors, nor murderer to magistrates, but declaring it to be in obedience to an oracle from Delphi that they made the asylum secure for all men. Therefore the city soon was full of people, for they say that the first houses numbered no more than a thousand. This, however, was later.

When they set out to establish their city, a dispute at once arose concerning the site. Romulus, accordingly, built Roma Quadrata[11] (which means "square"), and wished to have a city on that site, but Remus laid out a strong precinct on the Aventine Hill,[12] which was named from him Remonium, but now is called Rignarium. Agreeing to settle their quarrel by the flight of birds of omen,[13] and taking their seats on the ground apart from one another, six vultures, they say, were seen by Remus, and twice that number by Romulus. Some, however, say that whereas Remus truly saw his six, Romulus lied about his twelve, but that when Remus came to him, then he did see the twelve. Hence it is that at the present time also the Romans chiefly regard vultures when they take auguries from the flight of birds.

When Remus learned of the deceit he was enraged, and as Romulus was digging a trench where his city's wall was to run he ridiculed some parts of the work and obstructed others. At last, when he leaped across it, he was smitten by Romulus himself and fell dead there. Faustulus also fell in the battle. Romulus buried Remus and then set himself to building his city. A circular trench was dug around what is now the Comitium[14] and in this were deposited the first-fruits of all things the use of which was sanctioned by custom as good and by nature as necessary. Finally, every man brought a small portion of the soil of his native land and these were cast in among the first-fruits and mingled with them. Then, taking this as a center, they marked out the city in a circle around it. And the founder, having shod a plough with a bronze ploughshare and having yoked to it a bull and a cow, himself drove a deep furrow round the boundary lines while those who followed after him had to turn the clods, which the plough threw up, inward toward the city, and suffer no clod to lie turned outward. With this line they marked out the course of the wall, and it is called, by contraction, "pomerium."[15] And where they intended to put in a gate, there they took the share out of the ground, lifted the plough over, and left a vacant space. And this is the reason why they regard all the wall as sacred except the gates, for if they held the gates sacred it would not be possible, without religious scruples, to bring into and send out of the city things that are necessary and yet unclean.[16]

Now it is agreed that the city was founded on the twenty-first of April, and this day the Romans celebrate with a festival, calling it the birthday of their country. And at first, as it is said, they sacrificed no living creature at that festival, but thought they ought to keep it pure and without stain of blood, because it commemorated the birth of their country.

[10] To have a legal marriage, a couple needed to have the right of intermarriage in the society where they were getting married; because the early Romans did not have this with their neighbors, they had to kidnap their brides.

[11] "Square Rome."

[12] Later a center of the plebeian opposition to the patricians.

[13] A rite of divination known as "taking the auspices."

[14] The meeting place in the Forum of the Roman popular assemblies.

[15] That is, from "post murum," "beyond the wall."

[16] Such as corpses, which were buried outside the pomerium.

74

ROME OF THE KINGS (CA. 550 BCE): THE *LAPIS NIGER*

The oldest surviving written evidence from Rome, dating from ca. 550 BCE, the "Lapis niger" ("Black Stone"), named after a large black stone that covered the site where it was buried in the Roman Forum, preserved in the Terme Museum in Rome.

Only a single document survives from the period of Rome of the Kings, the so-called "Black Stone," a fragmentary inscription carved onto tufa, a volcanic stone common in the area, whose very archaic form of lettering uses the Etruscan alphabet, which, in turn, was based on the alphabet used by the Greeks of southern Italy. The inscription is written in what is called "boustrophedon" ("ox-turning") style, which alternates between left to right and right to left. Both the archaic form of Latin and the fact that half or more of each line is missing makes the inscription very difficult to understand, although it appears to concern religious prohibitions about bringing draft animals into a certain area of the Roman Forum. The following translation of necessity is rather fanciful.

Source: Paul MacKendrick, *The Mute Stones Speak* (New York: St. Martin's Press, 1960), 94.

Whosoever defiles this spot, let him be forfeit to the shades of the underworld, and whosoever contaminates this spot with refuse, it is right for the king after due process of law, to confiscate his property. Whatsoever persons the king shall discover passing on this road, let him order the summoner to seize their draft animals by the reins, that they may turn out of the road forthwith and take the proper detour. Whosoever persists in traveling this road, and fails to take the proper detour, by due process of law let him be sold to the highest bidder

75

THE VIOLATION OF LUCRETIA AND THE FOUNDING OF THE ROMAN REPUBLIC (509 BCE): LIVY, *FROM THE FOUNDING OF THE CITY*, BOOK 1, CHAPTERS 57–60

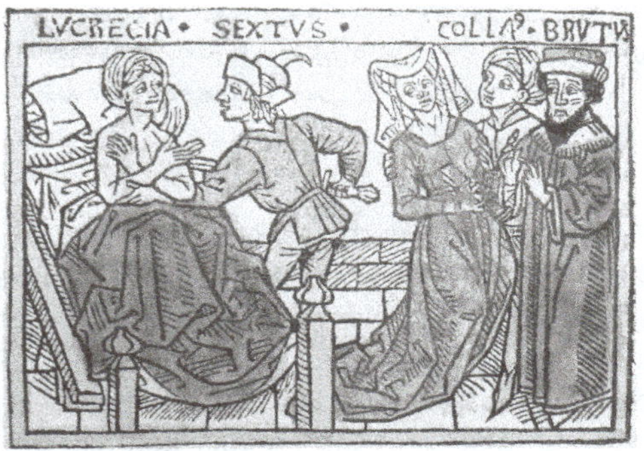

The story of the violation of the virtuous Lucretia by the evil Sextus Tarquin has struck a chord through the ages and often has served as an inspiration for artistic renditions. This woodcut appeared in Heinrich Steinhöwel's translation of Giovanni Boccaccio's *De mulieribus claris* ("On Famous Women") (Ulm: Johannes Zainer, ca. 1474).

The overthrow of Tarquinius Superbus ("Tarquin the Proud"), the last Etruscan king of Rome, and the establishment of the Roman Republic in 509 BCE was one of the most important events in Roman history. It therefore is no surprise that the Romans had a detailed account of how they believed this momentous change had occurred. The cast of characters in the version presented by the Roman historian Livy (ca. 60 BCE–17 CE) in his work "From the Founding of the

City" included patriotic Romans, despicable Etruscans, and a virtuous Roman matron. A close reading of the story suggests that the expulsion of the kings resulted not from a popular revolt but from a conspiracy involving the highest officials of the Roman government of the time.

Source: B. O. Foster, trans. *Livy, Books I and II* (Cambridge, MA: Harvard University Press, 1919).

Ardea[17] belonged to the Rutuli,[18] who were a nation of commanding wealth for that place and period. This very fact was the cause of the war, because the Roman king[19] was eager not only to enrich himself, impoverished as he was by the splendor of his public works, but also to appease with booty the feeling of the common people, who, besides the enmity they bore the monarch for other acts of pride, were especially resentful that the king should have kept them employed so long as artisans and doing the work of slaves.

An attempt was made to capture Ardea by assault. Having failed in this, the Romans invested the place with entrenchments, and began to besiege the enemy. Here in their permanent camp, as is usual with a war not sharp but long drawn out, furlough was rather freely granted, although more freely to the leaders than to the soldiers. The young princes[20] for their part passed their idle hours together at dinners and drinking bouts. It chanced, as they were drinking in the quarters of Sextus Tarquinius, where Tarquinius Collatinus,[21] son of Egerius, also was a guest, that the subject of wives came up. Every man fell to praising his own wife with enthusiasm, and, as their rivalry grew hot, Collatinus asserted that there was no need to talk about it, for it was in their power to know, in a few hours' time, how far the rest were excelled by his own Lucretia: "Come! If the vigor of youth is in us let us mount our horses and see for ourselves the disposition of our wives. Let every man regard as the surest test what meets his eyes when the woman's husband enters unexpected." They were heated with wine. "Agreed!," they all cried, and clapping spurs to their horses were off for Rome.

Arriving there at early dusk, they thence proceeded to Collatia,[22] where Lucretia was discovered behaving very differently from the daughters-in-law of the king. These they had seen at a luxurious banquet, whiling away the time with their young friends, whereas Lucretia, although it was late at night, was busily engaged upon her wool,[23] while her maidens toiled about her in the lamplight as she sat in the hall of her house. The prize of this contest in womanly virtues fell to Lucretia. When Collatinus and the Tarquinii approached they were graciously received, and the victorious husband courteously invited the young princes to his table.

It was there that Sextus Tarquinius was seized with a wicked desire to debauch Lucretia; not only her beauty but also her proved chastity provoked him. For the present, however, they ended the boyish prank of the night and returned to the camp. When a few days had gone by, Sextus Tarquinius, without letting Collatinus know, took a single attendant and went to Collatia. Being kindly welcomed, for no one suspected his purpose, he was brought after dinner to a guest-chamber. Burning with passion, he waited until it seemed to him that all about him was secure and everybody fast asleep. Then, drawing his sword, he came to the sleeping Lucretia. Holding the woman down he said, "Be still, Lucretia! I am Sextus Tarquinius. My sword is in my hand. Utter a sound, and you die!"

In fear the woman started out of her sleep. No help was in sight, but only imminent death. Then Tarquinius began to declare his love, to plead, to mingle threats with prayers, to bring every resource to bear upon her woman's heart. When he found her obdurate and not to be moved even by fear of death, he went

[17] A city, like Rome, founded in the eighth century BCE, about thirty-five kilometers southeast of Rome.
[18] An ancient Italic people.
[19] The Etruscan king Tarquinius Superbus ("Tarquin the Proud") (535–509 BCE).
[20] Tarquin had three sons, Titus, Arruns, and Sextus.
[21] A great-nephew of the first Etruscan king of Rome, Tarquinius Priscus ("Tarquin the Old").
[22] A town where Collatinus's father was stationed and which gave Collatinus his name.
[23] To spin wool for making the family clothing was the most virtuous act that a Roman matron could perform.

farther and threatened her with disgrace, saying that when she was dead he would kill his slave and lay him naked by her side, that she might be said to have been put to death in adultery with a man of base condition. At this dreadful prospect her resolute modesty was overcome by his victorious lust, and Tarquinius departed, exulting in his conquest of a woman's honor.

Lucretia, grieving at her great disaster, dispatched the same message to her father in Rome and to her husband at Ardea; she asked that they should each take a trusty friend and come, that they must do this and do it quickly, for a frightful thing had happened. Spurius Lucretius[24] came with Publius Valerius,[25] Volesus' son. Collatinus brought Lucius Junius Brutus,[26] with whom he chanced to be returning to Rome when he was met by the messenger from his wife. They found Lucretia sitting sadly in her chamber. The entrance of her friends brought the tears to her eyes, and to her husband's question, "Is all well?" She replied, "Far from it; for what can be well with a woman when she has lost her honor? The print of a strange man, Collatinus, is in your bed. Yet my body only has been violated. My heart is guiltless, as death shall be my witness. But pledge your right hands and your words that the adulterer shall not go unpunished. Sextus Tarquinius is he that last night returned hostility for hospitality, and brought ruin on me, and on himself no less, if you are men, when he worked his pleasure upon me."

They give their pledges, every man in turn. They seek to comfort her, sick at heart as she is, by diverting the blame from her to the doer of the wrong. They tell her it is the mind that sins, not the body, and that where purpose has been wanting there is no guilt. "It is for you to determine," she answers, "what is due to him. For my own part, although I acquit myself of the sin, I do not absolve myself from punishment, nor in time to come shall ever unchaste woman live through the example of Lucretia."

Taking a knife that she had concealed beneath her dress she plunged it into her heart, and sinking forward upon the wound, died as she fell. The wail for the dead was raised by her husband and her father. Brutus, while the others were absorbed in grief, drew out the knife from Lucretia's wound, and holding it up, dripping with gore, exclaimed, "By this blood, most chaste until a prince wronged it, I swear, and I take you, gods, to witness, that I will pursue Lucius Tarquinius Superbus and his wicked wife and all his children, with sword, with fire, aye with whatsoever violence I may, and that I will suffer neither them nor any other to be king in Rome!"

The knife he then passed to Collatinus, and from him to Lucretius and Valerius. They were dumbfounded at this miracle. Whence came this new spirit in the breast of Brutus? As he bade them, so they swore. Grief was swallowed up in anger; and when Brutus summoned them to make war from that very moment on the power of the kings, they followed his lead. They carried out Lucretia's corpse from the house and bore it to the market-place, where men crowded about them, attracted, as they were bound to be, by the amazing character of the strange event and its heinousness. Every man had his own complaint to make of the prince's crime and his violence. They were moved, not only by the father's sorrow, but by the fact that it was Brutus who chided their tears and idle lamentations and urged them to take up the sword, as befitted men and Romans, against those who had dared to treat them as enemies.

The boldest of the young men seized their weapons and offered themselves for service, and the others followed their example. Then, leaving Lucretia's father to guard Collatia, and posting sentinels so that no one might announce the rising to the royal family, the rest, equipped for battle and with Brutus in command, set out for Rome. Once there, wherever their armed band advanced it brought terror and confusion; but again, when people saw that in the van

[24] Spurius Lucretius Tricipitinus, Lucretia's father.

[25] A leading Roman aristocrat who later held four consulates and established many of the fundamental guiding principles of the Roman Republic; he gained the epithet "Publicola," or "Friend of the People."

[26] The nephew of Tarquin the Proud; although the king had executed his brother, Brutus remained second in command to the king. Brutus had visited the Oracle of Apollo at Delphi with Tarquin's sons to ask who would be the next king of Rome. The Oracle replied that it would be the first one to kiss his mother. On their return, Brutus pretended to trip and surreptitiously kissed the earth. The Brutus who helped to assassinate Julius Caesar in 44 BCE claimed descent from this Brutus.

were the chief men of the state, they concluded that whatever it was it could be no meaningless disturbance. And in fact there was no less resentment at Rome when this dreadful story was known than there had been at Collatia. So from every quarter of the city men came running to the Forum.

No sooner were they there than a crier summoned the people before the Tribune of the Celeres,[27] which office Brutus happened to be holding. There he made a speech by no means like what might have been expected of the mind and the spirit that he had feigned up to that day. He spoke of the violence and lust of Sextus Tarquinius, of the shameful defilement of Lucretia, and her deplorable death, of the bereavement of Tricipitinus,[28] in whose eyes the death of his daughter was not so outrageous and deplorable as was the cause of her death. He reminded them, besides, of the pride of the king himself and the wretched state of the commons, who were plunged into ditches and sewers and made to clear them out. The men of Rome, he said, the conquerors of all the nations round about, had been transformed from warriors into artisans and stone-cutters. He spoke of the shameful murder of King Tullius, and how his daughter had driven her accursed chariot over her father's body,[29] and he invoked the gods who punish crimes against parents.

With these and, I fancy, even fiercer reproaches, such as occur to a man in the very presence of an outrage, but are far from easy for an historian to reproduce, he inflamed the people, and brought them to abrogate the king's authority and to exile Lucius Tarquinius, together with his wife and children.[30] Brutus himself then enrolled the juniors,[31] who voluntarily gave in their names, and arming them set out for the camp at Ardea to arouse the troops against the king. The command at Rome he left with Lucretius, who had been appointed Prefect of the City[32] by the king some time before. During this confusion Tullia[33] fled from her house, cursed wherever she went by men and women, who called down upon her the furies that avenge the wrongs of kindred.

When the news of these events reached the camp, the king, in alarm at the unexpected danger, set out for Rome to put down the revolt. Brutus, who had perceived the king's approach, made a circuit to avoid meeting him, and at almost the same moment, although by different roads, Brutus reached Ardea and Tarquinius Rome. Against Tarquinius the gates were closed and exile was pronounced. The liberator of the city was received with rejoicings in the camp and the sons of the king were driven out of it. Two of them followed their father, and went into exile at Caere, in Etruria. Sextus Tarquinius departed for Gabii,[34] as though it had been his own kingdom, and there the revengers of old quarrels, which he had brought upon himself by murder and rapine, slew him.

Lucius Tarquinius Superbus ruled for five and twenty years. The rule of the kings at Rome, from its foundation to its liberation, lasted two hundred and forty-four years. Two Consuls were then chosen in the Centuriate Assembly,[35] under the presidency of the Prefect of the City, in accordance with the reforms of Servius Tullius.[36] These were Lucius Junius Brutus and Lucius Tarquinius Collatinus.[37]

[27] The commander of the king's bodyguard.

[28] Lucretia's father.

[29] Servius Tullius (575–535 BCE), the predecessor of Tarquin the Proud, was murdered by his daughter Tullia and her husband Tarquin, who went on to become king.

[30] The Tribune of the Celeres had the power to summon the popular assembly, so in the official Roman version of the story Tarquin had been legally deposed.

[31] The "juniors" of the Roman army were young men who fought in the field, whereas the "seniors" were older men who defended the city.

[32] An official who acted in place of the king when the king was not in Rome.

[33] The wife of King Tarquin.

[34] A Latin town eighteen kilometers east of Rome that Sextus had brought under Roman control.

[35] The assembled Roman army, which had the authority to choose its own commanders, in this case, the Consuls.

[36] In Roman legend it was believed that the establishment of the Centuriate Assembly, and other reforms, such as the building of the "Servian Wall," had been accomplished under King Servius Tullius; it now appears that these reforms actually occurred during the early Roman Republic.

[37] Collatinus, however, soon was forced to resign and go into exile because of his family relationship to the Etruscan kings.

76

THE ORIGINS OF ROMAN LAW (451–450 BCE): THE "TWELVE TABLES"

The monetary fines in later editions of the "Twelve Tables" were cited in "asses," large copper coins that were not introduced until ca. 280 BCE, attesting to the slowness with which the Romans adopted an actual currency. The "as" weighed one pound of copper. Such a cumbersome coin was not useful for large transactions but would have been suitable for the payment of ritualized amounts such as those found in the Twelve Tables.

Soon after the establishment of the Roman Republic in 509 BCE, the plebeians (the unprivileged citizens) began to agitate against the patricians (the Roman aristocrats) to have greater rights. One of their earliest demands was to know the laws. As a result, in 451 BCE the patricians appointed a board of ten men, the Decemvirs, who, analogous to the "lawgivers" of ancient Greece,[38] were charged with writing down the laws. After being reappointed for a second

[38] See Readings 53 and 54.

term in 450 BCE, the Decemvirs issued the famous "Twelve Tables" of Roman law, which, with few exceptions, did not create new law but merely recorded existing law. They stated the fundamental concepts of Roman law, such as "mancipatio" (transferring ownership over property), "stipulatio" (making a contract), "emancipatio" (freeing someone from slavery), and "nexum" (reducing someone to slavery). The code also covered criminal law, with crimes such as arson, casting spells, and stealing crops being punishable by death. Because there were no state police or prosecutors, criminal prosecutions had to be initiated by the wronged parties themselves. The Twelve Tables can be compared with other ancient law codes, such as those of Ur-Nammu and Hammurabi in Mesopotamia and of the Hebrews.[39]

Source: S. P. Scott, trans., *The Civil Law Including the Twelve Tables, the Institutes of Gaius, the Rules of Ulpian, the Opinions of Paulus, the Enactments*, Vol. 1 (Cincinnati: Central Trust, 1932).

Table I. Concerning the summons to court.

Law I. When anyone summons another before the tribunal of a judge, the latter must, without hesitation, immediately appear.

Law II. If, after having been summoned, he does not appear, or refuses to come before the tribunal of the judge, let the party who summoned him call upon any citizens who are present to bear witness. Then let him seize his reluctant adversary; so that he may be brought into court, as a captive, by apparent force.

Law III. When anyone who has been summoned to court is guilty of evasion, or attempts to flee, let him be arrested by the plaintiff.

Law IV. If bodily infirmity or advanced age should prevent the party summoned to court from appearing, let him who summoned him furnish him with an animal as a means of transport. If he is unwilling to accept it, the plaintiff cannot legally be compelled to provide the defendant with a vehicle constructed of boards or a covered litter.

Law V. If he who is summoned has either a sponsor or a defender, let him be dismissed, and his representative can take his place in court.

Law VI. The defender, or the surety[40] of a wealthy man, must himself be rich, but anyone who desires to do so can come to the assistance of a person who is poor and occupy his place.

Law VII. When litigants wish to settle their dispute among themselves, even while they are on their way to appear before the Praetor,[41] they shall have the right to make peace. Whatever agreement they enter into shall be considered just and shall be confirmed.

Law VIII. If the plaintiff and defendant do not settle their dispute, as above mentioned, let them state their cases either in the Comitium[42] or the Forum, by making a brief statement in the presence of the judge,[43] between the rising of the sun and noon, and, both of them being present, let them speak so that each party may hear.

Law IX. In the afternoon, let the judge grant the right to bring the action,[44] and render his decision in the presence of the plaintiff and the defendant.

Law X. The setting of the sun shall be the extreme limit of time within which a judge must render his decision.

Table II. Concerning judgments and thefts.

Law I. When issue has been joined in the presence of the judge, sureties and their substitutes for appearance at the trial must be furnished on both sides. The parties shall appear in person, unless prevented by disease of a serious character, or where

[39] See Readings 19, 20, and 35.

[40] Someone who ensures that a person will appear in court and abide by the settlement.

[41] The Roman magistrate who ranked just below the Consul and oversaw the Roman court system; this office was not created until 367 BCE.

[42] The area of the Forum where popular assemblies met.

[43] The Praetor.

[44] That is, the legal case.

vows that they have taken must be discharged to the gods, or where the proceedings are interrupted through their absence on business for the State, or where a day has been appointed by them to meet an alien.[45]

Law II. If any of the above mentioned occurrences takes place, that is, if one of the parties is seriously ill, or a vow has to be performed, or one of them is absent on business for the State, or a day has been appointed for an interview with an alien, so that the judge, the arbiter, or the defendant is prevented from being present, and the furnishing of security is postponed on this account, the hearing of the case shall be deferred.

Law III. Where anyone is deprived of the evidence of a witness let him call him with a loud voice in front of his house, on three market-days.[46]

Law IV. Where anyone commits a theft by night, and having been caught in the act is killed, he is legally killed.

Law V. If anyone commits a theft during the day, and is caught in the act, he shall be whipped, and given up as a slave to the person against whom the theft was committed. If he who perpetrated the theft is a slave, he shall be beaten with rods and hurled from the Tarpeian Rock.[47] If he is under the age of puberty, the Praetor shall decide whether he shall be whipped and surrendered by way of reparation for the injury.

Law VI. When any persons commit a theft during the day and in the light, whether they be freemen or slaves, of full age or minors, and attempt to defend themselves with weapons, or with any kind of implements, and the party against whom the violence is committed raises the cry of thief, and calls upon other persons, if any are present, to come to his assistance; and this is done, and the thieves are killed by him in the defense of his person and property, it is legal, and no liability attaches to the homicide.

Law VII. If a theft be detected by means of a dish and a girdle,[48] it is the same as manifest theft,[49] and shall be punished as such.

Law VIII. When anyone accuses and convicts another of theft that is not manifest, and no stolen property is found, judgment shall be rendered to compel the thief to pay double the value of what was stolen.

Law IX. Where anyone secretly cuts down trees belonging to another, he shall pay twenty-five *asses*[50] for each tree cut down.

Law X. Where anyone, in order to favor a thief, makes a compromise for the loss sustained, he cannot afterward prosecute him for theft.

Law XI. Stolen property shall always be his to whom it formerly belonged, nor can the lawful owner ever be deprived of it by long possession, without regard to its duration, nor can it ever be acquired by another, no matter in what way this may take place.

Table III. Concerning Property that is Lent.

Law I. When anyone, with fraudulent intent, appropriates property deposited with him for safe keeping, he shall be condemned to pay double its value.

Law II. When anyone collects interest on money loaned at a higher rate per annum than that of the *unciae*,[51] he shall pay quadruple the amount by way of penalty.

Law III. An alien cannot acquire the property of another by usucaption,[52] but a Roman citizen, who is

[45] A non-Roman.

[46] In the Roman calendar, market days occurred every eight days.

[47] A rocky prominence eighty feet high on the south side of the Capitoline Hill.

[48] Apparently someone making an accusation of theft could search the premises of the accused dressed only in a girdle, for decency's sake, and carrying a dish into which any stolen property could be put. This would ensure that the accuser was not perpetrating a false accusation by bringing in the supposedly stolen goods himself.

[49] Being caught in the act.

[50] The *as*, a copper coin initially weighing a pound of copper, was not introduced until ca. 280 BCE.

[51] The *uncia*, or ounce, was one-twelfth of a pound, or eight and one-third percent.

[52] To gain ownership of something by using it for a specified period of time.

the lawful owner of the property, always shall have the right to demand it from him.

Law IV. Where anyone, having acknowledged a debt, has a judgment rendered against him requiring payment, thirty days shall be given to him in which to pay the money and satisfy the judgment.

Law V. After the term of thirty days granted by the law to debtors who have had judgment rendered against them has expired, and in the meantime, they have not satisfied the judgment, their creditors shall be permitted to forcibly seize them and bring them again into court.

Law VI. When a defendant, after thirty days have elapsed, is brought into court a second time by the plaintiff, and does not satisfy the judgment, or, in the meantime, another party, or his surety does not pay it out of his own money, the creditor, or the plaintiff, after the debtor has been delivered up to him, can take the latter with him and bind him or place him in fetters, provided his chains are not of more than fifteen pounds weight; he can, however, place him in others that are lighter, if he desires to do so.

Law VII. If, after a debtor has been delivered up to his creditor, or has been placed in chains, he desires to obtain food and has the means, he shall be permitted to support himself out of his own property. But if he has nothing on which to live, his creditor, who holds him in chains, shall give him a pound of grain every day, or he can give him more than a pound, if he wishes to do so.

Law VIII. In the meantime, the party who has been delivered up to his creditor can make terms with him. If he does not, he shall be kept in chains for sixty days, and for three consecutive market-days he shall be brought before the Praetor in the place of assembly in the Forum, and the amount of the judgment against him shall be publicly proclaimed.

Law IX. After he has been kept in chains for sixty days, and the sum for which he is liable has been three times publicly proclaimed in the Forum, he shall be condemned to be reduced to slavery by him to whom he was delivered up; or, if the latter prefers, he can be sold beyond the Tiber.[53]

Law X. Where a party is delivered up to several persons, on account of a debt, after he has been exposed in the Forum on three market days, they shall be permitted to divide their debtor into different parts, if they desire to do so; and if anyone of them should, by the division, obtain more or less than he is entitled to, he shall not be responsible.

Table IV. Concerning the Rights of a Father, and of Marriage.

Law I. A father shall have the right of life and death over his son born in lawful marriage, and also shall have the power to render him independent, after he has been sold[54] three times.

Law II. If a father sells his son three times, the latter shall be free from paternal authority.

Law III. A father shall immediately put to death a son recently born who is a monster or has a form different from that of members of the human race.[55]

Law IV. When a woman brings forth a son within the next ten months after the death of her husband, he shall be born in lawful marriage, and shall be the legal heir of his estate.

Table V. Concerning Estates and Guardianships.

Law I. No matter in what way the head of a household may dispose of his estate, and appoint heirs to the same, or guardians; it shall have the force and effect of law.

Law II. Where a father dies intestate, without leaving any proper heir, his nearest agnate,[56] or, if there is none, the next of kin among his family, shall be his heir."

Law III. When a freedman dies intestate, and does not leave any proper heir, but his patron, or the children of the latter survive him; the inheritance of the estate of the freedman shall be adjudged to the next of kin of the patron.

[53] So as not to become an object of pity and create social unrest.

[54] And then set free.

[55] This practice can be compared to the inspection of new-born infants at Sparta; see Reading 53.

[56] "Agnates" were male relatives from the same "gens," or extended family.

Law IV. When a creditor or a debtor dies, his heirs can only sue, or be sued, in proportion to their shares in the estate; and any claims, or remaining property, shall be divided among them in the same proportion.

Law V. Where co-heirs desire to obtain their shares of the property of an estate, which has not yet been divided, it shall be divided. In order that this may be properly done and no loss be sustained by the litigants, the Praetor shall appoint three arbiters, who can give to each one that to which he is entitled in accordance with law and equity.

Law VI. When the head of a family dies intestate, and leaves a proper heir who has not reached the age of puberty, his nearest agnate shall obtain the guardianship.

Law VII. When no guardian has been appointed for an insane person, or a spendthrift, his nearest agnates, or if there are none, his other relatives, must take charge of his property.

Table VI. Concerning Ownership and Possession.

Law I. When anyone contracts a legal obligation with reference to his property, or sells it, by making a verbal statement or agreement concerning the same, this shall have the force and effect of law. If the party should afterward deny his statements, and legal proceedings are instituted, he shall, by way of penalty, pay double the value of the property in question.

Law II. Where a slave is ordered to be free by a will, upon his compliance with a certain condition, and he complies with the condition; or if, after having paid his price to the purchaser, he claims his liberty, he shall be free.

Law III. Where property has been sold, even though it may have been delivered, it shall by no means be acquired by the purchaser until the price has been paid, or a surety or a pledge has been given, and the vendor satisfied in this manner.

Law IV. Immovable property shall be acquired by usucaption after the lapse of two years; other property after the lapse of one year.

Law V. Where a woman, who has not been united to a man in marriage, lives with him for an entire year without the usucaption of her being interrupted for three nights, she shall pass into his power as his legal wife.[57]

Law VI. Where parties have a dispute with reference to property before the tribunal of the Praetor, both of them shall be permitted to state their claims in the presence of witnesses.

Law VII. Where anyone demands freedom for another against the claim of servitude, the Praetor shall render judgment in favor of liberty.

Law VIII. No material forming part of either a building or a vineyard shall be removed therefrom. Anyone who, without the knowledge or consent of the owner, attaches a beam or anything else to his house or vineyard shall be condemned to pay double its value.

Law IX. Timbers that have been dressed and prepared for building purposes, but which have not yet been attached to a building or a vineyard can legally be recovered by the owner, if they are stolen from him.

Law X. If a husband desires to divorce his wife, and dissolve his marriage, he must give a reason for doing so.

Table VII. Concerning Crimes.

Law I. If a quadruped causes injury to anyone, let the owner tender him the estimated amount of the damage, and if he is unwilling to accept it, the owner shall, by way of reparation, surrender the animal that caused the injury.

Law II. If you cause any unlawful damage accidentally and unintentionally, you must make good the loss, either by tendering what has caused it or by payment.

Law III. Anyone who, by means of incantations and magic arts, prevents grain or crops of any kind belonging to another from growing shall be sacrificed to Ceres.[58]

---

[57] That is, that he will gain legal authority over her; otherwise, she remained under the legal authority of her father or, if her father were deceased, of her father's male relatives.

[58] The goddess of grain, Demeter to the Greeks.

Law IV. If anyone who has arrived at puberty, secretly, and by night, destroys or cuts and appropriates to his own use the crop of another, which the owner of the land has obtained laboriously by plowing and the cultivation of the soil, he shall be sacrificed to Ceres, and hung.

If he is under the age of puberty, and not yet old enough to be accountable, he shall be whipped, in the discretion of the Praetor, and shall make good the loss by paying double its amount.

Law V. Anyone who turns cattle on the land of another, for the purpose of pasture, shall surrender the cattle by way of reparation.

Law VI. Anyone who, knowingly and maliciously, burns a building, or a heap of grain left near a building, after having been placed in chains and whipped shall be put to death by fire. If, however, he caused the damage by accident and without malice, he shall make it good, or, if he has not the means to do so, he shall receive a lighter punishment.

Law VII. When a person, in any way, causes an injury to another that is not serious he shall be punished with a fine of twenty *asses*.

Law VIII. When anyone publicly abuses another in a loud voice or writes a poem for the purpose of insulting him or rendering him infamous,[59] he shall be beaten with a rod until he dies.

Law IX. When anyone breaks a member of another, and is unwilling to come to make a settlement with him, he shall be punished by the law of retaliation.[60]

Law X. When anyone knocks a tooth out of the gum of a freeman, he shall be fined three hundred *asses*; if he knocks one out of the gum of a slave, he shall be fined a hundred and fifty *asses*.

Law XL If anyone, after having been asked, appears either as a witness or a balance-holder at a sale or the execution of a will and refuses to testify when this is required to prove the genuineness of the transaction, he shall become infamous[61] and cannot afterward give evidence.

Law XII. Anyone who gives false testimony shall be hurled from the Tarpeian Rock.

Law XIII. If anyone knowingly and maliciously kills a freeman, he shall be guilty of a capital crime. If he kills him by accident, without malice and unintentionally, let him substitute a ram to be sacrificed publicly by way of expiation for the homicide of the deceased and for the purpose of appeasing the children of the latter.

Law XIV. Anyone who annoys another by means of magic incantations or diabolical arts, and renders him inactive, or ill, or who prepares or administers poison to him, is guilty of a capital crime, and shall be punished with death.

Law XV. Anyone who kills an ascendant[62] shall have his head wrapped in a cloth, and, after having been sewed up in a sack, shall be thrown into the water.

Law XVI. Where anyone is guilty of fraud in the administration of a guardianship, he shall be considered infamous; and, even after the guardianship has been terminated, if any theft is proved to have been committed, he shall, by the payment of double damages, be compelled to make good the loss that he caused.

Law XVII. When a patron defrauds his client, he shall be dedicated to the infernal gods.[63]

Table VIII. Concerning the Laws of Real Property.

Law I. A space of two feet and a half must be left between neighboring buildings.

Law II. Societies and associations that have the right to assemble can make, promulgate, and confirm for themselves such contracts and rules as they may desire, provided nothing is done by them contrary to public enactments or which does not violate the common law.[64]

---

[59] Personal honor was very important and disrespect of one's personal honor was a grave offense.

[60] That is, by the imposition of the same injury, the "eye for an eye" law, as in the Code of Hammurabi (Reading 20) and the Hebrew laws (Reading 35).

[61] The punishment of *infamia* brought a diminution of one's citizenship rights.

[62] An older male relative.

[63] That is, sacrificed to the gods of the underworld.

[64] The right to form private associations was severely restricted in the future; see Reading 79.

Law III. The space of five feet shall be left between adjoining fields, by means of which the owners can visit their property, or drive and plow around it. No one shall ever have the right to acquire this space by usucaption.

Law IV. If any persons are in possession of adjoining fields and a dispute arises with reference to the boundaries of the same, the Praetor shall appoint three arbiters, who shall take cognizance of the case. After the boundaries have been established, he shall assign to each party that to which he is entitled.

Law V. When a tree overhangs the land of a neighbor so as to cause injury by its branches and its shade, it shall be cut off fifteen feet from the ground.

Law VI. When the fruit of a tree falls upon the premises of a neighbor, the owner of the tree shall have a right to gather and remove it.

Law VII. When rain falls upon the land of one person in such a quantity as to cause water to rise and injure the property of another, the Praetor shall appoint three arbiters for the purpose of confining the water and providing against damage to the other party.

Law VIII. Where a road runs in a straight line, it shall be eight feet, and where it curves, it shall be sixteen feet in width.

Law IX. When a man's land lies adjacent to the highway he can enclose it in any way that he chooses; but if he neglects to do so, any other person can drive an animal over the land wherever he pleases.[65]

Table IX. Concerning Public Law.

Law I. No privileges or statutes shall be enacted in favor of private persons, to the injury of others contrary to the law common to all citizens, and which individuals, no matter of what rank, have a right to make use of.

Law II. The same rights shall be conferred upon, and the same laws have been enacted for good and steadfast Roman citizens, shall be considered to have been enacted for all the people residing in and beyond Latium.[66]

Law III. When a judge, or an arbiter appointed to hear a case, accepts money, or other gifts, for the purpose of influencing his decision, he shall suffer the penalty of death.

Law IV. No decision with reference to the life or liberty of a Roman citizen shall be rendered except by the vote of the Greater Comitia.[67]

Law V. Public accusers in capital cases shall be appointed by the people.

Law VI. If anyone should cause nocturnal assemblies in the city, he shall be put to death.[68]

Law VII. If anyone should stir up war against his country, or delivers a Roman citizen into the hands of the enemy, he shall be punished with death.

Table X. Concerning Religious Law.

Law I. An oath shall have the greatest force and effect for the purpose of compelling good faith.

Law II. Where a family adopts private religious rites every member of it can, afterward, always make use of them.

Law III. No burial or cremation of a corpse shall take place in a city.

Law IV. No greater expenses or mourning than is proper shall be permitted in funeral ceremonies.

Law V. No one shall, hereafter, exceed the limit established by these laws for the celebration of funeral rites.

Law VI. Wood employed for the purpose of constructing a funeral pyre shall not be finished, but shall be rough and unpolished.

Law VII. When a corpse is prepared for burial at home, not more than three women with their heads covered with mourning veils shall be permitted to perform this service. The body may be enveloped in purple robes, and when borne outside, ten flute players, at the most, may accompany the funeral procession.

Law VIII. Women shall not during a funeral lacerate their faces, or tear their cheeks with their nails, nor shall they utter loud cries bewailing the dead.

Law IX. No bones shall be taken from the body of a person who is dead, or from his ashes after

[65] For a similar practice in ancient Egypt, see Reading 22.

[66] That is, Roman citizens who reside outside of Roman territory.

[67] The Centuriate, or Army, Assembly.

[68] As in Reading 79.

cremation, in order that funeral ceremonies may again be held elsewhere. When, however, anyone dies in a foreign country, or is killed in war, a part of his remains may be transferred to the burial place of his ancestors.

Law X. The body of no dead slave shall be anointed, nor shall any drinking take place at his funeral, nor shall a banquet of any kind be instituted in his honor.

Law XI. No wine flavored with myrrh, or any other precious beverage, shall be poured upon a corpse while it is burning, nor shall the funeral pyre be sprinkled with wine.

Law XII. Large wreaths shall not be borne at a funeral; nor shall perfumes be burned on the altars.

Law XIII. Anyone who has rendered himself deserving of a wreath as the reward of bravery in war or through his having been the victor in public contests or games, whether he has obtained it through his own exertions or by means of others in his own name, and by his own money, through his horses, or his slaves, shall have a right to have the said wreath placed upon his dead body, or upon that of any of his ascendants, as long as the corpse is at his home, as well as when it is borne away, so that, during his funeral rites he may enjoy the honor that in his lifetime he acquired by his bravery or his good fortune.

Law XIV. Only one funeral of an individual can take place, and it shall not be permitted to prepare several biers.

Law XV. Gold, no matter in what form it may be present, shall, by all means, be removed from the corpse at the time of the funeral, but if anyone's teeth should be fastened with gold, it shall be lawful either to burn or bury it with the body.[69]

Law XVI. No one, without the knowledge or consent of the owner, shall erect a funeral pyre or a tomb nearer than sixty feet to the building of another.

Law XVII. No one can acquire by usucaption either the vestibule or approach to a tomb or the tomb itself.

Law XVIII. No assembly of the people shall take place during the obsequies of any man distinguished in the State.

Table XI. Supplement to the Five Preceding Tables.

Law I. Affairs of great importance shall not be transacted without the vote of the people, with whom rests the power to appoint magistrates, to condemn citizens, and to enact laws. Laws subsequently passed always take preference over former ones.

Law II. Those who belong to the Senatorial Order and are styled Fathers shall not contract marriage with plebeians.[70]

Table XII. Supplement to the Five Preceding Laws.

Law I. No one shall render sacred[71] any property with reference to which there is a controversy in court, where issue has already been joined; and if anyone does render such property sacred, he shall pay double its value as a penalty.

Law II. If the claim of anyone in whose favor judgment was rendered after the property had been illegally seized, or after possession of the same had been delivered, is found to be false, the Praetor shall appoint three arbiters by whose award double the amount of the profits shall be restored by him in whose favor the judgment was rendered.

Law III. If a slave, with the knowledge of his master, should commit a theft, or cause damage to anyone, his master shall be given up to the other party by way of reparation for the theft, injury, or damage committed by the slave.

[69] The Romans had two forms of interment, inhumation (the burial of the body intact) and cremation (the burning of the body, followed by the gathering of the bones for burial).

[70] A very contentious ruling added to the lawcode in 450 BCE.

[71] Dedicate to the gods.

77

THE SACK OF ROME BY THE GAULS (390 BCE): LIVY, *FROM THE FOUNDING OF THE CITY*, BOOK 5, CHAPTERS 32–42

After the sack of Rome by the Gauls in 390 BCE, the Romans decided it would be a good idea to build a defensive wall around the city. The largest surviving portion of the resulting "Servian Wall," which centuries later was thought to have been built by King Servius Tullius in the seventh century BCE, stands next to the main train station in Rome.

It was not until 396 BCE, with the defeat of the Etruscan city of Veii, that the Romans were able markedly to increase their territory. Immediately after this victory, however, Roman fortunes took a decided turn for the worse. In 390 BCE, as graphically recounted by the Roman historian Livy (ca. 60 BCE–17 CE) in his work "From the Founding of the City," a raiding party of Gauls from the Po River valley attacked Rome. The Roman army, packed together in the traditional phalanx formation, was completely flabbergasted by the horrifying, undisciplined charge of the howling Celtic warriors. The Romans turned tail and ran, leaving the Gauls to occupy, sack, and burn the city of Rome, destroying in the process any written records, such as the original copy of the Twelve Tables, that existed. After the sack, it was only by paying a hefty ransom that the Romans were able to induce the Gauls to depart. According to one account, after the Romans complained that the ransom paid to the Gauls was too great, the Gallic chieftain Brennus threw his sword onto the scales and said, "Vae victis," that is, "Woe to the conquered." The Romans also patriotically claimed that under the Dictator Camillus they eventually regrouped and defeated the Gauls before they could depart with their treasure. The Romans vowed that such a disaster would never happen again.

Source: Canon Roberts, trans., *Titus Livius. The History of Rome*, Vol. 1 (London: Dent, 1905).

In this year[72] Marcus Caedicius, a member of the plebs, reported to the tribunes that while he was in the Via Nova[73] he heard in the silence of the night a voice more powerful than any human voice bidding the magistrates be told that the Gauls were approaching. No notice was taken of this, partly owing to the humble rank of the informant, and partly because the Gauls were a distant and therefore an unknown nation. Ambassadors came from Clusium[74] begging for assistance against the Gauls. The tradition is that this nation, attracted by the report of the delicious fruits and especially of the wine, a novel pleasure to them, crossed the Alps and occupied the lands formerly cultivated by the Etruscans. As a matter of fact, Gauls crossed into Italy two centuries before they attacked Clusium and took Rome. Nor were the Clusines the first Etruscans with whom the Gallic armies came into conflict; long before that they had fought many battles with the Etruscans who dwelt between the Apennines and the Alps.[75]

The people of Clusium were appalled by this strange war, when they saw the numbers, the extraordinary appearance of the men, and the kind of weapons they used, and heard that the armies of Etruria had been often routed by them on both sides of the Po. Although they had no claim on Rome, either on the ground of alliance or friendly relations, unless it was that they had not defended their kinsmen at Veii[76] against the Romans, they nevertheless sent ambassadors to ask the Senate for assistance. Active assistance they did not obtain. The three sons of M. Fabius Ambustus[77] were sent as ambassadors to negotiate with the Gauls and warn them not to attack those from whom they had suffered no injury, who were allies and friends of Rome, and who, if circumstances compelled them, must be defended by the armed force of Rome. They preferred that actual war should be avoided, and that they should make acquaintance with the Gauls, who were strangers to them, in peace rather than in arms.

A peaceable enough mission, had it not contained envoys of a violent temper, more like Gauls than

[72] 390 BCE.

[73] The "New Way," the second road built in Rome; it branched off from the first, the Via Sacra ("Sacred Way"), and ran along the base of the Palatine Hill.

[74] An Etruscan city.

[75] For the Celtic expansion into northern Italy, see Reading 72.

[76] An Etruscan city that had been conquered very recently, in 396 BCE, by the Romans.

[77] The "Pontifex Maximus" (Chief priest) of Rome. The Fabii were one of the most distinguished aristocratic families of Rome.

Romans.[78] After they had delivered their instructions in the council of the Gauls, the following reply was given: "Although we are hearing the name of Romans for the first time, we believe nevertheless that you are brave men, because the Clusines are imploring your assistance in their time of danger. Because you prefer to protect your allies against us by negotiation rather than by armed force, we on our side do not reject the peace you offer, on condition that the Clusines cede to us Gauls, who are in need of land, a portion of that territory that they possess to a greater extent than they can cultivate. On any other conditions peace cannot be granted. We wish to receive their reply in your presence, and if territory is refused us we shall fight, while you are still here, so that you may report to those at home how far the Gauls surpass all other men in courage."

The Romans asked them what right they had to demand, under threat of war, territory from those who were its owners, and what business the Gauls had in Etruria. The haughty answer was returned that they carried their right in their weapons, and that everything belonged to the brave. Passions were kindled on both sides; they flew to arms and joined battle. Thereupon, contrary to the Law of Nations,[79] the envoys seized their weapons, for the Fates[80] already were urging Rome to its ruin. The fact of three of the noblest and bravest Romans fighting in the front line of the Etruscan army could not be concealed, so conspicuous was the valor of the strangers. And what was more, Q. Fabius rode forward at a Gallic chieftain, who was impetuously charging right at the Etruscan standards, ran his spear through his side and slew him. While he was in the act of despoiling the body the Gauls recognized him, and the word was passed through the whole army that it was a Roman ambassador. Forgetting their rage against the Clusines, and breathing threats against the Romans, they sounded the retreat.

Some Gauls were for an instant advance on Rome. The older men thought that ambassadors should first be sent to Rome to make a formal complaint and demand the surrender of the Fabii as satisfaction for this violation of the Law of Nations. After the ambassadors had stated their case, the Senate, while disapproving of the conduct of the Fabii and recognizing the justice of the demand that the barbarians made, were prevented by political interests from placing their convictions on record in the form of a recommendation in the case of men of such high rank. In order, therefore, that the blame for any defeat that might be incurred in a war with the Gauls might not rest on them alone, they referred the consideration of the Gauls' demands to the people. Here personal popularity and influence had so much more weight that the very men whose punishment was under discussion were elected Consular Tribunes[81] for the next year.

The Gauls regarded this procedure as it deserved to be regarded, namely, as an act of hostility, and after openly threatening war, returned to their people. Burning with rage, for as a nation they cannot control their passions, they seized their standards and hurriedly set out on their march. At the sound of their tumult as they swept by, the affrighted cities flew to arms and the country folk took to flight. Horses and men, spread far and wide, covered an immense tract of country; wherever they went they made it understood by loud shouts that they were going to Rome. But although they were preceded by rumors and by messages from Clusium, and then from one town after another, it was the swiftness of their approach that created most alarm in Rome. An army hastily raised by a levy en masse marched out

[78] A stereotype of Gauls was that they were quick tempered and violent.

[79] The "Ius gentium" ("Law of Nations") were established customs that applied to all peoples. Ambassadors were supposed to be inviolate and were not supposed to engage in military conflicts while they were on their missions.

[80] Goddesses depicted as elderly women who control human destiny: Clotho spun the thread of life, Lachesis measured how long it would be, and Atropos cut it off at the end.

[81] In 444 BCE, when the plebs demanded the right to hold the office of Consul, the patricians abolished the consulate and replaced it with the office of Military Tribune with Consular Powers, which plebeians could hold.

to meet them. The two forces met hardly eleven miles from Rome, at a spot where the Allia River, flowing in a very deep channel from the Crustuminian Mountains, joins the river Tiber a little below the road to Crustumerium.[82] The whole country in front and around was now swarming with the enemy, who, being as a nation given to wild outbreaks, had by their hideous howls and discordant clamor filled everything with dreadful noise.

The Consular Tribunes had secured no position for their camp, had constructed no entrenchments behind which to retire, and had shown as much disregard of the gods as of the enemy, for they formed their order of battle without having obtained favorable auspices.[83] They extended their line on either wing to prevent their being outflanked, but even so they could not make their front equal to the enemy's, while by thus thinning their line they weakened the center so that it could hardly keep in touch. On their right was a small eminence that they decided to hold with reserves, and this disposition, although it was the beginning of the panic and flight, proved to be the only means of safety to the fugitives. For Brennus, the Gallic chieftain, fearing some ruse in the scanty numbers of the enemy, and thinking that the rising ground was occupied in order that the reserves might attack the flank and rear of the Gauls while their front was engaged with the legions, directed his attack upon the reserves, feeling quite certain that if he drove them from their position, his overwhelming numbers would give him an easy victory on the level ground. So not only Fortune but tactics also were on the side of the barbarians.

In the other army there was nothing to remind one of Romans either among the generals or the private soldiers. They were terrified and all they thought about was flight, and so utterly had they lost their heads that a far greater number fled to Veii, although the Tiber lay in their way, rather than by the direct road to Rome, to their wives and children. For a short time the reserves were protected by their position. In the rest of the army, no sooner was the battle-shout heard on their flank by those nearest to the reserves, and then by those at the other end of the line heard in their rear, than they fled, whole and unhurt, almost before they had seen their untried foe, without any attempt to fight or even to give back the battle-shout. None were slain while actually fighting; they were cut down from behind while hindering one another's flight in a confused, struggling mass. Along the bank of the Tiber, whither the whole of the left wing had fled, after throwing away their arms, there was great slaughter. Many who were unable to swim or were hampered by the weight of their cuirasses and other armor were sucked down by the current. The greater number, however, reached Veii in safety, yet not only were no troops sent from there to defend Rome but not even was a messenger dispatched to report the defeat to Rome. All the men on the right wing, which had been stationed some distance from the river and nearer to the foot of the hill, made for Rome and took refuge in the Citadel without even closing the city gates.

The Gauls for their part were almost dumb with astonishment at so sudden and extraordinary a victory. At first they did not dare to move from the spot, as though puzzled by what had happened, then they began to fear a surprise, at last they began to despoil the dead, and, as their custom is, to pile up the arms in heaps. Finally, as no hostile movement was anywhere visible, they commenced their march and reached Rome shortly before sunset. The cavalry, who had ridden on in front, reported that the gates were not shut, there were no pickets on guard in front of them, no troops on the walls. This second surprise, as extraordinary as the previous one, held them back, and fearing a nocturnal conflict in the streets of an unknown city, they halted and bivouacked between Rome and the Anio.[84] Reconnoitering parties were sent out to examine the circuit of the walls and the other gates, and to ascertain what plans their enemies were forming in their desperate plight.

As for the Romans, because the greater number had fled from the field in the direction of Veii instead

[82] A Latin town conquered by the Romans around 500 BCE.

[83] Religious rites intended to secure the good will of the gods before important undertakings.

[84] The modern Aniene River; it joins the Tiber River just north of Rome.

of Rome, it was universally believed that the only survivors were those who had found refuge in Rome, and the mourning for all who were lost, whether living or dead, filled the whole city with the cries of lamentation. But the sounds of private grief were stifled by the general terror when it was announced that the enemy were at hand. Presently the yells and wild war-whoops of the squadrons were heard as they rode round the walls. All the time until the next day's dawn the citizens were in such a state of suspense that they expected from moment to moment an attack on the city. They expected it first when the enemy approached the walls, for they would have remained at the Allia had not this been their object; then just before sunset they thought the enemy would attack because there was not much daylight left; and then when night was fallen they imagined that the attack was delayed until then to create all the greater terror. Finally, the approach of the next day deprived them of their senses; the entrance of the enemy's standards within the gates was the dreadful climax to fears that had known no respite.

But all through that night and the following day the citizens afforded an utter contrast to those who had fled in such terror at the Allia. Realising the hopelessness of attempting any defense of the city with the small numbers that were left, they decided that the men of military age and the able-bodied among the senators should, with their wives and children, withdraw into the Citadel[85] and the Capitol,[86] and after getting in stores of arms and provisions, should from that fortified position defend their gods, themselves, and the great name of Rome. The Flamen[87] and priestesses of Vesta[88] were to carry the sacred things of the State far away from the bloodshed and the fire, and their sacred cult should not be abandoned as long as a single person survived to observe it. If only the Citadel and the Capitol, the abode of gods; if only the Senate, the guiding mind of the national policy; if only the men of military age survived the impending ruin of the city, then the loss of the crowd of old men left behind in the city could be easily borne; in any case, they themselves were certain to perish. To reconcile the aged plebeians[89] to their fate, the men who had been Consuls and enjoyed triumphs gave out that they would meet their fate side by side with them, and not burden the scanty force of fighting men with bodies too weak to carry arms or defend their country.

Thus they sought to comfort one another, these aged men doomed to death. Then they turned with words of encouragement to the younger men on their way to the Citadel and Capitol, and solemnly commended to their strength and courage all that was left of the fortunes of a city that for 360 years[90] had been victorious in all its wars. As those who were carrying with them all hope and succor finally separated from those who had resolved not to survive the fall of the city the misery of the scene was heightened by the distress of the women. Their tears, their distracted running about as they followed first their husbands then their sons, their imploring appeals to them not to leave them[91] to their fate, made up a picture in which no element of human misery was wanting.

After all the arrangements that circumstances permitted had been made for the defense of the Capitol, the old men returned to their respective homes and, fully prepared to die, awaited the coming of the enemy. Those who had filled curule offices[92] resolved to meet their fate wearing the insignia of their former rank and honor and distinctions. They put on the splendid dress that they wore when conducting the chariots of the gods or riding in triumph through

[85] A high point on the north end of the Capitoline Hill.
[86] The Temple of "Jupiter the Best and Greatest" atop the Capitoline Hill.
[87] The Flamen dialis, the high priest of Jupiter.
[88] The six Vestal Virgins.
[89] Who at this point time still were not eligible to be Consuls.
[90] Rounded; actually 363 years from the founding of Rome in 753 BCE.
[91] The elderly men.
[92] Offices whose holders had the power of imperium (the power to command armies) and were permitted to use the curule chair; at this time, this included Consular Tribunes, Consuls, and Dictators.

the city, and thus arrayed, they seated themselves in their ivory chairs in front of their houses. Some writers record that, led by Marcus Fabius, the Pontifex Maximus, they recited the solemn formula in which they devoted themselves to death for their country.[93]

As the Gauls were refreshed by a night's rest after a battle that had at no point been seriously contested, and as they were not now taking the city by assault or storm, their entrance the next day was not marked by any signs of excitement or anger. Passing the Colline Gate,[94] which was standing open, they came to the Forum and gazed round at the temples and at the Citadel, which alone wore any appearance of war. They left there a small body to guard against any attack from the Citadel or Capitol while they were scattered, and then they dispersed in quest of plunder through streets in which they did not meet a soul. Some poured in a body into all the houses near, others made for the most distant ones, expecting to find them untouched and full of spoils.

Appalled by the very desolation of the place and dreading lest some stratagem should surprise the stragglers, they returned to the neighborhood of the Forum in close order. The houses of the plebeians were barricaded, the halls of the patricians stood open, but they felt greater hesitation about entering the open houses than those which were closed. They gazed with feelings of real veneration upon the men who were seated in the porticoes of their mansions, not only because of the superhuman magnificence of their apparel and their whole bearing and demeanor, but also because of the majestic expression of their countenances, wearing the very aspect of gods. So they stood, gazing at them as if they were statues, until, as it is asserted, one of the patricians, M. Papirius, roused the passion of a Gaul, who began to stroke his beard, which in those days was universally worn long, by smiting him on the head with his ivory staff. He was the first to be killed, the others were butchered in their chairs. After this slaughter of the magnates, no living being was thenceforth spared; the houses were rifled, and then set on fire.[95]

Now, whether it was that the Gauls were not all animated by a passion for the destruction of the city, or whether their chiefs had decided on the one hand to present the spectacle of a few fires as a means of intimidating the besieged into surrender from a desire to save their homes, and on the other, by abstaining from a universal conflagration, hold what remained of the city as a pledge by which to weaken their enemies' determination, it is certain that the fires were far from being so indiscriminate or so extensive as might be expected on the first day of a captured city. As the Romans beheld from the Citadel the city filled with the enemy who were running about in all the streets while some new disaster was constantly occurring, first in one quarter then in another, they could no longer control their eyes and ears, let alone their thoughts and feelings. In whatever direction their attention was drawn by the shouts of the enemy, the shrieks of the women and boys, the roar of the flames, and the crash of houses falling in, thither they turned their eyes and minds as though set by Fortune to be spectators of their country's fall, powerless to protect anything left of all they possessed beyond their lives.

---

[93] The ceremony of *devotio* ("devotion"), in which a contract was made with the gods; in exchange for sacrificing themselves, distinguished Romans expected that the gods would give their support to Rome.

[94] The site of a crucial battle in 83 BCE between the rebel general Sulla and supporters of the Senate.

[95] This would have destroyed many records of earlier Roman history.

78

THE BATTLE OF CANNAE (216 BCE): LIVY, *FROM THE FOUNDING OF THE CITY*, BOOK 22, CHAPTERS 34–57

A Carthaginian silver double shekel, now in the British Museum in London, issued by the general Hamilcar Barca, the father of Hannibal, in Spain ca. 230 BCE. The obverse depicts the god Melqart in the form of Hercules, with a club over his shoulder, and the reverse portrays a Carthaginian war elephant. Most of Hannibal's elephants died crossing the Alps; the survivors only participated in one battle, at the Trebia River in 218, and only one, nicknamed "The Syrian," survived the war.

The Battle of Cannae in 216 BCE was Rome's defining moment. After the Romans had lost fifty thousand soldiers in the first two years of the war, at Cannae Hannibal's smaller army surrounded the much larger Roman one and totally destroyed it. The Romans lost another fifty thousand men; only ten thousand escaped to tell the tale. It appeared that the Romans were about to lose the war. But not only did they continue the fight; they even expanded the theaters of operation. Livy's account of the battle begins with the contentiousness that arose over the Consular elections for 216 BCE, where two bitterly opposed Consuls were elected, Gaius Terentius Varro, an inexperienced rabble rousing plebeian whose emotional appeals to the plebs opposed the delaying tactics of the dictator Quintus Fabius Maximus and rashly promised a quick end to the war with Hannibal, and Lucius Aemilius Paullus, a distinguished, experienced, and cautious patrician implacably opposed to Varro and the plebeians. The two were at odds throughout the campaign, with disastrous results. The Roman historian Livy (ca. 60 BCE–17 CE) in his work "From the Founding of the City," described the events leading up to the battle and the battle itself in great detail.

Source: Canon Roberts, trans., *Titus Livius. The History of Rome*, Vol. 3 (London: Dent, 1905).

The elections[96] were held amid a bitter struggle between the patricians and the plebs. C. Terentius Varro,[97] a member of their own order, had ingratiated himself with the plebs by his attacks upon the leading men in the state and by all the tricks known to the demagogue. His success in shaking the influence of Fabius[98] and weakening the authority of the Dictator had invested him with a certain glory in the eyes of the mob, and they did their utmost to raise him to the consulship. The patricians opposed him with their utmost strength, dreading lest it should become a common practice for men to attack them as a means of rising to an equality with them. Q. Baebius Herennius, a relation of Varro's, strengthened the feeling in favor of his own candidate. "It was by the nobility," he declared, "who had for many years been trying to get up a war, that Hannibal was brought into Italy, and when the war might have been brought to a close, it was they who were unscrupulously protracting it. We shall never see the end of the war until we have elected as our Consul a man who is really a plebeian, that is, one from the ranks. The plebeian nobility[99] have all been initiated into the same mysteries; when they are no longer looked down upon by the patricians they at once begin to look down upon the plebs. One consulship at all events belongs to the Roman plebs; the people will freely dispose of it and give it to the man who prefers an early victory to prolonged command."

Harangues like these kindled intense excitement among the plebs. There also were three patrician candidates in the field, P. Cornelius Merenda, L. Manlius Vulso, and M. Aemilius Lepidus, and two plebeians who now were ennobled, C. Atilius Serranus and Q. Aelius Paetus. But the only one elected was C. Terentius Varro, so that the elections for appointing his colleague were in his hands. The nobility compelled L. Aemilius Paullus to come forward. On the next election day, after all Varro's opponents had retired, Paullus was given to him not so much to be his colleague as to oppose him on equal terms.

The armies were increased, but as to what additions were made to the infantry and cavalry, the authorities vary so much, both as to the numbers and nature of the forces, that I should hardly venture to assert anything as positively certain. Some say that 10,000 recruits were called out to make up the losses; others, that four new legions were enrolled so that they might carry on the war with eight legions. Some authorities record that both horse and foot in the legions were made stronger by the addition of 1000 infantry and 100 cavalry to each, so that they contained 5000 infantry and 300 cavalry, whereas the allies[100] furnished double the number of cavalry and

96 For the year 216 BCE.

97 Varro was a complete outsider, a "new man," that is, a person none of whose ancestors had held the office of Consul.

98 Quintus Fabius Maximus, who had been appointed Dictator after the disastrous Roman defeat at the Battle of Lake Trasimene in 217 BCE. By implementing his "Fabian Strategy" of restricting military operations to raids and guerilla warfare but not engaging Hannibal's main army, Fabius got the nickname "Cunctator," "The Delayer."

99 Plebeians who, unlike Varro, did have a Consul in their family background. The consulate had been open to plebeians since 367 BCE.

100 The "socii," or Italian allies, defeated peoples and cities of Italy not governed by Rome but expected to contribute troops for Rome's wars.

an equal number of infantry. Thus, according to these writers, there were 87,200 men in the Roman camp when the Battle of Cannae[101] was fought. One thing is quite certain; the struggle was resumed with greater vigor and energy than in former years, because the Dictator had given them reason to hope that the enemy might be conquered.[102] But before the newly raised legions left the city the Decemvirs[103] were ordered to consult the Sibylline Books[104] owing to the general alarm that had been created by fresh portents. It was reported that showers of stones had fallen simultaneously on the Aventine in Rome and at Aricia; that the statues of the gods among the Sabines had sweated blood, and cold water had flowed from the hot springs. This latter portent created more terror, because it had happened several times. In the colonnade near the Campus Martius[105] several men had been killed by lightning. The proper expiation of these portents was ascertained from the Sibylline Books.

After completing the enrolment the Consuls waited a few days for the contingents furnished by the Latins and the allies to come in. Then a new departure was made; the soldiers were sworn in by the Military Tribunes.[106] Up to that day there had only been the military oath binding the men to assemble at the bidding of the Consuls and not to disband until they received orders to do so. It had also been the custom among the soldiers, when the infantry were formed into companies of 100, and the cavalry into troops of 10, for all the men in each company or troop to take a voluntary oath to each other that they would not leave their comrades for fear or for flight, and that they would not quit the ranks save to fetch or pick up a weapon, to strike an enemy, or to save a comrade. This voluntary covenant was now changed into a formal oath taken before the tribunes.

Before they marched out of the city, Varro delivered several violent harangues, in which he declared that the war had been brought into Italy by the nobles, and would continue to feed on the vitals of the Republic if there were more generals like Fabius; he, Varro, would finish off the war the very day he caught sight of the enemy. His colleague, Paullus, made only one speech, in which there was much more truth than the people cared to hear. He passed no strictures on Varro, but he did express surprise that any general, while still in the city before he had taken up his command, or become acquainted with either his own army or that of the enemy, or gained any information as to the lie of the country and the nature of the ground, should know in what way he should conduct the campaign and be able to foretell the day on which he would fight a decisive battle with the enemy.

As for himself, Paullus said that he would not anticipate events by disclosing his measures, for, after all, circumstances determined measures for men much more than men made circumstances subservient to measures. He hoped and prayed that such measures as were taken with due caution and foresight might turn out successful; so far rashness, besides being foolish, had proved disastrous. He made it quite clear that he would prefer safe to hasty counsels, and in order to strengthen him in this resolve Fabius is said to have addressed him on his departure in the following terms:

"You are mistaken, Lucius Paullus, if you imagine that you will have less difficulty with Gaius Terentius than with Hannibal. I rather think the former will prove a more dangerous enemy than the latter. With the one you will only have to contend in the field, the opposition of the other you will have to meet everywhere and always. Against Hannibal and his legions you will have your cavalry and infantry, when Varro is in command he will use your own

[101] In Apulia in far southeastern Italy, the site of one of Rome's most disastrous military defeats.

[102] By his policy of harrassing but not directly confronting Hannibal.

[103] The "Ten Men in Charge of Carrying out Sacrificial Duties," five patricians and five plebeians. They were in charge of consulting the Sibylline Books.

[104] Books believed to have been purchased from a Sibyl (a prophetress) by King Tarquin the Proud. They were consulted in times of emergencies to find the proper expiatory rites needed to regain the favor of the gods.

[105] The "Field of Mars," where, in earlier Roman history, the army was accustomed to assemble.

[106] Each legion had six Military Tribunes, chosen by the Senate and by vote of the people.

men against you. If he carries out his threat and brings on an action at once, some place or other will be rendered more notorious by our defeat than even Trasimene.[107] The only rational method of carrying on war against Hannibal is the one that I have followed. We are carrying on war in Italy, in our own country on our own soil, everywhere round us are citizens and allies, and time and circumstance are making us more efficient, more circumspect, more self-reliant. Hannibal, on the other hand, is in a foreign and hostile land, far from his home and country, confronted everywhere by opposition and danger; nowhere by land or sea can he find peace; nowhere does he see anything that he can call his own, he has to live on each day's pillage. He has hardly a third of the army with which he crossed the Ebro.[108] He has lost more by famine than by the sword, and even the few he has cannot get enough to support life. Do you doubt then, that if we sit still we shall get the better of a man who is growing weaker day by day, who has neither supplies nor reinforcements nor money? Varro, although he is a Roman Consul, will desire just what Hannibal the Carthaginian commander desires. Hannibal will only feel contempt for a man who runs all risks; he will be afraid of one who never takes a rash step."

The Consul's reply was far from being a cheerful one, for he admitted that the advice given was true, but not easy to put into practice. What power or authority would a Consul have against a violent and headstrong colleague? With these words Paullus, it is said, set forward, escorted by the foremost men among the patricians; the plebeian Consul was attended by his plebeian friends, more conspicuous for their numbers than for the quality of the men who composed the crowd. When they came into camp the recruits and the old soldiers were formed into one army, and two separate camps were formed, the new camp, which was the smaller one, being nearer to Hannibal, while in the old camp the larger part of the army and the best troops were stationed.

An incident occurred that still further encouraged Varro's impetuous and headstrong temperament. Parties were sent to drive off the foragers; a confused fight ensued owing to the soldiers rushing forward without any preconcerted plan or orders from their commanders, and the contest went heavily against the Carthaginians. As many as 1700 of them were killed, the loss of the Romans and the allies did not amount to more than 100. The Consuls commanded on alternate days, and that day happened to be Paullus' turn. He checked the victors who were pursuing the enemy in great disorder, for he feared an ambuscade. Varro was furious, and loudly exclaimed that the enemy had been allowed to slip out of their hands, and if the pursuit had not been stopped the war could have been brought to a close. Hannibal did not very much regret his losses. On the contrary, he believed that they would serve as a bait to the impetuosity of the Consul and his newly-raised troops, and that he would be more headstrong than ever. What was going on in the enemy's camp was quite as well known to him as what was going on in his own; he was fully aware that there were differences and quarrels between the commanders, and that two-thirds of the army consisted of new recruits.

Owing to the want of grain, Hannibal decided to move into the warmer parts of Apulia, where the harvest was earlier and where, owing to the greater distance from the enemy, desertion would be rendered more difficult for the fickle-minded part of his force. He ordered campfires to be lighted, and a few tents left where they could be easily seen, in order that the Romans, remembering a similar stratagem,[109] might be afraid to move. Statilius, however, was sent to reconnoiter with his Lucanians.[110] He reported that he had caught a distant view of the enemy in line of march, and the question of pursuit was

[107] The Roman defeat at the Battle of Lake Trasimene the year before, where incompetent Roman generals had allowed the Roman army to be trapped between a mountain and a lake.

[108] The Spanish river that marked the northern boundary of Carthaginian territory. It was Rome's violation of the Ebro Treaty of 226 that had led to the Second Punic War.

[109] A stratagem previously used by the Dictator Fabius Maximus to escape from Hannibal.

[110] An Italic people of southern Italy.

discussed. As usual, the views of the two Consuls were opposed, but almost all present supported Varro, not a single voice was given in favor of Paullus, except that of Servilius, Consul in the preceding year. The opinion of the majority of the council prevailed, and so, driven by destiny, they went forward to render Cannae famous in the annals of Roman defeats. It was in the neighborhood of this village that Hannibal had fixed his camp with his back to the sirocco that blows from Mount Vulture[111] and fills the arid plains with clouds of dust. This arrangement was a very convenient one for his camp, and it proved to be extremely advantageous afterward, when he was forming his order of battle, for his own men, with the wind behind them, blowing only on their backs, would fight with an enemy who was blinded by volumes of dust.

The Consuls followed the Carthaginians, and when they reached Cannae and had the enemy in view they formed two entrenched camps. Hannibal now saw his hopes fulfilled, that the Consuls would give him an opportunity of fighting on ground naturally adapted for the movements of cavalry, the arm in which he had so far been invincible, and accordingly he placed his army in order of battle, and tried to provoke his foe to action by repeated charges of his Numidians.[112] The Roman camp was again disturbed by a mutinous soldiery and Consuls at variance, Paullus bringing up against Varro the fatal rashness of Sempronius and Flaminius,[113] Varro retorting by pointing to Fabius as the favorite model of cowardly and inert commanders, and calling gods and men to witness that it was through no fault of his that Hannibal had acquired, so to speak, a prescriptive right to Italy; he had had his hands tied by his colleague; his soldiers, furious and eager for fight, had had their swords and arms taken away from them. Paullus, on the other hand, declared that if anything happened to the legions flung recklessly and betrayed into an ill-considered and imprudent action, he was free from all responsibility for it, although he would have to share in all the consequences. "See to it," he said to Varro, "that those who are so free and ready with their tongues are equally so with their hands in the day of battle."

While time was thus being wasted in disputes instead of deliberation, Hannibal withdrew the bulk of his army, who had been standing most of the day in order of battle, into camp. He sent his Numidians, however, across the river[114] to attack the parties who were getting water for the smaller camp. They had hardly gained the opposite bank when with their shouting and uproar they sent the crowd flying in wild disorder, and galloping on as far as the outpost in front of the rampart, they nearly reached the gates of the camp. It was looked upon as such an insult for a Roman camp to be actually terrorized by irregular auxiliaries that one thing, and one thing alone, held back the Romans from instantly crossing the river and forming their battle line—the supreme command that day rested with Paullus. The following day Varro, whose turn it now was, without any consultation with his colleague, exhibited the signal for battle and led his forces drawn up for action across the river. Paullus followed, for although he disapproved of the measure, he was bound to support it. After crossing, they strengthened their line with the force in the smaller camp and completed their formation. On the right, which was nearest to the river, the Roman cavalry were posted, then came the infantry; on the extreme left were the cavalry of the allies, their infantry were between them and the Roman legions. The javelin men with the rest of the light-armed auxiliaries formed the front line. The Consuls took their stations on the wings, Terentius Varro on the left, Aemilius Paullus on the right.

As soon as it grew light Hannibal sent forward the Balearics[115] and the other light infantry. He then crossed the river in person and as each division was

[111] An extinct volcano in Lucania in southern Italy.

[112] A native North African people known for its excellent cavalry.

[113] Sempronius had lost the Battle of the Trebia River in 218 BCE and Flaminius had lost the Battle of Lake Trasimene in 217.

[114] The Aufidus River, just south of the battle site.

[115] From the Balearic Islands in the Mediterranean Sea east of Spain; known for their skill as slingers.

brought across he assigned it its place in the line. The Gallic and Spanish horse he posted near the bank on the left wing in front of the Roman cavalry; the right wing was assigned to the Numidian troopers. The center consisted of a strong force of infantry, the Gauls and Spaniards in the middle, the Africans at either end of them. You might fancy that the Africans were for the most part a body of Romans from the way they were armed, they were so completely equipped with the arms, some of which they had taken at the Trebia, but the most part at Trasimene. The Gauls and Spaniards had shields almost of the same shape but their swords were totally different, those of the Gauls being very long and without a point, the Spaniard, accustomed to thrust more than to cut, had a short handy sword, pointed like a dagger. These nations, more than any other, inspired terror by the vastness of their stature and their frightful appearance: the Gauls were naked above the waist, the Spaniards had taken up their position wearing white tunics embroidered with purple, of dazzling brilliancy. The total number of infantry in the field was 40,000, and there were 10,000 cavalry. Hasdrubal was in command of the left wing, Maharbal of the right; Hannibal himself with his brother Mago commanded the center. It was a great convenience to both armies that the sun shone obliquely on them, whether it was that they had purposely so placed themselves, or whether it happened by accident, because the Romans faced the north, the Carthaginans the south. The wind, called by the inhabitants the Vulturnus,[116] was against the Romans, and blew great clouds of dust into their faces, making it impossible for them to see in front of them.

When the battle shout was raised the auxiliaries ran forward, and the battle began with the light infantry. Then the Gauls and Spaniards on the left engaged the Roman cavalry on the right; the battle was not at all like a cavalry fight, for there was no room for maneuvering, the river on the one side and the infantry on the other hemming them in, compelled them to fight face to face. Each side tried to force their way straight forward, until at last the horses were standing in a closely pressed mass, and the riders seized their opponents and tried to drag them from their horses. It had become mainly a struggle of infantry, fierce but short, and the Roman cavalry was repulsed and fled. Just as this battle of the cavalry was finished, the infantry became engaged, and as long as the Gauls and Spaniards kept their ranks unbroken, both sides were equally matched in strength and courage. At length after long and repeated efforts the Romans closed up their ranks, echeloned their front,[117] and by the sheer weight of their deep column bore down the division of the enemy that was stationed in front of Hannibal's line and was too thin and weak to resist the pressure. Without a moment's pause they followed up their broken and hastily retreating foe until they took to headlong flight. Cutting their way through the mass of fugitives, who offered no resistance, they penetrated as far as the Africans who were stationed on both wings, somewhat further back than the Gauls and Spaniards who had formed the advanced center. As the latter fell back the whole front became level, and as they continued to give ground it became concave and crescent-shaped, the Africans at either end forming the horns. As the Romans rushed on incautiously between them, they were enfiladed[118] by the two wings, which extended and closed round them in the rear. On this, the Romans, who had fought one battle to no purpose, left the Gauls and Spaniards, whose rear they had been slaughtering, and commenced a fresh struggle with the Africans. The contest was a very one-sided one, for not only were they hemmed in on all sides, but wearied with the previous fighting they were meeting fresh and vigorous opponents.

By this time the Roman left wing, where the allied cavalry were fronting the Numidians, had become engaged, but the fighting was slack at first owing to a Carthaginian stratagem. About 500 Numidians, carrying, besides their usual arms and missiles, swords

[116] The Roman god of the east wind.

[117] By advancing in misaligned columns, a tactic made famous by the Theban general Epaminondas in the 370s and 360s BCE.

[118] Surrounded.

concealed under their coats of mail, rode out from their own line with their shields slung behind their backs as though they were deserters, and suddenly leaped from their horses and flung their shields and javelins at the feet of their enemy. They were received into their ranks, conducted to the rear, and ordered to remain quiet. While the battle was spreading to the various parts of the field they remained quiet, but when the eyes and minds of all were wholly taken up with the fighting they seized the large Roman shields that were lying everywhere among the heaps of slain and commenced a furious attack upon the rear of the Roman line. Slashing away at backs and hips, they made a great slaughter and a still greater panic and confusion. Amid the rout and panic in one part of the field and the obstinate but hopeless struggle in the other, Hasdrubal, who was in command of that arm, withdrew some Numidians from the center of the right wing, where the fighting was feebly kept up, and sent them m pursuit of the fugitives, and at the same time sent the Spanish and Gallic horse to the aid of the Africans, who were by this time more wearied by slaughter than by fighting.

Paullus was on the other side of the field. In spite of his having been seriously wounded at the commencement of the action by a bullet from a sling, he frequently encountered Hannibal with a compact body of troops, and in several places restored the battle. The Roman cavalry formed a bodyguard round him, but at last, as he became too weak to manage his horse, they all dismounted. It is stated that when someone reported to Hannibal that the Consul had ordered his men to fight on foot, he remarked, "I would rather he handed them over to me bound hand and foot." Now that the victory of the enemy was no longer doubtful this struggle of the dismounted cavalry was such as might be expected when men preferred to die where they stood rather than flee, and the victors, furious at them for delaying the victory, butchered without mercy those whom they could not dislodge. They did, however, repulse a few survivors exhausted with their exertions and their wounds.

All were at last scattered, and those who could regained their horses for flight. Cn. Lentulus, a military tribune, saw, as he rode by, the Consul covered with blood sitting on a boulder. "Lucius Aemilius," he said, "the one man whom the gods must hold guiltless of this day's disaster, take this horse while you have still some strength left." The Consul replied: "Cornelius, do not waste in useless pity the few moments left in which to escape from the hands of the enemy. Go, announce publicly to the Senate that they must fortify Rome before the victorious enemy approaches, and tell Q. Fabius privately that I have ever remembered his precepts in life and in death. Suffer me to breathe my last among my slaughtered soldiers." Lentulus escaped on horseback in the rush. The other Consul escaped with about fifty cavalry to Venusia. 45,500 infantry, 2700 cavalry, almost an equal proportion of Romans and allies, are said to have been killed.

Such was the battle of Cannae, a battle as famous as the disastrous one at the Allia River[119]; not so serious in its results, owing to the inaction of the enemy, but more serious and more horrible in view of the slaughter of the army. For the flight at the Allia saved the army although it lost the city, whereas at Cannae hardly fifty men shared the Consul's flight, nearly the whole army met their death in company with the other Consul.

Hannibal's officers all surrounded him and congratulated him on his victory, and urged that after such a magnificent success he should allow himself and his exhausted men to rest. Maharbal, however, the commandant of the cavalry, thought that they ought not to lose a moment. "That you may know," he said to Hannibal, "what has been gained by this battle I prophesy that in five days you will be feasting as victor in the Capitol. Follow me; I will go in advance with the cavalry; they will know that you are come before they know that you are coming." Hannibal told Maharbal that he commended his zeal, but he needed time to think out his plans. Maharbal replied, "You know how to win victory, Hannibal, but you do not how to use it."[120] That delay is believed to have saved the city and the nation.

---

[119] Where the Romans were defeated by the Gauls in 390 BCE; see Reading 77.

[120] One of the most famous quotations of antiquity.

The reports that reached Rome left no room for hope that even these remnants of citizens and allies were still surviving; it was asserted that the army with its two Consuls had been annihilated and the whole of the forces wiped out. Never before, while the city itself was still safe, had there been such excitement and panic within its walls. Over and above these serious disasters, considerable alarm was created by portents that occurred. Two Vestal virgins, Opimia and Floronia, were found guilty of unchastity. One was buried alive, as is the custom, at the Colline Gate,[121] the other committed suicide. L. Cantilius, one of the pontifical secretaries, now called "Minor Pontiffs," who had been guilty with Floronia, was whipped in the Comitium by the Pontifex Maximus so severely that he died under it. This act of wickedness, coming as it did among so many calamities, was regarded as a portent, and the Decemvirs were ordered to consult the Sibylline Books. Q. Fabius Pictor[122] was sent to consult the Oracle of Delphi as to what forms of prayer and supplication they were to use to propitiate the gods, and what was to be the end of all these terrible disasters. Meanwhile, in obedience to the Sibylline Books, some strange and unusual sacrifices were made, human sacrifices among them. A Gallic man and a Gallic woman and a Greek man and a Greek woman were buried alive under the Forum Boarium.[123] They were lowered into a stone vault, which had on a previous occasion also been polluted by human victims, a practice most repulsive to Roman feelings.

Yet, in spite of all their disasters, no one anywhere in Rome mentioned the word "Peace," either before the Consul's return or after his arrival. Such a lofty spirit did the citizens exhibit in those days that although the Consul[124] was coming back from a terrible defeat for which they knew he was mainly responsible, he was met by a vast concourse drawn from every class of society, and thanks were formally voted to him because he "had not despaired of the Republic." Had he been commander-in-chief of the Carthaginians there was no torture to which he would not have been subjected.[125]

---

[121] One of the gates of Rome.

[122] The first Roman writer of history, who wrote in Greek ca. 200 BCE.

[123] The "Cattle Forum" in Rome.

[124] Varro.

[125] For Carthaginian treatment of defeated generals, see Reading 71.

79

THE BACCHANALIAN SCANDAL AND A CRIMINAL INVESTIGATION OF THE IMPACT OF FOREIGN CULTURES ON ROME (186 BCE): LIVY, *FROM THE FOUNDING OF THE CITY*, BOOK 39, CHAPTERS 5–19, AND "THE RECOMMENDATION OF THE SENATE ON THE BACCHANALIANS"

An original copy of the "Recommendation of the Senate on the Bacchanalians," engraved on a bronze plate, still survives, preserved in the Kunsthistorisches Museum in Vienna.

Few examples survive of actual criminal investigations during the Roman Republic. One that does involves investigations into the activities of worshippers of the wine god Bacchus, another name for Dionysus, in the year 186 BCE. During the course of the inquiry, Roman concerns arose regarding threats to their way of life posed by exposure to foreign customs. Roman discomfort about illegal organizations, and especially those that met at night (see the "Twelve Tables," Reading 76), also surfaced. It is our good fortune that two detailed sources on this controversy survive, in the Roman historian Livy's "From the Founding of the City" and in an original copy of the Recommendation[126] of the Senate issued to the two Consuls. Many of the same concerns that arose regarding the Bacchanalians resurfaced centuries later with respect to the Christians; see Reading 107.

Source: Oliver J. Thatcher, ed., *The Library of Original Sources* (Milwaukee: University Research Extension Co., 1907), Vol. III: *The Roman World*, 65–77.

(a) Livy, *From the Founding of the City*, Book 39, Chapters 5–19

The following year diverted Spurius Postumius Albinus and Quintus Marcius Philippus[127] from the care of armies, and wars, and provinces, to the punishing of an intestine conspiracy. Both Consuls were advised to make an inquisition concerning clandestine meetings. A Greek of mean condition came into Etruria, a low operator in sacrifices, and a soothsayer, and a priest of secret and nocturnal rites. These mysterious rites were, at first, imparted to a few, but afterward communicated to great numbers, both men and women. To their religious performances were added the pleasures of wine and feasting, to allure a greater number of proselytes. When wine, lascivious discourse, night, and the mingling of the sexes had extinguished every sentiment of modesty, then debaucheries of every kind began to be practiced, as every person found at hand that sort of enjoyment to which he was disposed by the passion predominant in his nature.

Nor were they confined to one species of vice, the promiscuous mingling of free-born men and women, but from this store-house of villainy proceeded false witnesses, counterfeit seals, false evidences, and pretended discoveries. From the same place, too, proceeded poison and secret murders, so that in some cases, not even the bodies could be found for burial. Many of their audacious deeds were brought about by treachery, but most of them by force. It served to conceal the violence, that, on account of the loud shouting, and the noise of drums and cymbals, none of the cries uttered by the persons suffering violence or murder could be heard abroad.

The infection of this mischief, like that from the contagion of disease, spread from Etruria to Rome, where the size of the city affording greater room for such evils and more means of concealment, cloaked it at first, but information of it was at length brought to the Consul, Postumius, principally in the following manner. Publius Aebutius, whose father had held equestrian rank in the army,[128] was left an orphan, and his guardians having died, he was educated under the

[126] Traditionally, the Latin term "senatus consultum" has been translated as "Decree of the Senate." But the Senate was not a constitutional body and did not issue legislation. The most it could do was give advice and make recommendations. The advice usually was followed, and had the *de facto* force of law, but *de iure*, all the Senate did was issue "Consultationes" ("Recommendations").

[127] Consuls for the year 186 BCE.

[128] That is, that he had been granted a "public horse," a great honor.

eye of his mother Duronia, and his stepfather Titus Sempronius Rutilus. Duronia was entirely devoted to her husband; and Sempronius, having managed the guardianship in such a manner that he could not give an account of the property, wished that his ward should be either made away with, or bound to compliance with his will by some strong tie. The Bacchanalian rites were the only way to effect the ruin of the youth. His mother told him, that, "during his sickness, she had made a vow for him, that if he should recover, she would initiate him among the Bacchanalians."

There was a freedwoman called Hispala Fecenia, a noted courtesan, but deserving of a better lot than the mode of life to which she had been accustomed when very young and a slave, and by which she had maintained herself since her manumission. As they lived in the same neighborhood, an intimacy subsisted between her and Aebutius, which was far from being injurious to the young man's character or property, for he had been loved and wooed by her unsolicited, and as his friends supplied his wants ungenerously, he was supported by the generosity of this woman. To such a length did she go under the influence of her affection, that, on the death of her patron, because she was under the protection of no one, having petitioned the Tribunes and Praetors for a guardian[129] when she was making her will, she constituted Aebutius her sole heir.

As neither kept anything secret from the other, the young man, jokingly, bid her not be surprised if he separated himself from her for a few nights; as, on account of a religious duty, to discharge a vow made for his health, he intended to be initiated among the Bacchanalians. On hearing this, the woman, greatly alarmed, cried out, "May the gods will more favorably!" affirming that it would be better, both for him and her, to lose their lives than that he should do such a thing. She then imprecated curses, vengeance, and destruction on the head of those who advised him to such a step. The young man, surprised both at her expressions and at the violence of her alarm, bid her refrain from curses, for it was his mother who ordered him to do so, with the approbation of his stepfather. "Then," said she, "your stepfather is in haste to destroy, by that act, your chastity, your character, your hopes, and your life."

To him, now surprised by such language, and inquiring what was the matter, she said that when she was a slave, she had gone into that place of worship as an attendant on her mistress, but that, since she had obtained her liberty, she had never once gone near it: that she knew it to be the receptacle of all kinds of debaucheries; that it was well known that, for two years past, no one older than twenty had been initiated there. When any person was introduced he was delivered as a victim to the priests, who led him away to a place resounding with shouts, the sound of music, and the beating of cymbals and drums, lest his cries, while suffering violation, should be heard abroad. She then entreated and besought him to put an end to that matter in some way or other and not to plunge himself into a situation where he must first suffer, and afterward commit, everything that was abominable. Nor did she quit him until the young man gave her his promise to keep himself clear of those rites.

When he came home, he told his mother that he did not intend to be initiated. His stepfather was present at this discourse. His mother on one side and his stepfather on the other, loading him with reproaches, drove him out of the house, assisted by four slaves. The youth repaired to his aunt Aebutia, told her the reason of his being turned out by his mother, and the next day, by her advice, gave information of the affair to the Consul Postumius, without any witnesses of the interview.

The Consul dismissed him, with an order to come again on the third day following. In the mean time, he inquired of his mother-in-law Sulpicia, a woman of respectable character, whether she knew an old matron called Aebutia, who lived on the Aventine Hill. When she answered that she knew her well, and that Aebutia was a woman of virtue, and of the ancient purity of morals, he said that he required a conference with her, and that a messenger should be sent for her to come. Aebutia, on receiving the message, came to Sulpicia's house, and the Consul, soon after, coming in, as if by accident, introduced a conversation

[129] A temporary guardian, just for the purpose of filing the will. Women were not allowed to submit documents with their own hand, so courts had stand-in men to perform this service.

about Aebutius, her brother's son. The tears of the woman burst forth, and she began to lament the unhappy lot of the youth, who, after being robbed of his property by persons whom it least of all became, was then residing with her, being driven out of doors by his mother, because, being a good youth, he refused to be initiated in ceremonies devoted to lewdness, as report goes.

The Consul, thinking that he had made sufficient inquiries concerning Aebutius, and that his testimony was unquestionable, having dismissed Aebutia, requested his mother-in-law to send again to the Aventine, and bring from that quarter Hispala, a freedwoman, not unknown in that neighborhood, for there were some queries that he wished to make of her. Hispala being alarmed because she was sent for by a woman of such high rank and respectable character, and being ignorant of the cause, after that she saw the Lictors[130] in the porch, the multitude attending on the Consul and the Consul himself, was very near fainting. The Consul led her into a retired part of the house, and, in the presence of his mother-in-law, told her that she need not be uneasy, if she could resolve to speak the truth she might receive a promise of protection either from Sulpicia, a matron of such dignified character, or from himself. And that she ought to tell him what was accustomed to be done at the Bacchanalia, in the nocturnal orgies in the grove of Stimula.

When the woman heard this, such terror and trembling of all her limbs seized her, that for a long time she was unable to speak. But recovering, at length she then gave a full account of the origin of the mysteries. "At first," she said, "those rites were performed by women. No man used to be admitted. They had three stated days in the year on which persons were initiated among the Bacchanalians, in the daytime. The matrons used to be appointed priestesses, in rotation. Paculla Minia, a Campanian, when priestess, made an alteration in every particular, as if by the direction of the gods. For she first introduced men; changed the time of celebration, from day to night; and, instead of three days in the year, appointed five days of initiation in each month.

From the time that the rites were thus made common, and men were intermixed with women, and the licentious freedom of the night was added, there was nothing wicked, nothing flagitious, that had not been practiced among them. There was more frequent pollution of men with each other than with women. If any were less patient in submitting to dishonor, or more averse to the commission of vice, they were sacrificed as victims. To think nothing unlawful was the grand maxim of their religion.

The men, as if bereft of reason, uttered predictions, with frantic contortions of their bodies; the women, in the habit of *Bacchantes*, with their hair disheveled, and carrying blazing torches, ran down to the Tiber, where, dipping their torches in the water, they drew them up again with the flame unextinguished, being composed of native sulphur and charcoal. Their number was exceedingly great now, almost a second state in themselves, and among them were many men and women of noble families."

When she had completed her information, she entreated the Consul that he might send her out of the country. The Consul requested his mother-in-law to clear some part of the house, into which Hispala might remove. Accordingly, an apartment was assigned her in the upper part of it. Aebutius, also, was ordered to remove to the house of one of the Consul's clients. When both the informers were by these means in his power, Postumius represented the affair to the Senate. Great consternation seized on the senators, not only on the public account, lest such conspiracies and nightly meetings might be productive of secret treachery and mischief, but, likewise, on account of their own particular families, lest some of their relations might be involved in this infamous affair.

The Senate voted, moreover, that thanks should be given to the Consul because he had investigated the matter with singular diligence and without exciting any alarm. The senators then committed to the Consuls the holding of an inquiry, out of the common course, concerning the Bacchanals and their nocturnal orgies. They ordered them to take care that the

[130] Twelve attendants of the Consul who carried the fasces, bundles of wooden rods with an ax-head projecting from them, symbolizing the power of life and death. In the city proper, the ax-head was removed.

informers, Aebutius and Fecenia, might suffer no injury on that account, and to invite other informers in the matter, by offering rewards. They ordered that the officials in those rites, whether men or women, should be sought for, and be delivered over to the power of the Consuls; and also that proclamation should be made that no persons initiated in the Bacchanalian rites should presume to come together or assemble on account of those rites, or to perform any such kind of worship; and above all, that search should be made for those who had assembled or conspired for personal abuse, or for any other flagitious practices.

The Senate resolved these things. The Consuls directed the Curule Aediles[131] to make strict inquiry after all the priests of those mysteries, and to keep such as they could apprehend in custody until their trial; they at the same time charged the Plebeian Aediles[132] to take care that no religious ceremonies should be performed in private. To the Capitol Triumvirs[133] the task was assigned to post watches in proper places of the city and to use vigilance in preventing any meetings by night.

After dispatching these officers to their several employments, the Consuls mounted the rostrum; and, having summoned a *contio*[134] of the people. One of the Consuls, when he had finished the solemn form of prayer that the magistrates are accustomed to pronounce before they address the people, proceeded thus:

> Romans, to no former *contio* was this solemn supplication to the gods more suitable or even more necessary, as it serves to remind you, that these are the deities whom your forefathers pointed out as the objects of your worship, veneration, and prayers, and not those that infatuated men's minds with corrupt and foreign modes of religion, and drove them, as if goaded by the furies, to every lust and every vice. That the Bacchanalian rites have subsisted for some time past in every country in Italy, and are at present performed in many parts of this city also, I am sure you must have been informed, not only by report but also by the nightly noises and horrid yells that resound through the whole city, but still you are ignorant of the nature of that business. As regards the number, they are many thousands. A great part of them are women, and this was the source of the evil. The rest are males, but nearly resembling women, debauchers and the debauched, night revelers, driven frantic by wine, noises of instruments, and clamors. The conspiracy, as yet, has no strength, but it has abundant means of acquiring strength, for they are becoming more numerous every day.
>
> The impious assembly at present confines itself to outrages on private citizens because it has not yet acquired force sufficient to crush the Republic, but the evil increases and spreads daily. It already is too great for the private ranks of life to contain it, and aims its views at the body of the state. Unless you take timely precautions, Romans, their nightly assembly may become as large as this, held in open day, and legally summoned by a Consul. Now they one by one dread you collected together in the *contio*; presently, when you shall have separated and retired to your several dwellings, in town and country, they will again come together, and will hold a consultation on the means of their own safety, and, at the same time, of your destruction. Thus united, they will cause terror to every one of you.
>
> How often in the ages of our fathers was it given in charge to the magistrates to prohibit the performance of any foreign religious rites; to banish strolling sacrificers and soothsayers from the Forum, the circus, and the city; to search for, and burn, books of divination; and to abolish every mode of sacrificing that was not conformable to the Roman practice? We shall do all these things with the favor and approbation of the gods, who, because they were indignant that their divinity was dishonored by those people's lusts and crimes, have drawn forth their proceedings from hidden darkness into the open light and have directed them to be exposed, not that they may escape with impunity but in order that they may be punished and suppressed.

[131] Two junior magistrates elected from the patrician class to oversee the city infrastructure; they had imperium and were allowed two lictors each.

[132] Two junior magistrates chosen from among the plebeians to care for the city.

[133] Junior magistrates in charge of holding prisoners and executions; they oversaw the closest thing there was to a police force at this time.

[134] A general meeting of the entire population for informational purposes, as opposed to a meeting of a popular assembly.

> The Senate has committed to me and my colleague an extraordinary inquisition[135] concerning this affair. The charge of posting watches through the city during the night we have committed to the inferior magistrates, and, for your part, it is incumbent on you to execute vigorously whatever duties are assigned you, and in the several places where each will be placed, to perform whatever orders you shall receive, and to use your best endeavors that no danger or tumult may arise from the treachery of the party involved in the guilt.

They then ordered the Recommendation of the Senate to be read and published a reward for any discoverer who should bring any of the guilty before them, or give information against any of the absent. They then issued an edict,[136] that no person whatever should presume to buy or sell anything for the purpose of leaving the country; or to receive or conceal, or by any means aid the fugitives. On the *contio* being dismissed, great terror spread throughout the city; nor was it confined merely within the walls, or to the Roman territory, for everywhere throughout the whole of Italy alarm began to be felt when the letters from guest-friends[137] were received, concerning the Recommendation of the Senate, and what passed in the *contio*, and the edict of the Consuls.

During the night, great numbers, attempting to flee, were seized, and brought back by the Triumvirs, who had posted guards at all gates, and accusations were lodged against many, some of whom, both men and women, put themselves to death. Those who, as it appeared, had been only initiated, and had made after the priest, and in the most solemn form, the prescribed imprecations, in which the conspiracy for the perpetration of every crime and lust was contained, but who had not themselves committed, or compelled others to commit, any of those acts to which they were bound by the oath, all such they left in prison.[138] But those who had forcibly committed personal defilements or murders, or were stained with the guilt of false evidence, counterfeit seals, forged wills, or other frauds, all these they punished with death.

A greater number were executed than thrown into prison; indeed, the multitude of men and women who suffered in both ways was very considerable. The Consuls delivered the women who were condemned to their relations, or to those under whose guardianship they were, so that they might inflict the punishment in private. If there did not appear any proper person of the kind to execute the sentence, the punishment was inflicted in public.

With regard to the future, the Senate passed a recommendation that no Bacchanalian rites should be celebrated in Rome or in Italy, and ordering that, in case any person should believe some such kind of worship incumbent upon him, and necessary; and that he could not, without offense to religion, and incurring guilt, omit it, he should represent this to the Urban Praetor, and the Praetor should lay the business before the Senate. If permission were granted by the Senate, when not less than one hundred members were present, then he might perform those rites, provided that no more than five persons should be present at the sacrifice, and that they should have no common stock of money, nor any president of the ceremonies, nor priest.[139]

Spurius Postumius some time after came to Rome, and on his proposing the question, concerning the reward to be given to Publius Aebutius and Hispala Fecenia, because the Bacchanalian ceremonies were discovered by their exertions, the Senate passed a vote, that the City Quaestors should give to each of them, out of the public treasury, one hundred thousand *asses*; and that the Consuls should desire the Tribunes of the Plebs to propose to the plebs,[140] that

[135] Because the Roman government had no permanent officials, offices, or bodies to investigate crimes against the state, all such investigations were ad hoc in nature.
[136] Like Praetors, who could issue certain forms of law in the law courts, Consuls had the power, usually exercised only outside Rome, to issue edicts based on their power of imperium.
[137] Romans who had ties of friendship to Italians passed along reports of what had transpired at the meeting.
[138] Not as punishment, but to await trial.
[139] For the original "Recommendation of the Senate" on which this report is based, see Reading 79b.
[140] That is, to the Council of the Plebs.

Publius Aebutius should not become a soldier against his wishes.

They voted also, that Hispala Fecenia should enjoy the privileges of alienating her property by gift or deed; of marrying out of her rank, and of choosing a guardian, as if a husband had conferred these privileges by will; that she should be at liberty to wed a man of honorable birth[141]; and that there should be no disgrace or ignominy to him who should marry her, and that the Consuls and Praetors then in office, and their successors, should take care that no injury should be offered to that woman, and that she might live in safety. All these particulars were proposed to the Council of the Plebs, and executed, in accordance with the Recommendation of the Senate, and full permission was given to the Consuls to determine respecting the impunity and rewards of the other informers.[142]

(b) *Senatus Consultum de Bacchanalibus* ("Recommendation of the Senate on the Bacchanalians")

Quintus Marcius, the son of Lucius, and Spurius Postumius consulted the Senate on the Nones of October[143] at the Temple of Bellona.[144] Marcus Claudius, son of Marcus, Lucius Valerius, son of Publius, and Quintus Minucius, son of Gaius, were the committee for drawing up the report. Regarding the Bacchanalia, it was resolved to give the following directions to those who are in alliance with us. No one of them is to possess a place where the festivals of Bacchus are celebrated; if there are any who claim that it is necessary for them to have such a place, they are to come to Rome to the Urban Praetor, and the Senate is to decide on those matters after their claims have been heard, provided that not less than one hundred senators are present when the affair is discussed. No man is to be a Bacchantian, neither a Roman citizen, nor one of the Latin name, nor any of our allies unless they come to the Urban Praetor, and he in accordance with the opinion of the Senate expressed when not less than one hundred senators are present at the discussion, shall have given leave. Carried.

No man is to be a priest; no one, either man or woman, is to be an officer to manage the temporal affairs of the organization; nor is anyone of them to have charge of a common treasury; no one shall appoint either man or woman to be master or to act as master; henceforth they shall not form conspiracies among themselves, stir up any disorder, make mutual promises or agreements, or interchange pledges; no one shall observe the sacred rites either in public or private or outside the city, unless he comes to the Urban Praetor, and he, in accordance with the opinion of the Senate, expressed when no less than one hundred senators are present at the discussion, shall have given leave. Carried.

No one in a company of more than five persons altogether, men and women, shall observe the sacred rites, nor in that company shall there be present more

[141] There usually were severe restrictions against marriages between full Roman citizens and persons with a servile background.

[142] All grants of special privileges had to be approved by the Council of the Plebs.

[143] 7 October.

[144] Meetings of the Senate regarding warfare were held on the Capitoline Hill in the Temple of Bellona, an ancient war goddess sometimes said to be married to Mars.

Source: Nina Weston, trans., in Oliver Joseph Thatcher, ed., *The Ideas That Have Influenced Civilization, in the Original Documents*, Vol. III, *The Roman World* (Manchester, UK: Roberts-Manchester, 1901), 76–77.

than two men or three women, unless in accordance with the opinion of the Urban Praetor and the Senate as written above. See that you declare it in the assembly for not less than three market days, so that you may know the opinion of the Senate that this was their judgment. If there are any who have acted contrary to what was written above, they have decided that a proceeding for a capital offense should be instituted against them. The Senate has justly recommended that you should inscribe this on a bronze tablet, and that you should order it to be placed where it can be easiest to read. See to it that the revelries of Bacchus, if there be any, except in case there be concerned in the matter something sacred, as was written above, be disbanded within ten days after this letter shall be delivered to you.

In the Teuranian field.[145]

[145] A comment appended to the document attesting to the place where it was posted in Bruttium in southern Italy, where the tablet was found.

80

A ROMAN "NEW MAN" CONFRONTS GREEK CULTURE (234–149 BCE): PLUTARCH, *LIFE OF CATO THE ELDER*

A severely depicted portrait bust from the Museum of the Villa Torlonia in Rome and known as the "Patrizio Torlonia," ("The Torlonian Patrician,") is a second-century CE copy of an original dating to 80–70 BCE and is thought to represent Marcus Porcius Cato the Elder.

During the second century BCE, the Romans experienced intense cultural pressures as a result of Roman expansion, which brought exposure to different cultures and the assimilation of foreign populations. Some Romans, such as Scipio Aemilianus, the grandson of Scipio Africanus, who had defeated Hannibal, embraced Greek culture and welcomed Greek writers and scholars to Rome. But more conservative Romans were chary of excessive foreign contacts, fearing that old Roman values and virtues were threatened by what they viewed as Greek self-indulgence, immorality, frivolity, and general lack of respect for Roman values. No one was more conservative than Marcus Porcius Cato the Elder, a "new man" from a very undistinguished family who rose to the august offices of Consul in 195 BCE and Censor in 184 BCE. As a newcomer to the Roman nobility, Cato established a reputation for being more senatorial than the established senators by espousing the most extreme practice of what he considered old Roman virtues.

Source: John Dryden, *The Lives of the Noble Greeks and Romans*, revised by A. H. Clough, Vol. 1 (Boston: Little, Brown, 1910).

The family of Marcus Cato, it is said, was of Tusculan[146] origin. His ancestors commonly passed for men of no note whatever, but Cato himself extols his father, Marcus, as a brave man and good soldier. He also says that his grandfather, Cato, often won prizes for soldierly valor, and received from the state treasury, because of his bravery, the price of five horses which had been killed under him in battle. The Romans used to call men who had no family distinction, but were coming into public notice through their own achievements, "New Men," and such they called Cato.[147] But he himself used to say that as far as office and distinction went, he was indeed new, but having regard to ancestral deeds of valor, he was oldest of the old. Near his fields was the cottage which had once belonged to Manius Curius, a hero of three triumphs. To this he would often go, and the sight of the small farm and the mean dwelling led him to think of their former owner, who, although he had become the greatest of the Romans, had subdued the most warlike nations, and driven Pyrrhus out of Italy,[148] nevertheless tilled this little patch of ground with his own hands and occupied this cottage, after three triumphs.[149] He did not learn Greek until late in life, and was quite well on in years when he took to reading Greek books.[150] He never paid more than fifteen hundred denarii for a slave because he did not want them to be delicately beautiful, but sturdy workers, such as grooms and herdsmen, and these he thought it his duty to sell when they got oldish, instead of feeding them when they were useless.[151]

There was at Rome a certain man of the highest birth and greatest influence, who had the power to discern excellence in the bud, and the grace to cultivate it and bring it into general esteem. This man was Valerius Flaccus.[152] He had a farm next to that of Cato, and learned from Cato's servants of their master's laborious and frugal way of living. He was amazed to hear them tell how Cato, early in the morning, went on foot to the market-place and

[146] From Tusculum, a city of Latium, fifteen miles southeast of Rome.

[147] More specifically, "New Men" were individuals who gained the office of Consul after never having had a consular ancestor.

[148] The Roman war with Pyrrhus of Epirus lasted between 280 and 275 BCE. Even though he defeated the Romans several times in battle, he eventually returned to Greece because his extensive losses of manpower had nearly ruined him.

[149] It was believed that the greatest virtue that a Roman senator could manifest was to plow his own fields.

[150] Cato's aversion to Greek culture is discussed more extensively later in the text.

[151] This kind of callous behavior toward agricultural slaves was one of the reasons for the slave revolts of 135, 104, and especially that led by Spartacus in 70 BCE (see Reading 82).

[152] For a person from an undistinguished family to have political success, it was necessary to have powerful patrons. In Cato's case, it was the patrician Lucius Valerius Flaccus, whose father had been Consul in 227 BCE and with whom Cato shared the consulate in 195 BCE and the office of Censor in 183 BCE.

pleaded the cases of all who wished his aid[153]; then came back to his farm, where he worked with his servants and then sat down with them to eat of the same bread and drink of the same wine. They told Valerius many other instances of Cato's fairness and moderation, until at last Valerius gave command that Cato be invited to dine with him. After this, discovering by converse with him that his nature was gentle and polite, and needed, like a growing tree, only cultivation and room to expand, Valerius urged and at last persuaded him to engage in public life at Rome. Accordingly, taking up his abode in the city, his own efforts as an advocate at once won him admiring friends, and the favor of Valerius brought him great honor and influence, so that he was made Military Tribune first, and then Quaestor.[154] After this, being now launched on an eminent and brilliant career, he shared the highest honors with Valerius, becoming Consul with him, and afterwards Censor.

Ten years after his consulship, Cato stood for the censorship. This office towered, as it were, above every other civic honor, and was, in a way, the culmination of a political career. Therefore, when Cato stood for it, nearly all the best known and most influential men of the senatorial party united to oppose him. The men of noble parentage among them were moved by jealousy, thinking that nobility of birth would be trampled in the mire if men of ignoble origin forced their way up to the summits of honor and power, whereas those who were conscious of base practices and of a departure from ancestral customs feared the severity of the man, which was sure to be harsh and inexorable in the exercise of power. Therefore, after due consultation and preparation, they put up in opposition to Cato seven candidates for the office, who sought the favor of the multitude with promises of mild conduct in office, supposing that it wanted to be ruled with a lax and indulgent hand. Cato, on the contrary, threatened wrong-doers in his speeches, and loudly cried that the city had need of a great purification. He adjured the people, if they were wise, not to choose the most agreeable physician, but the one who was most in earnest. He himself, he said, was such a physician, and so was Valerius Flaccus, of the patricians. With him as colleague, he thought he could cut and sear the luxury and effeminacy of the time. So truly great was the Roman people, and so worthy of great leaders, that they elected Flaccus to the office along with Cato. As Censor, Cato made Lucius Valerius Flaccus, his colleague and friend, chief senator.[155] He also expelled many members of the Senate,[156] including a senator who was thought to have good prospects for the consulship, namely, Manilius, because he embraced his wife in open day before the eyes of his daughter. For his own part, he said, he never embraced his wife unless it thundered loudly and it was a pleasantry of his to remark that he was a happy man when it thundered.

Cato was not only his son's reading teacher, but also his tutor in law and his athletic trainer, and he taught his son not merely to hurl the javelin and fight in armor and ride the horse, but also to box, to endure heat and cold, and to swim lustily through the eddies and billows of the Tiber. His *History of Rome*, as he tells us himself, he wrote out with his own hand[157] and in large characters, that his son might have in his own home an aid to acquaintance with his country's ancient traditions. He declares that his son's presence, as much as that of the so-called Vestal Virgins,[158] put him on his guard against indecencies of speech, and that he never bathed with him. This, indeed, would seem to have been a general custom with the Romans, for even fathers-in-law avoided bathing with their

[153] Many newcomers to politics, such as Cicero (see Reading 83), initially made names for themselves as lawyers.

[154] The typical beginning of a senatorial career.

[155] That is, Cato repaid Flaccus for his support by granting him the title of "Princeps Senatus" ("First Man of the Senate"), the greatest honor a Roman senator could receive.

[156] Censors had the right both to admit new worthy members to the Senate and to expel those whom they thought were guilty of misbehavior. Cato used this power to revenge himself on some of his enemies, and in so doing he created for himself even more enemies.

[157] Cato wrote his history, which does not survive, in Latin, contrary to the existing custom of writing in Greek. Subsequently, Latin became a literary language in its own right.

[158] The six most distinguished women in Rome, in whose presence one always was on one's best behavior.

sons-in-law, because they were ashamed to uncover their nakedness. Afterward, however, when the Romans had learned from the Greeks their freedom in going naked, they in their turn infected the Greeks with the practice even when women were present.

When Cato was now well on in years, there came as ambassadors from Athens to Rome, Carneades the Academic,[159] and Diogenes, the Stoic philosopher,[160] to beg the reversal of a certain decision against the Athenian people, which imposed upon them a fine of five hundred talents. Upon the arrival of these philosophers, the most studious of the city's youth hastened to wait upon them, and became their devoted and admiring listeners. The charm of Carneades especially, which had boundless power, and a fame not inferior to its power, won large and sympathetic audiences, and filled the city, like a rushing mighty wind, with the noise of his praises. Report spread far and wide that a Greek of amazing talent, who disarmed all opposition by the magic of his eloquence, had infused a tremendous passion into the youth of the city, in consequence of which they forsook their other pleasures and pursuits and were "possessed" about philosophy. The other Romans were pleased at this, and glad to see their young men lay hold of Greek culture and consort with such admirable men.

Cato, however, at the very outset, when this zeal for discussion came pouring into the city, was distressed, fearing lest the young men, by giving this direction to their ambition, should come to love a reputation based on mere words more than one achieved by martial deeds. And when the fame of the visiting philosophers rose yet higher in the city, and their first speeches before the Senate were interpreted, at his own instance and request by so conspicuous a man as Gaius Acilius,[161] Cato determined, on some decent pretext or other, to rid and purge the city of them all. So he rose in the Senate and censured the magistrates for keeping in such long suspense an embassy composed of men who could easily secure anything they wished, so persuasive were they. "We ought," he said, "to make up our minds one way or another, and vote on what the embassy proposes, in order that these men may return to their schools and lecture to the sons of Greece, while the youth of Rome give ear to their laws and magistrates, as heretofore."

This he did, not, as some think, out of personal hostility to Carneades, but because he was wholly averse to philosophy, and made mock of all Greek culture and training, out of patriotic zeal. He said, for instance, that Socrates[162] was a mighty prattler, who attempted, as best he could, to be his country's tyrant, by abolishing its customs, and by enticing his fellow citizens into opinions contrary to the laws. He made fun of the school of Isocrates,[163] declaring that his pupils kept on studying with him until they were old men, as if they were to practice their arts and plead their cases before Minos in Hades.[164] And seeking to prejudice his son against Greek culture, he indulged in an utterance all too rash for his years, declaring, in the tone of a prophet or a seer, that Rome would lose her empire when she had become infected with Greek letters. But time has certainly shown the emptiness of this ill-boding speech of his, for while the city was at the zenith of its empire, she made every form of Greek learning and culture her own.[165]

It was not only Greek philosophers that he hated, but he also was suspicious of Greeks who practiced medicine at Rome. He had heard, it would seem, of

[159] Carneades was the head of the "Academy," the philosophical school founded in Athens by Plato (see Reading 60). He espoused "skepticism," the belief that it was impossible to know anything about anything exactly.

[160] A Greek from Seleucia in Babylonia and the head of the Stoic school in Athens; see Reading 66. A third Greek philosopher on the embassy was Critolaus, who represented the "Peripatetic" school based on the teachings of Aristotle, on whom see Reading 65.

[161] A Roman Senator who interpreted the speeches of the Greek philosophers and wrote, in Greek, a history of Rome.

[162] For Socrates, see Reading 60.

[163] A famous Athenian teacher of oratory in the first half of the fourth century BCE.

[164] Minos, the legendary king of Crete, became the judge of deceased spirits in Hades, the underworld.

[165] Plutarch, a Greek himself, naturally spoke here on behalf of Greek culture.

Hippocrates'[166] reply when the Great King of Persia consulted him, with the promise of a fee of many talents, namely, that he would never put his skill at the service of barbarians who were enemies of Greece. He said all Greek physicians had taken a similar oath, and urged his son to beware of them all. He himself, he said, had written a book of recipes, which he followed in the treatment and regimen of any who were sick in his family. He never required his patients to fast, but fed them on greens, and on bits of duck, pigeon, or hare. Such a diet, he said, was light and good for sick people, except that it often causes dreams. By following such treatment and regimen he said he had good health himself, and kept his family in good health.

He composed speeches, then, on all sorts of subjects, and histories, and as for farming, he followed it in earnest when he was young and poor, indeed, he says he then had only two ways of getting money, farming and frugality, but in later life he was only a theoretical and fancy farmer. He also composed a book on farming,[167] in which he actually gave recipes for making cakes and preserving fruit, so ambitious was he to be superior and peculiar in everything.

The last of his public services is supposed to have been the destruction of Carthage.[168] It was Scipio the Younger[169] who actually brought the task to completion, but it was largely in consequence of the advice and counsel of Cato that the Romans undertook the war. It was in this manner. Cato was sent on an embassy to the Carthaginians and to Masinissa the Numidian,[170] who were at war with one another, to inquire into the grounds of their quarrel. Masinissa had been a friend of the Roman people from the first, and the Carthaginians had entered into treaty relations with Rome after their defeat by the elder Scipio.[171] The treaty deprived them of their empire and imposed a grievous money tribute upon them. Cato, however, found the city by no means in a poor and lowly state, as the Romans supposed, but rather teeming with vigorous fighting men, overflowing with enormous wealth, filled with arms of every sort and with military supplies, and not a little puffed up by all this. He therefore thought it no time for the Romans to be ordering and arranging the affairs of Masinissa and the Numidians, but that unless they should repress a city which had always been their malignant foe, now that its power was so incredibly grown, they would be involved again in dangers as great as before.[172] Accordingly, he returned with speed to Rome, and advised the Senate that the former calamitous defeats of the Carthaginians had diminished not so much their power as their foolhardiness, and were likely to render them in the end not weaker, but more expert in war. Their present contest with Numidia was but a prelude to a contest with Rome, whereas peace and treaty were mere names wherewith to cover their postponement of war until a fit occasion offered.

In addition to this, it is said that Cato contrived to drop a Libyan fig in the Senate, as he shook out the folds of his toga, and then, as the senators admired its size and beauty, said that the country where it grew was only three days' sail from Rome. And in one thing he was even more savage, namely, in adding to his vote on any question whatsoever these words: "In my opinion, Carthage must be destroyed." In this way Cato is said to have brought to pass the third and last war against Carthage,[173] but it had no sooner begun than he died.

---

[166] The most famous Greek physician, from the Aegean island of Cos; he practiced just before and after 400 BCE.

[167] Cato's "On Agriculture" still survives.

[168] For Carthage, see Readings 71 and 78.

[169] Scipio Aemilianus, adopted by Scipio the son of Scipio Africanus, who had defeated Hannibal. He was a great supporter of Greek culture.

[170] The peace treaty between Rome and Carthage in 201 BCE had prohibited the Carthaginians from going to war without permission of the Romans. As a result, the native Numidians, led by King Masinissa, has been nibbling away at Carthaginian territory, but the Romans had refused to allow the Carthaginians to defend themselves.

[171] At the Battle of Zama in 202 BCE, where Scipio defeated Hannibal.

[172] A manifestation of the typical Roman paranoia about strong neighbors who might repeat the Sack of Rome by the Gauls in 390 BCE.

[173] From 149 to 146 BCE, when Carthage finally was captured and destroyed by Scipio Aemilianus.

CHAPTER 11

Crisis, Recovery, and the Creation of the Principate (150–21 BCE)

During the second century BCE, Rome became the most powerful state in the Mediterranean world, and, even though we still call it the Republic, it amassed an empire of provinces extending from Spain to Anatolia. The creation of this empire placed tremendous stress on administration and politics. Rome's city-state form of government was not designed to handle an overseas empire. The need to raise large professional armies was inconsistent with the Roman tradition of armies recruited from peasant farmers. And powerful ambitious senators, in command of these large armies, increasingly tended to put their own personal ambitions ahead of the best interests of the Roman state. Combined, these factors eventually led to the fall of the Republic as it initially had been established.

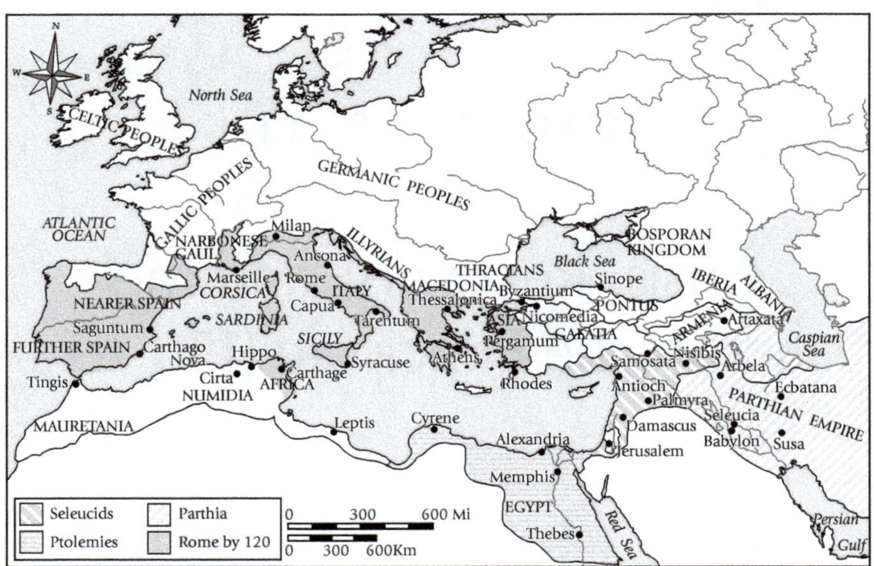

Map 11 The Roman Republic and Its Neighbors in 120 BCE

81

THE LAND LAW OF TIBERIUS GRACCHUS (133 BCE): PLUTARCH, *LIFE OF TIBERIUS GRACCHUS*

The reforms of the Gracchi brothers were facilitated by the introduction of a secret ballot in the popular assemblies in 139 BCE, only six years earlier. The law was intended to reduce bribery and intimidation, but a more significant result was that voters no longer could be observed directly by their patrons. On the reverse of this denarius, issued in 113 BCE, one voter receives a ballot from an attendant and another places his ballot in an urn.

In 133 BCE, Tiberius Gracchus was a decorated war hero with impeccable family credentials: he was the maternal grandson of Scipio Africanus, who had defeated Hannibal in 202 BCE, and his sister was married to Scipio Aemilianus, who had destroyed Carthage in 146 BCE. If he had worked within the system, he could have expected to have a stellar political career, but instead he chose to become a reformer. Realizing that it was becoming more and more difficult to find recruits for the Roman army who met the requirement for property ownership, as Tribune of the Plebs he proposed legislation to distribute Public Land (land owned by the government) to landless plebeians and thus make them eligible for military service. The introduction of this law brought a resurgence of the same class conflicts as had been manifested between the Consuls Paullus and Varro before the Battle of Cannae in 216 CE (Reading 78). The law was opposed vigorously by senators who had been renting the land and looked on it as their own. Tiberius therefore ignored tradition and took his law directly to the Council of the Plebs without consulting the Senate. The law passed. Soon thereafter, Tiberius again violated tradition for running for Tribune of the Plebs a second time in a row. This was too much for the senators, who instigated a riot and clubbed Tiberius to death. This was the first use of violence in Roman politics. It would not be the last. These reforms of Tiberius and the subsequent reforms of his brother Gaius Gracchus (123-121 BCE) marked the beginning of the end of the Roman Republic. Senators on both sides of issues were no longer able to reach behind-the-scenes compromises as they had in the past and were increasingly willing to put their own personal ideas about what was good for Rome ahead of the best interests of the state as a whole. As a result, the hard-won unity within the Senate that had allowed the Senate to govern effectively began to break down, and other groups, such as the Knights, the Italian allies, and the plebs, assumed greater roles in politics. The pursuit of senatorial self-interest would culminate with generals who were willing to use their armies to seize control of the government. Tiberius's career is fulsomely discussed by the second-century CE Greek biographer Plutarch.

Source: John Dryden, *The Lives of the Noble Greeks and Romans*, revised by A. H. Clough, Vol. 1 (Boston: Little, Brown, 1910).

Tiberius and Gaius were sons of Tiberius Gracchus, who, although he had been Censor[1] at Rome, twice Consul, and had celebrated two triumphs, derived his more illustrious dignity from his virtue. Therefore, after the death of the Scipio who conquered Hannibal, he was judged worthy to take Scipio's daughter Cornelia in marriage. A short time afterward he died, leaving Cornelia with twelve children by him. Cornelia took charge of the children and of the estate, and showed herself so discreet, so good a mother, and so magnanimous, that Tiberius was thought to have been made no bad decision when he elected to die. For when Ptolemy the king offered to share his crown with her and sought her hand in marriage, she refused him, and remained a widow. In this state she lost most of her children, but three survived; one daughter, who married Scipio the Younger,[2] and two sons, Tiberius and Gaius, whose lives I now relate. These sons Cornelia reared with such scrupulous care that although confessedly no other Romans were so well endowed by nature, they were thought to owe their virtues more to education than to nature. The younger Tiberius, accordingly, serving in Africa under the younger Scipio, who had married his sister, and sharing his commander's tent, soon learned to understand that commander's nature and soon led all the young men in discipline and bravery; yes, he was first to scale the enemies' wall.

While he remained with the army Tiberius was the object of much good will, and on leaving it he was greatly missed. Tiberius then began to agitate his agrarian laws. The occasion of this was as follows. Of the territory that the Romans won in war

[1] Two Censors were appointed every five years to take the census (a survey of property ownership), oversee the membership list of the Senate, and let out contracts for construction work. For the office of Censor, see also Reading 80.

[2] Cornelia's daughter Sempronia married her cousin, Scipio Aemilianus, grandson of Scipio Africanus.

from their neighbors, a part they sold, and part they made public land, and assigned it for occupation to the poor and indigent among the citizens on payment of a small rent into the public treasury. And when the rich began to offer larger rents and drove out the poor, a law was enacted forbidding the holding by one person of more than five hundred acres of land. For a short time this enactment gave a check to the rapacity of the rich, and was of assistance to the poor, who remained in their places on the land that they had rented and occupied the allotment that each had held from the outset. But later on the neighboring rich men, by means of fictitious personages, transferred these rentals to themselves and finally held most of the land openly in their own names. Then the poor, who had been ejected from their land, no longer showed themselves eager for military service and neglected the bringing up of children. Soon all Italy was conscious of a dearth of freemen and was filled with gangs of foreign slaves, by whose aid the rich cultivated their estates, from which they had driven away the free citizens. An attempt was therefore made to rectify this evil by Gaius Laelius the comrade of Scipio,[3] but the men of influence opposed his measures, and he, fearing the disturbance that might ensue, desisted, and received the surname of "The Wise" (for the Latin word "sapiens" has that meaning). Tiberius, however, on being elected Tribune of the Plebs, took the matter directly in hand. His brother Gaius, in a certain pamphlet, wrote that as Tiberius was passing through Tuscany[4] on his way to Numantia,[5] and observed the dearth of inhabitants in the country and that those who tilled its soil or tended its flocks there were barbarian slaves, he then first conceived the public policy that was the cause of countless ills to the two brothers. The energy and ambition of Tiberius, however, were most of all kindled by the people themselves, who posted writings on porticoes, house-walls, and monuments calling upon him to recover for the poor the public land.

[3] That is, Scipio Africanus.

[4] In northwestern Italy, homeland of the Etruscans.

[5] The final stronghold of rebels in Spain.

He did not, however, draw up his law by himself, but took counsel with the citizens who were foremost in virtue and reputation, among whom were Crassus the Pontifex Maximus, Mucius Scaevola the jurist,[6] who then was Consul, and Appius Claudius,[7] his father-in-law. And it is thought that a law dealing with such great injustice and rapacity never was drawn up in milder and gentler terms. For men who ought to have been punished for their disobedience and to have surrendered with payment of a fine the land that they were illegally enjoying, these men it merely ordered to abandon their unjust acquisitions upon being paid the value and to admit into ownership of them such citizens as needed assistance. But although the rectification of the wrong was so considerate, the people were satisfied to let bygones be bygones if they could be secure from such wrong in the future. The men of wealth and substance, however, were led by their greed to hate the law, and by their wrath and contentiousness to hate the law-giver, and tried to dissuade the people by alleging that Tiberius was introducing a re-distribution of land for the confusion of the body politic and was stirring up a general revolution.

But they accomplished nothing, for Tiberius, striving to support a measure that was honorable and just with an eloquence that would have adorned even a meaner cause, was formidable and invincible whenever, with the people crowding around the rostra,[8] he took his stand there and pleaded for the poor. "The wild beasts that roam over Italy," he would say, "have every one of them a cave or lair to lurk in, but the men who fight and die for Italy enjoy the common air and light, indeed, but nothing else. Houseless and homeless they wander about with their wives and children. And it is with lying lips that their imperators[9] exhort the soldiers in their battles to defend tombs and shrines from the enemy, for not a man of them has a hereditary altar, not one of all these many

[6] A legal expert.

[7] Appius Claudius Pulcher, Consul in 143 BCE and later a Censor.

[8] The speaker's platform in the Roman Forum.

[9] Victorious army generals.

Romans an ancestral tomb, but they fight and die to support others in wealth and luxury, and although they are styled masters of the world they have not a single clod of earth that is their own."

Such words as these, the product of a lofty spirit and genuine feeling, and falling upon the ears of a people profoundly moved and fully aroused to the speaker's support, no adversary of Tiberius could successfully withstand. Abandoning therefore all counter-pleading, they addressed themselves to Marcus Octavius,[10] another one of the Tribunes of the Plebs, a young man of sober character, discreet, and an intimate companion of Tiberius. On this account Octavius at first tried to hold himself aloof, out of regard for Tiberius, but he was forced from his position, as it were, by the prayers and supplications of many influential men, so he set himself in opposition to Tiberius and staved off the passage of the law. Now, the decisive power is in the hands of any Tribune who interposes his veto, for the wishes of the majority avail not if one Tribune is in opposition. Incensed at this procedure, Tiberius withdrew his considerate law, and introduced this time one that was more agreeable to the multitude and more severe against the wrongdoers, because it simply ordered them to vacate without compensation the land that they had acquired in violation of the earlier laws.

When the appointed day was come and Tiberius was summoning the people to the vote, the voting urns were stolen away by the party of the rich, and great confusion arose. The supporters of Tiberius, however, were numerous enough to force the issue, and were banding together for this purpose, when Manlius and Fulvius, men of consular dignity, fell down before Tiberius, clasped his hands, and with tears besought him to desist. Tiberius, conscious that the future was now all but desperate, and moved by respect for the men, asked them what they would have him do. They replied that they were not competent to advise in so grave a crisis, and urged him with entreaties to submit the case to the Senate. To this Tiberius consented.

But the Senate in its session accomplished nothing, owing to the prevailing influence of the wealthy class in it, and therefore Tiberius resorted to a measure that was illegal and unseemly, the ejection of Octavius from his office, for he was unable in any other way to bring his law to the vote. In the first place, however, he begged Octavius in public, addressing him with kindly words and clasping his hands, to give in and gratify the people, who demanded only their just rights, and would receive only a trifling return for great toils and perils. But Octavius rejected the petition, and therefore Tiberius, after premising that, because they were colleagues in office with equal powers and differed on weighty measures, it was impossible for them to complete their term of office without open war, said he saw only one remedy for this, and that was for one or the other of them to give up his office. Indeed, he urged Octavius to put to the people a vote on his own case first, promising to retire at once to private life if this should be the will of the citizens. But Octavius was unwilling, and therefore Tiberius declared that he would put the case of Octavius unless Octavius should change his mind upon reflection.

With this understanding, he dissolved the assembly for that day, but on the following day, after the people had come together, he mounted the rostra and once more attempted to persuade Octavius. When, however, Octavius was not to be persuaded, Tiberius introduced a law depriving him of his tribuneship, and summoned the citizens to cast their votes upon it at once. Now, there were five and thirty tribes,[11] and when seventeen of them had cast their votes, and the addition of one more would make it necessary for Octavius to become a private citizen, Tiberius called a halt in the voting, and again entreated Octavius, embracing him and kissing him in the sight of the people and fervently begging him not to allow himself to be dishonored, and not to attach to a friend responsibility for a measure so grievous and severe.

[10] An ancestor of Augustus, the first Roman emperor.

[11] Originally, Roman citizens were distributed among three tribes (from Latin tribus, "one third") based on family descent; subsequently thirty-five geographic tribes, based on place of residence, were used for political purposes.

On hearing these entreaties, we are told, Octavius was not altogether untouched or unmoved; his eyes filled with tears and he stood silent for a long time. But when he turned his gaze toward the men of wealth and substance who were standing in a body together, his awe of them, as it would seem, and his fear of ill repute among them, led him to take every risk with boldness and bid Tiberius do what he pleased. And so the law was passed, and Tiberius ordered one of his freedmen to drag Octavius from the rostra, for Tiberius used his freedmen as officers, and this made the sight of Octavius insultingly dragged along a more pitiful one. Moreover, people made a rush at him, and although the men of wealth ran in a body to his assistance and spread out their hands against the crowd, it was with difficulty that Octavius was snatched away and safely rescued from the crowd; and a trusty servant of his who stood in front of his master and protected him, had his eyes torn out, against the protest of Tiberius, who, when he perceived what had been going on, ran down with great haste to appease the tumult.

After this the agrarian law was passed, and three men were chosen for the survey and distribution of the public land, Tiberius himself, Appius Claudius his father-in-law, and Gaius Gracchus his brother, who was not at Rome, but was serving under Scipio[12] in the expedition against Numantia. These measures were carried out by Tiberius quietly and without opposition. The aristocrats,[13] however, who were vexed at these proceedings and feared the growing power of Tiberius, heaped insult upon him in the Senate. When he asked for the customary tent at public expense for his use when dividing up the public land, they would not give it, although other men often had obtained one for less important purposes, and they fixed his daily allowance for expenses at nine obols.[14] These things were done on motion of Publius Nasica,[15] who surrendered completely to his hatred of Tiberius. For he was a very large holder of public land, and bitterly resented his being forced to give it up.

And now Attalus Philometor[16] died, and Eudemus of Pergamum brought to Rome the king's last will and testament, by which the Roman people was made his heir. At once Tiberius courted popular favor by bringing in a bill that provided that the money of King Attalus, when brought to Rome, should be given to the citizens who received a parcel of the public land, to aid them in stocking and tilling their farms. And as regarded the cities that were included in the kingdom of Attalus, he said it did not belong to the Senate to deliberate about them, but he himself would submit a pertinent resolution to the people. By this proceeding he gave more offense than ever to the Senate, and Pompeius,[17] rising to speak there, said that he was a neighbor of Tiberius, and therefore knew that Eudemus of Pergamum had presented Tiberius with a royal diadem and purple robe, believing that he was going to be king in Rome.[18]

And now Tiberius' friends, observing the threats and the hostile combination against him, thought that he ought to be made Tribune again for the following year. Once more, therefore, Tiberius sought to win the favor of the multitude by fresh laws, reducing the time of military service, granting appeal to the people from the verdicts of the judges, adding to the judges, who at that time were composed of senators only, an equal number from the equestrian order, and in every way at length trying to maim the power of the Senate from motives of anger and contentiousness rather than from calculations of justice and the public good. And when, as the voting was going on, the friends of Tiberius perceived that their opponents were getting the better of the contest, because all the people were not present, and in the first place resorted to abuse of his fellow tribunes, and so protracted the time. Next,

[12] Scipio Aemilianus, who had been appointed when the Roman offensive against the Spaniards bogged down.

[13] The senators who opposed Tiberius.

[14] A small Greek silver coin; this was an insultingly small sum.

[15] Publius Scipio Nasica, a cousin of Scipio Aemilianus and Consul in 138 BCE.

[16] Attalus III (138–133 BE), king of Pergamum in western Anatolia.

[17] Elected Tribune of the Plebs in the next year, 132 BCE, and continued to oppose the Gracchi brothers.

[18] Claiming that a politician wanted to become "king" was the worst accusation that could be made.

they dismissed the assembly, and ordered that it should convene on the following day. Then Tiberius, going down into the Forum, at first supplicated the citizens in a humble manner and with tears in his eyes. Next, he declared he was afraid that his enemies would break into his house by night and kill him, and thereby so wrought upon his hearers that great numbers of them took up their station about his house and spent the night there on guard.

At break of day there came to the house the man who brought the birds with which auspices are taken, and he threw food before them. But the birds would not come out of the cage, with the exception of one, although the keeper shook the cage right hard and even the one that came out would not touch the food, but raised its left wing, stretched out its leg, and then ran back into the cage.[19] At the same time also many of his friends on the Capitol came running to Tiberius with urgent appeals to hasten thither, because matters there were going well. And in fact things turned out splendidly for Tiberius at first, as soon as he came into view the crowd raised a friendly shout, and as he came up the hill they gave him a cordial welcome and ranged themselves about him, that no stranger might approach.

But after Mucius[20] began once more to summon the tribes to the vote, none of the customary forms could be observed because of the disturbance that arose on the outskirt of the throng, where there was crowding back and forth between the friends of Tiberius and their opponents, who were striving to force their way in and mingle with the rest. Moreover, at this juncture Fulvius Flaccus, a senator, posted himself in a conspicuous place and because it was impossible to make his voice heard so far, indicated with his hand that he wished to tell Tiberius something meant for his ear alone. Tiberius ordered the crowd to part for Flavius, who made his way up to him with difficulty, and told him that at a session of the Senate the party of the rich, because they could not prevail upon the Consul to do so, were purposing to kill Tiberius themselves, and for this purpose had under arms a multitude of their friends and slaves.

Tiberius, accordingly, reported this to those who stood about him, and they at once girded up their togas, and breaking in pieces the spear-shafts with which the officers keep back the crowd, distributed the fragments among themselves, that they might defend themselves against their assailants. Those who were farther off, however, wondered at what was going on and asked what it meant. Whereupon Tiberius put his hand to his head, making this visible sign that his life was in danger, because the questioners could not hear his voice. But his opponents, on seeing this, ran to the Senate and told that body that Tiberius was asking for a crown; and that his putting his hand to his head was a sign having that meaning. All the senators, of course, were greatly disturbed, and Nasica demanded that the Consul should come to the rescue of the state and put down the tyrant. The Consul replied with mildness that he would resort to no violence and would put no citizen to death without a trial; if, however, the people, under persuasion or compulsion from Tiberius, should vote anything that was unlawful, he would not regard this vote as binding. Thereupon Nasica sprang to his feet and said: "Because, then, the chief magistrate[21] betrays the state, all you who wish to preserve the laws, follow me!" With these words he covered his head with the skirt of his toga and set out for the Capitol. All the senators who followed him wrapped their togas about their left arms[22] and pushed aside those who stood in their path, no man opposing them, in view of their dignity, but all taking to flight and trampling upon one another.

Now, the attendants of the senators carried clubs and staves that they had brought from home, and the senators themselves seized the fragments and legs of the benches that were shattered by the crowd in its flight, and went up against Tiberius, at the same time smiting those who were drawn up to protect him. Of these there was a rout and a slaughter, and as Tiberius

[19] This was a very bad omen.

[20] Publius Mucius Scaevola, one of the two Consuls and a legal expert.

[21] The Consul Mucius.

[22] To give themselves more room to maneuver because the toga was a very confining garment.

himself turned to flee, someone laid hold of his garments. So he let his toga go and fled in his tunic. But he stumbled and fell to the ground among some bodies that lay in front of him. As he strove to rise to his feet, he received his first blow, as everybody admits, from Publius Satyreius, one of his colleagues,[23] who smote him on the head with the leg of a bench. And of the rest more than three hundred were slain by blows from sticks and stones, but not one by the sword.

This is said to have been the first sedition at Rome, since the abolition of royal power, to end in bloodshed and the death of citizens; the rest although neither trifling nor raised for trifling objects, were settled by mutual concessions, the nobles yielding from fear of the multitude, and the people out of respect for the Senate. And it was thought that even on this occasion Tiberius would have given way without difficulty had persuasion been brought to bear upon him, and would have yielded still more easily if his assailants had not resorted to wounds and bloodshed, for his adherents numbered not more than three thousand. But the combination against him would seem to have arisen from the hatred and anger of the rich rather than from the pretexts that they alleged, and there is strong proof of this in their lawless and savage treatment of his dead body. For they would not listen to his brother's request that he might take up the body and bury it by night, but threw it into the river along with the other dead. Nor was this all; they banished some of his friends without a trial and others they arrested and put to death.

But the Senate, trying to conciliate the people now that matters had gone too far, no longer opposed the distribution of the public land, and proposed that the people should elect a commissioner in place of Tiberius. So they took a ballot and elected Publius Crassus, who was a relative of Gracchus. Moreover, because the people felt bitterly over the death of Tiberius and were clearly awaiting an opportunity for revenge, and because Nasica was already threatened with prosecutions, the Senate, fearing for his safety, voted to send him to Asia. For when people met Nasica they did not try to hide their hatred of him, but grew savage and cried out upon him wherever he chanced to be, calling him an accursed man and a tyrant, who had defiled with the murder of an inviolable and sacred person the holiest and most awe-inspiring of the city's sanctuaries. And so Nasica stealthily left Italy. He roamed and wandered about in foreign lands ignominiously, and after a short time ended his life at Pergamum.

[23] Another one of the Tribunes of the Plebs.

82

THE SLAVE REVOLT OF SPARTACUS (73–71 BCE): PLUTARCH, *LIFE OF CRASSUS*

An inscription put up by C. Popilius Laenas, Consul in 132 BCE, reports that as Praetor, perhaps the year before, he had rounded up 917 slaves in Sicily who belonged to absentee Italian owners. This would have been at the end of the first large Roman slave revolt, which took place in Sicily from 135 to 132 BCE.

Roman mistreatment of large numbers of agricultural slaves purchased at low costs led to several massive slave revolts, as in Sicily between 135 and 132 BCE and then again from 104 to 100 BCE. The greatest slave revolt began in 73 BCE right at home, in Italy, when Spartacus, a Thracian slave being trained as a gladiator, organized a massive revolt that eventually included more than 100,000 slaves. After defeating several Roman military units, the slaves finally were defeated in 71 BCE by the Roman general Crassus. Even though the revolt had failed, the Romans did learn their lesson, and the treatment of slaves generally improved. This also was the last of the Roman slave revolts.

Source: John Dryden, *The Lives of the Noble Greeks and Romans*, revised by A. H. Clough, Vol. 1 (Boston: Little, Brown, 1910).

The insurrection of the gladiators and the devastation of Italy, commonly called the War of Spartacus, began upon this occasion. One Lentulus Batiates trained up a great many gladiators in Capua,[24] most of them Gauls and Thracians,[25] who, not for any fault by them committed, but simply through the cruelty of their master, were kept in confinement for this object of fighting one with another. Two hundred of these formed a plan to escape, but being discovered, those of them who became aware of it in time to anticipate their master, being seventy-eight, got out of a cook's shop chopping-knives and spits, and made their way through the city, and meeting along the way several wagons carrying gladiators' arms to another city, they seized them and armed themselves. And occupying a defensible place, they chose three captains, of whom Spartacus was chief, a Thracian of one of the nomadic peoples, and a man not only of high spirit and valiant, but in understanding, also, and in gentleness superior to his condition, and more of a Grecian than the people of his country usually are. When he first came to be sold at Rome, they say a snake coiled itself upon his face as he lay asleep, and his wife, who at this latter time also accompanied him in his flight, his countrywoman, a kind of prophetess, and one of those possessed with the bacchanal[26] frenzy, declared that it was a sign portending great and formidable power to him with no happy event.

First, then, routing those that came out of Capua against them, and thus procuring a quantity of proper soldiers' arms, they gladly threw away their own as barbarous and dishonorable. Afterward Claudius,[27] the Praetor, took the command against them with a body of three thousand men from Rome and besieged them within a mountain, accessible only by one narrow and difficult passage, which Claudius kept guarded, encompassed on all other sides with steep and slippery precipices. Upon the top, however, grew a great many wild vines, and cutting down as many of their boughs as they had need of, they twisted them into strong ladders long enough to reach from thence to the bottom, by which, without any danger, they got down all but one, who stayed there to throw them down their arms, and after this succeeded in saving himself. The Romans were ignorant of all this, and, therefore, coming upon them in the rear, they assaulted them unawares and took their camp. Several shepherds and herdsmen that were there, stout and nimble fellows, also revolted over to them, to some of whom they gave complete arms, and made use of others as scouts and light-armed soldiers.

Publius Varinius,[28] the Praetor, was now sent against them, whose lieutenant, Furius, with two thousand men, they fought and routed. Then Cossinius[29] was sent with considerable forces to give his assistance and advice, and Spartacus barely missed but very capturing him in person, as he was bathing at Salinae.[30] With great difficulty he made his escape, while Spartacus possessed himself of his baggage, and following the chase with a great slaughter, stormed his camp and took it, where Cossinius himself was slain. After many successful skirmishes with the Praetor himself, in one of which Spartacus took his Lictors and his own horse, he began to be great and terrible, but wisely considering that he was not to expect to match the force of the Republic, he marched his army toward the Alps, intending, when he had passed them, that every man should go to his own home, some to Thrace, some to Gaul. But the slaves, grown confident in their numbers and puffed up with their success, would give no obedience to him and went about and ravaged Italy.

The Senate now not only was moved at the indignity and baseness, both of the enemy and of the insurrection, but also, looking upon it as a matter of alarm and of dangerous consequence, sent out both the Consuls,[31] as to a great and difficult enterprise.

---

[24] An ancient city inland from the Bay of Naples in Italy.

[25] From a rugged area of the Balkans northeast of Greece and Macedonia.

[26] For Bacchanalians, see Reading 79.

[27] Gaius Claudius Glaber, otherwise unknown.

[28] Another Roman officer largely unknown aside from his defeat by Spartacus.

[29] Another lieutenant of the Praetor Varinius.

[30] A spa at an unknown location.

[31] The two Consuls were Lucius Gellius Publicola and Gnaeus Cornelius Lentulus Clodianus.

The Consul Gellius, falling suddenly upon a party of Germans, who through contempt and confidence had straggled from Spartacus, cut them all to pieces. But when Lentulus with a large army besieged Spartacus, he sallied out upon him, and, joining battle, defeated his chief officers and captured all his baggage. As he made toward the Alps, Cassius, who was Praetor of that part of Gaul that lies about the Po, met him with ten thousand men, but being overcome in the battle, he had much ado to escape himself, with the loss of a great many of his men.

When the Senate understood this, it was displeased at the Consuls and, ordering them to meddle no further, it appointed Crassus[32] general of the war, and a great many of the nobility went as volunteers with him, partly out of friendship and partly to get honor. He stayed himself on the borders of Picenum,[33] expecting Spartacus would come that way, and sent his lieutenant, Mummius, with two legions, to wheel about and observe the enemy's motions, but upon no account to engage or skirmish. But Mummius, upon the first opportunity, joined battle, and was routed, having a great many of his men slain and a great many only saving their lives with the loss of their arms. Crassus rebuked Mummius severely, and arming the soldiers again, he made them find sureties[34] for their arms, that they would part with them no more, and five hundred that were the first to flee he divided into fifty tens, and one of each was to die by lot, thus reviving the ancient Roman punishment of decimation,[35] where ignominy is added to the penalty of death, with a variety of appalling and terrible circumstances, presented before the eyes of the whole army, assembled as spectators.

After he thus had reclaimed his men, he led them against the enemy; but Spartacus retreated through Lucania[36] toward the sea, and in the straits meeting with some Cilician[37] pirate ships, he had thoughts of attempting Sicily, where, by landing two thousand men, he hoped to new kindle the war of the slaves, which was but lately extinguished,[38] and seemed to need but little fuel to set it burning again. But after the pirates had struck a bargain with him, and received his earnest they deceived him and sailed away. He thereupon retired again from the sea and established his army in the peninsula of Rhegium.[39] There Crassus came upon him, and considering the nature of the place he set to work to build a wall across the isthmus, thus keeping his soldiers at once from idleness and his foes from forage. This great and difficult work he perfected in a space of time short beyond all expectation, making a ditch from one sea to the other, over the neck of land, three hundred furlongs[40] long, fifteen feet broad, and as much in depth, and above it built a wonderfully high and strong wall. All of which Spartacus at first slighted and despised, but when provisions began to fail and he found he was walled in and no more food was to be had in the peninsula, taking the opportunity of a snowy, stormy night, he filled up part of the ditch with earth and boughs of trees and so passed the third part of his army over.

Crassus was afraid lest Spartacus should march directly to Rome, but was soon eased of that fear when he saw many of his men break out in a mutiny and quit him and encamp by themselves upon the Lucanian lake. Crassus, falling upon these, beat them from the lake, but he could not pursue the slaughter because of Spartacus suddenly coming up and checking the flight. Now he began to repent that he had previously written to the Senate to call Lucullus out of Thrace[41] and Pompey out of Spain,[42] so that he did

[32] Marcus Licinius Crassus Dives ("The Rich"); given that there already were two Consuls, he was given the rank of Praetor.

[33] A region on the northeastern coast of Italy.

[34] Guarantors.

[35] A punishment where every tenth man is selected to be beaten to death by his own comrades.

[36] A region of southern Italy.

[37] Cicilia was a mountainous area on the coast of southern Anatolia known for its pirates.

[38] Actually, twenty-nine years earlier, in 101 BCE.

[39] On the top of the toe of Italy.

[40] A furlong equals 660 feet.

[41] Marcus Lucullus was Consul in 73 BCE and then in the following year was Proconsul of Macedonia, where he fought the Bessi in Thrace, northeast of Greece, before being recalled to assist in the campaign against Spartacus.

[42] The Roman general Gnaeus Pompey was in Spain mopping up the suppression of a revolt by the Roman general Sertorius.

all he could to finish the war before they came, knowing that the honor of the action would redound to him that came to his assistance. Resolving, therefore, first to set upon those that had mutinied and encamped apart, whom Gaius Cannicius and Castus commanded, he sent six thousand men before to secure a little eminence and to do it as secretly as possible. To do so, they covered their helmets, but having been discovered by two women who were sacrificing for the enemy, they would have been in great danger had not Crassus immediately appeared and engaged in a battle that proved a most bloody one. Of twelve thousand three hundred whom he killed, two only were found wounded in their backs, the rest all having died standing in their ranks and fighting bravely.

Spartacus, after this discomfiture, retired to the mountains of Petelia,[43] but Quintius, one of Crassus's officers, and Scrofa, the Quaestor, pursued and overtook him. But when Spartacus rallied and faced them, they were utterly routed and fled, and had much ado to carry off their Quaestor, who was wounded. This success, however, ruined Spartacus, because it encouraged the slaves, who now disdained any longer to avoid fighting or to obey their officers. While they were upon the march they came to their officers with their swords in their hands and compelled them to lead them back again through Lucania, against the Romans, the very thing that Crassus was eager for. For news already had arrived that Pompey was at hand, and people began to talk openly that the honor was reserved to him, who would come and at once oblige the enemy to fight and put an end to the war. Crassus, therefore, eager to fight a decisive battle, encamped very near the enemy, and began to make lines of circumvallation,[44] but the slaves made a sally and attacked the workers. Spartacus, seeing there was no avoiding it, set all his army in array and when his horse was brought him, he drew out his sword and killed him, saying that if he won the day he would have a great many better horses of the enemies and if he lost it he should have no need of a horse. And so making directly toward Crassus himself, through the midst of arms and wounds, he missed him, but slew two centurions that fell upon him together. At last being deserted by those that were about him, he himself stood his ground, and, surrounded by the enemy, bravely defending himself, he was cut in pieces.

Although Crassus had good fortune, and not only played the part of a good general but also gallantly exposed his person, yet Pompey received much of the credit of the action. For he met with many of the fugitives and slew them, and wrote to the Senate that Crassus indeed had vanquished the slaves in a pitched battle but that he had put an end to the war. Pompey was honored with a magnificent triumph for his conquest over Sertorius and Spain, whereas Crassus could not so much as desire a triumph in its full form, and it even was thought mean of him to accept of the lesser honor, called the ovation, for a servile war, and perform a procession on foot.[45]

---

[43] On the coast of southwestern Italy.

[44] A circular line of siege works.

[45] A triumph was granted for victories over foreign enemies; in an ovation, a lesser ceremony, the victorious general walked rather than being driven in a chariot.

83

CICERO, *FIRST SPEECH AGAINST CATILINE* (63 BCE)

A fresco by Cesare Maccari (1840–1919) in the Palazzo Madama in Rome, often reproduced in Latin textbooks, depicts Cicero denouncing Catiline, seated alone by himself at the right, before the Senate. In reality, however, Catiline was not actually present when Cicero delivered his famous Catilinarian speeches.

The late Roman Republican politician Marcus Tullius Cicero made his reputation as a good speaker, especially in court cases. By successfully defending influential Roman senators, he made them into his clients. In 64 BCE, he called in his favors and was elected Consul for the following year. In that year, Rome was faced with a crisis when Lucius Sergius Catilina, or Catiline, a failed candidate for Consul, formed a conspiracy to take control of the government. Cicero made several anti-Catiline speeches in the Senate, addressing Catiline as if he were present, when in reality he was in Etruria raising his army. Citing previous examples of when the Senate had caused the deaths of its political opponents, Cicero succeeded in having several of Catiline's co-conspirators executed without a trial. This act was completely contrary to Roman law and eventually led to Cicero's exile.

Source: Charles Duke Yonge, trans., *Select Orations of M. T. Cicero* (New York: Harper, 1877), 1–14.

When, O Catiline, do you mean to cease abusing our patience? How long is that madness of yours still to mock us? When is there to be an end of that unbridled audacity of yours, swaggering about as it does now? Do not the night guards placed on the Palatine Hill,[46] do not the watches posted throughout the city, does not the alarm of the people, and the union of all good men, does not the precaution taken of assembling the Senate in this most defensible place, do not the looks and countenances of this venerable body here present, have any effect upon you?[47] Do you not feel that your plans are detected? Do you not see that your conspiracy is already arrested and rendered powerless by the knowledge that every one here possesses of it? What is there that you did last night, what the night before, where it is that you were, who was there that you summoned to meet you, what design was there that was adopted by you, with which you think that any one of us is unacquainted?

Shame on the age and on its principles! The Senate is aware of these things; the Consul[48] sees them, and yet this man lives. Lives! Aye, he comes even into the Senate. He takes a part in the public deliberations; he is watching and marking down and checking off for slaughter every individual among us. And we, gallant men that we are, think that we are doing our duty to the Republic if we keep out of the way of his frenzied attacks. You ought, O Catiline, long ago to have been led to execution by command of the Consul. The destruction that you have been long plotting against us ought to have already fallen on your own head.

[46] The important hill adjoining the Forum and the site of many posh residences.

[47] Cicero pretends to address Catiline as if he were actually present, but he already had departed to his army in Etruria.

[48] That is, Cicero himself.

What? Did not that most illustrious man, Publius Scipio, the Pontifex Maximus, in his capacity of a private citizen, put to death Tiberius Gracchus, although but slightly undermining the constitution?[49] And shall we, who are the Consuls,[50] tolerate Catiline, openly desirous to destroy the whole world with fire and slaughter? For I pass over older instances, such as how Gaius Servilius Ahala with his own hand slew Spurius Maelius when he was plotting a revolution in the state.[51] There was, there was once such virtue in this Republic that brave men would repress mischievous citizens with severer chastisement than the most bitter enemy. For we have a resolution of the Senate, a formidable and authoritative recommendation against you, O Catiline; the wisdom of the Republic is not at fault, nor the dignity of this senatorial body. We, we alone, I say it openly, we, the Consuls, are wanting in our duty.

The Senate once passed a recommendation that Lucius Opimius, the Consul, should take care that the Republic suffered no injury.[52] Not one night elapsed. There was put to death, on some mere suspicion of disaffection, Gaius Gracchus, a man whose family had borne the most unblemished reputation

[49] Scipio Nasica (see Reading 81), whom, as a consequence of his implication in Tiberius's murder in 133 BCE, the Senate in fact sent away from Rome to Asia, where he died in the same year. Given the importance that Romans placed on following tradition, Cicero's acknowledgment that Nasica acted unconstitutionally at once raises a suspicion that Cicero himself plans to do the same.

[50] Cicero's colleague as Consul was Gaius Antonius Hybrida, the uncle of the Triumvir Mark Antony (see Reading 86).

[51] In 439 BCE; Ahala in fact was charged with murder and, like Nasica, escaped conviction only by going into exile.

[52] In 121 BCE during a protest organized by Gaius Gracchus, the brother of Tiberius; the first example, of the "Senatus consultum ultimum" ("The Last Resolution of the Senate"), which asks the Consuls to see to the safety of the Republic. Gaius and three thousand of his supporters were murdered.

for many generations. There was slain Marcus Fulvius, a man of consular rank, and all his children. By a like Recommendation of the Senate the safety of the Republic was entrusted to Gaius Marius and Lucius Valerius,[53] the Consuls. Did not the vengeance of the Republic, did not execution overtake Lucius Saturninus,[54] a Tribune of the Plebs, and Gaius Servilius,[55] the Praetor, without the delay of one single day? But we, for these twenty days, have been allowing the edge of the Senate's authority to grow blunt, as it were. For we are in possession of a similar Recommendation of the Senate, but we keep it locked up in its parchment, buried, I may say, in the sheath; and according to this recommendation you ought, O Catiline, to be put to death this instant. You live, and you live not to lay aside but to persist in your audacity.

I wish, O Conscript Fathers,[56] to be merciful; I wish not to appear negligent amid such danger to the state; but I do now accuse myself of remissness and culpable inactivity. A camp is pitched in Italy, at the entrance of Etruria, in hostility to the Republic; the number of the enemy increases every day and yet the general of that camp, the leader of those enemies, we see within the walls, aye, and even in the Senate, planning every day some internal injury to the Republic. If, O Catiline, I should now order you to be arrested, to be put to death, I should, I suppose, have to fear lest all good men should say that I had acted tardily, rather than that anyone should affirm that I acted cruelly. But yet this, which ought to have been done long since, I have good reason for not doing as yet. I will put you to death, then, when there shall be not one person possible to be found so wicked, so abandoned, as like yourself, as not to allow that it has been rightly done. As long as one person exists who can dare to defend you, you shall live; but you shall live as you do now, surrounded by my many and trusty guards, so that you shall not be able to stir one finger against the Republic. Many eyes and ears shall still observe and watch you, as they have hitherto done, although you shall not perceive them.

For what is there, O Catiline, that you can still expect, if night is not able to veil your nefarious meetings in darkness, and if private houses cannot conceal the voice of your conspiracy within their wall, if everything is seen and displayed? Change your mind. Trust me. Forget the slaughter and conflagration you are meditating. You are hemmed in on all sides; all your plans are clearer than the day to us; let me remind you of them. Do you recollect that on the 21st of October I said in the Senate, that on a certain day, which was to be the 27th of October, C. Manlius, the satellite and servant of your audacity, would be in arms? Was I mistaken, Catiline, not only in so important, so atrocious, so incredible a fact, but, what is much more remarkable, in the very day? I said also in the Senate that you had fixed the massacre of the nobles for the 28th of October, when many chief men of the Senate had left Rome, not so much for the sake of saving themselves as of checking your designs. Can you deny that on that very day you were so hemmed in by my guards and my vigilance that you were unable to stir one finger against the Republic, when you said that you would be content with the flight of the rest and the slaughter of us who remained? What? When you made sure that you would be able to seize Praeneste[57] on the first of November by a nocturnal attack, did you not find that that colony was fortified by my order, by my garrison, by my watchfulness and care? You do nothing, you plan nothing, you think of nothing that I not only do not hear but also that I do not see and know every particular of.

Listen while I speak of the night before. You shall now see that I watch far more actively for the safety than you do for the destruction of the Republic. I say that you came the night before into the Scythedealers'

---

[53] Consuls in 100 BCE.

[54] A rabble-rousing Tribune of the Plebs elected for the third time in 100 BCE.

[55] Gaius Servilius Glaucia; in 100 BCE when his candidacy for the office of Consul was failing, he and Saturninus engineered the murder of his opponent, which led the Senate to issue the "Last Resolution of the Senate." Both men then were killed.

[56] The members of the Senate.

[57] Modern Palestrina, twenty-two miles east of Rome.

street, to the house of Marcus Lecca; that many of your accomplices in the same insanity and wickedness came there too. Do you dare to deny it? Why are you silent? I will prove it if you do deny it, for I see here in the Senate some men who were there with you. O ye immortal gods, where on earth are we? In what city are we living? What constitution is ours? There are here, here in our body, O Conscript Fathers, in this the most holy and dignified assembly of the whole world, men who meditate my death, and the death of all of us, and the destruction of this city, and of the whole world. I, the Consul, see them; I ask them their opinion about the Republic, and I do not yet attack, even by words, those who ought to be put to death by the sword. You were, then, O Catiline, at Lecca's that night; you divided Italy into sections; you settled where every one was to go; you fixed whom you were to leave at Rome, whom you were to take with you; you portioned out the divisions of the city for conflagration; you undertook that you yourself would at once leave the city, and said that there was then only this to delay you, that I was still alive. Two Roman knights were found to deliver you from this anxiety, and to promise that very night, before daybreak, to slay me in my bed. All this I knew almost before your meeting had broken up. I strengthened and fortified my house with a stronger guard; I refused admittance, when they came, to those whom you sent in the morning to salute me, and of whom I had foretold to many eminent men that they would come to me at that time.

As, then, this is the case, O Catiline, continue as you have begun. Leave the city at last. The gates are open; depart. That Manlian camp[58] of yours has been waiting too long for you as its general. And lead forth with you all your friends, or at least as many as you can. Purge the city of your presence. You will deliver me from a great fear when there is a wall between me and you. Among us you can dwell no longer, I will not bear it, I will not permit it, I will not tolerate it. Great thanks are due to the immortal gods, and to this very Jupiter Stator,[59] in whose temple we are, the most ancient protector of this city, that we have already so often escaped so foul, so horrible, and so deadly an enemy to the Republic. But the safety of the Republic must not be too often allowed to be risked on one man. As long as you, O Catiline, plotted against me while I was the Consul Elect,[60] I defended myself not with a public guard, but by my own private diligence. When, in the next Consular Comitia,[61] you wished to slay me when I was actually Consul, and your competitors also, in the Campus Martius,[62] I checked your nefarious attempt by the assistance and resources of my own friends, without exciting any disturbance publicly. In short, as often as you attacked me, I by myself opposed you, and that, too, although I saw that my ruin was connected with great disaster to the Republic. But now you are openly attacking the entire republic.

You are summoning to destruction and devastation the temples of the immortal gods, the houses of the city, the lives of all the citizens; in short, all Italy. Wherefore, because I do not yet venture to do that which is the best thing, and which belongs to my office and to the discipline of our ancestors, I will do that which is more merciful if we regard its rigor, and more expedient for the state. For if I order you to be put to death, the rest of the conspirators will still remain in the Republic; if, as I have long been exhorting you, you depart, your companions, those worthless dregs of the Republic, will be drawn off from the city too. What is the matter, Catiline? Do you hesitate to do that when I order you what you were already doing of your own accord? The Consul orders an enemy to depart from the city. Do you ask me, are you to go into banishment? I do not order it, but, if you consult me, I advise it.

[58] Catiline's army in Etruria, under the command of Gaius Manlius, an ex-centurion of Sulla, who had seized control of the government in 88 and 82 BCE.

[59] The Senate was meeting not in the Senate house, but in the temple of Jupiter Stator ("Jupiter the Stayer from Flight") near the Forum.

[60] In late 64 BCE.

[61] The Centuriate, or Army, Assembly,

[62] A region outside the sacred boundary of the city, near the Tiber River.

But now, what is that life of yours that you are leading? For I will speak to you not so as to seem influenced by the hatred I ought to feel, but by pity, nothing of which is due to you. You came a little while ago into the Senate. In so numerous an assembly, who of so many friends and connections of yours saluted you? If this in the memory of man never happened to anyone else, are you waiting for insults by word of mouth, when you are overwhelmed by the most irresistible condemnation of silence? Is it nothing that at your arrival all those seats were vacated? That all the men of consular rank, who had often been marked out by you for slaughter, the very moment you sat down, left that part of the benches bare and vacant? With what feelings do you think you ought to bear this? On my honor, if my slaves feared me as all your fellow-citizens fear you, I should think I must leave my house. Do not you think you should leave the city? If I saw that I was even undeservedly so suspected and hated by my fellow-citizens, I would rather flee from their sight than be gazed at by the hostile eyes of every one. And do you, who, from the consciousness of your wickedness, know that the hatred of all men is just and has been long due to you, hesitate to avoid the sight and presence of those men whose minds and senses you offend? If your parents feared and hated you, and if you could by no means pacify them, you would, I think, depart somewhere out of their sight. Now, your country, which is the common parent of all of us, hates and fears you, and has no other opinion of you, than that you are meditating parricide in her case; and will you neither feel awe of her authority, nor deference for her judgment, nor fear of her power?

And yet, why am I speaking? So that anything may change your purpose? So that you may ever amend your life? So that you may meditate flight or think of voluntary banishment? I wish the gods may give you such a mind, although I see, if alarmed at my words you bring your mind to go into banishment, what a storm of unpopularity hangs over me, if not at present, while the memory of your wickedness is fresh, at all events hereafter. But it is worth while to incur that, as long as that is but a private misfortune of my own, and is unconnected with the dangers of the Republic. But we cannot expect that you should be concerned at your own vices, that you should fear the penalties of the laws, or that you should yield to the necessities of the Republic, for you are not, O Catiline, one whom either shame can recall from infamy, or fear from danger, or reason from madness.

You will go at last where your unbridled and mad desire has been long hurrying you. And this causes you no grief, but an incredible pleasure. Nature has formed you, desire has trained you, fortune has preserved you for this insanity. Not only did you never desire quiet, but you never even desired any war but a criminal one; you have collected a band of profligates and worthless men, abandoned not only by all fortune but even by hope. Then what happiness will you enjoy! With what delight will you exult! In what pleasure will you revel! When in so numerous a body of friends, you neither hear nor see one good man. All the toils you have gone through have always pointed to this sort of life; your lying on the ground not merely to lie in wait to gratify your unclean desires, but even to accomplish crimes; your vigilance, not only when plotting against the sleep of husbands, but also against the goods of your murdered victims, have all been preparations for this. Now you have an opportunity of displaying your splendid endurance of hunger, of cold, of want of everything, by which in a short time you will find yourself worn out. All this I effected when I procured your rejection from the consulship,[63] so that you should be reduced to make attempts on your country as an exile instead of being able to distress it as Consul, and so that which had been wickedly undertaken by you should be called piracy rather than war.

Now that I may remove and avert, O Conscript Fathers, any in the least reasonable complaint from myself, listen, I beseech you, carefully to what I say, and lay it up in your inmost hearts and minds. In truth,

[63] In the consular elections in 64 BCE, conservative senators preferred to support Cicero, a "new man" who was not a member of the nobility, against Catiline, a member of an ancient and distinguished patrician family who sought popularity among the plebeians by proposing to cancel all debts.

if my country, which is far dearer to me than my life, if all Italy, if the whole republic were to address me,

> Marcus Tullius, what are you doing? Will you permit that man to depart whom you have ascertained to be an enemy? Whom you see ready to become the general of the war? Whom you know to be expected in the camp of the enemy as their chief, the author of all this wickedness, the head of the conspiracy, the instigator of the slaves and abandoned citizens, so that he shall seem not driven out of the city by you, but let loose by you against the city? Will you not order him to be thrown into prison, to be hurried off to execution, to be put to death with the most prompt severity? What hinders you? Is it the customs of our ancestors? But even private men often in this Republic have slain mischievous citizens. Is it the laws that have been passed about the punishment of Roman citizens? But in this city those who have rebelled against the Republic have never had the rights of citizens. Do you fear odium with posterity? You are showing fine gratitude to the Roman people that has raised you, a man known only by your own actions, of no ancestral renown, through all the degrees of honor at so early an age to the very highest office, if from fear of unpopularity or of any danger you neglect the safety of your fellow-citizens. But if you have a fear of unpopularity, is that arising from the imputation of vigor and boldness, or that arising from that of inactivity and indecision most to be feared? When Italy is laid waste by war, when cities are attacked and houses in flames, do you not think that you will be then consumed by a perfect conflagration of hatred?

To this holy address of the Republic, and to the feelings of those men who entertain the same opinion, I will make this short answer: If, O Conscript Fathers, I thought it best that Catiline should be punished with death, I would not have given the space of one hour to this gladiator to live in. If, forsooth, those excellent men and most illustrious cities not only did not pollute themselves, but even glorified themselves by the blood of Saturninus, and the Gracchi, and Flaccus, and many others of old time, surely I had no cause to fear lest for slaying this parricidal murderer of the citizens any unpopularity should accrue to me with posterity. And if it did threaten me to ever so great a degree, yet I have always been of the disposition to think unpopularity earned by virtue and glory, not unpopularity. although there are some men in this body who either do not see what threatens, or dissemble what they do see; who have fed the hope of Catiline by mild sentiments, and have strengthened the rising conspiracy by not believing it; influenced by whose authority many, and they not wicked, but only ignorant, if I punished him would say that I had acted cruelly and tyrannically. But I know that if he arrives at the camp of Manlius to which he is going, there will be no one so stupid as not to see that there has been a conspiracy, no one so hardened as not to confess it. But if this man alone were put to death, I know that this disease of the Republic would be only checked for awhile, not eradicated for ever. But if he banishes himself, and takes with him all his friends, and collects at one point all the ruined men from every quarter, then not only will this full-grown plague of the Republic be extinguished and eradicated, but also the root and seed of all future evils.

We have now for a long time, O Conscript Fathers, lived among these dangers and machinations of conspiracy; but somehow or other, the ripeness of all wickedness, and of this long-standing madness and audacity, has come to a head at the time of my consulship. But if this man alone is removed from this piratical crew, we may appear, perhaps, for a short time relieved from fear and anxiety, but the danger will settle down and lie hid in the veins and bowels of the Republic. As it often happens that men afflicted with a severe disease, when they are tortured with heat and fever, if they drink cold water, seem at first to be relieved, but afterward suffer more and more severely; so this disease that is in the Republic, if relieved by the punishment of this man, will only get worse and worse, as the rest will be still alive.

Wherefore, O Conscript Fathers, let the worthless be gone, let them separate themselves from the good, let them collect in one place, let them, as I have often said before, be separated from us by a wall. Let them cease to plot against the Consul in his own house, to surround the tribunal of the Urban Praetor, to besiege the Senate house with swords, to prepare brands and torches to burn the city. Let it, in short, be written on the brow of every citizen, what are his sentiments about the Republic. I promise you this, O Conscript Fathers, that there shall be so much diligence in us the Consuls, so much authority in you, so much virtue in the Roman knights, so much unanimity in all good men, that you shall see everything made plain and manifest by the departure of Catiline, everything checked and punished.

With these omens, O Catiline, be gone to your impious and nefarious war, to the great safety of the Republic, to your own misfortune and injury, and to the destruction of those who have joined themselves to you in every wickedness and atrocity. Then do you, O Jupiter, who were consecrated by Romulus with the same auspices as this city, whom we rightly call the stay of this city and Republic, repel this man and his companions from your altars and from the other temples, from the houses and walls of the city, from the lives and fortunes of all the citizens; and overwhelm all the enemies of good men, the foes of the Republic, the robbers of Italy, men bound together by a treaty and infamous alliance of crimes, dead and alive, with eternal punishments.

84

CATULLUS, *POEMS* (CA. 60 BCE)

A wall fresco from Herculaneum, now in the National Archaeological Museum in Naples, depicts a well-to-do Roman couple enjoying each other's company in the same way that Catullus and his lady love "Lesbia," who probably is to be identified with Clodia, sister of the rabble-rousing politician Clodius, did. Curiously, the small female figure to the left has no legs; it has been suggested that this is not a person at all, but some kind of mechanical device, such as a clock, set on a pedestal.

The Roman poet Catullus was one of the so-called "New Poets" who composed avant garde poetry that focused on small-scale personal matters as opposed to more traditional poetry involving gods, heroes, and the Roman state. His poetry is characterized by much use of literary allusion, different meters, and refined vocabulary. His work greatly influenced Augustan poets such as Horace, Ovid, and Vergil.

Sources: Francis Warre Cornish, J. P. Postgate, and J. W. Mackail, trans., *Catullus. Tibullus. Pervigilium Veneris*, revised by G. P. Goold, Loeb Classical Library (Cambridge, MA: Harvard University Press, 1913); Francis Ware Cornish, *The Poems of Gaius Valerius Catullus with an English Translation* (Cambridge, UK: Cambridge University Press, 1904).

Poem 2: The Sparrow

Sparrow, my lady's pet, with whom she often plays while she holds you in her lap, or gives you her fingertip to peck and provokes you to bite sharply, whenever she, the bright-shining lady of my love, has a mind for some sweet pretty play, in hope, as I think, that when the sharper smart of love abates, she may find some small relief from her pain. Ah, might I but play with you as she does, and lighten the gloomy cares of my heart!

Poem 5: "Let Us Live"

Let us live and love, my Lesbia,[64] and a penny for all the talk of morose old sages! Suns may set and rise again; but we, when once our brief light has set, must sleep through a perpetual night. Give me a thousand kisses, then a hundred, then still another thousand, then a hundred. Then when we shall have made up many thousands, we shall confuse the reckoning, so that we ourselves may not know their amount, nor any spiteful person have it in his power to envy us when he knows that our kisses were so many.

Poem 39: Lampoon of Egnatius

Egnatius, because he has white teeth, is everlastingly smiling. If people come to the prisoner's bench, when the counsel for the defense is making everyone cry, he smiles. If they are wailing at the funeral of an affectionate son, when the bereaved mother is weeping for her only boy, he smiles. Whatever it is, wherever he is, whatever he is doing, he smiles. It is a malady he has, neither an elegant one as I think nor in good taste. So I must give you a bit of advice, my good Egnatius. If you were a Roman or a Sabine or a Tiburtine or a thrifty Umbrian or a plump Etruscan, or a black and tusky Lanuvian, or a Transpadane, to touch on my own people too,[65] or anybody else who washes his teeth with clean water, still I should not like you to be smiling everlastingly, for there is nothing more silly than a silly laugh. As it is, you are a Celtiberian,[66] now in the Celtiberian country. The natives rub their teeth and red gums every morning with what they have urinated, so that the cleaner your teeth are, the more urine you are shown to have drunk.

Poem 101: On the Burial of His Brother

Wandering through many countries and over many seas
I come, my brother, to these sorrowful obsequies,
To present you with the last guerdon of death,
And speak, although in vain, to your silent ashes,
Because fortune has taken your own self away from me
Alas, my brother, so cruelly torn from me!
Yet now meanwhile take these offerings, which by the custom of our fathers
Have been handed down—a sorrowful tribute—for a funeral sacrifice;
Take them, wet with many tears of a brother,
And for ever, O my brother, hail and farewell!

[64] The poetic name of the object of the poet Catullus's affections; she usually is identified as Clodia, the sister of the rabble-rousing politician Clodius who was murdered in 52 BCE. The name probably includes an allusion to the famous Greek woman poet Sappho of Lesbos (see Reading 49).

[65] These all are references to cities or regions in Italy.

[66] One of the Celts of Spain.

85

THE SIEGE OF ALESIA (52 BCE): CAESAR, *GALLIC WARS*, BOOK 7, CHAPTERS 68–89

A silver denarius issued in 48 BCE, four years after the defeat of Vercingetorix, depicts on the obverse not a Roman deity, but a Gallic warrior with his hair stiffened back with dried lime in typical Gallic fashion. On the reverse is a Gallic chariot with a driver and spear thrower. The chain around the neck suggests that this may be Vercingetorix himself, who at this time was imprisoned in Rome. He was strangled after Caesar's Gallic triumph in 46 BCE.

In 52 BCE, it seemed that Caesar's conquest of Gaul, which already had been formed into a Roman province, was complete. But the Gauls[67] then found an inspirational leader, Vercingetorix, a chief of the Arvernians, a people of central Gaul. A massive revolt left Caesar's ten-legion 60,000 man army besieging Vercingetorix and 80,000 Gauls in the hill fortress of Alesia at the same time that a relief army of 100,000 Gauls was on its way. To prevent being

[67] For the earlier history of the Gauls, or Celts, see Reading 72.

trapped between two forces, Caesar's army put its engineering talents to work and constructed massive siegeworks around Alesia.

Source: W. A. McDevitte and W. S. Bohn, trans., *Gaius Julius Caesar. Commentaries on the Gallic War* (New York: Harper, 1869).

After his cavalry had been routed, Vercingetorix immediately began to march to Alesia, which is a town of the Mandubii,[68] and ordered the baggage to be speedily brought forth from the camp and to follow him closely. Caesar,[69] having conveyed his baggage to the nearest hill, and having left two legions to guard it, pursued as far as the time of day would permit, and after slaying about three thousand of the rear of the enemy, encamped at Alesia on the next day. On reconnoitering the situation of the city, finding that the enemy were panic-stricken because the cavalry in which they placed their chief reliance had been beaten, he encouraged his men to endure the toil, and began to draw a line of circumvallation[70] around Alesia.

The town itself was situated on the top of a hill, in a very lofty position, so that it did not appear likely to be taken except by a regular siege. Two rivers, on two different sides, washed the foot of the hill. Before the town lay a plain of about three miles in length, and on every other side hills at a moderate distance, and of an equal degree of height, surrounded the town. The army of the Gauls had filled all the space under the wall, comprising a part of the hill that looked to the rising sun, and had drawn in front a trench and a stone wall six feet high. The circuit of the fortification commenced by the Romans extended eleven miles. The camp was pitched in a strong position, and twenty-three fortified places were raised in it, in which sentinels were placed by day, lest any sally should be made suddenly, and by night the same were occupied by watches and strong guards.

The work having been begun, a cavalry action ensues in that plain. The contest is maintained on both sides with the utmost vigor; Caesar sends the Germans to aid our troops when distressed, and draws up the legions in front of the camp, lest any sally should be suddenly made by the enemy's infantry. The courage of our men is increased by the additional support of the legions. The enemy, being put to flight, hinder one another by their numbers, and as only the narrower gates were left open, are crowded together in them. Then the Germans[71] pursue them with vigor even to the fortifications. A great slaughter ensues; some leave their horses and endeavor to cross the ditch and climb the wall. Caesar orders the legions that he had drawn up in front of the rampart to advance a little. The Gauls, who were within the fortifications, were no less panic-stricken, thinking that the enemy were coming that moment against them, and unanimously shout "to arms"; some in their alarm rush into the town. Vercingetorix orders the gates to be shut, lest the camp should be left undefended. The Germans retreat, after slaying many and taking several horses.

Vercingetorix adopts the design of sending away all his cavalry by night, before the fortifications should be completed by the Romans. He charges them when departing that each of them should go to his respective state and press for the war all who were old enough to bear arms. He states his own merits, and conjures them to consider his safety, and not surrender him who had deserved so well of the general freedom to the enemy for torture. He points out to them that, if they should be remiss, eighty thousand chosen men would perish with him, and that upon making a calculation, he had barely grain for thirty days, but could hold out a little longer by economy. After giving these instructions he silently dismisses the cavalry in the second watch,[72] at the point where our works were not completed. He orders all the grain to be brought to

[68] A group of Gallic peoples living in east central Gaul.

[69] So as to make his report seem more objective, Caesar always speaks of himself in the third person.

[70] A circular line of siegeworks; for this tactic, see also Reading 82.

[71] German allies of the Romans.

[72] From about 9:00 PM until midnight.

himself; he ordains capital punishment to such as should not obey; he distributes among them, man by man, the cattle, great quantities of which had been driven there by the Mandubii. He began to measure out the grain sparingly, and by little and little, he receives into the town all the forces that he had posted in front of it. In this manner he prepares to await the reinforcements from Gaul and to carry on the war.

Caesar, on learning of these proceedings from deserters and captives, adopted the following system of fortification: he dug a trench twenty feet deep, with perpendicular sides, in such a manner that the base of this trench should extend so far as the edges were apart at the top. He raised all his other works at a distance of four hundred feet from that ditch. He did that with this intention, lest a large number of the enemy should suddenly, or by night, sally against the fortifications, or lest they should by day cast weapons against our men while occupied with the works. Having left this interval, he drew two trenches fifteen feet broad, and of the same depth; the innermost of them, being in low and level ground, he filled with water conveyed from the river. Behind these he raised a rampart and wall twelve feet high; to this he added a parapet and battlements, with large stakes cut like stags' horns, projecting from the junction of the parapet and battlements, to prevent the enemy from scaling it, and surrounded the entire work with turrets, which were eighty feet distant from one another.

It was necessary, at one and the same time, to procure timber, to lay in supplies of grain, and to raise also extensive fortifications, and the available troops were in consequence of this reduced in number, because they used to advance to some distance from the camp, and sometimes the Gauls endeavored to attack our works and to make a sally from the town by several gates and in great force. Caesar thought that further additions should be made to these works, in order that the fortifications might be defensible by a small number of soldiers. Having, therefore, cut down the trunks of trees or very thick branches, and having stripped their tops of the bark, and sharpened them into a point, he drew a continued trench every where five feet deep. These stakes being sunk into this trench, and fastened firmly at the bottom, to prevent the possibility of their being torn up, had their branches only projecting from the ground. There were five rows in connection with, and intersecting each other; and whoever entered within them were likely to impale themselves on very sharp stakes. The soldiers called these "tombstones." Before these, which were arranged in oblique rows in the form of a quincunx,[73] pits three feet deep were dug, which gradually diminished in depth to the bottom. In these pits tapering stakes, of the thickness of a man's thigh; sharpened at the top and hardened in the fire, were sunk in such a manner as to project from the ground not more than four inches; at the same time for the purpose of giving them strength and stability, they were each filled with trampled clay to the height of one foot from the bottom: the rest of the pit was covered over with osiers and twigs, to conceal the deceit. Eight rows of this kind were dug, and were three feet distant from each other. They called this a "lily" from its resemblance to that flower. Stakes a foot long, with iron hooks attached to them, were entirely sunk in the ground before these, and were planted in every place at small intervals; these they called "spurs."

After completing these works and having enclosed an area of fourteen miles, he constructed, against an external enemy, fortifications of the same kind in every respect,[74] and separate from these, so that the guards of the fortifications could not be surrounded even by immense numbers, if such a circumstance should take place owing to the departure of the enemy's cavalry; and in order that the Roman soldiers might not be compelled to go out of the camp with great risk, he orders all to provide forage and grain for thirty days.

While those things are carried on at Alesia, the Gauls, having convened a council of their chief nobility, determine that all who could bear arms should not be called out, which was the opinion of Vercingetorix, but that a fixed number should be levied from each state lest, if too great a multitude assembled together,

[73] In the shape of the number five on dice.

[74] A wall of contravallation, facing outward rather than inward.

they could neither govern nor distinguish their men, nor have the means of supplying them with grain. Yet such was the unanimity of the Gauls in asserting their freedom and recovering their ancient renown in war, that all earnestly directed their energies and resources to that war, and they collected eight thousand cavalry, and about two hundred and forty thousand infantry.[75] All march to Alesia, sanguine and full of confidence, nor was there a single individual who imagined that the Romans could withstand the sight of such an immense host, especially in an action carried on both in front and rear, when the besieged would sally from the town and attack the enemy, and on the outside so great forces of cavalry and infantry would be seen.

But those who were blockaded at Alesia, the day being past on which they had expected auxiliaries from their countrymen, and all their grain being consumed ignorant of what was going on among the Aedui,[76] convened an assembly and deliberated on the exigency of their situation. After various opinions had been expressed among them, some of which proposed a surrender, others a sally, while their strength would support it. When different opinions were expressed, they determined that those who, owing to age or ill health, were unserviceable for war, should depart from the town. The Mandubii, who had admitted them into the town, are compelled to go forth with their wives and children. When these came to the Roman fortifications, weeping, they begged of the soldiers by every entreaty to receive them as slaves and relieve them with food. But Caesar, placing guards on the rampart, forbade them to be admitted.

In the meantime, Commius[77] and the rest of the leaders, to whom the supreme command had been entrusted, came with all their forces to Alesia, and encamped not more than a mile from our fortifications. The following day, having led forth their cavalry from the camp, they fill all that plain, which, we have related, extended three miles in length, and drew out their infantry a little from that place, and post them on the higher ground. The town Alesia commanded a view of the whole plain. The besieged run together when these auxiliaries were seen; mutual congratulations ensue, and the minds of all are elated with joy. Accordingly, drawing out their troops, they encamp before the town, and cover the nearest trench with hurdles[78] and fill it up with earth, and make ready for a sally and every casualty.

Caesar, having stationed his army on both sides of the fortifications, in order that, if occasion should arise, each should hold and know his own post, orders the cavalry to issue forth from the camp and commence action. There was a commanding view from the entire camp, which occupied a ridge of hills, and the minds of all the soldiers anxiously awaited the issue of the battle. The Gauls had scattered archers and light-armed infantry here and there among their cavalry to give relief to their retreating troops and sustain the impetuosity of our cavalry. Several of our soldiers were unexpectedly wounded by these, and left the battle. When the Gauls were confident that their countrymen were the conquerors in the action, and beheld our men hard pressed by numbers, both those who were hemmed in by the line of circumvallation and those who had come to aid them, they supported the spirits of their men by shouts and yells from every quarter. As the action was carried on in sight of all, neither a brave nor cowardly act could be concealed; both the desire of praise and the fear of ignominy urged on each party to valor. After fighting from noon almost to sunset, without victory inclining in favor of either, the Germans, on one side, made a charge against the enemy in a compact body, and drove them back, and the archers were surrounded and cut to pieces. In other parts, likewise, our men pursued to the camp the retreating enemy, and did not give them an opportunity of rallying. Those who had come forth from Alesia returned into the town dejected and almost despairing of success.

[75] Probably closer to 100,000 soldiers.

[76] The longest and oldest allies of the Romans in Gaul, who likewise had joined the revolt.

[77] King of the Atrebates, a Belgic people, who hitherto had been a loyal ally of Caesar.

[78] Wooden frames used to cover a ditch.

The relieving Gauls, after the interval of a day and after making, during that time, an immense number of hurdles, scaling-ladders, and iron hooks, silently went forth from the camp at midnight and approached the fortifications in the plain. Raising a shout suddenly, that by this intimation those who were besieged in the town might learn their arrival, they began to cast down hurdles and dislodge our men from the rampart by slings, arrows, and stones, and to execute the other movements that are requisite in storming.

While the Gauls were at a distance from the fortification they were more successful, owing to the immense number of their weapons. But after they came nearer, they either unawares impaled themselves on the spurs or were pierced by the darts from the ramparts and towers, and thus perished. After receiving many wounds on all sides, and having forced no part of the works, when day drew nigh, fearing lest they should be surrounded by a sally made from the higher camp on the exposed flank, they retreated to their countrymen. But those within, when they bring forward those things that had been prepared by Vercingetorix for a sally, fill up the nearest trenches. Having delayed a long time in executing these movements, they learned the retreat of their countrymen before they drew nigh to the fortifications. Thus they returned to the town without accomplishing their object.

The Gauls, having been twice repulsed with great loss, consult what they should do. They avail themselves of the information of those who were well acquainted with the country. From them they ascertain the position and fortification of the upper camp. There was, on the north side, a hill, which our men could not include in their works, on account of the extent of the circuit, and had necessarily made their camp in ground almost disadvantageous, and quite steep. Gaius Antistius Reginus, and Gaius Caninius Rebilus, two of the lieutenants, with two legions, were in possession of this camp. The leaders of the enemy, having reconnoitered the country by their scouts, select from the entire army sixty thousand men belonging to those states that bear the highest character for courage. They privately arrange among themselves what they wished to be done, and in what manner. They decide that the attack should take place when it should seem to be noon. They appoint over their forces Vergasillaunus, the Arvernian, one of the four generals and a near relative of Vercingetorix. He, having issued from the camp at the first watch and having almost completed his march a little before the dawn, hid himself behind the mountain and ordered his soldiers to refresh themselves after their labor during the night. When noon now seemed to draw nigh, he marched hastily against that camp that we have mentioned before, and, at the same time, the cavalry began to approach the fortifications in the plain and the rest of the forces to make a demonstration in front of the camp.

Vercingetorix, having beheld his countrymen from the citadel of Alesia, issues forth from the town. He brings forth from the camp long hooks, movable mantlets,[79] wall hooks, and other things that he had prepared for the purpose of making an attack. They engage on all sides at once and every expedient is adopted. They flocked to whatever part of the works seemed weakest. The army of the Romans is distributed along their extensive lines, and with difficulty meets the enemy in every quarter. The shouts that were raised by the combatants in their rear had a great tendency to intimidate our men, because they perceived that their own protection from danger depended on the bravery of others, for generally all evils that are distant most powerfully alarm men's minds.

Caesar, having selected a commanding situation, sees distinctly whatever is going on in every quarter, and sends assistance to his troops when hard pressed. The idea uppermost in the minds of both parties is that the present is the time in which they would have the fairest opportunity of making a struggle, the Gauls despairing of all safety unless they should succeed in forcing the lines, and the Romans expecting an end to all their labors if they should gain the day. The principal struggle is at the upper lines, to which as we have said Vergasillaunus was sent. The least elevation of ground, added to a declivity,[80] exercises a momentous influence. Some are casting missiles,

---

[79] Portable shelters that offer protection from arrow and slingstone fire.

[80] Low point in the terrain.

others, forming a testudo,[81] advance to the attack; fresh men by turns relieve the wearied. The earth, heaped up by all against the fortifications, gives the means of ascent to the Gauls, and covers those works that the Romans had concealed in the ground. Our men have no longer arms or strength. Caesar, on observing these movements, sends Labienus[82] with six cohorts to relieve his distressed soldiers. He orders him that if he should be unable to withstand them to draw off the cohorts and make a sally, but not to do this except through necessity. Caesar himself goes to the rest and exhorts them not to succumb to the toil. He shows them that the fruits of all former engagements depend on that day and hour.

The Gauls within, despairing of forcing the fortifications in the plains on account of the greatness of the works, attempt the places precipitous in ascent. Here they bring the engines that they had prepared. By the immense number of their missiles they dislodge the defenders from the turrets. They fill the ditches with clay and hurdles, then clear the way. They tear down the rampart and breast-work with hooks. Caesar sends at first young Brutus[83] with six cohorts, and afterward Gaius Fabius, his lieutenant, with seven others. Finally, as the Gauls fought more obstinately, he leads up fresh men to the assistance of his soldiers. After renewing the action, and repulsing the enemy, he marches in the direction in which he had sent Labienus, drafts four cohorts from the nearest redoubt, and orders part of the cavalry to follow him, and part to make the circuit of the external fortifications and attack the enemy in the rear. Labienus, when neither the ramparts or ditches could check the onset of the enemy, informs Caesar by messengers of what he intended to do. Caesar hastens to share in the action.

When his arrival becomes known from the color of his cloak,[84] and the troops of cavalry and the cohorts that he had ordered to follow him being seen, as these low and sloping grounds were plainly visible from the eminences, the enemy join battle. A shout being raised by both sides, it was succeeded by a general shout along the ramparts and whole line of fortifications. Our troops, laying aside their javelins, carry on the engagement with their swords. The cavalry is suddenly seen in the rear of the Gauls; the other cohorts advance rapidly; the enemy turn their backs; the cavalry intercept them in their flight, and a great slaughter ensues. Sedulius the general and chief of the Lemovices[85] is slain; Vergasillaunus the Arvernian is taken alive in the flight. Seventy-four military standards are brought to Caesar, and few out of so great a number return safe to their camp.

The besieged, beholding from the town the slaughter and flight of their countrymen and despairing of safety, lead back their troops from the fortifications. A flight of the Gauls from their camp immediately ensues on hearing of this disaster, and had not the soldiers been wearied by sending frequent reinforcements and the labor of the entire day, all the enemy's forces could have been destroyed. Immediately after midnight, the cavalry are sent out and overtake the rear, a great number are taken or cut to pieces, the rest by flight escape in different directions to their respective states.

Vercingetorix, having convened a council the following day, declares, that he had undertaken that war not on account of his own exigencies but on account of the general freedom, and because he must yield to fortune, he offered himself to them for either purpose, whether they should wish to atone to the Romans by his death, or surrender him alive. Ambassadors are sent to Caesar on this subject. He orders their arms to be surrendered, and their chieftains delivered up. He seated himself at the head of the lines in front of the camp. The Gallic chieftains are brought before him.

---

[81] The "tortoise," a formation the soldiers made by interlocking their rectangular shields over their heads.

[82] Caesar's second in command in Gaul, he later became one of Caesar's main opponents in the civil war with Pompey.

[83] A favorite cousin of Caesar who in 44 BCE brought Caesar to the meeting of Senate where Caesar was assassinated; it is this Brutus to whom Caesar referred in the Shakespeare play "Julius Caesar" when he uttered his last words, "Et tu, Brute?" ("And you too, Brutus?").

[84] The scarlet "paludamentum," or general's cloak.

[85] A Gallic people who gave their name to the city of Limoges.

They surrender Vercingetorix and lay down their arms. Reserving the Aedui and Arverni, to attempt to win over, through their influence, their respective states, he distributes one of the remaining captives to each soldier throughout the entire army as plunder. A supplication[86] of twenty-days is ordered by the Senate at Rome on learning of these successes from Caesar's dispatches.

86

CLEOPATRA, PHARAOH AND QUEEN OF EGYPT (48–31 BCE): PLUTARCH, *LIVES OF CAESAR AND ANTONY*

A silver denarius issued in 32 BCE depicts Cleopatra and Antony. The legend on the obverse reads, "Of Cleopatra, Queen of Kings, whose Sons are Kings," and the reverse reads, "Of Antony, after Armenia had been defeated." The coin thus tactfully remains silent about the defeat of Antony's invasion of Parthia.

Cleopatra VII was not only the last of the Ptolemaic rulers of Egypt but also the last of a line of Egyptian pharaohs that extended back to ca. 3000 BCE. Her career overlaid one of the most

[86] A "supplicatio" was a period of public prayer to the gods for salvation from a crisis.

portentous periods of Roman history, the period of civil wars that brought the end of the Roman Republic and the creation of the Roman Empire. As a Hellenistic ruler at a time when the domination of Rome extended across the entire Mediterranean, she exhibited ambition, skill, and tact as she attempted to carve out an Egyptian empire of her own. Plutarch's lives of Julius Caesar and Mark Antony, written in the mid-second century CE, have much to say about the relationship between Cleopatra and these two pre-eminent Roman generals. Cleopatra became, in succession, the lover of both of them, and adroitly used her relationships with them to expand her own authority and power. Antony in particular is portrayed as being completely smitten with Cleopatra and totally under her control. Cleopatra's suicide in 30 BCE, which followed on her and Antony's defeat by Julius Caesar's adopted son Octavian at the Battle of Actium in 31 BCE, brought the independent kingdom of Egypt to an end and helped to make her one of the most admired women of antiquity; a scene of her suicide even appeared in the Christian catacombs of Rome. In Plutarch's *Life of Caesar,* the discussion of Cleopatra picks up after Caesar has followed his defeated rival Pompey to Egypt. Caesar was compelled to spend the winter there and used that opportunity to reorganize the administration of the Ptolemaic kingdom. In the *Life of Antony,* the readings likewise commence after Caesar's victory over Pompey at the Battle of Pharsalus in 48 BCE. In his youth Antony had a reputation in public as an excellent general but in private life as a frivolous, loose-living spendthrift. Both reputations followed him throughout his life.

Source: John Dryden, *Plutarch: The Lives of the Noble Greeks and Romans*, revised by A. H. Clough, Vol. 1 (Boston: Little, Brown, 1910).

(Plutarch, Life of Caesar)

Caesar replied that he did not want Egyptians to be his counselors, and soon after privately sent for Cleopatra from her retirement.[87] She took a small boat and one only of her confidants, Apollodorus the Sicilian, along with her, and in the dusk of the evening landed near the palace. She was at a loss how to get in undiscovered until she thought of putting herself into the coverlet of a bed and lying at length while Apollodorus tied up the bedding and carried it on his back through the gates to Caesar's apartment. Caesar was first captivated by this proof of Cleopatra's bold wit and afterward was afterward so overcome by the charm of her society that he made a reconciliation between her and her brother, on the condition that she should rule as his colleague in the kingdom. There was a plot against Caesar by Achillas, general of the king's forces, who escaped to the army and raised a troublesome and embarrassing war against Caesar. The first difficulty Caesar met with was want of water. Another was, when the enemy endeavored to cut off his communication by sea, he was forced to set fire to his own ships, which, after burning the docks, spread on and destroyed the great library.[88] A third was when, in an engagement near Pharos, he threw himself into the sea and with much difficulty swam off. At last, the king having gone off to Achillas

[87] In 51 BCE, eighteen-year-old Cleopatra VII and her younger brother, ten-year-old Ptolemy XIII, had been made joint rulers of Egypt; following Egyptian tradition, the two also married. In 48 BCE Cleopatra was exiled as a result of a palace conspiracy. Caesar, who had pursued his rival Pompey to Egypt only to find him shockingly beheaded by the retinue of young Ptolemy, recalled Cleopatra from exile.

[88] The great library of Alexandria, founded by King Ptolemy I (323–283 BCE), was said to have been destroyed on several occasions: in 48 BCE; also when the city was recaptured by the emperor Aurelian in 272 CE; again when the temple of Serapis was burned by Christians in 391 CE (see Reading 111); and finally by the Arab general 'Amr in 641 CE (see Reading 125).

and his party, Caesar engaged and conquered them. Many fell in that battle, and the king himself was never seen again. Upon this, Caesar left Cleopatra Queen of Egypt, who soon after had a son by him, whom the Alexandrians called Caesarion, and then departed for Syria.[89]

(Plutarch, Life of Antony)l

Caesar cured Antony of most of his prodigality and folly by not allowing his errors to pass unnoticed. For Antony put away his reprehensible way of living and turned his thoughts to marriage, taking to wife Fulvia, the widow of Clodius the demagogue.[90] She was a woman who took no thought for spinning or housekeeping, nor would she deign to bear sway over a man of private station, but she wished to rule a ruler and command a commander. Therefore Cleopatra later was indebted to Fulvia for teaching Antony to endure a woman's sway, because she took him over quite tamed and schooled at the outset to obey women.

Such, then, was the nature of Antony, when as a crowning evil his love for Cleopatra supervened, roused, and drove to frenzy many of the passions that were still hidden and quiescent in him, and dissipated and destroyed whatever good and saving qualities still offered resistance. He was taken captive in this manner. As he was getting ready for the Parthian war,[91] he sent to Cleopatra, ordering her to meet him in Cilicia[92] in order to make answer to the charges made against her of giving to Cassius much money for the war.[93] But Dellius, Antony's messenger, when he saw how Cleopatra looked and noticed her subtlety and cleverness in conversation, at once perceived that Antony would not so much as think of doing such a woman any harm but that she would have the greatest influence with him. He therefore resorted to flattery and tried to induce the Egyptian to go to Cilicia "decked out in fine array," as Homer would say. She was persuaded, and judging by the proofs that she had had previously of the effect of her beauty upon Gaius Caesar and Gnaeus the son of Pompey,[94] she had hopes that she would more easily bring Antony to her feet. For Caesar and Gnaeus had known her when she was still a girl and inexperienced in affairs, but she was going to visit Antony at the very time when women have the most brilliant beauty and are at the acme of intellectual power.

Cleopatra therefore provided herself with many gifts, much money, and such ornaments as high position and prosperous kingdom made it natural for her to take, but she went putting her greatest confidence in herself and in the charms and sorceries of her own person. She so despised and laughed the man to scorn as to sail up the Cydnus River[95] in a barge with gilded poop,[96] its sails spread purple, its rowers urging it on with silver oars to the sound of the flute blended with pipes and lutes. She herself reclined beneath a canopy spangled with gold, adorned like Venus in a painting, while boys like Cupids in paintings stood on either side and fanned her. Likewise, the fairest of her serving-maidens, attired like Nereïds and Graces,[97] were stationed, some at the rudder-sweeps and others at the reefing-ropes.[98] Wondrous odors from countless incense-offerings diffused themselves along the river-banks. A rumor spread on every hand that Venus[99] had come to revel with Bacchus[100] for the

[89] In 47 BCE.

[90] A political ally of Julius Caesar killed during rioting in Rome in 52 BCE. For Clodius's sister Clodia, see Reading 84.

[91] In 41 BCE.

[92] At the city of Tarsus, on the coast of southeastern Anatolia.

[93] Cassius was one of the assassins of Julius Caesar in 44 BCE and had been defeated by the Triumvirs Octavian and Antony at the Battle of Philippi in 42 BCE.

[94] This is the only surviving reference to a love affair between Cleopatra and Gnaeus, who in 49 BCE had been sent by his father to obtain aid from Egypt in Pompey's civil war with Julius Caesar. He returned with sixty ships.

[95] The modern Berdan River, next to Tarsus.

[96] The back section of a ship.

[97] The Nereïds were sea nymphs who helped sailors during storms. The Graces, known in Greek as the Charites, were minor female goddesses connected to nature and fertility.

[98] The lines used to adjust the sails.

[99] The goddess of love, that is, Cleopatra.

[100] The dissipated god of wine, that is, Antony. For Bacchus worshippers, see Reading 79.

good of Asia. Antony, therefore, invited her to supper, but she thought it fitting that he should rather come to her. At once, then, Antony obeyed and went. Cleopatra observed in the jests of Antony much of the soldier and the common man and adopted this manner also toward him, boldly and without restraint.

Her beauty was in itself not altogether incomparable nor such as to strike those who saw her, but conversation with her had an irresistible charm, and her presence, combined with the persuasiveness of her discourse and the character that was somehow diffused about her behavior toward others, had something stimulating about it. There was sweetness also in the tones of her voice. Her tongue, like an instrument of many strings, she could readily turn to whatever language she pleased, so that in her interviews with barbarians she very seldom had need of an interpreter, but made her replies to most of them herself and unassisted, whether they were Ethiopians, Troglodytes,[101] Hebrews, Arabians, Syrians, Medes or Parthians. Nay, it is said that she knew the speech of many other peoples also, although the kings of Egypt before her had not even made an effort to learn the native language, and some actually gave up their Macedonian dialect.[102] Accordingly, she made such sport of Antony that, while Fulvia his wife was carrying on war at Rome with Caesar in defense of her husband's interests, and while a Parthian army was hovering about Mesopotamia, he suffered her to hurry him off to Alexandria. There, indulging in the sports and diversions of a young man of leisure, he squandered and spent upon pleasures that which Antiphon[103] calls the most costly outlay, namely, time.[104] They had an association called The Inimitable Livers, and every day they feasted one another, making expenditures of incredible profusion.

Cleopatra, ever contributing some fresh delight and charm to Antony's hours of seriousness or mirth, kept him in constant tutelage, and released him neither night nor day. She played at dice with him, drank with him, hunted with him, and watched him as he exercised himself in arms. When by night he would station himself at the doors or windows of the common folk and scoff at those within, she would go with him on his round of mad follies, wearing the garb of a serving maiden, for Antony also would try to array himself like a servant.

While Antony was indulging in such follies, he was surprised by reports from two quarters: one from Rome, that Lucius his brother and Fulvia his wife had waged war with Octavian Caesar, had lost, and were in flight from Italy, and another, that the Parthians were subduing Asia as far as Lydia and Ionia. He learned that Fulvia had been to blame for the war, being naturally a meddlesome and headstrong woman and hoping to draw Antony away from Cleopatra. It happened, however, that Fulvia fell sick and died at Sicyon.[105] Therefore there was an opportunity for a reconciliation with Caesar.[106] The friends of the two men reconciled them, and divided up the empire assigning the east to Antony, and the west to Caesar. These arrangements needed a stronger security, and this security Fortune offered. Octavia was a sister of Caesar. Her husband, Caius Marcellus, had died a short time before and she was a widow. Antony, too, was a widower; although he did not deny his relations with Cleopatra, he would not admit that she was his wife, for his reason was still battling with his love for the Egyptian. When both men were agreed, they went up to Rome and celebrated Antony's marriage to Octavia.[107]

Antony, after putting Octavia in Caesar's charge together with his children by her and Fulvia,[108] crossed over into Asia. But the dire evil that had been slumbering for a long time, namely, his passion

[101] A people from the African coast of the Red Sea.

[102] That is, they only spoke standard Greek.

[103] An Athenian orator of the late fifth century BCE.

[104] Antony spent the winter of the years 41–40 BCE with Cleopatra in Alexandria. At the end of 40 BCE Cleopatra gave birth to twins.

[105] A city in Greece.

[106] That is, Octavian.

[107] In the fall of 40 BCE.

[108] Antony and Octavia's daughter Antonia would become the mother of the emperor Claudius (41–54 CE), the grandmother of the emperor Caligula (37–41 CE), and the great-grandmother of the emperor Nero (54–68 CE).

for Cleopatra, which men thought had been put to rest by sensible considerations, blazed up again with renewed power as he drew near to Syria. Finally, he spurned away all saving and noble counsels and brought Cleopatra to Syria. When she had come, he made her a present of no insignificant addition to her dominions, namely, Phoenicia, Coele Syria, Cyprus, and a large part of Cilicia, and still further, the balsam-producing part of Judaea and all that part of Arabia Nabataea that slopes toward the outer sea.[109] These gifts particularly annoyed the Romans. He also made presents to many private persons of tetrarchies and realms of great peoples,[110] but the shamefulness of the honors conferred upon Cleopatra gave most offense. And he heightened the scandal by acknowledging his two children by her, and called one Alexander and the other Cleopatra, with the surname of "Sun" for the first and of "Moon" for the other.

After sending Cleopatra back to Egypt, Antony proceeded through Arabia and Armenia to the place where his forces were assembled.[111] And yet we are told that all this preparation and power, which terrified even the Indians beyond Bactria and made all Asia quiver, was made of no avail to Antony by reason of Cleopatra. For so eager was he to spend the winter with her that he began the war before the proper time and managed everything confusedly. He was not master of his own faculties, but, as if he were under the influence of drugs or of magic rites, was ever looking eagerly toward her and thinking more of his speedy return than of conquering the enemy.

[After some initial successes, Antony is forced to retreat until he finally reaches the Euphrates River.]
The front ranks advanced little by little, and the river[112] came in sight. On its bank Antony sent his sick and disabled soldiers across first. When the Parthians saw the river, they unstrung their bows and bade the Romans cross over with good courage, bestowing much praise also upon their valor. Antony held a review of his troops and found that twenty thousand of the infantry and four thousand of the cavalry had perished, not all at the hands of the enemy but more than half by disease. He himself went down to the sea and waited for Cleopatra to come. Because she was slow in arriving he was beside himself with distress, promptly resorting to drinking and intoxication, and in the midst of the drinking would often spring up to look out until she put into port. Afterward, Antony once more invaded Armenia and took Artavasdes[113] in chains down to Alexandria, where he celebrated a triumph. And herein particularly did he give offense to the Romans, because he bestowed the honorable and solemn rites of his native country upon the Egyptians for Cleopatra's sake.[114]

Meanwhile, at Rome Octavia was desirous of sailing to Antony, and Caesar[115] gave her permission to do so, not as a favor to her, but in order that, in case she were neglected and treated with scorn, he might have plausible ground for war. But Cleopatra was afraid that if Octavia added to the dignity of her character and the power of Caesar her assiduous attentions to Antony, she would become invincible and get complete control over her husband. She therefore pretended to be passionately in love with Antony herself and reduced her body by slender diet. She put on a look of rapture when Antony drew near and one of melancholy when he went away. She contrived often to be seen in tears and then would quickly wipe the tears away and try to hide them, as if she would not have Antony notice them. Her flatterers reviled Antony as hard-hearted and unfeeling, and as the destroyer of a mistress who was devoted only to him. Octavia, they said, had married him as a matter of public policy, but Cleopatra, who was queen of so many people, was called Antony's beloved. At last, Antony became fearful that Cleopatra would throw away her life and went back to Alexandria.

At Rome, Antony was hated for the distribution that he made to his children in Alexandria; it was

[109] The ocean, in this case the Indian Ocean.

[110] Apparently a reference to the installation of client rulers.

[111] For the war against Parthia.

[112] The westernmost loop of the Euphrates River.

[113] The King of Armenia.

[114] In 34 BCE.

[115] Octavian.

seen to evince hatred of Rome.[116] For after placing on a tribunal of silver two thrones of gold, one for himself and the other for Cleopatra, and other lower thrones for his sons, in the first place he declared Cleopatra to be Queen of Egypt, Cyprus, Libya, and Coele Syria, and she was to share her throne with Caesarion.[117] Caesarion was believed to be a son of the former Caesar, by whom Cleopatra was left pregnant. In the second place, he proclaimed his own sons by Cleopatra as Kings of Kings. To Alexander he allotted Armenia, Media, and Parthia (when he would have subdued it), and to Ptolemy Phoenicia, Syria, and Cilicia.[118] Cleopatra assumed a robe sacred to Isis and was addressed as the New Isis. By reporting these things to the Senate and by frequent denunciations before the people Caesar tried to inflame the multitude against Antony.

Antony heard of this while he was tarrying in Armenia, and at once he ordered Canidius[119] to take sixteen legions and go down to the sea, but he himself took Cleopatra with him and came to Ephesus.[120] Antony ordered Cleopatra to sail to Egypt and there await the result of the war.[121] Cleopatra, however, fearing that Octavia would again succeed in putting a stop to the war, said that it was neither just to drive away from the war a woman whose contributions to it were so large nor was it for the interest of Antony to dispirit the Egyptians, who formed a large part of his naval force. And besides, it was not easy to see how Cleopatra was inferior in intelligence to anyone of the princes who took part in the expedition, she who for a long time had governed so large a kingdom by herself and by long association with Antony had learned to manage large affairs. These arguments prevailed, and with united forces they sailed to Samos[122] and there made merry.

Meanwhile, Titius and Plancus, friends of Antony and men of consular rank, being abused by Cleopatra, ran away to Caesar and gave him information about Antony's will, which was on deposit with the Vestal Virgins. When Caesar asked for it, they would not give it to him, but if he wanted to, they told him to come and take it. So he assembled the Senate and read it aloud to them. Caesar laid most stress on the clause that directed that Antony's body, even if he should die in Rome, should be borne in state through the Forum and then sent away to Cleopatra in Egypt. And Calvisius, a companion of Caesar, brought forward charges against Antony that he had bestowed upon Cleopatra the libraries from Pergamum, in which there were two hundred thousand volumes[123]; that at a banquet he had stood up and rubbed Cleopatra's feet; that he had consented to have the Ephesians salute Cleopatra as mistress; and that many times, while he was seated on his tribunal and dispensing justice, he received love letters from her and read them.

When Caesar had made sufficient preparations, a vote was passed to wage war against Cleopatra and to take away from Antony the authority that he had surrendered to a woman. Caesar said in addition that Antony had been drugged and was not even master of himself. When the forces came together for the war,[124] Antony had no fewer than five hundred fighting ships, among which were many vessels of eight and ten banks of oars. He also had one hundred thousand infantry soldiers and twelve thousand horsemen. Caesar had two hundred and fifty ships of war, eighty thousand infantry, and about as many horsemen as his enemies.

To such an extent, now, was Antony an appendage of the woman that although he was far superior on

[116] The so-called "Donations of Alexandria," at the same time as Antony's triumph in 34 BCE.

[117] Caesarion thus became Ptolemy XV.

[118] In addition, Cleopatra Selene was allotted Cyrenaica and Libya.

[119] Antony's most important general; he later was executed by Octavian.

[120] A Greek city on the Ionian coast of Anatolia.

[121] Antony by now had realized that war with Octavian was inevitable.

[122] An island, and city, in the Aegean Sea off the coast of Ionia.

[123] To replace the books that had been burned during Caesar's stay; the library of Pergamum was second only to that of Alexandria.

[124] In 31 BCE, at Actium on the coast of western Greece.

land, he wished the decision to rest with his navy, to please Cleopatra, even though he saw that for lack of crews his trierarchs[125] were recruiting wayfarers, mule-drivers, harvesters, and teen-agers, and that even then their ships were not fully manned, but most of them were deficient and sailed wretchedly. Canidius, the commander of the land forces, advised Antony to send Cleopatra away and to decide the issue by a land battle, saying that it would be a strange thing for Antony, who was most experienced in land conflicts, not to avail himself of his numerous legionary soldiers but to distribute his forces among ships and fritter them away. Cleopatra, however, prevailed with her opinion that the war should be decided by the ships.

During that day, then, and the three following days the sea was tossed up by a strong wind and prevented the battle, but on the fifth, the weather becoming fine and the sea calm, they came to an engagement. The sea-fight was undecided and equally favorable to both sides when suddenly the sixty ships of Cleopatra were seen hoisting their sails for flight and making off through the midst of the combatants. The enemy looked on with amazement. Here, Antony made it clear to all the world that he was swayed neither by the sentiments of a commander nor of a brave man, nor even by his own, but he was dragged along by the woman as if he had become incorporate with her and must go where she did. No sooner did he see her ship sailing off than he forgot everything else, betrayed and ran away from those who were fighting and dying in his cause, got into a five-oared galley, and hastened after the woman who had already ruined him and would make his ruin still more complete. Cleopatra recognized him and raised a signal on her ship, so Antony came up and was taken on board, but he neither saw nor was seen by her. Instead, he went forward alone to the prow and sat down by himself in silence, holding his head in both hands. He spent three days by himself at the prow, either because he was angry with Cleopatra or because he was ashamed to see her, and then put in at Taenarum.[126] Here the women in Cleopatra's company persuaded them to eat and sleep together. After Antony had reached the coast of Libya and sent Cleopatra forward into Egypt from Paraetonium,[127] he had the benefit of solitude without end.

Antony tried to kill himself, but was prevented by his friends and brought to Alexandria. Here he found Cleopatra venturing upon a hazardous and great undertaking. The isthmus in Egypt that separates the Red Sea from the Mediterranean Sea and is considered to be the boundary between Asia and Libya, at its narrowest point measures three hundred furlongs. Here Cleopatra undertook to raise her fleet out of water and drag the ships across, and after launching them in the Arabian Gulf with much money and a large force, to settle outside of Egypt, thus escaping war and servitude. But because the Arabians about Petra[128] burned the first ships that were drawn up, and Antony still thought that his land forces at Actium were holding together, she desisted, and guarded the approaches to the country.

Canidius in person brought him word of the loss of his forces at Actium, but none of these things greatly disturbed him, for he gladly laid aside his hopes so that he also might lay aside his anxieties. After he had been received into the palace by Cleopatra, he turned the city to the enjoyment of suppers and drinking-bouts and distributions of gifts. Cleopatra and Antony now dissolved their famous society of Inimitable Livers and founded another, not at all inferior to that in extravagant outlay, which they called the society of Partners in Death. They passed the time delightfully in a round of suppers. Moreover, Cleopatra was getting together collections of all sorts of deadly poisons. She tested the painless working of each of them by giving them to prisoners under sentence of death. But when she saw that the speedy poisons enhanced the sharpness of death by the pain they caused, whereas the milder poisons were not quick, she made trial of venomous animals. She found that the bite of the asp alone

[125] Ship captains.

[126] A coastal city near Sparta in southern Greece.

[127] Modern Mersa Matruh on the Mediterranean coast of Egypt, now a major tourist destination.

[128] A powerful trading city of northern Arabia.

induced a sleepy torpor and sinking, where there was no spasm or groan but rather a gentle perspiration on the face, while the perceptive faculties were easily relaxed and dimmed, and resisted all attempts to rouse and restore them, as is the case with those who are soundly asleep.

When the winter was over, Caesar marched against his enemy through Syria, and his generals through Libya. When Caesar had taken up position near the hippodrome, Antony sallied forth against him and routed his cavalry. Then, exalted by his victory, he went into the palace and kissed Cleopatra, all armed as he was. Antony, conscious that there was no better death for him than that by battle, determined to attack by land and sea at once. He personally posted his infantry on the hills in front of the city and watched his ships as they attacked those of the enemy. But the crews of his ships saluted Caesar's crews with their oars and changed sides. No sooner had Antony seen this than he also was deserted by his cavalry, and after being defeated with his infantry he retired into the city, crying out that he had been betrayed by Cleopatra to those with whom he waged war for her sake. But she, fearing his anger and his madness, fled for refuge into her tomb. Then she sent messengers to tell Antony that she was dead. Antony believed that message, and saying to himself, "Why doest thou longer delay, Antony? Fortune has taken away thy sole remaining excuse for clinging to life," he went into his chamber. Here, as he unfastened his breastplate and laid it aside, he said: "O Cleopatra, I am not grieved to be bereft of thee, for I shall straightway join thee; but I am grieved that such an Imperator[129] as I am has been found to be inferior to a woman in courage." And running himself through the belly with his sword he dropped upon the couch. But the wound did not bring a speedy death.

Antony lay writhing and crying out until Diomedes the secretary came from Cleopatra with orders to bring him to her in the tomb. Having learned that Cleopatra was alive, Antony eagerly ordered his servants to raise him up, and he was carried to her tomb. Cleopatra, however, would not open the doors, but showed herself at a window, from which she let down ropes and cords, and she drew him up herself with the aid of the two women whom alone she had admitted with her. Smeared with blood and struggling with death he was drawn up, stretching out his hands to her even as he dangled in the air. For the task was not an easy one, and scarcely could Cleopatra, with clinging hands and strained face, pull up the rope. And when she had thus got him in and laid him down, she rent her garments over him, beat and tore her breasts with her hands, wiped some of his blood upon her face, and called him master, husband, and Imperator; indeed, she almost forgot her own ills in her pity for his. But Antony stopped her lamentations and asked for a drink of wine, either because he was thirsty or in the hope of a speedier release. When he had drunk, he advised her to consult her own safety, if she could do it without disgrace, and among all the companions of Caesar to put most confidence in Proculeius,[130] and not to lament him for his last reverses, but to count him happy for the good things that had been his, because he had become most illustrious of men, had won greatest power, and now had been not ignobly conquered, a Roman by a Roman.

Scarcely was he dead when Caesar sent Proculeius, bidding him, if possible, above all things to get Cleopatra into his power alive, for he was fearful about the treasures in her funeral pyre, and he thought it would add greatly to the glory of his triumph if she were led in the procession. Proculeius applied a ladder and went in through the window. One of the women imprisoned with Cleopatra cried out, "Wretched Cleopatra, thou art taken alive," whereupon the queen turned about, saw Proculeius, and tried to stab herself, for she had at her girdle a dagger such as robbers wear. Proculeius ran swiftly to her, threw both his arms about her, and said: "O Cleopatra, thou art wronging both thyself and Caesar by trying to rob him of an opportunity to show great kindness." At the same time he took away her weapon, and shook

[129] A general who has won an important victory.

[130] A knight and good friend of Octavian, known for his powers of persuasion.

out her clothing, to see whether she was concealing any poison. And there was also sent from Caesar one of his freedmen, Epaphroditus, with injunctions to keep the queen alive by the strictest vigilance.

After a few days Caesar himself came to talk with her and give her comfort. She was lying on a mean pallet-bed, clad only in her tunic, but she sprang up as he entered and threw herself at his feet. Her hair and face were in terrible disarray, her voice trembled, and her eyes were sunken. There were also visible many marks of the cruel blows upon her bosom; in a word, her body seemed to be no better off than her spirit. Nevertheless, the charm for which she was famous and the boldness of her beauty were not altogether extinguished, but, although she was in such a sorry plight, they shone forth from within and made themselves manifest in the play of her features. Caesar told her that he would give her more splendid treatment than she could possibly expect. Then he went off, supposing that he had deceived her, but he rather had been deceived by her.

Cleopatra begged Caesar that she might be permitted to pour libations for Antony; and when the request was granted, she had herself carried to the tomb, and embracing the urn that held his ashes, she said: "Dear Antony, I buried thee but lately with hands still free; now, however, I pour libations for thee as a captive, and so carefully guarded that I cannot either with blows or tears disfigure this body of mine, which is a slave's body and closely watched so that it may grace the triumph over thee. Do not expect other honors or libations; these are the last from Cleopatra the captive. For although in life nothing could part us from each other, in death we are likely to change places, with thee, the Roman, lying buried here, while I, the hapless woman, lie in Italy. But if indeed there is any might or power in the gods of that country (for the gods of this country have betrayed us), do not abandon thine own wife while she lives, nor permit a triumph to be celebrated over myself in my person, but hide and bury me here with thyself, because out of all my innumerable ills not one is so great and dreadful as this short time that I have lived apart from thee."

After such lamentations, she wreathed and kissed the urn and then ordered a bath to be prepared for herself. After her bath, there came a man from the countryside carrying a basket, and when the guards asked him what he was bringing there, he opened the basket and showed them a dish full of leaves and figs. The guards were amazed at the great size and beauty of the figs, whereupon the man smiled and asked them to take some, so they felt no mistrust and bade him take them in. After her meal, Cleopatra took a tablet that was already written upon and sealed and sent it to Caesar. When Caesar opened the tablet, he found there supplications of one who begged that he would bury her with Antony and quickly knew what had happened. He ordered messengers to go with all speed and investigate. But the mischief had been swift. When they opened the doors they found Cleopatra lying dead upon a golden couch, arrayed in royal state. Of her two women, the one called Iras was dying at her feet, while Charmion, already tottering and heavy-handed, was trying to arrange the diadem that encircled the queen's brow. Then somebody said in anger: "A fine deed, this, Charmion!" "It is indeed most fine," she said, "and befitting the descendent of so many kings." Not a word more did she speak, but fell there by the side of the couch. It is said that a cobra[131] was brought with those figs and leaves and lay hidden beneath them. When she took away some of the figs and saw it, she said, "There it is, you see," and baring her arm she held it out for the bite. Caesar, although vexed at the death of the woman, admired her lofty spirit; and he gave orders that her body should be buried with that of Antony in splendid and regal fashion.

[131] The word used here, "aspis," meaning simply a poisonous snake, does not refer to the European snake called the asp, as it commonly is rendered, but to the Egyptian cobra. Ironically, a rearing cobra known as the "uraeus" was affixed to the forehead of the Pharaoh.

87

AN EXEMPLARY ROMAN WOMAN (CA. 20 BCE): THE "PRAISE OF TURIA"

A section of the "Praise of Turia," engraved on a stone tombstone in the late first century BCE.

The "Laudatio Turiae," or "Praise of Turia," is an inscription on a tombstone that preserves a husband's lengthy and very touching eulogy on the virtues of his wife. The woman's name is not preserved on the fragmentary inscription, but she often has been identified with the Turia who was married to Q. Lucretius Vespillo, who was proscribed by the Second

Triumvirate in 43 BCE but later rose to become Consul in 19 BCE. His deeds during the proscriptions were described by the authors Valerius Maximus and Appian.

Source: *ILS* 8393; Erik Wistrand, *The So-Called Laudatio Turiae* (Berlingska Boktryckeriet, 1976)

(Heading)

[---] of my wife

(Left-hand column)

(line 1) [---] through the honesty of your character [---] you remained [---]
You became an orphan suddenly before the day of our wedding, when both your parents were murdered together in the solitude of the countryside. It was mainly due to your efforts that the death of your parents was not left unavenged, for I had left for Macedonia, and your sister's husband Cluvius[132] had gone to the province of Africa.

So strenuously did you perform your filial duty by your insistent demands and your pursuit of justice that we could not have done more if we had been present. These merits you have in common with that most virtuous lady your sister.

While you were engaged in these things, having secured the punishment of the guilty, you immediately left your own house in order to guard your modesty and you came to my mother's house, where you awaited my return. Then pressure was brought to bear on you and your sister to accept the view that your father's will, by which you and I were heirs, had been invalidated by his having contracted a *coemptio*[133] with his wife. If that was the case, then you together with all your father's property would necessarily come under the guardianship of those involved, and your sister would be left without any share at all of that inheritance, because she had been transferred to the *potestas* of Cluvius.[134] How you reacted to this, with what presence of mind you offered resistance, I know full well, although I was absent.

You defended our common cause by asserting the truth, namely, that the will had not in fact been broken, so that we should both keep the property, instead of your getting all of it alone.[135] It was your firm decision that you would defend your father's written word; you would do this anyhow, you declared, by sharing your inheritance with your sister, if you were unable to uphold the validity of the will. And you maintained that you would not come under the state of legal guardianship,[136] because there was no such right against you in law, for there was no proof that your father belonged to any gens that could by law compel you to do this. For even assuming that your father's will had become void, those who prosecuted had no such right because they did not belong to the same gens.[137] They gave way before your firm resolution and did not pursue the matter any further. Thus you on your own brought to a successful conclusion

[132] Otherwise unknown.

[133] That is, the property had been put into trust. Guardians would have been appointed, and Turia and her husband would not have had direct access to the property.

[134] That is, she had entered a marriage "cum manu" ("with authority"), in which she came under the legal authority of her husband. Doing so disqualified her from being an heir of her father.

[135] If the will had been disallowed, Turia would have inherited everything as the only surviving child still under the *potestas* (legal authority) of her father, which indicates that her marriage must have been "sine manu" ("without authority"), in which she remained under her own legal authority.

[136] Having the property put under someone else's guardianship was to be avoided because guardians sometimes mismanaged the property put in their care, as in Reading 79.

[137] In Roman law, guardians were to be appointed from among a person's nearest agnates, that is, male relatives from the same "gens" (extended family); see Reading 76. Given that the accusers were not agnates, they had no legal right to bring a case, and the will thus stood.

the defense you took up because of your duty to your father, your devotion to your sister, and your faithfulness toward me.

Marriages as long as ours are rare, marriages that are ended by death and not broken by divorce. For we were fortunate enough to see our marriage last without disharmony for fully forty years. I wish that our long union had come to its final end through something that had befallen me instead of you; it would have been more just if I as the older partner had had to yield to fate through such an event.

Why should I mention your domestic virtues: your loyalty, obedience, affability, reasonableness, industry in working wool,[138] religion without superstition, sobriety of attire, modesty of appearance? Why dwell on your love for your relatives, your devotion to your family? You have shown the same attention to my mother as you did to your own parents, and have taken care to secure an equally peaceful life for her as you did for your own people, and you have innumerable other merits in common with all married women who care for their good name. It is your very own virtues that I am asserting, and very few women have encountered comparable circumstances to make them endure such sufferings and perform such deeds. Providentially Fate has made such hard tests rare for women.

We have preserved all the property you inherited from your parents under common custody, for you were not concerned to make your own what you had given to me without any restriction. We divided our duties in such a way that I had the guardianship of your property and you had the care of mine. Concerning this side of our relationship I pass over much, in case I should take a share myself in what is properly yours. May it be enough for me to have said this much to indicate how you felt and thought.

Your generosity you have manifested to many friends and particularly to your beloved relatives. On this point someone might mention with praise other women, but the only equal you have had has been your sister. For you brought up your female relations who deserved such kindness in your own houses with us. You also provided dowries for them so that they could obtain marriages worthy of your family. The dowries you had decided upon Cluvius and I by common accord took upon ourselves to pay,[139] and because we approved of your generosity we did not wish that you should let your own patrimony suffer diminution but substituted our own money and gave our own estates as dowries. I have mentioned this not from a wish to commend ourselves but to make clear that it was a point of honor for us to execute with our means what you had conceived in a spirit of generous family affection.

A number of other benefits of yours I have preferred not to mention [---]

(several lines missing)

(Right-hand column)

You provided abundantly for my needs during my flight[140] and gave me the means for a dignified manner of living, when you took all the gold and jewelry from your own body and sent it to me and over and over again enriched me in my absence with servants, money, and provisions, showing great ingenuity in deceiving the guards posted by our adversaries.

You begged for my life when I was abroad—it was your courage that urged you to this step—and because of your entreaties I was shielded by the clemency of those against whom you marshaled your words. Whatever you said was always said with undaunted courage.

Meanwhile when a troop of men collected by Milo,[141] whose house I had acquired through purchase when he was in exile, tried to profit by the

[138] The pre-eminent virtue of Roman women; see Reading 75.

[139] Because Turia's sister was under the legal authority of Cluvius, the latter had control of her inheritance.

[140] A supporter of Pompey during the latter's civil war with Julius Caesar, he again chose the wrong side and was proscribed by the Second Triumvirate in 43 BCE. He later returned to favor and was named Consul for 19 BCE.

[141] A rabble-rousing Tribune of the Plebs who opposed Julius Caesar; he was exiled in 52 BCE after the murder of Clodius.

opportunities provided by the civil war and break into our house to plunder, you beat them back successfully and were able to defend our home.

(About 12 lines missing)

[---] exist [---] that I was brought back to my country by him[142] for if you had not, by taking care for my safety, provided what he could save, he would have promised his support in vain. Thus I owe my life no less to your devotion than to Caesar.

Why should I now hold up to view our intimate and secret plans and private conversations. How I was saved by your good advice when I was roused by startling reports to meet sudden and imminent dangers; how you did not allow me imprudently to tempt providence by an overbold step but prepared a safe hiding-place for me when I had given up my ambitious designs, choosing as partners in your plans to save me your sister and her husband Cluvius, all of you taking the same risk? There would be no end, if I tried to go into all this. It is enough for me and for you that I was hidden and my life was saved.

But I must say that the bitterest thing that happened to me in my life befell me although what happened to you. When thanks to the kindness and judgment of the absent Caesar Augustus I had been restored to my county as a citizen, Marcus Lepidus,[143] his colleague, who was present, was confronted with your request concerning my recall, and you lay prostrate at his feet, and you were not only not raised up but were dragged away and carried off brutally like a slave. But although your body was full of bruises, your spirit was unbroken and you kept reminding him of Caesar's edict with its expression of pleasure at my reinstatement, and although you had to listen to insulting words and suffer cruel wounds, you pronounced the words of the edict in a loud voice, so that it should be known who was the cause of my deadly perils. This matter was soon to prove harmful for him.[144] What could have been more effective than the virtue you displayed? You managed to give Caesar an opportunity to display his clemency and not only to preserve my life but also to brand Lepidus' insolent cruelty by your admirable endurance.

But why go on? Let me cut my speech short. My words should and can be brief, lest by dwelling on your great deeds I treat them unworthily. In gratitude of your great services toward me let me display before the eyes of all men my public acknowledgement that you saved my life. When peace had been restored throughout the world and the lawful political order reestablished, we began to enjoy quiet and happy times. It is true that we did wish to have children, who had for a long time been denied to us by an envious fate. If it had pleased Fortune to continue to be favorable to us as she was wont to be, what would have been lacking for either of us? But Fortune took a different course, and our hopes were sinking. The courses you considered and the steps you attempted to take because of this would perhaps be remarkable and praiseworthy in some other women, but in you they are nothing to wonder at when compared to your other great qualities and I will not go into them.

When you despaired of your ability to bear children and grieved over my childlessness, you became anxious lest by retaining you in marriage I might lose all hope of having children and be distressed for that reason. So you proposed a divorce outright and offered to yield our house free to another woman's fertility. Your intention was in fact that you yourself, relying on our well-known conformity of sentiment, would search out and provide for me a wife who was worthy and suitable for me, and you declared that you would regard future children as joint and as your own, and that you would not effect a separation of our property that hitherto had been held in common, but that it would still be under my control and, if I wished so, under your administration: nothing would be kept apart by you, nothing separate, and you

[142] Octavian Augustus.

[143] Marcus Aemilius Lepidus, one of the members of the Second Triumvirate; during Antony's and Octavian's campaign against Caesar's assassins in 43 BCE, Lepidus was left in charge back in Rome.

[144] Lepidus was forced into retirement by Octavian and Antony in 36 BCE.

would thereafter take upon yourself the duties and the loyalty of a sister and a mother-in-law.[145]

I must admit that I flared up so that I almost lost control of myself; so horrified was I by what you tried to do that I found it difficult to retrieve my composure. To think that separation should be considered between us before fate had so ordained, to think that you had been able to conceive in your mind the idea that you might cease to be my wife while I was still alive, although you had been utterly faithful to me when I was exiled and practically dead!

What desire, what need to have children could I have had that was so great that I should have broken faith for that reason and changed certainty for uncertainty? But no more about this! You remained with me as my wife, for I could not have given in to you without disgrace for me and unhappiness for both of us.

But on your part, what could have been more worthy of commemoration and praise than your efforts in devotion to my interests: when I could not have children from yourself, you wanted me to have them through your good offices, and because you despaired of bearing children, to provide me with offspring by my marriage to another woman.

Would that the life-span of each of us had allowed our marriage to continue until I, as the older partner, had been borne to the grave—that would have been more just—and you had performed for me the last rites, and that I had died leaving you still alive and that I had had you as a daughter to myself in place of my childlessness.

Fate decreed that you should precede me. You bequeathed me sorrow through my longing for you and left me a miserable man without children to comfort me. I on my part will, however, bend my way of thinking and feeling to your judgments and be guided by your admonitions.

But all your opinions and instructions should give precedence to the praise you have won so that this praise will be a consolation for me and I will not feel too much the loss of what I have consecrated to immortality to be remembered forever.

What you have achieved in your life will not be lost to me. The thought of your fame gives me strength of mind and from your actions I draw instruction so that I shall be able to resist Fortune. Fortune did not rob me of everything because it permitted your memory to be glorified by praise. But along with you I have lost the tranquility of my existence. When I recall how you used to foresee and ward off the dangers that threatened me, I break down under my calamity and cannot hold steadfastly by my promise.

Natural sorrow wrests away my power of self-control and I am overwhelmed by sorrow. I am tormented by two emotions: grief and fear—and I do not stand firm against either. When I go back in time to my previous misfortunes and when I envisage what the future may have in store for me, fixing my eyes on your glory does not give me strength to bear my sorrow with patience. Rather I seem to be destined to long mourning.

The conclusions of my speech will be that you deserved everything but that it did not fall to my lot to give you everything as I ought. Your last wishes I have regarded as law; whatever it will be in my power to do in addition, I shall do.

I pray that your *Di manes*[146] will grant you rest and protection.

[145] To the new wife, that is.

[146] "The Remaining Gods," deities that embody the spirits of deceased loved ones; Roman tombstones often began their epitaphs with the large letters "DM," "To spirits that remain."

CHAPTER 12

The Roman Peace (27 BCE–192 CE)

The Principate—the Roman Empire as established by Augustus—inaugurated a period of more than two hundred years of peace and prosperity for the Roman world. For the most part, the Roman army not only was successfully kept out of politics but also maintained a secure frontier defense system that prevented foreign invasions at the same time that it permitted commerce and immigration across the borders. As the Roman Empire became more socially, culturally, and economically integrated, it embraced all of the manifold peoples living within its diffuse frontiers and provided opportunities for advancement to all of its residents. The evolution of a Mediterranean Culture created the most cohesive and successful empire that the world had yet known. In general, the first and second centuries are known as the period of the *Pax Romana*, or Roman Peace. The most unified culture and society yet known extended from Britain to Arabia.

Map 12 The Roman Empire at Its Greatest Extent at the Death of Trajan, 117 CE

88

ANCHISES PROPHESIZES THE FUTURE OF ROME (19 BCE): VERGIL, *AENEID*, BOOK 6

A mosaic from Hadrumetum in North Africa depicts Vergil with two of the muses, Clio, the muse of history, and Melpomene, the muse of poetry. Preserved now in the Bardo Museum in Tunis.

The *Aeneid* of Vergil, which told of the ten years of wandering by Aeneas as he made his way around the Mediterranean world from burning Troy to a settlement not far from the later site of Rome, was the national poem of Rome during the Roman Empire. It was the first work of literature that anyone learning to read and write Latin studied. In the sixth book, Aeneas visits the Cumaean Sibyl, who utters prophesies on behalf of the god Apollo. The Sibyl leads Aeneas through the underworld, where he eventually meets his father, Anchises, who predicts the future greatness of Rome, including the greatness of the emperor Augustus. In Vergil's view, then, the rise of Augustus and the Roman Empire had been preordained by the gods. The story begins here with Aeneas's arrival in Italy.

Source: H. R. Fairclough, trans., *Vergil. Eclogues, Georgics, Aeneid*, Loeb Classical Library, 2 vols. (Cambridge, MA: Harvard University Press, 1916).

Thus Aeneas at last glides up to the shores of Euboean Cumae.[1] Dutiful[2] Aeneas seeks the heights, where Apollo sits enthroned, and a vast cavern hard by, hidden haunt of the dread Sibyl,[3] into whom the Delian seer[4] breathes a mighty mind and soul, revealing the future. The huge side of the Euboean rock is hewn into a cavern, into which lead a hundred wide mouths, a hundred gateways, from which rush as many voices, the answers of the Sibyl. They had come to the threshold, when the maiden cries: "Tis time to ask the oracles; the god, lo! the god!" As thus she spoke before the doors, suddenly not countenance nor color was the same, nor stayed her tresses braided, but her bosom heaves, her heart swells with wild frenzy, and she is taller to behold, nor has her voice a mortal ring, because now she feels the nearer breath of deity. "Are you slow to vow and to pray?" she cries. "Are you slow, Trojan Aeneas? For until then the mighty mouths of the awestruck house will not gape open." So she spoke and was mute. A chill shudder ran through the Teucrians'[5] sturdy frames, and their king[6] pours forth prayers from his inmost heart: "Phoebus,[7] who never failed to pity Troy's sore agony,[8] who guided the Dardanian[9] shaft and hand of Paris against the body of Aeacus' son,[10] under your guidance did I enter so many seas, skirting mighty lands, now at last is Italy's ever receding shore within our grasp. Thus far only may Troy's fortune have followed us! You, too, may now fitly spare the people of Pergamus,[11] you gods and goddesses[12] all, to whom Troy and Dardania's great glory were an offense. And you, most holy prophetess, who foreknow the future, grant that the Teucrians may rest in Latium,[13] with the wandering gods and storm-tossed powers of Troy. Then to Phoebus and Trivia[14] will I set up a temple of solid marble, and festal days in Phoebus' name. You also a stately shrine awaits in our realm, for here I will place your oracles and mystic utterances, told to my people, and ordain chosen men, O gracious one. Only trust not your verses to leaves, lest they fly in disorder, the sport of rushing winds; chant them yourself, I pray." His lips ceased speaking.

But the prophetess, not yet acknowledging the authority of Phoebus, storms wildly in the cavern, as if to shake the mighty god from her breast, but he tires her raving mouth, tames her wild heart, and molds her by constraint. And now the hundred mighty mouths of the house have opened of their own will, and bring through the air the seer's reply: "O you that have at length survived the great perils of the sea—yet by land more grievous woes lie in wait—into the realm of Lavinium[15] the sons of Dardanus shall come, relieve your heart of this care. Yet they shall not also rejoice in their coming. Wars, grim wars I see, and the Tiber foaming with streams of blood. Even now in Latium a new Achilles[16] has been born, himself a goddess's son, nor shall Juno[17] anywhere

[1] The Italian city of Cumae had been founded by the Greek settlers from the island of Euboea.

[2] The Latin word is "pius," the customary epithet applied to Aeneas; to do one's duty was the greatest virtue that any Roman could display. As of the second century CE, Roman emperors also bore the epithet Pius.

[3] A woman who makes prophecies under the influence of some god, often Apollo.

[4] Apollo, who was born on the island of Delos in the Aegean Sea.

[5] The Trojans, named after Teucer, the legendary first king of Troy.

[6] Aeneas.

[7] An epithet of the god Apollo.

[8] The fall of Troy, on which see also Reading 58.

[9] Dardanus was the son of the god Zeus and Electra, the daughter of Atlas. He founded the city of Dardanus near Troy.

[10] Achilles, who was killed by an arrow shot by Paris, son of Priam, the King of Troy.

[11] The citadel of the city of Troy.

[12] The gods and goddesses of the Greeks, such as Athena and Juno, who had been bringing ruin on the Trojans.

[13] The fertile plain south of the lower Tiber River, where Rome later would be founded.

[14] Goddess of witchcraft, Hecate in Greek, identified by the Romans with Artemis, sister of Apollo.

[15] A new city named by Aeneas in honor of Lavinia, the daughter of Latinus, King of the Latins.

[16] Turnus, King of the Rutili in Italy, who would be the main antagonist of Aeneas in the *Aeneid*.

[17] The sister and wife of Zeus; she opposed the Trojans during the Trojan War because Paris had judged Venus, and not her, to be the most beautiful of all the goddesses.

fail to dog the Trojans, while you, a suppliant in your need, what peoples, what cities of Italy will you not implore! The cause of all this Trojan woe is again an alien bride, again a foreign marriage![18] Yield not to ills, but go forth all the bolder to face them as far as your destiny will allow!"

In these words the Cumaean Sibyl chants from the shrine her dread enigmas and booms from the cavern, wrapping truth in darkness. As soon as the frenzy ceased and the raving lips were hushed, Aeneas the hero begins: "For me, no form of toils arises, O maiden, that is strange or unlooked for. All this have I foreseen and debated in my mind. One thing I pray: because here is the famed gate of the nether king[19] and the gloomy marsh from Acheron's[20] overflow, be it granted me to pass into my dear father's sight and presence; show the way and open the hallowed portals! Amid flames and a thousand pursuing spears, I rescued him on these shoulders, and brought him safe from the enemy's midst. He it was who prayed and charged me humbly to seek you and draw near to your threshold. Pity both son and sire, I beseech you, gracious one!"

In such words he prayed and clasped the altar, when thus the prophetess began to speak: "Sprung from blood of gods, son of Trojan Anchises, easy is the descent to Avernus.[21] Night and day the door of gloomy Dis[22] stands open. But to recall one's steps and pass out to the upper air, this is the task, this the toil! In all the mid-space lie woods, and Cocytus[23] girds it, gliding with murky folds. But if such love is in your heart, if such a yearning, twice to swim the Stygian[24] lake, twice to see black Tartarus.[25] and if you are pleased to give rein to the mad endeavor, hear what must first be done. There lurks in a shady tree a bough, golden leaf and pliant stem, held consecrate to nether Juno.[26] It is not given to pass beneath earth's hidden places before someone has plucked from the tree the golden-tressed fruitage. Search then with eyes aloft and, when found, duly pluck it with your hand. Only so will you survey the Stygian groves and realms the living may not tread." She spoke, and with closed lips was silent.

With sad countenance Aeneas wends his way, and ponders in his mind the dark issues, gazing on the boundless forest. He prays, "O if now that golden bough would show itself to us on the tree in the deep wood!" Scarce had he said these words when twin doves came flying from the sky and lit on the green grass. Then the great hero knew them for his mother's[27] birds, and prays with joy: "Be my guides and through the air steer a course into the grove, where the rich bough shades the fruitful ground! And you, goddess-mother, fail not my dark hour!" So speaking, he checked his steps, marking where they direct their course. Then, when they came to the jaws of noisome Avernus, they perch side by side on their chosen goal, a tree, through whose branches flashed the contrasting glimmer of gold. Forthwith Aeneas plucks it and greedily breaks off the clinging bough, and carries it beneath the roof of the prophetic Sibyl.

He fulfils with haste the Sibyl's behest. A deep cave there was, yawning wide and vast, of jagged rock, and sheltered by dark lake and woodland gloom, over which no flying creatures could safely wing their way; such a vapor from those black jaws was wafted to the vaulted sky whence the Greeks spoke of Avernus, the Birdless Place.[28] Here first the

[18] The first alien marriage had been that of Helen of Sparta to the Trojan Paris; the second would be the marriage of Aeneas to Lavinia, the daughter of the Latin king Latinus.

[19] The god Hades, king of the underworld.

[20] The "River of Woe," along with the Styx, Lethe, Cocytus, and Pyriphlegethon, one of the five rivers of the underworld.

[21] A volcanic crater near the city of Cumae, believed to be the entrance to the underworld.

[22] Hades, god of the underworld.

[23] The "River of Lamentation," one of the rivers of the underworld.

[24] The Styx was another of the rivers of the underworld.

[25] The deepest section of the underworld, where the most dangerous creatures were imprisoned.

[26] Proserpina, Persephone in Greek, queen of the underworld.

[27] The goddess Venus.

[28] From a Greek word meaning "without birds," perhaps because the volcanic fumes killed any birds that flew over the crater.

priestess set in line four dark-backed heifers, and pours wine upon their brows.[29] Then, plucking the topmost bristles from between the horns, she lays them on the sacred fire for first offering, calling aloud on Hecate, supreme both in Heaven and in Hell. Others set knives to the throat and catch the warm blood in bowls. Aeneas himself sacrifices with the sword a black-fleeced lamb, an offering to the mother of the Eumenides[30] and her great sister,[31] and to you, Proserpina, a barren heifer. But just before the rays and dawning of the early sun the ground rumbled underfoot, the wooded ridges began to quiver, and through the gloom dogs seemed to howl as the goddess[32] drew nigh. The seer shrieks, "Rush on the road and unsheathe your sword! Now, Aeneas, is the hour for courage!" So much she said, and plunged madly into the opened cave. He, with fearless steps, keeps pace with his advancing guide.

On they went dimly, beneath the lonely night amid the gloom, through the empty halls of Dis and his phantom realm. Just before the entrance, even within the very jaws of Hell, Grief and avenging Cares have set their bed; there pale Diseases dwell, sad Age, and Fear, and Hunger, temptress to sin, and loathly Want, shapes terrible to view, and Death and Distress. Next, Death's own brother Sleep, and the soul's Guilty Joys, and, on the threshold opposite, the death-dealing War, and the Furies' iron cells, and maddening Strife, her snaky locks entwined with bloody ribbons.

A road leads to the waters of Tartarean Acheron. Here, a whirlpool seethes and belches into Cocytus all its sand. A grim ferry man guards these waters and streams. Charon, on whose chin lies a mass of unkempt hoary hair. His eyes are staring orbs of flame; his squalid garb hangs by a knot from his shoulders. Unaided, he poles the boat, tends the sails, and in his murky craft convoys the dead. Hither rushed all the throng, streaming to the banks; mothers and men and bodies of high-souled heroes, their life now done, boys and unwedded girls, and sons placed on the pyre before their fathers' eyes. They stood, pleading to be the first ferried across, and stretched out hands in yearning for the farther shore. But the surly boatman takes now these, now those, while others he thrusts away, back from the brink.

Then aroused and amazed by the disorder, Aeneas cries, "Tell me, maiden, what means the crowding to the river? What seek the spirits? By what rule do these leave the banks, and those sweep the lurid stream with oars?" To him thus briefly spoke the aged priestess, "Anchises' son, true offspring of gods, all this crowd is helpless and graveless; yonder ferryman is Charon; those whom the flood carries are the buried.[33] He may not carry them over the dreadful banks and hoarse-voiced waters until their bones have found a resting place. A hundred years they roam and flit about these shores; then only are they admitted and revisit the longed-for pools."

They pursue the journey, and draw near to the river. But when the boatman saw them he rebukes them: "Whoever you are who come to our river in arms, tell me, even from there, why you come, and check your step. Living bodies I may not carry in the Stygian boat." In answer the soothsayer spoke briefly: "Trojan Aeneas, famous for piety and arms, descends to his father, to the lowest shades of Erebus.[34] If the picture of such piety in no wise moves you, yet know this bough," and she shows the bough, hidden in her robe. At this his swelling breast subsides from its anger. No more is said, but he, marveling at the dread gift, turns his blue barge and nears the shore. Then other souls that sat on the long thwarts he routs out and at once he takes aboard giant Aeneas. The seamy craft groaned under the weight and through its chinks took in marshy flood. At last, across the water, he lands seer and soldier unharmed on the ugly mire.

[29] Before any great undertaking, sacrifices to the gods had to be performed.

[30] The Furies, avenging goddesses who pursued and punished disrespectful people. They were the daughters of the goddess Night; see Reading 5.

[31] Earth.

[32] Hecate.

[33] Only the dead who have been buried are permitted to pass immediately to the underworld; the unburied must wait a hundred years.

[34] Another name for Tartarus and the underworld.

These realms huge Cerberus[35] makes ring with his triple-throated baying, his monstrous bulk crouching in a cavern opposite. To him, seeing the snakes now bristling on his necks, the seer flung a morsel drowsy with honey and drugged meal. He, opening his triple throat in ravenous hunger, catches it when thrown and, with monstrous frame relaxed, sinks to earth and stretches his bulk over the entire den. The warder buried in sleep, Aeneas wins the entrance, and swiftly leaves the bank of that stream whence none return.

Not far from here, outspread on every side, are shown the Mourning Fields; such is the name they bear. Here those whom stern Love has consumed with cruel wasting are hidden. Among them, with wound still fresh, Phoenician Dido[36] was wandering in the great forest, and soon as the Trojan hero stood near and knew her, he shed tears, and spoke to her in tender love, "Unhappy Dido! Was the tale true then that came to me, that you were dead and had sought your doom with the sword? Was I, alas! the cause of your death? I swear by whatever is sacred that unwillingly, queen, I parted from your shores. Stay your step and withdraw not from our view." With these words Aeneas strove to soothe the wrath of the fiery, fierce-eyed queen. She, turning away, kept her looks fixed on the ground. At length she flung herself away and, still his foe, fled back to the shady grove where Sychaeus,[37] her lord of former days, responds to her sorrows and gives her love for love. Yet none the less, stricken by her unjust doom, Aeneas pities her as she goes.

At length they came to a land of joy, the pleasant lawns of the Elysian Fields.[38] Here an ampler ether clothes the meadows with roseate light, and they know their own sun, and stars of their own. Some disport their limbs on the grassy wrestling ground, vie in sports, and grapple on the yellow sand; some tread the rhythm of a dance and chant songs. Others he sees, to right and left, feasting on the sward, and chanting in chorus a joyous paean within a fragrant laurel grove, whence the full flood of the Eridanus[39] rolls upward through the forest. From afar Aeneas marvels at their phantom arms and chariots. These, as they streamed round, the Sibyl thus addressed, Musaeus[40] before all: "Say, happy souls, and you, best of bards, what land, what place holds Anchises? For his sake are we come." And to her the hero thus made brief reply, "No one has a fixed home. We dwell in shady groves and in meadows fresh with streams. But if the wish, surmount this ridge, and soon I will set you on an easy path." He spoke and stepped on before, and from above points out the shining fields.

Deep in a green vale father Anchises was surveying with earnest thought the imprisoned souls and counting over the full number of his people and beloved children, their fates and fortunes, their works and ways. And as he saw Aeneas coming toward him over the meadow, he eagerly stretched forth both hands while tears streamed from his eyes and a cry fell from his lips, "Have you come at last, and has the duty that your father expected vanquished the toilsome way? Is it given me to see your face, my son, and hear and utter familiar tones? Over what lands, what wide seas have you journeyed to my welcome? What dangers have beset you, my son? How I feared the realm of Libya might work you harm!" And he answered: "Your sad shade, father, meeting me repeatedly, drove me to seek these portals. Grant me to clasp your hand, father, and withdraw not from my embrace!" So he spoke, his face wet with flooding tears. Thrice there he strove to throw his arms about his neck; thrice the form, vainly clasped, fled from his hands.

Meanwhile, in a retired vale, Aeneas sees a sequestered grove and rustling forest thickets, and the river Lethe[41] drifting past those peaceful homes. About it

[35] The three-headed dog who guards the underworld.

[36] The queen of Carthage, a native of Tyre in Phoenicia, who killed herself after Aeneas abandoned her, creating a pretext for the later enmity between the Carthaginians and Romans.

[37] A priest of Tyre and former husband of Dido; he was murdered by Dido's brother Pygmalion, who wanted to steal his treasure.

[38] The resting place of heroes and those who had led virtuous lives.

[39] A river often associated with the Po River in northern Italy; Vergil speaks of it as if it is in the underworld.

[40] A legendary philosopher and poet of Athens.

[41] The River of Forgetfulness.

hovered peoples and nations unnumbered. Aeneas is startled by the sudden sight and asks the cause, "What is that river yonder, and who are the men thronging the banks in such a host?" Then said father Anchises, "Spirits they are to whom second bodies are owed by Fate. At the water of Lethe's stream they drink the soothing draught and long forgetfulness." "But, father, must we think that any souls pass aloft from here to the world above and return a second time to bodily fetters?" "I will surely tell you, my son, and keep you not in doubt," Anchises replies, "All these that you see, when they have rolled time's wheel through a thousand years, the god summons in vast throng to Lethe's river, so that, their memories effaced, they may once more revisit the vault above and conceive the desire of return to the body."

Anchises paused, and drew his son and with him the Sibyl into the heart of the assembly and buzzing throng, then chose a mound whence he might scan face to face the whole of the long procession, saying,[42] "Now then, the glory henceforth to attend the Trojan people, what children of Italian stock are held in store by fate, glorious souls waiting to inherit our name, this shall I reveal in speech and inform you of your destiny. The youth you see leaning on an untipped spear holds the most immediate place. The first to rise into the upper air with Italian blood in his vein will be Silvius[43] of Alban name, last-born of your children, whom late in your old age your wife Lavinia shall rear, a king and father of kings, with whom our people shall hold sway in Alba Longa. He next is Procas, pride of the Trojan nation, then Capys and Numitor, and he who will resurrect you by his name, Aeneas Silvius, no less eminent in goodness and in arms, if ever he come to reign over Alba.[44] What fine young men are these! Further, a son of Mars shall keep his grandsire company, Romulus, whom his mother Ilia shall bear of Assaracus' stock.[45] Lo, under Romulus' auspices, my son, shall that glorious Rome extend her empire to earth's ends, her ambitions to the skies, and shall embrace seven hills with a single city's wall, blessed in a brood of heroes."

"Turn hither now your two-eyed gaze, and behold this nation, the Romans that are yours. Here is Caesar and all the seed of Iulus[46] destined to pass under heaven's spacious sphere. And this in truth is he whom you so often hear promised you, Augustus Caesar, son of a god,[47] who will again establish a Golden Age in Latium amid fields once ruled by Saturn. He will advance his empire beyond the Garamantes[48] and Indians to a land that lies beyond our stars, where sky-bearing Atlas wheels on his shoulders the blazing star-studded sphere. Against his coming Caspian[49] realms and the Maeotic land[50] even now shudder at the oracles of their gods, and the mouths of sevenfold Nile[51] quiver in alarm."

"But who is he apart, crowned with sprays of live, offering sacrifice? Ah, I recognize the hoary hair and beard of that king of Rome[52] who will make the infant city secure on a basis of laws. Him shall Tullus[53] next succeed, the breaker of his country's peace, who will rouse to war an inactive folk and armies long unused

[42] Anchises now prophesies what the future of Aeneas and, descended from him, the Roman people will be.

[43] The son either of Aeneas himself or of Aeneas's son Ascanius; he succeeded Ascanius as king of Alba Longa.

[44] This list of kings is different from the traditional list, which has Aeneas Silvius as the son of Silvius, then Capys four generations, then Procas six generations after him, followed by his son Numitor.

[45] Romulus was the grandson of Numitor and son of Rhea Silvia, also known as Ilia. Assaracus was the brother of Illus, the founder of Troy; see Reading 73.

[46] Iulus (Julius) was another name for Ascanius, the son of Aeneas. The Julian family of Julius Caesar and Octavian claimed descent from this Iulus and thus from Aeneas and the goddess Venus.

[47] Augustus was the adopted son of Julius Caesar, who was deified after his assassination in 44 BCE.

[48] A people of the western Sahara Desert.

[49] The Caspian Sea, to the east of the Black Sea.

[50] The Maeotian Lake, the modern Sea of Azov, a northern extension of the Black Sea.

[51] So called because the Nile had seven mouths in the Nile delta.

[52] Numa Pompilius (716–672 BCE), the second king of Rome, known for establishing Roman religion.

[53] Tullus Hostilius (672–640 BCE), the third king of Rome, known for wars.

to triumphs. Hard on his heels follows over-boastful Ancus,[54] who even now enjoys too much the breeze by popular favor. Would you also see the Tarquin kings,[55] the proud spirit of Brutus the Avenger,[56] and the fasces regained? He first shall receive a Consul's power and the cruel axes, and when his sons would stir up revolt, the father will hale them to execution in fair freedom's name, unhappy man, however later ages will extol that deed; yet shall a patriot's love prevail and unquenched thirst for fame.

"Now behold over there the Decii and the Drusi,[57] Torquatus[58] of the cruel axe and Camillus[59] bringing the standards home! But they whom you see, resplendent in matching arms, souls now in harmony and as long as they are imprisoned in night, alas, if once they attain the light of life, what mutual strife, what battles and bloodshed will they cause, the bride's father swooping from Alpine ramparts and Monoecus' fort, her husband confronting him with forces from the east![60] Steel not your hearts, my sons, to such wicked war nor vent violent valor on the vitals of your land. And you who draw your lineage from heaven, be you the first to show mercy; cast the sword from your hand, child of my blood!"

"He yonder,[61] triumphant over Corinth, shall drive a victor's chariot to the lofty Capitol, famed for Achaeans he has slain. Yon other[62] shall uproot Argos, Agamemnon's Mycenae, and even an heir of Aeacus, seed of mighty Achilles: he will avenge his Trojan sires and Minerva's polluted shrine.[63] Who, lordly Cato,[64] could leave you unsung, or you, Cossus,[65] who the Gracchan[66] family or the two Scipios,[67] two thunderbolts of war and the ruin of Carthage, or Fabricius,[68] in penury a prince, or you, Serranus,[69] sowing seed in the soil? Whither, O Fabii, do ye hurry me all

[54] Ancus Martius (640–616 BCE), also known for wars.

[55] Two Etruscan kings, Tarquinius Priscus ("Tarquin the Old") (616–578 BCE) and Tarquinius Superbus ("Tarquin the Proud") (534–509 BCE), the last king of Rome. Omitted from Vergil's list is Servius Tullius (578–534), who reigned between the two Tarquins.

[56] Lucius Junius Brutus, who in 509 BCE avenged the violation of Lucretia at the hands of Sextus Tarquin by masterminding the overthrow of the monarchy (see Reading 75) and became one of the first two Roman consuls. He had his sons executed for trying to overthrow the Republic.

[57] Two famous Roman families.

[58] Titus Manlius Torquatus, who in 361 defeated a huge Gaul in single combat, decapitated him, and thus acquired the torque that he wore around his neck, thus gaining the epithet "Torquatus" ("Torque-wearer") for himself and his descendants.

[59] Marcus Furius Camillus who, in a popular legend, was believed to have recaptured the Roman military standards from the Gauls who sacked Rome in 390 BCE.

[60] A reference to the civil war between Julius Caesar, who in 49 BCE invaded Italy via the Alps, and Pompey, who had married Caesar's daughter Julia. The town of Portus Monoeci is modern-day Monaco.

[61] Lucius Mummius, the Roman general who destroyed Corinth in 146 BCE.

[62] Lucius Aemilius Paullus, who defeated Perseus of Macedon at the Battle of Pydna in 168 BCE.

[63] A reference to the enmity between Romans and Greeks that supposedly went back to the Trojan War; the Greek hero Ajax the Lesser polluted the temple of Minerva (Athena) by carrying off Cassandra, daughter of King Priam of Troy, who had taken refuge there; see Reading 58.

[64] Marcus Porcius Cato the Elder, Consul in 195 BCE and Censor in 184 BCE, whose constant advice that "Carthage must be destroyed" incited Rome to the Third Punic War (149–146 BCE); see Reading 80.

[65] Aulus Cornelius Cossus, who in the mid-fifth century BCE became one of only three Roman generals to win the "spolia opima" for defeating an enemy commander in single combat.

[66] Represented by the brothers Tiberius and Gaius Gracchus, who in the years 133–121 BCE began the changes that led to the fall of the Roman Republic; see Reading 81.

[67] Scipio Africanus, who defeated Hannibal in 202 BCE, and his grandson Scipio Aemilianus, who ended the Third Punic War in 146 BCE.

[68] Gaius Fabricius Luscinus, Consul in 282 and 278 and Censor in 275 BCE, known for his austerity and morality.

[69] Gaius Atilius Regulus Serranus, Consul during the First Punic War, in 257 and 250 BCE, who was said to have received the news of his election as Consul while he was sowing.

breathless? You are he, the mightiest,[70] who could, as no one else, through inaction preserve our state. Others, I doubt not, shall with softer lines beat out the breathing bronze, coax from the marble features to life, plead cases with greater eloquence, and with a pointer trace heaven's motions and predict the risings of the stars: you, Roman, be sure to rule the world, for these are your arts: to crown peace with justice, to spare the vanquished and beat down the proud."

Thus Father Anchises adds, "Behold how Marcellus[71] advances, graced with the spoils of the chief he slew, and towers triumphant over all! When the Roman state is reeling under a brutal shock, he will steady it, will ride down Carthaginians and the insurgent Gaul, and offer up to Father Quirinus[72] a third set of spoils."

They wander at large over the whole region in the wide airy plain, taking note of all. After Anchises had led his son over every scene, kindling his soul with longing for the glory that was to be, he then tells of the wars that the hero next must wage.

Two gates of Sleep there are. One, they say, is horn and offers a ready exit to true shades, the other shines with the sheen of polished ivory, but delusive dreams issue upward through it from the world below. Thither Anchises, discoursing thus, escorts his son and with him the Sibyl, and sends them forth by the ivory gate. Aeneas speeds his way to the ships and rejoins his comrades, then straight along the shore he sails. The anchor is cast from the prow; the sterns stand ranged on the shore.

---

[70] Quinus Fabius Maximus, named dictator after the Roman defeat at the Battle of Cannae in 216 BCE by the Carthaginian Hannibal; see Reading 78.

[71] Marcus Claudius Marcellus was Consul five times in the last quarter of the third century BCE. During a war with the Gauls, Marcellus killed the opposing general and thus won the "spolia opima." Marcellus is glorified here because he was an ancestor of the Marcus Claudius Marcellus who was the nephew of the emperor Augustus and an early choice to be Augustus's successor.

[72] An early god of the Roman state, being nearly on a par with Jupiter.

89

HORACE, "THE SECULAR HYMN" (17 BCE)

In 86 CE the emperor Domitian celebrated the next secular games after those that Augustus had held in 17 BCE, not quite 110 years later. On the reverse of this sestertius, Domitian, on a dais, distributes to a man and child combustibles to be used for making ceremonial torches. The legend on the right reads "Ludi saeculares" ("Secular Games"), and the letters "SVEPD" are thought to mean "combustibles being distributed to the people."

In 17 BCE, as part of his attempt to normalize life in the Roman world, solidify his own position, and create a system of government that we know as the Roman Empire, Augustus celebrated a ceremony that was only held every 110 years or so, the Secular Games, a festival of renewal and purification that was held at a time when no one who was alive during the previous celebration was still alive. The poet Horace was commissioned to compose a hymn to commemorate the event.

Source: Stephen De Vere translation, in William Stearns Davis, *Rome and the West* (Boston/New York/Chicago, Allyn & Bacon: 1913), no. 58, 174–176.

Phoebus,[73] and Diana,[74] you whose sway,
Mountains and woods obey!
Twin glories of the skies,[75] forever worshiped,
hear!
Accept our prayer this sacred year

[73] Another name of the sun god Apollo.

[74] Goddess of the moon, Artemis to the Greeks.

[75] The sun and moon.

When, as the Sibyl's[76] voice ordained
For ages yet to come,
Pure maids and youths unstained
Invoke the gods who love the sevenfold hills of
Rome.
All bounteous Sun![77]
Forever changing, and forever one!
Who in your lustrous car bear'st forth light,
And hid'st it, setting, in the arms of Night,
Look down on worlds outspread, yet nothing see
Greater than Rome, and Rome's high
sovereignty.
You Ilithyia,[78] too, whatever name,
Goddess, you do approve,
Lucina, Genitalis,[79] still the same
Aid destined mothers with a mother's love;
Prosper the Senate's wise recommendation,
Fertile of marriage faith and countless progeny![80]
As centuries progressive wing their flight
For you the grateful hymn shall ever sound;
Thrice by day, and thrice by night
For you the choral dance shall beat the ground.
Fates! whose unfailing word
Spoken from Sibylline lips shall abide,
Ordained, preserved, and sanctified
By Destiny's eternal law, accord
To Rome new blessings that shall last
In chain unbroken from the Past.
Mother of fruits and flocks, prolific Earth!
Bind wreaths of spiked grain round Ceres'[81] hair:
And may soft showers and Jove's[82] benignant air
Nurture each infant birth!

[76] A Sibyl (a prophetress) sold to king Tarquin the Proud a book of prophecies that were consulted in times of emergencies to find the proper expiatory rites needed to regain the favor of the gods.
[77] Apollo.
[78] Goddess of childbirth.
[79] Other names for the goddess of childbirth.
[80] Acting through the Senate, Augustus issued legislation favoring those who had children and penalizing those who did not; see Reading 97.
[81] The goddess of grain; Demeter to the Greeks.
[82] Another name for Jupiter.

Lay down your arrows, god of day!
Smile on your youths elect who singing pray.
You, Crescent Queen,[83] bow down your
star-crowned head
And on your youthful choir a kindly influence
shed.
If Rome be all your work, if Troy's[84] sad band
Safe sped by you attained the Etruscan strand,
A chosen remnant, vowed [85]
To seek new Lares,[86] and a changed abode.
A remnant for whom through Ilium's[87] blazing
gate
Aeneas,[88] orphan of a ruined State,
Opened a pathway wide and free
To happier homes and liberty.
Ye gods! If Rome be yours, to placid age
Give timely rest: to docile youth
Grant the rich heritage
Of morals, modesty, and truth.
On Rome herself bestow a teaming race
Wealth, empire, faith, and all befitting grace
Deliver to Venus' and Anchises' heir,[89]
Who offers at your shrine
Due sacrifice of milk-white kine,
Justly to rule, to pity and to dare,
To crush insulting hosts, the prostrate foeman
spare.
The haughty Mede[90] has learned to fear

[83] Diana, Greek Artemis, goddess of the moon, was depicted with a lunar crescent in her hair.
[84] For the Trojan refugees who were ancestors of the Romans, see Reading 88.
[85] The same sentiment as that expressed toward the end of Reading 88.
[86] Household gods.
[87] Another name for Troy.
[88] For the Trojan hero Aeneas, the ancestor of Augustus, see Reading 88.
[89] Aeneas was the son of the goddess Venus and the Trojan hero Anchises.
[90] The Parthians, who ruled a huge empire east of the Roman Empire; see Reading 69. Three years earlier Augustus had recovered from the Parthians the military standards lost by the general Crassus in 53 BCE, a huge propaganda coup.

The Alban[91] axe, the Latian[92] spear,
And Scythians,[93] suppliant now, await
The conqueror's doom, their coming fate.
Honor and peace, and pristine shame,
And virtue's oft dishonored name,
Have dared, long exiled, to return,
And with them Plenty[94] lifts her golden horn.
Augur Apollo! Bearer of the bow!
Warrior and prophet! Loved one of the Nine!
Healer in sickness! Comforter in woe!
If still the templed crags of Palatine[95]
And Latium's fruitful plains to you are dear,
Perpetuate for cycles yet to come,
Mightier in each advancing year,
The ever growing might and majesty of Rome.
You, too, Diana, from your Aventine,[96]
And Algidus[97] deep woods, look down
and hear
The voice of those who guard the books divine,[98]
And to your youthful choir incline a loving ear.
Return we home! We know that Jove
And all the gods our song approve
To Phoebus and Diana given;
The virgin hymn is heard in Heaven.

[91] From Alba Longa, the town founded by Aeneas not far from the future site of Rome.

[92] Latium, the fertile plain on which Rome was situated.

[93] Augustus recently had received an embassy from the nomadic "Scythians" of southern Russia, for whom see Reading 68.

[94] Ops, the goddess of plenty and fertility.

[95] A hill of Rome that rises above the Forum; it was a posh residential district and the later site of imperial palaces.

[96] One of the hills of Rome, just southwest of the Palatine Hill.

[97] Part of a dormant volcano twelve miles southeast of Rome, site of a famous battle between Rome and the Aequi in 457 BCE.

[98] The Sibylline Books.

90

DEEDS OF THE DEIFIED AUGUSTUS (14 CE)

The "Deeds of the Deified Augustus" as it survives inscribed on the wall of the Temple of Augustus in Ankara, Turkey.

One of the most historically significant texts preserved on stone, and one of the most effective pieces of propaganda ever produced, is the "Res gestae divi Augusti," or "Deeds of the Deified Augustus," an autobiographical account of his own achievements that Augustus wrote when he was seventy-six and instructed the Senate to post throughout the empire, in both Latin and Greek, after his death. This was done, but the "Res gestae" do not survive intact anywhere. The original bronze copy from the Forum in Rome is lost, and the surviving version had been pieced together from stone fragments found in Anatolia at Ancyra, where the best copy survives; Apollonia; Sardis; and Antioch in Pisidia.

Source: Frederick W. Shipley, trans., *Velleius Paterculus and Res Gestae Divi Augusti* (Cambridge, MA: Harvard University Press, 1924), 344–405.

Below is a copy of the acts of the Deified Augustus by which he placed the whole world under the sovereignty of the Roman people, and of the amounts that he expended upon the state and the Roman people, as engraved upon two bronze columns[99] that have been set up in Rome.

[99] These columns no longer survive.

At the age of nineteen, on my own initiative and at my own expense, I raised an army by means of which I restored liberty to the Republic, which had been oppressed by the tyranny of a faction.[100] For which service the Senate, with complimentary resolutions, enrolled me in its order, in the consulship of Gaius Pansa and Aulus Hirtius,[101] giving me at the same time consular precedence in voting[102]; it also gave me the imperium.[103] As Propraetor[104] it ordered me, along with the Consuls, "to see that the Republic suffered no harm."[105] In the same year, moreover, as both Consuls had fallen in war, the people elected me Consul and a Triumvir[106] for settling the constitution. Those who slew my father I drove into exile, punishing their deed by due process of law, and afterward when they waged war upon the Republic I twice defeated them in battle.[107] Wars, both civil and foreign, I undertook throughout the world, and when victorious I spared all citizens who sued for pardon. The foreign nations that could with safety be pardoned I preferred to save rather than to destroy. The number of Roman citizens who bound themselves to me by military oath was about 500,000. Of these I settled in colonies or sent back into their own towns after their term of service, something more than 300,000, and to all I assigned lands or gave money as a reward for military service. The dictatorship offered me by the people and the Roman Senate, in my absence and later when present, in the consulship of Marcus Marcellus and Lucius Arruntius[108] I did not accept. I did not decline at a time of the greatest scarcity of grain the charge of the grain-supply, which I so administered that, within a few days, I freed the entire people, at my own expense, from the fear and danger in which they were. The consulship, either yearly or for life, then offered me I did not accept. I refused to accept any power offered me that was contrary to the traditions of our ancestors. Those things that the Senate at that time wished me to administer I carried out by virtue of my tribunician power.[109] To the day of writing this I have been Princeps Senatus[110] for forty years. I have been Pontifex Maximus,[111] Augur,[112] a member of the Fifteen Commissioners for Performing Sacred Rites, one of the Seven for Sacred Feasts, an Arval Brother,[113] a *Sodalis Titius*,[114] and a Fetial priest.[115] By Recommendation of the Senate my name was included in the Salian Hymn,[116] and it was enacted by law that my person should be sacred in perpetuity and that so long as I lived I should hold the tribunician power. When I returned from Spain and Gaul, in the consulship of Tiberius Nero and

[100] Encompassing all of Augustus's enemies, including the assassins of Julius Caesar and the supporters of Mark Antony (see Reading 86).

[101] In 43 BCE.

[102] Voting in the Senate was done in rank order; thus, those with the status of Consuls voted before those with the status of Praetors, and so on.

[103] The power to command armies.

[104] At this point in his career, Octavian never had held any office, but there were precedents for this kind of irregular grant, as when the later triumvir Pompey was given the power of a Proconsul in 78 BCE in Spain.

[105] The "Last Recommendation of the Senate"; see Readings 81 and 83.

[106] The "Second Triumvirate"; the other two Triumvirs were Mark Antony and Marcus Aemilius Lepidus.

[107] At Philippi in Macedonia in 42 BCE Augustus, with critical assistance from his comrade Agrippa and Mark Antony, defeated the assassins Brutus and Cassius.

[108] In 22 BCE.

[109] A power that gave Augustus the right to introduce legislation, veto power, and the sacrosanctity of his person. It was renewed every year and later provided a means to date the years of an emperor's reign.

[110] The first person listed on the official list of the Senate, in rank order.

[111] Chief Priest of the Roman people.

[112] The Augurs were Roman priests charged with taking the auspices, that is, seeing the will of the gods in the flights of birds.

[113] The Arval Brothers were an ancient college of twelve priests who made sacrifices to ensure good harvests.

[114] Priests initially appointed by the Sabine king Titus Tatius.

[115] In the Roman Republic, the Fetials were priests were responsible for declaring war.

[116] A song sung in March of every year by the Salian priests.

Publius Quinctilius,[117] after successful operations in those provinces, the Senate voted in honor of my return the consecration of an altar[118] to Pax Augusta in the Campus Martius, and on this altar it ordered the magistrates and priests and Vestal virgins to make annual sacrifice. I made twelve distributions of food from grain bought at my own expense, and in the twelfth year of my tribunician power I gave for the third time four hundred sesterces[119] to each man. To the municipal towns I paid money for the lands that I assigned to soldiers in my own fourth consulship[120] and afterward in the consulship of Marcus Crassus and Gnaeus Lentulus the Augur.[121] The sum that I paid for estates in Italy was about six hundred million sesterces, and the amount that I paid for lands in the provinces was about two hundred and sixty million. I was the first and only one to do this of all those who up to my time settled colonies of soldiers in Italy or in the provinces. And later, in the consulship of Tiberius Nero and Gnaeus Piso, likewise in the consulship of Gaius Antistius and Decimus Laelius, and of Gaius Calvisius and Lucius Passienus, and of Lucius Lentulus and Marcus Messalla, and of Lucius Caninius and Quintus Fabricius,[122] I paid cash gratuities to the soldiers whom I settled in their own towns at the expiration of their service, and for this purpose I expended four hundred million sesterces as an act of grace. I furnished from my own purse and my own patrimony tickets for grain and money, sometimes to a hundred thousand persons, sometimes to many more. I built the curia[123] and the Chalcidicum[124] adjoining it, the temple of Apollo on the Palatine with its porticoes, the temple of the deified Julius,[125] I restored the channels of the aqueducts that in several places were falling into disrepair through age, and doubled the capacity of the aqueduct called the Marcia by turning a new spring into its channel. I completed the Julian Forum.[126] On my own ground I built the temple of Mars Ultor and the Augustan Forum[127] from the spoils of war. Three times in my own name I gave a show of gladiators, and five times in the name of my sons or grandsons; in these shows there fought about ten thousand men. I conducted the Secular Games[128] in the consulship of Gaius Furnius and Marcus Silanus. In my own name, or that of my sons or grandsons, on twenty-six occasions I gave to the people, in the circus, in the Forum, or in the amphitheater, hunts of African wild beasts, in which about three thousand five hundred beasts were slain. I gave the people the spectacle of a naval battle beyond the Tiber, at the place where now stands the grove of the Caesars, the ground having been excavated for a length of eighteen hundred and a breadth of twelve hundred feet. In this spectacle thirty beaked ships, triremes or biremes, and a large number of smaller vessels met in conflict. In these fleets there fought about three thousand men exclusive of the rowers. I freed the sea from pirates. About thirty thousand slaves, captured in that war, who had run away from their masters and had taken up arms against the Republic, I delivered to their

[117] In 13 BCE. In 9 CE Publius Quinctilius Varus was defeated and killed by the Germans at the disastrous Battle of the Teutoberg Forest.

[118] The Altar of Peace, which still survives.

[119] About three months wages for an ordinary worker.

[120] In 30 BCE.

[121] In 14 BCE.

[122] Between 7 and 2 BCE.

[123] Augustus actually merely completed the rebuilding of the Curia Julia, or Julian Senate house, in Rome, which had been begun under Julius Caesar.

[124] An annex or addition to a building.

[125] After his assassination, Julius Caesar, the great-uncle and adoptive father of Augustus, was deified, that is, made into a god.

[126] The Forum of Julius Caesar, which adjoined the Republican Forum on one side and the even newer Forum of Augustus on the other side.

[127] The Forum of Augustus, built next to the Forum of Caesar, contained a temple to "Mars the Avenger" that Augustus had vowed to build if he was able to defeat the assassins of Caesar.

[128] A purification festival, held every 110 years or so, at a time when everyone alive at the time of last one was dead. Augustus celebrated it in 19 BCE and the poet Horace composed a celebratory hymn (see Reading 89).

masters for punishment.[129] I extended the boundaries of all the provinces that were bordered by peoples not yet subject to our empire.[130] The provinces of the Gauls, the Spains, and Germany, bounded by the ocean from Gades[131] to the mouth of the Elbe,[132] I reduced to a state of peace.[133] The Alps, from the region that lies nearest to the Adriatic as far as the Etruscan Sea, I brought to a state of peace without waging on any people an unjust war. My fleet sailed from the mouth of the Rhine eastward as far as the lands of the Cimbri[134] to which, up to that time, no Roman had ever penetrated either by land or by sea, and the Cimbri and Charydes and Semnones and other peoples of the Germans of that same region through their envoys sought my friendship and that of the Roman people. On my order and under my auspices two armies were led, at almost the same time, into Ethiopia and into Arabia that is called the "Happy,"[135] and very large forces of the enemy of both peoples were cut to pieces in battle and many towns were captured. Ethiopia was penetrated as far as the town of Napata, which is next to Meroë.[136] In Arabia the army advanced into the territories of the Sabaeans to the town of Mariba.[137] I settled colonies of soldiers in Africa, Sicily, Macedonia, both Spains, Achaea, Asia, Syria, Narbonese Gaul, and Pisidia.[138] Moreover, Italy has twenty-eight colonies founded under my auspices. The Parthians I compelled to restore to me the spoils and standards of three Roman armies,[139] and to seek as suppliants the friendship of the Roman people. These standards I deposited in the inner shrine that is in the Temple of Mars Ultor. The peoples of the Pannonians,[140] to which no army of the Roman people had ever penetrated before my Principate, having been subdued by Tiberius Nero who was then my stepson and my legate, I brought under the sovereignty of the Roman people, and I pushed forward the frontier of Illyricum as far as the bank of the river Danube. Embassies were often sent to me from the kings of India, a thing never seen before in the camp of any general of the Romans. Our friendship was sought, through ambassadors, by the Bastarnae[141] and Scythians,[142] and by the kings of the Sarmatians who live on either side of the river Tanaïs,[143] and by the Kings of the Albani[144] and of the Iberians[145] and of the Medes.[146] In my sixth and seventh consulships,[147] when

[129] The "pirates" and "slaves" are an allusion to Augustus's war with Sextus Pompey, the son of Pompey the Great, who occupied Sicily and competed with Augustus for power between 42 and 36 BCE.

[130] Augustus added more territory to the Roman Empire, especially in Pannonia (modern Hungary), than any earlier Roman. After his conquests, the empire went into a defensive posture and, with only a few exceptions, under the emperors Claudius (41–54) and Trajan (98–117), further wars of conquests virtually ceased.

[131] Modern Cadiz in Spain.

[132] A river running through Germany into the North Sea.

[133] Augustus's attempt to expand to the Elbe River in Germany in fact failed disastrously in 9 CE when the charismatic German leader Arminius destroyed three legions at the Battle of the Teutoburg Forest.

[134] A voyage of exploration led by Augustus's stepson Tiberius in 5 CE.

[135] "Arabia Felix" ("Happy Arabia"); modern Yemen.

[136] In the Kingdom of Kush, on the Nile River south of Egypt.

[137] In modern Yemen; the Sabaeans lived in the ancient kingdom of Sheba, whence came the Queen of Sheba who visited Solomon (Reading 38). Augustus neglects to mention that the invasion of Arabia and siege of Marib of 26–24 BCE were total disasters; most of the Roman army was lost to disease and battle.

[138] In Anatolia.

[139] The standards lost by the Roman Crassus at the Battle of Carrhae (53 BCE), recovered by Augustus in a treaty of 20 BCE, a huge propaganda coup.

[140] In modern Hungary.

[141] An ancient Celtic people dwelling north of the lower Danube River.

[142] Peoples of the southern Russian steppes; see Reading 68.

[143] The Don River in southern Russia, flowing south into the Sea of Azov north of the Black Sea.

[144] A nomadic people living near the Caspian Sea.

[145] Inhabitants of Iberia (modern Georgia) in the Caucasus Mountains between the Black and Caspian seas.

[146] That is, the Parthians.

[147] 28–27 BCE.

I had extinguished the flames of civil war, after receiving by universal consent the absolute control of affairs, I transferred the Republic from my own control to the will of the Senate and the Roman people. For this service on my part I was given the title of Augustus by Recommendation of the Senate, and the doorposts of my house were covered with laurels by public act, and a civic crown[148] was fixed above my door, and a golden shield was placed in the Curia Julia[149] whose inscription testified that the Senate and the Roman people gave me this in recognition of my Valor, my Clemency, my justice, and my Piety.[150] After that time I took precedence of all in rank, but of power I possessed no more than those who were my colleagues in any magistracy.

[148] A crown of oak leaves awarded for saving the life of Roman citizens.

[149] The Senate house in Rome; construction was begun by Caesar and finished by Augustus.

[150] "Pietas," or "Dutifulness," was the greatest virtue that a Roman could demonstrate.

91

THE TRIAL OF JESUS BEFORE PONTIUS PILATE (CA. 28/37 CE): THE *NEW TESTAMENT*, MATTHEW 27:11–16, MARK 5:1–30, JOHN 18:28–40 AND 19:1–24, AND LUKE 23:1–25

The Rossano Gospels, an illustrated manuscript produced in Italy in the sixth century CE, depict the trial of Jesus before Pontius Pilate. Pilate is shown as a late Roman governor sitting on a raised dais and flanked by attendants holding standards bearing the portraits of two emperors. To his left lawyers make their case and to his right the crowd shouts its opinions. A stenographer records the proceedings as two imperial officials in military robes present Jesus and two underlings present the robber Barabbas.

During the early years of the Principate, Judaea was racked by dissension. Various Jewish popular leaders, such as Simon of Peraea, an ex-slave of King Herod the Great, Judas the Galilean, and the shepherd Athronges, laid claim to be, or were thought to be, the "messiah," the person that many Jews believed would unify the Jewish people, give the Jews back their independence, and bring a new era of world peace. The Jewish teacher Yeshua bar Yosef Nazareth, known as Jesus in English and Christos ("the annointed one") in Greek, was believed by many to be the messiah. He caused so much anxiety for the established Jewish hierarchy that he was put on trial before the Sanhedrin, the Jewish high court, and was condemned when he declined to deny that he was the son of God. Because the Jewish court was located in the Roman province of Judaea, it had no authority to pass the death sentence. Only the Roman governor, in this case the Prefect of Judaea Pontius Pilate, had the authority to do that. So Caïaphas, the Jewish High Priest, turned Jesus over to the Romans for an additional trial. During the proceedings, Pilate made several attempts to distance himself from what he saw as purely local bickering. The date of Jesus's trial is uncertain, but the book of Luke states that Jesus's baptism occurred at some time after the beginning of the ministry of John the Baptist, "In the fifteenth year of the reign of Tiberius Caesar," that is, in 28 CE. Pontius Pilate was replaced as governor ca. 36 BCE. This would place Jesus's trial sometime between 28 and 36 BCE. The story of Jesus's trial before Pilate presented here is a conflation of the accounts given in all four of the New Testament gospels: the three synoptic gospels, Matthew (27:11–16), Mark (5:1–30), and Luke (23:1–25), repeat similar versions of the same account; the book of John gives a longer report. For other accounts of Roman trials, see Readings 100, 103, and 113.

Source: *The Bible, American Standard Version* (New York, 1901).

They led Jesus therefore from Caïaphas[151] into the Praetorium[152]; and it was early, and they themselves entered not into the Praetorium, that they might not be defiled, but might eat the Passover.[153] Pilate[154] therefore went out unto them, and saith, "What accusation bring ye against this man?" They answered unto him, "If this man were not an evildoer, we should not have delivered him up unto thee." And they began to accuse him, saying, "We found this man perverting our nation and forbidding to give tribute to Caesar, and saying that he himself is Christ a king." And Pilate asked him, saying, "Art thou the King of the Jews?" And he answered him, "Thou sayest."[155] And Pilate said unto the chief priests and the multitudes, "I find no fault in this man." But they were the more urgent, saying, "He stirreth up the people, teaching throughout all Judaea, and beginning from Galilee[156] even unto this place." But when Pilate heard it he asked whether the man were a Galilaean. And when he knew that he was of Herod's jurisdiction, he sent him unto Herod,[157] who himself also was at Jerusalem in these days. Now when Herod saw Jesus he was exceeding glad, for he was of a long time desirous to see him because he had heard about him, and he hoped to see some miracle done by him. And he questioned Jesus in many words, but he answered him nothing. And the chief priests and the scribes stood, vehemently accusing him. And Herod with his soldiers set him at nought, and mocked him, and arraying him in gorgeous apparel sent him back to Pilate. And Herod and Pilate became friends with

[151] The High Priest of the Jews in Jerusalem.

[152] The headquarters building of a Roman army camp.

[153] The Jews had many regulations relating to ritual purity, especially at the time of the celebration of festivals; see Reading 35.

[154] Pontius Pilate, the Equestrian Prefect (Governor) of the Roman province of Judaea ca. 26–36 CE.

[155] Throughout the proceedings, Jesus refuses to speak to the Jewish officials and in so doing acknowledge their authority; he speaks only to Pilate.

[156] A region of Judaea neighboring the Sea of Galilee, north of Jerusalem.

[157] Herod Antipas, son of Herod the Great and Tetrarch of Galilee and Perea ca. 6–39 CE.

each other that very day: for before they were at enmity between themselves.

And Pilate called together the chief priests and the rulers and the people, and said unto them, "Ye brought unto me this man as one that perverteth the people, and behold, I having examined him before you, found no fault in this man touching those things whereof ye accuse him, no, nor yet Herod, for he sent him back unto us, and behold, nothing worthy of death hath been done by him. I will therefore chastise him, and release him." And when the chief priests and elders accused Jesus of many things, he answered nothing. And Pilate again asked Jesus, saying, "Answerest thou nothing? Behold how many things they accuse thee of." But Jesus no more answered anything, insomuch that Pilate marveled. Pilate therefore said unto them, "Take him yourselves and judge him according to your law." The Jews said unto him, "It is not lawful for us to put any man to death."

Pilate therefore entered again into the Praetorium, and called Jesus, and said unto him, "Art thou the King of the Jews?" Jesus answered, "Sayest thou this of thyself, or did others tell it to thee concerning me?" Pilate answered, "Am I a Jew? Thine own nation and the chief priests delivered thee unto me. What hast thou done?" Jesus answered, "My kingdom is not of this world. If my kingdom were of this world, then would my servants fight so that I should not be delivered to the Jews, but my kingdom is not from here." Pilate therefore said unto him, "Art thou a king then?" Jesus answered, "Thou sayest that I am a king. To this end have I been born and to this end am I come into the world, that I should bear witness unto the truth. Every one that is of the truth heareth my voice." Pilate saith unto him, "What is truth?"

And when he had said this, he went out again unto the Jews, and saith unto them, "I find no crime in him. But ye have a custom, that I should release unto you one prisoner at the Passover." And there was one called Barabbas, who for a certain insurrection made in the city, and for murder, was cast into prison.[158] Pilate said unto them, "Whom will ye that I release unto you? Barabbas, or Jesus who is called Christ and the King of the Jews?" For he knew that it was for envy that they had delivered Jesus up. And while he was sitting on the judgment-seat, his wife sent unto him, saying, "Have thou nothing to do with that righteous man, for I have suffered many things this day in a dream because of him." Now the chief priests and the elders persuaded the multitudes that they should ask for Barabbas, and destroy Jesus. The governor said unto them, "Which of the two will ye that I release unto you?" They cried out therefore again, saying, "Not this man, but Barabbas." Pilate saith unto them, "What then shall I do unto Jesus who is called Christ?" They all say, "Let him be crucified."

And he said unto them the third time, "Why, what evil hath this man done? I have found no cause of death in him. I will therefore chastise him and release him." But they were urgent with loud voices, asking that he might be crucified. And their voices prevailed. So when Pilate saw that he achieved nothing, but rather that a tumult was arising, he took water and washed his hands before the multitude, saying, "I am innocent of the blood of this righteous man. See ye to it." And all the people answered and said, "His blood be on us, and on our children." And Pilate gave sentence that what they asked for should be done. And he released the one who for insurrection and murder had been cast into prison, whom they asked for. Then Pilate therefore took Jesus and whipped him.

And the soldiers plaited a crown of thorns and put it on his head, and arrayed him in a purple garment, and they came unto him, and said, "Hail, King of the Jews!," and they struck him with their hands. And Pilate went out again, and saith unto them, "Behold, I bring him out to you, that ye may know that I find no crime in him." Jesus therefore came out, wearing the crown of thorns and the purple garment. And Pilate saith unto them, "Behold, the man!" When therefore the chief priests and the officers saw him, they cried out, saying, "Crucify him, crucify him!" Pilate saith unto them, "Take him yourselves, and crucify him, for I find no crime in him." The Jews answered him, "We have a law, and by that law he ought to die, because he made himself the Son of

[158] This from the books of Mark and Luke; according to the book of John, Barabbas was a robber.

God." When Pilate therefore heard this saying, he was the more afraid, and he entered into the Praetorium again and saith unto Jesus, "Whence art thou?" But Jesus gave him no answer. Pilate therefore saith unto him, "Speakest thou not unto me? Knowest thou not that I have power to release thee, and have power to crucify thee?" Jesus answered him, "Thou wouldest have no power against me except it were given thee from above. Therefore he that delivered me unto thee hath greater sin." Upon this Pilate sought to release him, but the Jews cried out, saying, "If thou release this man, thou art not Caesar's friend. Every one that maketh himself a king speaketh against Caesar." When Pilate therefore heard these words, he brought Jesus out and sat down on the judgment-seat at a place called The Pavement, but in Hebrew, Gabbatha. Now it was the Preparation of the Passover; it was about the sixth hour. And he saith unto the Jews, "Behold, your king!" They therefore cried out, "Away with him, away with him, crucify him!" Pilate saith unto them, "Shall I crucify your king?" The chief priests answered, "We have no king but Caesar."

Then therefore he delivered him unto them to be crucified. Therefore they took Jesus, and he went out, bearing the cross for himself, unto the place called the place of a skull, which is called in Hebrew, Golgotha. There they crucified him, and with him two others, on either side one, and Jesus in the middle. And Pilate wrote a title also, and put it on the cross. And there was written, "Jesus of Nazareth, the King of the Jews." This title therefore many of the Jews read, for the place where Jesus was crucified was nigh to the city; and it was written in Hebrew, in Latin, and in Greek. The chief priests of the Jews therefore said to Pilate, "Write not, 'The King of the Jews,' but that he said, 'I am King of the Jews.'" Pilate answered, "What I have written I have written." The soldiers therefore, when they had crucified Jesus, took his garments and made four parts, to every soldier a part, and also the coat. Now the coat was without seam, woven from the top throughout. They said therefore one to another, let us not rend it, but cast lots for it, whose it shall be, that the scripture might be fulfilled, which saith, They parted my garments among them, And upon my vesture did they cast lots.

92

THE EMPEROR CALIGULA (37–41 CE): SUETONIUS, *LIFE OF CALIGULA*

A sestertius of the emperor Caligula depicts his three sisters, Agrippina, Drusilla, and Julia, on the reverse. Caligula was undeniably very fond of them and subsequently was accused of incest with all of them.

In 37 CE, at the age of twenty-four, Gaius Julius Caesar Augustus Germanicus succeeded Tiberius as emperor. He was the first, but by no means the last, emperor to have had no formal training for the position and whose only qualification was to be a member of the right family. He was known either as Gaius, his praenomen, or as Caligula, a nickname given him as a toddler by soldiers who had made little boots for him modeled on the *caligae* (boots) of the soldiers. In the course of his brief four-year reign he became known for bizarre behavior, especially after he suffered and recovered from a mysterious illness, which was gleefully reported by Suetonius, an imperial biographer and court gossip who wrote in the 130s CE.

Source: J. C. Rolfe, trans., *Suetonius. Volume I: The Lives of the Caesars* (Cambridge, MA: Harvard University Press, 1914).

He began from that time[159] on to lay claim to divine majesty, for after giving orders that such statues of the gods as were especially famous for their sanctity or their artistic merit, including that of Jupiter of Olympia, should be brought from Greece in order to remove their heads and put his own in their place, he built out a part of the palace as far as the Forum, and making the temple of Castor and Pollux its vestibule he often took his place between the divine brethren, and exhibited himself there to be worshipped by those who presented themselves; some hailed him as Jupiter Latiaris. At night he used constantly to invite the full and radiant moon to his embraces and his bed, whereas in the daytime he would talk confidentially with Jupiter Capitolinus, now whispering and then in turn putting his ear to the mouth of the god, now in louder and even angry language, for he was heard to make the threat, "Lift me up, or I'll lift you." Finally won by entreaties, as he reported, and even invited to live with the god, he built a bridge over the temple of the Deified Augustus, and thus joined his palace to the Capitol.[160] When his grandmother Antonia[161] asked for a private interview, he refused it except in the presence of the Prefect Macro,[162] and by such indignities and annoyances he caused her death, although some think that he also gave her poison. After she was dead, he paid her no honor, but viewed her burning pyre from his dining-room. He had his brother Tiberius put to death without warning, suddenly sending a Tribune of the Soldiers to do the deed; besides driving his father-in-law Silanus to end his life by cutting his throat with a razor. As for his uncle Claudius,[163] he spared him merely as a laughingstock.

He lived in habitual incest with all his sisters, and at a large banquet he placed each of them in turn below him whereas his wife reclined above.[164] Of these he is believed to have violated Drusilla when he was still a minor, and even to have been caught lying with her by his grandmother Antonia, at whose house they were brought up in company. Afterward, when she was the wife of Lucius Cassius Longinus, an ex-Consul, he took her from him and openly treated her as his lawful wife. When ill, he made her heir to his property and the throne. The rest of his sisters he did not love with so great affection, nor honor so highly, but often prostituted them to his favorites, so that he was the readier at the trial of Aemilius Lepidus[165] to condemn them as adulteresses and privy to the conspiracies against him.

It would be trivial and pointless to add to this an account of his treatment of his relatives and friends, Ptolemy, son of king Juba, his cousin, for he was the grandson of Marcus Antonius by Antonius' daughter Selene,[166] and in particular Macro himself and even Ennia, who helped him to the throne[167]; all these were rewarded for their kinship and their faithful services by a bloody death. He was no whit more respectful or mild toward the Senate, compelling some who had held the highest offices to run in their togas for several miles beside his chariot and to wait on him at table, standing napkin in hand either at the head of his couch, or at his feet. Others he secretly put to death, yet continued to send for them as if they were alive, and after a few days falsely asserting that they had committed suicide.

The following are special instances of his innate brutality. When cattle to feed the wild beasts that he

[159] After recovering from some kind of mystery illness.

[160] The Temple of Jupiter atop the Capitoline Hill.

[161] The daughter of Mark Antony and Octavia, sister of Augustus.

[162] The Praetorian Prefect, commander of the ten thousand elite troops stationed just outside Rome.

[163] Roman emperor 41–54 CE, the successor of Caligula.

[164] At a Roman dinner party, three couches were arranged in a "∩" shape; here, Caligula occupied the "low" couch on the left, where the host reclined, whereas his wife was on the "high" couch on the right.

[165] Initially a confidant of Caligula and even named as his heir, he fell out of favor and was executed for conspiracy in 39 CE.

[166] Grandson of Cleopatra and Mark Antony, he was the last King of Mauretania (modern Morocco) at the time of his assassination by Caligula in 40 CE.

[167] The Praetorian Prefect Macro initially had sponsored Caligula as emperor in 37 BCE; Caligula soon felt threatened by him and coerced him and his wife Ennia, who had been Caligula's mistress, into committing suicide.

had provided for a gladiatorial show were rather costly, he selected criminals to be devoured. Many men of honorable rank were first disfigured with the marks of branding-irons and then condemned to the mines, to work at building roads, or to be thrown to the wild beasts, or else he shut them up in cages on all fours, like animals, or had them sawn into pieces. Not all these punishments were for serious offenses, but merely for criticizing one of his shows, or for never having sworn by his Genius.[168]

He seldom had anyone put to death except by numerous slight wounds, his constant order, which soon became well-known, being, "Strike so that he may feel that he is dying." When a different man than he had intended had been killed, through a mistake in the names, he said that the victim too had deserved the same fate. He often uttered the familiar line of the tragic poet, "Let them hate me, so long as they fear me."[169] Angered at the rabble for applauding a faction[170] that he opposed, he cried, "I wish the Roman people had but a single neck." At one of his more sumptuous banquets he suddenly burst into a fit of laughter, and when the Consuls, who were reclining next him, politely inquired at what he was laughing, he replied, "What do you suppose, except that at a single nod of mine both of you could have your throats cut on the spot?" After inviting Ptolemy, whom I have mentioned before, to come from his kingdom, and receiving him with honor, he suddenly had him executed for no other reason than that when giving a gladiatorial show he noticed that Ptolemy on entering the theater attracted general attention by the splendor of his purple cloak.

He respected neither his own chastity nor that of anyone else. He is said to have had unnatural relations with Marcus Lepidus, the pantomimic actor Mnester, and certain hostages. Valerius Catullus, a young man of a consular family, publicly proclaimed that he had violated the emperor and worn himself out in commerce with him. To say nothing of his incest with his sisters and his notorious passion for the concubine Pyrallis, there was scarcely any woman of rank whom he did not approach. These as a rule he invited to dinner with their husbands, and as they passed by the foot of his couch, he would inspect them critically and deliberately, as if buying slaves, even putting out his hand and lifting up the face of anyone who looked down in modesty. Then, as often as the fancy took him he would leave the room, sending for the one who pleased him best, and returning soon afterward with evident signs of what had occurred, he would openly commend or criticize his partner, recounting her charms or defects and commenting on her conduct. To some he personally sent a bill of divorce in the name of their absent husbands and had it entered in the public records.

Having thus impoverished himself, from very need he turned his attention to pillage through a complicated and cunningly devised system of false accusations, auction sales, and imposts. He levied new and unheard of taxes, at first through the publicans[171] and then, because their profit was so great, through the centurions and tribunes of the Praetorian Guard. There was no class of commodities or men on which he did not impose some form of tariff. On all eatables sold in any part of the city he levied a fixed and definite charge; on lawsuits and legal processes begun anywhere, a fortieth part of the sum involved, adding a penalty in case anyone was found guilty of compromising or abandoning a suit; on the daily wages of porters, an eighth; on the earnings of prostitutes, as much as each received for one embrace; and a clause was added to this chapter of the law, providing that those who ever had been prostitutes or pimps should be liable to this public tax, and that even matrimony should not be exempt.

He had but one experience with military affairs or war, and then on a sudden impulse. Having gone to Mevania to visit the river Clitumnus[172] and its grove, he was reminded of the necessity of recruiting his

[168] The emperor's guardian spirit.

[169] A quotation from the play "Atreus" of the mid-second century BCE Latin tragedian Accius.

[170] A chariot-racing team.

[171] Tax collectors.

[172] A small river in Umbria that flowed to the town of Mevania; the site of sacred shrines.

body-guard of Batavians[173] and was seized with the idea of an expedition to Germania. So without delay he assembled legions and auxiliaries from all quarters, holding levies everywhere with the utmost strictness and collecting provisions of every kind on an unheard of scale. On reaching his camp, to show his vigilance and strictness as a commander, he dismissed in disgrace the generals who were late in bringing in the auxiliaries from various places, and in reviewing his troops he deprived many of the chief centurions who were well on in years of their rank, in some cases only a few days before they would have served their time, giving as a reason their age and infirmity; then railing at the rest for their avarice, he reduced the rewards given on completion of full military service to six thousand sesterces.[174] All that he accomplished was to receive the surrender of Adminius, son of Cunobellinus,[175] King of the Britons, who had been banished by his father and had deserted to the Romans with a small force. Presently, finding no one to fight with, he had a few Germans of his bodyguard taken across the river[176] and concealed there, and word brought him after luncheon with great bustle and confusion that the enemy were close at hand. Upon this he rushed out with his friends and a part of the praetorian cavalry to the woods close by, and after cutting the branches from some trees and adorning them like trophies, he returned by torchlight, taunting those who had not followed him as timorous and cowardly, and presenting his companions and the partners in his victory with crowns.

Finally, as if he intended to bring the war to an end, he drew up a line of battle on the shore of the ocean,[177] arranging his ballistas[178] and other artillery, and when no one knew or could imagine what he was going to do, he suddenly bade them gather shells and fill their helmets and the folds of their gowns, calling them spoils from the ocean, due to the Capitol and Palatine.[179]

Then turning his attention to his triumph,[180] in addition to a few captives and deserters from the barbarians he chose all the tallest of the Gauls, and as he expressed it, those who were "worthy of a triumph," as well as some of the chiefs. These he reserved for his parade, compelling them not only to dye their hair red and to let it grow long, but also to learn the language of the Germans and assume barbarian names.

He was very tall and extremely pale, with an unshapely body and very-thin neck and legs. His eyes and temples were hollow, his forehead broad and grim, his hair thin and entirely gone on the top of his head, although his body was hairy. Because of this to look upon him from a higher place as he passed by, or for any reason whatever to mention a goat, was treated as a capital offense. He was sound neither of body nor mind. As a boy he was troubled with the falling sickness.[181] While in his youth he had some endurance, yet at times because of sudden faintness he was hardly able to walk, to stand up, to collect his thoughts, or to hold up his head. He himself realized his mental infirmity, and thought at times of going into retirement and clearing his brain. It is thought that his wife Caesonia[182] gave him a drug intended for a love potion, which, however, had the effect of driving him mad. He was especially tormented with sleeplessness; for he never rested more than three hours at night, and even

[173] A people of the lower Rhine River often recruited for service in the imperial bodyguard.

[174] Reducing the rewards given to the soldiers always was a potentially dangerous undertaking.

[175] King of several peoples of Britain. Caligula used the appeal of Cunobellinus's exiled son Adminius as a pretext to lay claim to Britain. Cunobellinus was the title character in Shakespeare's play, *Cymbeline, King of Britain.*

[176] The Rhine River.

[177] The Atlantic Ocean.

[178] Torsion weapons, like giant bows, used for shooting spears or stones.

[179] A good example of how Caligula's actions were misrepresented; the shells would have been crushed and used to make waterproof cement for constructing harbor facilities.

[180] Ostensibly for a victory over the Germans.

[181] Epilepsy.

[182] Milonia Caesonia, Caligula's fourth and last wife, to whom he was quite devoted. She was murdered shortly after Caligula's assassination in 41 CE.

for that length of time he did not sleep quietly but was terrified by strange apparitions.

In his clothing, his shoes, and the rest of his attire he did not follow the usage of his country and his fellow-citizens, not always even that of his sex, or in fact, that of an ordinary mortal. He often appeared in public in embroidered cloaks covered with precious stones, with a long-sleeved tunic and bracelets; sometimes in silk and in a woman's robe, now in slippers or buskins, again in boots, such as the emperor's body-guard wear, and at times in the low shoes that are used by females.

He was so passionately devoted to the green faction[183] that he constantly dined and spent the night in their stables, and in one of his revels with them he gave the driver Eutychus two million sesterces in gifts. In order to prevent the horse Incitatus from being disturbed he used to send his soldiers on the day before the games and order silence in the neighborhood. Along with a stall of marble, a manger of ivory, purple blankets and a collar of precious stones, he even gave this horse a house, a troop of slaves, and furniture for the more elegant entertainment of the guests invited in his name. It is also said that he planned to make him Consul.

During this frantic and riotous career several thought of attempting his life. But when one or two conspiracies had been detected and the rest were waiting for a favorable opportunity, two men made common cause and succeeded, with the connivance of his most influential freedmen and the officers of the Praetorian Guard, for although the charge that these last were privy to one of the former conspiracies was false, they realized that Caligula hated and feared them. In fact, he exposed them to great odium by once taking them aside and declaring, drawn sword in hand, that he would kill himself if they too thought he deserved death, and from that time on he never ceased accusing them one to the other and setting them all at odds. When they had decided to attempt his life at the exhibition of the Palatine games, as he went out at noon, Cassius Chaerea, Tribune of a cohort of the Praetorian Guard, claimed for himself the principal part, for Gaius used to taunt him, a man already well on in years, with voluptuousness and effeminacy by every form of insult. When he asked for the watch word Gaius would give him "Priapus" or "Venus," and when Chaerea had occasion to thank him for anything, he would hold out his hand to kiss, forming and moving it in an obscene fashion.

On the ninth day before the Kalends of February[184] at about the seventh hour he hesitated whether or not to get up for luncheon because his stomach was still disordered from excess of food on the day before, but at length he came out at the persuasion of his friends.[185] In the covered passage through which he had to pass, some boys of good birth, who had been summoned from Asia to appear on the stage, were rehearsing their parts, and he stopped to watch and encourage them. Had not the leader of the troop complained that he had a chill, he would have returned and had the performance given at once. From this point there are two versions of the story. Some say that as he was talking with the boys, Chaerea came up behind and gave him a deep cut in the neck, having first cried, "Take that," and that then the Tribune Cornelius Sabinus, who was the other conspirator and faced Gaius, stabbed him in the breast. Others say that Sabinus, after getting rid of the crowd by means of centurions who were in the plot, asked for the watchword, as soldiers do, and that when Gaius gave him "Jupiter," he cried "So be it," and as Gaius looked around, he split his jawbone with a blow of his sword. As he lay upon the ground and with writhing limbs called out that he still lived, the others dispatched him with thirty wounds, for the general signal was "Strike again." Some even thrust their swords through his privates. At the beginning of the disturbance his bearers ran to his aid with their litter poles and presently the Germans of his body-guard, and they slew several of his assassins along with some inoffensive senators. Gaius lived twenty-nine years and ruled three years, ten months, and eight days.

[183] The fan club of the "Greens," a chariot-racing team.

[184] 24 January 41 CE.

[185] A similar story was told about Julius Caesar, who had to be persuaded to attend the Senate meeting where he was assassinated in 44 BCE.

93

EXPANDING THE MEMBERSHIP OF THE SENATE (48 CE): THE "CLAUDIAN RECOMMENDATION OF THE SENATE REGARDING THE RIGHT OF HONORS FOR THE GAULS," H. DESSAU, *SELECTED LATIN INSCRIPTIONS*, NO. 212, AND TACITUS, *ANNALS*, BOOK 11, CHAPTERS 23–25

The bottom half of a bronze tablet preserves approximately the first half of the speech of Claudius expanding Senate membership to Gauls in 48 CE. It was discovered in 1528 and is displayed in the Musée des Beaux Arts in Lyon.

This speech of the emperor Claudius (41–54 CE) to the Senate in Rome in 48 CE, engraved on a bronze tablet erected in Lyon in Gaul, is one of the very few surviving copies of the original words of an imperial speech. In it, Claudius admitted some Roman citizens from Gaul into the Senate and thus began the process by which the Senate came to represent all the populations of the Empire. The speech was an official transcript and even preserved the words of interruptions from the audience, one of the typical means by which the public could make its views known directly to an emperor. Claudius had a reputation as a historian before becoming emperor, and the examples used in the speech support this impression. The speech also is reported in the "Annals" of Tacitus, allowing one to compare the original text with the slant given to it by a historian.

(a) Claudius, Speech to the Senate

Sources:
Column 1: E. Mary Smallwood, *Documents Illustrating the Principates of Gaius Claudius and Nero* (Cambridge, UK: Cambridge University Press, 1967), 369.
Column 2: William Stearns Davis, ed., *Readings in Ancient History: Illustrative Extracts from the Vol. II: Rome and the West* (Boston: Allyn & Bacon, 1912–13), 186–188.

[Column I]
"I should say at the outset that I reject the first thought that will, I am sure, be the very first thing to stand in my way: namely that you will recoil from my suggestion as though I were introducing some revolutionary innovation. Think, instead, of how many changes have taken place over the years in this state and how many forms and constitutions our state has had, from the time of its very foundation.

At one time this city was held by kings,[186] although they did not pass it along to successors from their own families. People from other families came to the throne and even some foreigners. Numa, for example, succeeded Romulus, and was a Sabine; that made him a neighbor, certainly, but at the time he also was a foreigner. Another example is Tarquinius Priscus, who succeeded Ancus Martius: his father was the Corinthian Demaratus and his mother was from Tarquinii, so Tarquinius Priscus supposedly had a Greek father and an Etruscan mother. And although well-born she was very poor, which is why she was forced to marry such a husband. Tarquinius was kept from positions of honor in his own land and thus emigrated to Rome, where he became king. Between Tarquinius and either his son or his grandson (for our authorities disagree on this point) there came Servius Tullius. According to the Roman sources Servius Tullius had as a mother a prisoner-of-war, Ocresia; according to the Etruscans he had been the faithful companion of Caelius Vibenna[187] and took part in his adventures, and later, when he was driven out by a change of fortune, he left Etruria with all the surviving troops of Caelius and seized the Caelian hill, which thus takes its name from his leader Caelius, and after changing his name, for his Etruscan name was Mastarna, he was given the name I have already mentioned, and became king, to the very great advantage of the state. Then, after the behavior of Tarquinius Superbus[188] came to be hated by our city, and not only his behavior but that of his sons, the people obviously became tired of monarchy, and the administration of state was transferred to the Consuls, who were annual magistrates.

[186] Claudius indulges his interest in ancient history with these historical excurses on the kings of Rome; see Readings 73 and 88.

[187] An Etruscan chieftain who aided Romulus in his wars against the Sabines.

[188] Tarquin the Proud, the last king of Rome: see Reading 75.

Why need I mention the dictatorship, more powerful even than the consulship, which was what our ancestors came up with when wars were particularly hard or there was serious civil disturbance? Or why need I mention the creation of Tribunes of the Plebs, to provide assistance for the plebs? Why mention transfer of imperium from Consuls to the Decemvirs, and at the end of the reign of the Decemvirs the return of imperium back to the Consuls?[189] Why mention the distribution of the consular power to multiple recipients, called Military Tribunes with Consular Power,[190] who were first six and then eight in number? Why should I mention the fact that offices that once were patrician ones eventually were shared with the plebeians, religious ones as well as military?

If I were to tell of the wars that our ancestors started with and that have continued down to the present day, I fear that I would appear too boastful and look as though I wanted to boast about my glory in extending the empire beyond the Ocean.[191] But let me instead return to my original point. Citizenship can [---]." [192]

[Column II]

[Claudius]: "It surely is an innovation of the divine Augustus,[193] my great-uncle, and of Tiberius Caesar,[194] my uncle, to desire that particularly the flower of the colonies and of the municipal towns,[195] that is to say, all those that contain men of breeding and wealth, should be admitted to this assembly."

[Interruption, seemingly by a senator]: "How now? Is not an Italian senator to be preferred to a provincial senator?"

[Claudius]: "I will soon explain this point to you, when I submit that part of my acts that I performed as Censor,[196] but I do not conceive it needful to repel even the provincials who can do honor to the Senate House. Here is this splendid and powerful colony of Vienna[197] is it so long since it sent senators to us? From that colony comes Lucius Vestinus,[198] one of the glories of the equestrian order, my personal friend, whom I keep close to myself for the management of my private affairs. Let his sons be suffered, I pray you, to become priests of the lowest rank, while waiting until, with the lapse of years, they can follow the advancement of their dignity. As for that robber[199] from Vienna, I will pass over his hateful name. For I detest this hero of the gymnasium, who brought the consulship into his family before even his colony had obtained the full rights of Roman citizenship. I could say as much of his brother, stamped as unworthy by this unlucky relationship, and incapable henceforth of being a useful member of your body."

[Interrupting shout]: "Here now, Tiberius Caesar Germanicus! It is time to let the Conscript Fathers[200] understand what your talk is driving at! Already you've reached the very limits of Narbonnese Gaul![201]"

[Claudius]: "All these young men of rank, on whom I cast my glance, you surely do not regret to see among the number of the senators, any more than Persicus, that most high-born gentleman and my friend, is ashamed when he meets upon the images

[189] In the years 451 and 450 BCE, when the Twelve Tables of Roman law were crafted; see Reading 76.

[190] Lasting from 444 until 367 BCE.

[191] The Atlantic Ocean; in 43 CE Claudius had begun the Roman occupation of Britain; see Reading 94.

[192] Some text is lost here.

[193] The first emperor, Augustus (27 BCE–14 CE).

[194] Tiberius (14–37 CE), second Roman emperor and adopted son of Augustus.

[195] Colonies and municipalities were cities of Roman citizens that had formal Roman organizational charters.

[196] The ancient Republican magistrate with the authority to adlect (admit) new members to the Senate.

[197] Modern Vienne, on the Rhône River in central France.

[198] Otherwise unknown but probably an ancestor of the Lucius Vestinus who was Consul in 112 CE.

[199] Valerius Asiaticus, whose family had received Roman citizenship ca. 80 BCE. A famous athlete, friendly with the Julio-Claudian emperors, he was the first Gaul to enter the Senate and became Consul in 46 CE. In 47 CE he was accused of adultery and forced by Claudius to commit suicide.

[200] A term for senators.

[201] The original Roman province in southern Gaul, as of ca. 120 BCE; the remainder of Gaul was not annexed by Julius Caesar until 54 BCE.

of his ancestors the name Allobrogius.[202] And if such is your thought, what would you desire more? Do I have to point it out to you? Even the territory that is located beyond the province of Narbonese Gaul, has it not already sent you senators? For surely we have no regrets in going clear up to Lugdunum[203] for the members of our order. Assuredly, Conscript Fathers, it is not without some hesitation that I cross the limits of the provinces that are well known and familiar to you, but the moment is come when I must plead openly the cause of Further Gaul.[204] It will be objected that Gaul sustained a war against the divine Julius for ten years.[205] But let there be opposed to this the memory of a hundred years of steadfast fidelity, and a loyalty put to the proof in many trying circumstances. My father, Drusus,[206] was able to force Germany to submit because behind him reigned a profound peace assured by the tranquillity of the Gauls. And note well, that at the moment he was summoned to that war, he was busy instituting the census[207] in Gaul, a new institution among them, and contrary to their customs. And how difficult and perilous to us is this business of the census, although all we require is that our public resources should be known, we have learned by all too much experience."

(b) Tacitus, *Annals*, Book 11, Chapters 23–25

Source: Alfred John Church and William Jackson Brodribb, trans., *Annals of Tacitus* (London: Macmillan, 1876).

In the consulship of Aulus Vitellius and Lucius Vipstanus[208] the question of filling up the Senate was discussed, and the chief men of Gallia Comata,[209] as it was called, who had long possessed the rights of allies and of Roman citizens, sought the privilege of obtaining public offices at Rome. There was much talk of every kind on the subject, and it was argued before the emperor with vehement opposition. "Italy," it was asserted, "is not so feeble as to be unable to furnish its own capital with a Senate. Once our native-born citizens sufficed for peoples of our own kin, and we are by no means dissatisfied with the Rome of the past. To this day we cite examples, which under our old customs the Roman character exhibited as to valor and renown. Is it a small thing that Veneti and Insubres[210] already have burst into the Senate house, unless that now a mob of foreigners, a troop of captives, so to say, is forced upon us? What distinctions will be left for the remnants of our noble houses, or for any impoverished senators from Latium? Every place will be crowded with these millionaires, whose ancestors of the second and third generations at the head of hostile peoples destroyed

[202] A joke. The Allobroges were a famous Gallic people; Persicus's ancestor got the name not because he was one of them, but because he defeated them.

[203] Modern Lyon, just north of Vienne on the Rhône River in central France.

[204] The part of Gaul on the far side of the Alps, contrasted to Cisalpine Gaul, "Gaul on the Near Side of the Alps."

[205] Not quite; from 58 to 50 BCE at the latest.

[206] Nero Claudius Drusus Germanicus, stepson of the emperor Augustus and brother of the emperor Tiberius. After successful campaigns against the Germans, he died in 9 BCE after a fall from his horse.

[207] The cataloguing of property ownership for the purposes of tax assessment.

[208] Consuls in 48 CE.

[209] "Long Haired Gaul," the name given to the areas of Gaul annexed by Julius Caesar in 54 BCE, the same as the "Further Gaul" cited by Claudius in the previous passage.

[210] Peoples of far northern Italy; the Insubres were Celts, the Veneti native peoples.

our armies with fire and sword, and actually besieged the divine Julius at Alesia.[211] These are recent memories. What if there were to rise up the remembrance of those who fell in Rome's citadel and at her altar by the hands of these same barbarians![212] Let them enjoy indeed the title of citizens, but let them not vulgarize the distinctions of the Senate and the honors of office."

These and like arguments failed to impress the emperor. He at once addressed himself to answer them, and thus harangued the assembled Senate.

> My ancestors, the most ancient of whom was made at once a citizen and a noble of Rome, encourage me to govern by the same policy of transferring to this city all conspicuous merit, wherever found. And indeed I know, as facts, that the Julii came from Alba,[213] the Coruncanii from Camerium,[214] the Porcii from Tusculum,[215] and not to inquire too minutely into the past, that new members have been brought into the Senate from Etruria and Lucania and the whole of Italy, that Italy itself was at last extended to the Alps, to the end that not only single persons but entire countries and peoples might be united under our name.[216] We had unshaken peace at home; we prospered in all our foreign relations, in the days when Italy beyond the Po was admitted to share our citizenship,[217] and when, enrolling in our ranks the most vigorous of the provincials, under color of settling our legions throughout the world, we recruited our exhausted empire. Are we sorry that the Balbi came to us from Spain, and other men not less illustrious from Narbonese Gaul? Their descendents are still among us, and do not yield to us in patriotism.
>
> What was the ruin of Sparta and Athens,[218] but this, that mighty as they were in war they spurned from them as aliens those whom they had conquered? Our founder Romulus, on the other hand, was so wise that he fought as enemies and then hailed as fellow-citizens several nations on the very same day. Strangers have reigned over us. That freedmen's sons should be entrusted with public offices is not, as many wrongly think, a sudden innovation, but was a common practice in the old Republic. But, it will be said, we have fought with the Senones.[219] I suppose then that the Volsci and Aequi[220] never stood in array against us. Our city was taken by the Gauls. Well, we also gave hostages to the Etruscans, and passed under the yoke of the Samnites.[221] On the whole, if you review all our wars, never has one been finished in a shorter time than that with the Gauls. Thenceforth they have preserved an unbroken and loyal peace. United as they now are with us by manners, education, and intermarriage, let them bring us their gold and their wealth rather than enjoy it in isolation. Everything, Senators, that we now hold to be of the highest antiquity once was new. Plebeian magistrates came after patrician; Latin magistrates after plebeian; magistrates of other Italian peoples after Latin. This practice too will establish itself, and what we are this day justifying by precedents, will be itself a precedent."

The emperor's speech was followed by a Recommendation of the Senate, and the Aedui[222] were the first to obtain the right of becoming senators at Rome. This compliment was paid to their ancient alliance, and to the fact that they alone of the Gauls cling to the name of brothers of the Roman people.

---

[211] Actually it was Julius Caesar who besieged the Gauls at Alesia; see Reading 85.

[212] During the Sack of Rome by the Gauls in 390 BCE; see Reading 77.

[213] Claudius's own ancestors, the descendants of Iulus, or Ascanius, the son of the Trojan hero Aeneas, who had founded the city of Alba Longa; see Reading 88.

[214] An ancient colony of Alba Longa near Rome.

[215] An ancient Latin town.

[216] Claudius again indulges his interests in ancient history.

[217] Cisalpine Gaul received citizenship from Julius Caesar in 49 BCE.

[218] For the disastrous consequences of the warfare between Sparta and Athens, see Reading 56.

[219] Gauls of northern Italy.

[220] Italic peoples who fought the Romans during the early Roman Republic.

[221] After a Roman army was trapped at the Caudine Forks in 321 BCE.

[222] An important people of central Gaul.

94

THE REBELLION OF BOUDICCA (60–61 CE): TACITUS, *ANNALS*, BOOK 14, CHAPTERS 31–37

A silver coin of the Iceni, a Celtic people of Britain, dated to the middle of the first century CE. This coin type often is attributed to Queen Boudicca. In typical Celtic abstract style, it displays a head on the obverse that some claim is Boudicca herself and a horse on the reverse with a wheel above.

In 43 CE the emperor Claudius (41–54 CE) began the conquest of Britain, which proceeded smoothly until 60 CE, when Roman heavy-handedness provoked a revolt led by Boudicca, the charismatic Queen of the Iceni, who had united the hitherto disunified Celtic peoples. Initially, the Romans were caught off guard. In particular, the able Roman commander in Britain, Suetonius Paulinus, was occupied in the far west subduing the island of Mona (Anglesey), which had become a refuge for rebels and Celtic priests known as Druids. Boudicca's Celts destroyed the Roman colony of Camulodunum (Colchester). London received similar treatment; a ten-inch layer of red clay from the burned city still lies beneath London streets. After one cowardly legion refused to march, Suetonius could assemble only ten thousand soldiers to face the hundred thousand Celts. At the Battle of Watling Street, Paulinus lined up his troops with his rear and flanks protected by forests. The Celts spent their energy on fruitless assaults on the Roman shield wall, and then the slaughter started. Eighty thousand Celts were killed and Boudicca poisoned herself. Having failed in their revolt, the Celts of Britain, like those of Spain, Pannonia, and Gaul, then accommodated themselves to Roman rule.

Source: Arthur Murphy, *The Works of Tacitus* (Dublin: White, 1794).

During the consulship of Lucius Caesennius Paetus and Publius Petronius Turpilianus,[223] a dreadful calamity befell the army in Britain. Paulinus Suetonius succeeded to the command; an officer of distinguished merit. His military talents gave him pretensions, and the voice of the people, who never leave exalted merit without a rival, raised him to the highest eminence. By subduing the mutinous spirit of the Britons he hoped to equal the brilliant success of Corbulo in Armenia.[224] With this view, he resolved to subdue the island of Mona[225]; a place inhabited by a warlike people, and a common refuge for all the discontented Britons. In order to facilitate his approach to a difficult and deceitful shore, he ordered a number of flat-bottomed boats to be constructed. In these he transported over the infantry, while the cavalry, partly by fording over the shallows and partly by swimming their horses, advanced to gain a footing on the island.

On the opposite shore stood the Britons, close embodied, and prepared for action. Women were seen running through the ranks in wild disorder, their hair loose to the wind, in their hands flaming torches, and their whole appearance resembling the frantic rage of the Furies. The Druids were ranged in order, with hands uplifted, invoking the gods, and pouring forth horrible imprecations. The novelty of the fight struck the Romans with awe and terror. The exhortations of the general diffused new vigor through the ranks, and the men, by mutual reproaches, inflamed each other to deeds of valor. They felt the disgrace of yielding to a troop of women and a band of fanatic priests. They advanced their standards, and rushed on to the attack with impetuous fury.

The Britons perished in the flames that they themselves had kindled. The island fell, and a garrison was established to retain it in subjection. The religious groves,[226] dedicated to superstition and barbarous rites, were levelled to the ground. In those recesses, the natives stained their altars with the blood of their prisoners, and in the entrails of men explored the will of the gods.[227] While Suetonius was employed in making his arrangements to secure the island, he received intelligence that Britain had revolted and that the whole province was up in arms.

Prasutagus, the late King of the Iceni,[228] in the course of a long reign had amassed considerable wealth. By his will he left the whole to his two daughters and the emperor in equal shares, conceiving, by that stroke of policy, that he should provide at once for the tranquility of his kingdom and his family. The event was otherwise. His dominions were ravaged by the centurions, the slaves pillaged his house, and his effects were seized as lawful plunder. His wife, Boudicca, was disgraced with a cruel whipping, her daughters were ravished, and the most illustrious of the Iceni were, by force, deprived of the

[223] 60–61 CE.

[224] Corbulo occupied Armenia in 58 CE and it became a Roman client state. In 67 CE he was ordered by the emperor Nero (54–68) to commit suicide.

[225] Anglesey, off the northwestern coast of Wales.

[226] The Druids were believed to worship in groves of oak trees.

[227] In the same way that the Romans practiced the haruspices, the inspection of the livers of sacrificial animals, to ascertain the will of the gods.

[228] A Celtic people of eastern Britain.

positions that had been transmitted to them by their ancestors. The whole country was considered as a legacy bequeathed to the plunderers. The relations of the deceased king were reduced to slavery.

Exasperated by their acts of violence, and dreading worse calamities, the Iceni had recourse to arms. The Trinobantes[229] joined in the revolt. The neighboring states, not as yet taught to crouch in bondage, pledged themselves, in secret councils, to stand forth in the cause of liberty. What chiefly fired their indignation was the conduct of the veterans, lately planted as a colony at Camulodunum.[230] These men treated the Britons with cruelty and oppression. They drove the natives from their habitations, and calling them by the shameful names of slaves and captives, added insult to their tyranny. In these acts of oppression, the veterans were supported by the common soldiers, a class of men, by their habits of life, trained to licentiousness, and, in their turn, expecting to reap the same advantages. The temple built in honor of Claudius was another cause of discontent. In the eye of the Britons it seemed the citadel of eternal slavery. The priests appointed to officiate at the altars, with a pretended zeal for religion, devoured the whole substance of the country. To overrun a colony, which lay quite naked and exposed without a single fortification to defend it, did not appear to the incensed and angry Britons an enterprise that threatened either danger or difficulty. The fact was that the Roman generals attended to improvements to taste and elegance but neglected the useful. They embellished the province and took no care to defend it.

While the Britons were preparing to throw off the yoke, the statue of victory, erected at Camulodunum, fell from its base without any apparent cause and lay extended on the ground with its face averted, as if the goddess yielded to the enemies of Rome. Women in restless ecstasy rushed among the people and with frantic screams denounced impending ruin. By these portents the Romans were sunk in despair whereas the Britons anticipated a glorious victory. Suetonius, in the meantime, was detained on the isle of Mona. In this alarming crisis, the veterans at the colony sent to Catus Decianus, the Procurator of the province,[231] for a reinforcement. Two hundred men, and those not completely armed, were all that officer could spare. The colony had but a handful of soldiers. Their temple was strongly fortified and there they hoped to make a stand. But even for the defense of that place no ditch was made and no palisade thrown up, nor were the women and those disabled by age or infirmity sent out of the garrison. Unguarded and unprepared, they were taken by surprise, and, in the moment of profound peace, overpowered by the barbarians in one general assault. The colony was laid waste with fire and sword.

The temple held out, but, after a siege of two days, was taken by storm. Petilius Cerealis, who commanded the Ninth Legion, marched to the relief of the place. The Britons, flushed with success, advanced to give him battle. The legion was routed and the infantry cut to pieces. Cerealis escaped with the cavalry to entrenchments of his camp. Catus Decianus, alarmed at the scene of carnage that he beheld on every side, and further dreading the indignation of a people whom by rapine and oppression he had driven to despair, betook himself to flight and crossed over into Gaul.

Suetonius, undismayed by this disaster, marched through the heart of the country as far as London, a place not dignified with the name of a colony but the chief residence of merchants and a great center of trade and commerce. At that place he meant to fix the feat of war, but reflecting on the scanty numbers of his little army and the fatal rashness of Cerealis, he resolved to quit the station, and, by giving up one post, secure the rest of the province. Neither supplications nor the tears of the inhabitants could induce him to change his plan. The signal for the march was given. All who chose to follow his banners were taken under his protection. Of all who, on account of their advanced age, the weakness of their sex, of the attractions of the situation, thought proper to remain

[229] A Celtic people dwelling south of the Iceni.

[230] Colchester.

[231] An imperial official in charge of tax collection.

behind, not one escaped the rage of the barbarians. The inhabitants of Verulamium,[232] a municipal town,[233] in like manner were put to the sword. The genius[234] of a savage people leads them always in quest of plunder, and, accordingly, the Britons left behind them all places of strength. Wherever they expected feeble resistance and considerable booty, there they were sure to attack with the fiercest rage. Military skill was not the talent of barbarians. The number massacred in the places that have been mentioned amounted to no less than seventy thousand, all citizens or allies of Rome. To make prisoners and reserve them for slavery or exchange them was not in the character of a people who despised all the laws of war. They hastened to inflict death, whipping, burning, and crucifixion as if aware they were going to receive retribution but in the meantime were taking their revenge.

The Fourteenth Legion, with the veterans of the Twentieth Legion,[235] and the auxiliaries from the adjacent stations, having joined Suetonius, his army amounted to little less than ten thousand men. Thus reinforced, he resolved, without loss of time, to bring on a decisive action. For this purpose he chose a spot encircled with woods, narrow at the entrance, and sheltered in the rear by a thick forest. In that situation he had no fear of an ambush. The enemy, he knew, had no approach but in front. An open plain lay before him. He drew up his men in the following order: the legions in close array formed the center; the light-armed troops were stationed at hand to serve as occasion might require; the cavalry took post in the wings.[236] The Britons brought into the field an incredible multitude. They formed no regular line of battle. Detached parties and loose battalions displayed their numbers, in frantic transport bounding with exultation, and so sure of victory, that they placed their wives in wagons at the extremity of the plain where they might survey the scene of action, and behold the wonders of British valor.

Boudicca, in a chariot, with her two daughters before her, drove through the ranks. She harangued the different nations in their turn: "This," she said, "is not the first time that the Britons have been led to battle by a woman. But now she did not come to boast the pride of a long line of ancestry, nor even to recover her kingdom and the plundered wealth of her family. She took the field, like the meanest among them, to assert the cause of public liberty, and to seek revenge for her body seamed with ignominious stripes, and her two daughters infamously ravished. From the pride and arrogance of the Romans nothing is sacred. All persons are subject to violation; the old endure the whip and the virgins are violated. But the vindictive gods now are at hand. A Roman legion dared to face the warlike Britons. With their lives they paid for their rashness. Those who survived the carnage of that day lie poorly hid behind their entrenchments, meditating nothing but how to save themselves by an ignominious flight.[237] From the din of preparation and the shouts of the British army the Romans, even now, shrink back with terror. What will be their case when the assault begins? Look round, and view your numbers. Behold the proud display of warlike spirits, and consider the motives for which we draw the avenging sword. On this spot we must either conquer, or die with glory. There is no alternative. Although a woman, my resolution is fixed. The men, if they please, may survive with infamy, and live in bondage."

Suetonius, in a moment of such importance, did not remain silent. He expected every thing from the valor of his men and yet urged every topic that could inspire and animate them to the attack. "Despise," he said, "the savage uproar, the yells and shouts of undisciplined barbarians. In that mixed multitude, the women outnumber the men. Void of spirit, unprovided with arms, they are not soldiers who come to offer battle; they are bastards, runaways, the refuse of your swords, who often have fled before you, and

[232] St. Albans.

[233] That is, a city of Roman citizens with a municipal charter.

[234] Guiding spirit.

[235] Another of the four legions stationed in Britain.

[236] The standard offensive formation of an ancient army.

[237] The Ninth Legion of Cerialis. Another, the Second Legion under Poenius Postumius, also refused to fight.

will again betake themselves to flight when they see the conqueror flaming in the ranks of war. In all engagements it is the valor of a few that turns the fortune of the day. It will be your immortal glory that with a scanty number you can equal the exploits of a great and powerful army. Keep your ranks, discharge your javelins, rush forward to a close attack, bear down all with your shields, and hew a passage with your swords. Pursue the vanquished and never think of spoil and plunder. Conquer, and victory gives you everything." This speech was received with warlike acclamations. The soldiers burned with impatience for the onset, the veterans brandished their javelins and the ranks displayed such an intrepid countenance that Suetonius, anticipating the victory, gave the signal for the charge.

The engagement began. The Roman legion presented a close embodied line. The narrow defile gave them the shelter of a rampart. The Britons advanced with ferocity and discharged their darts at random. In that instant, the Romans rushed forward in the form of a wedge. The auxiliaries followed with equal ardor. The cavalry, at the same time, bore down upon the enemy, and, with their pikes, overpowered all who dared to make a stand. The Britons betook themselves to flight, but their wagons in the rear obstructed their passage. A dreadful slaughter followed. Neither sex nor age was spared. The cattle, falling in one promiscuous carnage, added to the heaps of slain. The glory of the day was equal to the most splendid victory of ancient times. According to some writers, not less than eighty thousand Britons were put to the sword. The Romans lost about four hundred men, and the wounded did not exceed that number. Boudicca, by a dose of poison, ended her life. Poenius Postumius, the Prefect on the Camp of the Second Legion,[238] as soon as he heard of the brave exploits of the Fourteenth and Twentieth legions, felt the disgrace of having, in disobedience to the orders of his general, robbed the soldiers under his command of their share in so complete a victory.[239] Stung with remorse, he fell upon his sword and expired on the spot.

---

[238] It is unclear why the Prefect of the Camp, who ranked beneath the Legate of the Legion and the Military Tribune, was in command of the legion.

[239] Thus, of the four British legions, only two, the Second and the Fourteenth, actually participated in Boudicca's defeat.

95

THE FALL OF MASADA (74 CE): JOSEPHUS, *THE WARS OF THE JEWS*, BOOK 7, CHAPTER 9

An aerial view of the site of Masada, showing the Herodian fortress atop the bluff, the Roman ramp up the side, and the remains of Roman siege camps scattered around the base of the escarpment.

In spite of Roman efforts to accommodate the religious sensibilities of the Jews of Palestine, there always were religious incompatibilities between the Jews and the Roman government and the Jews easily were the most restive of all the peoples included in the Roman Empire. Large-scale Jewish revolts against Roman authority occurred in 66, 115, and 131 CE, after which the Jews were expelled from Palestine, thus augmenting the already extensive Jewish diaspora. The first of these rebellions occurred under the emperor Nero and resulted in a massive Roman response. The general Vespasian was appointed to suppress the revolt. In 69 CE, after Vespasian had been declared emperor, he left the revolt in the hands of his son, Titus. In the next year, Jerusalem was captured and sacked, but Jewish Sicarii, or Dagger-Carriers, a fanatic group of the Jewish Zealots who had attempted to expel the Romans, had retreated to and occupied what was thought to be the impregnable fortress of Masada, built atop a precipitous bluff in the Judaean desert by King Herod the Great in the 30s BCE. In 73 CE the Roman army besieged Masada and began the construction of a massive earthen ramp to the top. The work initially was done by Roman soldiers, but when the besieged Jews bombarded them with rocks from the top of the bluff, the Romans also put captured Jews to work, and the Jews stopped throwing stones. After three months, the ramp was complete. The Romans broke into the fortress to find that 960 Jews had committed suicide; only 7 survived to report what had happened. The Jewish historian Josephus provides a detailed account of the siege.

Source: From William Whiston, trans., *The Works of Josephus* (Peabody, MA: Hendrickson, 1987).

Now as Eleazar[240] was proceeding on in his exhortations, they all cut him off short[241] and made haste to do the work, full of an unconquerable ardor of mind and moved with a demoniacal fury. So they went their ways, with each one still endeavoring to be before the others, and as if they were thinking that this eagerness would be a demonstration of their courage and good conduct. So great was the zeal they were in to slay their wives and children, and themselves also! Nor, indeed, when they came to the work itself, did their courage fail them, as one might imagine it would have done. Then they held fast to the same resolution, without wavering, that they had upon hearing of Eleazar's speech, while every one of them still retained the natural passion of love for their families, because the reasoning they depended upon appeared to them to be very just, even with regard to those that were dearest to them. The husbands tenderly embraced their wives and took their children into their arms, and gave the longest parting kisses to them, with tears in their eyes. Yet at the same time did they complete what they had resolved on, as if they had been executed by the hands of strangers, and they had nothing else for their comfort but the necessity they were in of doing this execution to avoid that prospect they had of the miseries they were to suffer from their enemies. Nor was there at length any one of these men found that scrupled to act their part in this terrible execution, but every one of them dispatched his dearest relations.

Miserable men indeed were they, whose distress forced them to slay their own wives and children with their own hands, as the lightest of the evils that were before them. So, being not able to bear the grief they were under for what they had done any longer, and esteeming it an injury to those they had slain to live even the shortest space of time after them, they presently laid all their possessions in a heap and set fire to it. They then chose ten men by lot out of them to slay all the rest, every one of whom laid himself down by his wife and children on the ground, and threw his arms about them, and they offered their necks to the stroke of those who by lot executed that melancholy office. And when these ten had, without fear, slain them all, they made the same rule for casting lots for themselves, that he whose lot it was should first kill the other nine, and after all, should kill himself. Accordingly, all these had courage sufficient to be no way behind one another in doing or

[240] Eleazar ben Ya'ir, the leader of the Jewish Sicarii ("knife-bearers") who had occupied Masada.

[241] When it became clear that the Romans had completed their ramp and were about to storm the fortress, Eleazar spoke in favor of committing suicide. His supporters needed no speeches to be convinced to do this.

suffering. So, for a conclusion, the nine offered their necks to the executioner, and he who was the last of all took a view of all the other bodies, lest perchance some or other among so many that were slain should want his assistance to be quite dispatched, and when he perceived that they were all slain, he set fire to the palace, and with the great force of his hands ran his sword entirely through himself and fell down dead near to his own relations.

So these people died with this intention, that they would leave not so much as one soul among them all alive to be subject to the Romans. Yet there was an ancient woman, and another who was of kin to Eleazar, and superior to most women in prudence and learning, with five children, who had concealed themselves in caverns under ground, and had carried water thither for their drink, and were hidden there when the rest were intent upon the slaughter of one another. Those others were nine hundred and sixty in number, the women and children being withal included in that computation. This calamitous slaughter was made on the fifteenth day of the month Xanthicus.[242]

Now for the Romans, they expected that they should be fought in the morning, when accordingly they put on their armor and laid bridges of planks upon their ladders from their ramp, to make an assault upon the fortress, which they did, but saw nobody as an enemy, but a terrible solitude on every side, with a fire within the place as well as a perfect silence. So they were at a loss to guess at what had happened. At length they made a shout, as if it had been at a blow given by the battering-ram, to try whether they could bring anyone out that was within. The women heard this noise and came out of their underground cavern and informed the Romans what had been done, as it was done, and the second of them clearly described both all that was said and what was done, and the manner of it. Yet the Romans did not easily give their attention to such a desperate undertaking, and did not believe it could be as the women said. They also attempted to put the fire out, and quickly cutting themselves a way through it, they came within the palace, and so met with the multitude of the slain, but could take no pleasure in the fact, although it was done to their enemies. Nor could they do other than wonder at the courage of their resolution and the immovable contempt of death that so great a number of them had shown, when they went through with such an action as that was.

[242] The first month in the Macedonian calendar, equivalent to the Jewish month of Nisan, or April.

96

HADRIAN INSPECTS THE TROOPS (128 CE): THE LAMBAESIS INSCRIPTION

On the detailed reverse of this sestertius, the emperor Hadrian (117–138), in the course of his travels around the empire, delivers an *adlocutio*, or formal speech of greeting, to the British army, represented by an *aquilifer* (eagle bearer), *signifer* (standard bearer), and common soldier.

In the summer of 128 CE, during a tour of North Africa, the emperor Hadrian visited the legionary fortress at Lambaesis in Numidia (modern Algeria), the headquarters of the Third

Augustan Legion. As was his practice, during the two-week visit he observed army units doing prepared maneuvers and then after each exercise he made an "adlocutio," a formal address, in which he commented on what he had seen. The *adlocutio* made on this occasion is the only one to survive from antiquity, preserved on the base of a column erected to commemorate Hadrian's visit. The inscription began with a dedication by the legion and was followed by the text of the emperor's speech. Hadrian began by praising Quintus Fabius Catullinus, the "Legate of the Legion." Then, after a few words about the value of military exercise that he no doubt repeated in all such speeches, the inscription continued with Hadrian's comments on each unit in turn, in which the emperor mixed praise with occasional criticism, just enough to validate the praise. The text is fragmentary, so only the best-preserved sections are quoted here.

Source: Michael Speidel, *Emperor Hadrian's Speeches to the African Army. A New Text* (Mainz: Römisch-Germanischen Zentralmuseums, 2006).

[Dedication]
The Third Augustan Legion to the Imperator Caesar Trajan Hadrian Augustus, bravest and most generous emperor, after the encampment and the army had passed inspection.

[Hadrian's adlocutio]
After the exercises had been observed, the Imperator Caesar Trajan Hadrian Augustus spoke these words that are written below, on the Kalends of July while Torquatus for the second time and Libo were Consuls.[243]

To the *pili*.[244]

Catullinus, my Legate,[245] is keen in your support. Indeed, everything that you might have had to put to me he has himself told me on your behalf; that a cohort[246] is away because, taking turns, one is sent every year to the staff of the Proconsul[247]; that two years ago you gave a cohort and five men from each century to the fellow Third Legion; that many far-flung outposts keep you scattered, that twice within our memory you have not only changed fortresses but built new ones. For this I would have forgiven you if something had come to a halt in your training. But nothing seems to have halted, nor is there any reason why you should need my forgiving.

To the cavalry of the legion.

Military exercises somehow have their own laws by which, if anything is added or taken away, the exercise gets either easier or harder. And the harder one makes it, the less graceful it becomes. You have made the hardest out of a hard task by throwing spears while wearing the *lorica*,[248] and thereby you lost in elegance. But I do approve the spirit in which you did this.

To the *principes*.[249]

Work that others would have spread out over several days you took only one day to finish. You have built a lengthy wall, made as if for permanent winter-quarters, in nearly as short a time as if it were built from turf that is cut in even pieces, easily carried and handled, and laid without difficulty, being naturally smooth and flat. You built with big, heavy, uneven stones that no one can carry, lift, or lay

[243] 1 July 128 CE.

[244] The "spear carriers," that is, the legionaries stationed in the first rank.

[245] The "Legatus legionis," that is, the "Legate of the Legion," the commander of the legion.

[246] A subdivision of a legion, which had ten cohorts of rather less than six hundred men each.

[247] Because Africa was a senatorial province, its governor was a Proconsul, not a "Legate of Augustus."

[248] Roman body armor, made of metal scales or plates.

[249] The "leaders," the legionaries of the second rank.

without their unevenness becoming evident. You dug a straight ditch through hard and rough gravel and scraped it smooth. Your work approved, you quickly entered camp, took your food and weapons, and followed the horse who had been sent out, hailing them with a great shout as they came back.

To the second cohort of the Hamii.[250]

Because you do not shoot at a signal, the foe being already upon you, your Prefect makes you try and shoot oftener and sharper, so that among the many missiles the foe dare not lift his head above the shield. You were slow to close ranks . . .

To the *ala*[251] . . .

I praise him[252] for having brought you over to this maneuver that has taken on the looks of true fighting, and for training you so well that I can praise you. Your Prefect Comelianus has done his duty undauntedly. I do not like counter-wheelings,[253] nor did the deified Trajan,[254] my model. A horseman should ride out from cover. If he does not see where he is going, or cannot rein in his horse when he wishes, he may come to grief from hidden traps and trenches he does not see. If you want to attack, you must charge across the middle of the field, as when facing the foe. Nothing ever must be done recklessly.

The third day before the Ides of July.[255]

To the first squadron of the Pannonians.

You did everything according to the book. You filled the training ground with your wheelings, you threw spears not ungracefully, although with short and stiff spears.

Several of you hurled *lancea* spears with skill. Your jumping onto the horses here was lively and yesterday was swift. Had anything been lacking, I would note it; had anything stood out, I would mention it. You pleased equally throughout the whole maneuver. Noble Catullinus, my deputy, gives the same care to all.

To the cavalry of the sixth cohort of the Commagenians.[256]

It is hard for horsemen of a cohort to please, even as they are, and harder still not to displease after a show by horsemen of an *ala*: the training field differs in size, spear throwers are fewer, the right-wheel is tight, the Cantabrian formation[257] is cramped, the condition of the horses and the maintenance of the equipment in keeping with the pay level. But you have banished weariness by your eagerness, by doing briskly what had to be done. Moreover, you shot stones from slings and fought with javelins; everywhere you jumped nimbly onto your horses. The outstanding manhood of noble Catullinus, my legate, shows itself in that under this man you are such men.

[250] Hadrian now has moved on to the units of the *auxilia*, commanded by Prefects and composed of specialized troops such as cavalry and archers.

[251] A squadron of cavalry.

[252] Presumably Catullinus.

[253] Circling movements that do not allow a rider to see clearly what is ahead.

[254] The emperor Trajan (98–117 CE), Hadrian's predecessor.

[255] 13 July.

[256] Named after Commagene, a region in the southeastern corner of Anatolia.

[257] A tactic in which cavalry rode in a continuously rotating circle and thus kept up a steady stream of arrow, spear, or sling-stone fire.

97

ROMAN MISOGYNY (CA. 100 CE): JUVENAL, *SATIRE* 6

A fresco from the "House of the Chaste Lovers" in Pompeii shows men and women enjoying each other's company at a banquet. The kinds of pleasures being enjoyed here would have seemed tame compared to the kinds of activities in which, according to the Roman satirist Juvenal, upper-class Roman women indulged around 100 CE.

The Roman satirist Juvenal's Sixth Satire, which nominally attempts to dissuade Juvenal's friend Postumus from getting married, usually is taken as evidence for Roman attitudes toward gender in general and misogeny in particular, as Juvenal expounds on women's fundamental lack of morality. But the Satire also includes the famous line, "Who will guard the guards?," making the point that it is impossible to impose standards of morality if those doing the imposing are themselves immoral. For example, men who divorce older wives in order to marry younger ones also are condemned. The Satire thus can be taken as being equally against the men who themselves have encouraged, participated in, and enabled immoral behavior. At the same time, the Satire also is full of jokes and mythological allusions—only some of which can be commented on here—that an educated audience would have appreciated.

Source: G. G. Ramsay, trans., *Juvenal and Persius*, Loeb Classical Library (London: Heinemann, New York, Putnam, 1918).

In the days of Saturn,[258] I believe, Chastity still lingered on the earth, and was to be seen for a time. These were the days when men were poorly housed in chilly caves; when one common shelter enclosed hearth and household gods, herds and their owners; when the hill-bred wife spread her sylvan bed with leaves and straw and the skins of her neighbors the wild beasts, a wife not like to thee, O Cynthia,[259] nor to thee, Lesbia,[260] whose bright eyes were clouded by a sparrow's death, but one whose breasts gave suck to lusty babes, often more unkempt herself than her acorn-belching spouse. For in those days, when the world was young, and the skies were new, men born of the riven oak, or formed of dust, lived differently from now, and had no parents of their own. Under Jove,[261] perchance, some few traces of ancient modesty may have survived, But that was before he had grown his beard, before the Greeks had learned to swear by someone else's head, when men feared not thieves for their cabbages or apples, and lived with unwalled gardens. After that Astraea[262] withdrew by degrees to heaven, with Chastity[263] as her comrade, the two sisters taking flight together.

To set your neighbor's bed a-shaking, Postumus,[264] and to flout the Genius[265] of the sacred couch, is now an ancient and long-established practice. All other sins came later, the products of the Age of Iron; but it was the Silver Age that saw the first adulterers. Nevertheless, in these days of ours, you are preparing for a covenant, a marriage-contract, and a betrothal; you are by now getting your hair cut by a master barber; you have also perhaps given a pledge to her finger. What! Postumus, are you, you who once had your wits, taking to yourself a wife? Tell me what Tisiphone, what snakes are driving you mad?[266] Can you submit to a she-tyrant when there is so much rope to be had, so many dizzy heights of windows standing open, and when the Aemilian Bridge[267] offers itself to hand? Or if none of all these modes of exit hits your fancy, how much better to take some boy bedfellow, who would never wrangle with you over nights, never ask presents of you when in bed, and never complain that you took your ease and were indifferent to his solicitations!

But Ursidius[268] approves of the Julian Law.[269] He purposes to bring up a dear little heir, although he will thereby have to do without the fine turtles, the bearded mullets, and all the legacy-hunting[270] delicacies of the meat-market. What can you think impossible if Ursidius takes to himself a wife? If he, who has long been the most notorious of gallants, who has so often found safety in the grain-bin of the luckless Latinus,[271] puts his head into the connubial noose? And what think you of his searching for a wife of the good old virtuous sort? O doctors, lance his over-blooded veins. A pretty fellow you! Why, if you have the good luck to find a modest spouse, you should prostrate yourself before the Tarpeian threshold and sacrifice a heifer with gilded horns to Juno,[272] so few are the wives worthy to handle the fillets of Ceres,[273] or from whose kisses their own

---

258 The "Golden Age" of Hesiod; see Reading 47.
259 The paramour of the Augustan poet Propertius.
260 The paramour of the late Roman Republican poet Catullus; see Reading 84.
261 Another name for Jupiter; the "Bronze Age" of Hesiod.
262 The virgin goddess of innocence; she fled from the earth and became the constellation Virgo ("the virgin").
263 Pudicitia, the goddess of chastity.
264 A friend of Juvenal; the Satire purportedly is intended to dissuade him from getting married.
265 Guardian spirit.
266 One of the Furies, the avengers of crimes; she had snakes for hair. See Reading 5.
267 A bridge across the Tiber River near the Aventine Hill, more usually known as the Milvian Bridge.
268 A notorious adulterer who finally decided to get married and raise a family.
269 A law of Augustus against adultery.
270 Marriages often were contracted with inheritances in mind; once he was married, Ursidius would have to give this up.
271 In Roman comedies "Latinus," a stock character, often had to hide anyplace that was on hand to avoid being caught in the act of adultery.
272 A shrine to Juno, part of the Capitoline temple, was near the Tarpeian Rock, from which unfaithful Vestal Virgins sometimes were flung, on the Capitoline Hill.
273 Only chaste women were supposed to participate in the rites of the grain goddess Ceres.

father would not shrink! Weave a garland for thy doorposts, and set up wreaths of ivy over thy lintel![274]

But will Hiberina[275] be satisfied with one man? Sooner compel her to be satisfied with one eye! You tell me of the high repute of some maiden, who lives on her paternal farm. Well, let her live at Gabii, at Fidenae,[276] as she lived in her own country, and I will believe in your paternal farm. But will anyone tell me that nothing ever took place on a mountain side or in a cave?[277] Have Jupiter and Mars become so senile? Can our arcades[278] show you one woman worthy of your vows? Do all the tiers in all our theaters hold one whom you may love without misgiving, and pick out thence? When the soft Bathyllus[279] dances the part of the gesticulating Leda,[280] Tuccia[281] cannot contain herself; your Apulian maiden heaves a sudden and longing cry of ecstasy, as though she were in a man's arms. Other women pay great prices for the favors of a comedian. Hispulla[282] has a fancy for tragedians; but do you suppose that any one will be found to love Quintilian?[283] If you marry a wife, it will be so that the flute player Ambrosius may become a father. Adorn your doors and doorposts with wreaths of laurel, so that your highborn son may exhibit, in his tortoiseshell cradle, the lineaments of a murmillo![284]

When Eppia, the senator's wife, ran off with a gladiator to Pharos[285] and the Nile, Canopus[286] itself cried shame upon the monstrous morals of our town. Forgetful of home, of husband, and of sister, without thought of her country, she shamelessly abandoned her weeping children. Although born in wealth, although as a babe she had slept in an ornamented cradle on the paternal down, she made light of the sea, just as she had long made light of her good name. And so with stout heart she endured the tossing and the roaring of the Tyrrhenian and Ionian Seas,[287] and all the many seas she had to cross. Now, when danger comes in an honorable way, a woman's heart grows chill with fear, and she cannot stand upon her trembling feet: but if she be doing a bold, bad thing, her courage fails not. For a husband to order his wife on board ship is cruelty; the bilge-water sickens her. But if she is running away with a lover, she feels no qualms. In the first case, she vomits over her husband, but in the second she flirts with the sailors, roams about the deck, and delights in hauling at the hard ropes.

And what were the youthful charms that captivated Eppia? What did she see in him to allow herself to be called "a she-Gladiator"? Her dear Sergius[288] already had begun to shave[289]; a wounded arm gave promise of a discharge,[290] and there were sundry deformities in his face: a scar caused by the helmet, a huge boil upon his nose, a nasty humor always trickling from his eye. But then he was a gladiator! It is this that transforms these fellows into Hyacinths![291] It was this that she preferred to

[274] Decorations put on the homes of newlyweds.
[275] The putative fiancée of Postumus. This section turns to a discussion of unfaithfulness.
[276] Towns outside Rome.
[277] Juvenal refers to mythological sexual escapades that took place in the countryside.
[278] Fashionable Roman women promenading in sheltered arcades could see and be seen.
[279] A male slave who introduced pantomime, where stories were told accompanied only by movements.
[280] The mortal woman whom Jupiter visited disguised as a swan.
[281] A Vestal Virgin who cleared herself of a charge of fornication by drawing water in a sieve.
[282] A Roman noblewoman.
[283] A famous rhetorician.
[284] A type of gladiator.
[285] The famous lighthouse at Alexandria in Egypt.
[286] An Egyptian city on the eastern edge of Alexandria.
[287] The Tyrrhenian Sea was just west of the boot of Italy and the Ionian Sea just east of it.
[288] The gladiator that she had run off with.
[289] At this time, Roman men often did not begin to shave until forty years of age.
[290] A discharge from service as a gladiator.
[291] A beautiful boy loved by Apollo, who changed him into a flower after he was accidentally killed.

children and to country, to sister, and to husband. What these women love is the sword!

Do the concerns of a private household and the doings of Eppia affect you? Just look at those who rival the gods, and hear what Claudius[292] endured. As soon as his wife[293] perceived that her husband was asleep, this august harlot was shameless enough to prefer a common mat to the imperial couch. Assuming a night-cowl and attended by a single maid, she went out. Then she took her place in a brothel reeking with long-used coverlets. Entering an empty cell reserved for herself, she there took her stand, under the feigned name of Lycisca, her nipples bare and gilded, and exposed to view the womb that bore thee, O nobly-born Britannicus![294] Here she graciously received all comers, asking from each his fee, and when at length the keeper dismissed the rest, she remained to the very last before closing her cell, and with passion still raging hot within her went sorrowfully away. Then exhausted but unsatisfied, with soiled cheeks and begrimed with the smoke of lamps, she took back to the imperial pillow all the odors of the bordello.

But tell me why is Censennia,[295] on her husband's testimony, the best of wives? "She brought him a million sesterces; that is the price at which he calls her chaste. He has not pined under the darts of Venus; he was never burnt by her torch. It was the dowry that lit his fires, the dowry that shot those arrows! That dowry bought liberty for her: she may make what signals, and write what love letters she pleases, before her husband's face. The rich woman who marries a money-loving husband is as good as unmarried.

[292] Roman emperor, 41–54 CE.

[293] Claudius's third wife Valeria Messalina, who had a reputation for promiscuity.

[294] The son of Claudius and Messalina; murdered by the emperor Nero (54–68) when he was fourteen.

[295] Not a clearly Roman name; Juvenal's point may be that as long as a woman has money, she can find a respectable, but perhaps impoverished, high-ranking Roman husband.

If you are not to love the woman betrothed and united to you in due form, what reason have you for marrying? Why waste the supper and the wedding cakes to be given to the well-filled guests when the company is slipping away? If you are honestly devoted to one woman, then bow your head and submit your neck to the yoke. Never will you find a woman who spares the man who loves her; for although she be herself aflame, she delights to torment and plunder him. So the better the man, the more desirable he is as a husband, the less good will he get out of his wife. No present will you ever make if your wife forbids; nothing will you ever sell if she objects; nothing will you buy without her consent. She will arrange your friendships for you; she will turn your now-aged friend from the door that saw the beginnings of his beard. Panders and trainers can make their wills as they please, as also can the gentlemen of the arena, but you will have to write down among your heirs more than one rival of your own.

"Crucify that slave!" says the wife. Thus does she lord it over her husband. But before long she vacates her kingdom; she flits from one home to another, wearing out her bridal veil. Then back she flies again and returns to her own imprints in the bed that she has abandoned, leaving behind her the newly decorated door, the festal hangings on the walls, and the garlands still green over the threshold. Thus does the tale of her husbands grow; there will be eight of them in the course of five autumns, a fact worthy of commemoration on her tomb![296]

There never was a case in court in which the quarrel was not started by a woman. If Manilia[297] is not a defendant, she will be the plaintiff. She will herself frame and adjust the pleadings; she will be ready to instruct Celsus[298] himself how to open his case, and how to urge his points.

[296] For the epitaph of a respectable Roman woman, see Reading 87.

[297] A plebeian woman of this name was prosecuted for hitting a magistrate with a stone.

[298] A legal scholar during the reign of Tiberius (14–37 CE).

Why need I tell of the wrestling-oils used by women? Who has not seen one of them smiting a tree stump, piercing it through and through with a sword, lunging at it with a shield, and going through all the proper motions? A matron truly qualified to blow a trumpet at the Floralia![299] Unless, indeed, she is nursing some further ambition in her bosom, and is practicing for the real arena. What modesty can you expect in a woman who wears a helmet, abjures her own sex, and delights in feats of strength? Yet she would not choose to be a man, knowing the superior joys of womanhood. What a fine thing for a husband, at an auction of his wife's effects, to see her belt and armlets and plumes put up for sale, with a gaiter that covers half the left leg; or if she fight another sort of battle, how charmed you will be to see your young wife disposing of her greaves! Yet these are the women who find the thinnest of thin robes too hot for them; whose delicate flesh is chafed by the finest of silk tissue. See how she pants as she goes through her prescribed exercises; how she bends under the weight of her helmet; how big and coarse are the bandages that enclose her thighs; and then laugh when she lays down her arms and shows herself to be a woman!

I hear all this time the advice of my old friends: keep your women at home and put them under lock and key. Yes, but who will watch the watchers?[300] Wives are crafty. High or low their passions are all the same. She who wears out the black cobble-stones with her bare feet is no better than she who rides[301] upon the necks of eight stalwart Syrians. Ogulnia hires clothes to see the games; she hires attendants, a litter, cushions, female friends, a nurse, and a fair-haired girl to run her messages; yet she will give all that remains of the family plate, down to the last flagon, to some smooth-faced athlete. Many of these women are poor, but none of them pay any regard to their poverty, or measure themselves by the standard that that prescribes and lays down for them. Men, on the other hand, do sometimes have an eye to utility, but your extravagant woman is never sensible of her dwindling means; she never gives a thought to what her pleasures cost her.

Yes, I know well the advice and warnings of my old friends: Put on a lock and keep your wife indoors. And yes, just who will guard the guards? They get paid in kind for holding their tongues as to their young lady's escapades. The wily wife arranges accordingly, and begins with them. If your wife is musical, none of those who sell their voices to the Praetor can compete with her charms. Better, however, that your wife should be musical than that she should be rushing boldly about the entire city, attending men's meetings, talking with unflinching face and hard breasts to generals in their military cloaks, with her husband looking on! This same woman knows what is going on all over the world: what the Thracians[302] and Chinese are after; she knows who loves whom, what gallant is the rage; she will tell you who got the widow with child, and in what month; how every woman behaves to her lovers, and what she says to them.

She frequents the baths by night; she loves all the bustle of the hot bath, when her arms drop exhausted by the heavy weights,[303] the anointer passes his hand skilfully over her body, bringing it down at last with a resounding smack upon her thigh. Meanwhile her unfortunate guests are overcome with sleep and hunger, until at last she comes in with a flushed face and tosses off a couple of pints before her dinner to create a raging appetite; then she brings it all up; the stream runs over the marble pavement and the gilt basin reeks of Falernian,[304] for she drinks and vomits like a big snake that has tumbled into a vat. The sickened husband closes his eyes and so keeps down his bile.

[299] A six-day festival, held in late April, in honor of the fertility goddess Flora. It was marked by theater performances and the participation of prostitutes and was known for its licentiousness.

[300] "Quis custodiet ipsos custodes," one of the most famous ancient quotations.

[301] In a litter.

[302] Thrace was a mountainous Balkan region northeast of Greece; modern Bulgaria.

[303] After a workout in the weight room.

[304] The most famous Roman wine, produced from grapes of Mt. Falernus in Latium.

If the woman be of humble rank, she will promenade between the turning-posts of the Circus.[305] Wealthy women will pay for answers from a Phrygian or Indian augur[306] well skilled in the stars and the heavens. These poor women, moreover, endure the perils of child-birth and all the troubles of nursing to which their lot condemns them; but how often does a gilded bed contain a woman that is lying in?[307] So great is the skill, so powerful the drugs, of the abortionist, paid to murder mankind within the womb. Rejoice, poor wretch, give her the stuff to drink whatever it be, with your own hand, for were she willing to get big and trouble her womb with bouncing babes, you might perhaps find yourself the father of an Ethiopian, and some day a colored heir would fill all the places in your will.

A wife hates the children of a concubine, let none demur or forbid, seeing that it has long been deemed right and proper to slay a stepson. But I warn you wards, you who have a good estate, keep watch over your lives; trust not a single dish, for those hot cakes are black with the poison of a mother's baking. Whatever is offered you by the mother, let someone taste it first; let your trembling tutor[308] take the first taste of every cup. Now think you that all this is a fancy tale, and that our satire is taking to herself the high heels of tragedy? Think you that I have out-stepped the limits and the laws of those before me? Would indeed that my words were idle! But here is Pontia proclaiming "I did the deed; I gave aconite,[309] I confess it, to my own children; the crime was detected, and is known to all." "What, you most savage of vipers? You killed two, did you, two, at a single meal?" "Aye, and seven too, had there chanced to be seven to kill!"

305 The Circus Maximus ("Great Circus"), the chariot-racing track, with turning posts at each end.

306 In this case, a fortune teller.

307 Waiting to give birth.

308 In this case, a child-care worker.

309 An extremely poisonous plant, also known as wolfsbane; the poison also was associated with rabid dogs.

98

PRAISE OF THE ROMAN EMPIRE (CA. 155 CE): PUBLIUS AELIUS ARISTIDES THEODORUS, *TO ROME*

A bronze statue of the first century BCE found at Perugia in Tuscany portrays an orator wearing a Roman toga. The inscription on the toga's hem, written in Etruscan, reads "To Aule Meteli, son of Vel and Vesi. This statue was erected by deliberation of the people." The statue now is in the National Archaeological Museum in Florence.

Publius Aelius Aristides Theodorus was a Greek orator of the mid-second century CE who is considered a primary example of the period known as the "Second Sophistic," a revival of Greek rhetoric and oratory lasting from about 60 to 230 CE. During this period, Roman emperors such as Hadrian (117–138) and Marcus Aurelius (161–180) served as patrons for and participated in literary activities. Aristides flourished during the reigns of Hadrian and Antoninus Pius (138–161). After a visit to Rome in 143 CE, Aristides returned to his native Smyrna in

Anatolia. In the 150s CE he toured Greece and Rome, where he delivered his best known speech, "To Rome," probably before the emperor Antoninus Pius. The speech glorified the emperors as having created an ideal world where opportunities were open to all, which no doubt is exactly what the emperors wanted to hear.

Source: James H. Oliver, *The Ruling Power. A Study of the Roman Empire in the Second Century after Christ through the Roman Oration of Aelius Aristides* (Philadelphia: American Philosophical Society, 1953), 895–907.

It is an age-old tradition that travelers who journey forth on land or water offer a prayer whereby they pledge to fulfill some vow—something they have on their mind—on reaching their destination safely. The vow I took as I journeyed here was not the usual silly and irrelevant sort, nor was it one unrelated to the art I profess. I simply vowed that, if I arrived safely, I would salute your city with a public address.

Some writer referring to Asia asserted that one man ruled as much territory as the sun passed over, but his statement was false, because he placed all of Africa and Europe outside of the area where the sun rises in the east and sets in the west. Now, however, it has become fact. The land you possess equals what the sun can pass over, and the sun does encompass your land. You do not reign within fixed boundaries and another state does not dictate the limits of the land you control[310]; rather, the sea[311] extends like a belt, situated in the middle of the civilized world and in the middle of the land over which you rule. Around that sea lie the great continents[312] massively sloping down to it, forever offering you in full measure what they possess. Whatever each culture grows and manufactures cannot fail to be here[313] at all times and in great profusion. Here merchant vessels arrive carrying these many commodities from every region in every season and even at every equinox,[314] so that the city takes on the appearance of a sort of common market for the world. One can see cargoes from India and even, if you will, from southern Arabia in such numbers that one must conclude that the trees in those lands have been stripped bare and if the inhabitants of those lands need anything, they must come here to beg for a share of what they have produced. Your farmlands are Egypt, Sicily, and all of cultivated Africa. Seaborne arrivals and departures are ceaseless, to the point that the wonder is, not so much that the harbor[315] has insufficient space for all these merchant vessels, but that the sea has enough space, if it really does. Just as there is a common channel where all waters of the Ocean[316] have a single source and destination, so there is a common channel to Rome and all meet here: trade, shipping, agriculture, metallurgy, all the arts and crafts that are or ever were and all things that are produced or spring from the earth. What one does not see here does not exist. So it is not easy to decide which is the greater: the superiority of this city relative to cities that presently exist, or the superiority of this empire relative to all empires that ever existed.

As vast and comprehensive as its size is, your empire is much greater for its perfection than for the area its borders encircle. The entire civilized world prays with one voice that this empire will endure forever. For of all who ever have gained an empire, you alone rule over free men. You conduct public business throughout the whole civilized world exactly as if it were one city-state, you appoint governors, as if it were by election, to protect and care for the governed, not to act as slave masters over them. One could say

[310] Reflecting the official view that the Roman Empire ruled, in reality or potentiality, the whole world.
[311] The Mediterranean.
[312] That is, Asia, Africa, and Europe.
[313] In Rome.
[314] The two moments during the solar year, roughly 21 March and 21 September, when night and day are of equal length.

[315] Ostia, the port of Rome at the mouth of the Tiber River.
[316] The great ocean that it was believed encircled all of the continents.

that the people of today are ruled by governors sent out to them only to the degree that they wish to be ruled.

You have divided into two parts all men throughout your empire, everywhere giving citizenship to all those who are more accomplished, noble, and powerful, even as they retain their native-born identities, whereas the rest you have made subjects and the governed. Neither the sea nor the great expanse of intervening land keeps one from being a citizen, and there is no distinction between Europe and Asia. No one is a foreigner who deserves to hold an office or is worthy of trust. Rather, there is here a common "world democracy" under the rule of one man, the best ruler and director.

You have divided humanity into Romans and non-Romans, and because you have divided people in this manner, in every city throughout the empire there are many who share citizenship with you, no less than they share citizenship with their fellow natives. And some of these Roman citizens have not even seen this city! There is no need for troops to garrison the strategic high points of these cities because the most important and powerful people in each region guard their native lands for you. Yet there is not a residue of resentment among those excluded. Because your government is both universal and like that of a single city-state, its governors rightly rule not as foreigners but, as it were, their own people. Additionally, all of the masses of subjects under this government have protection against the more powerful of their native countrymen, by virtue of your anger and vengeance, which would fall upon the more powerful without delay should they dare to break the law. Thus, the present government serves rich and poor alike, and your constitution has developed a single, harmonious, all-embracing union. What in former days seemed impossible has in your time come to pass. You control a vast empire with a rule that is firm but not unkind.

As on a holiday, the entire civilized world lays down the weapons that were its ancient burden and has turned to adornment and all glad thoughts, with the power to realize them. Cities glisten with radiance and charm, and the entire earth has been made beautiful like a garden. Like a perpetual sacred flame, the celebration is unending. You, better than anyone else, have proved the truth of the proverb: "The earth is everyone's mother and our common fatherland." It now is possible for Hellene[317] and non-Hellene, with or without property, to travel with ease wherever he wishes, as though passing from homeland to homeland. As far as security is concerned, it suffices to be a Roman citizen, or rather one of those people united under your rule.

Let us pray that all the gods and their children grant that this empire and this city flourish forever and never cease until stones float on water and trees cease to put forth shoots in spring, and that the Great Governor and his sons[318] be preserved and obtain blessings for all.

---

[317] Technically, a Greek, but here probably referring to Roman citizens.

[318] The emperor; Antoninus Pius had two adopted sons, Lucius Verus and Marcus Aurelius, both of whom became emperor when he died in 161 CE.

99

THE JEWS CONFRONT ROME (133–180 CE): BABYLONIAN TALMUD, SANHEDRIN 39A, SABBATH 33B, ME'ILAH 17B

A silver shekel of the Bar Kochba revolt, the third Jewish revolt against the Roman Empire, struck in 133–134 CE, depicts a temple facade that might be the Jewish temple destroyed by the Romans in 70 CE at the end of the first Jewish revolt. The reverse depictions of a lulav (palm branch, myrtle, and willow) and ethrog (citron fruit) refer to the Jewish feast of Sukkot (the Feast of the Tabernacles) and the legend reads "Year Two of the Freedom of Israel." After the suppression of the revolt in 135 CE, anti-Jewish legislation prohibited the use of Torah law and the Jewish calendar and many Jews departed, expanding the Jewish diaspora. The remaining rabbis attempted to prevent further emigration.

Under Roman rule, the Jews maintained their identity by the creation and circulation of the Talmud, a massive and comprehensive guidebook for Jewish life compiled beginning in the third century CE. It comprised oral tradition, interpretations of Mosaic Law, observations on faith and morality, Bible commentaries, and historical narratives. One version of the Talmud was completed in the late fourth century in Palestine and a Babylonian version was completed by ca. 500. The Talmud illustrated the complex and conflicted relationship that the Jews had with the Romans. For example, stories circulated about how Jewish rabbis had carried out theological debates with the emperor or the emperor's daughter. One individual who was caught in the middle was rabbi Simeon ben Yoḥai. Simeon's teacher, rabbi Akiba ben Yoseph, had supported the Bar Kochba Revolt (131–133 CE), and after the defeat of the revolt, Akiba's followers, including Simeon, were discredited. Circa 140 CE, Simeon lost the election to be head of the Sanhedrin, the Jewish governing body, which only existed by sufferance of the Romans and could not offend them. At a subsequent Sanhedrin meeting, ben Yoḥai criticized rabbi Yehudah ben Ilai, who praised Roman achievements. When this exchange was reported to the Romans, Yehudah was rewarded and Simeon was sentenced to death. After many years hiding in a cave, Simeon emerged and became a great Jewish teacher. He gained a reputation as a wonder worker and stories were told about his spiritual authority. In one story, he was said to have been sent to the emperor, perhaps Marcus Aurelius (180–192), to have the anti-Jewish legislation of the emperor Hadrian (117–138) rescinded. He accomplished the mission by having the emperor's daughter become possessed by a demon and then releasing her from it, a motif similar to later Christian traditions of holy men and women who released people from demonic possession.

Source: I. Epstein, trans., *Contents of the Soncino Babylonian Talmud*, 26 volumes (London: Soncino, 1935–1948).

The emperor once said to rabbi Gamaliel,[319] "Your God is a thief, for it is written, 'And the Lord God caused a deep sleep to fall upon Adam and he slept, and he took one of his ribs.'" Thereupon the emperor's daughter replied, "Leave him to me and I will answer him,"[320] and said, "Give me a military guard commander." "Why do you need him?," he asked. "Thieves visited us last night and robbed us of a silver pitcher, leaving a golden one in its place." "Would that such thieves visited us every day!," the emperor exclaimed. "Ah!," she retorted, "was it not to Adam's gain that he was deprived of a rib and a handmaid presented to him in its stead to serve him?" The emperor replied: "This is what I mean: he should have taken it from him openly, when he was awake." Said she to him, "Let me have a piece of raw meat." It was given to her. She placed it under her armpit, then took it out and offered it to him to eat. "I find it loathsome," he exclaimed. "Even so would Eve have been to Adam had she been taken from him openly,"[321] she retorted.

The emperor proposed to rabbi Tanhum,[322] "Come, let us all be one people." "Very well," he answered, "but we who are circumcised cannot possibly become like you unless you become circumcised like us." The emperor replied, "You have spoken well; nevertheless, anyone who gets the better of the king in debate must be thrown into the vivarium."[323] So they threw him in, but he was not eaten. Thereupon a heretic remarked, "The reason they did not eat him is that they are not hungry." They then threw the heretic in, and he was eaten . . .

[319] A rabbi known to have visited Rome at least twice, during the reigns of Domitian (81–96) and Nerva (96–98). Neither of these had a known daughter.

[320] That is, she would deal with the emperor's question in place of the rabbi.

[321] And he thus had known where she had come from.

[322] Tanḥum ben Ḥanilai, a rabbi of the third century CE.

[323] Enclosures where the Romans kept wild animals to be used in the games.

Rabbi Judah, rabbi Yose, and rabbi Simeon were sitting, and Judah, a son of proselytes,[324] was sitting near them. Rabbi Judah commenced by observing, "How fine are the works of the Romans. They have made streets, they have built bridges, they have erected baths." Rabbi Yose was silent. Rabbi Simeon ben Yoḥai answered and said, "All that they made they made for themselves; they built market-places, to set harlots in them; baths, to rejuvenate themselves; bridges, to levy tolls for them." Now, Judah the son of proselytes went and repeated this conversation, which was heard by the Roman government. The Romans decreed: "Judah, who exalted us, shall be rewarded by having the privilege to speak first on all occasions. Yose, who was silent, shall be exiled to Sepphoris[325]; Simeon, who censured, let him be executed. Simeon and his son went and hid themselves in the Beth Hamidrash[326] and his wife brought him bread and a mug of water and they dined. But when the decree became more severe he said to his son, "Women are of unstable temperament; she may be put to the torture[327] and expose us." So they went and hid in a cave. The whole day they studied. When it was time for prayers they robed, covered themselves, prayed, and then put off their garments again, so that they should not wear out. Thus they dwelt twelve years in the cave. Then Elijah[328] came and stood at the entrance to the cave and exclaimed, "Who will inform the son of Yoḥai that the emperor is dead and his decree annulled?"[329] So they emerged. Seeing a man ploughing and sowing, they exclaimed, "They forsake life eternal and engage in life temporal!" Whatever they cast their eyes upon was immediately burnt up. Thereupon a Heavenly Echo came forth and cried out, "Have ye emerged to destroy My world? Return to your cave!'"[330] So they returned and dwelt there twelve months, saying, "The punishment of the wicked in Gehenna is limited to twelve months."[331] A Heavenly Echo then came forth and said, "Go forth from your cave!" Thus, they issued forth: wherever rabbi Eleazar[332] wounded, rabbi Simeon healed. Said he to him, "My son! You and I are sufficient for the world." Rabbi Phinchas ben Ya'ir his son-in-law went out to meet him. He took him into the baths and massaged[32] his flesh. Seeing the clefts in his body he wept and the tears streamed from his eyes. "Woe to me that I see you in such a state!," he cried out "Happy are you that you see me thus," he retorted, "for if you did not see me in such a state you would not find me so learned."[333] For originally, when rabbi Simeon ben Yoḥai raised a difficulty, rabbi Phinehas ben Ya'ir would give him thirteen answers, but subsequently when rabbi Phinehas ben Ya'ir raised a difficulty, rabbi Simeon ben Yoḥai would give him twenty-four answers . . .

The government[334] once issued a decree that Jews might not keep the sabbath, circumcise their children, and that they should have intercourse with menstruant women. The Jews then conferred as to who should go to Rome to work for the annulment of the decrees. "Let rabbi Simeon ben Yoḥai go for he is experienced in miracles," said rabbi Eleazar son of rabbi Yose. "And who should accompany him?," they asked. Said rabbi Yose to them, "I shall accompany him." Then

[324] Converts to Judaism.

[325] A desert city west of the Sea of Galilee and a center of rabbinical activity at this time.

[326] A place for Jewish religious study.

[327] Jews who were not Roman citizens, such as Joshua ben Yoseph (Jesus of Nazareth) in the previous century, would be liable to torture should they be brought in for questioning by the Roman government; see Reading 91.

[328] A prophet who lived in the northern Hebrew kingdom of Israel during the reign of King Ahab (ca. 885–850 BCE).

[329] Presumably the emperor Antoninus Pius (138–161); this would date Simeon's original condemnation to around 148 CE.

[330] This story is a rebuke of excessively pious Jews who believed they should only study religion and not do practical work.

[331] In general, Judaism had no concept of eternal punishment in Hell, but rather of limited, regenerative punishment in Gehenna.

[332] Eleazar ben Simeon, the son of Simeon; another disciple of Akiba. He later held office under the Romans.

[333] Making the point that he spent all his time studying.

[334] Rulings of the emperor Hadrian (117–138 CE).

ben Temalion[335] came to meet them and said, "Is it your wish that I accompany you?" Thereupon rabbi Simeon wept and said, "Let the miracle be performed, no matter how." Thereupon ben Temalion went ahead and entered into the emperor's daughter. When rabbi Simeon arrived in Rome he called out,[336] "Ben Temalion leave her, ben Temalion leave her," and as he proclaimed this the demon left her. The emperor said to them, "Request whatever you desire." They were led into the treasure house to take whatever they chose. They found that edict[337] took it and tore it to pieces. It was with reference to this visit that rabbi Eleazar, son of rabbi Yose, related: "I saw it[338] in the city of Rome and there were on it several drops of blood."

[335] A demon, also known as Asmodeus.

[336] After having been invited to cure the emperor's daughter based on his reputation as a wonder worker.

[337] That is, the anti-Jewish legislation.

[338] The curtain from the Jewish Temple in Jerusalem that had been carried off in the sack by the Romans in 70 CE.

100

DEALING WITH CHRISTIANS (CA. 112 CE): PLINY, *LETTERS* 10.96–97

In the early Principate, many misconceptions about the Christians were current in the Roman world. One of them is portrayed on a graffito, dating to the third century CE, discovered on the Palatine Hill in Rome in 1857. It depicts a human figure with a donkey head attached to a cross. Another figure stands to the left, and an inscription in Greek reads, "Alexamenos worships his god." Next to it, in another hand, Alexamenos himself replied, in another graffito, this time in Latin, "Alexamenos is faithful." These kinds of exchanges between pagans and Christians would have been more and more commonplace as Christianity became increasingly widespread.

The Jews were not the only followers of a monotheistic religion that caused problems for the Romans. Around 112 CE, Gaius Plinius Secundus, or Pliny, the governor of the Roman province of Bithynia-Pontus on the southern coast of the Black Sea, wrote to the emperor Trajan (98–117) asking his advice about how to deal with a curious religious sect known as "Christians," who seemed to reject Roman religious practices and often to refuse to participate in the Roman loyalty oath. Trajan's brief reply spelled out the Roman government's "don't ask, don't tell" principle regarding the Christians, a rather more sympathetic policy than had been that of the Senate with respect to the Bacchanalians nearly three hundred years earlier (see Reading 79).

Source: William Melmoth, trans., *Pliny: Letters*, revised by W. M. L. Hutchinson. 2 vols., Loeb Classical Library, (London: Heinemann; New York: Macmillan, 1915).

Pliny to the Emperor Trajan.
It is my practice, my lord, to refer to you all matters concerning which I am in doubt. For who can better give guidance to my hesitation or inform my ignorance? I have never participated in trials of Christians. I therefore do not know what offenses it is the practice to punish or investigate, and to what extent. And I have been not a little hesitant as to whether there should be any distinction on account of age or no difference between the very young and the more mature; whether pardon is to be granted for repentance, or, if a man has once been a Christian, it does him no good to have ceased to be one; whether the name itself, even without offenses, or only the offenses associated with the name are to be punished.

Meanwhile, in the case of those who were denounced to me as Christians, I have observed the following procedure: I interrogated these as to whether they were Christians; those who confessed I interrogated a second and a third time, threatening them with punishment; those who persisted I ordered executed. For I had no doubt that, whatever the nature of their creed, stubbornness and inflexible obstinacy surely deserve to be punished. There were others possessed of the same folly, but because they were Roman citizens, I signed an order for them to be transferred to Rome.[339]

Soon accusations spread, as usually happens, because of the proceedings going on, and several incidents occurred. An anonymous document was published containing the names of many persons. Those who denied that they were or had been Christians, when they invoked the gods in words dictated by me, offered prayer with incense and wine to your image, which I had ordered to be brought for this purpose together with statues of the gods, and moreover cursed Christ, something that none of which those who are really Christians, it is said, can be forced to do, these I thought should be discharged. Others named by the informer declared that they were Christians, but then denied it, asserting that they had been but had ceased to be, some three years before, others many years, some as much as twenty-five years. They all worshipped your image and the statues of the gods, and cursed Christ.

They asserted, however, that the sum and substance of their fault or error had been that they were accustomed to meet on a fixed day before dawn and sing responsively a hymn to Christ as to a god, and to bind themselves by oath, not to some crime but rather not to commit fraud, theft, or adultery, not falsify their trust, nor to refuse to return a trust when called upon to do so.[340] When this was over, it was their custom to depart and to assemble again to partake of food, but ordinary and innocent food.[341] Even this, they affirmed, they had ceased to do after my edict by which, in accordance with your instructions, I had forbidden political associations. Accordingly, I judged it all the more necessary to find out what the truth was by torturing two female slaves who were

[339] Roman citizens automatically had the right of appeal regarding accusations that could carry the death penalty, as occurred with the Christian leader Paul, who was sent from Judaea to Rome for trial during the reign of Nero (54–68) after it was discovered that he was a Roman citizen.

[340] The same crimes of which the Bacchanalians had been accused in 186 BCE (see Reading 79).

[341] Contradicting the popular belief that Christians were cannibals because they ate flesh and drank blood during their religious rites.

called deaconesses.[342] But I discovered nothing else but depraved, excessive superstition.[343]

I therefore postponed the investigation and hastened to consult you. For the matter seemed to me to warrant consulting you, especially because of the number involved. For many persons of every age, every rank, and also of both sexes are and will be endangered. For the contagion of this superstition has spread not only to the cities but also to the villages and farms. But it seems possible to check and cure it. It is certainly quite clear that the temples, which had been almost deserted, have begun to be frequented, that the established religious rites, long neglected, are being resumed, and that from everywhere sacrificial animals are coming, for which until now very few purchasers could be found. Hence it is easy to imagine what a multitude of people can be reformed if an opportunity for repentance is afforded.

Trajan to Pliny.

You observed proper procedure, my dear Pliny, in sifting the cases of those who had been denounced to you as Christians. For it is not possible to lay down any general rule to serve as a kind of fixed standard. They are not to be sought out. If they are denounced and proved guilty, they are to be punished, with this reservation, that whoever denies that he is a Christian and really proves it, that is, by worshiping our gods, even though he was under suspicion in the past, shall obtain pardon through repentance. But anonymously posted accusations ought to have no place in any prosecution. For this is both a dangerous kind of precedent and out of keeping with the spirit of our age.

[342] Demonstrating that in early Christianity women were admitted to the clergy and that even slaves could be clerics.

[343] For the Romans, "superstition" was not believing in the gods, that is, atheism.

CHAPTER 13

Crisis, Recovery, and the Creation of the Late Roman Empire (192–337)

Beginning in the third century, the carefully constructed Roman Empire began to disintegrate as a result of economic, political, and military problems that the Roman government found increasingly difficult to deal with. A fifty-year Imperial Crisis that threatened the empire's very existence finally was brought to an end when Diocletian and Constantine reestablished the empire in a new form. The Late Roman Empire was very different from the Principate, and the changes it brought marked the onset of Late Antiquity, the fourth and final phase of the ancient world. The world of Late Antiquity would be characterized by the breakdown of the unity of the Mediterranean world that had evolved ever since the days of the ancient Phoenicians and Greeks. At the same time, many of the defining characteristics of the modern world, such as the genesis of the western European nations and the appearance and expansion of new religious movements, such as Christianity and Islam, also are to be sought here.

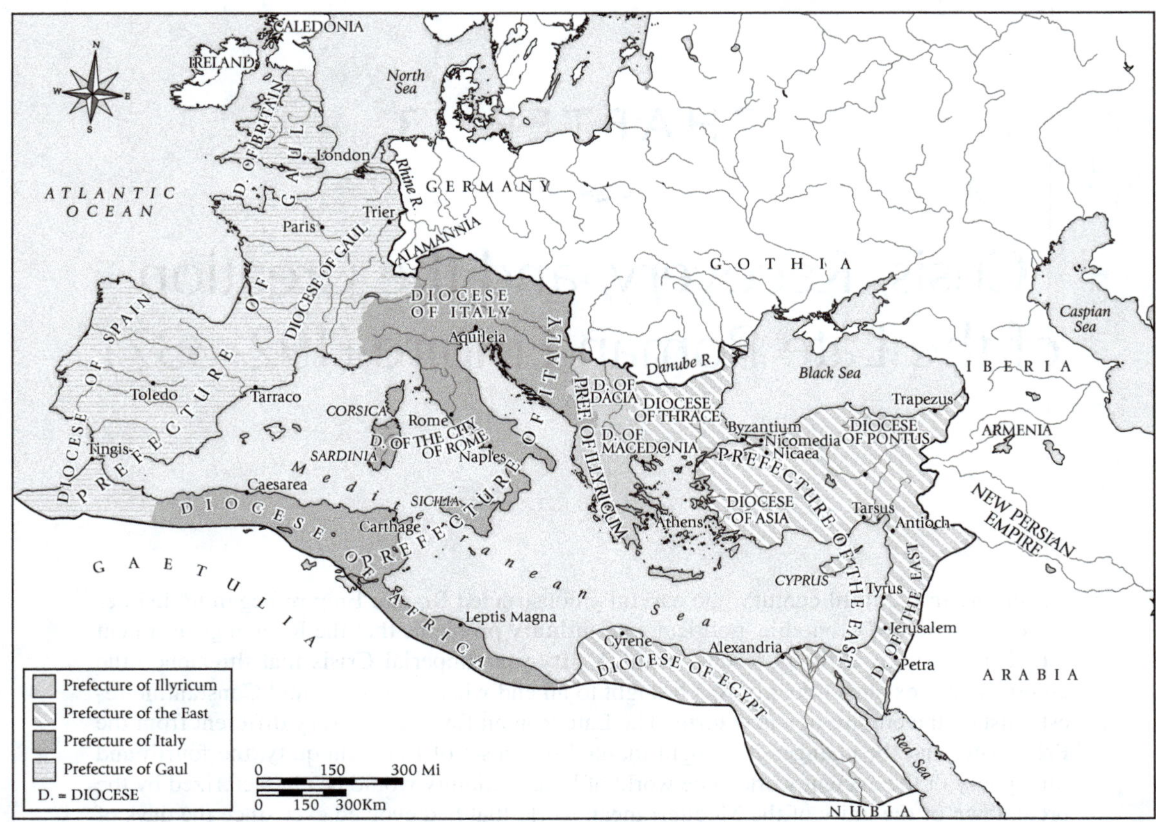

Map 13 The Reorganized Empire of Diocletian, Divided into Prefectures and Dioceses

101

THE ANTONINE CONSTITUTION (212 CE): *PAPYRUS GISSENSIS* 40; CASSIUS DIO, *ROMAN HISTORY*, BOOK 78, CHAPTER 9

The only surviving original version of the Antonine Constitution issued by the emperor Caracalla (211–217), also known as Antoninus, is preserved on a fragmentary papyrus copy now in Giessen in Germany. Although enough of the text survives to provide a general idea of what was in Caracalla's edict, there also remain areas of uncertainly as to the exact contents.

In 212 CE the emperor Caracalla (211–217), whose full legal name was Marcus Aurelius Severus Antoninus, issued an edict that made all of the inhabitants of the Roman Empire except slaves and "dediticii" (legally disadvantaged freedmen) into Roman citizens. Far from creating legal equality for all Romans, this edict merely acknowledged two realities: (1) by this time, well over half of all Romans already were citizens, which created complications in navigating among Roman, provincial, and local laws, and (2) by now, other legal distinctions, those between "honestiores" ("more distinguished people") and "humiliores" ("more humble people"), had replaced the distinctions between citizens and noncitizens. Caracalla's edict, therefore, had the benefits of simplifying legal procedures and raising a bit of extra tax income because some taxes, such as taxes on inheritances and slave manumissions, applied only to Roman citizens. Those persons enfranchised by Caracalla's law then took the name

"Aurelius," the extended family name of Caracalla. It is unclear what "danger" Caracalla is referring to; it could be a purported conspiracy that led to his murder of his younger brother Geta at the end of 211 CE. The law attracted surprisingly little attention in antiquity. The edict survives only in a single ragged piece of papyrus and is mentioned in only four other ancient sources. The only contemporary historian to discuss it any length was Cassius Dio, a senator from Bithynia who served under emperors from Commodus (180–192) to Severus Alexander (222–235). After antagonizing the Praetorian Guard in 227 CE, Dio escaped into an honorable retirement. He is known primarily for his massive eighty-book "Roman History," which ran from Aeneas until 229 CE. Dio's history is especially important for the invaluable information that it provides based on Dio's personal experiences and knowledge.

Source: Allan Johnson, Paul Coleman-Norton, and Frank Bourne, *Ancient Roman Statutes* (Austin: University of Texas Press, 1961), no. 277, 225–226.

(a) *Papyrus Gissensis* 40

Emperor Caesar Marcus Aurelius Severus Antoninus Augustus proclaims: It is most fitting that, as I ascribe the causes and the reasons of events to divine origin, I should attempt to render thanks to the immortal gods for their preservation of me in so great a danger. I believe, therefore, that most magnificently and reverently I can perform a service not unworthy of their majesty,[1] if I make my offerings to the gods in company with the foreigners[2] who at any time have entered the number of my subjects, as well as with my own people. I grant, therefore, the Roman citizenship to all foreigners throughout the Empire [. . .] except the for *dediticii*. For it is proper that the populace not only should [. . .] everything, but also should share in the victory. This edict will enhance the majesty of the Roman people.

[1] Not a reference to barbarians who had surrendered, as often is thought, but to stigmatized freedman who had been branded or tortured or had fought in the arena.

[2] Latin "peregrini," referring to any "foreigner," including Roman provincials and barbarian immigrants.

(b) Cassius Dio, *Roman History*, Book 78, Chapter 9

Now this great admirer of Alexander,[3] Antoninus,[4] was fond of spending money upon the soldiers, great numbers of whom he kept in attendance upon him, alleging one excuse after another and one war after another; but he made it his business to strip, despoil, and grind down all the rest of mankind, and the senators by no means least. In the first place, there were

[3] Alexander the Great; see Readings 62 and 63.

[4] The son of Septimius Severus (193–211), more usually known by his nickname "Caracalla," the word for a Gallic cloak that he liked to wear.

Source: Earnest Gary, trans., *Dio's Roman History*, 9 vols. (Cambridge, MA: Harvard University Press, 1927).

the gold crowns[5] that he was repeatedly demanding, on the constant pretext that he had conquered some enemy or other. And I am not referring, either, to the actual manufacture of the crowns—for what does that amount to?—but to the vast amount of money constantly being given under that name by the cities for the customary "crowning," as it is called, of the emperors. Then there were the provisions that we were required to furnish in great quantities on all occasions, and this without receiving any remuneration and sometimes actually at additional cost to ourselves, all of which supplies he either bestowed upon the soldiers or else peddled out. There also were the gifts that he demanded from the wealthy citizens and from the various communities; and the taxes, especially the new ones that he promulgated, and the ten percent tax that he instituted in place of the five percent tax applying to the emancipation of slaves, to bequests, and to all inheritances, for he abolished the right of succession and exemption from taxes that had been granted in such cases to those who were closely related to the deceased. This was the reason why he made all the people in his empire Roman citizens. Nominally he was honoring them, but his real purpose was to increase his revenues by this means, inasmuch as aliens did not have to pay most of these taxes. But apart from all these burdens, we also were compelled to build at our own expense all sorts of houses for him whenever he set out from Rome, and costly lodgings in the middle of even very shortest journeys; yet he not only never lived in them, but in some cases was not destined even to see them. Moreover, we constructed amphitheaters and racecourses wherever he spent the winter or expected to spend it, all without receiving any contribution from him; and they were all promptly demolished, the sole reason for their being built in the first place being, apparently, that we might become impoverished.

[5] What was known as "crown gold"; emperors expected the cities of the empire to provide gold crowns after victories over a foreign enemy, which led emperors to declare victories of dubious value.

102

PERVIGILIUM VENERIS ("THE VIGIL OF VENUS") (CA. 200/300 CE)

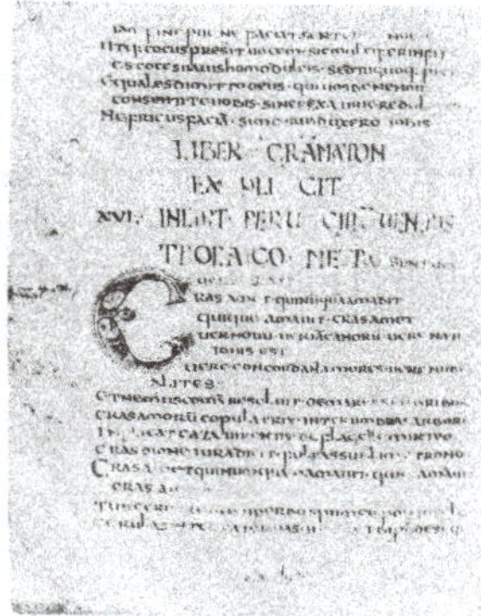

The first page of the "Pervigilium Veneris" ("Vigil of Venus") as preserved in the Codex Salmasianus ("Salmasian Manuscript"), now in Paris, a famous collection of late antique poetry copied around the year 700 CE.

The "Pervigilium Veneris," or "Vigil of Venus," was written by an unknown author and is variously dated to between the second and fifth centuries CE; a third-century date certainly would fit its themes and presentation. It is preserved in only two manuscripts, both in Paris. It was written for a festival in honor of the goddess Venus that lasted for three nights, 1–3 April, and reflects the deep and lasting hold that traditional religious practices could have on the popular mentality. The focus on the reawakening of plant and animal life in the spring makes it different from the typical poetry of antiquity and more of a harbinger of the Middle Ages. The repetitious refrain "Cras amet qui nunquam amavit; quique amavit cras amet" ("May one love tomorrow, who never has loved; may whoever has loved, love tomorrow") conveys the sense of longing that underlies the poem. This anonymous versified translation from 1843 uses archaic word forms and verbal elisions, such as "'tis" for "it is," "twill" for "it will," and so on.

Source: "The Vigil of Venus. Translated from the Latin," *Blackwood's Edinburgh Magazine* 53.332 (June 1843).

May one love tomorrow, who never has loved;
may whoever has loved, love tomorrow.
Spring, new spring, with song and mirth,
Spring is on the newborn earth.
Spring is here, the time of love—
The merry birds pair in the grove,
And the green trees hang their tresses,
Loosen'd by the rain's caresses.
Tomorrow she who joins lovers all,
Where the woodland shadows fall,
On bowers of myrtle intertwined,[6]
Many a band of love she'll bind.
Tomorrow Dione[7] speaks her laws,
Seated in her justice hall.
May one love tomorrow, who never has loved;
may whoever has loved, love tomorrow.
Tomorrow is the day when first
From the foam-world of ocean burst,
Like one of his own waves, the bright
Dione, queen of love and light,
Amid the sea-gods' azure train,
'Mid the strange horses of the sea.[8]
May one love tomorrow, who never has loved;
may whoever has loved, love tomorrow.
She[9] it is that lends the Hours[10]
Their crimson glow, their jewel-flowers:
At her command the buds are seen,
Where the west-wind's breath hath been,
To swell within their dwellings green.
She abroad those dewdrops flings,
Dew that night's cool softness brings;
How the bright tears hang declining,
And glisten with a tremulous shining,

[6] During the festivals of Venus her statues were crowned with myrtle leaves.

[7] A Titaness, daughter of Oceanus, personification of the sea, and mother of Venus (Greek Aphrodite), often, as here, identified with Venus herself.

[8] Seahorses. Venus was born from the sea foam that arose around the god Uranus's castrated testicles; see Reading 5.

[9] Venus.

[10] The goddesses that control the sequence and attributes of the seasons.

Almost of weight to drop away,
And yet too light to leave the spray.
Hence the tender plants are bold
Their blushing petals to unfold:
'Tis that dew, which through the air
Falls from heaven when night is fair,
That unbinds the moist green vest
From the floweret's maiden breast.
'Tis Venus' will, when morning glows,
'Twill be the bridal of each rose.
Then the bride-flower[11] shall reveal,
What her veil cloth now conceal,
The blush divinest, which of old
She caught from Venus' trickling blood,
With Love's kisses mix'd, I think,
With blaze of fire, and rubies' pink,
And with many a crimson ray
Stolen from the birth of day.
May one love tomorrow, who never has loved;
may whoever has loved, love tomorrow.
All the nymphs[12] the Queen of Love[13]
Summons to the myrtle-grove;
And see ye, her wanton boy,[14]
Comes with them to share our joy?
Yet, if Love[15] be arm'd, they say,
Love can scarce take a holiday,
Not without his bow laid down!
Come, ye nymphs, Love says now,
His torch, his shafts, are now deferred,
From them no harm shall you incur,
Yet, I advise ye, nymphs, beware,
For your foe is passing fair;
Love is mighty, ye'll confess,
Mighty e'en in nakedness;
And most panoplied for fight
When his charms are bared to sight.
May one love tomorrow, who never has loved;

[11] The rose, the flower of Venus.

[12] Young nubile female nature deities who live in woods, mountains, streams, and oceans.

[13] That is, Venus.

[14] Cupid, son of Venus.

[15] Cupid, who was armed with a bow and arrow. Before lovemaking can take place, Cupid must put down his bow.

may whoever has loved, love tomorrow.
Diana[16] a petition we,
By Venus sent, proffer to thee:
Virgin envoys, it is meet,
Should the Virgin huntress greet:
Quit the grove, nor it profane
With the blood of quarry slain.
She would ask thee, might she dare
Hope a maiden's thought to share—
She would bid thee join us now,
Might cold maids our sport allow.
For three nights[17] thou may'st have seen,
Wandering through thine alleys green,
Troops of joyous friends, with flowers
Crown'd, amid their myrtle bowers.
Ceres and Bacchus[18] us attend,
And great Apollo[19] is our friend;
All night we must our vigil keep—
Night by song redeem'd from sleep.
Let Venus in the woods bear sway,
Dian, quit the grove, we pray.
May one love tomorrow, who never has loved;
may whoever has loved, love tomorrow.
Of Hybla's[20] flowers, so Venus will'd,
Venus' judgment-seat we build.
She is judge supreme; the Graces,[21]
As assessors, take their places.
Hybla, render all thy store
All the season sheds thee o'er,
Till a hill of bloom be found
Wide as Enna's[22] flowery ground.
Attendant nymphs shall here be seen,
Those who delight in forest green,
Those who on mountain-top abide,
And those whom sparkling fountains hide.
All these the queen of joy and sport
Summons to attend her court,
And bids them all of Love beware,
Although the guise of peace he wear.
May one love tomorrow, who never has loved;
may whoever has loved, love tomorrow.
Fresh be your coronals of flowers,
And green your overarching bowers,
To-morrow brings us the return
Of Aether's[23] primal marriage-morn.
In amorous showers of rain he came
T' embrace his bride's mysterious frame,
To generate the blooming year,
And all the produce Earth does bear.
Venus still through vein and soul
Bids the genial current roll;
Still she guides its secret course
With interpenetrating force,
And breathes through heaven, and earth,
and sea,
A reproductive energy.
May one love tomorrow, who never has loved;
may whoever has loved, love tomorrow.
She old Troy's[24] extinguish'd glory
Revived in Latium's later story,
When, by her auspices, her son
Laurentum's[25] royal damsel won.
She vestal Rhea's spotless charms
Surrender'd to the War-god's arms;[26]
She for Romulus that day

[16] The virgin goddess of hunting.
[17] April was the month of Venus; her festival lasted three nights, 1–3 April.
[18] Ceres, goddess of the harvest, and Bacchus (Dionysus), god of wine.
[19] The sun god, brother of Diana.
[20] The name of several cities in Sicily, which has led to suggestions that the poem may have originated there.
[21] Known in Greek as the Charites, the Graces were minor female goddesses connected to nature and fertility; in some myths they are the companions of Venus.
[22] A city in central Sicily.
[23] In Greek mythology, the god of the upper atmosphere, the son of Darkness and Night and the brother of Day, thought to give the spark of life to all creatures.
[24] Venus favored Troy in the Trojan War because the Trojan prince Paris had declared her most beautiful in the competition with the goddesses Hera and Athena.
[25] Aeneas, the son of Venus married Lavinia, daughter of the Latin king Latinus, whose capital city was Laurentum; see Reading 88.
[26] The Vestal Virgin Rhea Silvia claimed that Mars was the father of the twins Romulus and Remus; see Reading 73.

The Sabine daughters bore away;[27]
Thence sprung the Ramnes'[28] lofty name,
Thence the old Quirites[29] came;
And thence the stock of high renown,
The blood of Romulus, handed down
Through many an age of glory pass'd,
To blaze in Caesar's at last.[30]
May one love tomorrow, who never has loved;
may whoever has loved, love tomorrow.
All rural nature feels the glow
Of quickening passion through it flow.
Love, in rural scenes of yore,
They say, his goddess-mother bore;
Received on Earth's sustaining breast,
Th' ambrosial infant[31] sunk to rest;
And him the wild-flowers, o'er his head
Bending, with sweetest kisses fed.
May one love tomorrow, who never has loved;
may whoever has loved, love tomorrow.
On yellow field out yonder, see,
The mighty bulls lie peacefully.
Each animal of field or grove
Owns faithfully the bond of love.
The flocks of ewes, beneath the shade,
Around their gallant rams are laid;
And Venus bids the birds awake
To pour their song o'er plain and lake.
Hark! the noisy pools reply
To the swan's hoarse harmony;
And Philomel[32] is vocal now,
Perch'd upon a poplar-bough.
Thou scarce would'st think that dying fall
Could ought but love's sweet griefs recall;
Thou scarce would'st gather from her song
The tale of brother's barbarous wrong.
She sings, but I must silent be:—
When will the spring-tide come for me?
When, like the swallow, spring's own bird,
Shall my faint twittering notes be heard?
Alas! the muse, while silent I
Remain'd, hath gone and pass'd me by,
Nor Phoebus[33] listens to my cry.
And thus forgotten, I await,
By silence lost, Amyclae's[34] fate.

[27] In legend, the Sabines were an Italic people living near the original foundation of Rome; Romulus organized the kidnaping of Sabine women in order to provide wives for Roman men.

[28] One of the original three tribes (thirds) of Rome, their name supposedly derived from "Romulus."

[29] A name for Roman citizens, from the ancient Roman god Quirinus.

[30] Venus and her son Aeneas were the ancestors of the Julian family, which included Julius Caesar and Augustus.

[31] Cupid, son of Venus, who ate ambrosia, the food of the gods.

[32] Philomela, Greek mythology, a daughter of Pandion, king of Athens, who after being violated and having her tongue cut out by her brother-in-law was turned by the gods into a nightingale.

[33] An epithet of the god Apollo.

[34] A village conquered by the Spartans early in their history.

103

THE MARTYRDOM OF PERPETUA AND FELICITAS (7 MARCH 203 CE)

A gold aureus of the emperor Elagabalus (218–222 CE) depicts the transfer of the sacred black stone of the sun god Elagabal from Emesa in Syria to Rome. The legend reads, "To the Blessed Sun God Elagabal." This scene reflects the increasing trend in the Roman Empire toward monotheism based on various forms of sun worship.

During the course of the Principate, traditional religious beliefs and practices were increasingly threatened by the expansion of Christianity, a new religion that better met the needs and desires of larger and larger numbers of people. Christianity offered a multitude of benefits, including a moral code for guiding one's life, easy access (compared to the Jewish requirement that male converts be circumcised), a community experience and social support system, the forgiveness of sins, and, in particular, an afterlife. Initially, Christianity often had been greeted by the Romans with hostility and skepticism that even could result in execution by the Roman government (see Reading 100), but during the second and third centuries, Christianity developed the look and feel of a more mainstream religion. In the Severan period (193–235 CE), for example, a form of pagan monotheism focused on sun worship became increasingly popular and even was promoted by Roman emperors. In spite of increasing popular sympathy toward Christianity, Christians still could run afoul of the Roman government if they refused to take the loyalty oath to Rome and the emperor by participating in the imperial cult, which they believed was contrary to their monotheistic religious beliefs. As a consequence, many Christians suffered execution and became martyrs (from the Greek word for "witnesses") to their Christian beliefs. They were believed to receive the "crown of martyrdom" and to go directly to heaven, where they could intercede with God on behalf of persons who still were alive. Christian communities preserved many authentic accounts of martyrdoms that were intended to provide examples of commendable behavior to other members of the community. These "martyrs' acts" often included the verbatim minutes of the trial before a Roman magistrate. These accounts demonstrate that many Roman judges were sympathetic to the accused Christians, attempting to reason with them and offering them extra time to reconsider. One of the most famous Christian martyrs was Vibia Perpetua, an aristocratic woman of Carthage, who was married and nursing a child. Felicitas, a pregnant slave, was martyred with her. The account of the martyrdom, written in Latin, purportedly was a form of prison diary by Perpetua herself, making it one of the earliest surviving pieces of writing by a Christian woman. Additional material was added after her death. The account is viewed as being completely authentic.

Source: Walter H. Shewring, trans., *The Passion of SS. Perpetua and Felicity* (London: Sheed and Ward, 1931).

If ancient examples of faith kept, both testifying to the grace of God and working for the edification of man, have to this end been set in writing, that by their reading God may be glorified and man strengthened, why should not new witnesses also be so set forth which likewise serve either end? There were apprehended the young catechumens, Revocatus and Felicitas his fellow servant, Saturninus, and Secundulus. With them also was Vibia Perpetua, nobly born, reared in a liberal manner, wedded honorably, and having a father and mother and two brothers, one of them a catechumen likewise, and a son, a child at the breast; and she herself was about twenty-two years of age. What follows here shall she tell herself; the whole order of her martyrdom as she left it written with her own hand and in her own words.

At that time when, she said, we were still with our companions and my father was liked to vex me with his words and continually strove to hurt my faith because of his love,[35] "Father," said I, "Do you see, for example, this vessel lying, a pitcher or whatsoever it may be?" And he said, "I see it." And I said to him, "Can it be called by any other name than that which it is?" And he answered, "No." "So can I call myself nought other than that which I am, a Christian." Then my father, angry with this word, came upon me to tear out my eyes, but he only vexed me, and he departed, vanquished, he and the arguments of the devil. Then, because I was without my father for a few days I gave thanks unto the Lord and I was comforted because of his absence. In this same space of a few days we were baptized, and the spirit[36] declared to me that I must pray for nothing else after that water[37] save only endurance of the flesh. After a few days we were taken into prison, and I was much afraid because I never had known such darkness. O bitter day! There was a great heat because of the press, there was cruel handling by the soldiers. Lastly I was tormented there by care for the child.

[35] Because he knew that being a Christian could be dangerous.

[36] The Holy Spirit.

[37] Of baptism.

Then Tertius and Pomponius, the blessed deacons[38] who ministered to us, obtained with money that for a few hours we should be taken forth to a better part of the prison and be refreshed. Then, when all of them went out from the dungeon and took their pleasure, I suckled my child who now was faint with hunger. And being careful for him, I spoke to my mother and strengthened my brother and commended my son unto them. I pined because I saw they pined for my sake. Such cares I suffered for many days, and I obtained that the child should abide with me in prison,[39] and straightway I became well and was lightened of my labor and care for the child, and suddenly the prison was made a palace for me, so that I would sooner be there than anywhere else.

Then said my brother to me, "Lady my sister, you are now in high honor, even such that you might ask for a vision, and it should be shown you whether this be a passion[40] or else a deliverance." And I, as knowing that I conversed with the Lord, for whose sake I had suffered such things, did promise him nothing, doubting, and I said, "Tomorrow I will tell you." And I asked,[41] and this was shown me. I beheld a ladder of bronze, marvelously great, reaching up to heaven; and it was narrow, so that not more than one might go up at one time. And in the sides of the ladder were planted all manner of things of iron. There were swords there, spears, hooks, and knives, so that if any that went up took not good heed or looked not upward, he would be torn and his flesh cling to the iron. And there was right at the ladder's foot a serpent lying, marvelously great, which lay in wait for those that would go up, and frightened them that they might not go up. Now Saturus went up first. And he came to the ladder's head, and he turned and said, "Perpetua, I await you, but take care that serpent bites you not." And I said, "It shall not hurt me, in the name of Jesus Christ." And from beneath the ladder, as though it feared me, it softly put forth its head, and as though I trod on the first step I trod on its head. And I went up, and I saw a very great space of garden, and in the midst a man sitting, white-headed, in shepherd's clothing, tall milking his sheep, and standing around in white were many thousands. And he raised his head and beheld me and said to me, "Welcome, child." And all that stood around said, "Amen." And at the sound of that word I awoke, yet eating I know not what of sweet. And at once I told my brother, and we knew it should be a passion, and we began to have no hope any longer in this world.

A few days after, the report went abroad that we were to be tried. In addition, my father returned from the city spent with weariness, and he beseeched me to cast down my faith, saying, "Have pity, daughter, on my grey hairs, have pity on your father, if I am worthy to be called father by you. If with these hands I have brought you unto this flower of youth and have preferred you before all your brothers, give me not over to the reproach of men. Look upon your brothers, look upon your mother and mother's sister; look upon your son, who will not endure to live after you. Give up your resolution. Do not destroy us all together, for none of us will speak openly against men again if you suffer anything."

This he said, fatherly in his love, kissing my hands and grovelling at my feet, and with tears he named me, not daughter, but lady. And I was grieved for my father's case because, out of all my kin, he would not rejoice at my passion, and I comforted him, saying, "That shall be done at this tribunal,[42] whatsoever God shall please, for know that we are not established in our own power, but in God's." And he went from me very sorrowful.

Another day as we were at meal we were suddenly snatched away to be tried, and we came to the forum. Therewith a report spread abroad through the parts near to the forum, and a very great multitude gathered together.[43] We went up to the tribunal. The others

[38] Christian clerics who managed the resources of the church.

[39] Roman prisons were used as holding areas for persons awaiting trial, not as places to which one was sentenced for punishment.

[40] That is, a martyrdom.

[41] For a vision.

[42] The court of the magistrate.

[43] Criminal trials were a popular form of public entertainment; see also Reading 113.

being asked, confessed. So they came to me. And my father appeared there also, with my son, and would draw me from the step, saying, "Perform the sacrifice,[44] have mercy on the child." And Hilarian the Procurator,[45] who at that time, in the place of the deceased Proconsul[46] Minucius Timinianus, had received the right of the sword,[47] said, "Spare your father's grey hairs; spare the infancy of the boy. Make sacrifice for the emperor's[48] prosperity." And I answered, "I am a Christian." And when my father stood by me yet to cast down my faith, he was bidden by Hilarian to be cast down and was smitten with a rod. And I sorrowed for my father's harm as though I had been smitten myself; so sorrowed I for his unhappy old age. Then Hilarian passed sentence upon us all and condemned us to the beasts, and cheerfully we went down to the dungeon. Then, because my child had been used to being breastfed and to staying with me in the prison, straightway I sent Pomponius the deacon to my father, asking for the child. But my father would not give him. And as god willed, neither did he wish to be suckled any more, nor did I take fever, so that I might not be tormented by care for the child and by the pain of my breasts.

A few days after, while we were all praying, suddenly in the midst of the prayer I uttered a word and named Dinocrates, and I was amazed because he had never come to my mind save then, and I sorrowed, remembering his fate. And straightway I knew that I was worthy, and that I ought to ask for him. And I began to pray for him long, and to groan unto the Lord. Forthwith the same night, this was shown me.[49] I beheld Dinocrates coming forth from a dark place, where there were many others also, both hot and thirsty, his raiment foul, his color pale, and the wound on his face which he had when he died. This Dinocrates had been my brother in the flesh, seven years old, who being diseased with ulcers of the face had come to a horrible death, so that his death was abominated of all men. For him therefore I had made my prayer, and between him and me was a great gulf, so that either might not go to the other. There was, moreover, in the same place where Dinocrates was, a font full of water, having its edge higher than was the boy's stature, and Dinocrates stretched up as though to drink. I was sorry that the font had water in it, and yet for the height of the edge he might not drink. And I awoke, and I knew that my brother was in travail. Yet I was confident I should ease his travail, and I prayed for him every day until we passed over into the camp prison, for it was in the camp games that we were to fight, and the time was the anniversary of Geta Caesar.[50] And I made supplication for him day and night with groans and tears, that he might be given me.

On the day when we were in chains, this was shown me.[51] I saw that place that I had seen before, and Dinocrates clean of body, finely clothed, in comfort; and where the wound was before, I saw a scar; and the font I had seen before, the edge of it being drawn down to the boy's navel, and he drew water thence which flowed without ceasing. And on the edge was a golden cup full of water; and Dinocrates came up and began to drink therefrom, and the cup failed not. And being satisfied he departed away from the water and began to play as children will, joyfully. And I awoke. Then I understood that he was translated from his pains.

Then a few days after, Pudens the adjutant, in whose charge the prison was, who also began to magnify us because he understood that there was much grace in us, let in many to us that both we and

[44] On behalf of the imperial cult; it involved dropping a pinch of incense on a fire.

[45] An official who usually had financial duties.

[46] The governors of the province of Africa still had the Republican office of Proconsul.

[47] The power to inflict the death sentence.

[48] In 203 CE there were three emperors, the Augustus Septimius Severus, and his sons, Caracalla, also Augustus, and the Caesar Geta.

[49] Perpetua has another vision.

[50] Either his birthday, 7 March, or the day when he was proclaimed Caesar in 197 CE. The celebration would have been marked by entertainments ranging from gladiatorial contests to the execution of condemned criminals.

[51] Perpetua has a third vision.

they in turn might be comforted.[52] Now, when the day of the games drew near, there came in my father to me, spent with weariness, and began to pluck out his beard and throw it on the ground and to fall on his face cursing his years and saying such words as might move all creation. I was grieved for his unhappy old age.

The day before we fought, I saw in a vision[53] that Pomponius the deacon had come hither to the door of the prison, and knocked hard upon it. And I went out to him and opened to him. He was clothed in a white robe ungirdled, having shoes curiously wrought. And he said to me, "Perpetua, we await you. Come." And he took my hand, and we began to go through rugged and winding places. At last with much breathing hard we came to the amphitheater, and he led me into the midst of the arena. And he said to me, "Be not afraid. I am here with you and labor together with you." And he went away. And I saw many people watching closely. And because I knew that I was condemned to the beasts I marvelled that beasts were not sent out against me. And there came out against me a certain ill-favored Egyptian with his helpers, to fight with me. Also there came to me comely young men, my helpers and aiders. And I was stripped naked, and I became a man. And my helpers began to rub me with oil as their custom is for a contest, and over against me I saw that Egyptian wallowing in the dust. And there came forth a man of very great stature, so that he overpassed the very top of the amphitheater, wearing a robe ungirdled, and beneath it between the two stripes over the breast a robe of purple, having also shoes curiously wrought in gold and silver, bearing a rod like a master of gladiators, and a green branch whereon were golden apples. And he besought silence and said, "The Egyptian, if shall conquer this woman, shall slay her with the sword, and if she shall conquer him, she shall receive this branch." And he went away. And we came nigh to each other, and began to buffet one another. He tried to trip up my feet, but I with my heels smote upon his face. And I rose up into the air and began so to smite him as though I trod not the earth. But when I saw that there was yet delay, I joined my hands, setting finger against finger of them. And I caught his head, and he fell upon his face, and I trod upon his head. And the people began to shout, and my helpers began to sing. And I went up to the master of gladiators and received the branch. And he kissed me and said to me, "Daughter, peace be with you. And I began to go with glory to the gate called the Gate of Life."[54] And I awoke, and I understood that I should fight, not with beasts but against the devil. But I knew that mine was the victory.

Thus far I have written this, until the day before the games, but as to the carrying out of the games themselves, if anyone wishes, let him write.

And blessed Saturus[55] too delivered this vision which he himself wrote down. We had suffered, he said, and we passed out of the flesh, and we began to be carried toward the east by four angels whose hand touched us not. And we went not as though turned upwards upon our backs, but as though we went up an easy hill. And passing over the world's edge we saw a very great light, and I said to Perpetua, for she was at my side, "That which the Lord promised us, we have received his promise." And while we were being carried by these same four angels a great space opened before us, having rose-trees and all kinds of flowers. The height of the trees was after the manner of the cypress, and their leaves sang without ceasing. And there in the garden were four other angels, more glorious than the rest, who when they saw us gave us honor and said to the other angels, "Lo, here are they, here are they," and marvelled. And the four angels who bore us set us down trembling, and we passed on foot by a broad way over a plain. There we found Jocundus and Saturninus and Artaxius, who in the same persecution had

[52] Many of these persons also were Christians, but because they had not been accused or denounced they could freely go in and out of the prisons and care for the condemned persons.

[53] A fourth vision.

[54] Victorious gladiators exited the arena through the Gate of Life on the eastern side, whereas dead gladiators were carried out the Gate of Death on the western side.

[55] Who also had been condemned.

been burned alive, and Quintus, a martyr also, who in prison had departed this life, and we asked of them where were the rest. The other angels said to us, "Come first, go in, and salute the Lord."

And we came near to a place, of which the walls were such that they seemed built of light, and before the door of that place stood four angels who clothed us when we went in with white raiment. And we went in, and we heard as it were one voice crying "Holy, holy, holy" without any end. And we saw sitting in that same place as it were a man, white-headed, having hair like snow; youthful of countenance; whose feet we saw not. And on his right hand and on his left, four elders, and behind them stood many other elders. And we went in with wonder and stood before the throne, and the four angels raised us up and we kissed him, and with his hand he passed over our faces. And the other elders said to us, "Stand you." And we stood, and gave the kiss of peace. And the elders said to us, "Go you and play." And I said to Perpetua, "You have that which you desire." And she said to me, "Yes, God be thanked," so that I that was glad in the flesh am now more glad.

And we went out, and we saw before the doors, on the right Optatus the bishop,[56] and on the left Aspasius the priest and teacher, being apart and sorrowful. And they cast themselves at our feet and said, "Make peace between us,[57] because you departed and left us thus." And we said to them, "Are not you our father, and you our priest, that you should throw yourselves at our feet?" And we were moved, and embraced them. And Perpetua began to talk with them in Greek,[58] and we set them apart in the arboretum beneath a rose tree. And while we yet spoke with them, the angels said to them, "Let them cool down, and whatsoever dissensions you have between you, put them away from you each for each." And they made them to be confounded. And they said to Optatus, "Correct your people, for they come to you as those that return from the games and arguing about the racing clubs."[59] And it seemed to us as though they would shut the gates. And we began to know many brothers there, martyrs also. And we were all sustained there with a savor inexpressible which satisfied us. Then in joy I awoke. These were the glorious visions of those martyrs themselves, the most blessed Saturus and Perpetua, that they themselves wrote down. But Secundulus by an earlier end God called from this world while he was yet in prison, not without grace, so that he should escape the beasts. Yet if not his soul, his flesh at least knew the sword.

As for Felicitas, she too received this grace of the lord. For because she was already eight months with child, for she was pregnant when she was arrested, she was very sorrowful as the day of the games drew near, fearing lest because of the child she would be kept back, for it is not permitted that pregnant women be presented for torment, and lest she should shed her holy and innocent blood after the rest, among strangers and malefactors.[60] Also her fellow martyrs were much afflicted lest they should leave behind them so good a friend and as it were their fellow-traveler on the road of the same hope. Therefore with joint and united groaning they poured out their prayer to the Lord three days before the games. Immediately after their prayer her pains came upon her. And when by reason of the natural difficulty of the eighth month she was oppressed with her travail and made complaint, there said to her one of the servants of the keepers of the door, "You that thus make complaint now, what wilt you do when you are thrown to the beasts, for whom you showed contempt when you would not sacrifice?" And she answered, "I myself now suffer that which I suffer, but there another shall be in me who shall suffer for me, because I am to suffer for him." So she was delivered of a daughter, whom a sister reared up to be her own daughter.

Because therefore the Holy Spirit permitted this, and by permitting it has willed that the account of

[56] Bishop of an unknown North African city.

[57] It was not uncommon for bishops to be defied by their clergy.

[58] The "Passion of Perpetua" circulated in both Latin and Greek.

[59] Generally, there were four chariot-racing factions, or clubs, identified by their colors, blue, green, red, and white; see Reading 123.

[60] Christians were executed along with any other criminals who had been sentenced to death.

the games also should be written, even if though we are unworthy of describing such great glory as a supplement, nevertheless we follow the, so to speak, mandate[61] of the most holy Perpetua, or rather her trust, adding one testimony more of her own steadfastness and height of spirit. When they were being more cruelly handled by the Tribune[62] because through the advice of certain most despicable men he feared lest by magic charms they might be withdrawn secretly from the prison house, Perpetua answered him to his face, "Why do you not allow us, the most noble guilty ones, the property, certainly, of Caesar, to take some comfort, and about to fight on his anniversary? Or is it not your glory that we should be taken out thither fatter of flesh?" The Tribune trembled and blushed, and gave order that they should be more gently handled, granting that her brothers and the rest should come in and rest with them. Also the adjutant of the prison now believed.

Likewise on the day before the games, when at the last feast which they call "free" they made, as far as they might, not a Free Feast[63] but a Love Feast,[64] with like hardihood they cast these words at the people, threatening the judgment of the Lord, witnessing to the felicity of their passion, setting at nought the curiosity of those that ran together. And Saturus said, "Is not tomorrow sufficient for you? Why do you favorably behold that which you hate? You are friends today, foes tomorrow. Yet mark our faces diligently, that you may know us again on that day." So they began all to go away thence astonished, of whom many believed.

Now dawned the day of their victory, and they went forth from the prison into the amphitheater as it were into heaven, cheerful and bright of countenance. If they trembled at all, it was for joy, not for fear. Perpetua followed behind, glorious of presence, as a true spouse of Christ and darling of God, at whose piercing look all cast down their eyes. Felicitas likewise, rejoicing that she had borne a child in safety so that she might fight with the beasts, came now from blood to blood, from the midwife to the gladiator, to wash after her travail in a second baptism. And when they had been brought to the gate and were being compelled to put on, the men the dress of the priests of Saturn, the women the dress of the priestesses of Ceres,[65] the noble Perpetua remained of like firmness to the end, and would not. She said, "For this cause came we willingly unto this, that our liberty might not be obscured. For this cause have we devoted our lives, that we might do no such thing as this. This we agreed with you." Injustice acknowledged justice; the Tribune suffered that they should be brought forth as they were, without more ado. Perpetua began to sing, as if already treading on the Egyptian's head. Revocatus and Saturninus and Saturus threatened the people as they gazed. Then when they came into Hilarian's sight, they began to say to Hilarian, stretching forth their hands and nodding their heads, "You judge us, they said, and God judges you." At this the people, being enraged, sought that they should be vexed with scourges before the line of the beast-fighters. Then truly they gave thanks because they had received somewhat of the sufferings of the Lord.

But he who had said, "Ask and you shall receive,"[66] granted them that end that each had desired. For whenever they spoke together of their desire in their martyrdom, Saturninus for his part would declare that he wished to be thrown to every kind of beast, that so indeed he might wear the more glorious crown. At the beginning of the spectacle therefore, Revocatus himself and Saturninus first had suffered a leopard and then were torn by a bear on a scaffold. Now, Saturus detested nothing more than a bear, but was confident already that he should die by one bite of a leopard. Therefore when he was being given to a boar, the gladiator instead who had bound

[61] A "mandate" was an imperial command issued to an imperial official.

[62] A junior officer, not a Military Tribune or Tribune of the Plebs.

[63] The "cena libera," or "free meal," of gladiators. All of those who would be taking part, including condemned criminals and gladiators, were together, many of whom would be fighting against each other on the next day.

[64] The "agape," a Christian communal meal that included taking communion.

[65] Saturn and Ceres were harvest deities.

[66] John 16:24.

him to the boar was torn asunder by the same beast and died after the days of the games; nor was Saturus more than dragged. Moreover, when he had been tied on a bridge to be assaulted by a bear, the bear would not come forth from his den. So Saturus was called back unharmed a second time.

But for the women the devil had made ready a most savage cow, prepared for this purpose against all custom, for even in the beast he mocked their sex. They were stripped therefore and made to put on nets, and so they were brought forth. The people shuddered, seeing one a tender girl, the other her breasts yet dropping from her late childbearing. So they were called back and clothed in loose robes.[67] Perpetua was first thrown and fell upon her loins. And when she had sat upright, her robe being rent at the side, she drew it over to cover her thigh, mindful rather of modesty than of pain. Next, looking for a pin, she likewise pinned up her disheveled hair, for it was not meet that a martyr should suffer with hair disheveled, lest she should seem to grieve in her glory. So she stood up; and when she saw Felicitas smitten down, she went up and gave her her hand and raised her up. And both of them stood up together and, the hardness of the people being now subdued, were called back to the Gate of Life. There Perpetua being received by one named Rusticus, then a catechumen,[68] who stood close at her side, and as now awakening from sleep, so much was she in the Spirit and in ecstasy, she began first to look about her; and then, which amazed all there, she asked, "When, indeed, are we to be thrown to the cow?" And when she heard that this had been done already, she would not believe until she perceived some marks of mauling on her body and on her dress. Thereupon she called her brother to her, and that catechumen, and spoke to them, saying, "Stand fast in the faith, and love you all one another; and be not offended because of our passion."

Saturus also at another gate exhorted Pudens the soldier, saying, "So then indeed, as I trusted and foretold, I have felt no assault of beasts until now. And now believe with all your heart. Behold, I go out thither and shall perish by one bite of the leopard." And immediately at the end of the spectacle, the leopard being released, with one bite of his Saturus was covered with so much blood that the people, in witness to his second baptism, cried out to him returning, "Well washed, well washed." Truly it was well with him who had washed in this wise. Then said he to Pudens the soldier, "Farewell. Remember the faith and me, and let not these things trouble you, but strengthen you." And therewith he took from Pudens' finger a little ring, and dipping it in his wound gave it back again for an heirloom, leaving him a pledge and memorial of his blood. Then as the breath left him he was cast down with the rest in the accustomed place for his throat to be cut.[69] And when the people besought that they should be brought forward, that when the sword pierced through their bodies their eyes might be joined thereto as witnesses to the slaughter, they rose of themselves and moved, whither the people willed them, first kissing one another, that they might accomplish their martyrdom with the rites of peace. The rest not moving and in silence received the sword. Saturus much earlier gave up the ghost, for he had gone up earlier also, and now he waited for Perpetua likewise. But Perpetua, that she might have some taste of pain, was pierced between the bones and shrieked out, and when the swordsman's hand wandered still, for he was a novice, herself set it upon her own neck. Perchance so great a woman could not else have been slain, being feared by the unclean spirit,[70] had she not herself so willed it.

O most valiant and blessed martyrs! O truly called and elected unto the glory of Our Lord Jesus Christ! Which glory he that magnifies, honors and adores, ought to read these witnesses likewise, as being no less than the old, unto the Church's edification; that these new wonders also may testify that one and the same Holy Spirit works ever until now, and with Him God the Father Almighty, and His Son Jesus Christ Our Lord, to Whom is glory and power unending for ever and ever. Amen.

[67] Because they had gained the sympathy of the crowd; see also Reading 113.

[68] An unbaptized Christian.

[69] To end his suffering and ensure that he actually was dead.

[70] The Devil.

104

THE NEW PERSIAN EMPIRE (CA. 270 CE): THE SHAPUR I INSCRIPTION

In this cliff carving, Shapur I, with the Roman emperor Philip kneeling in front of him and holding the emperor Valerian by hand, tramples the emperor Gordian III. Bishapur. The high priest Kartir and a Sasanian general stand on the right.

Like the kings of the Old Persian Empire (550–331 BCE), the kings of the New Persian, or Sasanid, Empire advertised their achievements with monumental reliefs and inscriptions carved on the sides of cliffs (see Reading 44). A trilingual rock carving, in Parthian, Middle Persian, and Greek, at Naqsh-I Rustam in Iran gives a detailed account of the reign of the

Sasanid king Shapur I (241–272 CE). Shapur describes himself as "The Mazda worshipping lord Shapur, King of Kings of Iran and non-Iran, whose lineage is from the gods, son of the Mazda worshipping divinity Ardashir, King of Kings of Iran, whose lineage is from the gods, grandson of king Papak." Like the Roman emperors, Shapur I claimed to rule the entire world. Among other projects, he built the city of Bishapur using enslaved Roman soldiers, many of whom were captured after the defeat of Valerian in 260.

Source: R. N. Frye *The History of Ancient Iran*, Vol. 7 (Beck: Munich, 1983), 370–373.

I, the Mazda-worshipping lord Shapur, King of Kings of Iran and non-Iran, whose lineage is from the gods, son of the Mazda worshipping divinity Ardashir,[71] King of Kings of Iran, whose lineage is from the gods, grandson of King Papak,[72] am ruler of Iranshahr and these lands[73]: Persis, Parthia, Khuzistan, Characene, Assyria, Adiabene, Arabia, Azerbaijan, Armenia, Georgia, Segan, Arran, Balasakan, up to the Caucasus mountains and the Gates of Albania, and all of the mountain chain of Pareshwar, Media, Gurgan, Merv, Herat and all of Aparshahr, Kerman, Seistan, Turan, Makuran, Paradene, Sind, the Kushanshahr up to Peshawar, and up to Kashgar, Sogdiana and to the mountains of Tashkent, and on the other side of the sea, Oman. And we have given to a village district the name Peroz-Shapur and we made Hormizd-Ardashsir by name Shapur. And these many lands, and rulers and governors, all have become tributary and subject to us.

When at first we had become established in the empire, Gordian Caesar[74] raised in all of the Roman Empire a force from the Gothic and German realms[75] and marched on Asuristan[76] against the Empire of Iran and against us. On the border of Babylonia at Misikhe, a great "frontal" battle occurred. Gordian Caesar was killed and the Roman force was destroyed.[77] And the Romans made Philip Caesar.[78] Then Philip Caesar came to us for terms, and to ransom their lives, gave us 500,000 denarii, and became tributary to us. For this reason we have renamed Misikhe Peroz-Shapur.[79]

And Caesar lied again and did wrong to Armenia.[80] Then we attacked the Roman Empire and annihilated at Barbalissos a Roman force of 60,000 and Syria and the environs of Syria we burned, ruined, and pillaged.[81] In this one campaign we conquered of the Roman Empire the following fortresses and towns: the town of Anatha with surroundings, Birtha of Arūpān with surroundings, Birtha of Asporakan, the town of Sura, Barbalissos, Manbuk, Aleppo, Qennisrin, Rhephania, Zeugma, Urima, Gindaros, Armenaza, Seleucia, Antioch[82], Cyrrhe,

[71] Ardashir I (224–241 CE) overthrew the Parthians and established the New Persian Empire in 224 CE.

[72] A Persian prince, the son of Sāsān, who gave his name to the Sasanian Dynasty.

[73] Regions extending from Arabia to western India.

[74] Roman emperor from 238 until 244.

[75] Auxiliary troops serving in the Roman army.

[76] Babylonia.

[77] In reality, after Shapur had invaded Roman territory he was defeated by Gordian at the Battle of Resaena in 243. Gordian was not killed there.

[78] Gordian III was assassinated in 244 and succeeded by Philip the Arab (244–249).

[79] Philip's offensive against the New Persians later in 244 was initially successful but ultimately defeated at the Battle of Misikhe.

[80] Armenia lay on the frontier between the Roman and New Persian Empires and was a constant bone of contention between them, just as it had been between the Romans and Parthians.

[81] This Roman incursion in 253 is known only from this inscription; Shapur probably took advantage of the troubled times relating to the fall of the emperor Trebonianus Gallus (251–253) and the proclamation of Valerian (253–260). The victory opened the way to the Persian capture of Dura Europa and Antioch in 256 CE.

[82] The most important Roman city of Syria and the Levant.

another town of Seleucia, Alexandretta, Nicopolis, Sinzara, Hama, Rastan, Dikhor, Dolikhe, Dura,[83] Circusium, Germanicia, Batna, and Khanar, and in Cappadocia[84] the towns of Satala, Domana, Artangil, Suisa, Sinda, and Phreata, a total of thirty-seven towns with surroundings.

In the third campaign, when we were besieging Carrhae and Edessa, Valerian Caesar[85] marched against us. He had with him a force of 70,000 from Germany, Raetia, Noricum, Dacia, Pannonia, Moesia, Istria, Spain, Africa, Thrace, Bithynia, Asia, Pamphylia, Isauria, Lycaonia, Galatia, Lycia, Cilicia, Cappadocia, Phrygia, Syria, Phoenicia, Judaea, Arabia, Mauritania, Germania, Rhodes, Osrhoëne, and Mesopotamia.[86] And beyond Carrhae and Edessa we had a great battle with Valerian Caesar.[87] We made prisoner ourselves with our own hands Valerian Caesar and the others, chiefs of that army, the Praetorian Prefect, and senators; we made all prisoners and deported them to Persis.[88] Syria, Cilicia, and Cappadocia we burned, ruined and pillaged. In that campaign we conquered from the Roman Empire[89] the town of Samosata, Alexandria on the Issus, Katabolos, Aegaea, Mopsuestia, Mallos, Adana, Tarsus, Augustinia, Zephyrion, Sebaste, Korykos, Anazarba, Kastabala, Neronias, Flavias, Nicopolis, Epiphaneia, Celenderis, Anemurion, Selinus, Mzd, Antioch, Seleucia, Dometiopolis, Tyana, Caesarea, Komana, Kybistra, Sebasteia, Birtha, Rakundia, Laranda, and Iconium, altogether all these cities with their surroundings.

Men of the Roman Empire, of non-Iranians, we deported. We settled them in the Empire of Iran in Persis, Parthia, Khuzistan, Babylonia, and other lands where there were domains of our father, grandfathers, and of our ancestors. We searched out for our conquest many other lands, and we acquired fame for heroism that we have not engraved here, except for the preceding. We ordered it written so that whoever comes after us may know of our fame, heroism, and power. Thus, for this reason, that the gods have made us their ward, and with the aid of the gods we have searched out and taken so many lands, so that in every land we have founded many Bahram fires[90] and have conferred benefices upon many magians,[91] and we have magnified the cult of the gods. And here by this inscription, we founded a fire Khosro-Shapur by name for our soul and to perpetuate our name, a fire called Khosro-Aduranahid by name for the soul of our daughter Aduranahid, Queen of Queens, to perpetuate her name, a fire called Khosro-Hormizd-Ardashir by name for the soul of our son, Hormizd-Ardashir, Great King of Armenia, to perpetuate his name, another fire called Khosro-Shapur by name, for the soul of our son Shapur, King of Characene, to perpetuate his name, and a fire called Khosro-Narseh by name, for the soul of our son, the noble, Mazda worshipping Narseh, King of Sind, Seistan, and Turan to the edge of the sea, to perpetuate his name.

And that which we have donated to these fires, and which we have established as a custom, all of that we have written upon the document of guaranty. Of those 1,000 lambs, of which custom gives us the excess, and which we have donated so these fires, we have ordered as follows[92]: for our soul each day a lamb, one and a half measures of bread and four quantities of wine; for that of Sāsān the Lord[93]; King

---

[83] Dura Europa, the site of major modern archaeological excavations.

[84] A Roman province of western Anatolia.

[85] Emperor from 253 until 260; he made his son Gallienus (253–268) his co-emperor.

[86] A catalogue of many of the Roman provinces; this information probably came from Roman prisoners of war.

[87] In 268 CE.

[88] In southwestern Iran.

[89] Some of these places were announced as having been captured previously, but in the interim had been retaken by the Romans.

[90] New Persian fire temples.

[91] Priests of the god Ahura Mazda.

[92] To stress his own legitimacy, Shapur lists the royal genealogy, from Sāsān, who gave his name to the Sasanid Dynasty, up to his own family, many of whom have royal titles in their own right attesting to the desire of the New Persian rulers to keep the real power within their own family circle.

[93] A priest of a fire temple of the water goddess Anahita and the first member of the Sasanid Dynasty.

Papak[94]; King Shapur, son of Papak; King of Kings Ardashir[95]; the Empire's Queen Khoranzim; Queen of Queens Aduranahid; Queen Dinak, King of Gilan; Bahram, King of Characene Shapur; Great King of Armenia Hormizd-Ardashir; King of the Saka[96] Narseh; Queen of the Saka Shapurdukhtak; Lady of the Saka Narsehdukht; Lady Ćašmak; Prinz Peroz; Lady Mirdut, mother of King of Kings Shapur; Prince Narseh, Princess Rud-dukhtak, daughter of Anošak, Varazdukht, daughter of Khoranzim, Queen Stahyrad; Hormizdak, son of the King of Armenia Hormizd; Hormizdak; Odabakht; Bahram; Shapur; Peroz, son of the King of Characene; Shapurdukhtak, daughter of the King of Characene; and Hormizd-dukhtak, daughter of the King of the Saka, for their souls a lamb, a measure and a half of bread and four quantities of wine.

Now as we serve and worship the gods with zeal, because we are the wards of the gods and with the aid of the gods we have searched out these peoples, have dominated them, and have acquired fame for bravery, also whoever comes after us and rules, may he also serve and worship the gods with zeal, so the gods may aid him and make him their ward.

This is the writing by my hand, Hormizd, the scribe, son of Shirak, the scribe.[97]

---

[94] A Persian prince, son of Sāsān and grandfather of Ardashir.

[95] Ardashir I (224–241 CE), who revolted against the Parthians (Reading 69) and founded the Sasanid, or New Persian, Empire.

[96] A generic term for the peoples of the Asian steppe east of the Caspian Sea.

[97] The subscription appears only in the Parthian version of the inscription.

105

ZENOBIA AND THE EMPIRE OF PALMYRA (266–274 CE): *THE AUGUSTAN HISTORY*, "ODENATHUS" AND "ZENOBIA"

A debased silver antoninianus of Queen Zenobia depicts her as Augusta, or empress, with the legend "Zenobia Aug(usta)" on the obverse and a standing figure of the goddess Juno Regina, "Juno the Queen (of the Gods)," on the reverse, emphasizing Zenobia's royal status.

Zenobia, queen of the powerful trading city of Palmyra in Syria on the eastern frontier of the Roman Empire, was the wife of Odenathus, a Palmyrene prince who drove off the New Persians after their defeat and capture of the emperor Valerian in 268 CE. As a reward, Odenathus was placed in charge of the east by Valerian's son Gallienus. After further defeats of the Persians, Odenathus took the title "King of Kings" in 264. But when he appeared to be on the verge of declaring himself emperor in 267, Zenobia organized a conspiracy against him and he was assassinated. Zenobia then assumed his position as ruler of Palmyra. She took advantage of Roman weakness—Gaul, Spain, and Britain already had created an "Empire of Gaul" in 259 CE—to take the title of Augusta (Empress) and create an Empire of Palmyra, which included the Levant, part of Anatolia, and Egypt. Zenobia's story is told most fully in the sections "Odenathus" and "Zenobia" in the *Augustan History*, a compilation of the 390s CE that is part fact and part historical fiction.

Source: David Magie, trans., *Historia Augusta*, Vol. I (Cambridge, MA: Harvard University Press, 1921).

[Augustan History, "Odenathus"]
Had not Odenathus, Prince of the Palmyrenes, seized the imperial power after the capture of Valerian,[98] when the strength of the Roman state was exhausted, all would have been lost in the east. He assumed, therefore, as the first of his line, the title of King, and after gathering together an army he set out against the Persians, having with him his wife Zenobia, his elder son, whose name was Herodes, and his younger sons, Herennianus and Timolaus. First of all, he brought under his power Nisibis[99] and most of the east together with the whole of Mesopotamia; next, he defeated the king himself and compelled him to flee. Finally, he pursued Shapur[100] and his children even as far as Ctesiphon,[101] and captured his concubines and also a great amount of booty;

When Gallienus[102] learned that Odenathus had ravaged the Persians, brought Nisibis and Carrhae[103] under the sway of Rome, made all of Mesopotamia ours, and finally arrived at Ctesiphon, put the king to flight, captured the satraps and killed large numbers of Persians, he gave him a share in the imperial power, conferred on him the name Augustus, and ordered coins to be struck in his honor that showed him haling the Persians into captivity.[104] This measure the Senate, the city, and men of every age received with approval.

Then, after he had for the most part put in order the affairs of the east, Odenathus was killed by his cousin Maeonius, who also had seized the imperial power together with his son Herodes, who, also, after returning from Persia along with his father, had received the title of emperor.[105] Some god, I believe, was angry with the Republic, who, after Valerian's death, was unwilling to preserve Odenathus alive. For of a surety he, with his wife Zenobia, would have restored not only the east, which he had already brought back to its ancient condition, but also all parts of the whole world. Hardened by these feats, he was able to bear the sun and the dust in the wars with the Persians, and his wife, too, was inured to hardship and in the opinion of many was held to be more brave than her husband, being, indeed, the noblest of all the women of the east, and, as Cornelius Capitolinus[106] declares, the most beautiful.

Then Zenobia, his wife, because the sons who remained, Herennianus and Timolaus, were still very young, assumed the power herself and ruled for a long time, not in feminine fashion or with the ways of a woman, but surpassing in courage and skill not merely Gallienus, than whom any girl could have

[98] In 268 CE; see Reading 104.
[99] A powerful fortress on the border between the Roman and Sasanid empires.
[100] Shapur I (241–272 CE), King of Kings of the New Persian Empire.
[101] The western capital of the New Persian Empire, on the Tigris River in Mesopotamia.
[102] Roman emperor from 253 until 268 CE, the son of the emperor Valerian.
[103] A city on the frontier of the Roman and Sasanid Empire that had been captured by Shapur (see Reading 104).
[104] No such coins are known to exist.
[105] There is no other evidence that Maeonius or Herodes ever did so.
[106] An otherwise unknown Roman author.

ruled more successfully, but also many an emperor. As for Gallienus, indeed, when he learned that Odenathus was murdered, he made ready for war with the Persians, an over-tardy vengeance for his father,[107] and, gathering an army with the help of the general Heraclianus, he played the part of a skilful prince. This Heraclianus, however, on setting out against the Persians, was defeated by the Palmyrenes and lost all the troops he had gathered, for Zenobia was ruling Palmyra and most of the east with the vigor of a man.

[Augustan History, "Zenobia"]
Now all shame is exhausted, for in the weakened state of the Republic things came to such a pass that, while Gallienus conducted himself in the most evil fashion, even women ruled most excellently. For, in fact, even a foreigner, Zenobia by name, about whom much already has been said, boasting herself to be of the family of the Cleopatras[108] and the Ptolemies, proceeded upon the death of her husband Odenathus to cast about her shoulders the imperial mantle; and arrayed in the robes of Dido[109] and even assuming the diadem, she held the imperial power in the name of her sons Herennianus and Timolaus, ruling longer than could be endured from one of the female sex. For this proud woman performed the functions of a monarch both while Gallienus was ruling and afterward when Claudius[110] was busied with the war against the Goths, and in the end could scarcely by conquered by Aurelian[111] himself, under whom she was led in triumph and submitted to the sway of Rome.

There is still in existence a letter of Aurelian that bears testimony concerning this woman, then in captivity. For when some found fault with him, because he, the bravest of men, had led a woman in triumph, as though she were a general, he sent a letter to the senate and the Roman people, defending himself by the following justification:

> I have heard, Conscript Fathers, that men are reproaching me for having performed an unmanly deed in leading Zenobia in triumph. But in truth those very persons who find fault with me now would accord me praise in abundance, did they but know what manner of woman she is, how wise in counsels, how steadfast in plans, how firm toward the soldiers, how generous when necessity calls, and how stern when discipline demands. I might even say that it was her doing that Odenathus defeated the Persians and, after putting Shapur to flight, advanced all the way to Ctesiphon. I might add thereto that such was the fear that this woman inspired in the peoples of the east and also the Egyptians that neither Arabs nor Saracens nor Armenians ever moved against her. Nor would I have spared her life had I not known that she did a great service to the Roman state when she preserved the imperial power in the east for herself or for her children. Therefore let those whom nothing pleases keep the venom of their own tongues to themselves. For if it is not meet to vanquish a woman and lead her in triumph, what are they saying of Gallienus, in contempt of whom she ruled the empire well? What of the Deified Claudius, that revered and honored leader? For he, because he was busied with his campaigns against the Goths, suffered her, or so it is said, to hold the imperial power, doing it of purpose and wisely, in order that he himself, while she kept guard over the eastern frontier of the empire, might the more safely complete what he had taken in hand.

This speech shows what opinion Aurelian held concerning Zenobia.

Such was her continence, it is said, that she would not know even her own husband save for the purpose of conception. For when once she had lain with him, she would refrain until the time of menstruation to see if she were pregnant; if not, she would again grant him an opportunity of begetting children. She lived in regal pomp. It was rather in the manner of the Persians that she received worship and in the manner of the Persian kings that she banqueted; but it was in the manner of a Roman emperor that she came forth to public assemblies, wearing a helmet and girt with a purple headband, which had gems hanging from the lower edge whereas its center was

---

[107] Valerian, who had been defeated and captured in 268.
[108] See Reading 86.
[109] The Queen of Carthage who was spurned by Aeneas and committed suicide; see Reading 88.
[110] Emperor Claudius II Gothicus (268–270).
[111] Emperor from 270 to 275.

fastened with the jewel called cochlis,[112] used instead of the brooch worn by women, and her arms were frequently bare. Her face was dark and of a swarthy hue, her eyes were black and powerful beyond the usual wont, her spirit divinely great, and her beauty incredible. So white were her teeth that many thought that she had pearls in place of teeth. Her voice was clear and like that of a man.

Her sternness, when necessity demanded, was that of a tyrant, her clemency, when her sense of right called for it, that of a good emperor. Generous with prudence, she conserved her treasures beyond the wont of women. She made use of a carriage, and rarely of a woman's coach, but more often she rode a horse; it is said, moreover, that frequently she walked with her foot-soldiers for three or four miles. She hunted with the eagerness of a Spaniard. She often drank with her generals, although at other times she refrained, and she drank, too, with the Persians and the Armenians, but only for the purpose of getting the better of them. At her banquets she used vessels of gold and jewels, and she even used those that had been Cleopatra's.[113] As servants she had eunuchs of advanced age and but very few maidens. She ordered her sons to speak Latin, so that, in fact, they spoke Greek but rarely and with difficulty. She herself was not wholly conversant with the Latin tongue, but nevertheless, mastering her timidity she would speak it; Egyptian, on the other hand, she spoke very well. In the history of Alexandria and the Orient she was so well versed that she even composed an epitome, so it is said. Roman history, however, she read in Greek.

After Aurelian took her prisoner he caused her to be led into his presence and then asked her, "Why is it, Zenobia, that you dared to show insolence to the emperors of Rome?" To this she replied, it is said: "You, I know, are an emperor indeed, for you win victories, but Gallienus and Aureolus[114] and the others I never regarded as emperors. Believing Victoria[115] to be a woman like me, I desired to become a partner in the royal power, should the supply of lands permit." And so she was led in triumph with such magnificence that the Roman people had never seen a more splendid parade. For, in the first place, she was adorned with gems so huge that she labored under the weight of her ornaments; for it is said that this woman, courageous although she was, halted very frequently, saying that she could not endure the load of her gems. Furthermore, her feet were bound with shackles of gold and her hands with golden fetters, and even on her neck she wore a chain of gold, the weight of which was borne by a Persian guardsman. Her life was granted her by Aurelian, and they say that thereafter she lived with her children in the manner of a Roman matron on an estate that had been presented to her at Tibur, which even to this day is still called Zenobia, not far from the palace of Hadrian.[116]

[112] An agate-like gem from Arabia.

[113] Presumably after her conquest of Egypt.

[114] A general who revolted against Gallienus in 268 and later was murdered by the Praetorian Guard.

[115] The goddess Victory.

[116] At Tivoli, nineteen miles east of Rome.

106

DIOCLETIAN'S "EDICT ON MAXIMUM PRICES" (301 CE)

Diocletian's lengthy "Edict on Maximum Prices" was posted in Latin and Greek on stone inscriptions throughout the Roman Empire. The largest surviving portions have been found in Turkey, Egypt, and Greece, and pieces have been found in no less than thirty different places, nearly all in the eastern part of the empire.

When the emperor Diocletian came to power in 284 CE, the Roman economy was in a shambles, primarily because of enormous pay raises given to soldiers by Septimius Severus (193–211) and his son Caracalla (211–217) that had resulted in the debasement of the silver coinage. When millions of these coins flooded the marketplace, the empire was struck by massive inflation, not only because of the lowered value of the coins, but also because the economy could not absorb the great increase in the money supply and because people hoarded good silver coins and paid their taxes in the debased silver coins. Diocletian initially attempted to solve the problem by reissuing good silver and gold coins, but there was not enough silver available for this to work. So in 301 Diocletian adopted the usual late Roman method for addressing problems: he issued a law to deal with it, a "Maximum Price Edict" that established not only the maximum prices that could be charged for a large list of items but also the maximum wages that could be paid for a long list of jobs. Prices and wages were given in "denarii." Although the denarius was no longer issued, it remained a standard unit of account and had to be converted into whatever currency one was using. Thus, the silver-coated copper coin called the "follis" was valued at twenty-five denarii, and a gold aureus was technically worth one thousand denarii (although it is doubtful that anyone would exchange a gold aureus for forty copper folles). The law was a total failure. It simplistically attributed inflation to greedy merchants and took no account of either a merchant's need to make a profit or differential prices that had to be charged for items manufactured in one place and sold hundreds or thousands of miles away. In any event, moreover, the emperors had no means of enforcing laws; all they could do was hope that people obeyed the laws of their own volition. Goods that could not be sold openly were simply sold on the black market. Acknowledging the failure of the law, Diocletian then introduced the "annona" system, the payment of taxes and expenditures in kind. It was cumbersome, but it worked.

Source: Elsa R. Graser, trans., "The Edict of Diocletian on Maximum Prices," in T. Frank, *An Economic Survey of Ancient Rome Volume V: Rome and Italy of the Empire* (Baltimore: Johns Hopkins University Press, 1940), 307–421.

Diocletian, Maximianus, Constantius, and Galerius[117] declare:

As we recall the wars that we successfully have fought, we must be grateful for a world that is tranquil and reclining in the embrace of the most profound calm, and for the blessings of peace that was won with great effort. That the fortune of our Republic be faithfully disposed and suitably adorned is the demand of public opinion and the dignity and majesty of Rome. Therefore, we, who by the gracious favor the gods have repressed the former tide of ravages of barbarian nations by destroying them, must guard by due defenses of justice a peace that was established for eternity.

If, indeed, any self-restraint might check the excesses with which limitless and furious avarice rages, avarice that, with no thought for mankind, hastens to its own gain and increase, not by years or months or days but by hours and even by minutes, or, if the general welfare could endure undisturbed the riotous license by which it, in its misfortune, is from day to day most grievously injured, there would perhaps be left some room for dissimulation and silence, since human forbearance might alleviate the detestable cruelty of a pitiable situation. Because those whose extremes of need have brought us to an appreciation of their most unfortunate situation, so that we no longer can close our eyes to it, we, the protectors of the human race, viewing have agreed that justice should intervene[118] as arbiter, so that the long-hoped-for solution that mankind itself could not supply might, by the remedies of our foresight, be applied to the general betterment of all.

We, therefore, hasten to apply the remedies long demanded by this situation, satisfied that there can be no complaints that the intervention of our remedy may be considered untimely or unnecessary, trivial, or unimportant by the unscrupulous who, in spite of perceiving in our silence of so many years a lesson in restraint, have been unwilling to copy it. For who are so insensitive and so devoid of human feeling that cannot know, or rather, have not perceived, that in the commerce carried on in the markets or involved in the daily life of cities immoderate prices are so widespread that the uncurbed passion for gain is lessened neither by abundant supplies nor by fruitful years;

It is our pleasure, therefore, that the prices listed in the subjoined summary be observed in the whole of our empire in such fashion that everyone may know that whereas permission to exceed them has been forbidden, the blessing of low prices has in no case been restricted in those places where supplies are seen to abound, because special provision is made for these when avarice is definitely quieted. It is our pleasure that anyone who shall have resisted the form of this statute shall for this daring be

[117] The four emperors who were members of the "Tetrarchy," or "Rule by Four."

[118] The standard method used by late Roman emperors to try to solve problems was to issue laws.

subject to a capital penalty. And let no one consider the penalty harsh because there is at hand a means of avoiding the danger by observance of moderation. We, therefore, urge upon the loyalty of all our people that a law constituted for the public good may be observed with willing obedience[119] and due care, especially because in such a statute provision has been made, not for single states and peoples and provinces, but for the whole world.[120]

The prices for the sale of individual items that no one may exceed are listed below.

Wheat	1 army *modius*[121]	*den.*100[122]
Barley	1 army *modius*	*den.* 60
Rye	1 army *modius*	*den.* 60
Millet, ground	1 Sarmy *modius*	*den.* 100
Millet, whole	1 army *modius*	*den.* 50
Panic grass	1 army *modius*	*den.* 50
Spelt, hulled	1 army *modius*	*den.* 100
. . . .		
Beans, crushed	1 army *modius*	*den.* 100
Beans, not ground	1 army *modius*	*den.* 60
Lentils	1 army *modius*	*den.* 100
Pulse	1 army *modius*	*den.* 80
Peas, split	1 army *modius*	*den.* 100
Peas, not split	1 army *modius*	*den.* 60
. . . .		
Rice, cleaned	1 army *modius*	*den.* 200
Barley grits, cleaned	1 *modius*	*den.* 100
Spelt grits, cleaned	1 *modius*	*den.* 200
Sesame	1 army *modius*	*den.* 200
. . . .		
Likewise, for wines:		
Picene	1 Italian *sextarius*[123]	*den.* 30
Tiburtine	1 Italian *sextarius*	*den.* 30
Sabine	1 Italian *sextarius*	*den.* 30
. . . .		
Falernian	1 Italian *sextarius*	*den.* 30
Aged wine, first quality	1 Italian *sextarius*	*den.* 24
Aged wine, second quality	1 Italian *sextarius*	*den.* 16
Ordinary	1 Italian *sextarius*	*den.* 8
Beer, Gallic or Pannonian[124]	1 Italian *sextarius*	*den.* 4
Beer, Egyptian	1 Italian *sextarius*	*den.* 2
. . . .		
Likewise, for oil:		
From unripe olives	1 Italian *sextarius*	*den.* 40
Second quality	1 Italian *sextarius*	*den.* 24
Salt	1 army *modius*	*den.* 100
Spiced salt	1 Italian *sextarius*	*den.* 8
Honey, best quality	1 Italian *sextarius*	*den.* 40
Honey, second quality	1 Italian *sextarius*	*den* 24
Likewise, for meat:		
Pork	1 Italian pound	*den.* 12
Beef	1 Italian pound	*den.* 8
Leg of pork, Menapic[125] or Cerritane,[126] best	1 Italian pound	*den.* 20
Pork mincemeat	1 ounce	*den.* 2
Beef mincemeat	1 Italian pound	*den.* 10
Pheasant, fattened		*den.* 250

[119] This because the government had no institutionalized means of enforcing the laws.

[120] In legal theory, the Romans claimed to rule the entire world.

[121] A civilian *modius* was a dry measure unit equivalent to about eight liters, two gallons, or one peck. An "army modius" was about one and a half times a civilian "Italian modius."

[122] Prices still were given in terms of the denarius ("den."), the old silver coin, which had become a simple unit of account and was no longer issued in coin form, much like the modern "mill," one-tenth of a cent in the United States, is not issued as an actual coin but is used in the calculation of property taxes.

[123] A sextarius was a liquid measure equivalent to about a half liter or a half quart.

[124] That is, French or Hungarian.

[125] The Menapii were a Celtic people of Belgium.

[126] The Cerritani were a Pyrenaean people of northeastern Spain.

Pheasant, wild		*den.* 125
Chickens	1 brace	*den.* 60
Venison	1 Italian pound	*den.* 12
Butter	1 Italian pound	*den.* 16

Likewise, for fish:

Sea fish with rough scales	1 Italian pound	*den.* 24
Fish, second quality	1 Italian pound	*den.* 16
River fish, best quality	1 Italian pound	*den.* 12
River fish, second quality	1 Italian pound	*den.* 8
Salt fish	1 Italian pound	*den.* 6
Oysters	100	*den.* 100

Regarding the prices of slaves.

For a masculine slave, either a eunuch or a male, from the age of seventeen years to forty years,	35,000 denarii.
For a female slave of the aforementioned age,	25,000 denarii.
Likewise, for a man from the age of forty to sixty,	25,000 denarii.
For a woman of the aforementioned age,	20,000 denarii.
For a boy from the age of eight to sixteen and a girl of the aforementioned age,	15,000 denarii.
For a man over sixty years and less than nine years,	15,000 denarii.
For a woman of the aforementioned age,	10,000 denarii.

For a slave skilled in an occupation, with regard to the type and the age and the quality of the skills it is suitable that there be an agreement between the buyer and the seller about the price to the extent that it is not at all permitted to exceed double the statutory price.

For wages:

Farm laborer, with maintenance (daily)	*den.* 25
Carpenter, as above (daily)	*den.* 50
Wall painter, as above (daily)	*den.* 75
Picture painter, as above (daily)	*den.* 150
Baker, as above (daily)	*den.* 50
Shipwright working on a seagoing ship, as above (daily)	*den.* 60
Shipwright working on a river boat, as above (daily)	*den.* 50
Muleteer, with maintenance (daily)	*den.* 25
Veterinary, for clipping and preparing hoofs (per animal)	*den.* 6
Veterinary, for bleeding and cleaning the head (per animal)	*den.* 20
Barber (per man)	*den.* 2
Sewer cleaner, working a full day, with maintenance (daily)	*den.* 25
Scribe, for the best writing (100 lines)	*den.* 25
Scribe, for second-quality writing (100 lines)	*den.* 20
Notary, for writing a petition or legal document (100 lines)	*den.* 10
Elementary teacher per boy (monthly)	*den.* 50
Teacher of arithmetic, per boy (monthly)	*den.* 75
Teacher of shorthand, per boy (monthly)	*den.* 75
Teacher of Greek or Latin language and literature, and teacher of geometry, per pupil (monthly)	*den.* 200
Teacher of rhetoric or public speaking, per pupil (monthly)	*den.* 250
Advocate or jurist, fee for a complaint	*den.* 250
Advocate or jurist, fee for pleading	*den.* 1000
Teacher of architecture, per boy (monthly)	*den.* 100
Check room attendant, per bather	*den.* 2

107

THE REFORMS OF DIOCLETIAN AND THE "GREAT PERSECUTION" (303–311 CE): LACTANTIUS, *ON THE DEATHS OF THE PERSECUTORS*, 1–35

This sculpture made from porphyry, a purple igneous stone that came from a single Egyptian quarry, depicts the emperors embracing each other, thus emphasizing the idealized cooperation among the four emperors of the Tetrarchy. The sculpture was looted from Constantinople and taken to Venice when the city was sacked by Crusaders in 1204. Its original site is unknown, and it now is erected in a corner of St. Mark's basilica in Venice.

Although the four emperors of the Tetrarchy emphasized that they worked together in harmony and that there was only one empire, in practice, they did not always agree on policy. This is seen most clearly in the efforts of Diocletian (284–305) to use religion to unify the empire. Throughout the history of the Roman Empire, beginning with Augustus and the "Cult of Rome and Augustus," emperors used religion as a means of uniting the empire's otherwise disparate peoples. Participation in the imperial cult was meant to be a purely political act, a means of declaring one's loyalty to Rome and the emperor. Jews and Christians, however, saw things differently and often refused to participate, an act that would have been seen as treasonous and subject to a capital penalty. Jews, because of their long history of monotheism, received an exemption (for Rome and the Jews see Readings 95 and 99), but not Christians. As Christianity became more widespread, greater numbers of Christians were punished for refusing to sacrifice in the imperial cult (see Readings 100 and 103). As Diocletian attempted to reorganize the empire to meet the needs of the times, his colleague Galerius, an ardent anti-Christian, prevailed on him to see the Christians as disloyal and thus worthy of extreme punishment. In 303, Diocletian thus undertook what was called the "Great Persecution," the only concerted effort during the entire history of the Roman Empire to suppress Christianity. The persecution was a complete failure. By then, Christianity was too firmly entrenched. In the realms of Diocletian and, especially, Galerius (293–311) there were some efforts to enforce the legislation, but by and large it was ignored. The western emperors Maximianus (286–305) and, in particular, Constantius (293–306) participated either in a lukewarm manner or not at all. In 311 Galerius, racked by a wasting disease, rescinded the anti-Christian legislation, but this did not keep him from an agonizing death, gleefully described in the work "On the Deaths of the Persecutors" by the Christian rhetorician Lactantius. Lactantius also commented on what he saw as the problems with Diocletian's reform attempts.

Source: William Fletcher, trans. *Lactantius. Of the Manner in That the Persecutors Died* (Buffalo, NY: Christian Literature Publishing, 1886).

The Lord has heard those supplications that you, my best beloved Donatus,[127] pour forth in his presence all the day long, and the supplications of the rest of our brethren, who by a glorious confession have obtained an everlasting crown, the reward of their faith.[128] Behold, all the adversaries are destroyed, and tranquility having been re-established throughout the Roman Empire, the late oppressed church arises again, and the temple of God, overthrown by the hands of the wicked, is built with more glory than before. For God has raised up princes[129] to rescind the impious and sanguinary edicts[130] of the tyrants and provide for the welfare of mankind, so that now the cloud of past times is dispelled, and peace and serenity gladden all hearts. And after the furious whirlwind and black tempest, the heavens now have become calm, and the wished-for light has shone forth. God, the hearer of prayer, by his divine aid now has lifted his prostrate and afflicted servants from the ground, has brought to an end the united devices of the wicked, and wiped off the tears from the faces of those who mourned. They who insulted the divinity lie low; they who cast down the holy temple are fallen with more tremendous ruin; and the tormentors of just men have poured out their guilty souls amid plagues inflicted by heaven and amid deserved tortures. For God delayed to punish them so that, by great and marvelous examples, he might teach posterity that he alone is God, and that with fit vengeance he executes judgment on the proud, the impious, and the persecutors.

Of the end of those men I have thought good to publish a narrative, so that all who are far off and all

[127] The dedictee of Lactantius work; he had been tortured three times for his Christian beliefs.

[128] A reference to the "crown of martyrdom."

[129] Including the emperors Constantine I and Licinius, who in early 313 issued the Edict of Milan, which legalized Christianity.

[130] Edicts were imperial laws addressed to the entire population that had empirewide validity.

who shall arise hereafter may learn how the Almighty manifested his power and sovereign greatness in rooting out and utterly destroying the enemies of his name. And this will become evident, when I relate who were the persecutors of the church from the time of its first constitution, and what were the punishments by which the divine judge, in his severity, took vengeance on them.

While Diocletian,[131] that author of ill and deviser of misery, was ruining all things, he could not withhold his insults, not even against God. This man, by avarice partly, and partly by timid counsels, overturned the Roman Empire. For he chose three persons to share the government with him, and thus, the empire having been quartered, armies were multiplied and each of the four princes strove to maintain a much more considerable military force than any sole emperor had done in times past.[132] There began to be fewer men who paid taxes than there were who received wages, so that, with the means of the farmer exhausted by enormous impositions, the farms were abandoned, cultivated grounds became woodland, and universal dismay prevailed. The provinces, moreover, were divided into minute portions, and many governors and a multitude of inferior officers lay heavy on each territory, and almost on each city. There also were many stewards of different degrees, and deputies of Prefects.[133] Very few civil causes came before them, but there were criminal condemnations daily, and confiscations frequently inflicted, taxes on numberless commodities, and those not only often repeated, but perpetual, and, in exacting them, intolerable wrongs.

Whatever was laid on for the maintenance of the soldiery might have been endured, but Diocletian, through his insatiable avarice, would never allow the sums of money in his treasury to be diminished. He constantly was heaping together extraordinary aids and free gifts[134] so that his original hoards might remain untouched and inviolable. He also, when by various extortions he had made all things exceedingly dear, attempted by an ordinance to limit their prices. Then men were afraid to expose anything for sale, and the scarcity became more excessive and grievous than ever, until, in the end, the ordinance, after having proved destructive to multitudes, was from mere necessity abrogated.

I omit mentioning how many perished on account of their possessions or wealth, for such evils were exceedingly frequent, and through their frequency appeared almost lawful. But this was peculiar to him, that whenever he saw a field remarkably well cultivated, or a house of uncommon elegance, a false accusation and a capital punishment were straightway prepared against the proprietor; so that it seemed as if Diocletian could not be guilty of rapine without also shedding blood. I pass over Constantius,[135] a prince unlike the others, and worthy to have had the sole government of the empire.

Diocletian, as being of a timorous disposition, was a searcher into futurity and during his abode in the east he began to slay victims, so that from their livers he might obtain a prognostic of events,[136] and while he sacrificed, some attendants of his, who were Christians, stood by, and they put the immortal sign on their foreheads.[137] At this the demons were chased away and the holy rites interrupted. The soothsayers trembled, unable to investigate the wonted marks on the entrails of the victims. They frequently repeated the sacrifices, but the victims afforded no tokens for divination. At length Tages, the chief of the soothsayers, said, "There are profane persons here, who obstruct the rites." Then Diocletian, in furious

[131] Roman emperor from 284 to 305, he commenced the Great Persecution in 303 CE.

[132] In 293, Diocletian created the "Tetrarchy," or "Rule by Four," in which the eastern and western halves of the empire each had an Augustus (senior emperor) and a Caesar (junior emperor).

[133] Diocletian subdivided the 50 provinces into 102 and created additional levels of bureaucracy, such as Vicars who stood intermediate between Praetorian Prefects and provincial governors.

[134] Such as the "crown gold," on which see Reading 101.

[135] The father of Constantine I, Constantius (293–306) was the only member of the Tetrarchy to be praised by Lactantius.

[136] The Roman rite of taking the haruspices, the inspection of the livers of sacrificial animals, to ascertain the will of the gods.

[137] A sign of the cross made with chrism, or consecrated oil.

passion, ordered all who resided within the palace to sacrifice, and, in case of their refusal, to be whipped. And further, he enjoined that all soldiers should be forced to perform the same impiety, under pain of being dismissed the service. Thus far his rage proceeded, but at that season he did nothing more against the law and religion of God.

After an interval of some time he went to winter in Bithynia,[138] and presently Galerius Caesar[139] came thither, inflamed with furious resentment and planning to excite the empty-headed old man to carry on that persecution that he had begun against the Christians. I have learned that the cause of his fury was as follows. The mother of Galerius, a woman exceedingly superstitious, was a votary of the gods of the mountains. She made sacrifices almost every day and she feasted her servants on the meat offered to idols, but the Christians of her family would not partake of those entertainments. On this account she conceived ill-will against the Christians and by woman-like complaints instigated her son, no less superstitious than herself, to destroy them. So, during the whole winter, Diocletian and Galerius held councils together, at which no one else assisted. The old man long opposed the fury of Galerius, arguing how pernicious it would be to raise disturbances throughout the world and to shed so much blood, and suggesting that the Christians were wont with eagerness to meet death, and that it would be enough for him to exclude persons of that religion from the court and the army. Yet he could not restrain the madness of that obstinate man.[140] Diocletian determined above all to consult his gods; and he dispatched a soothsayer to inquire of Apollo at Miletus,[141] whose answer was such as might be expected from an enemy of the divine religion.

An edict was published, depriving the Christians of all honors and dignities, ordaining also that, without any distinction of rank or degree, they should be subjected to tortures and that every suit at law should be received against them, while, on the other hand, they were debarred from being plaintiffs in questions of wrong, adultery, or theft; and, finally, that they should neither be capable of freedom, nor have right of suffrage. A certain person tore down this edict and cut it in pieces, improperly indeed, but with high spirit, saying in scorn, "These are the triumphs of Goths and Sarmatians."[142] Having been instantly seized and brought to judgment he not only was tortured but also burnt alive, in accordance with the laws, and having displayed admirable patience under sufferings, he was consumed to ashes.

And now Diocletian raged, not only against his own domestics, but indiscriminately against all, and he began by forcing his daughter Valeria and his wife Prisca[143] to be polluted by sacrificing. Eunuchs, once the most powerful, and who had chief authority at court and with the emperor, were slain. Priests and other officers of the church were seized, without evidence by witnesses or confession, condemned, and together with their families led to execution. In burning alive, no distinction of sex or age was regarded, and because of their great multitude they were not burnt one after another but a herd of them were encircled with the same fire. Servants, having millstones tied about their necks, were cast into the sea. Nor was the persecution less grievous on the rest of the people of God; for the judges, dispersed through all the temples, sought to compel every one to sacrifice. The prisons were crowded; tortures, hitherto unheard of, were invented; and lest justice should be inadvertently administered to a Christian, altars were placed in the courts of justice, hard by the tribunal, that every litigant might offer incense before his cause could be heard.

Mandates[144] also had gone to Maximianus Herculius[145] and Constantius, requiring their concurrence

[138] A province on the southern coast of the Black Sea.

[139] Galerius (293–311) was the Caesar, or designated successor, of the Augustus Diocletian in the eastern half of the empire.

[140] Galerius.

[141] The location of another famous oracle.

[142] That is, of barbarians.

[143] Both of whom were Christians, attesting the degree to which Christianity now had infiltrated the highest levels of society.

[144] Mandates were administrative instructions sent to imperial officials; they, too, had the force of law.

[145] Maximianus (286–305) was the Augustus of the western part of the empire; Constantius was his Caesar.

in the execution of the edicts even though, in matters even of such mighty importance, their opinion never once was asked. Herculius, a person of no merciful temper, yielded ready obedience, and enforced the edicts throughout his dominions of Italy.[146] Constantius, on the other hand, lest he should have seemed to dissent from the injunctions of his superiors, permitted the demolition of churches—mere walls, and capable of being built up again—but he preserved entire that true temple of God, which is the human body.[147]

Having thus attained the highest power,[148] Galerius bent his mind to afflict the empire. Crucifixion was the punishment ready prepared in capital cases, and for lesser crimes, fetters. Matrons of honorable station were dragged into workhouses, and when any man was to be whipped, there were four posts fixed in the ground and to them he was tied, after a manner unknown even in the chastisement of slaves. He kept bears, most resembling himself in fierceness and bulk, that he had collected together during the course of his reign. As often as he chose to indulge his humor, he ordered some particular bear to be brought in and men were thrown to that savage animal rather to be swallowed up than devoured, and when their limbs were torn asunder, he laughed with excessive complacency. Men of private station were condemned to be burnt alive, and he began this mode of execution by edicts against the Christians, commanding that, after torture and condemnation, they should be burnt at a slow fire. They were fixed to a stake, and first a moderate flame was applied to the soles of their feet, until the muscles, contracted by burning, were torn from the bones. Then torches, lighted and put out again, were directed to all the members of their bodies, so that no part had any exemption. Meanwhile cold water was continually poured on their faces and their mouths moistened, lest, by reason of their jaws being parched, they should expire. At length they did expire, when, after many hours, the violent heat had consumed their skin and penetrated into their intestines.

Already the judgment of God approached him and that season ensued in which his fortunes began to droop and to waste away. While occupied in the manner that I have described above, he did not set himself to subvert or expel Constantius, but waited for his death, not imagining, however, that it was so nigh.[149] And now, when Galerius was in the eighteenth year of his reign,[150] God struck him with an incurable plague. A malignant ulcer formed itself in the lower part of his genitals and spread by degrees. The physicians attempted to eradicate it and healed up the place affected. But the sore, after having been skinned over, broke out again. A vein burst, and the blood flowed in such quantity as to endanger his life. The blood, however, was stopped, although with difficulty. He grew emaciated, pallid, and feeble, and the bleeding then stanched. The ulcer began to be insensible to the remedies applied and a gangrene seized all the neighboring parts. It diffused itself the wider the more the corrupted flesh was cut away, and everything employed as the means of cure served but to aggravate the disease. Already approaching to its deadly crisis, it had occupied the lower regions of his body. His bowels came out and his entire buttocks putrefied. The distemper attacked his intestines and worms were generated in his body. The stench was so foul as to pervade not only the palace but even the whole city. And no wonder, for by that time the passages from his bladder and bowels, having been devoured by the worms, became indiscriminate, and his body, with intolerable anguish, was dissolved into one mass of corruption.

They applied warm flesh of animals to the chief seat of the disease, so that the warmth might draw out those minute worms, and accordingly, when the dressings were removed, there issued forth an innumerable swarm. Nevertheless, the prolific disease

[146] Other sources suggest that Maximianus only half-heartedly enforced the persecution.

[147] Other sources state that Constantius did not participate in the persecution at all.

[148] Diocletian retired in 305 and Galerius was promoted to Augustus, senior emperor, in the eastern half of the empire.

[149] Constantius died in 306 CE, the year after he had been promoted to the rank of Augustus.

[150] 310 CE.

had hatched swarms much more abundant to prey upon and consume his intestines. Already, through a complication of distempers, the different parts of his body had lost their natural form. The upper part was dry, meager, and haggard, and his ghastly-looking skin had settled itself deep among his bones while the inferior, distended like bladders, retained no appearance of joints. At length, overcome by calamities, he was obliged to acknowledge God, and he cried aloud, in the intervals of raging pain, that he would rebuild the church that he had demolished, and make atonement for his misdeeds; and when he was near his end, he published an edict of the tenor following:[151]

> Among our other regulations for the permanent advantage of the Republic, we have hitherto studied to reduce all things to a conformity with the ancient laws and public discipline of the Romans. It has been our aim in a special manner, that the Christians also, who had abandoned the religion of their forefathers, should return to right opinions. For such willfulness and folly had, we know not how, taken possession of them, that instead of observing those ancient institutions, which possibly their own forefathers had established, they, through caprice, made laws to themselves and drew together into different societies many men of widely different persuasions. After the publication of our edict, ordaining the Christians to betake themselves to the observance of the ancient institutions, many of them were subdued through the fear of danger and moreover many of them were exposed to jeopardy. Nevertheless, because great numbers still persist in their opinions, and because we have perceived that at present they neither pay reverence and due adoration to the gods, nor yet worship their own God, therefore we, from our wonted clemency in bestowing pardon on all, have judged it fit to extend our indulgence to those persons and to permit them again to be Christians, and to establish the places of their religious assemblies, yet so as that they offend not against good order. By another mandate we purpose to signify unto magistrates how they ought herein to conduct themselves. Wherefore it will be the duty of the Christians, in consequence of this our toleration, to pray to their God for our welfare, and for that of the public, and for their own, so that the Republic may continue safe in every quarter, and that they themselves may live securely in their habitations. This edict was promulgated at Nicomedia[152] on the day preceding the Kalends of May, in the eighth consulship of Galerius and the second of Maximinus Daia.[153]

Then the prison-gates having been thrown open, you, my best beloved Donatus, together with the other confessors for the faith, were set at liberty from the prison that had been your residence for six years. Galerius, however, did not, by publication of this edict, obtain the divine forgiveness. In a few days after he was consumed by the horrible disease that had brought on a universal putrefaction.

I relate all those things on the authority of well-informed persons; and I thought it proper to commit them to writing exactly as they happened, lest the memory of events so important should perish, and lest any future historian of the persecutors should corrupt the truth, either by suppressing their offenses against God, or the judgment of God against them. To his everlasting mercy ought we to render thanks, that, having at length looked on the earth, he deigned to collect again and to restore his flock, partly laid waste by ravenous wolves, and partly scattered abroad, and to extirpate those noxious wild beasts who had trod down its pastures, and destroyed its resting-places. Where now are the surnames of the Jovii and the Herculii, once so glorious and renowned among the nations; surnames insolently assumed at first by Diocles and Maximianus, and afterward transferred to their successors? The Lord has blotted them out and erased them from the earth. Let us therefore with exultation celebrate the triumphs of God, and oftentimes with praises make

[151] The "Edict of Toleration," issued in 311 CE.

[152] The capital city of Diocletian, in Anatolia just east of the future site of Constantinople.

[153] 311 CE. Maximinus Daia was Caesar of Galerius, appointed in 305 on the retirement of Diocletian. After the death of Galerius in 311 he became the Augustus of the eastern half of the empire.

mention of his victory; let us in our prayers, by night and by day, beseech him to confirm for ever that peace that, after a warfare of ten years, he has bestowed on his own: and do you, above all others, my best beloved Donatus, who so well deserve to be heard, implore the Lord that it would please him propitiously and mercifully to continue his pity toward his servants, to protect his people from the machinations and assaults of the devil, and to guard the now flourishing churches in perpetual felicity.

108

THE EDICT OF MILAN (312/313 CE): LACTANTIUS, *ON THE DEATHS OF THE PERSECUTORS*, 45–48

Although Licinius shared in the promulgation of the Edict of Milan, there is no evidence that he had any Christian convictions himself. His coinage, for example, reveals only an allegiance to the traditional gods, as shown on this gold aureus, with the reverse legend, "To Jupiter, the Preserver of the Augustus Licinius."

After Constantine's victory over Maxentius at the Battle of the Milvian Bridge on 28 October 312 he traveled to Milan, where he met Licinius, Caesar of the eastern half of the empire. There, the two emperors sealed an alliance by the marriage of Constantine's half-sister

Constantia to Licinius. At the same time, the two emperors issued an edict that did not make Christianity into a merely tolerated religion, as Galerius's Edict of Toleration had done in 311, but made Christianity a fully legal and even favored religion. At the time, Licinius was engaged in a war with the eastern Augustus Maximinus Daia, who, like Galerius, was a devoted pagan. The Edict of Milan provided not only freedom of worship for Christians, but also the restitution of Christian property that had been confiscated by the imperial treasury or acquired by private persons, with the latter being provided compensation by the state. This marked the first time that the imperial government recognized the Christian church as a lawful institution. As reported by Lactantius, the only text of the Edict survives in a letter sent by Licinius to provincial governors ordering its publication. Embedded in Lactantius's account is a story about one of the many wars between the successors of Diocletian, a battle of Licinius against Maximinus Daia that is similar to the story of Constantine's victory over Maxentius.

Source: William Fletcher, trans. *Lactantius. Of the Manner in which the Persecutors Died* (Buffalo, NY: Christian Literature Publishing, 1886).

Constantine having settled all things at Rome, went to Milan about the beginning of winter. Thither also Licinius came to receive his wife Constantia.[154] When Daia[155] understood that they were busied in solemnizing the nuptials, he moved out of Syria in the depth of a severe winter, and by forced marches he came into Bithynia. Daia did not halt in his own territories; but immediately crossed the Bosphorus,[156] and in a hostile manner approached the gates of Byzantium.[157] Licinius by expeditious marches had reached Adrianople,[158] but with forces not numerous. The armies, thus approaching each other, seemed on the eve of a battle. Then Daia made this vow to Jupiter, that if he obtained victory he would extinguish and utterly efface the name of the Christians. And on the following night an angel of the Lord seemed to stand before Licinius while he was asleep, admonishing him to arise immediately, and with his whole army to put up a prayer to the Supreme God, and assuring him that by so doing he should obtain victory.[159] At this all men took fresh courage, in the confidence that victory bad been announced to them from heaven. Accounts came that Daia was in motion; the soldiers of Licinius armed themselves; and advanced. A barren and open plain called Campus Serenus lay between the two armies. The troops of Licinius charged.[160] The enemies, panic stricken, could neither draw their swords nor throw their javelins. After great numbers had fallen, Daia perceived that everything went contrary to his hopes. He threw aside the purple and, having put on the habit of a slave, hasted across the Bosphorus. One half of his army perished in battle and the rest either surrendered to the victor or fled. Not many days after his victory, Licinius, having received part of the soldiers of Daia into his service and properly distributed them, transported his army into Bithynia, and having made his entry into Nicomedia,[161] he returned thanks to God, through whose aid he had

[154] The sister of Constantine; her tomb in Rome survives as the church of Santa Costanza.

[155] Maximinus Daia (305–313), the other Augustus in the eastern part of the empire.

[156] The eastern strait linking the Aegean Sea to the Black Sea.

[157] An ancient Greek city on the south end of the Bosporus; soon to become Constantinople.

[158] A city just northwest of Byzantium; in 378 the location of a disastrous Roman defeat by the Visigoths; see Reading 114.

[159] Likewise, just before the Battle of the Milvian Bridge against Maxentius (306–312) the previous year Constantine also was said to have had a similar visit from an angel (that is, a "messenger") in a dream.

[160] The Battle of Tzirallum on 30 April 313.

[161] Capital city of the province of Bithynia.

overcome. On the Ides of June, while he and Constantine were Consuls for the third time,[162] he commanded the following letter[163] for the restoration of the church, directed to the governor of the province,[164] to be promulgated:

> When we, Constantine and Licinius, emperors, met at Milan and conferred together with respect to the good and security of the Republic, it seemed to us that, among those things that are profitable to mankind in general, the reverence paid to the divinity merited our first and chief attention, and that it was proper that the Christians and all others should have liberty to follow that mode of religion that to each of them appeared best, so that that God, who is seated in heaven, might be benign and propitious to us and to every one under our government. And therefore we judged it a salutary measure, and one highly consonant to right reason, that no man should be denied leave of attaching himself to the rites of the Christians, or to whatever other religion his mind directed him, that thus the supreme divinity, to whose worship we freely devote ourselves, might continue to grant his favor and beneficence to us. And accordingly we give you to know that, without regard to any provisos in our former orders to you concerning the Christians all who choose that religion are to be permitted, freely and absolutely, to remain in it, and not to be disturbed any ways or molested. And we thought fit to be thus special in the things committed to your charge, that you might understand that the indulgence that we have granted in matters of religion to the Christians is ample and unconditional; and perceive at the same time that the open and free exercise of their respective religions is granted to all others, as well as to the Christians.
>
> For it befits the well-ordered state and the tranquility of our times that each individual be allowed, according to his own choice, to worship the divinity, and we mean not to remove anything from the honor due to any religion or its votaries. Moreover, with respect to the Christians, we formerly gave certain orders concerning the places appropriated for their religious assemblies, but now we desire that all persons who have purchased such places, either from our treasury or from anyone else, shall restore them to the Christians, without money demanded or price claimed, and that this be performed peremptorily and unambiguously. And we desire also that those who have obtained any right to such places by form of gift do forthwith restore them to the Christians, reserving always to such persons, who either have purchased them for a price or gratuitously have acquired them, to make application to the judge of the district if they look on themselves as entitled to any compensation from our beneficence.
>
> All those places are, by your[165] intervention, to be restored immediately to the Christians. And because it appears that, besides the places appropriated to religious worship, the Christians possessed other places that belonged not to individuals but to their society in general, that is, to their churches, we include all such within the aforesaid regulation. We command that you cause them all to be restored to the society or churches without hesitation or controversy, always provided that the persons making restitution without a price paid shall be at liberty to seek indemnification from our bounty. In furthering all these things for the benefit of the Christians you are to use your utmost diligence, so that our orders are speedily obeyed and our gracious purpose in securing the public tranquility be promoted. So shall that divine favor that, in affairs of the mightiest importance, we have already experienced, continue to give success to us and in our successes make the Republic happy. And that the tenor of this our gracious ordinance may be made known unto all, we desire that you cause it by your authority to be published everywhere.

Having published this letter, Licinius made a harangue in which he exhorted the Christians to rebuild their religious edifices. And thus, from the overthrow of the church until its restoration, there was a space of ten years and about four months.[166]

---

[162] 13 June 313.

[163] Not an "edict," as in many translations, but a "letter," or "mandate," directed to a provincial governor that authorized the publication of the actual edict that had been promulgated by Licinius and Constantine previously at Milan.

[164] The same letter would have been forwarded to the governors of other eastern provinces.

[165] The governor.

[166] That is, from 303, the beginning of the Great Persecution, until 313.

109

THE COUNCIL OF NICAEA (325 CE): EUSEBIUS OF CAESAREA, *LIFE OF CONSTANTINE*, 2.61–71, 3.6–14

Although Constantine continued to issue coins in honor of Sol Invictus, the "Unconquered Son," he also struck coins with clearly Christian motifs. This copper coin, one of the first to be issued at Constantinople, 327, portrays an army standard bearing three dots, representing the equality of the Christian Trinity, and topped by a Christogram, the monogram of Christ. The base of the standard pierces a serpent, which represents heresy. The legend reads "Public Hope."

In 324 Constantine defeated Licinius and gained control of the entire Roman Empire. At the same time, he became responsible for refereeing the many quarrels regarding church authority, church practices, and church teachings that had arisen among competing Christian factions. The most serious theological issue related to the teachings of the priest Arius of Alexandria, who taught that Christ the son was of a different substance from and not co-eternal with

God the Father. Other Christians taught that Christ and God were made of the same substance and were co-eternal, that is, had existed together since the beginning of time. In an attempt to force unity on the Christians, Constantine first naively suggested that the dispute was of little significance and that the disputants should simply make up. Finally realizing how serious the matter was, in 325 Constantine summoned an ecumenical (that is, worldwide) council of Christian bishops from both within and outside the Roman Empire to meet at the city of Nicaea in northwestern Anatolia. Around 318 of approximately 1,800 bishops, mostly from the eastern provinces, attended and were required to remain until they had reached an agreement. The resulting "Nicene Creed" condemned Arianism and became a Christian statement of belief that is still used in most Christian churches. The council also issued other regulations that mark the beginning of Christian "canon law," such as establishing a standard date for Easter and a model for Christian administration based on the administration of Roman provinces. Constantine's initiative began the process of placing the Roman emperor, in effect, at the head of the Christian church, and thus, paradoxically, in the process of gaining imperial favor, the Christian church lost control of its own destiny. In his "Life of Constantine," the historian Eusebius, bishop of Caesarea, provided his version of the events surrounding the Council of Nicaea. Eusebius, a confidant of Constantine, had access to many official documents that are not preserved by any other author.

Source: Arthur Cushman McGiffert, trans., *Eusebius Pamphilius: Church History, Life of Constantine, Oration in Praise of Constantine* (New York: Christian Literature Publishing, 1890).

The emperor, like a powerful herald of God, addressed himself by his own letter to all the provinces, at the same time warning his subjects against superstitious error and encouraging them in the pursuit of true godliness. But in the midst of his joyful anticipations of the success of this measure, he received tidings of a most serious disturbance that had invaded the peace of the church. This intelligence he heard with deep concern, and at once he endeavored to devise a remedy for the evil. The origin of this disturbance may be thus described. The people of God were in a truly flourishing state. No terror from without assailed them, but a bright and most profound peace, through the favor of God, encompassed his church on every side. Meantime, however, the spirit of envy at first crept in unperceived but soon reveled in the midst of the assemblies of the saints. At length it reached the bishops themselves, and arrayed them in angry hostility against each other, on pretense of a jealous regard for the doctrines of divine truth. Hence it was that a mighty fire was kindled, originating in the first instance in the Alexandrian church, and overspread the whole of Egypt and Libya. Eventually it extended its ravages to the other provinces and cities of the empire, so that not only the prelates of the churches might be seen encountering each other in the strife of words, but the people themselves were completely divided, some adhering to one faction and others to another. So notorious did the scandal of these proceedings become, that the sacred matters of inspired teaching were exposed to the most shameful ridicule in the very theaters of the unbelievers.

As soon as the emperor was informed, he forthwith selected from the Christians in his train one whom he well knew to be approved for the sobriety and genuineness of his faith and sent him to negotiate peace between the dissentient parties at Alexandria. He also made him the bearer of a most needful and appropriate letter to the original movers of the strife, and this letter, as exhibiting a specimen of his watchful care over God's people, it may be well to introduce into this our narrative of his life. Its purport was as follows:

Victor Constantinus, Maximus Augustus, to Alexander and Arius.[167] I call God to witness that I had a twofold reason for undertaking the duty that I now have performed. My design was, first, to bring the diverse judgments formed by all nations respecting the deity to a condition of settled uniformity, and, secondly, to restore to health the system of the world, then suffering under the malignant power of a grievous distemper. I sought to accomplish the one by the secret eye of thought and the other by the power of military authority. For I was aware that if I should succeed in establishing, according to my hopes, a common harmony of sentiment among all the servants of God, the general course of affairs also would experience a change correspondent to the pious desires of them all.

Finding, then, that the whole of Africa[168] was pervaded by an intolerable spirit of mad folly through the influence of those who with heedless frivolity had presumed to rend the religion of the people into diverse sects, I was anxious to check this disorder, and could discover no other remedy equal to the occasion, except in sending some of yourselves to aid in restoring mutual harmony among the disputants, after I had removed that common enemy of mankind who had interposed his lawless sentence for the prohibition of your holy synods.[169] As soon, therefore, as I had secured my decisive victory and unquestionable triumph over my enemies, my first enquiry was concerning that object that I felt to be of paramount interest and importance.

But, O glorious Providence of God! How deep a wound did not only my ears only but also my very heart receive in the report that divisions existed among yourselves more grievous still than those that continued in your country. And yet, having made a careful enquiry into the origin and foundation of these differences, I find the cause to be of a truly insignificant character, and quite unworthy of such fierce contention. Feeling myself, therefore, compelled to address you in this letter and to appeal at the same time to your unanimity and sagacity, I interrupt your dissension in the character of a minister of peace. For if I might expect to be able by a judicious appeal to the pious feelings of those who heard me to recall them to a better spirit, even though the occasion of the disagreement were a greater one, how can I refrain from promising myself a far easier and more speedy adjustment of this difference, when the cause that hinders general harmony of sentiment is intrinsically trifling and of little moment?

I understand, then, that the origin of the present controversy is this. When you, Alexander, demanded of the priests what opinion they maintained respecting a certain passage in the divine law, then you, Arius, inconsiderately insisted on what ought never to have been conceived at all. Hence it was that a dissension arose between you, fellowship was withdrawn,[170] and the holy people, rent into diverse parties, no longer preserved the unity of the one body. Now, therefore, do ye both exhibit an equal degree of forbearance, and receive the advice that your fellow-servant[171] righteously gives. What then is this advice? It was wrong in the first instance to propose such questions as these. For those points of discussion that are enjoined by the authority of no law, but rather suggested by the contentious spirit that is fostered by misused leisure, even though they may be intended merely as an intellectual exercise, ought certainly to be confined to the region of our own thoughts, and not hastily produced in the popular assemblies or unadvisedly entrusted to the general ear. For how very few are there able either accurately to comprehend, or adequately to explain subjects so sublime and abstruse in their nature? Or, granting that one were fully competent for this, how many people will he convince? Or, who, again, in dealing with questions of such subtle nicety as these can secure himself against a dangerous

[167] Alexander was bishop of Alexandria; Arius was one of his priests.

[168] That is, Egypt and Libya.

[169] A reference to Licinius (308–324), who had prohibited the holding of church councils.

[170] That is, the dissenting parties excommunicated each other.

[171] Constantine himself.

declension from the truth? It is incumbent therefore on us in these cases to be sparing of our words, lest, in case we ourselves are unable, through the feebleness of our natural faculties, to give a clear explanation of the subject before us, or, on the other hand, in case the slowness of our hearers' understandings disables them from arriving at an accurate apprehension of what we say, from one or other of these causes the people to be reduced to the alternative either of blasphemy or schism.

Let therefore both the unguarded question and the inconsiderate answer receive your mutual forgiveness. For the cause of your difference has not been any of the leading doctrines or precepts of the divine law, nor has any new heresy respecting the worship of God arisen among you. You are in truth of one and the same judgment: you may therefore well join in communion and fellowship.

We are not all of us like-minded on every subject, nor is there such a thing as one disposition and judgment common to all alike. As far, then, as regards the divine providence, let there be one faith, and one understanding among you, one united judgment in reference to God. But as to your subtle disputations on questions of little or no significance, although you may be unable to harmonize in sentiment, such differences should be consigned to the secret custody of your own minds and thoughts. And now, let the preciousness of common affection, let faith in the truth, let the honor due to God and to the observance of his law continue immovably among you. Resume, then, your mutual feelings of friendship, love, and regard: restore to the people their wonted embracing; and do ye yourselves, having purified your souls, as it were, once more acknowledge one another. For it often happens that when a reconciliation is effected by the removal of the causes of enmity, friendship becomes even sweeter than it was before.

Then as if to bring a divine array against this enemy, he convoked a general council,[172] and invited the speedy attendance of bishops from all quarters, in letters expressive of the honorable estimation in which he held them. Nor was this merely the issuing of a bare command but the emperor's good will contributed much to its being carried into effect, for he allowed some the use of the public means of conveyance whereas he afforded to others an ample supply of horses for their transport.[173] The place, too, selected for the synod, the city Nicaea, named from "Victory," in Bithynia[174] was appropriate to the occasion. As soon as the imperial injunction was generally made known, all[175] with the utmost willingness hastened thither, for they were impelled by the anticipation of a happy result to the conference and the desire of beholding something new and strange in the person of so admirable an emperor. When they were all assembled, it appeared evident that the proceeding was the work of God, inasmuch as men who had been most widely separated, not merely in sentiment but also personally, and by difference of country, place, and nation, were here brought together and comprised within the walls of a single city.

In effect, the most distinguished of God's ministers from all the churches that abounded in Europe, Libya,[176] and Asia were here assembled. And a single house of prayer, as though divinely enlarged, sufficed to contain at once Syrians and Cilicians, Phoenicians and Arabians, delegates from Palestine, and others from Egypt, Thebans and Libyans, with those who came from Mesopotamia. A Persian bishop too was present at this conference, nor was even a Scythian[177] found wanting to the number. Pontus, Galatia, and Pamphylia, Cappadocia, Asia, and Phrygia, furnished their most distinguished prelates, whereas those who dwelt in the remotest districts of Thrace and Macedonia, of Achaea and Epirus, were notwithstanding in attendance. Even from Spain itself,

172 Clearly after his personal efforts at reconciliation had failed.

173 The government provided warrants so the bishops could use the public post system, which was used only for official business.

174 A province on the southwestern coast of the Black Sea. Nicaea was not far from the imperial capital city at Nicomedia.

175 Actually, 318 of the approximately 1,800 Christian bishops attended.

176 That is, Africa.

177 A Gothic bishop from the Crimea.

one whose fame was widely spread took his seat as an individual in the great assembly.[178] The prelate of the imperial city[179] was prevented from attending by extreme old age, but his priests were present and took his place. Constantine is the first prince of any age who bound together such a garland as this with the bond of peace and presented it to his savior as a thank-offering for the victories he had obtained over every foe. For the maintenance of all ample provision was daily furnished by the emperor's command.

When the appointed day arrived on which the council met each member was present in the central building of the palace.[180] On each side of the interior of this were many seats disposed in order, which were occupied by those who had been invited to attend according to their rank. As soon as the whole assembly had seated themselves a general silence prevailed, in expectation of the emperor's arrival. First of all, three of his immediate family entered in succession, then others also preceded his approach, not the soldiers or guards who usually accompanied him but only friends in the faith. And then, all rising at the signal that indicated the emperor's entrance, at last he himself proceeded through the midst of the assembly, clothed in raiment that glittered as it were with rays of light, reflecting the glowing radiance of a purple robe, and adorned with the brilliant splendor of gold and precious stones. Such was the external appearance of his person. With regard to his mind, he was distinguished by piety and godly fear as was indicated by his downcast eyes, the blush on his countenance, and his gait. He surpassed all present in height of stature and beauty of form as well as in majestic dignity of mien and invincible strength and vigor. As soon as he had advanced to the upper end of the seats, at first he remained standing, and when a low chair of wrought gold had been set for him, he waited until the bishops had beckoned to him, and then sat down, and after him the whole assembly did the same.

The bishop[181] who occupied the chief place in the right division of the assembly then rose, and, addressing the emperor, delivered a concise speech in a strain of thanksgiving to Almighty God on his behalf. When he had resumed his seat, silence ensued and all regarded the emperor with fixed attention, on which he looked serenely round on the assembly with a cheerful aspect, and, having collected his thoughts, in a calm and gentle tone gave utterance to the following words:

> It once was my chief desire, dearest friends, to enjoy the spectacle of your united presence, and now that this desire is fulfilled, I feel myself bound to render thanks to God because he has permitted me to see you all assembled together, united in a common harmony of sentiment. I pray therefore that no malignant adversary may henceforth interfere to mar our happy state. I pray that, now the impious hostility of the tyrants[182] has been forever removed, that spirit who delights in evil may devise no other means for exposing the divine law to blasphemous calumny, for, in my judgment, intestine strife within the church of God, is far more evil and dangerous than any kind of war or conflict, and these our differences appear to me more grievous than any outward trouble.[183] Accordingly, when, by the will of God, I had been victorious over my enemies, I thought that nothing more remained but to sympathize in the joy of those whom he had restored to freedom through my instrumentality. As soon as I received the news of your dissension, I judged it to be of no secondary importance. With the earnest desire that a remedy for this evil also might be found through my means, I immediately sent to require your presence. And now I rejoice in beholding your assembly, and I feel that my desires will be most completely fulfilled

[178] Hosius, bishop of Cordova. Few westerners attended; Hosius just happened to be there by chance.

[179] The bishop of Rome Silvester (314–335), who declined to attend.

[180] The so-called "Senatus Palace," actually a church.

[181] Eusebius of Caesarea, the author of this account.

[182] Maxentius, Licinius, Maximinus Daia, and Constantine's other rivals for power. Defeated emperors traditionally were stigmatized as "tyrants."

[183] Emperors always were much more concerned about internal trouble, from usurpers or other kinds of unrest, than about foreign attacks.

> when I can see you all united in one judgment, and that common spirit of peace and concord prevailing among you all. Delay not, then, ye ministers of God. Begin from this moment to discard the causes of that disunion that has existed among you and remove the perplexities of controversy by embracing the principles of peace. For by such conduct you will at the same time be acting in a manner most pleasing to the supreme God, and you will confer an exceeding favor on me, your fellow-servant.

As soon as the emperor had spoken these words in the Latin tongue, which another translated,[184] he gave permission to those who presided in the council to deliver their opinions.

On this, some began to accuse their neighbors, who defended themselves and recriminated in their turn. In this manner numberless assertions were put forth by each party, and a violent controversy arose at the very commencement. Notwithstanding this, the emperor gave patient audience to all alike and received every proposition with steadfast attention. By occasionally assisting the argument of each party in turn,[185] he gradually disposed even the most vehement disputants to a reconciliation. At the same time, by the affability of his address to all and his use of the Greek language, with which he was not altogether unacquainted, he appeared in a truly attractive and amiable light, persuading some, convincing others by his reasoning, praising those who spoke well, and urging all to unity of sentiment, until at last he succeeded in bringing them to one mind and judgment respecting every disputed question.

The result was that they not only were united as concerning the faith,[186] but also that the time for the celebration of the salutary feast of Easter[187] was agreed on by all. Those points also which were sanctioned by the resolution of the whole body were committed to writing, and received the signature of each several member.[188] Then the emperor, believing that he had thus obtained a second victory over the adversary of the church, proceeded to solemnize a triumphal festival in honor of God.

[184] Into Greek, the language of most of the participants.

[185] That is, by participating directly in the theological discussions.

[186] That is, the condemnation of Arianism.

[187] A major point of contention was the means by which the date of Easter, which did not occur on the same day each year, was calculated.

[188] In fact, two Libyan bishops refused to subscribe.

CHAPTER 14

The Christian Empire and the Late Roman World (337–476)

The late Roman world looked very different from the Principate. The most significant change was the evolution of Christianity into the primary religion of the Roman world. Even though emperors continued to be confronted by religious controversy, by the end of the fourth century, Christianity had prevailed and had become the only fully legal religion. Christianity muscled its way into every nook and cranny of the Roman world, and Christian culture became inextricably intertwined with virtually every aspect of Roman society, culture, and politics. At the same time, other trends led to a continued breakdown of the carefully constructed unity of the Principate. One of the greatest changes was the arrival and settlement of various barbarian peoples, who by the 480s had established independent kingdoms in the western half of the Roman Empire.

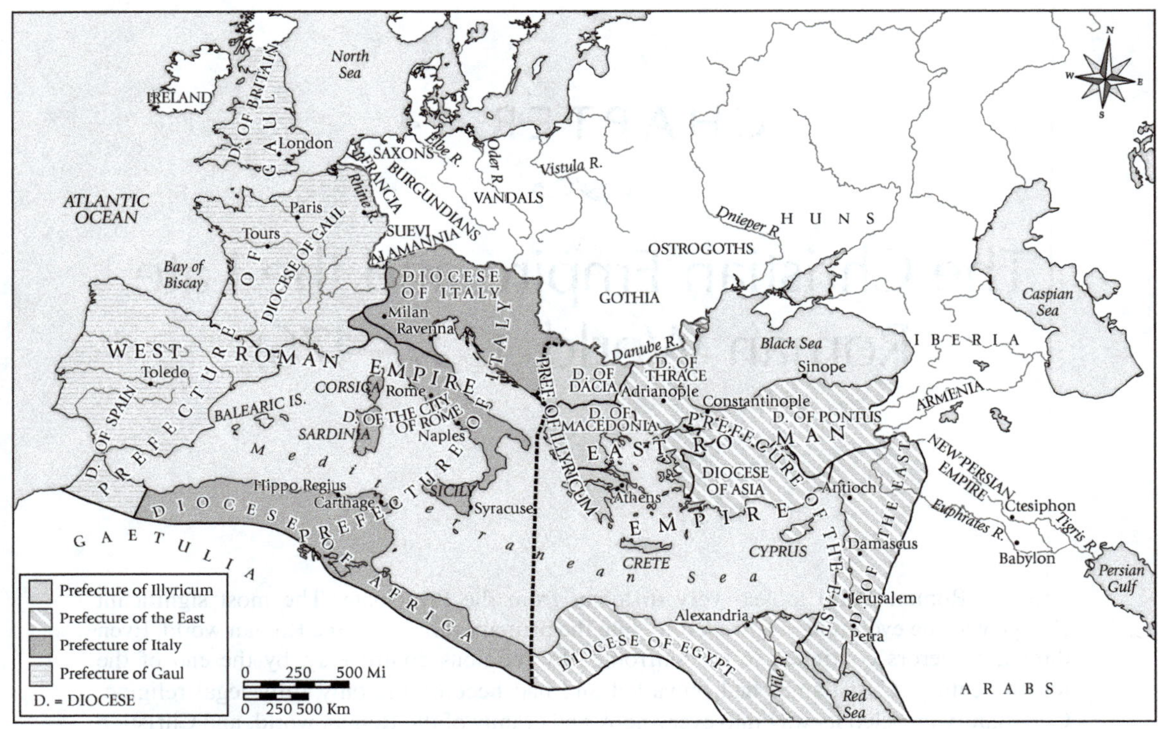

Map 14 The Divided Empire as of 395 CE

110

THE IMPERIAL OPPRESSION OF PAGANS, JEWS, AND HERETICS: THEODOSIAN CODE (437 CE); CODE OF JUSTINIAN (534 CE)

A portrait bust, now in the Louvre Museum in Paris, depicts the emperor Theodosius II (402–450), who in 437 issued the Theodosian Code, a compilation of all the significant Roman laws going back to the time of Constantine. It provides a wealth of information about Roman administration and society and the economy and gives us insight into what the emperors thought were some of the most important issues confronting them.

During the late Roman Empire, emperors issued thousands of constitutions (a generic word for laws) of various types, including edicts (laws addressed to the entire empire, akin to legislation of the U.S. Congress); mandates (instructions to imperial officials, akin to the "Executive Orders" of the U.S. president); decrees (the emperors' decisions in courts cases, akin to decisions of the U.S. Supreme Court); and rescripts (replies to petitions addressed to the emperor, which have no modern equivalent). There was no standard method for archiving and accessing all this legislation, and it quickly became unmanageable. In 429 CE the eastern emperor Theodosius II (402–450) undertook a massive project to codify all imperial legislation going back to the reign of Constantine I (306–337), the first Christian emperor. Imperial constitutions dating from 18 January 313 to 16 March 437 were collected from both central and provincial archives and edited by an imperial commission of officials and legal experts in Constantinople. The final compilation of more than 2,500 entries (some constitutions were subdivided into multiple entries), organized into sixteen books, was issued in the eastern empire in November 437, on the occasion of the marriage of the young emperor Valentinian III (425–455) to Theodosius's daughter Licinia Eudoxia (see Reading 117). In this legislation, the full weight of government authority was brought to bear against persons who did not subscribe to what the government deemed to be Orthodox (or Catholic) Christian beliefs, that is, beliefs that at some point had been agreed on at an imperial-sponsored church council, such as that at Nicaea in 325 CE (see Reading 109). Hundreds of laws preserved not only in the Theodosian Code but also in the Code of Justinian, issued in ten books under the emperor Justinian (527–565) in 534, supported Orthodox Christians and disadvantaged everyone else, including pagans, Jews, and, in particular, Christian heretics (Christians with non-Orthodox beliefs) and schismatics (Christians who did not recognize the authority of government-supported Christian authorities). The penalties against heretics, schismatics, Jews, and pagans included the imposition of "infamia" ("infamy"), which brought loss of social rank, the inability to act or appear for someone else at law (such as, to serve as a guardian or a witness), the inability to make or receive testamentary bequests, and the inability to initiate a civil case. Other penalties were dependent on one's social status: persons of "more humble" status could suffer corporeal punishment, whereas "more distinguished" people had to pay a fine. In both law codes, the topic of religion was allocated an entire book, subdivided into sections with multiple entries on the same topic, attesting to the significant place that Christianity had assumed in the life of the empire. For each constitution cited below, its date and place of issue, where known, also are given.

Sources: J. C. Ayer, ed., *A Source Book for Ancient Church History* (New York: Scribner, 1913); Oliver J. Thatcher, ed., *The Library of Original Sources*, Vol. IV, *The Early Medieval World* (Milwaukee: University Research Extension, 1907).

Theodosian Code, Book 2, Section 1, "On Jurisdiction, and Where It Is Fitting for Anyone to Assemble"

(1) THEODOSIAN CODE, BOOK 2, SECTION 1, ENTRY 10 (CONSTANTINOPLE: 11 FEBRUARY 398)

Even though imperial legislation generally penalized non-Orthodox Christians, Jews were permitted to continue to practice their ancestral religion so long as doing so did not conflict with the administration of Roman law.

The Imperators[1] Arcadius and Honorius[2] Augustuses to Eutychianus, Praetorian Prefect.[3] Jews who are living under Roman common law shall attend the courts in the usual way in those cases that do not concern so much their superstition[4] as court, laws, and rights, and all of them shall bring actions and defend themselves under the Roman laws. In sum, they shall be under our laws. Certainly, if some shall deem it necessary to litigate before the Jews or the patriarchs[5] through mutual agreement, in the manner of arbitration with the consent of both parties, at least in civil matters, they shall not be prohibited by public law from accepting their verdict, the governors of the provinces shall even execute their sentences as if they were appointed arbiters through the award of a judge.

Theodosian Code, Book 9, Section 9, "On Evil Doers and Astrologers and Other Similar Persons"

(2) THEODOSIAN CODE, BOOK 9, SECTION 16, ENTRY 2 (15 MAY 319)

The prohibition of private pagan sacrifices; public sacrifices still were allowed.

The Imperator Constantine Augustus to the people. Haruspices[6] and priests and those accustomed to minister in their rite we forbid to enter any private house, or under the pretence of friendship to cross the threshold of another, under the penalty established against them if they disobey the law.[7] But those of you who choose to participate may approach public altars and shrines and celebrate the solemnities of your custom, for we do not indeed prohibit the duties of the old usurpation to be performed in broad daylight.

Source: Ayer, 386.

[1] The ancient Roman Republican title given to victorious army generals; it remained part of the titulature of Roman emperors.
[2] The sons of the emperor Theodosius I (379–395), with Arcadius holding office in the eastern part of the empire from 395 to 408 and Honorius in the west from 395 until 423.
[3] The Praetorian Prefect was the highest-ranking official in the empire after the emperor and was the emperor's chief executive officer. Thus, much imperial legislation was addressed to the Praetorian Prefects, who then were expected to put it into effect.
[4] Any form of religion that was not Orthodox Christianity was conventionally referred to by the government as a "superstition."
[5] Jewish leaders recognized by the Roman government.
[6] Priests who read signs in the entrails of sacrificial animals, usually sheep.
[7] For Roman concern about the performance of prohibited religious rites, see also Reading 79.

Theodosian Code, Book 11, Section 7, "On Taxation"

(3) THEODOSIAN CODE, BOOK 11, SECTION 7, ENTRY 13 (AQUILEIA: 3 NOVEMBER 386)

The conducting of business and legal cases is prohibited on Sunday.

The Imperators Gratian,[8] Valentinian,[9] and Theodosius Augustuses to Principius, Praetorian Prefect. Let the course of all law suits and all business cease on Sunday, which our fathers rightly have called the Lord's day, and let no one try to collect either a public or a private debt, and let there be no hearing of disputes by any judges, either those required to serve by law or those voluntarily chosen by disputants. And he is to be held not only infamous[10] but sacrilegious who has turned away from the service and observance of holy religion on that day.

Source: Thatcher, 69–71.

Theodosian Code, Section 15.5, "On Public Spectacles"

(4) THEODOSIAN CODE, BOOK 15, SECTION 5, ENTRY 5 (CONSTANTINOPLE: 1 FEBRUARY 425)

The celebration of Christian festivals is not to be inhibited by the holding of public shows or spectacles or by the performance of Jewish or pagan rituals.

The Imperators Theodosius Augustus and Valentinian Caesar[11] to Asclepiodotus, Praetorian Prefect. On the Lord's day, which is the first day of the week, on Christmas,[12] and on the days of Epiphany,[13] Easter,[14] and Pentecost,[15] inasmuch as then the garments[16]

[8] The son of Valentinian (364–375) and emperor in the western empire from 375 until 383.

[9] Valentinian II (375–392), younger brother of Gratian.

[10] The legal status of "infamia" ("infamy") encompassed legal restrictions, such as the inability to make contracts or bequeath property.

[11] The emperor Valentinian III (425–455), who was appointed briefly to the rank of Caesar in 424 before being promoted to Augustus in 425.

[12] A Christian festival celebrated in the modern day on 25 December in the Gregorian calendar, used by the Roman Catholic, Protestant, and some Orthodox churches, which translates to 7 January in the Julian calendar, used by the Russian and some other Orthodox churches.

[13] A Christian festival celebrated on 6 January in the Gregorian calendar which translates to 19 January in the Julian calendar.

[14] A Christian festival of varying date celebrated in March or April.

[15] A Christian festival celebrated seven weeks after Easter.

[16] The white garb of Christians.

symbolizing the light of heavenly cleansing bear witness to the new light of holy baptism, and at the time also of the suffering of the apostles, the example, for all Christians, the pleasures of the theaters and games are to be kept from the people in all cities, and all the thoughts of Christians and believers are to be occupied with the worship of God. And if any are kept from that worship through the madness of Jewish impiety or the error and insanity of foolish paganism, let them know that there is one time for prayer and another for pleasure. And lest anyone should think he is compelled by the honor of Our Godliness[17] as if by a certain greater necessity of imperial ceremony, or that, unless he attempted to hold the games in contempt of the religious prohibition, he might offend Our Serenity in showing less than the usual devotion toward us,[18] let no one doubt that our clemency is revered in the highest degree by humankind when the worship of the whole world is paid to the might and goodness of God.

Theodosian Code, Section 16.1, "On the Catholic Faith"

Book 16 of the Theodosian code dealt with matters of religion, and it covered in great detail the relative statuses of orthodox Christians, heretical and schismatic Christians, Jews, and pagans. Late Roman emperors took responsibility for ensuring the predominance of Orthodox Christianity, so the first section of the book contained four rulings relating to how Orthodox belief was to be established. Methods for establishing a person's orthodox status ranged from accepting a permitted statement of faith to being in communion with a senior prelate whose orthodoxy was recognized by the government.

(5) THEODOSIAN CODE, BOOK 16, SECTION 1, ENTRY 2 (THESSALONICA[19]: 27 FEBRUARY 380)

One of the means of establishing orthodoxy was to be in communion with persons of proven orthodoxy. In this case, the bishops of Rome and Alexandria are declared to be the touchstones through which the orthodoxy of others can be tested.

The Imperators Gratian, Valentinian, and Theodosius Augustuses to the people of the city of Constantinople. We desire that all the peoples whom the moderation of our clemency rules should abide in this type of religion, a religion that, having penetrated all the way to the present through him[20], declares that the divine Peter the Apostle[21] transmitted it to the Romans, a religion that, it is clear, the pontiff Damasus[22]

[17] The emperors, who referred to themselves by a variety of titles manifesting personal qualities.

[18] Customarily, celebrations in honor of the emperors were held throughout the year, and individuals and officials could be concerned about appearing to be disrespectful if they did not perform these celebrations.

[19] Modern Salonica, on the northeastern coast of Greece.

[20] That is, the apostle Peter.

[21] One of the disciples of Jesus Christ (see Reading 91); in later church tradition, Peter was the first bishop of Rome.

[22] Bishop of Rome from 366 until 384.

follows along with Peter, bishop of Alexandria,[23] a man of apostolic sanctity, that is, that we should believe, according to the apostolic teaching and the doctrine of the gospel, in the single deity of the father, Son, and Holy Spirit, in equal majesty and under the devout Trinity. We order those following this law to embrace the name of catholic Christians, and judging that others are demented and insane, we order that they endure the infamy of their heretical belief, nor can their gatherings be called churches, having been punished first of all by divine vengeance and subsequently even by the revenge of our initiative, which we will have undertaken through celestial authority.

(6) THEODOSIAN CODE, BOOK 16, SECTION 1, ENTRY 3 (HERACLEA[24]: 30 JULY 381)

The churches of those declared to be heretics are to be confiscated. Orthodox Christians are declared to be those who are in communion with the bishops listed here. As was the secular world, the ecclesiastical world was very status conscious. Thus, the bishops of Constantinople and Alexandria, who had the rank of "patriarch," were listed first.

The Imperators Gratian, Valentinian, and Theodosius, Augustuses, to Auxonius, Proconsul of Asia. We command that all churches be forthwith delivered up to the bishops who confess the Father, the Son, and the Holy Spirit to be of one majesty and power, of the same glory and of one splendor, making no distinction by any profane division, but rather harmony by the assertion of the Trinity of the persons and the unity of the godhead, to the bishops who are associated in communion with Nectarius, bishop of the church of Constantinople, and with Timotheus in Egypt, bishop of the city of Alexandria; in the parts of the Orient,[25] who are in communion with Pelagius, bishop of Laodicaea and Diodorus, bishop of Tarsus; in Proconsular Asia and in the diocese of Asiana,[26] who are in communion with Amphilochius, bishop of Iconium, and Optimus, bishop of Antioch; in the diocese of Pontus,[27] who are in communion with Helladius, bishop of Caesarea, and Otreius, bishop of Melitina, and Gregory, bishop of Nyssa, Terennius, bishop of Scythia, and Marmarius, bishop of Marcianopolis. Those who are of the communion and fellowship of approved priests ought to be permitted to possess the catholic churches, but all who dissent from the communion of the faith of those whom the special list has named ought to be expelled from the churches as manifest heretics, and no opportunity whatsoever ought to be allowed them henceforth of obtaining episcopal churches that the priestly orders of the true and Nicene faith[28] may remain pure and no place be given to evil cunning, according to the evident form of our precept.

Source: Ayer, 351.

[23] Bishop of Alexandria from 373 until 381.

[24] On the Black Sea coast east of Constantinople.

[25] The imperial diocese that included the easternmost provinces of the empire plus a few provinces in southeastern Anatolia.

[26] A diocese that included the provinces of southwestern Anatolia.

[27] A diocese that included the provinces of northwestern Anatolia.

[28] That is, based on the Creed of Nicaea, issued in 325 CE.

(7) THEODOSIAN CODE, BOOK 16, SECTION 1, ENTRY 4 (MILAN: 23 JANUARY 386)

Many barbarian soldiers in the Roman army were "homoians," following the Creed of Rimini, issued in 359 CE, which declared that "the Son was like ('homoios') the Father according to scripture," as opposed to the Creed of Nicaea of 325, which stated that the Son and Father were of the same substance. In the modern day, this divergence from the orthodox Nicene belief has resulted in the followers of the Creed of Rimini wrongly being labelled "Arians." The Roman government may have legitimated this divergence because of the need to conciliate its barbarian soldiers.

The Imperators Valentinian, Theodosius, and Arcadius Augustuses to Eusignius, Praetorian Prefect. We grant a full right of gathering to those who believe according to those things that during the times of Constantius[29] of blessed memory were decreed, to remain valid for eternity, at the Council of Rimini and indeed were confirmed at Constantinople.[30] Indeed, we command that the opportunity of assembling shall be open to them. They are to know this, that whoever thinks that so much of an opportunity of gathering has been granted only to them, if they think that anything disruptive should be done against the precept of Our Tranquility, that as the authors of sedition and the disturbed peace of the church and even of treason, they are going to suffer punishments of capital punishment and bloodshed, with no lesser punishment awaiting those who attempt anything secretly or surreptitiously against this our disposition.

Theodosian Code, Book 16, Section 2, "On Bishops, Churches, and Clerics"

The forty-seven entries contained in the second section of Book 16 dealt with church clergy and practices.

(8) THEODOSIAN CODE, BOOK 16, SECTION 2, ENTRY 3 (20 OCTOBER 319)

Beginning with the emperor Constantine, Christian clergy gained many privileges, such as, in this ruling, exemption from the performance of public services.

[29] A son and successor of Constantine I, Constantius II (337–361 CE) had preferred the homoian interpretation of the relationship between the Father and Son.

[30] A confirmation of the Creed of Rimini in 360 CE.

The Imperator Constantine Augustus to Octavianus, Corrector[31] of Lucania and Bruttium.[32] Those who engage in divine worship through the ministry of religion, that is, those who are called clergy, are altogether excused from public obligations, so that they may not be called away from divine services by the sacrilegious malice of certain persons.

(9) THEODOSIAN CODE, BOOK 16, SECTION 2, ENTRY 5 (25 MAY 323)

Christians are not to be forced to perform pagan rituals.

The Imperator Constantine Augustus to Helpidius. Because we have heard that ecclesiastics and others belonging to the catholic religion are compelled by men of different religions to celebrate the sacrifices of the lustrum,[33] we, by this decree, do ordain that if anyone believes that those who observe the most sacred law[34] ought to be compelled to take part in the rites of a strange superstition, let him, if his condition permits,[35] be beaten with staves, but if his rank exempts him from such rigor, let him bear the most severe condemnation, which will confiscate his property to the treasury.

Source: Ayer, 384.

Theodosian Code, Book 16, Section 5, "On Heretics"

As the enforcers of Christian orthodoxy, the emperors saw it as their duty to repress non-Orthodox beliefs by a series of increasingly detailed and restrictive measures, as illustrated by the sixty-six entries in this section.

(10) THEODOSIAN CODE, BOOK 16, SECTION 5, ENTRY 1 (GERASTUM[36]: 1 SEPTEMBER 326)

Privileges granted to Christians are only for Orthodox Christians, not for heretics and schismatics.

[31] The type of provincial governor found only in Italy.
[32] Provinces of southern Italy.
[33] A purification ceremony.
[34] The Christian religion.
[35] Persons of "more humble" status suffered corporeal punishment, whereas those of "more distinguished" status generally paid fines.
[36] In Greece.

Imperator Constantine Augustus to Dracilianus. It is proper that privileges that have been granted in consideration of religion ought to profit only the adherents of catholic law. We desire, moreover, that heretics and schismatics not only are to be denied these privileges but even are to be bound by and subjected to diverse public duties.

(11) THEODOSIAN CODE, BOOK 16, SECTION 5, ENTRY 2 (SPOLETO: 25 SEPTEMBER 326)

At the end of the Decian Persecution in 251 CE, a schism arose in the church of Rome when two rival candidates, the learned Novatian, who opposed the readmission of lapsed Christians into the church, and Cornelius, who had a more moderate policy, both were consecrated as bishops of Rome. Although Cornelius soon prevailed, a separate, more hard-line Novatian church persisted into the fifth century. Because it had no non-Orthodox theological beliefs, the emperors generally tolerated its existence.

Imperator Constantine Augustus to Bassus. We have learned that up until now the Novatians have not been condemned in such a way that we believe that they should not be granted those things that they seek. Therefore, we command that they can resolutely possess the buildings of their church and places suitable for burials without any interference, those properties, that is, that they have possessed for an extensive period or by purchase or that they lay claim to for any reason. Clearly it must be seen to lest they attempt to usurp for themselves anything from those things that belonged to the churches of perpetual sanctity[37] prior to the schism.

(12) THEODOSIAN CODE, BOOK 16, SECTION 5, ENTRY 3 (TRIER: 2 MARCH 372)

The Manichaeans, a dualistic sect descended from Persian Zoroastrians (see Reading 44), were the most persecuted of all the Christian heresies.

The Imperators Valentinian and Valens Augustuses to Ampelius, Prefect of the City.[38] Whenever an assembly or a crowd of Manichaeans is discovered, with their teachers having been punished with a heavy assessment and with those too, who assembled, having been segregated from the company of people as being dishonored[39] and shameful, indubitably let their houses and habitations, in which this profane belief is taught, be confiscated by the forces of the treasury.

[37] That is, to churches that the emperors considered to be fully Orthodox.

[38] Rome.

[39] That is, to suffer "infamy."

(13) THEODOSIAN CODE, BOOK 16, SECTION 5, ENTRY 11 (CONSTANTINOPLE: 25 JULY 383)

The emperors not uncommonly issued catalogs of heresies, all of which had inflicted on them the same kinds of legal disabilities and penalties.

The Imperators Gratian, Valentinian, and Theodosius Augustuses to Postumianus, Praetorian Prefect. All those altogether, whomever the error of diverse heresies disquiets, that is, the Eunomians, the Arians, the Macedonians, the Pneumatomachi, the Manichaeans, the Encratites, the Apotactitae, the Saccofori, the Hydroparastatae, shall come together in no assemblies, shall gather no multitude, shall draw no people to themselves, nor shall they present private houses in the guise of churches. They shall carry out nothing publicly or privately that could possibly obstruct catholic sanctity. And if anyone appears who so obviously surpasses forbidden things, with the opportunity permitted to all whom the beauty and worship of proper observance delights, let him be exiled by means of a shared feeling of all the good people.

(14) THEODOSIAN CODE, BOOK 16, SECTION 5, ENTRY 40 (ROME: 22 FEBRUARY 407)

As time went on, the penalties against heretics became more numerous and more specific. This ruling was particularly directed against the Manichaeans, along with two other heresies that were thought to share many of their practices.

The Imperators Arcadius, Honorius, and Theodosius[40] Augustuses to Senator, Prefect of the City.[41] What we have thought concerning the Donatists[42] we recently have set forth. Especially do we pursue, with well-merited severity, the Manichaeans, the Phrygians, and the Priscillianists. Therefore, there is nothing in custom, nothing in laws that is common for these kinds of people. And first we declare that their crime is against the state, because what is committed against the divine religion is held to be an injury of all. And we will take vengeance upon them by the confiscation of their goods, which, however, we command shall fall to whomsoever is nearest of their kindred, in ascending or descending lines or cognates of collateral branches to the second degree, as the order is in succession to goods.[43] Finally, it shall be so that we allow to them the right to receive the goods only if they themselves are not in the same way polluted by the same belief. And it is our will that they be deprived of every grant or succession from whatever title derived. In addition, we do not leave to anyone convicted of this crime the right of giving, buying, selling, or finally of making a contract. The investigation shall continue until death. For if in the case of the crime of treason it is lawful to attack the memory of the deceased, not without desert ought this one to endure judgment.

Therefore let his last will and testament be invalid, whether he leave property by testament, codicil, epistle, or by any sort of will, if ever he has been convicted of being a Manichaean, Phrygian, or Priscillianist, and in this case the same order is to

[40] Theodosius II (402–450 CE).

[41] Rome.

[42] A schismatic African sect that was heavily persecuted by the western government.

[43] That is, according to standard Roman legal procedures relating to inheritances.

be followed as in the grades above stated, and we do not permit sons to succeed as heirs unless they forsake the paternal depravity, for we grant forgiveness of the offence to those repenting. We will that slaves be without harm if, rejecting their sacrilegious master, they pass over to the catholic church by a more faithful service. The property on which a congregation of men of this sort assembled, with the owner knowing but not prohibiting, even if not implicated in participation in the crime, is to be confiscated to our patrimony.[44] If the owner was ignorant, let the agent or steward of the property, having been scourged with a lead-weighted whip, be sent to labor in the mines. The tenant, if he is of sufficient status, will be deported. If the governors of provinces by fraud or favor defer what has been reported or fail to carry out the sentences, let them know that they will be inflicted by a fine of twenty pounds of gold.[45] A penalty of ten pounds of gold also will constrain the defenders[46] and principals[47] of individual cities, and also the provincial office staffs unless they provide the most sagacious care and the most skillful labor in pursuing those matters that were commanded by the governors regarding this law.

(15) THEODOSIAN CODE, BOOK 16, SECTION 5, ENTRY 59 (CONSTANTINOPLE: 9 APRIL 423)

Because the government lacked effective means of enforcement, Roman laws against heretics in particular, and all Roman laws in general, tended not to be obeyed. As a consequence, laws often were reissued and repeated many times over, as in this ruling that merely reiterates previous antiheretic legislation.

The Imperators Honorius and Theodosius Augustuses to Asclepiodotus, Praetorian Prefect. After other matters. Let the Manichaeans and Phrygians, who, by a more disguised word are called Pepyzites or Priscillianists, the Arians likewise, the Macedonians and Eunomians, the Novatians and Sabbatiani, and other heretics know that by this constitution too all things are denied to them that the authority of general legislation prohibits to them. Those persons who attempt to go against the interdicts of general constitutions must be punished.

(16) THEODOSIAN CODE, BOOK 16, SECTION 5, ENTRY 65 (CONSTANTINOPLE: 30 MAY 428)

The longest and most exhaustive list of heresies, accompanied by lists of penalties, came in 428, when the last of the reiterated condemnations of heresy contained in the Theodosian Code was issued. It is primarily eastern; only three groups cited here, the Priscillianists,

[44] The branch of the imperial treasury that oversaw the personal property of the emperor.

[45] Extreme fines such as this—twenty pounds of gold amounted to 1,440 gold solidi, about 480 years' wages for an ordinary worker—would seem to have been intended primarily as deterrents.

[46] The "Defender of the City" was an imperial official whose responsibility was to protect local inhabitants from oppression by city council members, but because the Defenders often were members of the city council, the practice was not always effective.

[47] The "principals" were the highest ranking and most influential members of the city council.

Donatists, and Novatians, originated in the west. Other western groups that in the past had received imperial condemnation, such as the Pelagians, however, are omitted.

The Imperators Theodosius and Valentinian[48] Augustuses to Florentius, Praetorian Prefect. The insanity of heretics must be repressed to such an extent that there is no doubt that, before everything, the churches they hold everywhere that have been taken from orthodox believers must be surrendered immediately to the catholic church, because it cannot be tolerated that those who do not deserve to have their own property should any longer maintain possession of properties that were possessed or established by orthodox believers and were occupied by their temerity. Next, if they recruit to themselves other clerics or, as they style themselves, bishops, let a fine of ten pounds of gold be wrested away to our treasury for each violation from the one who did this or who allowed it to be done, or, if they claim poverty, from the common body of the clerics of the same superstition or even from the sanctuaries themselves.

In addition, because not all of them should be afflicted with the same harshness, it is permitted to the Arians certainly, and the Macedonians and Apollinarians, whose crime is this, that, having been deceived by harmful contemplation they believe lies about the fountain of truth, to have a church within no city; to the Novatians[49] and Sabbatians, however, all freedom of new construction is removed,[50] if perchance they might attempt this. The Eunomians, truly, the Valentinians, the Montanists or Priscillianists, the Phrygians, the Marcianists, the Borborians, the Messalians, the Euchitae or Enthusiastae, the Donatists, the Audians, the Hydroparastatae, the Tascodrogitae, the Photinians, the Paulians, the Marcellians, and those who have come all the way to the lowest wickedness of crimes, the Manichaeans, nowhere on Roman soil are to have the opportunity for gathering and praying—indeed, the Manichaeans are to be expelled from cities—because no place must be left to all of these in which injury could occur to the fundamental principles[51] themselves.

No official office is permitted to them at all beyond that of a clerk in provincial offices or military service,[52] with the right granted to no one, in turn, of making a donation, to no one at all of a final testament or will, and with all the laws that were once issued and promulgated at diverse times against these and others who oppose our faith to remain valid with enthusiastic observance,[53] whether regarding donations made to the churches of heretics, or regarding property of any kind bequeathed in a last will, or regarding private buildings, in which they meet with the permission or connivance of the owner, being surrendered to the catholic church, revered by us, or regarding a procurator,[54] who did this without the knowledge of the owner, suffering a fine of ten pounds of gold or exile, if he is freeborn, or the mines after a whipping if he was of servile status, thus so that they should dare to contemplate neither meeting in a public place nor building churches for themselves nor regarding any overreaching of the laws. They must be prohibited from receiving civil and military assistance, from city councils and even from defenders and governors, under threat of a fine of twenty pounds of gold.

Indeed, with all of these regulations remaining in their firmness, which have been promulgated about diverse heretics regarding official position and the right of donating property and the making of a will, which are completely denied or barely

[48] Theodosius II (402–450), emperor in the east, and Valentinian II (425–455), emperor in the west.

[49] As above, the Novatians, now joined by the Sabbatians, as schismatics rather than heretics, receive the most lenient treatment.

[50] That is, they were permitted to keep existing churches.

[51] That is, Orthodox beliefs.

[52] The emperors were so desperate for soldiers that even heretics were permitted to enlist.

[53] Another indication that the laws were not being obeyed.

[54] The manager of the property; much property was held by absentee landlords.

conceded only to certain persons, in this manner, no special exception received against the laws shall be valid.

To no heretic must be given the freedom of conducting to his own baptism either freeborn persons or his own slaves who have been initiated into the mysteries of orthodox believers, nor indeed those whom they, prohibited from following the religion of the catholic church, acquired or in some manner have not yet associated with their superstition. But if anyone does this, or, because he is freeborn, allowed this to be done to himself or did not avoid it being done, he will be condemned to exile and a fine of ten pounds of gold, with the freedom of making a will and a donation denied to each one.

We command that all these rulings are to be enforced thus, so that it is permitted to no judge to order for an accusation placed before him a lesser or no punishment, unless he wishes to suffer that which he conceded to others by his dissimulation.

Theodosian Code, Book 1, Section 10: "On Pagans, Sacrifices, and Temples"

Another section of Book 16 was devoted to dealing with, and suppressing, pagan practices. During the course of the fourth century the opportunity to engage in pagan ceremonies was increasingly restricted.

(17) THEODOSIAN CODE, BOOK 16, SECTION 10, ENTRY 4 (1 DECEMBER 346)

Pagan temples are closed and pagan sacrifices are forbidden; violators are punished.

The Imperators Constantius and Constans[55] Augustuses to Taurus, Praetorian Prefect. It is our pleasure that in all places and in all cities the temples be henceforth closed, and access having been forbidden to all, freedom to sin be denied to the wicked. We command that all abstain from sacrifices; that if anyone should commit any such act, let him fall before the vengeance of the sword. Their goods, we decree, shall be taken away entirely and recovered to the fisc,[56] and likewise rectors of provinces are to be punished if they neglect to punish for these crimes.

Source: Ayer, 323.

[55] Constans succeeded his father Constantine I in 337 and ruled until 350.

[56] The imperial treasury.

(18) THEODOSIAN CODE, BOOK 16, SECTION 10, ENTRY 12 (CONSTANTINOPLE: 8 NOVEMBER 392)

This constitution often is seen as the definitive ruling prohibiting pagan practices and making Christianity into the only fully legal Roman religion. The prohibitions cited here may be compared with the prohibitions against the Bacchanalians cited in Reading 79.

The Imperators Theodosius, Arcadius, and Honorius Augustuses to Rufinus, Praetorian Prefect. No one at all of whatever sort or rank of people or offices, either serving in office or retired with honor, whether empowered by circumstances of birth or humble in nature, condition, and fortune, shall in any place or in any city sacrifice an innocent victim, or, on behalf of images lacking sense, in a more hidden shrine, having venerated the Lar with fire, the Genius with wine, or the Penates[57] with smoke, kindle lights, place incense or suspend garlands.

If anyone, about to sacrifice, dares to burn an offering, or to consult the smoking entrails, let him, as guilty of treason, receive the appropriate sentence, having been accused by a lawful indictment, even if he has not sought anything against the safety of the princes[58] or concerning their welfare. It constitutes a crime of this nature to wish to repeal the laws, to spy into unlawful things, to reveal secrets, or to attempt things forbidden, to seek the end of another's welfare, or to promise the hope of another's ruin.

If anyone venerates, with incense placed upon them and in a laughable display, images made by mortal labor and intended to be permanent, suddenly fearing what he himself has made, or, with a tree encircled with garlands or an altar erected from excavated pieces of turf, attempts to worship empty images, even if with a humble reward for the service nevertheless with a great injury to religion,[59] he, just like one guilty of a religious violation, will be fined by the house or property in which it is established that he was a servant to pagan superstition. For we command that all places that are proven to have smoked with the vapor of incense, if moreover they are proven to be the lawful possessions of those burning the incense, are to be confiscated to our treasury.

But if in temples or public sanctuaries or in buildings and fields belonging to another anyone should venture to carry out this sort of sacrifice, if it should be established that the unlawful acts were performed with the owner being ignorant, let him be compelled to pay twenty-five pounds of gold in the form of a fine, and let an equal penalty constrain anyone conniving at this crime and anyone sacrificing.

We also desire that this ruling be enforced by governors, defenders, and decurions[60] of individual cities, so that things learned by them immediately will be brought to judgment and the matters reported through them shall be punished. Furthermore, if they think that anything should be passed over on account of personal favor or carelessness, they shall be subjected to a judicial action. Truly, after they have been warned, if they defer punishment by dissimulation, they will be fined by an exaction of thirty pounds of gold, with their office staffs also being constrained by a like punishment.

[57] The Lar, Genius, and Penates were household gods who looked after a home's welfare.

[58] The emperors.

[59] That is, Christianity.

[60] Members of city councils, who oversaw local administration.

(19) THEODOSIAN CODE, BOOK 16, SECTION 10, ENTRY 24 (CONSTANTINOPLE: 8 JUNE 423)

The full weight of imperial authority is imposed on the Manichaeans and others who dissent regarding the date of Easter, but restraint is ordered with respect to law-abiding Jews and pagans.

The Imperators Arcadius and Honorius Augustuses to Asclepiodotus, Praetorian Prefect. The Manichaeans and those who are called Pepyzites[61] and also those who in this one persuasion are worse than all the heretics, because they dissent from everyone regarding the venerable day of Easter. If they persevere in this same madness, we impose the same punishment, confiscation of property and exile. But this we especially demand of Christians, those who truly are such and those who are called such, that on the Jews and pagans living in peace and attempting nothing seditious contrary to the laws they dare not lay their hands, having abused the authority of religion. For if they act violently against those who are peaceful or seize their property, they are to be compelled to restore not only those things alone that they carried off but also the things that they seized, assessed at threefold or fourfold. Indeed, the governors of the provinces and their office staffs and the provincials should understand that, if they permit this, they themselves must be punished just as those who do this.

Code of Justinian, Book 1, Section 5: "On the Highest Trinity and the Catholic Faith and so That No One May Dare to Argue about It in Public

The Code of Justinian, issued in 534 CE, was organized in much the same way as the Theodosian Code, although whereas the Theodosian Code covered the period 313–437 CE, the Code of Justinian included legislation from the reign of Hadrian (117–138 CE) to 534.

(20) CODE OF JUSTINIAN, BOOK 1, SECTION 5, ENTRY 18 (CONSTANTINOPLE: ca. 529)

Much of the legislation directed against pagans, Jews, and heretics in the Theodosian Code was repeated in the Code of Justinian, which made some new additions of its own.

Justinian Augustus. Looking after all things useful to our subjects, we see to it above all, as the first and most necessary thing, so as to save their souls, that all sincerely revere the catholic faith, adore and believe in the holy and consubstantial Trinity, and acknowledge and venerate the holy, glorious, every virgin Mary, the Mother of God.

[61] Another name for Montanists.

Because, therefore, we have learned that very many people meander about in various heresies, we zealously have essayed to guide them, along with our associates serving god, to a better sentiment and with sacred edicts as well as laws, to emend the opinion that descended wrongly into their spirits, and to promote, understand, and revere the true and sole salubrious faith of the Christians. All of which was done both with respect to other heresies, and in particular against the impious Manichaeans, part of whom are the Boboritae, regarding whom sanctions were issued by name.

The things, truly, that we have established against the Samaritans,[62] we also sanction against the Montanists, Tascodrogae, and Ophites, that is, that they not be permitted to have any synagogue, in which they meet, assembling with impious and laughable words and deeds, nor shall they be able to transmit their property as an inheritance or trust by testament or on intestacy, whether the person be a cognate relative or an outside heir, unless perchance the person called to the succession, or who is instituted as an heir or is honored by a trust, embraces the catholic faith.

In regard to all the other heresies—we mean all different from the catholic faith—we desire the law heretofore enacted by us and our father of blessed memory[63] to be in force, in which are defined the proper things not only concerning heresies but also concerning the Samaritans and pagans, namely that those affected by such frenzy shall not be in the imperial service or enjoy any position of rank, or under any pretense of professor of any branch of learning divert the minds of the simple to their own error. We permit only those to teach and receive public salary who are of the catholic faith.

But if anyone, in order to obtain any position in the imperial service or as an advocate or a position of rank, or a public charge, embraces the true and catholic faith only in pretense, and, promoted to such position by reason of such pretense, is found to have a wife and children who are adherents of a clear heresy, and fails to lead them to knowledge of truth, we order him to be removed from such advocate's position, service, or public charge. If he secretly remains, he may not transfer anything to a heretic by a gift or by any contract or last will and the inheritance left by him to a heretic shall be taken by the fisc. But truly catholic Christians my receive property from him while he lives or may become his heirs after he is dead.

Only persons who are catholic Christians shall be heirs to those occupying, or those who have occupied, positions of rank, or in the imperial service, or as an advocate, and all those who have enjoyed any kind whatsoever of public charge or favor, shall have only catholic Christians as heirs.

Indeed, we totally prohibit sharing with these people, that is to say, those things that are transferred to a heretic by inheritance or gift or by any reason. But if it appears that someone has done anything of this nature, those things that in this manner were given or bequeathed shall be surrendered to the treasury.

And plainly if anyone of those who were forbidden by us, that is to say, pagans or Manichaeans or Samaritans or heretics related to them should, perchance, seek a position in the imperial service or one of rank or as an advocate, or any public charge, or should attempt to teach or receive a public salary, or, finally, do any prohibited act, and he is not denounced by every office, whether military or civil, here or in the provinces, to which these prohibitions pertain, the offender himself shall, after he has been apprehended, be subjected to the punishment above laid down, the persons who have failed to report him shall pay a fine of twenty pounds of gold, and a fine of thirty pounds of gold shall be imposed on every office staff, civil or military, here and in the provinces.

But if he,[64] has pursued the heretic and has demanded the penalty and has shown himself to have

[62] Descendants of the Hebrews who resided in the northern Hebrew kingdom of Israel when it separated from the southern Hebrew kingdom of Judah after the death of King Solomon in 930 BCE.

[63] Justin I (518–527).

[64] The official concerned.

Source: Fred H. Blume, *Annotated Justinian Code* (Laramie: University of Wyoming, 1920/1952).

been diligent in the things ordered, but has failed to collect the penalty due from any person or in any cause, the illustrious Count of the Crown Domain[65] shall collect and receive it and turn it into the crown domain, knowing that if he, through the corps of palace officials under him, and the corps itself, fail to investigate such matters and to summon the guilty, the former shall pay a fine of 50 pounds of gold, and the members of the corps itself, aside from the corporal punishment which is due in such case, will incur the risk of a fine imposed on them if they do not pay attention to our orders.

The same duty is imposed on the pious bishop of each city, who shall investigate in the different cities the attempts made by anyone in violation of this, our imperial law, and shall make them known to the honorable governor of the province, so that the latter may enforce our pious orders. If the reverend bishops find that the moderator of the province[66] is negligent, he should report the matter to us, so that we may subject the negligent ones to the same punishment, to which we have ordered the violators of the foregoing provisions to be subjected.

And be it known to the pious bishops that if they are negligent they will come before the Lord God and his judgment seat; and if they are convicted of negligence they stand in danger of losing their bishopric.

[65] The imperial official who administered the personal property of the emperor.

[66] The governor.

111

THE MURDER OF HYPATIA OF ALEXANDRIA (415 CE): SOCRATES SCHOLASTICUS, *ECCLESIASTICAL HISTORY*, BOOK 7, CHAPTER 15, AND JOHN OF NIKIÛ, *CHRONICLE*, CHAPTER 84

An illustration from the "Alexandrian World Chronicle," written on papyrus in the early fifth century, shows bishop Theophilus of Alexandria standing on top of the Serapeum, the famous temple of Serapis in Alexandria, at the time of its demolition in 391 CE. The temple housed part of the Library of Alexandria and was a symbol of the pagan resistance to Christianity. A large number of other pagan monuments also subsequently were destroyed.

The final triumph of Christianity came under the emperor Theodosius I (379–395), who definitively outlawed the performance of public pagan rituals and made Christianity the only fully legal religion in the empire (see Reading 110). Zealous Christians then struck back and began to persecute both pagans and Jews with acts ranging from the destruction of pagan temples and monuments to the murder of professed pagans. A marquee example of this occurred in

Alexandria, where at the Museum, the university that had been established in the third century BCE under the Ptolemies, the female philosopher and mathematician Hypatia was the head of the school of Neoplatonism. She was the teacher of later Christian bishops such as Synesius of Cyrene. In 415 a quarrel broke out between Orestes, the imperial Prefect of Egypt, and Cyril, the ambitious bishop of Alexandria. Hypatia was accused of arousing Orestes against Cyril and, as a consequence, she was assaulted and gruesomely murdered by a band of fanatical Christian monks. Two accounts of the murder, both by Christian authors, provide rather different views of Hypatia. Socrates Scholasticus, who had received a classical education and wrote an "Ecclesiastical History" in the 440s CE, painted a sympathetic picture of Hypatia, but the hard-line Monophysite (anti-Chalcedonian) bishop John of Nikiû, who wrote a chronicle shortly after the Muslim capture of Alexandria in 640, portrayed her as a devotee of Satanism.

(a) Socrates Scholasticus, *Ecclesiastical History*, Book 7, Chapter 15

Source: A. C. Zenos, Chester D. Hartranft, trans., *Socrates, Sozomenus. Church Histories* (New York: Christian Literature, 1890).

There was a woman at Alexandria named Hypatia, daughter of the philosopher Theon,[67] who made such attainments in literature and science so as to surpass by far all the philosophers of her own time. Having succeeded to the school of Plato and Plotinus, she explained the principles of philosophy to her students, many of whom came from a distance to receive her instructions. On account of the self-possession and ease of manner that she had acquired in consequence of the cultivation of her mind she not infrequently appeared in public in presence of the magistrates. Nor did she feel abashed in coming to an assembly of men, for all men on account of her extraordinary dignity and virtue admired her all the more. Yet even she fell a victim to the political jealousy that at that time prevailed. For as she had frequent interviews with Orestes,[68] it was calumniously reported among the Christian populace that it was she who prevented Orestes from being reconciled to the bishop.[69] Some of them therefore, whose ringleader was a Reader[70] named Peter, hurried away with a fierce and bigoted zeal. They waylaid her returning home, and, dragging her from her carriage, took her to the church called Caesareum, where they completely stripped her and then murdered her with tiles. After tearing her body in pieces, they took her mangled limbs to a place called Cinaron and there burnt them. This affair brought not the least opprobrium upon Cyril or upon the whole Alexandrian church. But surely nothing can be farther from the spirit of Christianity than the allowance of massacres, fights, and transactions of that sort. This happened in the month of March during Lent, in the fourth year of Cyril's episcopate, under the tenth consulate of Honorius, and the sixth of Theodosius.[71]

[67] A Greek scholar who edited the works of the mathematician Euclid.

[68] The Augustal Prefect, the highest civil official of Roman Egypt.

[69] Cyril, the powerful and ambitious bishop of Alexandria from 412 until 444.

[70] The position of Lector (Reader) was a minor clerical position in the church.

[71] 415 CE.

(b) John of Nikiu, *Chronicle*, Chapter 84

Source: R. H. Charles, *The Chronicle of John, Bishop of Nikiu* (London: Williams & Norgate, 1916).

And in those days there appeared in Alexandria a female philosopher, a pagan named Hypatia, and she was devoted at all times to magic, astrolabes,[72] and instruments of music, and she beguiled many people with her Satanic wiles. The governor of the city[73] honored her exceedingly, for she had captivated him through her magic. He ceased attending church as had been his custom. He also went once under circumstances of danger, and he not only did this, but he also drew many believers to her and he himself received the unbelievers[74] at his house. And on a certain day when the unbelievers were making merry over a theatrical exhibition connected with dancers, the governor of the city published an edict regarding the public exhibitions in the city of Alexandria, and all the inhabitants of the city had assembled in the theater.

Now Cyril, who had been appointed Patriarch[75] after Theophilus,[76] was eager to gain exact intelligence regarding this edict. And there was a man named Hierax, a Christian possessing understanding and intelligence, who used to mock the pagans and was a devoted adherent of the illustrious father, the Patriarch, and was obedient to his monitions. He was also well versed in the Christian faith. Now this man attended the theater to learn the nature of this edict. But when the Jews saw him in the theater they cried out and said: "This man has not come with any good purpose, but only to provoke an uproar." And Orestes the Prefect was displeased with the children of the holy church and had Hierax seized and subjected to punishment publicly in the theater, although he was wholly guiltless. And Cyril was angry with the governor of the city for doing so, and likewise for his putting to death an illustrious monk of the convent of Pernôdj named Ammonius, and other monks also.

And when the chief magistrate of the city[77] heard this, he sent word to the Jews as follows, "Cease your hostilities against the Christians." But they refused to hearken to what they heard, for they gloried in the support of the Prefect[78] who was with them, and so they added outrage to outrage and plotted a massacre through a treacherous device. And they posted beside them at night in all the streets of the city certain men, while others cried out and said: "The church of the apostolic Athanasius[79] is on fire: come to its succor, all ye Christians." And the Christians on hearing their cry came forth quite ignorant of the treachery of the Jews. And when the Christians came forth, the Jews arose and wickedly massacred the Christians and shed the blood of many even though they were guiltless. And in the morning, when the surviving Christians heard of the wicked deed that the Jews had wrought, they betook themselves to the Patriarch. And the Christians mustered all together and went and marched in wrath to the synagogues of the Jews and took possession of them, and purified them and converted them into churches. And one of them they named after the name of Saint George. And as for the Jewish assassins they expelled them from the city and pillaged all their possessions and drove them forth wholly despoiled, and Orestes the Prefect was unable to render them any help.

[72] A scientific device for measuring the angular distance above the horizon of stars and planets.

[73] Orestes, the Augustal Prefect of Egypt.

[74] The non-Christians.

[75] Only the bishops of Alexandria, Antioch, Jerusalem, Constantinople, and Rome ranked as "Patriarchs."

[76] In 391 CE, Theophilus, bishop of Alexandria, had overseen the destruction of the Serapaeum, the great temple of the god Serapis and a symbol of Egypt's past respect for the traditional gods.

[77] Perhaps the official who presided over the city council.

[78] That is, Orestes.

[79] A famous fourth-century bishop of Alexandria who was instrumental in combating Arianism.

And thereafter a multitude of believers in God arose under the guidance of Peter the magistrate[80]—now this Peter was a perfect believer in all respects in Jesus Christ—and they proceeded to seek out the pagan woman who had beguiled the people of the city and the Prefect through her enchantments. And when they learned the place where she was, they proceeded to her and found her seated on a lofty chair, and having made her descend they dragged her along until they brought her to the great church, named Caesareum.[81] Now this was in the days of the fast.[82] And they tore off her clothing and dragged her through the streets of the city until she died. And they carried her to a place named Cinaron and they burned her body with fire. And all the people surrounded the Patriarch Cyril and named him "the new Theophilus," for he had destroyed the last remains of idolatry in the city.

[80] In the preceding account of Socrates, Peter is merely a minor Christian cleric.

[81] A large temple of the imperial cult that rather than being destroyed had been converted into a Christian church.

[82] Lent.

112

THE MONASTIC LIFE ON THE EASTERN FRONTIER (CA. 350/390 CE): JEROME, *THE LIFE OF MALCHUS THE CAPTIVE MONK*

A low-relief carving on basalt shows the stylite (pillar sitter) Simeon, a shepherd's son, atop his fifty-foot (sixteen-meter) high column near Aleppo, Syria, where he resided on a nine-foot (one-meter) square platform in all kinds of weather, never coming down, between 422 and 459 CE. As a result of his ascetic lifestyle, he gained a reputation for great sanctity, and his advice and blessings were sought by rich and poor alike. By adopting lives of extreme deprivation, ordinary people were able to attain great authority. Most persons who took up the monastic life, however, did not go to such extremes to gain holiness.

During the late Roman Empire, many individuals abandoned the secular world and adopted the monastic life. Some did so purely for reasons of piety, others to evade secular responsibilities, to flee barbarian incursions, or, especially women, to escape problematic domestic situations. Some monasteries were located conveniently close to cities, whereas others were in more isolated regions, such as deserts, islands, or mountains. Around 390 CE, Jerome of Bethlehem, one of the greatest Christian intellectuals, told the story of Malchus, a young man who abandoned his family to become a monk. Eventually, Malchus decided to return home. On the way he got rather more than he had bargained for.

Source: Philip Schaff and Henry Wace, trans., *Jerome: Letters and Selected Works* (New York: Christian Literature, 1893).

Maronia is a little hamlet some thirty miles to the east of Antioch in Syria. After having many owners or landlords at the time when I was staying as a young man in Syria it came into the possession of my intimate friend, the bishop Evagrius,[83] whose name I now give in order to show the source of my information. Well, there was at the place at that time an old man by name Malchus, a Syrian by nationality and speech, in fact a genuine son of the soil. His companion was an old woman very decrepit who seemed to be at death's door. Both of them were zealously pious and constant frequenters of the church. With some curiosity I asked the neighbors what was the link between them; was it marriage, or kindred, or the bond of the spirit? All with one accord replied that they were holy people, well pleasing to God, and gave me a strange account of them. Longing to know more I began to question the man with much eagerness about the truth of what I heard, and learnt as follows.

My son, said he, I used to farm a bit of ground at Nisibis[84] as an only son. My parents regarding me as the heir and the only survivor of their family, wished to force me into marriage, but I said I would rather be a monk. How my father threatened and my mother coaxed me to betray my chastity requires no other proof than the fact that I fled from home and parents. I could not go to the east because Persia was close by and the frontiers were guarded by the soldiers of Rome; I therefore turned my steps to the west, taking with me some little provision for the journey, but barely sufficient to ward off destitution. To be brief, I came at last to the desert of Chalcis, which is situated between Immae and Beroea[85] farther south. There, finding some monks, I placed myself under their direction, earning my livelihood by the labor of my hands and curbing the wantonness of the flesh by fasting. After many years the desire came over me to return to my country, and stay with my mother and cheer her widowhood while she lived (my father, as I had already heard, was dead) and then to sell the little property and give part to the poor, settle part on the monasteries and, I blush to confess my faithlessness, keep some to spend in comforts for myself.

My abbot began to cry out that it was a temptation of the devil, and that under fair pretexts some snare of the old enemy[86] lay hid. It was, he declared, a case of the dog returning to his vomit. Many monks, he said, had been deceived by such suggestions, for the devil never showed himself openly. When he failed to convince me he fell upon his knees and besought me not to forsake him, nor ruin myself by looking back after putting my hand to the plough. Unhappily for myself I had the misfortune to conquer my adviser. I thought he was seeking not my salvation but his own comfort. So he followed me from the monastery as if he had been going to a funeral, and at last bade me farewell, saying, "I see that you bear the brand of a son of Satan. I do not ask your reasons nor take your excuses. The sheep that forsakes its fellows is at once exposed to the jaws of the wolf."

On the road from Beroea to Edessa[87] adjoining the high-way is a waste over which the Saracens[88] roam to and fro without having any fixed abode. Through fear of them travelers in those parts assemble in numbers, so that by mutual assistance they may escape impending danger. There were in my company men, women, old men, youths, children, altogether about seventy persons. All of a sudden the Ishmaelites[89] on horses and camels made an assault upon us, with

[83] Bishop of Antioch from 388 to 392.

[84] A powerful fortress on the border between the Roman and Sasanid empires; see Reading 104.

[85] Modern Aleppo in Syria.

[86] Satan.

[87] Modern Şanlıurfa in Turkey, northeast of Beroea.

[88] A Roman name for Arabs.

[89] That is, Arabs. Traditionally, Arabs were the descendants of Ishmael, Abraham's son by his handmaid Hagar.

their flowing hair bound with fillets, their bodies half-naked, with their broad military boots, their cloaks streaming behind them, and their quivers slung upon the shoulders. They carried their bows unstrung and brandished their long spears, for they had come not to fight but to plunder. We were seized, dispersed, and carried in different directions. I, meanwhile, repenting too late of the step I had taken, and far indeed from gaining possession of my inheritance, was assigned, along with another poor sufferer, a woman, to the service of one and the same owner. We were led, or rather carried, high upon the camel's back through a desert waste, every moment expecting destruction, and suspended, I may say, rather than seated. Flesh half raw was our food, camel's milk our drink.

At length, after crossing a great river[90] we came to the interior of the desert, where, being commanded after the custom of the people to pay reverence to the mistress and her children, we bowed our heads. Here, as if I were a prisoner, I changed my dress, that is, learnt to go naked, the heat being so excessive as to allow of no clothing beyond a covering for the loins. Some sheep were given to me to tend, and, comparatively speaking, I found this occupation a comfort, for I seldom saw my masters or fellow slaves. I fed on fresh cheese and milk, prayed continually, and sang psalms that I had learnt in the monastery. I was delighted with my captivity, and thanked God because I had found in the desert the monk's estate that I was on the point of losing in my country.

But no condition can ever shut out the Devil. How manifold past expression are his snares! Hid although I was, his malice found me out. My master, seeing his flock increasing and finding no dishonesty in me and wishing to reward me in order to secure my greater fidelity, gave me the woman who once was my fellow servant in captivity. On my refusing and saying I was a Christian, and that it was not lawful for me to take a woman to wife so long as her husband was alive (her husband had been captured with us, but carried off by another master), my owner was relentless in his rage, drew his sword and began to make at me. If I had not without delay stretched out my hand and taken possession of the woman, he would have slain me on the spot. Well, by this time a darker night than usual had set in and, for me, all too soon. I led my bride into an old cave. Sorrow was bride's-maid; we shrank from each other but did not confess it.

Then I really felt my captivity; I threw myself down on the ground and began to lament the monastic state that I had lost, and said, "Wretched man that I am! Have I been preserved for this? Has my wickedness brought me to this, that in my gray hairs I must lose my virgin state and become a married man? What is the good of having abandoned my parents, country, and property for the Lord's sake, if I do the thing I wished to avoid doing when I abandoned them? Turn your weapon against yourself. I must fear your death, my soul, more than the death of the body. Chastity preserved has its own martyrdom. Let the witness for Christ lie unburied in the desert."

Thus speaking I drew my sword that glittered even in the dark, and turning its point toward me said, "Farewell, unhappy woman, receive me as a martyr not as a husband." She threw herself at my feet and exclaimed, "I pray you by Jesus Christ, and adjure you by this hour of trial, do not shed your blood and bring its guilt upon me. If you choose to die, first turn your sword against me. Let us rather be united upon these terms. Supposing my husband should return to me. I would preserve the chastity that I have learnt in captivity. I would even die rather than lose it. Why should you die to prevent a union with me? I would die if you desired it. Take me then as the partner of your chastity and love me more in this union of the spirit than you could in that of the body only. Let our master believe that you are my husband. Christ knows you are my brother. We shall easily convince them that we are married when they see us so loving." I confess, I was astonished and, much as I had before admired the virtue of the woman, I now loved her as a wife still more. Yet I never gazed upon her naked person, I never touched her flesh, for I was afraid of losing in peace what I had preserved in the conflict. In this strange wedlock many days passed away. Marriage had made us more pleasing to our masters,

[90] The Euphrates, which lay between Beroea and Edessa.

and there was no suspicion of our flight. Sometimes I was absent for even a whole month like a trusty shepherd traversing the wilderness.

After a long time as I sat one day by myself in the desert with nothing in sight save earth and sky, I began quickly to turn things over in my thoughts, and among others called to mind my friends the monks, and especially the look of the father who had instructed me, kept me, and lost me. I began to tire of captivity and to miss the monk's cell, where toil is for the community, and, because nothing belongs to anyone, all things belong to all.

When I returned to my chamber, my wife met me. My looks betrayed the sadness of my heart. She asked why I was so dispirited. I told her the reasons, and exhorted her to escape. She did not reject the idea. We constantly spoke to one another in whispers, and we floated in suspense between hope and fear. I had in the flock two very fine he-goats: these I killed, made their skins into bottles, and from their flesh prepared food for the way. Then in the early evening when our masters thought we had retired to rest we began our journey, taking with us the bottles and part of the flesh. When we reached the river that was about ten miles off, having inflated the skins and got astride upon them, we entrusted ourselves to the water, slowly propelling ourselves with our feet, that we might be carried down by the stream to a point on the opposite bank much below that at which we embarked and that thus the pursuers might lose the track. But meanwhile the flesh became sodden and partly lost, and we could not depend on it for more than three days' sustenance. We drank until we could drink no more by way of preparing for the thirst we expected to endure, then hastened away, constantly looking behind us, and advanced more by night than day, on account both of the ambushes of the roaming Saracens, and of the excessive heat of the sun. I grow terrified even as I relate what happened, and, although my mind is perfectly at rest, yet my frame shudders from head to foot.

Three days after we saw in the dim distance two men riding on camels approaching with all speed. At once foreboding ill I began to think my master purposed putting us to death, and our sun seemed to grow dark again. In the midst of our fear, and just as we realized that our footsteps on the sand had betrayed us, we found on our right hand a cave that extended far underground. Well, we entered the cave, but we were afraid of venomous beasts such as vipers, basilisks,[91] scorpions, and other creatures of the kind, which often resort to such shady places so as to avoid the heat of the sun. We therefore barely went inside and took shelter in a pit on the left, not venturing a step farther, lest in fleeing from death we should run into death. We thought thus within ourselves: If the Lord helps us in our misery, we have found safety; if he rejects us for our sins, we have found our grave. What was our terror, when in front of the cave, close by, there stood our master and fellow-servant, brought by the evidence of our footsteps to our hiding place. How much worse is death expected than death inflicted! Again, my tongue stammers with distress and fear; it seems as if I heard my master's voice, and I hardly dare mutter a word. He sent his servant to drag us from the cavern while he himself held the camels and, sword in hand, waited for us to come. Meanwhile the servant entered about three or four cubits,[92] and we in our hiding place saw his back although he could not see us, for the nature of the eye is such that those who go into the shade out of the sunshine can see nothing. His voice echoed through the cave, "Come out, you felons; come out and die. Why do you stay? Why do you delay? Come out, your master is calling and patiently waiting for you." He still was speaking when lo! through the gloom we saw a lioness seize the man, strangle him, and drag him, covered with blood, farther in. Good Jesus! How great was our terror now, how intense our joy! We beheld, although our master knew not of it, our enemy perish. He, when he saw that he was long in returning, supposed that the fugitives being two to one were offering resistance. Impatient in his rage, and sword still in hand, he came to the cavern, and shouted like a madman as he chided the slowness of his slave, but was seized upon by the wild beast before he reached

[91] A very poisonous small snake.

[92] The cubit was the length of a forearm, about eighteen inches.

our hiding place. Who ever would believe that before our eyes a brute would fight for us?

One cause of fear was removed, but there was the prospect of a similar death for ourselves, although the rage of the lion was not so bad to bear as the anger of the man. Our hearts failed for fear. Without venturing to stir a step we awaited the issue, having no wall of defense in the midst of so great dangers except the consciousness of our chastity. Then, early in the morning, the lioness, afraid of some snare and aware that she had been seen took up her cub in her teeth and carried it away, leaving us in possession of our retreat. Our confidence was not restored all at once. We did not rush out, but waited for a long time; for as often as we thought of coming out we pictured to ourselves the horror of falling in with her.

At last we got rid of our fright. When that day was spent we sallied forth toward evening and saw the camels, called "dromedaries"[93] on account of their great speed, quietly chewing the cud. We mounted, and with the strength gained from the new supply of grain, after ten days traveling through the desert arrived at the Roman camp.[94] After being presented to the Tribune[95] we told all, and from thence were sent to Sabinianus,[96] who commanded in Mesopotamia, where we sold our camels. My dear old abbot now was sleeping in the Lord. I betook myself therefore to this place, and returned to the monastic life, whereas I entrusted my companion here to the care of the virgins, for although I loved her as a sister, I did not commit myself to her as if she were my sister.

[93] From the Greek word "dromas," or "runner."

[94] On the frontier between Roman and Persian territory.

[95] The commander of the legion.

[96] A Roman general said to have sought the aid of the "Martyrs of Edessa" against the New Persians in 359 CE. The two escapees would have been debriefed regarding their knowledge of the Saracens.

113

THE LATE ROMAN CRIMINAL LEGAL PROCESS (CA. 370 CE): JEROME, *LETTER* 1

A late Roman Coptic tapestry from Egypt, now in the Bode Museum in Berlin, depicts an execution scene. Here, the biblical sacrifice of Isaac by his father Abraham is depicted, with Abraham portrayed as a *carnifex* (executioner), with his military cloak pinned at the shoulder, about to apply *jugulatio* (throat slitting) to a condemned criminal.

Jerome of Bethlehem provides a detailed account of the public trial and attempted execution of a woman who was tried before a Consular governor ca. 375 CE at Vercellae in northern Italy. His tendentious account, written in the form of a letter, relates how "a certain little woman" was accused by her husband of adultery with a young man. The subsequent investigation and trial demonstrates that legal proceedings were public and provided a popular spectacle, with the audience sometimes getting directly involved in the proceedings. After a botched execution attempt, the woman received a pardon from the emperor through the intercession of Evagrius, a priest, and later bishop, of Antioch (see Reading 112).

Source: W. H. Fremantle, G. Lewis, and W. G. Martley, trans., *St. Jerome: Letters and Select Works*, Nicene and Post-Nicene Fathers, second series, Vol. 6. (New York: Christian Literature Publishing, 1893).

To Innocent. You frequently have asked me, dearest Innocent, not to pass over in silence the marvelous event that has happened in our own day. To begin, then, Vercellae is a Ligurian town, situated not far from the base of the Alps, once important, but now sparsely peopled and fallen into decay. When the Consular[97] was holding his visitation there, a certain little woman[98] and her paramour were brought before him—the charge of adultery had been fastened upon them by the husband—and were both consigned to the penal horrors of a prison. Shortly after an attempt was made to elicit the truth by torture, and when the blood-stained hook smote the young man's livid flesh and tore furrows in his side, the unhappy wretch sought to avoid prolonged pain by a speedy death. Falsely accusing his own passions, he involved another in the charge. It appeared that he was of all men the most miserable and that his execution was just inasmuch as he had left to an innocent woman no means of self-defense. But the woman, stronger in virtue if weaker in sex, although her frame was stretched upon the rack, and although her hands, stained with the filth of the prison, were tied behind her, looked up to heaven with her eyes, which alone the torturer had been unable to bind, and while the tears rolled down her face, said, "Thou art witness, Lord Jesus, that it is not to save my life that I deny this charge. I refuse to lie because to lie is sin. And as for you, unhappy man, if you are bent on hastening your death, why must you destroy not one innocent person, but two? I also, myself, desire to die. I desire to put off this hated body, but not as an adulteress. I offer my neck. I welcome the shining sword without fear, yet I will take my innocence with me."

The Consular, who had been feasting his eyes upon the bloody spectacle, now, like a wild beast ordered the torture to be doubled, and threatened the executioner with like punishment if he failed to extort from the weaker sex a confession that a man's strength had not been able to keep back. Every species of torture is devised. She is bound by the hair to a stake, her whole body is fixed more firmly than ever on the rack, fire is brought and applied to her feet, her sides quiver beneath the executioner's probe. Still the woman remains unshaken and, triumphing in spirit over the pain of the body, enjoys the happiness of a good conscience. The cruel judge rises, overcome with passion. Her limbs are wrenched from their sockets. Another confesses what is thought their common guilt. She, for the confessor's sake, denies the confession, and, in peril of her own life, tries to clear one who is in peril of his.

She has but one thing to say, "Beat me, burn me, tear me, if you will. I have not done it. If you will not believe my words, a day will come when this charge shall be carefully sifted. I have one who will judge me.[99]" Wearied out at last, the torturer sighed in response to her groans; nor could he find a spot on which to inflict a fresh wound. Immediately the Consular cried, in a fit of passion, "Why does it surprise you, bystanders,[100] that a woman prefers torture to death? It takes two people, most assuredly, to commit adultery, and I think it more credible that a guilty woman should deny a sin than that an innocent young man should confess one."

Like sentence, accordingly, was passed on both, and the condemned pair were dragged to execution. The entire people poured out to see the sight. Indeed, so closely were the gates thronged by the out-rushing crowd that you might have fancied the city itself to be migrating. At the very first stroke of the sword the head of the hapless youth was cut off and the headless trunk rolled over in its blood. Then came the woman's turn. She knelt down upon the ground, and the shining sword was lifted over her quivering neck. But although the executioner summoned all his strength, the moment it touched her flesh the fatal blade stopped short, and, lightly glancing over the skin, merely grazed it sufficiently to draw blood. The striker saw, with terror, his hand unnerved, and, amazed at his defeated skill and at his drooping sword, he whirled it aloft for another stroke. Again the blade fell forceless on the woman, sinking

[97] A governor who had the rank of a Consul.

[98] A diminutive term suggesting unprivileged legal status.

[99] That is, God.

[100] As often happened in Roman courtrooms, the audience was drawn into the proceedings.

harmlessly on her neck, as though the steel feared to touch her. The enraged and panting officer, who had thrown open his cloak at the neck to give his full strength to the blow, shook to the ground the brooch[101] that clasped the edges of his mantle, and not noticing this, began to poise his sword for a fresh stroke. "See," cried the woman, "Your jewel has fallen from your shoulder. Pick up what you have earned by hard toil, that you may not lose it."

What, I ask, is the secret of such confidence as this? Death draws near, but it has no terrors for her. When smitten she exults, and the executioner turns pale. Her eyes see the brooch, they fail to see the sword. And, as if intrepidity in the presence of death were not enough, she confers a favor upon her cruel foe. And now the mysterious power of the Trinity rendered even a third blow vain. The terrified soldier, no longer trusting the blade, proceeded to apply the point to her throat,[102] in the idea that although it might not cut, the pressure of his hand might plunge it into her flesh. Marvel unheard of through all the ages! The sword bent back to the hilt, and in its defeat looked to its master, as if confessing its inability to slay.

Now at length the populace rise in arms to defend the woman. Men and women of every age join in driving away the executioner, shouting round him in a surging crowd. Hardly a man dares trust his own eyes. The disquieting news reaches the city close at hand, and the entire force Lictors[103] is mustered. The officer who is responsible for the execution of criminals bursts from among his men, and staining his grey hair with soiling dust, exclaims, "What? Citizens, do you mean to seek my life? Do you intend to make me a substitute for her? However much your minds are set on mercy, and however much you wish to save a condemned woman, yet assuredly I, I who am innocent, ought not to perish.[104]" His tearful appeal tells upon the crowd, they are all benumbed by the influence of sorrow, and an extraordinary change of feeling is manifested. Before it had seemed a duty to plead for the woman's life, now it seemed a duty to allow her to be executed.

Accordingly a new sword is fetched, a new executioner appointed. The victim takes her place. The first blow makes her quiver, beneath the second she sways to and fro, by the third she falls wounded to the ground.[105] She who previously had received four strokes without injury, now, a few moments later, seems to die that an innocent man may not perish in her stead.

Those of the clergy whose duty it is to wrap the blood-stained corpse in a winding-sheet dig out the earth and, heaping together stones, form the customary tomb. Sunset comes on quickly. Suddenly the woman's bosom heaves, her eyes seek the light, her body is quickened into new life. A moment after she sighs, she looks round, she gets up and speaks. At last she is able to cry: "The Lord is on my side; I will not fear. What can man do unto me?" Meantime an aged woman, supported out of the funds of the church, gave back her spirit to heaven from which it came. It seemed as if this thus purposely had been ordered, for her body took the place of the other beneath the mound. In the gray dawn the devil appears in the form of a Lictor, asks for the corpse of her who had been slain, and desires to have her grave pointed out to him. The clergy show him the fresh turf and meet his demands by pointing to the earth lately heaped up, taunting him with such words as these, "Yes, of course, tear up the bones that have been buried! Pluck her limb from limb for birds and beasts to mangle! Mere dying is too good for one whom it took seven strokes to kill."

Before such opprobrious words the executioner retires in confusion, whereas the woman is secretly revived at home. Then, lest the frequency of the doctor's visits to the church might give occasion for suspicion, they cut her hair short and send her in the company of some virgins to a sequestered country house. There she changes her dress for that of a man

[101] The *fibula*, or pin, that was a badge of rank for imperial officials, as depicted in the illustration.

[102] The executioner thus turns from beheading to throat slitting as a means of execution.

[103] The axe-bearing attendants of the consular governor.

[104] For failing to do his duty

[105] The executioner still is pulling his punches.

and scars form over her wounds. Yet even after the great miracles worked on her behalf, the laws still rage against her. It is so true that where there is the most law, there, there is also the most injustice.

But now see where the progress of my story has brought me. We come upon the name of our friend Evagrius.[106] Who can fittingly praise the vigilance that enabled him to bury before his death Auxentius of Milan,[107] that curse brooding over the church? Or who can sufficiently extol the discretion with which he rescued the Roman bishop[108] from the toils of the net in which he was entangled? I now am satisfied to record the conclusion of my tale. Evagrius sought a special audience of the emperor,[109] importuned him with his entreaties, won his favor by his services, and finally gained his cause through his earnestness. The emperor restored to liberty the woman whom God had restored to life.

[106] A priest of Antioch who took refuge in Italy in 363; Jerome accompanied him back to the east in 373. In 388 he was named a competing bishop of Antioch.

[107] Arian bishop of Milan until his death in 374 CE; a metaphorical burial.

[108] Bishop Damasus of Rome, whose election in 367 involved much violence and controversy.

[109] The western emperor Valentinian I (364–375).

114

THE BATTLE OF ADRIANOPLE (378 CE): AMMIANUS MARCELLINUS, *HISTORIES*, BOOK 31, CHAPTERS 12–14

This nine-solidus gold medallion of Valens would have been a special presentation piece, probably to a high-ranking subordinate or a barbarian chieftain. The obverse depicts Valens in a general's cloak holding a globe topped by the goddess Victory crowning him with a wreath, and the reverse shows Valens in a chariot, this time being crowned by two winged Victories. The reverse legend grandiosely proclaims Valens as "Perpetual Victor," a denotation belied by the disastrous defeat he suffered at the Battle of Adrianople in 378. In 2009, this medallion sold for more than half a million dollars.

In 376 CE, one year after the death of his elder and much abler brother, Valentinian I (364–375), the emperor Valens (364–378) allowed groups of Visigoths who were fleeing the Huns to settle in Roman territory south of the Danube River on the understanding that they would become tax-paying farmers and serve in the Roman army. Because of Roman mismanagement, the Visigoths revolted and in 378 Valens assembled the eastern Roman army to subdue them. The subsequent Roman defeat at the Battle of Adrianople, chronicled by Ammianus Marcellinus, an army officer who became, with Livy and Tacitus, one of Rome's three greatest historians, was as disastrous as the previous Roman defeats at Cannae (216 BCE) and the Teutoberg Forest (9 CE). It also has been seen as marking the beginning of the "barbarian invasions" of the Roman Empire.

Source: C. D. Yonge, trans., *The Roman History of Ammianus Marcellinus during the Reigns of the Emperors Constantius, Julian, Jovianus, Valentinian, and Valens* (London: Bell, 1911), 609–618.

At this time Valens[110] was disturbed by a twofold anxiety,[111] having learned that the Lentienses[112] had been defeated and also because Sebastianus,[113] in the letters that he sent from time to time, exaggerated what had taken place by his pompous language. Therefore he advanced from Melanthias,[114] being eager by some glorious exploit to equal his youthful nephew,[115] by whose virtue he was greatly excited. He was at the head of a numerous force, neither unwarlike nor contemptible, and had united with them many veteran bands, among whom were several officers of high rank, especially Trajan,[116] who a little while before had been commander of the forces. And as by means of spies and observation it was ascertained that the enemy were intending to blockade the different roads by which the necessary supplies must come, with strong divisions he sent a sufficient force to prevent this, dispatching a body of the archers of the infantry and a squadron of cavalry, with all speed, to occupy the narrow passes in the neighborhood.

Three days afterward, when the barbarians, who were advancing slowly because they feared an attack in the unfavorable ground that they were traversing, arrived within fifteen miles from the station of Nicaea,[117] which was the aim of their march, the emperor, with wanton impetuosity, resolved on attacking them instantly, because those who had been sent forward to reconnoiter (what led to such a mistake is unknown) affirmed that their entire body did not exceed ten thousand men. Marching on with his army in battle array, he came near the suburb of Adrianople,[118] where he pitched his camp, strengthening it with a rampart of palisades, and then impatiently waited for Gratian. While here, Richomer, Count of the Domestics,[119] arrived, who had been sent on by that emperor with letters announcing his immediate approach and imploring Valens to wait a little while for him that he might share his danger, and not rashly face the danger before him single handed, he took counsel with his officers as to what was best to be done.

Some, following the advice of Sebastianus, recommended with urgency that he should at once go forth to battle, whereas Victor, Master of the Cavalry, a Sarmatian[120] by birth and a man of slow and cautious temper, recommended that he wait for his imperial colleague, and this advice was supported by

[110] Named co-emperor by Valentinian I (364–375) in 364, he became senior emperor when Valentinian died in 375.
[111] Resulting from his envy of the military successes of others.
[112] An Alamannic people of southern Germany, mentioned only by Ammianus, defeated by the western Roman army.
[113] A Roman general whose task it was to organize the Roman armies in Thrace and who won a few minor skirmishes with the Visigoths.
[114] An imperial villa in Thrace.
[115] Valens was jealous of the successes of the western emperor Gratian (367–383), who had succeeded his father Valentinian I as western Augustus in 375.
[116] A Roman general who previously had defeated the New Persians.
[117] A city in Thrace, not the Nicaea in Anatolia.
[118] A city in Thrace west of Constantinople.
[119] The "Protectors and Domestics" were elite palace guards attendant on the emperor.
[120] A barbarian people of the southern Russian steppes.

several other officers, who suggested that the reinforcement of the Gallic army would be likely to awe the fiery arrogance of the barbarians. The fatal obstinacy of the emperor, however, prevailed, fortified by the flattery of certain barbarian chieftains, who advised him to hasten with all speed so that Gratian might have no share in a victory that, as they fancied, already almost was gained.

And while all necessary preparations were being made for the battle, a priest of the Christian religion, as he called himself, having been sent by Fritigern[121] as his ambassador, came, with some colleagues of low rank, to the emperor's camp. Having been received with courtesy, he presented a letter from that chieftain, openly requesting that the emperor would grant to him and to his followers, who now were exiles from their native homes, from which they had been driven by the rapid invasions of savage nations,[122] Thrace,[123] with all its flocks and all its crops, for a habitation. And if Valens would consent to this, Fritigern would agree to a perpetual peace. In addition to this message, the same Christian, as one acquainted with his commander's secrets, and well trusted, produced other secret letters from his chieftain who, being full of craft and every resource of deceit, informed Valens, as one who was hereafter to be his friend and ally, that he had no other means to appease the ferocity of his countrymen, or to induce them to accept conditions advantageous to the Roman state, unless from time to time he showed them an army under arms close at hand, and by frightening them with the name of the emperor, recalled them from their mischievous eagerness for fighting. The ambassadors retired unsuccessful, having been looked on as suspicious characters by the emperor.

When the day broke that the annals mark as the fifth before the Ides of August,[124] the Roman standards were advanced with haste, the baggage having been placed close to the walls of Adrianople under a sufficient guard of soldiers of the legions. The treasures and the chief insignia of the emperor's rank were within the walls, with the Prefect and the principal members of the council.[125] Then, having traversed the broken ground that divided the two armies, as the burning day was progressing toward noon, at last, after marching eight miles, our men came in sight of the wagons of the enemy, which had been stated by the scouts to be all arranged in a circle. According to their custom, the barbarian host raised a fierce and hideous yell while the Roman generals marshaled their line of battle. The right wing of the cavalry was placed in front; the chief portion of the infantry was kept in reserve. But the left wing of the cavalry, of which a considerable number were still straggling on the road, were advancing with speed, although with great difficulty. While this wing was deploying, not as yet meeting with any obstacle, the barbarians being alarmed at the terrible clang of their arms and the threatening crash of their shields, because a large portion of their own army was still at a distance, under Alatheus and Saphrax,[126] and, although sent for, had not yet arrived, again sent ambassadors to ask for peace.

The emperor was offended at the lowness of their rank, and replied that if they wished to make a lasting treaty they must send him nobles of sufficient dignity. They designedly delayed, in order by the fallacious truce that subsisted during the negotiation to give time for their cavalry to return, whom they looked upon as close at hand, and for our soldiers, already suffering from the summer heat, to become parched and exhausted by the conflagration of the vast plain, for the enemy had, with this object, set fire to the crops by means of burning faggots and fuel. To this evil another was added, that both men and cattle were suffering from extreme hunger.

In the meantime Fritigern, being skilful in divining the future and fearing a doubtful struggle, on his own authority sent one of his men as a herald,

[121] One of the leaders of the Visigoths who had crossed the Danube.
[122] The Huns.
[123] A Balkan region south of the lower Danube River.
[124] 9 August.
[125] The most important officials of the imperial court traveled with the emperor.
[126] Regents for the boy Viderichus, chieftain of another band of Goths.

requesting that some nobles and picked men should at once be sent to him as hostages for his safety, whereas he himself would fearlessly bring us both military aid and supplies. The proposition of this formidable chief was received with praise and approbation, and the Tribune Equitius, a relation of Valens who was at that time Caretaker of the Palace, was appointed, with general consent, to go with all speed to the barbarians as a hostage. But he refused, because he had once been taken prisoner by the enemy, and had escaped from Dibaltum,[127] so that he feared their vengeful anger. Upon this Richomer voluntarily offered himself, and willingly undertook to go, thinking it a bold action, and one becoming a brave man; and so he set out, bearing vouchers of his rank and high birth. As he was on his way toward the enemy's camp, the accompanying archers and the Scutarii,[128] who on that occasion were under the command of Bacurius, a native of Iberia,[129] and of Cassio, yielded, while on their march, to an indiscreet impetuosity, and on approaching the enemy first attacked them rashly and then by a cowardly flight disgraced the beginning of the campaign. This ill-timed attack frustrated the willing services of Richomer, as he was not permitted to proceed. In the meantime the cavalry of the Goths had returned with Alatheus and Saphrax, and with them a battalion of Alans.[130] These, descending from the mountains like a thunderbolt, spread confusion and slaughter among all whom in their rapid charge they encountered.

And while arms and missiles of all kinds were meeting in fierce conflict and Bellona,[131] blowing her mournful trumpet, was raging more fiercely than usual to inflict disaster on the Romans, our men began to retreat. But presently, roused by the reproaches of their officers, they made a fresh stand, and the battle increased like a conflagration, terrifying our soldiers, numbers of whom were pierced by strokes from the javelins hurled at them and from arrows. Then the two lines of battle dashed against each other, like the beaks or rams of ships, and thrusting with all their might were tossed to and fro, like the waves of the sea. Our left wing had advanced actually up to the wagons, with the intent to push on still further if they were properly supported, but they were deserted by the rest of the cavalry and so pressed upon by the superior numbers of the enemy that they were overwhelmed and beaten down, like the ruin of a vast rampart. Presently, our infantry also was left unsupported and the different companies became so huddled together that a soldier could hardly draw his sword or withdraw his hand after he had once stretched it out. And by this time such clouds of dust arose that it was scarcely possible to see the sky, which resounded with horrible cries; and in consequence, the darts, which were bearing death on every side, reached their mark, and fell with deadly effect, because no one could see them beforehand so as to guard against them.

But when the barbarians, rushing on with their enormous host, beat down our horses and men and left no spot to which our ranks could fall back to deploy, while they were so closely packed that it was impossible to escape by forcing a way through them, our men at last began to despise death, and again took to their swords and slew all they encountered, while with mutual blows of battle-axes, helmets and breastplates were dashed in pieces. Then, you might see the barbarian towering in his fierceness, hissing or shouting, fall with his legs pierced through, or his right hand cut off, sword and all, or his side transfixed, and still, in the last gasp of life, casting round him defiant glances. The plain was covered with carcasses, strewing the mutual ruin of the combatants and the groans of the dying or of men fearfully wounded were intense, and caused great dismay all around.

[127] An ancient Roman military colony in modern Bulgaria on the Black Sea, site of a Roman defeat by the Visigoths in 376.

[128] Shield-bearing cavalry.

[129] Not Spanish Iberia but the Iberia north of Armenia between the Black and Caspian seas. The Christian Kingdom of Iberia was sometimes independent, sometimes a client state of Rome, and sometimes a vassal of the New Persians.

[130] Iranian steppe nomads living north of the Black Sea who often served in the Roman army.

[131] An ancient Italian war goddess.

Amid all this great tumult and confusion our infantry were exhausted by toil and danger, until at last they had neither strength left to fight nor spirits to plan anything. Their spears were broken by the frequent collisions, so that they were forced to content themselves with their drawn swords, which they thrust into the dense battalions of the enemy, disregarding their own safety and seeing that every possibility of escape was cut off from them. The ground, covered with streams of blood, made their feet slip, so that all that they endeavored to do was to sell their lives as dearly as possible, and with such vehemence did they resist their enemies who pressed on them, that some were even killed by their own weapons. At last one black pool of blood disfigured everything and wherever the eye turned, it could see nothing but piled-up heaps of dead and lifeless corpses trampled on without mercy.

The sun being now high in the heavens scorched the Romans, who were emaciated by hunger, worn out with toil, and scarcely able to support even the weight of their armor. At last our columns were entirely beaten back by the overpowering weight of the barbarians, and so they took to disorderly flight, which is the only resource in extremity, each man trying to save himself as well as he could. While they were all flying and scattering themselves over roads with which they were unacquainted, the emperor, bewildered with terrible fear, made his way over heaps of dead and fled to the battalions of the Lancearii and the Mattiarii,[132] who, until the superior numbers of the enemy became wholly irresistible, stood firm and immovable. As soon as he saw him, Trajan exclaimed that all hope was lost, unless the emperor, thus deserted by his guards, could be protected by the aid of his foreign allies.

When this exclamation was heard, a Count named Victor hastened to bring up with all speed the Batavians,[133] who were placed in the reserve and who ought to have been near at hand, to the emperor's assistance; but as none of them could be found, he too retreated, and in a similar manner Richomer and Saturninus[134] saved themselves from danger. So now, with rage flashing in their eyes, the barbarians pursued our men, who were in a state of torpor. Many were slain without knowing who smote them, some were overwhelmed by the mere weight of the crowd that pressed upon them, and some were slain by wounds inflicted by their own comrades. The barbarians spared neither those who yielded nor those who resisted. Besides these, many half slain lay blocking up the roads, unable to endure the torture of their wounds, and heaps of dead horses were piled up and filled the plain with their carcasses. At last a dark moonless night put an end to the irremediable disaster that cost the Roman state so dear.

Just when it first became dark, the emperor being among a crowd of common soldiers, as it was believed, for no one said either that he had seen him, or been near him, was mortally wounded with an arrow, and, very shortly after, died, although his body was never found. For as some of the enemy loitered for a long time about the field in order to plunder the dead, none of the defeated army or of the inhabitants ventured to go to them. A similar fate befell the Caesar Decius,[135] when fighting vigorously against the barbarians, for he was thrown by his horse falling, which he had been unable to hold, and was plunged into a swamp, out of which he could never emerge, nor could his body be found.

Others report that Valens did not die immediately, but that he was borne by a small body of picked soldiers and eunuchs to a cabin in the neighborhood, which was strongly built, with two stories; and that while these unskillful hands were tending his wounds, the cottage was surrounded by the enemy, although they did not know who was in it. Still, however, he was saved from the disgrace of being made a prisoner. For when his pursuers, while vainly

[132] Elite units of the Roman army.

[133] A Roman military unit named after peoples from the mouth of the Rhine River.

[134] Roman Master of Soldiers who eventually negotiated a treaty with the Visigoths in 382 and was named Consul for 383.

[135] Trajan Decius (249–251), killed by the Goths at the Battle of Abritus on the lower Danube, was the first Roman emperor to die in battle.

attempting to force the barred doors, were assailed with arrows from the roof, they, not to lose by so inconvenient a delay the opportunity of collecting plunder, gathered some faggots and stubble and setting fire to them, burnt down the building along with those who were in it. But one of the soldiers dropped from the windows, and, being taken prisoner by the barbarians, revealed to them what had taken place, which caused them great concern, because they looked upon themselves as defrauded of great glory in not having taken the ruler of the Roman state alive. This same young man afterward secretly returned to our people and gave this account of the affair. When Spain had been recovered after a similar disaster, we are told that one of the Scipios was lost in a fire, the tower in which he had taken refuge having been burnt.[136] At all events it is certain that neither Scipio nor Valens enjoyed that last honor of the dead, a regular funeral.

Many illustrious men fell in this disastrous defeat, and among them one of the most remarkable was Trajan, and another was Sebastian. There perished also thirty-five unassigned Tribunes, many unit commanders, and Valerianus and Equitius, one of whom was Master of the Horse and the other Caretaker of the Palace. Potentius, too, Tribune of the Promoti,[137] fell in the flower of his age, a man respected by all persons of virtue, and recommended by the merits of his father, Ursicinus,[138] who had formerly been Master of Soldiers, as well as by his own. Scarcely one-third of the whole army escaped.

Nor, except the Battle of Cannae,[139] is so destructive a slaughter recorded in our annals, although even in the times of their prosperity, the Romans have more than once had to deplore the uncertainty of war and have for a time succumbed to evil fortune. Such was the death of Valens, when he was about fifty years old and had reigned rather less than fourteen years.

[136] Gnaeus Scipio, the uncle of Scipio Africanus, killed in Spain in 211 BCE when, pursued by the Carthaginians, he took refuge in a tower and was burned to death.

[137] A cavalry unit.

[138] A high-ranking Roman general during the 350s, highly praised by Ammianus.

[139] In 216 BCE, when the Romans were defeated by Hannibal; see Reading 78.

115

THE SACK OF ROME BY THE VISIGOTHS (410 CE): OROSIUS, *HISTORY AGAINST THE PAGANS*, BOOK 7, CHAPTERS 38–40

An ivory diptych (a bifolded placque) portrays in the right panel the Master of Soldiers Stilicho, in military attire, and on the left his wife Serena and son Eucherius. The murder of Stilicho in 408 on the orders of the emperor Honorius (395–423) opened the way for the Sack of Rome by Alaric and the Visigoths in 410.

In the early years of the fifth century, barbarian groups made their way into the western empire. In 401, the Visigoths invaded Italy, and on the last day of 406, a barbarian horde crossed the frozen Rhine. For a time, the crafty western general Stilicho was able to keep the barbarians at bay, but after the emperor Honorius had Stilicho executed for treason in 408, the fall of the west began in earnest, punctuated by the Visigothic Sack of Rome in 410. Although the sack caused little or no actual architectural damage and was more akin to some rowdy soldiers getting out of hand, the psychological damage was immense. "Roma invicta," "Unconquered Rome," was no longer unconquered. Encouraged by bishop Augustine of Hippo, the Christian historiographer Orosius painted a rather biased picture of Rome's past military history, arguing that throughout its history, when the pagan gods still were worshipped, Rome had suffered military defeats, a point already acknowledged, however, by Ammianus at the end of Reading 114.

Source: Irving W. Raymond, trans., *Seven Books of History against the Pagans. The Apology of Paulus Orosius* (New York: Columbia University Press, 1936).

Meanwhile Count Stilicho,[140] who was sprung from the Vandals, that unwarlike, greedy, treacherous, and crafty people, thought it a small matter that he held the rule under the emperor, and, as was reported by many, was attempting in some manner to place upon the throne his own son Eucherius, who had been planning the persecution of the Christians ever since he was a boy and a private citizen. Hence, when Alaric and the whole Gothic nation begged humbly and straightforwardly for peace on very favorable terms and also for some place to settle, Stilicho supported them by a secret alliance, but in the name of the state refused them the opportunity of either making war or peace, reserving them to wear down and to intimidate the state. Moreover, other nations irresistible in numbers and might who are now oppressing the provinces of Gaul and Spain, namely, the Alans, Suevi, and Vandals, as well as the Burgundians,[141] were induced by Stilicho to take arms on their own initiative and were aroused when once their fear of Rome was removed. Stilicho's plan was to batter the Rhine frontier and strike against the Two Gauls.[142] This wretched man hoped that in this dangerous situation he could thereby wrest the imperial dignity from his son-in-law[143] and give it to his son, and that it would be as easy to repress the barbarian nations as it was to arouse them.

When the character of these crimes was openly revealed to the emperor Honorius and to the Roman army, the soldiers very properly mutinied and killed Stilicho, who, in order to clothe one boy with the royal purple had imperiled the blood of the whole human race. Eucherius also was slain, who for the sake of gaining the favor of the pagans had threatened that he would celebrate the beginning of his reign by the restoration of the temples and by the overthrow of the churches. Several accomplices also were punished for their wicked plots. Thus the churches of Christ and the devout emperor were freed as well as avenged with very little trouble and with the punishment of but a few persons.

After this great increase of blasphemies without any evidence of repentance, the final, long-impending doom overtook the City.[144] Alaric appeared before trembling Rome, laid siege, spread confusion, and broke into the City. He first, however, gave orders that all those who had taken refuge in sacred places, especially in the basilicas of the holy Apostles Peter and Paul, should be permitted to remain inviolate and unmolested. He allowed his men to devote themselves to plunder as much as they wished, but he gave orders that they should refrain from bloodshed. A further proof that the storming of the City was due to the wrath of God rather than to the bravery of the enemy is shown by the fact that the blessed Innocent, the bishop of Rome, who at that time was at Ravenna

[140] Stilicho was the son of a Roman mother and a Roman general of Vandal origin; although in the modern literature he often is portrayed as a barbarian, he was thoroughly Roman.

[141] All of whom crossed the frozen Rhine River into Gaul on the last day of the year 406.

[142] The two imperial dioceses of Gaul, "Viennensis" and "Gallia."

[143] The emperor Honorius (395–423), who married, in succession, Stilicho's two daughters Maria and Thermantia. Stilicho himself was married to Honorius's cousin Serena.

[144] Rome was referred to simply as "the City."

[145] The bishop of Rome Innocent (401–417) fled Rome and took refuge with the emperor Honorius in Ravenna before the sack, an act that, despite Orosius's spin, rather damaged his credibility.

through the hidden providence of God,[145] even as Lot the Just[146] was withdrawn from the Sodomites, did not witness the destruction of the sinful populace.

While the barbarians were roaming through the City, one of the Goths, a powerful man and a Christian, chanced to find in a church building a virgin advanced in years who had dedicated herself to God. When he respectfully asked her for gold and silver, she declared with the firmness of her faith that she had a large amount in her possession and that she would bring it forth at once. She did so. Observing that the barbarian was astonished at the size, weight, and beauty of the riches displayed, even though he did not know the nature of the vessels, the virgin of Christ then said to him: "These are the sacred vessels of the Apostle Peter. Presume, if you dare! You will have to answer for the deed. As for me, because I cannot protect them, I dare not keep them."

The barbarian, stirred to religious awe through the fear of God and by the virgin's faith, sent word of the incident to Alaric. He ordered that all the vessels, just as they were, should be brought back immediately to the basilica of the Apostle, and that the virgin also, together with all Christians who might join the procession, should be conducted thither under escort. The building, it is said, was at a considerable distance from the sacred places, with half the city lying between. Consequently the gold and silver vessels were distributed, each to a different person. They were carried high above the head in plain sight, to the wonder of all beholders. The pious procession was guarded by a double line of drawn swords; Romans and barbarians in concert raised a hymn to God in public. In the sacking of the City the trumpet of salvation sounded far and wide and smote the ears of all with its invitation, even those lying in hiding. From every quarter the vessels of Christ mingled with the vessels of Peter, and many pagans even joined the Christians in making profession, although not in true faith. In this way they escaped, but only for a time, that their confusion might afterward be the greater.

The more densely the Roman refugees flocked together, the more eagerly their barbarian protectors surrounded them. O sacred and inscrutable discernment of the divine judgment! O glorious trumpet of Christian warfare that, inviting by its sweet notes all without distinction to life, leaves those who, for want of obedience, cannot be roused to salvation, to meet their death for want of excuse!

The third day after they had entered the City, the barbarians departed of their own accord. They had, it is true, burned a certain number of buildings, but even this fire was not so great as that which had been caused by accident in the seven hundredth year of Rome. Indeed, if I review the conflagration produced during the spectacles of Nero, her own emperor, this later fire, brought on by the anger of the conqueror, will surely bear no comparison with the former, which was kindled by the wantonness of the prince. Nor do I need in a comparison of this sort to mention the Gauls, who, after burning and sacking the City, camped upon her ashes for almost an entire year.[147] Moreover, to remove all doubt that the enemy were permitted to act in this manner in order to chastise the proud, wanton, and blasphemous City, it may be pointed out that her most magnificent sites, which the Goths were unable to set on fire, were destroyed at this time by lightning.[148]

It was in the one thousand one hundred and sixty-fourth year of the City that Alaric stormed Rome. Although the memory of the event is still fresh, anyone who saw the numbers of the Romans themselves and listened to their talk would think that "nothing had happened," as they themselves admit, unless perhaps he were to notice some charred ruins still remaining. When the City was stormed, Placidia,[149] the

[146] In the Bible, Lot was given by God the opportunity to flee with his family from the city of Sodom before it was destroyed.

[147] The Sack of Rome by the Gauls in 390 BCE, in this interpretation the last time that Rome had been captured by a foreign enemy; see Reading 77.

[148] This is the only evidence for lightning strikes during this sack.

[149] Galla Placidia, mother of the emperor Valentinian III (425–455) and virtual ruler of the western empire during much of his reign.

daughter of the princely Theodosius[150] and sister of the emperors Arcadius and Honorius, was captured and taken to wife by Alaric's kinsman,[151] as if she had been a hostage given by Rome as a special pledge, according to divine decree. Thus, through her alliance with the powerful barbarian king, Placidia did much to benefit the state.

Meanwhile, as I have said, the Alans, Suevi, and Vandals, as well as many others with them, overwhelmed the Franks, crossed the Rhine, invaded Gaul, and advanced in their onward rush as far as the Pyrenees. Checked for the time being by this barrier, they poured back over the neighboring provinces.[152]

[150] The emperor Theodosius I (379–395), who was succeeded by his sons Arcadius (395–408) in the eastern empire and Honorius in the west.

[151] In 414, Galla Placidia married the Gothic king Athaulf (410–415); their son Theodosius died in infancy.

[152] Actually, theVandals and Alans crossed into Spain in 409 CE, the year before the Sack of Rome, when the Pyrenees passes were left undefended.

116

THE SACK OF ROME BY THE VISIGOTHS IN GOD'S PLAN (410 CE): AUGUSTINE, *CITY OF GOD*, BOOK 1

The popular perception of the Sack of Rome by the Visigoths in 410, as portrayed in this 1962 depiction in *National Geographic*, is one of hulking, savage barbarians looting property, burning buildings, and harassing respectable Roman matrons. The reality, as portrayed by Orosius above and Augustine below, was rather different.

After the sack of Rome in 410, dedicated pagans argued that Rome was suffering misfortunes because of the abandonment of the old Roman gods who had made Rome great. These arguments were very convincing, so in response, bishop Augustine of Hippo in North Africa wrote his massive work, *On the City of God*, in which he made the counterargument that everything that happened on earth was part of God's plan and that people should be more concerned not with the earthly city but with the heavenly city. He proposed that the barbarian sack of Rome in fact had been quite genteel, as far as sacks went, as a result of God's influence because any show of mercy or clemency during wartime must have come from God. In the course of discussing the question of why the good and the wicked suffered equally, Augustine argued that the misfortunes that he acknowledged were besetting the Roman world were the fault of sinful Christians, not only those who were guilty of gross wickedness but also those who were guilty of petty sins. Thus, Augustine proposed that Christian virgins deserved blame for their own violation at the hands of barbarians because they supposedly indulged in secret pride about their chastity.

Source: Marcus Dods, trans., *The Works of Augustine, Bishop of Hippo. The City of God* (Edinburgh: Clark, 1871).

PREFACE

The glorious City of God is my theme in this work, which you, my dearest son Marcellinus,[153] suggested, and which is due to you by my promise. I have undertaken its defense against those who prefer their own gods to the founder of this city, a city surpassingly glorious, whether we view it as it still lives by faith in this fleeting course of time, and sojourns as a stranger in the midst of the ungodly, or as it shall dwell in the fixed stability of its eternal seat, which it now with patience waits for. A great work this, and an arduous one, but God is my helper. For I am aware of what ability is requisite to persuade the proud how great is the virtue of humility, which raises us, not by a quite human arrogance but by a divine grace above all earthly dignities that totter on this shifting scene. For the king and founder of this city of which we speak has in scripture uttered to his people a dictum of the divine law in these words, "God resisteth the proud, but giveth grace unto the humble."[154] But this, which is God's prerogative, the inflated ambition of a proud spirit also affects, and dearly loves that this be numbered among its attributes, to "show pity to the humbled soul, and crush the sons of pride."[155] And therefore, as the plan of this work we have undertaken requires, and as occasion offers, we must speak also of the earthly city, which, although it be mistress of the nations, is itself ruled by its lust of rule.

CHAPTER 1: OF THE ADVERSARIES OF THE NAME OF CHRIST, WHOM THE BARBARIANS FOR CHRIST'S SAKE SPARED WHEN THEY STORMED THE CITY

For to this earthly city belong the enemies against whom I have to defend the City of God. Many of them, indeed, being reclaimed from their ungodly error have become sufficiently creditable citizens of this city,[156] but many are so inflamed with hatred

[153] An imperial Notary (all-purpose functionary) who oversaw the Council of Carthage in 411, which condemned the Donatists, a schismatic Christian sect that had originated during the Great Persecution of Diocletian.
[154] From the book of James 4:6 in the New Testament.

[155] A quotation from Vergil's *Aeneid*, where, in the underworld, Aeneas's father Anchises advises the Romans to "spare the vanquished and beat down the proud"; see Reading 88.
[156] A reference to barbarian Christians, perhaps even to those who espoused the so-called "Arian" creed.

against it and are so ungrateful to its redeemer for his signal benefits as to forget that they would now be unable to utter a single word to its prejudice had they not found in its sacred places, as they fled from the enemy's steel, that life in which they now boast themselves.[157] Are not those very Romans, who were spared by the barbarians through their respect for Christ, become enemies to the name of Christ? The reliquaries of the martyrs and the churches of the apostles bear witness to this, for in the sack of the city they were open sanctuary for all who fled to them, whether Christian or pagan. To their very threshold the bloodthirsty enemy raged; there his murderous fury owned a limit. Thither did such of the enemy as had any pity convey those to whom they had given quarter, lest any less mercifully disposed might fall upon them. And, indeed, when even those murderers who everywhere else showed themselves pitiless came to those spots where that was forbidden which the license of war permitted in every other place, their furious rage for slaughter was bridled and their eagerness to take prisoners[158] was quenched.

Thus escaped multitudes who now reproach the Christian religion, and impute to Christ the ills that have befallen their city. But the preservation of their own life, a boon that they owe to the respect entertained for Christ by the barbarians, they attribute not to our Christ but to their own good luck. They ought rather, had they any right perceptions, to attribute the severities and hardships inflicted by their enemies to the divine providence that is accustomed to reform the depraved manners of men by chastisement and that exercises with similar afflictions the righteous and praiseworthy, either translating them, when they have passed through the trial, to a better world, or detaining them still on earth for other purposes. And they ought to attribute it to the spirit of these Christian times, that, contrary to the custom of war, these bloodthirsty barbarians spared them, and spared them for Christ's sake, whether this mercy actually was shown in random places or was manifested in those places specially dedicated to Christ's name, of which the very largest were selected as sanctuaries, so that full scope thus might be given to the expansive compassion that desired that a large multitude might find shelter there. Therefore they ought to give God thanks and with sincere confession flee for refuge to his name, so that they may escape the punishment of eternal fire, they who with lying lips took upon them this name so that they might escape the punishment of present destruction. For of those whom you see insolently and shamelessly insulting the servants of Christ, there are numbers who would not have escaped that destruction and slaughter had they not pretended that they themselves were Christ's servants. Yet now, in ungrateful pride and most impious madness, and at the risk of being punished in everlasting darkness, they perversely oppose that name under which they fraudulently protected themselves for the sake of enjoying the light of this brief life.

CHAPTER 4: OF THE CHURCHES OF THE APOSTLES THAT PROTECTED FROM THE BARBARIANS ALL WHO FLED TO THEM

Troy itself, the mother of the Roman people, was not able to protect its own citizens in the sacred places of their gods from the fire and sword of the Greeks, although the Greeks worshipped the same gods.[159] The place consecrated to a great goddess was chosen not so that no one might be led out from it as a captive but so that all the captives might be detained in it.[160] Compare now this "asylum," the asylum not of an ordinary god, not of one of the rank and file of gods, but of Jupiter's own sister and wife, the queen of all the gods, with the churches built in memory of the apostles. Into it were collected the spoils rescued from the blazing temples and snatched from the gods, not that

[157]Pagans who took refuge in Christian churches in order to be secure from barbarians.

[158]Captives, who could be held for ransom or sold as slaves, were another form of loot.

[159]See Readings 58 and 88.

[160]In Vergil's *Aeneid*, when Aeneas was looking for his wife Creusa, he saw Trojan captives being kept in the temple of Juno (Greek Hera).

they might be restored to the vanquished but to be divided among the victors, whereas into the churches was carried back, with the most religious observance and respect, everything that belonged to them, even though found elsewhere. There liberty was lost; here preserved. There bondage was strict; here it was strictly excluded. Into that temple men were driven to become the chattels of their enemies; into these churches people were led by their relenting foes so that they might be at liberty. In sum, the "gentle" Greeks appropriated that temple of Juno to the purposes of their own avarice and pride, whereas these churches of Christ were chosen even by the savage barbarians as the fit scenes for humility and mercy.

CHAPTER 7: THAT THE CRUELTIES THAT OCCURRED IN THE SACK OF ROME WERE IN ACCORDANCE WITH THE CUSTOM OF WAR, WHEREAS THE ACTS OF CLEMENCY RESULTED FROM THE INFLUENCE OF CHRIST'S NAME

All the despoiling that Rome was exposed to in the recent calamity, all the slaughter, plundering, burning, and misery, was the result of the custom of war. But what was novel was that savage barbarians showed themselves in so gentle a guise, that the largest churches were chosen and set apart for the purpose of being filled with the people to whom quarter was given, and that in them none were slain, from them none forcibly dragged. That into them many were led by their relenting enemies to be set at liberty, and that from them none were led into slavery by merciless foes. Whoever does not see that this is to be attributed to the name of Christ, and to the Christian temper, is blind. Whoever sees this, and gives no praise, is ungrateful. Whoever hinders anyone from praising it is mad. Far be it from any prudent man to impute this clemency to the barbarians. Their fierce and bloody minds were awed and bridled and marvelously tempered by him who so long before said by his prophet, "I will visit their transgression with the rod, and their iniquities with stripes; nevertheless my loving-kindness will I not utterly take from them."[161]

CHAPTER 8: OF THE ADVANTAGES AND DISADVANTAGES THAT OFTEN INDISCRIMINATELY ACCRUE TO GOOD AND WICKED MEN

As for the good things of this life, and its ills, God has willed that these should be common to both, that we might not too eagerly covet the things that wicked men are seen equally to enjoy, nor shrink with an unseemly fear from the ills that even good men often suffer. If every sin were now visited with manifest punishment, nothing would seem to be reserved for the final judgment; on the other hand, if no sin received a plainly divine punishment, it would be concluded that there is no divine providence at all. And so of the good things of this life. If God did not by a very visible liberality confer these on some of those persons who ask for them, we should say that these good things were not at his disposal. And if he gave them to all who sought them, we should suppose that such were the only rewards of his service, and such a service would make us not godly, but greedy rather, and covetous. Wherefore, although good and bad people suffer alike, we must not suppose that there is no difference among the people themselves because there is no difference in what they both suffer. And thus it is that in the same affliction the wicked detest God and blaspheme, whereas the good pray and praise. So material a difference does it make, not what ills are suffered, but what kind of person suffers them.

CHAPTER 9: OF THE REASONS FOR ADMINISTERING CORRECTION TO BAD AND GOOD TOGETHER

What, then, have the Christians suffered in that calamitous period that would not profit every one who

[161] Psalms 89:32–33.

duly and faithfully considered the following circumstances? First of all, they must humbly consider those very sins that have provoked God to fill the world with such terrible disasters, for although they be far from the excesses of wicked, immoral, and ungodly persons, yet they do not judge themselves so clean removed from all faults as to be too good to suffer for these even temporal ills. For all persons, however laudably they live, yet yield in some points to the lust of the flesh. Even if they do not fall into gross enormity of wickedness, and abandoned viciousness, and abominable profanity, yet they slip into some sins, either rarely or so much the more frequently as the sins seem of less account. But not to mention this, where can we readily find anyone who holds in fit and just estimation those persons on account of whose revolting pride, luxury, and avarice, and cursed iniquities and impiety, God now smites the earth as his predictions threatened? Where is the person who deals with them in the manner in which it becomes us to deal with them? For often we wickedly blind ourselves to opportunities for teaching and admonishing them, sometimes even for reprimanding and chiding them, either because we shrink from the labor or are ashamed to offend them, or because we fear to lose good friendships, lest this should stand in the way of our advancement, or injure us in some worldly matter, which either our covetous disposition desires to obtain, or our weakness shrinks from losing. So that, although the conduct of wicked men is distasteful to the good, and therefore they do not fall with them into that damnation which in the next life awaits such persons, yet, because they spare their damnable sins through fear, therefore, even though their own sins be slight and venial, they are justly whipped with the wicked in this world, although in eternity they quite escape punishment. Justly, when God afflicts them in common with the wicked, do they find this life bitter, through love of whose sweetness they declined to be bitter toward these sinners.

CHAPTER 28: BY WHAT JUDGMENT OF GOD THE ENEMY WAS PERMITTED TO INDULGE HIS LUST ON THE BODIES OF CONTINENT CHRISTIANS

Even faithful women, I say, must not complain that permission was given to the barbarians so grossly to outrage them, nor must they allow themselves to believe that God overlooked their character when he permitted acts that no one with impunity commits. For some most flagrant and wicked desires are allowed free play at present by the secret judgment of God, and are reserved to the public and final judgment. Moreover, it is possible that those Christian women, who are unconscious of any undue pride on account of their virtuous chastity, whereby they sinlessly suffered the violence of their captors, had yet some lurking infirmity that might have betrayed them into a proud and contemptuous bearing, had they not been subjected to the humiliation that befell them in the taking of the city. As, therefore, some men were removed by death, so that no wickedness might change their disposition, so these women were outraged lest prosperity should corrupt their modesty. Neither those women then, who were already puffed up by the circumstance that they were still virgins, nor those who might have been so puffed up had they not been exposed to the violence of the enemy, lost their chastity, but rather gained humility; the former were saved from pride already cherished, the latter from pride that would shortly have grown upon them.

117

THE SACK OF ROME BY THE VANDALS (455 CE): PROCOPIUS, *HISTORY OF THE WARS*, BOOK 3, CHAPTER 5

A gold solidus of the short-lived emperor Petronius Maximus (455), who had the misfortune to be emperor during the Vandal Sack of Rome in 455. The obverse legend reads "Our Lord Petronius Maximus Dutiful and Fortunate Augustus," whereas the reverse reads "Victory of the Emperors" and shows Maximus holding a long cross in one hand and the goddess Victory in the other and trampling the serpent of heresy. The letters "RM" denote the Rome mint, and "COMOB" is an abbreviation for the "Count of Pure Gold," who was responsible for the gold content in the coin.

As the fifth century progressed, barbarian kingdoms coalesced in the western Roman Empire: the Visigoths in Aquitania in Gaul, the Vandals in North Africa, and the Burgundians in central Gaul. It appeared that barbarians were taking over. Paradoxically, however, this barbarian expansion was not accomplished by military means. There were only a few marquee battles, and most of those, such as the Battle of the Mauriac Plain in 451 against the Huns, were won by the Romans. But the western empire was clearly weakened, as seen in the much less well-attested sack of Rome by the Vandals in 455 CE, which demonstrated that the Roman government no longer could protect even the city of Rome. This sack lasted some eighteen days and was much more lengthy and more thorough than the genteel sack by the Visigoths in 410, which went on for only three days. By 455 it was clear that the western Roman Empire was failing fast, not to barbarian invasion but because of its own weaknesses. One more sack of the venerable city simply did not have the same shock-and-awe factor that it had forty-five years earlier. The account of the sack given nearly a century later by the Byzantine historian Procopius begins with a typical attempt to blame it on personal animus, the result of the lust of Valentinian III for the virtuous wife of the senator Petronius Maximus, in much the same way that the creation of the Roman Republic resulted from the lust of Sextus Tarquin for the virtuous Lucretia (Reading 75).

Source: H. B. Dewing, trans., *Procopius. History of the Wars, Books III and IV* (Cambridge, MA: Harvard University Press, 1916), 57–49.

And I shall now relate in what manner Valentinian died. There was a certain Maximus,[162] a Roman senator, of the house of that Maximus,[163] who, while usurping the imperial power, was overthrown by the elder Theodosius and put to death, and on whose account also the Romans celebrate the annual festival named from the defeat of Maximus. This younger Maximus was married to a woman discreet in her ways and exceedingly famous for her beauty. For this reason a desire came over Valentinian to have her to wife. And because it was impossible, much as he wished it, to meet her, he plotted an unholy deed and carried it to fulfillment. For he summoned Maximus to the palace and sat down with him to a game of dice, and a certain sum was set as a penalty for the loser. The emperor won in this game, and receiving Maximus' ring as a pledge for the agreed amount. He sent it to Maximus' house, instructing the messenger to tell the wife of Maximus that her husband bade her come as quickly as possible to the palace to salute the queen Eudoxia.[164] And she, judging by the ring that the message was from Maximus, entered her litter and was conveyed to the emperor's court. She was received by those who had been assigned this service by the emperor and led into a certain room far removed from the women's apartments, where Valentinian met her and violated her.[165] She, after this outrage, went to her husband's house weeping and feeling the deepest possible grief because of her misfortune, and she cast many curses upon Maximus as having provided the cause for what had been done. Maximus, accordingly, became exceedingly aggrieved at what had come to pass and straightway entered into a conspiracy against the emperor.

Maximus slew the emperor[166] with no trouble and secured the tyranny, and he married Eudoxia against

[162] Petronius Maximus, a powerful Roman senator who was twice Consul and became emperor for a few months in 455 after the murder of Valentinian III.

[163] Magnus Maximus, commander in Britain who seized the throne in 383 and was defeated and executed by Theodosius I (379–395) in 388.

[164] Licinia Eudoxia, the daughter of the eastern emperor Theodosius II (402–450), who had married the young Valentinian III in 437.

[165] This entire tale has striking parallels with the story of the Violation of Lucretia in 509 CE, which led to a conspiracy against the Etruscan kings of Rome and the creation of the Roman Republic (see Reading 75).

[166] Valentinian III actually was murdered in 455 by two comrades of the Patrician and Master of Soldiers Flavius Aëtius, whom Valentinian had murdered the year before.

her will. For the wife to whom he had been wedded had died not long before. And on one occasion in private he made the statement to Eudoxia that it was all for the sake of her love that he had carried out all that he had done. And because she felt a repulsion for Maximus even before that time, and had been desirous of exacting vengeance from him for the wrong done Valentinian, his words made her swell with rage still more against him, and led her on to carry out her plot, because she had heard Maximus say that on account of her the misfortune had befallen her husband. And as soon as day came, she sent to Carthage entreating Geiseric to avenge Valentinian,[167] who had been destroyed by an unholy man, in a manner unworthy both of himself and of his imperial station, and to deliver her, because she was suffering unholy treatment at the hand of the tyrant. And she impressed it upon Geiseric that, because he was a friend and ally and so great a calamity had befallen the imperial house, it was not a holy thing to fail to become an avenger. For from Byzantium she thought no vengeance would come, because Theodosius[168] already had departed from the world and Marcian[169] had taken over the empire.

And Geiseric, for no other reason than that he suspected that much money would come to him, set sail for Italy with a great fleet. And going up to Rome, because no one stood in his way, he took possession of the palace. Now while Maximus was trying to flee, the Romans threw stones at him and killed him, and they cut off his head and each of his other members and divided them among themselves. But Geiseric took Eudoxia captive, together with Eudocia and Placidia, the children of herself and Valentinian, and placing an exceedingly great amount of gold and other imperial treasure in his ships sailed to Carthage, having spared neither bronze nor anything else whatsoever in the palace. He plundered also the temple of Jupiter Capitolinus and tore off half of the roof.[170] Now this roof was of bronze of the finest quality, and because gold was laid over it exceedingly thick, it shone as a magnificent and wonderful spectacle. But of the ships with Geiseric, one, which was bearing the statues, was lost,[171] they say, but with all the others the Vandals reached port in the harbor of Carthage. Geiseric then married Eudocia to Huneric,[172] the elder of his sons, but the other of the two women, being the wife of Olybrius,[173] a most distinguished man in the Roman Senate, he sent to Byzantium[174] together with her mother, Eudoxia, at the request of the emperor.[175] Now the power of the east had by now fallen to Leo, because Marcian had already passed from the world.

[167] In the same manner that Justa Grata Honoria, the sister of the emperor Valentinian III, was said to have sent for Attila the Hun in 451.

[168] Eudoxia's father, the eastern emperor Theodosius II (402–450).

[169] The eastern emperor Marcian (450–457), the successor of Theodosius II.

[170] The temple of Jupiter on the top of the Capitoline Hill.

[171] This ship also was said by some to have carried the temple treasures taken when the Jewish Temple in Jerusalem was sacked by Titus in 70 CE.

[172] King of the Vandals, 477–484.

[173] Olybrius later became a short-lived emperor in the year 472.

[174] That is, Constantinople.

[175] The emperor Leo I (457–474).

118

THE LAST EMPEROR IN ROME (476 CE)

A gold solidus of Romulus struck at Rome in 475 or 476. The obverse legend reads "Romulus Augustus, Dutiful and Happy Emperor." The reverse depicts an angel (or the goddess Victory) holding a long cross with the legend "Victory of the Emperors." The letters "R M" indicate that the coin was minted at Rome, and the abbreviation "COMOB" refers to the "Count of Pure Gold," who attested to the coin's purity.

In 475, the western emperor Julius Nepos (474–480) was forced into exile in Dalmatia on the Greek Adriatic coast by his Master of Soldiers Orestes, formerly secretary of Attila the Hun. Even though Nepos continued to be recognized as western Roman emperor by the eastern emperor Zeno (474–491), Orestes then had his son Romulus, perhaps fourteen years old, named as western emperor, albeit a usurper. In 476, just a year later, young Romulus was forced into retirement by the barbarian Master of Soldier Odovacar, who, rather than setting up another emperor or declaring allegiance to Nepos, had Romulus announce to the eastern emperor Zeno that the west no longer needed its own emperor and that Odovacar would rule as "King of Italy" in Zeno's name. Although Romulus has gone down in history as the last western Roman emperor—historians, beginning with Count Marcellinus in the mid-sixth century, just could not pass up the opportunity to have Rome begin and end with someone named Romulus—Nepos remained the last legal emperor of the western empire until his death in 480. Meanwhile, the story of the rise and fall of little Romulus and even of the final extinction of the western Roman Empire passed with barely a mention in the ancient sources and must be pieced together from stray bits and snippets of information.

Source: Ralph W. Mathisen, "Romulus Augustulus (475–476)," *De imperatoribus Romanis. An Online Encyclopedia of Roman Emperors.*

(1) "And another emperor, Nepos,[176] upon taking over the empire and living to enjoy it only a few days, died of disease, and Glycerius[177] after him entered into this office and suffered a similar fate. And after him Augustulus[178] assumed the imperial power. There were, moreover, still other emperors in the west before this time, but although I know their names well, I shall make no mention of them whatsoever. For it so fell out that they lived only a short time after attaining the office and as a result of this accomplished nothing worthy of mention."[179] (Procopius, *Vandal War* 7.15–17: H. B. Dewing, trans., *Procopius. History of the Wars, Books III and IV* [Cambridge, MA: Harvard University Press, 1916], 69.)

(2) "Orestes,[180] having taken charge of the army and having departed from Rome against the enemies, arrived at Ravenna,[181] and remaining there he made his son Augustulus emperor. When he learned this, Nepos fled to Dalmatia"[182] (Jordanes, *Gothic History* 241).

[176] The legal western Roman emperor from 474 until 480 CE; he had been appointed western emperor by the eastern emperor Leo.

[177] Procopius has confused Nepos with Olybrius; the emperor who actually ruled a few days and died of disease was Olybrius (472); he was succeeded by Glycerius (473–474), who in turn was succeeded by Nepos.

[178] That is, Romulus (475–476), who followed Nepos.

[179] A sad epitaph for the last emperors of the western Roman Empire.

[180] The Patrician and Master of Soldiers, the highest-ranking western Roman general; he previously had been the secretary of Attila the Hun.

[181] The imperial capital on the coast of the Adriatic Sea in northeastern Italy.

(3) "Soon Nepos arrived at Ravenna, pursued by the Patrician Orestes and his army. Fearing the arrival of Orestes, Nepos boarded a ship and fled to Salona"[183] (*Anonymous Valesianus* 7.36, year 474).

(4) "While Nepos was in the city,[184] the Patrician Orestes was sent against him with the main force of the army. But because Nepos dared not undertake the business of resisting in such desperate conditions, he fled to Dalmatia in his ships. When Nepos had fled Italy and departed from the city, Orestes assumed the primacy and all the authority for himself and made his son Augustulus emperor at Ravenna" (*Auctuarii Hauniensis ordo prior*, year 475).

(5) "After Augustulus had been established as emperor at Ravenna by his father Orestes, not long afterward Odovacar, King of the Turcilingi,[185] who had with him the Scirians, Heruls,[186] and auxiliaries from diverse peoples, occupied Italy and, after killing Orestes, deposed his son Augustulus from the rule and condemned him to exile in the Castle of Lucullus[187] in Campania" (Jordanes, *Gothic History* 242).

(6) "Odovacar, King of the Goths, occupied Rome. Odovacar immediately killed Orestes. Odovacar condemned Augustulus, the son of Orestes, to exile in the Castle of Lucullus in Campania" (Count Marcellinus, *Chronicle*, year 476).

[182] Just across the Adriatic Sea on the western coast of Greece.

[183] A city in Dalmatia.

[184] That is, Ravenna.

[185] A poorly known barbarian people who might have been part of the horde of Attila the Hun.

[186] Peoples who had been part of the horde of Attila the Hun.

[187] Sometimes identified as the estate of the Roman Republican general Lucullus.

(7) "Entering Ravenna, Odovacar deposed Augustulus from the rule, and taking pity on his youth he granted him his life, and because he was comely he even granted to him an income of six thousand solidi and sent him to Campania to live freely with his relatives" (*Anonymous Valesianus* 8.38).

(8) "In this year, Orestes and his brother Paulus were killed by Odovacar, and Odovacar assumed the title of King, although he made use of neither the purple nor the imperial regalia" (Cassiodorus, *Chronicle*, year 476, no. 1303).

(9) "When Augustus,[188] the son of Orestes, heard that Zeno, having expelled Basiliscus,[189] had again gained the kingship of the east, he caused the Senate to send an embassy to tell Zeno that they had no need of a separate empire but that a single common emperor would be sufficient for both territories. And also to say that Odovacar had been chosen by the Senate as a suitable man to safeguard their affairs because he had political understanding along with military skill. They asked Zeno to award Odovacar the patrician honor and grant him the government of the Italies. The men from the Senate in Rome reached Byzantium carrying these messages. On the same day messengers from Nepos also came to congratulate Zeno on the recent events concerning this restoration, and at the same time to ask him zealously to help Nepos, a man who had suffered equal misfortunes, in the recovery of his empire. They asked that he grant money and an army for this purpose and that he co-operate in his restoration in any other ways that might be necessary. Nepos had sent the men to say these things. Zeno gave the following answer to those arrivals and to the men from the Senate: the western Romans had received two men from the eastern Empire and had driven one out, Nepos, and killed the other, Anthemius.[190] Now, he said, they knew what ought to be done. While their emperor was still alive they should hold no other thought than to receive him back on his return. To the barbarians he replied that it would be well if Odovacar were to receive the patrician rank from the emperor Nepos and that he himself would grant it unless Nepos granted it first. He commended him in that he had displayed this initial instance of guarding good order, suitable to the Romans, and trusted for this reason that, if he truly wished to act with justice, he would quickly receive back the emperor[191] who had given him his position of honor. He sent a royal letter about what he desired to Odovacar and in this letter named him a Patrician. Zeno gave this help to Nepos, pitying his sufferings because of his own, and holding to the principle that the common lot of fortune is to grieve with the unfortunate.[192] At the same time Verina[193] also joined in urging this, giving a helping hand to the wife of Nepos, her relative" (Malchus, *Chronicle*, fragment 10: Gordon trans., *Age of Attila*, 127–128).

(10) "The western empire of the Roman people, which first began in the seven hundred and ninth year after the founding of the City with Octavian Augustus, the first of the emperors, perished with this Augustulus, in the five-hundred and twenty-second year of the reign of Augustus' successor emperors. From this point on Gothic kings held power in Rome."[194] (Count Marcellinus, *Chronicle*, year 476).

[188] Young Romulus.

[189] The brother of Verina, the wife of Zeno's predecessor Leo; Basiliscus had rebelled against Zeno in 475.

[190] Named western Roman emperor in 467 by the eastern emperor Leo; he was killed in 472 during a civil war with the barbarian Patrician and Master of Soldiers Ricimer.

[191] Nepos.

[192] Zeno had been expelled by Basiliscus in the same year as Julius Nepos, although he regained his throne the next year.

[193] The wife of Zeno's predecessor as eastern emperor Leo (457–474) and mother of Zeno's wife Ariadne.

[194] In was not until 489, in fact, that the Ostrogoths under Theoderic the Great entered Italy; in 493 he defeated and killed Odovacar.

CHAPTER 15

The End of Antiquity (476–640)

By the end of the fifth century, the Roman world looked very different from the way it had appeared at the time of Augustus. The hard-won political unity of the Mediterranean world had been fractured. The western part of the empire had been partitioned among several barbarian peoples. But in the east, the Roman Empire, now known to modern historians as the Byzantine Empire, continued to survive and even flourish, adapting to changing times just as it had done in the past. During the seventh century, the ancient world was even more dramatically changed with the appearance of a new religion, Islam, in Arabia. The Persian Empire disappeared and Muslims soon occupied much of the ancient world. The ancient world was drawing to a close, soon to be replaced by three separate political, religious, and cultural worlds of the Middle Ages.

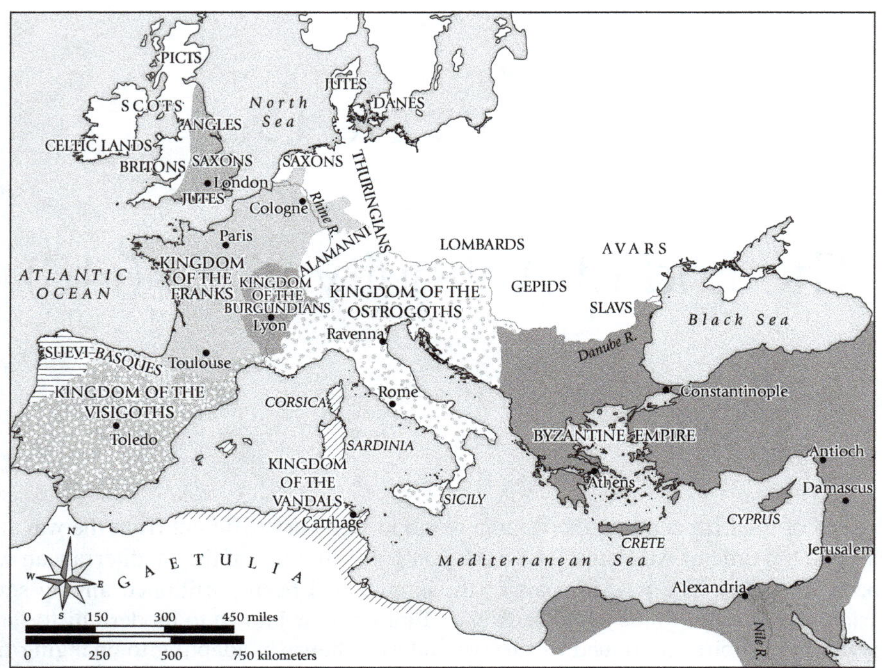

Map 15 Barbarian Settlements as of 526 CE

119

A VISIGOTHIC KING AND HIS COURT (CA. 455/465 CE): SIDONIUS APOLLINARIS, *LETTERS* 2.1

The remains of the Visigothic palace in Toulouse, built during the fifth century and large enough to include all the amenities described by Sidonius in his letter about king Theoderic II, were discovered in 1988 during the demolition of an old military hospital

In the early 450s, the blue-blooded Gallo-Roman aristocrat Sidonius Apollinaris, a native of Lyon, married Papianilla, the daughter of the emperor Eparchius Avitus (455–456). Sidonius later served first as Prefect of Rome in 468 and then bishop of Clermont from ca. 469 until his death ca. 485. He thus experienced the last years of

Very soon after its discovery in 1988, in an act of archaeological vandalism, the remains of the Visigothic palace in Toulouse were bulldozed to make way for the construction of these apartment buildings.

the Roman Empire and the rise of the Visigothic kingdom of Toulouse. Like most Roman aristocrats, he had to make his peace with the barbarian settlers. In a letter to his brother-in-law Agricola, he provided a description of the court of the Visigothic king Theoderic II (453–484 CE).

Source: O. M. alton, trans., *The Letters of Sidonius*, two vols. (Oxford: Clarendon, 1915).

Sidonius to Agricola. You often have begged a description of Theoderic the Gothic king, whose gentle breeding fame commends to every nation. You want him in his quantity and quality, in his person, and the manner of his existence. I gladly accede, as far as the limits of my page allow, and highly approve so fine and ingenuous a curiosity. Well, he is a man worth knowing, even by those who cannot enjoy his close acquaintance, so happily have providence and nature joined to endow him with the perfect gifts of fortune. His way of life is such that not even the envy that lies in wait for kings can rob him of his proper praise.

First as to his person. He is well set up, in height above the average man, but below the giant. His head is round, with curled hair retreating somewhat from brow to crown. His nervy neck is free from disfiguring knots. The eyebrows are bushy and arched; when the lids droop, the lashes reach almost half-way down the cheeks. The upper ears are buried under overlying locks, after the fashion of his people. The nose is finely aquiline; the lips are thin and not enlarged by undue distension of the mouth. Every day the hair springing from his nostrils is cut back; that on the face springs thick from the hollow of the temples, but the razor has not yet come upon his cheek, and his barber is assiduous in eradicating the rich growth on the lower part of the face. Chin, throat, and neck are full, but not fat, and all of fair complexion. Seen close, their color is fresh as that of youth, they often flush, but from modesty and not from anger. His shoulders are smooth, the upper- and forearms strong and hard; hands broad, breast prominent; waist receding. The spine dividing the broad expanse of back does not project, and you can see the springing of the ribs; the sides swell with salient muscle, the well-girt flanks are full of vigor. His thighs are like hard horn; the knee-joints firm and masculine; the knees themselves the comeliest and least wrinkled in the world. A full ankle supports the leg, and the foot is small to bear such mighty limbs.

Now for the routine of his public life. Before daybreak he goes with a very small retinue to attend the service of his priests.[1] He prays with assiduity, but, if

I may speak in confidence, one may suspect more of habit than conviction in this piety. Administrative duties of the kingdom take up the rest of the morning. Armed nobles stand about the royal seat; the mass of guards in their garb of skins are admitted that they may be within call, but kept at the threshold for quiet's sake; only a murmur of them comes in from their post at the doors, between the curtain and the outer barrier.

And now the foreign envoys are introduced. The king hears them out, and says little. If a thing needs more discussion he puts it off, but he accelerates matters ripe for dispatch. The second hour[2] arrives; he rises from the throne to inspect his treasure-chamber or stable. If the chase is the order of the day, he joins it, but never carries his bow at his side, considering this derogatory to royal state. When a bird or beast is marked for him, or happens to cross his path, he puts his hand behind his back and takes the bow from a page with the string all hanging loose; for as he deems it a boy's trick to carry it in a case, so he considers it effeminate to receive the weapon ready strung. When it is given to him, he sometimes holds it in both hands and bends the extremities toward each other; at others he sets it, knot-end downward, against his lifted heel and runs his finger up the slack and wavering string. After that, he takes his arrows, adjusts, and lets fly. He will ask you beforehand what you would like him to transfix; you choose, and he hits. If there is a miss through either's error, your vision will mostly be at fault and not the archer's skill.

On ordinary days, his table resembles that of a private person. The board does not groan beneath a mass of dull and unpolished silver set on by panting servitors; the weight lies rather in the conversation than in the plate; there is either sensible talk or none. The hangings and draperies used on these occasions are sometimes of purple silk, sometimes only of linen. Art, not costliness, commends the fare, as spotlessness rather than bulk does the silver. Toasts are few, and you will oftener see a thirsty guest impatient than a full one refusing cup or bowl. In short, you will find the elegance of Greece, the good cheer of Gaul, Italian nimbleness, the state of public banquets with the attentive service of a private table, and everywhere the discipline of a king's house. What need for me to describe the pomp of his feast days? No man is so unknown as not to know of them.

But to my theme again. The siesta after lunch is always slight and sometimes omitted. When inclined for the board game, he is quick to gather up the dice, examines them with care, shakes the box with expert hand, throws rapidly, humorously addresses them, and patiently waits the issue. Silent at a good throw, he makes merry over a bad, annoyed by neither fortune and always the philosopher. He is too proud to ask or to refuse a revenge;[3] he disdains to avail himself of one if offered and if it is used by an opponent he will quietly go on playing. You effect recovery of your own gaming pieces without obstruction on his side; he recovers his without collusion upon yours. You see the strategist when he moves the pieces; his one thought is victory. Yet at play he puts off a little of his kingly rigor, inciting all to good fellowship and the freedom of the game: I think he is afraid of being feared. Vexation in the man whom he beats delights him; he will never believe that his opponents have not let him win unless their annoyance proves him really victor. You would be surprised at how often the pleasure born of these little happenings may favor the march of great affairs. Petitions that some wrecked influence had left derelict come unexpectedly to port. I myself am gladly beaten by him

[1] The Visigoths subscribed to the homoian form of Christianity, which often, but mistakenly, is referred to as "Arianism" (see Reading 109). Homoian Christianity stated that God and Christ were of a similar substance "according to the scriptures," whereas Nicene Christianity stated that God and Christ were of the same substance (see Reading 110, Section 7).

[2] During antiquity and the Middle Ages, the day's activities started at sunrise and daylight was divided into twelve parts. Thus, the "second hour" began at approximately 5:00 AM in the summer and 8:00 AM in the wintr.

[3] Apparently an opportunity to retake a throw.

vwhen I have a favor to ask, because the loss of my game may mean the gaining of my cause.

About the ninth hour,[4] the burden of government begins again. Back come the appellants, back the ushers to remove them. On all sides buzz the voices of petitioners, a sound that lasts until evening and does not diminish until interrupted by the royal repast. Even then they only disperse to attend their various patrons among the courtiers, and are astir until bedtime. Sometimes, although this is rare, supper is enlivened by sallies of mimes,[5] but no guest is ever exposed to the wound of a satirical tongue. On the other hand, there is no noise of a hydraulic organ or a choir with its conductor intoning a set piece. You will hear no lyre or flute players, no director of the music, no girls with tambourine or lute. The king cares for no strains but those that no less charm the mind with virtue than the ear with melody. When he rises to withdraw, the treasury watch begins its vigil; armed sentries stand on guard during the first hours of slumber.

But I am wandering from my subject. I never promised a whole chapter on the kingdom, but a few words about the king. I must stay my pen; you asked for nothing more than one or two facts about the person and the tastes of Theoderic; and my own aim was to write a letter, not a history. Farewell.

[4] About 2:00 PM in summer and 1:00 PM in winter.

[5] A popular form of entertainment.

120

THE CONVERSION OF CLOVIS (496 CE): GREGORY OF TOURS, *HISTORIES*, BOOK 2, CHAPTERS 28–31

A manuscript of the Flemish poet Jacob van Maerlant copied CA 1335–1355 depicts the baptism of Clovis by Remigius, bishop of Reims, ca. 496 CE. The Holy Spirit, as a dove, brings the holy oil.

Circa 496 CE, during a hard-fought battle with the Alamanni, it was said that Clovis (481–511), the pagan king of the Franks, promised to become a Christian if he won. After the Frankish victory, Clovis, encouraged by his Nicene Christian wife, the Burgundian princess Clotilda, was baptized as a Nicene Christian by Remigius, the Roman bishop of Reims. As a result, barbarians and Romans in the Frankish kingdom shared the same religious beliefs and practices, greatly facilitating the integration of the two populations. His Nicene faith gained Clovis valuable Roman support during his subsequent war with the Visigoths, who espoused a non-Nicene form of Christianity (see Reading 110, Section 7). At the pivotal Battle of Vouillé in 507, Clovis defeated and killed the Visigothic king Alaric II (484–507), and the

Franks occupied most of the Visigothic territories in Gaul, thus becoming the primary barbarian power in Gaul.

Source: Ernest Brehaut, *History of the Franks, by Gregory, Bishop of Tours* (Oxford: Oxford University Press, 1916), 38–41.

Now the king of the Burgundians was Gundioc, of the family of king Athanaric[6] the persecutor. He had four sons: Gundobad,[7] Godegisel, Chilperic, and Godomar. Gundobad killed his brother Chilperic with the sword and sank his wife in water with a stone tied to her neck. His two daughters he condemned to exile; the older of these, who became a nun, was called Chrona, and the younger Clotilda. And as Clovis[8] often sent embassies to Burgundy,[9] the maiden Clotilda was found by his envoys. And when they saw that she was of good bearing and wise, and learned that she was of the family of the king, they reported this to King Clovis, and he sent an embassy to Gundobad without delay asking her in marriage. Gundobad was afraid to refuse and surrendered her to the men. They took the girl and brought her swiftly to the king. The king was very glad when he saw her, and married her, having already by a concubine a son named Theoderic.[10]

He had a first-born son by queen Clotilda, and as his wife wished to consecrate him in baptism, she tried unceasingly to persuade her husband, saying, "The gods you worship are nothing, and they will be unable to help themselves or anyone else. For they are graven out of stone or wood or some metal. And the names you have given them are names of men and not of gods, such as Saturn, who is declared to have fled in fear of being banished from his kingdom by his son; such as Jupiter[11] himself, the foul perpetrator of all shameful crimes, committing incest with men, mocking at his kinswomen, not able to refrain from intercourse with his own sister."[12]

But the spirit of the king was by no means moved to belief, and he said, "It was at the command of our gods that all things were created and came forth, and it is plain that your God has no power and, what is more, he is proven not to belong to the family of the gods." Meantime the faithful queen made her son ready for baptism. She gave command to adorn the church with hangings and curtains, in order that he who could not be moved by persuasion might be urged to belief by this mystery. The boy, whom they named Ingomer, died after being baptized, still wearing the white garments in which he became reborn. At this the king was violently angry and reproached the queen harshly, saying: "If the boy had been dedicated in the name of my gods he would certainly have lived; but as it is, because he was baptized in the name of your god, he could not live at all." After this she bore another son, whom she named Chlodomer[13] at baptism, and when he fell sick, the king said, "It is impossible that anything else should happen to him than what happened to his brother, namely, that being baptized in the name of your Christ, he should die at once." But through the prayers of his mother, and the Lord's command, he became well.

The queen did not cease to urge him to recognize the true God and cease worshipping idols. But he could not be influenced in any way to this belief, until at last a war arose with the Alamanni,[14] in which he was driven by necessity to confess what before he had of his free will denied. It came about that as the two armies were fighting fiercely, there was much slaughter, and Clovis's army began to be in danger of destruction.

---

[6] There is no other evidence that the Burgundian king Gundioc was related to the Visigothic chieftain Athanaric, who lived more than a century earlier and died as an exile in Constantinople in 381. Athanaric had persecuted Gothic Christians.

[7] King of the Burgundians from 473 until 516.

[8] King of the Franks from 481 until 511 CE.

[9] The Burgundian kingdom, the region around Lyon in France.

[10] Later the Frankish king Theoderic I (511–534 CE).

[11] Jupiter, Greek Zeus, overcame his father Saturn, Greek Cronus, and became king of the gods; see Reading 6.

[12] Juno, Greek Hera, the sister and wife of Jupiter.

[13] Later king of the Franks from 511 to 524.

[14] A people living between the upper Rhine and upper Danube rivers.

He saw it and raised his eyes to heaven, and with remorse in his heart he burst into tears and cried, "Jesus Christ, whom Clotilda asserts to be the son of the living God, who art said to give aid to those in distress and to bestow victory on those who hope in thee, I beseech the glory of thy aid, with the vow that if thou wilt grant me victory over these enemies and I shall know that power that she says that people dedicated in thy name have had from thee, I will believe in thee and be baptized in thy name. For I have invoked my own gods but, as I find, they have withdrawn from aiding me, and therefore I believe that they possess no power, because they do not help those who obey them. I now call upon thee, I desire to believe thee only let me be rescued from my adversaries." And when he said thus, the Alamanni turned their backs and began to disperse in flight. And when they saw that their king was killed, they submitted to the dominion of Clovis, saying, "Let not the people perish further, we pray. We are yours now." And he stopped the fighting, and after encouraging his men, he retired in peace and told the queen how he had had merited to win the victory by calling on the name of Christ. This happened in the fifteenth year of his reign.[15]

Then the queen asked saint Remigius, bishop of Reims, to summon Clovis secretly, urging him to introduce the king to the word of salvation. And the bishop sent for him secretly and began to urge him to believe in the true God, maker of heaven and earth, and to cease worshipping idols, which could help neither themselves nor anyone else. But the king said, "I gladly hear you, most holy father; but there remains one thing: the people who follow me cannot endure to abandon their gods; but I shall go and speak to them according to your words." He met with his followers, but before he could speak the power of God anticipated him, and all the people cried out together, "O pious king, we reject our mortal gods and we are ready to follow the immortal God whom Remigius preaches." This was reported to the bishop, who greatly rejoiced and bade them get ready the baptismal font. The squares were shaded with tapestried canopies, the churches adorned with white curtains, the baptistery set in order, the aroma of incense spread, candles of fragrant odor burned brightly, and the whole shrine of the baptistery was filled with a divine fragrance and the Lord gave such grace to those who stood by that they thought they were placed amid the odors of paradise.

The king was the first to ask to be baptized by the bishop. Another Constantine[16] advanced to the baptismal font, to terminate the disease of ancient leprosy and wash away with fresh water the foul spots that long had been borne. And when he entered to be baptized, the saint of God began with ready speech, "Gently bend your neck, Sicamber,[17] worship what you burned; burn what you worshipped." The holy bishop Remigius was a man of excellent wisdom and especially trained in rhetorical studies, and of such surpassing holiness that he equaled the miracles of Silvester.[18] For there is extant a book of his life that tells that he raised a dead man. So the king confessed all-powerful God in the Trinity, and was baptized in the name of the Father, Son, and Holy Spirit, and was anointed with the holy ointment with the sign of the cross of Christ. And of his army more than 3000 were baptized. His sister also, Albofleda, was baptized, who not long after passed to the Lord. And when the king was in mourning for her, the holy Remigius sent a letter of consolation that began in this way, "The reason of your mourning pains me, and pains me greatly, that Albofleda your sister, of good memory, has passed away. But I can give you this comfort, that her departure from the world was such that she ought to be envied rather than be mourned." Another sister also converted, Lanthechildis by name, who had fallen into the heresy of the Arians,[19] and she confessed that the Son and the holy Spirit were equal to the Father, and was anointed.

---

[15] That is, in 496 CE. Other dates also have been proposed for the battle.

[16] Constantine I (306–337), who likewise had adopted Christianity after being raised as a pagan.

[17] The Sicambrians were one of the peoples who made up the Franks.

[18] The bishop of Rome (314–335), who was said to have baptized Constantine and to have issued the "Donation of Constantine," a forged document that granted dominion of the western Roman Empire to the bishop of Rome.

[19] The derogatory name used by Gregory for the homoian Christians.

121

THE ACCLAMATIONS OF THE SENATE OF ROME (438 CE): THEODOSIAN CODE, "ACTS OF THE SENATE"

The surviving "Julian Curia," the Senate house in Rome, was initially constructed by Julius Caesar in 44 BCE, subsequently renovated by the emperors Domitian (81–96 CE) and Diocletian (284–305), and last remodeled in 412 CE. It was used as a church in the Middle Ages and thus escaped being demolished for building materials.

In December 438, the Theodosian Code (see Reading 110) was officially introduced to the western empire at a meeting of the Senate in Rome. The verbatim minutes of the meeting were preserved and prefaced to the official copies of the code that were circulated throughout the west. This process shows the continuing role of the Senate, no longer in policy making, but in distributing information received from the emperors. The only remaining means that the Senate had of communicating its desires to the emperors was by shouting acclamations after they had heard the emperors' wishes.

Source: Clyde Pharr, trans., *The Theodosian Code and Novels, and the Sirmondian Constitutions* (Princeton, NJ: Princeton University Press, 1952), 5–7.

Acts of the Senate.

In the year of the sixteenth consulship of Our Lord Flavius Theodosius Augustus[20] and the consulship of the Most Noble Anicius Acilius Glabrio Faustus.[21]

When the Most Noble and Illustrious Anicius Acilius Glabrio Faustus, thrice Ex-Prefect of the City, Praetorian Prefect, and Ordinary Consul,[22] in his home, which is at Palma,[23] and the Most Noble and Illustrious Flavius Paulus, Prefect of the City, the Respectable Junius Pompolius Publianus, Vicar of the Eternal City, men of noble rank, and the Most August Order of the Senate had assembled and conferred together for a considerable time, and the Constitutionaries[24] Anastasius and Martinus had entered pursuant to an order, the Most Noble and Illustrious Anicius Acilius Glabrio Faustus, thrice Ex-Prefect of the City, Praetorian Prefect, and Consul Ordinary, spoke as follows: "The felicity that emanates from our immortal emperors proceeds in its increase to the point that it arrays with the ornaments of peace those whom it defends in the fortunes of war.[25] Last year when I attended, as a mark of devotion, the most felicitous union of all the sacred ceremonies, after the nuptials had been felicitously solemnized,[26] the most sacred emperor, Our Lord Theodosius, desired to add the following high honor also to his world, namely, that he should order to be established the regulations that must be observed throughout the world,[27] in accordance with the precepts of the laws that had been gathered together in a compendium of sixteen books and these books he had desired to be consecrated by his most sacred name. The immortal emperor, Our Lord Valentinian, with the loyalty of a colleague and the affection of a son, approved this undertaking.[28]

The Assembly shouted:

"Thou art newly eloquent! Truly eloquent!"

The Most Noble and Illustrious Anicius Acilius Glabrio Faustus, thrice Ex-Prefect of the City, Praetorian Prefect, and Ordinary Consul, said, "Therefore, the most sacred emperor summoned me and the illustrious man who was Prefect of the East at that time and ordered copies of the Code to be delivered from his own divine hand, one to each of us, in order that they might be dispatched throughout the world with all due reverence. Thus, it was among the first of his provisions that his forethought should be brought to the knowledge of Your Sublimity.[29] The Code as directed by the order of both emperors was received into our hands. The Constitutionaries are present. If it please Your Magnificence, let Your Magnificence order that these very laws be read to you with which the emperors ordered that this undertaking should be performed, in order that we may obey with proper devotion the most carefully considered precepts of the immortal emperors."

---

20 The emperor Theodosius II (402–450).

21 The year 438 CE.

22 The first Consul appointed during any given year, who gave his name to the year; subsequent appointees were called Suffect Consuls.

23 An area near the center of Rome. The Senate often met not in the Curia (Senate house), which was rather spartan and small, but in the luxurious city house of a distinguished senator, which was a great honor and not, as suggested by Pharr (*Theodosian Code*, 3), "one of the many indications of the low status of the Senate."

24 Officials responsible for making and preserving official copies of the Code.

25 A rather optimistic statement because, in the east, the Huns were becoming a serious problem and in the west the Vandals had invaded Africa and were on the verge of capturing Carthage.

26 The marriage in 437 at Constantinople between Theodosius's cousin, the young western emperor Valentinian III (425–455), and Theodosius's daughter, Licinia Eudoxia.

27 In theory, the Romans claimed to rule the whole world.

28 The principle of "unanimity of Empire." Even though the Roman Empire now was effectively split into eastern and western halves, in legal practice there was still only a single empire and laws issued in one part of the empire were issued also in the name of the other emperor(s).

29 High-ranking officials were endowed with elaborate titles of address, such as "Your Sublimity" and "Your Magnificence."

The assembly shouted, "It is right! So be it! So be it!"

The Most Noble and Illustrious Anicius Acilius Glabrio Faustus, thrice Ex-Prefect of the City, Praetorian Prefect, and Ordinary Consul, read from the first book of the Theodosian Code, under the title, "Constitutions and Edicts of the Emperors"[30]:

"The emperors Theodosius and Valentinian Augustuses to the Senate. We decree that, after the pattern of the Gregorian and Hermogenian Codes,[31] a collection shall be made of all the constitutions that were issued by the renowned Constantine, by the sainted emperors after him, and by us and that rest upon the force of edicts or sacred imperial law of general force. First, the titles, which are the definite designations of the matters therein, shall be so divided that when the various headings have been expressed, if one constitution should pertain to several titles, the materials shall be assembled wherever each is fitting.[32] Second, if any diversity should cause anything to be stated in two ways, it shall be tested by the order of the headings, and not only shall the year of the consulship be considered and the time of the reign be investigated, but also the arrangement of the work itself shall show that the laws that are later are more valid.[33] Furthermore, the very words themselves of the constitutions, in so far as they pertain to the essential matter, shall be preserved, but those words that were added, not from the very necessity of sanctioning the law, shall be omitted.[34]

Although it would be simpler and more in accordance with law to omit those constitutions that were invalidated by later constitutions and to set forth only those that must be valid, let us recognize that this Code and the previous ones were composed for more diligent men, to whose scholarly efforts it is granted to know those laws also that have been consigned to silence and have passed into desuetude, because they were destined to be valid for cases of their own time only.

Moreover, from these three Codes and from the treatises and responses of the jurists that are attached to each of the titles, through the services of the same men who shall arrange the third code there shall be produced another Code of ours.[35] This Code shall permit no error, no ambiguities; it shall be called by our name, and shall show what must be followed and what must be avoided by all. For the consummation of so great a work and the composition of the Codes, the first of which shall collect all the diversity of general constitutions,[36] shall omit none outside itself that now are permitted to be cited in court,[37] and shall reject only an empty copiousness of words, and the other of which shall exclude every contradiction of the law and shall undertake the guidance of life—men must be chosen of singular trustworthiness, of the most brilliant genius. When they have presented

[30] Faustus then read out verbatim the legislation that had authorized the compilation of the Code. As can be seen, not all of it actually was put into effect.

[31] The existing Gregorian and Hermogenian codes were not "compilations of imperial enactments or constitutions," as Pharr (*Theodosian Code*, 4), but were collections of rescripts, that is, replies to petitions; and they were compiled under Diocletian in the 290s, not "in the early fourth century."

[32] That is, the laws were dismembered so different sections pertaining to different topics could be added to the appropriate sections of the Code.

[33] A full record of laws on any given topic was included, even laws that had been overridden or superseded by subsequent laws. So these overridden laws, too, could be cited in court.

[34] The authors of late Roman laws could be quite verbose, and the editors were instructed to omit material, sometimes a great amount, not directly relevant to the law being issued.

[35] A comprehensive code consisting of the Gregorian, Hermogenian, and Theodosian codes along with the writings of jurists (legal scholars) was not produced until the publication of the *Corpus iuris civilis* ("Body of Civil Law") under the emperor Justinian in the early 530s.

[36] That is, the existing Theodosian Code, which only included statute law issued by emperors.

[37] Once the Code had been issued, any laws that had not been included in it, even by inadvertence, no longer were valid.

the first Code[38] to our wisdom and to the public authority, they shall undertake the other, which must be worked over until it is worthy of publication.[39] Let Your Magnificence acknowledge the men who have been selected: the Illustrious Antiochus, Ex-Quaestor and Ex-Prefect; the Illustrious Antiochus, Quaestor of the Sacred Imperial Palace[40]; the Respectable Theodorus, Count and Master of the Bureau of Memorials[41]; the Respectable Eudicius and Eusebius, Masters of the Bureaux; and the Respectable Johannes, Ex-Count of our Sacred Consistory; the Respectable Comazon and Eubulus, Ex-Masters of the Bureaux; and Apelles, most eloquent jurist.

We are confident that these men who have been selected by Our Eternity will employ every exceptionally learned man in order that by their common study a reasonable plan of action may be apprehended and fallacious laws may be excluded.

Furthermore, if in the future it should be our pleasure to promulgate any law in one part of this very closely united empire, it shall be valid in the other part on condition that it does not rest upon doubtful trustworthiness or upon a private assertion. From that part of the empire in which it will be established, it shall be transmitted with the most sacred imperial letters, it shall be received in the bureaux of the other part of the empire also, and it shall be published with the due formality of edicts. For a law that has been sent must be accepted and must undoubtedly be valid, and the power to emend and to revoke shall be reserved to Our Clemency. Moreover the laws must be mutually announced, and they must not be admitted otherwise.

Given on the seventh day before the Kalends of April at Constantinople in the year of the consulship of Florentius and Dionysius.[42]"

The assembly shouted:

"Augustuses of Augustuses, the Greatest of Augustuses!"	Repeated[43] 8 times.
"God gave you to us! God save you for us!"	Repeated 27 times.
"As Roman Emperors, pious and felicitous, may you rule for many years!"	Repeated 22 times.
"For the good of the human race, for the good of the Senate, for the good of the state, for the good of all!"	Repeated 24 times.
"Our hope is in you, you are our salvation!"	Repeated 22 times.
"May it please our Augustuses to live forever!"	Repeated 22 times.
"May you pacify the world and triumph here in person!"	Repeated 24 times.
"There are the prayers of the Senate, these are the prayers of the Roman people!"	Repeated 10 times.
"Dearer than our children, dearer than our parents!"	Repeated 16 times.
"Suppressors of informers, suppressors of trickery!"[44]	Repeated 28 times.

[38] That is, the Theodosian Code, also referred to above as the "third Code," to distinguish it from the earlier Gregorian and Hermogenian codes.

[39] Only the first of these two codes ever was completed. The second was not assembled until a hundred years later as the *Digest* of the emperor Justinian, which compiled the opinions of Roman jurists.

[40] The chief legal official at the imperial court.

[41] The Bureaux were all of the high-ranking, specialized secretarial and office staffs in charge of correspondence, archives, and record-keeping.

[42] 26 March 429.

[43] The acclamations would be repeated in unison until no one continued. The number of repetitions then was reported to the emperors.

[44] This and the next acclamation, which received the greatest number of repetitions, reflect two of the Senate's greatest concerns: (1) a fear of informers and (2) the acknowledgment that the ranks, titles, and honors that the senators valued so much came from the emperors.

"Through you our honors, through you our patrimonies, through you our all!"	Repeated 28 times.
"Through you, our military strength; through you, our laws!"	Repeated 20 times.
"We give thanks for this regulation of yours!"	Repeated 23 times.
"You have removed the ambiguities of the imperial constitutions!"	Repeated 23 times.
"Dutiful emperors act wisely in this manner!"	Repeated 26 times.
"You wisely provide for lawsuits, you provide for the public peace!"	Repeated 25 times.
"Let many copies of the Code be made to be kept in the governmental office!"	Repeated 10 times.
"Let them be kept under seal in the public bureaux!"[45]	Repeated 20 times.
"In order that the established laws not be falsified, let many copies be made!	Repeated 25 times.
"In order that the established laws may not be falsified, let all copies be written out in letters!"[46]	Repeated 12 times.
"To this copy that will be made by the Constitutionaries let no annotations be added to the law!"	Repeated 12 times.
"We request that the copies to be kept in the bureaux shall be made at public expense!"[47]	Repeated 16 times.
"Hail, Faustus!"[48]	Repeated 17 times.
"A second term for you in the consulship!"	Repeated 15 times.
"You regulate everything, you harm no man!"	Repeated 13 times.
"Let copies be made and dispatched to the provinces!"	Repeated 11 times.
"Worthy purveyor of such great benefits"	Repeated 10 times.
"Hail Paulus!"[49]	Repeated 12 times.
"A Consulship for you!"	Repeated 11 times.
"We request that the Codes be kept in the public bureaux!"	Repeated 15 times.
"Let this duty be assigned to the office of the Prefects!"[50]	Repeated 12 times.
"Let each Prefect affix his own seal"	Repeated 15 times
"Let each have a copy in his own office!"	Repeated 12 times.
"We ask that no laws be promulgated in reply to supplications"[51]	Repeated 21 times.
"Hail Aëtius"[52]	Repeated 15 times.
"A third term for you in the consulship"	Repeated 13 times.
"Through your vigilance we are safe and secure"	Repeated 12 times.
"Through your vigilance, through your labors"	Repeated 15 times.

[45] So unauthorized changes could not be made.

[46] Written out in full without abbreviations that could be misconstrued.

[47] Roman laws were full of unfunded mandates, so the senators did not want to be made responsible for paying for the copies.

[48] The senator who made the opening address. He never received a second consulship.

[49] A senator who, with Faustus, had convoked the meeting.

[50] The Praetorian Prefects were the highest-ranking civil officials, ranking just below the emperor.

[51] Many late Roman laws were issued in response to requests from special interest groups: the emperors had a hard time saying "no" to these kinds of requests.

[52] The Patrician and Master of Soldiers and, along with Valentinian's mother Galla Placidia, the virtual ruler of the western empire. He did get a third consulship.

"Hail, Faustus!"	Repeated 13 times.
"A second term for you in the consulship!"	Repeated 10 times.
"We ask that you report to the emperors the desires of the Senate!"[53]	Repeated 20 times.
"Preserver of the laws, preserver of the decrees"	Repeated 16 times
"All the rights of landholders are thrown into confusion by such surreptitious actions"	Repeated 17 times.

The Most Noble and Illustrious Anicius Acilius Glabrio Faustus, thrice Ex-Prefect of the City, Praetorian Prefect, and Ordinary Consul, said, "Pursuant to the orders of Our Lords and the desires of Your Eminences, it now shall be an object of my care to provide for the transcription of this code in three copies, through the reliable services of the Respectable Veronicianus, who was selected by agreement between Your Magnificences and me, and by the reliable services of the Constitutionaries Anastasius and Martinus, whom we already have approved as having given long and faultless services to this office. Then, whereas the copy that I have presented shall remain in the exalted office of the praetorian[54] archives, the bureau of the magnificent Prefect of the City, a man of equal trustworthiness, shall hold the second, and the Constitutionaries shall be ordered to retain the third in their own custody faithfully and at their own risk, in order that they may publish it to the people, with this provision, that no copies may be published except such as have been transcribed from this copy by the Constitutionaries, in their own hand. Likewise it shall be an object of my care to arrange for this also, that another copy of the Code shall be transcribed by these men and shall be dispatched with like devotion to the Province of Africa,[55] in order that there, too, a model of equal reliability may be preserved."

The assembly shouted,

"Hail Faustus!"	Repeated 16 times.
"A second term for you in the consulship!"	Repeated 15 times.
"To a man of all virtues!"	Repeated 10 times.

And by another hand.[56] I, Flavius Laurentius, Secretary of the Most August Senate, have published this on the eighth day before the Kalends of January.[57]

[53] This was important because the reporting of such acclamations was the only remaining institutionalized way that the Senate of Rome had of communicating its desires to the emperors.

[54] Of the Praetorian Prefects.

[55] The senators could not have known that less than a year later, on 19 October 439, Carthage and the Roman province of North Africa would fall to the Vandals. After less than a hundred years, however, North Africa would be reconquered by the Romans; see Reading 122.

[56] A formula that indicates a scribal addendum.

[57] 25 December 438, Christmas Day.

122

THE END OF THE VANDAL KINGDOM (533 CE): PROCOPIUS, *HISTORY OF THE WARS*, BOOK 3, CHAPTERS 10–20

Silver siliqua of Gelimer (530–534), the last king of the Vandals. The legend on the obverse reads, "Our Lord King Geilamir." The reverse shows a Christian cross in a wreath, along with the number "L" and the abbreviation "D N," signifying the coin's value as "50 denarii." The denarius by this time was strictly a notional value and had no direct connection with the denarius of the Roman Principate.

Traditional accounts of the Fall of the Western Roman Empire leave the reader supposing that as of 476 the barbarians had "won," having established kingdoms throughout the old western empire. But appearances, and popular perceptions, can be deceiving. A mere seventy-five years later, much of the western Roman Empire had been reconquered by the Roman emperor Justinian (527–565), thus recreating an empire that extended from the cataracts of the Nile to the Strait of Gibraltar. The reconquest began in 533, when Justinian sent his general Belisarius to North Africa in an effort to conquer the Vandals and their king, Gelimer (530–534). At the Battle of Ad Decimum the Vandal army was destroyed and Gelimer put to flight. Belisarius then occupied Carthage, just as the Vandals themselves had done almost a century earlier. Later in the same year, the remaining Vandal resistance was mopped up at the Battle of Tricamarum, which effectively brought the Vandal Kingdom to an end. After being displayed in Justinian's triumph in Constantinople, Gelimer spent the rest of his life in honorable retirement on estates granted to him in Galatia. A detailed account of the war was written by the historian Procopius, who, as an Assessor, or legal expert, accompanied Belisarius on his campaigns.

Source: H. B. Dewing, trans., *Procopius. History of the Wars, Books III and IV* (Cambridge, MA: Harvard University Press, 1916).

And when the emperor Justinian[58] considered that the situation was as favorable as possible, both as to domestic affairs and as to his relations with Persia,[59] he took under consideration the situation in Libya.[60] But when he disclosed to the magistrates that he was gathering an army against the Vandals and Gelimer,[61] most of them began immediately to show hostility to the plan, and they lamented it as a misfortune, recalling the expedition of the emperor Leo and the disaster of Basiliscus,[62] and reciting how many soldiers had perished and how much money the state had lost. The emperor Justinian, hearkening, checked his eager desire for the war. But one of the priests whom they call bishops, who had come from the east, said that he wished to have a word with the emperor. And when he met Justinian, he said that God had visited him in a dream, and bidden him go to the emperor and rebuke him, because, after undertaking the task of protecting the Christians in Libya from tyrants, he had for no good reason become afraid. "And yet," God had said, "I will myself join with him in waging war and make him lord of Libya."

58 Byzantine emperor from 527 until 565; often looked on as a model Byzantine emperor.

59 The Sasanid, or New Persian, Empire to the east, which often was in a state of war with the Byzantine Empire.

60 In this case, a reference to the Vandal Kingdom in modern Tunisia and Algeria in North Africa.

61 The last King of the Vandals (530–534 CE).

62 A failed attempt made in 468 CE to reconquer North Africa by the eastern emperor Leo (457–474) was led by Leo's incompetent brother-in-law Basiliscus.

When the emperor heard this, he was no longer able to restrain his purpose, and he began to collect the army and the ships, and to make ready supplies of weapons and of food, and he announced to Belisarius[63] that he should be in readiness, because he was very soon to act as general in Libya. He had in readiness the expedition against Carthage, ten thousand foot-soldiers and five thousand horsemen,[64] gathered from the regular troops and from the "foederati." Now at an earlier time only barbarians were enlisted among the foederati, those, namely, who had come into the Roman political system, not in the condition of slaves, because they had not been conquered by the Romans, but on the basis of complete equality. For the Romans call treaties with their enemies "foedera." But at the present time there is nothing to prevent anyone from assuming this name.[65]

And after this the general Belisarius and Antonina,[66] his wife, set sail. And there was with them also Procopius, who wrote this history. When they came

63 Justinian's best and most reliable general.

64 A remarkably small number compared to the much larger armies of antiquity.

65 The "foederati" were still random auxiliary units.

66 The wife of Belisarius. She came from a family of entertainers; her father and grandfather were charioteers and her mother an actress, an occupation that often involved prostitution. Like Theodora, the wife of the emperor Justinian, who also had been an entertainer (Reading 123), Antonia manifests the opportunities for social advancement, especially for able women, that characterized Late Antiquity.

near the shore, the general bade them furl the sails, throw out anchors from the ships, and make a halt. They made the disembarkation as quickly as possible, about three months later than their departure from Byzantium. And indicating a certain spot on the shore the general bade both soldiers and sailors dig the trench and place the stockade about it.

And Belisarius, having arrayed his army as for battle in the following manner, began the march to Carthage. And accomplishing eighty stades[67] each day, we completed the whole journey to Carthage, passing the night either in a city, should it so happen, or in a camp made as thoroughly secure as the circumstances permitted. Thus we passed through the city of Leptis[68] and Hadrumetum[69] and reached the place called Grasse, three hundred and fifty stades distant from Carthage. But Gelimer, as soon as he heard in Hermione[70] that the enemy were at hand, wrote to his brother Ammatas in Carthage to kill Hilderic[71] and all the others, connected with him either by birth or otherwise, whom he was keeping under guard. He commanded him to make ready the Vandals and all others in the city serviceable for war, in order that, when the enemy got inside the narrow passage at the suburb of the city that they call Ad Decimum,[72] they might come together from both sides and surround them and, catching them as in a net, destroy them. Belisarius commanded Archelaus, the Prefect, and Calonymus, the Admiral, not to put in at Carthage, but to remain about two hundred stades away until he himself should summon them. And departing from Grasse we came on the fourth day to Ad Decimum, seventy stades distant from Carthage.

Belisarius, seeing a place well adapted for a camp, thirty-five stades distant from Ad Decimum, surrounded it with a stockade that was very well made, and placing all the infantry there and calling together the whole army, he spoke as follows:

> Fellow-soldiers, the decisive moment of the struggle is already at hand, for I perceive that the enemy are advancing upon us. The ships have been taken far away from us by the nature of the place, and it has come round to this that our hope of safety lies in the strength of our hands. For there is not a friendly city, no, nor any other stronghold, in which we may put our trust and have confidence concerning ourselves. But if we should show ourselves brave men, we shall overcome the enemy, but if we should weaken at all, we will fall under the hand of the Vandals and be destroyed disgracefully. And yet there are many advantages on our side to help us on toward victory; for we have with us both justice, with which we have come against our enemy, for we are here in order to recover what is our own, and the hatred of the Vandals toward their own tyrant. For the alliance of God follows naturally those who put justice forward, and a soldier who is ill-disposed toward his ruler knows not how to play the part of a brave man. And apart from this, we have been engaged with Persians and Scythians[73] all the time, but the Vandals, since the time they conquered Libya, have seen not a single enemy except naked Moors.[74] And who does not know that in every work practice leads to skill, whereas idleness leads to inefficiency? Now the stockade, from which we shall have to carry on the war, has been made by us in the best possible manner. And we are able to deposit here our weapons and everything else that we are not able to carry when we go forth; and when we return here again, no kind of provisions can fail us. And I pray that each one of you, calling to mind his own valor and those whom he has left at home, may so march with contempt against the enemy."

[67] A "stade" was approximately six hundred feet, making eighty stades about nine and a half miles.

[68] Leptis Magna, a Roman city on the Libyan coast eighty miles east of modern Tripoli.

[69] A Phoenician trading colony of the ninth century BCE that predated Carthage.

[70] A small inland city.

[71] Grandson of the Vandal king Geiseric, and son of Geiseric's son Huneric and Eudocia, daughter of the emperor Valentinian III. Hilderic served as king of the Vandals from 523 until 530, when he was deposed by his cousin Gelimer. Gelimer's rude responses to Justinian's protests gave Justinian the pretext for invading North Africa.

[72] A town located at the tenth mile post of one of the Roman roads leading out of Carthage.

[73] Huns.

[74] The native inhabitants of North Africa.

After speaking these words and uttering a prayer after them, Belisarius left his wife and the barricaded camp to the infantry, and himself set forth with all the horsemen. For it did not seem to him advantageous for the present to risk an engagement with the whole army, but it seemed wise to skirmish first with the horsemen and make trial of the enemy's strength, and later to fight a decisive battle with the whole army. Sending forward, therefore, the commanders of the foederati, he himself followed with the rest of the force, and his own spearmen and guards.[75] And when the foederati and their leaders reached Ad Decimum, they saw the corpses of the twelve comrades from the forces of John and near them Ammatas and some of the Vandals.[76] Hearing from the inhabitants of the place the whole story of the fight, they were vexed, being at a loss as to where they ought to go. But while they were still at a loss and from the hills were looking around over the whole country thereabouts, a dust appeared from the south and a little later a very large force of Vandal horsemen. They sent to Belisarius urging him to come as quickly as possible because the enemy were bearing down upon them. The opinions of the commanders were divided. Some thought that they ought to close with their assailants, but the others said that their force was not sufficient for this.

While they were debating thus among themselves, the barbarians drew near under the leadership of Gelimer, who was following a road between the one that Belisarius was traveling and the one by which the Massagetae who had encountered Gibamundus had come. But the land was hilly on both sides and did not allow him to see either the disaster of Gibamundus or Belisarius' stockade nor even the road along which Belisarius' men were advancing. But when they came near each other, a contest arose between the two armies as to which should capture the highest of all the hills there, for it seemed a suitable one to encamp upon, and both sides preferred to engage with the enemy from there. The Vandals, coming first, took possession of the hill by crowding off their assailants and routed the enemy, having already become an object of terror to them. And the Romans in flight came to a place seven stades distant from Ad Decimum, where, as it happened, Uliaris, the personal guard of Belisarius, was, with eight hundred guardsmen. All supposed that Uliaris would receive them and hold his position, and together with them would go against the Vandals, but when they came together, these troops all unexpectedly fled at top speed and went on the run to Belisarius.

From then on I am unable to say what happened to Gelimer because, having the victory in his hands, he willingly gave it up to the enemy. For if, on the one hand, he had made the pursuit immediately, I do not think that even Belisarius would have withstood him and our cause would have been utterly and completely lost, so numerous appeared the force of the Vandals and so great the fear they inspired in the Romans. Or if, on the other hand, he had even ridden straight for Carthage, he would easily have killed all John's men,[77] who, heedless of everything else, were wandering about the plain one by one or by twos and stripping the dead. He would have preserved the city with its treasures and captured our ships, which had come rather near, and he would have withdrawn from us all hope both of sailing away and of victory. But in fact he did neither of these things. Instead, he descended from the hill at a walk, and when he reached the level ground and saw the corpse of his brother, he turned to lamentations, and, in caring for his burial, he blunted the edge of his opportunity, an opportunity that he was not able to grasp again.

Meantime Belisarius, meeting the fugitives, bade them stop and arrayed them all in order and rebuked them at length. Then, after hearing of the death of Ammatas and the pursuit of John and learning what he wished concerning the place and the enemy, he proceeded at full speed against Gelimer and the

[75] The Roman generals of Late Antiquity had attendant on them large numbers of personal retainers.

[76] In one skirmish on the previous day, Roman Massagetae, a barbarian people of the central Asian steppes. had defeated a Vandal force led by Gibamundus, and in another Roman forces led by John the Armenian had killed Gelimer's brother Ammatus.

[77] From the battle the day before.

Vandals. The barbarians, having already fallen into disorder and being now unprepared, could not withstand the onset of the Romans, but fled with all their might, losing many there, and the battle ended at night. Now the Vandals were in flight, not to Carthage nor to Byzacium,[78] whence they had come, but to the plain of Boulla and the road leading into Numidia.[79] So the men with John and the Massagetae returned to us about dusk, and after learning all that had happened and reporting what they had done, they passed the night with us in Ad Decimum.

On the following day the infantry with the wife of Belisarius came up and we all proceeded together on the road toward Carthage, which we reached in the late evening. We passed the night in the open, although no one hindered us from marching into the city at once. For the Carthaginians opened the gates and burned lights everywhere and the city was brilliant with the illumination that whole night, and those of the Vandals who had been left behind were sitting as suppliants in the sanctuaries. But Belisarius prevented the entrance in order not only to guard against any ambush being set for his men by the enemy but also to prevent the soldiers from having freedom to turn to plundering, as they might under the concealment of night.

On the following day Belisarius commanded those on the ships to disembark, and after marshalling the whole army and drawing it up in battle formation, he marched into Carthage; for he feared lest he should encounter some snare set by the enemy. There he reminded the soldiers at length of how much good fortune had come to them because they had displayed moderation toward the Libyans, and he exhorted them earnestly to preserve good order with the greatest care in Carthage. Because no enemy was seen by them, he went up to the palace and seated himself on Gelimer's throne.

[78] A coastal region south of Carthage.

[79] A region of North Africa to the west of Carthage.

123

THE CHARACTER OF JUSTINIAN AND THEODORA (527–548 CE): PROCOPIUS, *SECRET HISTORY*, PROLOGUE, 1–12

The retinues of Justinian and Theodora are depicted in this composite view of a mosaic dating to 546 CE in the church of San Vitale in Ravenna. Theodora is just as resplendent, if not even more so, than Justinian, attesting to the important role that she played in the imperial hierarchy.

During the Roman Empire it always was potentially dangerous for writers to speak too candidly about current events. One had to wait until after the death of a problematic ruler, as Tacitus waited for the death of Domitian (81–96), before one could express oneself more freely. This also was the case for the historian Procopius, who glorified the emperor Justinian while the latter was alive, but vilified him and his wife, Theodora, after their deaths. After a lengthy character assassination of Belisarius, punctuated by the liaisons and schemes of his wife, Antonina (see Reading 122), Procopius turns to extravagant tales of the character flaws and misdeeds of Justinian and Theodora, who predeceased her husband in 548 CE. As in the case of the salacious tales retailed in the second century CE by the biographer Suetonius (see Reading 92), one must be cautious about accepting the literal truth of of Propopius's stories.

Source: Richard Atwater, trans., *The Secret History of Procopius* (New York: Covici-Friede, 1927).

It was not possible, during the life of certain persons, to write the truth of what they did, as a historian should. If I had, their hordes of spies would have found out about it, and they would have put me to a most horrible death. I could not even trust my nearest relatives. These secrets it is now my duty to tell and reveal the remaining hidden matters and motives. Yet when I approach this different task, I find it hard indeed to have to stammer and retract what I have written before about the lives of Justinian and Theodora. Worse yet, it occurs to me that what I am now about to tell will seem neither probable nor plausible to future generations, especially as time flows on and my story becomes ancient history. I fear they may think me a writer of fiction, and even put me among the poets. But I was constrained to proceed with this history, for the reason that future tyrants may see also that those who thus err cannot avoid retribution in the end. For who now would know of the unchastened life of Semiramis[80] or the madness of Sardanapalus[81] or Nero,[82] if the record had not thus been written by men of their own times?

I now come to the tale of what sort of beings Justinian and Theodora were, and how they brought confusion on the Roman State. During the rule of the emperor Leo[83] in Constantinople, three young farmers of Illyrian birth, named Zimarchus, Ditybistus, and Justin of Bederiana, after a desperate struggle with poverty, left their homes to try their fortune in the army. They made their way to Constantinople on foot, carrying on their shoulders their blankets in which were wrapped no other equipment except the biscuits they had baked at home. When they arrived and were admitted into military service, the emperor chose them for the palace guard; for they were all three fine-looking men.

As time went on, this Justin came to great power. The emperor Anastasius[84] appointed him Count of the Palace Guard; and when the emperor departed from this world, by the force of his military power Justin seized the throne. By this time he was an old man on the verge of the grave, and so illiterate that he could neither read nor write, which never before could have been said of a Roman ruler. It was the custom for an emperor to sign his edicts with his own hand, but he neither made decrees nor was able to understand the business of state at all. The man on whom it befell to assist him as Quaestor[85] was named Proclus, and he managed everything to suit himself. But so that he might have some evidence of the emperor's hand, he invented the following device for his clerks to construct. Cutting out of a block of wood the shapes of the four letters required to make the Latin word, they dipped a pen into the ink used by emperors for their signatures,[86] and put it in the emperor's fingers. Laying the block of wood I have described on the paper to be signed, they guided the emperor's hand so that his pen outlined the four letters, following all the curves of the stencil, and thus they withdrew with the "FIAT"[87] of the emperor. This is how the Romans were ruled under Justin. His wife was named Lupicina, a slave and a barbarian who was bought to be his concubine. With Justin, as the

[80] A legendary Assyrian queen said to have been the daughter of the fertility goddess Astarte, to have fought many wars as far away as India, and to have constructed many Near Eastern monuments.

[81] The legendary last king of Assyria whose decadent pleasure-seeking lifestyle led to the fall of the Assyrian Empire.

[82] Roman emperor from 54 to 68 CE, known for his decadent lifestyle.

[83] Leo I (457–474 CE).

[84] East Roman emperor from 491 until 518.

[85] Quaestor of the Sacred Palace, the chief legal official.

[86] The emperors used purple ink.

[87] Latin for "let it be so." The same urban legend was told about the Ostrogothic king Theoderic the Great (493–525 CE).

sun of his life was about to set, she ascended the throne.[88]

[The Character of Justinian]

Now Justin was able to do his subjects neither harm nor good. For he was simple, unable to carry on a conversation or make a speech, and utterly bucolic. His nephew Justinian, while still a youth, was the virtual ruler and the cause of more and worse calamities to the Romans than anyone man in all their previous history. He had no scruples, against murder or the seizing of other person's property, and it was nothing to him to make away with myriads of men, even when they gave him no cause. He had no care for preserving established customs, but was always eager for new experiments, and, in short, was the greatest corrupter of all noble traditions.

When the plague attacked the whole world, no fewer men escaped than perished of it, for some never were taken by the disease, and others recovered after it had smitten them.[89] But this man not one of all the Romans could escape. As if he were a second pestilence sent from heaven, he fell on the nation and left no man untouched. For some he slew without reason, and some he released to struggle with penury, and their fate was worse than that of those who had perished, so that they prayed for death to free them from their misery. Others he robbed of their property and their lives together. When there was nothing left to ruin in the Roman state, he determined the conquest of Libya and Italy, for no other reason than to destroy the people there, as he had those who were already his subjects. Justinian was very complacent and resembled most the silly ass, which follows, only shaking its ears, when one drags it by the bridle. As such Justinian acted, and threw everything into confusion.

As soon as he took over the rule from his uncle, his measure was to spend the public money without restraint, now that he had control of it. He gave much of it to the Huns who, from time to time, entered the state, and in consequence the Roman provinces were subject to constant incursions, for these barbarians, having once tasted Roman wealth, never forgot the road that led to it. He gathered to himself the private estates of Roman citizens from all over the empire, some by accusing their possessors of crimes of which they were innocent, others by juggling their owners' words into the semblance of a gift to him of their property. And many, caught in the act of murder and other crimes, turned their possessions over to him and thus escaped the penalty for their sins.

This emperor, then, was deceitful, devious, false, hypocritical, two-faced, cruel, skilled in dissembling his thought, never moved to tears by either joy or pain, although he could summon them artfully at will when the occasion demanded, a liar always, not only offhand but also in writing and when he swore sacred oaths to his subjects in their very hearing. Then he would immediately break his agreements and pledges, like the vilest of slaves, whom indeed only the fear of torture drives to confess their perjury. A faithless friend, he was a treacherous enemy, insane for murder and plunder, quarrelsome and revolutionary, easily led to anything evil but never willing to listen to good counsel, quick to plan mischief and carry it out but finding even the hearing of anything good distasteful to his ears.

How could anyone put Justinian's ways into words? These and many even worse vices were disclosed in him as in no other mortal nature seemed to have taken the wickedness of all other men combined and planted it in this man's soul. And besides this, he was too prone to listen to accusations and too quick to punish. For he decided such cases without full examination, naming the punishment when he had heard only the accuser's side of the matter. Without hesitation he wrote decrees for the plundering of countries, sacking of cities, and slavery of whole nations, for no cause whatever. So that if one wished to take all the calamities that had befallen the Romans before this time and weigh them against his crimes,

[88] As Augusta she took the name Euphemia, that of a Christian saint, perhaps because of the association of the name Lupicina with prostitution; see Reading 73.

[89] The Plague of Justinian (541–542 CE) afflicted much of Near Eastern and Mediterranean worlds, killing an estimated twenty-five million people; for ancient plagues, see also Reading 56.

I think it would be found that more men had been murdered by this single man than in all previous history.

He had no scruples about appropriating other people's property, and did not even think any excuse necessary, legal or illegal, for confiscating what did not belong to him. And when it was his, he was more than ready to squander it in insane display, or give it as an unnecessary bribe to the barbarians. In short, he neither held on to any money himself nor let anyone else keep any, as if his reason were not avarice but jealousy of those who had riches. Driving all wealth from the country of the Romans in this manner, he became the cause of universal poverty. Now this was the character of Justinian, so far as I can portray it.

[The Character of Theodora]

Justinian took a wife, and in what manner she was born and bred, and, wedded to this man, tore up the Roman Empire by the very roots, I now shall relate. Acacius was the keeper of wild beasts used in the amphitheater in Constantinople. He belonged to the Green faction[90] and was nicknamed the Bearkeeper. This man, during the rule of Anastasius, fell sick and died, leaving three daughters named Comito, Theodora, and Anastasia, of whom the eldest was not yet seven years old. When these children reached the age of girlhood, their mother put them on the local stage, for they were fair to look upon. Forthwith, Theodora became a courtesan, for she was not a flute or harp player, nor was she even trained to dance, but only gave her youth to anyone she met, in utter abandonment. She took part in the low comedy scenes, for she was very funny and a good mimic, and immediately became popular in this art. Frequently, she conceived but as she employed every artifice immediately, a miscarriage was straightway effected.

Later, she followed Hecebolus, a Tyrian[91] who had been made governor of Pentapolis,[92] serving him in the basest of ways, but finally she quarreled with him and was sent summarily away. Consequently, she found herself destitute of the means of life, which she proceeded to earn by prostitution, as she had done before this adventure. She came thus to Alexandria, and then traversing all the east, worked her way to Constantinople; in every city plying a trade as if the devil were determined there be no land on earth that should not know the sins of Theodora.

Thus was this woman born and bred. But when she came back to Constantinople, Justinian fell violently in love with her. At first he kept her only as a mistress, although he raised her to patrician[93] rank. Through him, Theodora was able immediately to acquire an unholy power and exceedingly great riches. She seemed to him the sweetest thing in the world, and like all lovers, he desired to please his charmer with every possible favor and requite her with all his wealth. The extravagance added fuel to the flames of passion. With her now to help spend his money he plundered the people more than ever, not only in the capital, but throughout the Roman Empire.

Justin, doting and utterly senile, now was the laughing stock of his subjects. He was disregarded by everyone because of his inability to oversee state affairs; but Justinian they all served with considerable awe. His hand was in everything, and his passion for turmoil created universal consternation. It was then that he undertook to complete his marriage with Theodora. Because it was impossible for a man of senatorial rank to make a courtesan his wife, this being forbidden by ancient law, Justinian made the emperor nullify this ordinance by creating a new one, permitting him to wed Theodora and consequently making it possible for anyone else to marry a courtesan.[94] Immediately after this he seized the power of the emperor, veiling his usurpation with a transparent

[90] The two most popular chariot-racing fan clubs were known as the "Blues" and the "Greens" from the colors the charioteers wore. These "circus factions" provided an outlet for popular political expression, often by shouting orchestrated acclamations (as in Reading 121) and slogans during performances in the hippodrome (chariot race track).

[91] From the Phoenician city of Tyre.

[92] A province in Libya, west of Egypt.

[93] Patricians outranked even Consuls.

[94] A law issued by Justin between 520 and 523.

pretext, for he was proclaimed colleague[95] of his uncle as emperor of the Romans by the questionable legality of an election inspired by terror.

So Justinian and Theodora ascended the imperial throne three days before Easter, a time, indeed, when even making visits or greeting one's friends is forbidden. And not many days later Justin died of an illness,[96] after a reign of nine years. Justinian now was sole monarch, together, of course, with Theodora. Thus it was that Theodora, although born and brought up as I have related, rose to royal dignity over all obstacles. What she and her husband did together must now be briefly described, for neither did anything without the consent of the other. For some time it was generally supposed they were totally different in mind and action, but later it was revealed that their apparent disagreement had been arranged so that their subjects might not unanimously revolt against them, but instead be divided in opinion.

As soon as Justinian came into power he turned everything upside down. As the Romans were now at peace with all the world and he had no other means of satisfying his lust for slaughter, he set the barbarians all to fighting each other. And for no reason at all he sent for the Hun chieftains and with idiotic magnanimity gave them large sums of money, alleging he did this to secure their friendship. This, as I have said, he also had done in Justin's time. These Huns, as soon as they had got this money, sent it together with their soldiers to others of their chieftains, with the word to make inroads into the land of the emperor, so that they might collect further tribute from him, to buy them off in a second peace. Thus the Huns enslaved the Roman Empire, and were paid by the emperor to keep on doing it.

To me, and many others of us, these two seemed not to be human beings but veritable demons, and what the poets call vampires. They laid their heads together to see how they could most easily and quickly destroy the race and deeds of men, and assuming human bodies, became man-demons, and so convulsed the world. Some of those who have been with Justinian at the palace late at night, men who were pure of spirit, have thought they saw a strange demoniac form taking his place. One man said that the emperor suddenly rose from his throne and walked about, and indeed he was never wont to remain sitting for long, and immediately Justinian's head vanished, while the rest of his body seemed to ebb and flow, whereat the beholder stood aghast and fearful, wondering if his eyes were deceiving him. But presently he perceived the vanished head filling out and joining the body again as strangely as it had left it. Another said he stood beside the emperor as he sat, and suddenly the face changed into a shapeless mass of flesh, with neither eyebrows nor eyes in their proper places nor any other distinguishing feature, and after a time the natural appearance of his countenance returned. I write these instances not as one who saw them myself, but heard them from men who were positive they had seen these strange occurrences at the time.

[95] On 1 April 527.

[96] On 1 August 527.

124

THE RISE OF ISLAM (627–629 CE): AL-TABARI, *HISTORY OF THE PROPHETS AND KINGS*, 1619

This manuscript illustration comes from "The Universal History" of Rashid Al-Din Hamadani, created in Tabriz, Persia, for the Mongol Ilkhanate in the early fourteenth century CE. It depicts the encounter in Syria of the ten-year-old Muhammad with the Arab Nestorian Christian monk Bahira, otherwise known as Sergius the Monk. The historian al-Tabari reported that Bahira saw a vision above Muhammad's head and foretold to Muhammad's uncle his future role as the Prophet and warned him to protect Muhammad from the Byzantines.

The Persian scholar Abu Ja'far Muhammad ibn Jarir al-Tabari (839–923 CE), one of the earliest Islamic historians, was the author of the "Tarikh al-Rusul wa al-Muluk" ("History of the Prophets and Kings"), which covered the period from the creation to 915 CE. The "Tarikh al-Tabari," its short title, meticulously cites its sources and is considered one of the most accurate accounts of early Islamic history. The section on the rise of Islam discusses the processes by which Muhammad extended his authority over the peoples of Arabia. Ancient Arabia was a welter of many different clans who were identified by the word "Banu," that is, "the descendants of," because each clan was believed to have had a single original progenitor. The clans all were interrelated to a closer or more distant degree and interacted with each other on many different levels, both friendly and hostile. In 627 CE, after Muhammad had fled from Mecca and established himself in Medina in 622 CE (the Hijra), the two sides made peace. But this did not last. It was only a matter of time before the quarrels among the different clans led to a further outbreak of hostilities. In 629 CE, fighting broke out between the Khuza'ah clan, which supported Muhammad, and the Banu Bakr clan, which supported Mecca. As a result, the peace collapsed, and in the next year Muhammad was able to gain control of Mecca. al-Tabari also wrote that Christians had deleted from the original Christian gospels references to the coming of Muhammad.

Source: Michael Fishbein, trans., *The History of Al-Tabari: The Victory of Islam*, Vol. 8 (Albany: State University of New York Press, 1997), 160–163.

After sending his expedition to Mut'ah,[97] the Messenger of God[98] stayed in Medina[99] during Jumada II and Rajab.[100] Then the Banu Bakr bin "Abd Manat bin Kinanah[101] assaulted the Khuza'ah[102] while the latter were at a watering place called al-Watir belonging to the Khuza'ah in Lower Mecca. The cause of the strife between Banu Bakr and the Banu Khuza'ah was a man from the Banu al-Hadrami[103] named Malik bin "Abbad. This man of the Banu al-Hadrami had a covenant of protection[104] at that time with al-Aswad bin Razn. Malik set out on a journey as a merchant. When he was in the middle of Khuza'ah territory, the Khuza'ah assaulted him, killed him, and took his property. The Banu Bakr therefore attacked and killed a man from Khuza'ah.[105] Just before Islam, the Khuza'ah in turn assaulted Salma, Kulthum, and Dhu'ayb, the sons of al-Aswad bin Razn al-Dili—they were the leading men and dignitaries of the Banu Bakr—and killed them at 'Arafah, by the border markers of the sacred territory.

According to Ibn Humayd, Salamah, and Muhammad bin Ishaq,[106] a man from the Banu al-Dil, said, "In pagan times two payments of blood money would be paid for each of the sons of al-Aswad, whereas a single payment of blood money would be paid for us, and that because of their excellence compared with us."[107]

Matters stood thus between the Banu Bakr and the Khuza'ah when Islam intervened to separate them and occupy people's minds. When the peace of al-Hudaybiyah[108] was concluded between the Messenger of God and the Quraysh[109] (this information is according to Ibn Humayd, Salamah, Muhammad bin Ishaq, Muhammad bin Muslim bin 'Abdallah bin Shihab al-Zuhri, 'Urwah bin al-Zubayr, al-Miswar bin Makhramah, Marwan bin al-Hakam, and other learned men of ours), among the terms they imposed on the Messenger of God and that he granted to them

[97] A town in eastern Jordan.
[98] Muhammad.
[99] The city to which Muhammad had fled after being expelled from Mecca in 622 CE.
[100] The sixth and seventh months of the Muslim calendar.
[101] A people of western Arabia south of Mecca. The word "bin," "son of," indicates the family lineage of the person believed originally to have established the clan.
[102] The Banū Khuza'a, an Arab people of west central Arabia who once ruled Mecca.
[103] A people of the Hadramat area of Yemen in southern Arabia.
[104] A promise not to attack or kill each other.
[105] The standard "law of retaliation" in force at the time.
[106] Earlier sources cited by al-Tabari.
[107] Blood money was paid to bring the cycles of retaliation to an end.
[108] Following several battles, the Treaty of Hudaybiyyah in March 628 specified a ten-year peace between Muhammad and the city of Medina on the one hand and the Quraysh clan of Mecca on the other.
[109] The clan that controlled the city of Mecca at this time.

was that whoever wanted to enter into a treaty and pact with the Messenger of God might do so, and whoever wanted to enter into a treaty with the Quraysh might do so. The Banu Bakr entered into a pact with the Quraysh, and the Khuza'ah entered into a pact with the Messenger of God.

The truce having been concluded, the Banu al-Dil of the Banu Bakr took advantage of it against Khuza'ah. To retaliate for the sons of al-Aswad bin Razn they wanted to kill the persons from Khuza'ah who had killed their men. Nawfal bin Mu'awiyah al-Dili set out with the Banu al-Dil (at that time he was a leader of the Banu al-Dil, although not all the Banu Bakr followed him). He made a night raid on the Khuza'ah while the latter were at their watering place of al-Watir, and they killed a man. They tried to drive each other away and fought. The Quraysh aided the Banu Bakr with weapons, and some members of the Quraysh fought on their side under cover of darkness until they drove the Khuza'ah into the sacred territory.[110]

According to al-Waqidi: Among the members of the Quraysh who helped the Banu Bakr against Khuza'ah that night, concealing their identity, were Safwan bin Umayyah, 'Ikrimah bin Abi Jahl, Suhayl bin 'Amr, and others, along with their slaves.

Resumption of the account of Ibn Ishaq, who said: When they reached the sacred territory, the Banu Bakr said, "Nawfal, we have entered the sacred territory. Be mindful of your God! Be mindful of your God!" To which Nawfal replied blasphemously, "Today he has no God! Banu Bakr, take your revenge! By my life you steal in the sacred territory; will you not take your revenge in it?"

The night that the Banu Bakr attacked the Khuza'ah at al-Watir, they killed a man of the Khuza'ah named Munabbih. Munabbih was a man with a weak heart. He had gone out with a clansman of his named Tamim bin Asad. Munabbih said to him, "Tamim, save yourself! As for me, by God, I am a dead man whether they kill me or spare me, for my heart has ceased beating." Tamim ran away and escaped; Munabbih they caught and killed. When the Khuza'ah entered Mecca, they took refuge in the house of Budayl bin Waqa' al-Khuza'i and the house of one of their *mawlas*[111] named Rafi'.

When the Quraysh leagued together with the Banu Bakr against the Khuza'ah and killed some of their men, breaking the treaty and covenant that existed between them and the Messenger of God by violating the Khuza'ah, who had a pact and treaty with him, 'Amr bin Salim al-Khuza'i, one of the Banu Ka'b, went to the Messenger of God in Medina. 'Amr stood before the Messenger of God while he was in the mosque sitting among the people, and he recited, "Oh God, I will remind Muhammad of the venerable alliance of our father and his father. Parent were we, and you were child."[112] This was one of the things that prompted the conquest of Mecca.

[110] The territory of Mecca, marked out by sacred stones.

[111] Patrons, protectors, or supporters.

[112] Arab peoples were very aware of family relationships going back for generations and were expected to preserve ancient loyalties.

125

THE MUSLIM CONQUEST OF EGYPT (640 CE): JOHN OF NIKIÛ, *CHRONICLE*, CHAPTERS 111–120

A gold solidus of the Byzantine emperor Heraclius (610–641) depicts on the obverse Heraclius with his son and short-lived successor, Heraclius Constantine (641). The legend reads "Our Lords Heraclius and Heraclius Constantinus, Perpetual Augustuses." On the reverse is a cross on steps and the legend "Victory of the emperors," with the abbreviation for "Count of Gold" below. After repelling and disastrously defeating the New Persians in the 620s, the weakened Heraclius was unable to withstand the onslaught of the Muslim Arabs during the 630s.

In late 639 CE, Byzantine Egypt was invaded by the Muslim general 'Amr. After a series of small victories, 'Amr completely destroyed the Roman army at the Battle of Heliopolis on 6 July 640. Any hope of reinforcements and continued resistance ended with the death of the Byzantine emperor Heraclius in February 641. After additional defeats, what was left of the Roman forces congregated in Alexandria. After a further nine-month siege, with further resistance having become futile, Cyrus, the Melchite (eastern supporters of the Council of Chalcedon in 451) Patriarch of Alexandria, who also had been appointed Prefect of Egypt, made a humiliating treaty with 'Amr that surrendered Alexandria to the Muslims. With the loss of Alexandria, the Romans had no hope of holding Egypt, and thus the richest of all the Roman provinces was abandoned to the Muslims and, with it, any hope of being able to recover the eastern provinces. This account is given by John, the Monophysite (anti-Chalcedonian) bishop of Nikiû in the Nile Delta, whose later seventh-century chronicle is often the only source for these events. The tale begins in the spring of 640.

Source: R. H. Charles, *The Chronicle of John, Bishop of Nikiu* (London: Williams & Norgate, 1916).

Now, Theodorus was Master of Soldiers in Egypt. And when the messengers of Theodosius the Prefect of Arcadia[113] informed him regarding the death of John, general of the local levies, he thereupon turned with all the Egyptian troops and his auxiliary forces and marched to Lôkjôn,[114] which is an island. Moreover he feared lest, owing to the dissensions prevailing among the inhabitants of that district, the Muslims should come and seize the coast of Lôkjôn and dislodge the communities of the servants of God who were subjects of the Roman emperor. His lamentations were more grievous than the lamentations of David over Saul when he said, "How are the mighty fallen, and the weapons of war perished!"[115] For not only had John the Master of Soldiers perished when the Arabs took Bahnasâ[116] and attacked Arsinoë,[117] but likewise John the general, who was of the city of Mârôs, had been slain in battle and fifty horsemen with him.

I will acquaint you briefly with what befell the former inhabitants of Arsinoë.

John and his troops had been appointed by the Romans to guard the district. They posted other guards near the rock of the city of Lâhûn in order to keep guard continually and to give information to the chief of the forces of the movements of their enemies. And subsequently they got ready some horsemen and a body of soldiers and archers, and these marched out to fight the Muslim, purposing to prevent their advance. And these Ishmaelites[118] came and slew without mercy the commander of the troops and all his companions. And forthwith they compelled the city of Arsinoë to open its gates, and they put to the sword all that surrendered, and they spared none, whether old men, babe, or woman. And they proceeded against the general John.

Tidings of these events were brought to the general Theodosius and to Anastasius,[119] who were then twelve miles distant from Nikiû.[120] And they betook themselves immediately to the citadel of Babylon,[121] and they remained there. And such Romans as were in Egypt sought refuge in the citadel of Babylon. And they also were awaiting the arrival of the general Theodorus in order to join with him in attacking the Ishmaelites before the rise of the river and the time of sowing.

[The Battle of Heliopolis]

Theodosius and Anastasius went forth to the city of Heliopolis,[122] on horseback, together with a large

[113] A Roman province in the northernmost part of Upper Egypt.

[114] All of the locations in this account, some of which are otherwise unknown, are located in Lower Egypt.

[115] 2 Samuel 1:27.

[116] A Christian episcopal see.

[117] Arsinoë in Arcadia, the capital city of the Fayum district. Known to the Egyptians as Shedet and the Greeks as Crocodilopolis, it was renamed Arsinoë by the Ptolemaic king Ptolemy II (309–246 BCE) in honor of his sister and wife, Arsinoë.

[118] In the Bible, the descendants of Ishmael, the son of Abraham and his handmaid Hagar. By the time of Muhammad, the Arabs were thought to be the descendants of Ishmael.

[119] The military governor of Alexandria.

[120] The episcopal see of the author of this account.

[121] The most important Roman fortress in Lower Egypt, on the Nile River south of modern Cairo.

[122] Lunu to the ancient Egyptians and On in the Bible, the worship center of the Egyptian gods Atum and Ra, located just north of modern Cairo near the border between Lower and Upper Egypt.

body of foot soldiers, in order to attack ‘Amr the son of Al-As.[123] And ‘Amr showed great vigilance and strenuous thought in his attempts to capture the city of Babylon. But he was troubled because of his separation from a part of the Muslim troops, who being divided into two corps on the east of the river were marching toward Heliopolis, which was situated on high ground. And ‘Amr the son of Al-As sent a letter to Omar the son of Al-Khattab in the province of Palestine to this effect, “If thou dost not send Muslim reinforcements, I shall not be able to take Babylon.” And Omar sent him 4,000 Muslim warriors whose general's name was Walwarja. He was of barbarian descent. And ‘Amr divided his troops into three corps. One corps he placed near Tendunias,[124] the second to the north of Babylon in Egypt, and he made his preparations with the third corps near the city of Heliopolis. And he gave the following orders, “Be on the watch, so that when the Roman troops come out to attack us, you may rise up in their rear, while we shall be on their front, and so having got them between us, we shall put them to the sword.”

And thus when the Roman troops, unaware, set out from the fortress to attack the Muslims, these Muslims thereupon fell upon their rear, as they had arranged, and a fierce engagement ensued. And when the Muslims came in great numbers against them, the Roman troops fled to their ships. And the Muslim army took possession of the city of Tendunias, for its garrison had been destroyed, and there survived only 300 soldiers. And these fled and withdrew into the fortress and closed the gates. But when they saw the great slaughter that had taken place, they were seized with panic and fled by ship to Nikiû in great grief and sorrow. And when Domentianus[125] heard of these events, he set out by night without informing the inhabitants of Abûît that he was fleeing to escape the Muslims, and they proceeded to Nikiû by ship. And when the Muslims learnt that Domentianus had fled, they marched joyously and seized the city of Abûît, and they shed much blood there.

Such of the governors as were in the city of Nikiû fled and betook themselves to the city of Alexandria, leaving Domentianus with a few troops to guard the city. Then a panic fell on all the cities of Egypt and all their inhabitants took to flight and made their way to Alexandria, abandoning all their possessions and wealth and cattle. And when those Muslims, accompanied by the Egyptians who had apostatized from the Christian faith and embraced the faith of the beast, had come up, the Muslims took as booty all the possessions of the Christians who had fled, and they designated the servants of Christ enemies of God. And ‘Amr the chief of the Muslims spent twelve months in warring against the Christians of northern Egypt, but failed nevertheless in reducing their cities.

And when the Muslims saw the weakness of the Romans and the hostility of the people to the emperor Heraclius[126] because of the persecution he had visited on all the land of Egypt in regard to the catholic faith, at the instigation of Cyrus the Chalcedonian Patriarch,[127] they became bolder and stronger in the war. And the inhabitants of the city of Antinoë[128] sought to concert measures with John their Prefect with a view to attacking the Muslim, but he refused, and arose with haste with his troops, and, having collected all the imposts of the city, betook himself to Alexandria, for he knew that he could not resist the Muslims and he feared lest he should meet with the same fate as the

[123] ‘Amr ibn al-‘As, an early enemy of Islam who converted in 620 CE and became one of Muhammad's chief generals. After the Muslim conquest of Syria, he proposed an invasion of Roman Egypt, which he led in late 639 CE.

[124] Muslim Umm Dûnayn, a Roman fortress on the Nile River.

[125] A Roman patrician and general known for his cowardice and love of intrigue.

[126] Emperor from 610 to 641 CE.

[127] A supporter of the ecumenical Council of Chalcedon, which in 451 CE had condemned the Monophysite view that Christ had a single divine nature as opposed to an equally divine and human nature, Cyrus had been made Patriarch of Alexandria by Heraclius in 631 in opposition to the exiled Monophysite patriarch Benjamin. Most of Egypt was Monophysite, and many Egyptians therefore welcomed the Muslim invasion, thinking they could thus gain greater religious tolerance.

[128] City in Upper Egypt built by the emperor Hadrian (117–138) in honor of his lover Antinoüs.

garrison of Arsinoë. Indeed, all the inhabitants of the province submitted to the Muslim and paid them tribute. And the Muslims put to the sword all the Roman soldiers whom they encountered.

Heraclius fell ill with fever and died in the thirty-first year of his reign in the month Yakâtîtof the Egyptians, that is, February of the Roman months, in the 357th year of Diocletian.[129] Pyrrhus, the Patriarch of Constantinople, nominated Constantine the son of the empress Eudocia[130] and made him head of the empire in succession to his father.[131] Constantine mustered a large number of ships and entrusted them to Kîrjûs and Salâkriûs and sent them to bring the Patriarch Cyrus to him so that he might take counsel with him as to the Muslims as to whether he should fight, if he were able, or, if not, should pay tribute.[132] Constantine sent orders to Theodorus to come to him and leave Anastasius to guard the city of Alexandria and the cities on the coast. And he held out hopes to Theodorus that he would send him a large force in the autumn in order to war with the Muslim.

And 'Amr the chief of the Muslim forces had encamped before the citadel of Babylon and besieged the troops that garrisoned it. Now the latter received his promise that they should not be put to the sword and undertook to deliver up to him all the munitions of war, which were considerable. And thereupon he ordered them to evacuate the citadel. And they took a small quantity of gold and set out. And it was in this way that the citadel of Babylon in Egypt was taken.[133]

'Amr and the Muslim army, on horseback, then proceeded by land until they came to the city of Kebrias of Abâdjâ. And on this occasion he attacked the general Domentianus. When the latter learned of the approach of the Muslim troops he embarked on a ship and fled and abandoned the army and their fleet and entered the city of Alexandria. Now when the soldiers saw that their commander had taken flight, they cast away their arms and threw themselves into the river in the presence of their enemies. And the Muslim troops slaughtered them with the sword in the river. Thereupon the Muslims made their entry into Nikiû, and took possession, and finding no soldiers they proceeded to put to the sword all whom they found in the streets and in the churches, men, women, and infants, and they showed mercy to none. And after they had captured the city, they marched against other localities and sacked them and put all they found to the sword.

And Egypt became enslaved to Satan. A great strife had broken out between the inhabitants of Lower Egypt, and these were divided into two parties. Of these, one sided with Theodorus, but the other wished to join the Muslims. And straightway the latter party rose against the other, and they plundered their possessions and burnt their city. But the Muslims distrusted them. And 'Amr sent a large force of Muslims against Alexandria, and they captured Kariun, which lies outside the city. And Theodorus and his troops who were in that locality fled and withdrew into Alexandria. And the Muslims began to attack them but were not able to approach the walls of the city, for stones were hurled against them from the top of the walls and they were driven far from the city.

Subsequently, Constantine gave Cyrus power and authority to make peace with the Muslims and check any further resistance against them, and to establish a system of administration suitable to the government

[129] 11 February 641, counting from the accession of Diocletian (284–305), who had reorganized the administration of Egypt.

[130] The first wife of Heraclius; after her death in 612 CE, Heraclius married his niece, Martina.

[131] Heraclius Constantine died only four months later of tuberculosis and was succeeded by his younger half-brother and co-emperor, Heracleonas. He, in turn, soon was deposed by his brother Constans II (641–668). This instability grievously affected the Byzantine ability to resist the Arabs.

[132] By now, Cyrus also had been appointed Prefect of Egypt, an extraordinary union of religious and secular authority and an indication of how serious the situation in Egypt was.

[133] On 21 December 640.

of the land of Egypt. Now, not only Cyrus the Chalcedonian Patriarch desired peace with the Muslim but also all the people and the patricians and Domentianus, who had enjoyed the favor of the empress Martina.[134] So all these assembled and took counsel with Cyrus the Patriarch with a view to making peace with the Muslim. And all the inhabitants of Alexandria, men and women, old and young, gathered together to meet the Patriarch Cyrus, rejoicing and giving thanks for the arrival of the Patriarch of Alexandria.[135]

And the Patriarch Cyrus set out and went to Babylon to the Muslim, seeking by the offer of tribute to procure peace from them and put a stop to war in the land of Egypt.[136] And 'Amr welcomed his arrival, and said unto him, "Thou hast done well to come to us." And Cyrus answered and said unto him, "God has delivered this land into your hands. Let there be no enmity from henceforth between you and Rome. Hitherto there has been no persistent strife with you." And they fixed the amount of tribute to be paid. And as for the Ishmaelites, they were not to intervene in any matter, but were to keep to themselves for eleven months. The Roman troops in Alexandria were to carry off their possessions and their treasures and proceed home by sea, and no other Roman army was to return. And the Romans were to cease warring against the Muslim and the Muslims were to desist from seizing Christian churches and were not to meddle with any concerns of the Christians. And the Jews were to be permitted to remain in the city of Alexandria. The Egyptians, who, through fear of the Muslim, had fled and taken refuge in the city of Alexandria, made the following request to the Patriarch, "Get the Muslim to promise that we may return to our cities and become their subjects." And he negotiated for them according to their request. And the Muslims took possession of all the land of Egypt, southern and northern.

[134] Widow of the deceased emperor Heraclius.
[135] After his return from consulting with the emperor.
[136] 8 November 641.

126

THE PERSISTENCE OF THE CLASSICAL TRADITION IN BARBARIAN EUROPE (CA. 575 CE): THE POEM OF EUCHERIA

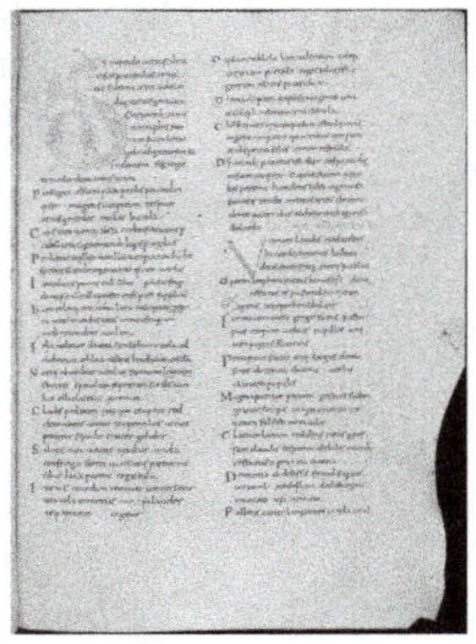

After the fall of the western Roman Empire, even barbarian kings assisted in the preservation of the classical poetic tradition, as when the Frankish king Chilperic (561–584) authored a poem in honor of Saint Medardus, the only surviving copy of which is found in a tenth-century manuscript preserved in Zurich, Switzerland: the subscription reads, "King Chilperic composed this hymn." Chiliperic was so engaged with literature and learning that he even ordered four letters to be added to the alphabet.

After the fall of the western Roman Empire, the classical tradition continued in the barbarian kingdoms. The only surviving poem of the author Eucheria was written in Gaul around the last quarter of the sixth century and is preserved in a collection of secular poems known as the "Latin Anthology." It is unclear what her connection is to the Rusticus, named in the last line, to whom the poem is addressed; he could be a paramour, or perhaps "Rusticus" is a nickname for her husband, the patrician Dynamius of Marseille, who served in Provence in the mid to late sixth century. The poem exhibits many of the characteristic traits of late Roman poetry, such as overblown rhetoric; obscure allusions, especially to mythology and the heroic Roman past; and the use of such literary tricks as antithesis (opposites), alliteration, and rhyme. Eucheria survived Dynamius by eight years and died ca. 605. Their epitaph, in the church of St. Hippolytus at Marseille, was erected by a grandson, also named Dynamius. Eucheria's literary activities demonstrate the continued survival and vitality of the Roman secular literary tradition in barbarian Europe into the late sixth century CE and beyond.

Source: Ralph W. Mathisen, *People, Personal Expression, and Social Relations in Late Antiquity*, Vol. I, *With Translated Texts from Gaul and Western Europe* (Ann Arbor: University of Michigan Press, 2003), 38–40.

I wish to fuse golden threads, shining with harmonious metal,
with masses of bristles.
Silken coverings, gem-studded Laconian[137] fabrics,
I say, must be matched with goat skins.
Let noble purple be joined with a frightful red jacket;
let the gleaming gemstone be joined to ponderous lead.
Let the pearl now be held captive by its own brightness,
and let it shine enclosed in dark steel.
Likewise, let the emerald be enclosed in Leuconian[138] bronze,
and let now hyacinth[139] be the equal of flint.
Let jasper be said to be like rubble and rocks;
let now the moon embrace the nether void.
Now, indeed, let us decree that lilies are to be joined with nettles,
and let the menacing hemlock oppress the scarlet rose.
Now, similarly, let us therefore, spurning the fish, choose
to disdain the delicacies of the great sea.
Let the rock-dwelling toad love the golden serpent,
and likewise let the female trout seek for herself the male snail.
And let the lofty lioness be joined with the foul fox;
let the ape embrace the sharp-eyed lynx.
Now let the doe be joined to the donkey, and the tigress to the wild ass;
now let the fleet deer be joined to the torpid bull.
Let now the foul silphium juice[140] taint the nectared rose-wine,
and let now honey be mixed with vile poisons.
Let us associate sparkling water with the muddy cesspool;
let the fountain flow saturated with a mixture of filth.
Let the swift swallow cavort with the funereal vulture;
let now the nightingale serenade with the doleful owl.
Let the unhappy coop-dweller[141] abide with the pellucid partridge,
and let the beautiful dove lie coupled with the crow.
Let the times manipulate these monstrosities with uncertain consequences,
and in this way let the slave Rusticus seek Eucheria.

137 From Laconia, in Greece, the homeland of Sparta.

138 A reference to Leuci (modern Toul) in Gaul.

139 A gemstone, possibly a kind of sapphire or dark amethyst, the color of the hyacinth flower (perhaps a larkspur).

140 A bad-smelling gum resin obtained from the silphium plant and used medicinally as an antispasmodic drug.

141 The inhabitant of a bird coop.

CREDITS

Text Credits

1.1: Republished with permission of Brill Publishers, from W.G. Ambert, "Mesopotamian Creation Stories," in Markham J. Geller, Mineke Schipper, eds., Imagining Creation, IJS Studies in Judaica 5, 2008; permission conveyed through Copyright Clearance Center, Inc.

1.2: Copyright © J.A. Black, G. Cunningham, E. Robson, and G. Zólyomi 1998, 1999, 2000; J.A. Black, G. Cunningham, E. Flückiger-hawker, E. Robson, J. Taylor, and G. Zólyomi 2001. The authors have asserted their moral rights.

1.3: Copyright © 1985, 1989 by the Board of Trustees of the Leland Standord University Press, sup.org.

1.5: Hugh G. Evelyn-White, Hesiod, the Homeric Hymns and Homerica (Cambridge, MA, 1924), 2–64.

1.9: The Holy Bible, King James Version. Cambridge Edition: 1769; King James Bible Online, 2016. www.kingjamesbibleonline.org.

1.10: The Holy Bible, King James Version. Cambridge Edition: 1769; King James Bible Online, 2016. www.kingjamesbibleonline.org.

1.11: Yusuf Ali, trans, The Holy Qur-an, Text, Translation and Commentary (Lahore, Cairo, Riyadh, 1934).

2.1: Copyright © J.A. Black, G. Cunningham, E. Robson, and G. Zólyomi 1998, 1999, 2000; J.A. Black, G. Cunningham, E. Flückiger-Hawker, E. Robson, J. Taylor, and G. Zólyomi 2001; J.A. Black, G. Cunningham, J. Ebeling, E. Robson, J. Taylor, and G. Zólyomi 2002, 2003, 2004, 2005; G. Cunningham, J. Ebeling, E. Robson, and G. Zólyomi 2006. The authors have asserted their moral rights.

2.2: William Ellery Leonard, trans., Gilgamesh. Epic of Old Babylonia (New York: Viking, 1934).

2.3: Copyright © J.A. Black, G. Cunningham, E. Robson, and G. Zólyomi 1998, 1999, 2000; J.A. Black, G. Cunningham, E. Flückiger-Hawker, E. Robson, J. Taylor, and G. Zólyomi 2001; J.A. Black, G. Cunningham, J. Ebeling, E. Robson, J. Taylor, and G. Zólyomi 2002, 2003, 2004, 2005; G. Cunningham, J. Ebeling, E. Robson, and G. Zólyomi 2006. The authors have asserted their moral rights.

2.5: Copyright © J.A. Black, G. Cunningham, E. Robson, and G. Zólyomi 1998, 1999, 2000; J.A. Black, G. Cunningham, E. Flückiger-Hawker, E. Robson, J. Taylor, and G. Zólyomi 2001; J.A. Black, G. Cunningham, J. Ebeling, E. Robson, J. Taylor, and G. Zólyomi 2002, 2003, 2004, 2005; G. Cunningham, J. Ebeling, E. Robson, and G. Zólyomi 2006. The authors have asserted their moral rights.

2.6: Copyright © J.A. Black, G. Cunningham, E. Robson, and G. Zólyomi 1998, 1999, 2000; J.A. Black, G. Cunningham, E. Flückiger-Hawker, E. Robson, J. Taylor, and G. Zólyomi 2001; J.A. Black, G. Cunningham, J. Ebeling, E. Robson, J. Taylor, and G. Zólyomi 2002, 2003, 2004,

2005; G. Cunningham, J. Ebeling, E. Robson, and G. Zólyomi 2006. The authors have asserted their moral rights.

2.7: J.J. Finkelstein, trans., in James Bennet Pritchard, ed., Ancient Near Eastern Texts Relating to the Old Testament (Princeton, 1950).

3.7: Miriam Lichtheim. ed., Ancient Egyptian Literature: A Book of Readings. Vol.2. The New Kingdom (London: 1976). Republished with permission of University of California Press - Books; permission conveyed through Copyright Clearance Center, Inc.

3.8: Michael V. Fox, Song of Songs and the Ancient Egyptian Love Songs (Madison: Univ. of Wisconsin Press, 1983), p. 7–8.

4.1: Excerpt(s) from THE ARCHIVES OF EBLA: AN EMPIRE INSCRIBED IN CLAY by Giovanni Pettianto, copyright © 1981 by Doubleday, an imprint of Penguin Random House LLC. Used by permission of Doubleday, an imprint of the Knopf Doubleday Publishing Group, a division of Penguin Random House LLC. All rights reserved.

4.2: John Chadwick, The Decipherment of Linear B, 2nd ed. (Cambridge, 1967), 158–161.

7.5: E. C. Marchant, G. W. Bowersock, eds., Pseudo-Xenophon. Constitution of the Athenians. In Xenophon VII. Scripta minora, Loeb Classical Library (Cambridge, MA: Harvard University Press, 1968), 459–507.

8.4: John Selby Watson, trans., Marcus Junius Justinus, Epitome of the Philippic History of Pompeius Trogus (London: Bohn, 1853).

8.5: Benjamin Jowett, trans., The Politics of Aristotle (Colonial Press, 1900).

8.6: Elizabeth Carter, trans., The Works of Epictetus, Translated from the Original Greek (London, 1758), reprinted in W.H.D. Rouse, ed., The Moral Discourses of Epictetus, (London-Toronto, Dent: 1910).

8.7: New Revised Standard Version Bible, copyright © 1989 National Council of the Churches of Christ in the United States of America. Used by permission. All rights reserved.

9.1: George Rawlinson, Henry Rawlinson, John Gardner Wilkinson, tr., The History of Herodotus. A New English Version (London: Murray, 1862).

9.2: John Selby Watson, Marcus Junius Justinus, Epitome of the Philippic History of Pompeius Trogus (London: Bohn, 1853).

9.3: James Henry Breasted, "The Piankhi Stela," in Ancient Records of Egypt ; Vol.4 (Chicago: 1906).

9.4: Benjamin Jowett, trans., The Politics of Aristotle (Colonial Press, 1900), pp. 49–51.

9.5: John Selby Watson, Marcus Junius Justinus, Epitome of the Philippic History of Pompeius Trogus (London: Bohn, 1853).

10.1: John Dryden, The Lives of the Noble Greeks and Romans, revised by A.H. Clough, vol. 1 (Boston: Little Brown, 1910).

10.3: B.O. Foster, trans. Livy, Books I and II (Cambridge, MA: Harvard Univ Press, 1919).

10.4: S.P. Scott, tr., The Civil Law Including the Twelve Tables, the Institutes of Gaius, the Rules of Ulpian, the Opinions of Paulus, the Enactments, vol.1 (Cincinnati, 1932).

10.5: Titus Livius. The History of Rome, vol. 1 (London: Dent, 1905).

10.6: Canon Roberts, trans., Titus Livius. The History of Rome, vol. 3 (London: Dent, 1905).

10.7: Oliver J. Thatcher, ed., The Library of Original Sources (Milwaukee: University Research Extension Co., 1907), Vol. III: The Roman World, 65–77.

11.1: John Dryden, The Lives of the Noble Greeks and Romans, revised by A.H. Clough, vol. 1 (Boston: Little Brown, 1910).

11.2: John Dryden, The Lives of the Noble Greeks and Romans, revised by A.H. Clough, vol. 1 (Boston: Little Brown, 1910).

11.3: Charles Duke Yonge, trans., Select Orations of M.T. Cicero (New York: Harper, 1877), 1–14.

11.4: Francis Warre Cornish, J. P. Postgate, J. W. Mackail, trans., Catullus. Tibullus. Pervigilium Veneris, Revised by G. P. Goold, Loeb Classical Library (Cambridge, MA: Harvard University Press, 1913).

11.5: W.A. McDevitte, W.S. Bohn, trans., Gaius Julius Caesar. Commentaries on the Gallic War (New York: Harper, 1869).

11.6: John Dryden, Plutarch: The Lives of the Noble Greeks and Romans, revised by A.H. Clough, Vol. 1 (Boston: Little Brown, 1910).

11.7: Wistrand, Erik Karl Hilding. The so-called Laudatio Turiae: introduction, text, translation, commentary. [Göteborg]: Acta Universitatis Gothoburgensis, 1976.

12.1: H.R. Fairclough, trans., Virgil. Eclogues, Georgics, Aeneid, Loeb Classical Library, 2 vols. (Cambridge, MA: Harvard University Press, 1916).

12.2: Stephen De Vere trans., in William Stearns Davis, Rome and the West (Boston: Allyn and Bacon, 1913), no.58, 174–176.

12.3: Frederick W. Shipley, Velleius Paterculus and Res Gestae Divi Augusti. Loeb Classical Library (London: Heinemann, 1924).

12.5: J.C. Rolfe, trans., Suetonius. Volume I: The Lives of the Caesars (Cambridge, MA: Harvard Univ. Press, 1914).

12.6a: Column 1: E. Mary Smallwood, Documents Illustrating the Principates of Gaius Claudius and Nero (Cambridge: Cambridge Univ. Press, 1967), 369.

12.6b: Alfred John Church, William Jackson Brodribb, trans., Annals of Tacitus (London: Macmillan & Co., 1876), book 11.

12.7: Arthur Murphy, The Works of Tacitus (Dublin, 1794).

12.8: Taken from The Works of Josephus © Copyright 1978 by William Whiston, trans. Published by Kregel Publications, Grand Rapids, MI. Used by permission of the publisher. All rights reserved.

12.10: James H. Oliver, The Ruling Power: A Study of the Roman Empire. Transactions of the American Philosophical Society, vol. 43, part 4 (1953), pp. 895–907. Reprinted with permission.

12.11: G.G. Ramsay, trans., Juvenal and Persius, Loeb Classical Library (London: Heinemann, New York, Putnam, 1918).

12.12: William Melmoth, trans., Pliny: Letters, revised by W. M. L. Hutchinson. 2 vols., Loeb Classical Library, (London: Wm. Heinemann; New York: The Macmillan Co., 1915).

13.1a: Allan Johnson, Paul Coleman-Norton, Frank Bourne, Ancient Roman Statutes: Corpus of Roman Law no. 277, (Austin: Univ. of Texas Press, 1961), pp. 225–226.

13.1b: Earnest Cary, trans., Dio's Roman History, 9 vols. (Cambridge, MA: Harvard University Press, 1917).

13.2: "The Vigil of Venus. Translated from the Latin," Blackwood's Edinburgh Magazine 53.332 (June, 1843). Retrieved from Project Gutenberg http://www.gutenberg.org/cache/epub/12511/pg12511.txt.

13.3: R. N. Frye The History of Ancient Iran, vol.7 (Beck: Munich, 198)

13.4: David Magie, trans., Historia Augusta, Volume I (Cambridge, MA: Harvard Univ. Press, 1921)

13.5: Elsa R. Graser, trans., "The Edict of Diocletian on Maximum Prices," in T. Frank, An Economic Survey of Ancient Rome Volume V: Rome and Italy of the Empire, 1st ed. (Octagon, 1940), 307–421.

14.5: Republished with permission of Columbia University Press, from Seven Books of History Against the Pagans: The Apology of Paulus Orosius, Irving W. Raymond, trans., 1936; permission conveyed through Copyright Clearance Center, Inc.

14.8: Ralph W. Mathisen, "Romulus Augustulus (475–476)," De imperatoribus Romanis. An Online Encyclopedia of Roman Emperors; http://www.luc.edu/roman-emperors/auggiero.htm

15.3: Republished with permission of Princeton University Press, from The Theodosian code and novels: and the Sirmondian constitutions, Clyde Pharr (trans.), 1952; permission conveyed through Copyright Clearance Center, Inc.

15.6: Reprinted by permission from Michael Fishbein, trans., The History of Al-Tabari: The Victory of Islam, vol.8, State University of New York Press © 1997, State University of New York. All rights reserved.

15.8: Ralph W. Mathisen, People, Personal Expression, and Social Relations in Late Antiquity. Volume I. With Translated Texts from Gaul and Western Europe (Ann Arbor: Univ. of Michigan Press, 2003).

Photo Credits

1.1: © The Trustees of the British Museum. All rights reserved.

1.3: © The Trustees of the British Museum. All rights reserved.

1.4: CC-by-A 3.0 Loïc Evanno

1.8: CC-by-A 3.0 Till F. Teenck

2.1: BabelStone

2.2: The Schoyen Collection, Oslo and London: MS 1989, Photo: Tom Jensen

2.3: Ashmolean Museum, Oxford; number: AN1923.444

2.4: Iraqi Directorate General of Antiquities

2.5: Courtesy of Penn Museum, image #B16665

2.6: CC BY-SA 2.0 fr Rama
2.7: © The Trustees of the British Museum. All rights reserved.
3.1: Eugene Grebaut
3.2: © The Trustees of the British Museum. All rights reserved.
3.3: © The Trustees of the British Museum. All rights reserved.
3.6: "Hatshepsut's Temple Inscription at Speos Artemidos," (1981) 7 Biblical Archaeology Review.
4.2: Copyright © Hellenic Ministry of Culture and Sports/Archaeological Receipts Fund.
4.3: М. Коростовцев: Путешествие Ун-Амуна в Библ. 1960 (M. Korostovtsev: Die Reise des Wenamun nach Byblos, 1960), S. 135.
4.5: Courtesy of the Israel Antiquities Authority
4.6: CC-by-A 3.0 WebScribe
4.7: Copyright: Griffith Institute, University of Oxford
4.8: CC-by-A 2.0 Wayne McLean
5.3: Erich Lessing / Art Resource, NY
5.4: Speculum Humanae Salvationis, Westfalen oder Köln, um 1360. ULB Darmstadt, Hs 2505, fol. 56v
5.5: Marseille - BM - ms. 0089, f. 004v
6.1: © 2002 J. Paul Getty Trust. A. J. Clark, M. Elston, M. L. Hart. Understanding Greek vases: a guide to terms, styles, and techniques. Los Angeles, 2002, p. 41, fig. 29.
6.3: Badisches Landesmuseum, Karlsruhe
6.4: © Marie-Lan Nguyen/Wikimedia Commons/ CC-BY 2.5
6.5: Beazley, ARV2, 385, 228
6.6: CC-by-A 3.0
6.7: Tampa 86.24. Photograph by Maria Daniels, courtesy of the Tampa Museum of Art
7.1: Chicago Art Institute
7.2: © The British Library Board, Papyrus 131
7.3: CC-BY-SA Marsyas (2006)
7.4: Museo Pio-Clementino, Muses Hall Inv. 269
7.5: CC BY-SA 3.0 Classical Numismatic Group SNG Copenhagen 39.
7.6: Barbara McManus, 1979
7.7: © ACE STOCK LIMITED / Alamy Stock Photo
8.1: CC-BY-SA 3.0 Philipp Pilhofer
8.4: Classical Numismatic Group, Inc. SNG Cop. 266
8.5: National Museum of Rome Inv. 8575
8.7: CC BY-SA 3.0 Classical Numismatic Group, Inc. http://www.cngcoins.com
9.1: Beazley, Attic Red-figured Vase-Painters (1963), 78, 93; CAVI 4497
9.4: © Manuel Cohen
10.1: Finds.org.uk/Julian Waters BH-1A66B4
10.2: Wikimedia Commons/Saiko
10.3: Penn Libraries call number: Inc B-720
10.5: CC-by-Wikivoyage
10.6: © Trustees of the British Museum. All rights reserved.
11.3: Palazzo Madama, Rome
11.4: CC-BY-SA www.hellenica.de
11.6: CC-by-A 2.5 Classical Numismatic Group
11.7: VRoma
12.1: VRoma
12.2: American Numismatic Society/Mike Gasvoda
12.6: Cc-by-sa-2.0-fr Rama
12.7: Wildwinds SE 434
12.8: CC-BY-2.0 Israel Tourism
12.9: Picture courtesy of Geoffrey Cope
12.10: VRoma: Archaeological Museum, Florence: Barbara McManus
12.11: Marisa Ranieri Panetta (ed.): Pompeji. Geschichte, Kunst und Leben in der versunkenen Stadt. Belser, Stuttgart 2005, ISBN 3-7630-2266-X, p. 206
12.12: AKG-images / André Held
12.13: CC-BY-SA 3.0 CNG
12.14: CC-BY-SA 3.0 via CNG
13.1: Geissen, Universitaetsbibliothek, P. Giss. 40.
13.3: David Dorren
13.4: CC-by-SA 3.0 Classical Numismatic Group, Inc. http://www.cngcoins.com
13.5: Antikensammlung Berlin/Pergamonmuseum, Property of the Münzkabinett Berlin/MatthiasKabel
13.6: CC-by-SA 3.0 Nino Barbieri
13.9: Louvre Museum, Ma 1036, OA 9056
14.5: ullstein bild/Getty Images
14.6: Andre Durenceau/National Geographic Creative
15.1b: R. de Filippo/INRAP
15.2: The Hague, KB, KA 20 (51–60 of 72) © Koninklijke Bibliotheek National Library of the Netherland
15.3: © Marie-Lan Nguyen / Wikimedia Commons
15.7: Downies Coins Pty Ltd, Melbourne Australia.
15.8: CC-BY-ND 4.0 Zürich, Zentralbibliothek, Ms. C 10i, f. 69r – Passionarius maior, http://www.e-codices.unifr.ch/de/zbz/C0010i/69r